Modern Orthodox Judaism

The Jewish Publication Society
expresses its gratitude for the generosity
of the sponsors of this book.

In honor of our beloved parents and
grandparents—
Rabbi Aaron (z"l) and Sora Landes
Rabbi Wilfred and Miriam (z"l) Shuchat

Joshua Landes and Bryna Shuchat
and Family

JPS ANTHOLOGIES
OF JEWISH THOUGHT

University of Nebraska Press | Lincoln

Modern Orthodox Judaism

A Documentary History | ZEV ELEFF

Foreword by Jacob J. Schacter

The Jewish Publication Society | Philadelphia

Acknowledgments for the use of copyrighted
material appear on pages 425–40, which
constitute an extension of the copyright page.
All rights reserved. Published by the University
of Nebraska Press as a Jewish Publication
Society book. Manufactured in the United
States of America. ∞

Library of Congress Control Number: 2016938772

Set in Arno Pro by L. Auten.

For Jack,

together with Meital,

my greatest contribution
to Modern Orthodoxy

Contents

List of Illustrations   xxiv

Foreword   xxv
by Jacob J. Schacter

Preface   xxix

Acknowledgments   xli

PART 1. *Orthodox Judaism and the Modern American Experience*

1. Engaging Reform   3

INTRODUCTION   3

SECTION 1 | Charleston Clamorings and Other "Heresies"

"Retrograde Instead of Advancing"   5
Mordecai Noah | 1825

New Lights and Old Lights   6
A Member of the Reformed Society of Israelites | 1825

This Happy Land   7
Isaac Harby | 1825

A Jewish Luther   9
Jacob Mordecai | 1826

An Open Letter to Gustavus Poznanski   12
Isaac Leeser | 1843

"Some Wolves Clothed in Sheep's-Cover"   16
Abraham Rice | 1848

What Prevails among the Jewish People?   18
Mordecai Noah | 1850

SECTION 2 | Living Orthodox Judaism

This Is Religious Liberty in America   19
Abraham Kohn | 1843

Our Holy Place   20
Trustees of the Congregation Shearith Israel | 1847

Strange Misbehavior   21
Max Lilienthal | 1854

An Aunt's Admonishment   24
Anna Marks Allen | 1858

CONCLUSION   25

2. **The Traditional Talmud and Response**
   to Reform Prayer Books   27

INTRODUCTION   27

SECTION 1 | Talking Talmud

"The Talmud Is Not Divine"   28
Benjamin Cohen Carillon | 1843

At the Risk of Being Considered Hyper-orthodox   31
Henry Goldsmith | 1843

A Return to the Maimonidean View?   33
Abraham Rice | 1844

The Cleveland Conference   35
Isaac Leeser | 1855

It Is Decidedly Heretical   38
Morris J. Raphall | 1856

SECTION 2 | The Modified Mahzor

An Ornament for Parlor-Tables   39
Bernard Illowy | 1855

A Letter from an "Enlightened Orthodox" Jew   41
Benjamin Franklin Peixotto | 1859

On Burning Reform Prayer Books   43
Eliyahu Holzman | 1865

Minhag Ashkenaz and Minhag Reform   45
Samuel Myer Isaacs | 1866

CONCLUSION   47

3. An Orthodox Ministry   48

INTRODUCTION   48

SECTION 1 | The Impaired and Itinerant "Rabbi"

Rabbinic Tenure   49
Max Lilienthal | 1854

A New Calling   52
Palestine | 1862

Isaac Leeser's Successor   54
Alfred T. Jones | 1869

SECTION 2 | Defenders of Tradition

The Ethics   56
Alexander Kohut | 1885

Backward or Forward?   59
Kaufmann Kohler | 1885

What Is Progress?   61
Alexander Kohut | 1885

SECTION 3 | An Orthodox Seminary?

To the Hebrews of America   63
Henry Pereira Mendes | 1886

A School for the Intelligent Orthodox   65
Sabato Morais | 1887

To Preserve Judaism Above All Else   68
Jacob H. Schiff | 1900

CONCLUSION   73

PART 2. *The Contest for Modern Orthodox Judaism*

4. The Arrival of Eastern European Immigrants   77

INTRODUCTION   77

SECTION 1 | Resisting a Treifene Medine

Sabbath at the Polish Shul   79
William M. Rosenblatt | 1872

The Chief Rabbi's Sermon   82
Abraham Cahan | 1888

The Charleston Responsum   85
Naftali Zvi Yehudah Berlin | 1894

Father and Mother   86
Anzia Yezierska | 1890

Daughter of the Ramaz   88
S. N. Behrman | 1893

The Bylaws of the Agudath Ha-Rabbonim   92
The Union of Orthodox Rabbis of America | 1902

SECTION 2 | Accommodating to a Goldene Medine

The Orthodox Convention   94
Orthodox Jewish Congregational Union of America | 1898

What Is Orthodoxy?   96
Henry Pereira Mendes | 1898

Modern Orthodoxy in the Light of Orthodox Authorities   98
Gotthard Deutsch | 1898

Pictures of Jewish Home Life   101
Esther J. Ruskay | 1902

Young Israel   103
Hebrew Standard | 1913

Proposal for a Five-Day Work Week   104
Bernard Drachman | 1915

The Synagogue Council of America 107
Abraham Burstein | 1927

CONCLUSION 109

5. Trailblazers 111

INTRODUCTION 111

SECTION 1 | The Revel Revolution

An Orthodox High School 112
Solomon T. H. Hurwitz | 1916

The Question of the Time 116
Eliezer Ladizinksy | 1926

Yeshiva College 118
Bernard Revel | 1928

The Hebrew Theological College of Chicago 122
Hyman L. Meites | 1924

SECTION 2 | Solomon Schechter and the Orthodox

Is Schechter Orthodox? 124
Emanuel Schreiber | 1902

The "General Religious Tendency" of the Seminary 127
Solomon Schechter | 1902

A Dangerous Situation 130
American Hebrew | 1904

The Orthodox Rabbis and the Seminary 132
Judah David Eisenstein | 1904

A Reaffirmation of Traditional Judaism 134
Max Drob | 1929

CONCLUSION 137

6. The Parting of the Ways: Orthodox and
Conservative Judaism 139

INTRODUCTION 139

SECTION 1 | What's in a Name?

A Definition of Modern Orthodox   140
Henry Pereira Mendes | 1913

The "Modern Orthodox" Rabbi   142
Solomon Zucrow | 1928

What Is Orthodox Judaism?   144
Leo Jung | 1930

The Rabbinical Council of America   147
Solomon Reichman | 1935

Orthodox–Traditional–Torah-True Judaism   149
Joseph Lookstein | 1940

SECTION 2 | Mixed Seating and "Modern Orthodox"

"A Modern Orthodox Congregation"   152
Joseph Rudnick | 1925

May Men and Women Sit Together in Shul?   154
Joseph B. Soloveitchik | 1954

A "Family Seated" Orthodox Synagogue   157
Julius Katz | 1956

SECTION 3 | Heresy Hunting

A New Religious Group in American Judaism?   159
S. Felix Mendelsohn | 1943

The Excommunication of Mordecai Kaplan   160
Agudath Ha-Rabbonim | 1945

The Conservative Beth Din   161
Fabian Schoenfeld | 1954

The Synagogue Council Ban   163
Eleven Roshei Yeshiva | 1956

A Conservative Converts to Orthodox Judaism   164
C. E. Hillel Kauvar | 1958

A Convert within Your Gates   165
Samson R. Weiss | 1958

CONCLUSION   166

PART 3. *A Modern Orthodox Movement*

7. Becoming Modern Orthodox Jews   **171**

INTRODUCTION   171

SECTION 1 | The New Orthodox Left

The Search for a Modern Orthodox "Ideologist"   172
Charles S. Liebman | 1965

Making Orthodoxy Relevant in America   174
Irving "Yitz" Greenberg | 1966

Dear Yitzchak   178
Aharon Lichtenstein | 1966

The Radicals   182
Walter Wurzburger | 1967

SECTION 2 | A Modern Orthodox Movement

The College Bowl *Sensation*   186
Yeshivah of Flatbush Student Government | 1963

Watching with Great Enthusiasm and Excitement   187
Fifth Graders of Hillel Day School | 1963

Modern Orthodoxy Is Not a Movement   188
Emanuel Rackman | 1969

A Modern Orthodox Movement   189
Norman Lamm | 1969

CONCLUSION   194

8. Orthodox, Inc.   **196**

INTRODUCTION   196

SECTION 1 | The Day School

Maimonides School   197
Shulamith Meiselman | 1941

A Rabbinical Supervisory Council for Day Schools   199
Torah Umesorah | 1944

Orthodox Student Pride   200
Gwendolyn R. Buttnick | 1967

SECTION 2 | Beyond the School
_____

Camp Moshava   202
Lillian X. Frost | 1945

National Conference of Synagogue Youth   203
Abraham I. Rosenberg | 1956

Drisha Institute for Jewish Education   206
Soshea Leibler | 1980

SECTION 3 | Yeshiva University
_____

Synthesis   207
Samuel Belkin | 1944

A New Beginning   209
Yeshiva University Office of Admissions | 1978

SECTION 4 | Industrializing Kashrut
_____

The "OU" Symbol   211
Herbert S. Goldstein | 1933

How Kosher Is OU?   212
Alexander Rosenberg | 1958

SECTION 5 | Interfaith Dialogue
_____

The Self-Appointed Spokesman   218
National Council of Young Israel | 1964

Confrontation   219
Joseph B. Soloveitchik | 1964

The New Encounter   225
Irving "Yitz" Greenberg | 1967

CONCLUSION   227

9. The Orthodox Synagogue and Rabbinate   229

INTRODUCTION   229

SECTION 1 | Rites of Passage

The Friday Night Bat Mitzvah   231
Oscar Z. Fasman | 1944

Fancy Parties and Busy Fathers   233
Joseph Speiser | 1961

SECTION 2 | A More Orthodox Sanctuary?

Law Is Law   235
William N. Ciner | 1952

The Reacculturation of the "Yeshiva Student"   236
Ralph Pelcovitz | 1960

The Social Politics of Shul   238
Samuel C. Heilman | 1976

SECTION 3 | The "New" Orthodox Rabbi

My Return to the Rabbinate   240
Anonymous | 1968

A Hero for the "Religiously Apathetic"   245
Steven "Shlomo" Riskin | 1972

Needed: Clinical Pastoral Training   247
Sherman P. Kirshner | 1988

CONCLUSION   248

10. **The State of Orthodox Belief**   250

INTRODUCTION   250

SECTION 1 | What Does Orthodoxy Believe?

The Core of Judaism   251
Herman Wouk | 1959

Minimal Set of Principles   253
Leonard B. Gewirtz | 1961

The State of Orthodox Belief—An Open View   256
Marvin Fox | 1966

The State of Orthodox Belief—A Less-Open View   260
Immanuel Jakobovits | 1966

SECTION 2 | Halakhah, the Modern Orthodox Way?

Halakhic Man and the Mathematician   264
Joseph B. Soloveitchik | 1944

Authentic Halakhah and the "Teleological Jurist"   267
Emanuel Rackman | 1954

The Letter and the Spirit of the Law   270
Immanuel Jakobovits | 1962

New York's Most Powerful Rabbi?   274
Ronald I. Rubin | 1979

CONCLUSION   275

11. **Responding to Tragedies and Triumphs**   277

INTRODUCTION   277

SECTION 1 | The Holocaust

Never Again!   278
Meir Kahane | 1971

The Voluntary Covenant   282
Irving Greenberg | 1982

SECTION 2 | Zionism and the State of Israel

*The Religious Zionist's Responsibilities in
"Galut" to "Eretz Israel"*   285
Bessie Gotsfeld | 1941

A Few Words of Confession   289
Joseph B. Soloveitchik | 1962

An Expression of the "Jewish Soul"   290
Joel B. Wolowelsky | 1970

The Six-Day War   292
Eliezer Berkovits | 1973

SECTION 3 | Communism, Vietnam, and Soviet Jewry

The Rosenberg Case   295
National Council of Young Israel | 1953

The Student Struggle for Soviet Jewry   296
Jacob Birnbaum | 1964

Rabbi Ahron Soloveichik's Opposition to the Vietnam War   298
Hamevaser | 1968

A Prayer for Soviet Jews   301
Haskel Lookstein | 1981

CONCLUSION   302

12. The Orthodox Family   304

INTRODUCTION   304

SECTION 1 | Ritual Purity and Birth Control

Five Reasons Why Every Jewish Woman Should
Adhere to Family Purity   305
Women's Branch of the Union of Orthodox Jewish
Congregations of America | 1941

Hedge of Roses   307
Norman Lamm | 1966

Commandment Number One: Birth Control   310
Herbert S. Goldstein | 1959

SECTION 2 | Tay-Sachs: An Ashkenazic "Disease"

Tay-Sachs Disease   312
Allan Kaplan | 1973

An Official Policy for Genetic Screening   314
Association of Orthodox Jewish Scientists | 1973

The Pros and Cons of "Mass Hysteria"   315
Moshe D. Tendler | 1977

SECTION 3 | The Prenuptial Agreement

Creativity in "Family Law"   316
Emanuel Rackman | 1973

In the Matter of Prenuptial Agreements   318
Rabbinical Council of America | 1993

Why Orthodox Rabbis Should Insist on a
Prenuptial Agreement   319
Saul J. Berman | 1993

CONCLUSION   322

13. **From Rebbetzin to Rabbah**   324

INTRODUCTION   324

SECTION 1 | The Rabbi's Wife

The Rabbi's Wife   325
Sara Hyamson | 1925

"My Occult Powers"   330
Channa Gerstein | 1947

The Role of the Rabbi's Wife   332
Theodore L. Adams | 1959

A Rebbitzen Respectfully Dissents   335
Helen Felman | 1959

SECTION 2 | A Female Synagogue Leader

Is Now the Time for Orthodox Women Rabbis?   336
Blu Greenberg | 1993

The Female "Congregational Educator"   339
Richard Kestenbaum | 1997

New Roles for Rebbetzins   341
Abby Lerner | 1998

Yes, We Are Orthodox, and Yes, We Hired a
Female Member of Our Clergy!   343
Adam Scheier | 2013

CONCLUSION   346

14. **Sliding to the Right and to the Left**   348

INTRODUCTION   348

SECTION 1 | The Center under Siege
_____

An American Zionist Lives a "Schizoid Life"   350
David Landesman | 1976

A Modern Orthodox Utopia Turned to Ashes   351
David Singer | 1982

"Centrist Orthodoxy"   354
Gilbert Klaperman | 1984

Gifter Slaughters Lamm for Passover   355
Mordechai Gifter | 1988

Baruch Lanner Will Be Your Rabbi   358
Elie Hiller | 1989

"Frum from Birth"   361
Anonymous | 1993

SECTION 2 | Sliding to the Right
_____

An "Unorthodox" Ad?   364
Haskel Lookstein | 1984

The Misleading Salesmen of Torah u-Madda   367
Paul Eidelberg | 1988

Trashing Torah u-Madda   369
Behnam Dayanim and Dov Pinchot | 1988

The Israel Experience   371
Esther Krauss | 1990

"I Never Saw the Rav Read a Secular Book"   373
Abba Bronspigel | 1993

SECTION 3 | Sliding to the Left
_____

Modern Orthodoxy Goes to Grossinger's   375
Shlomo Riskin | 1976

The RIETS Responsum on Women's Prayer Groups   377
Five Yeshiva University Roshei Yeshiva | 1984

The Affairs of the Rabbinical Council   380
Louis Bernstein | 1985

Piety Not Rebellion   381
Rivka Haut | 1985

"Very Little Halachic Judaism"   385
Eliezer Berkovits | 1985

"Modern Orthodox" and "Traditional Conservative":
Is an Alliance Possible?   386
Avi Weiss | 1989

Jewish Women Hear Muffled Voices   387
Laura Shaw | 1990

Take Rav Soloveitchik at Full Depth   391
Aharon Lichtenstein | 1999

CONCLUSION   395

15. **Reconsidering Modern Orthodox**
    Judaism in a New Century   397

    INTRODUCTION   397

    SECTION 1 | Loosening Grip

    Modern Orthodox Gedolim   398
    Dena Freundlich | 2004

    Stalemate at Stern College   401
    Cindy Bernstein and Norman Lamm | 2006

    Modern Orthodoxy's Demise   403
    Gary Bauman | 2011

    Social Orthodoxy   406
    Jay P. Lefkowitz | 2014

    The Freundel Affair   407
    Kesher Israel Board of Directors | 2014

    SECTION 2 | Modern Orthodoxy Reclaimed?

    Open Orthodox Judaism   409
    Dov Linzer and Avi Weiss | 2003

The Close of Edah   411
Saul J. Berman | 2006

Shirah Hadashah   413
Tova Hartman | 2007

A Statement of Principles   415
Nathaniel Helfgot | 2010

Taking Back Modern Orthodox Judaism   419
Asher Lopatin | 2014

CONCLUSION   423

Source Acknowledgments   425

Notes   441

Author's Note on Sources   489

Selected Bibliography   495

Index   501

Illustrations

1. Yeshiva University flyer inviting single women and men to a matchmaking program   xxxix

2. Eliyahu Holzman's 1865 pamphlet attacking Jewish reformers   44

3. "Pioneering" Yeshiva College undergraduates, 1929   122

4. Rabbis Tobias Geffen and Harry Epstein appeal to Atlanta Jews   144

5. Yeshiva University's *College Bowl* team, 1963   187

6. A "mifkad" flag ceremony in 1953 at Camp Moshava in Gelatt, Pennsylvania   204

7. Rabbi Joseph B. Soloveitchik delivering the inaugural Talmud class at Stern College, 1977   210

8 & 9. Advertisements from the Sunshine Company promoting their kosher products   214

10. Rabbi Shlomo Carlebach's song "Am Yisrael Chai"   299

11. Agudath Ha-Rabbonim's advertisement in *Jewish Week*, September 28, 1984   367

12. Yeshiva College student newspaper's cartoon of Rabbi Joseph B. Soloveitchik   374

13. Advertisements promoting Miami Beach hotels for Passover, 1980   378

14. Ban against women's prayer groups by a group of Queens Orthodox rabbis, 1997   390

15. Program cover of Jewish Orthodox Feminist Alliance conference, 1997   392

16. Cover of Rabbi Shmuel Herzfeld's "Open Orthodox" Passover Haggadah, 2015   422

Foreword | JACOB J. SCHACTER

In the last decade of the eighteenth century, Rebecca Samuel, then living in Petersburg, Virginia, wrote a letter to her parents in Hamburg, Germany, in which she explained why she was moving from that city to Charleston, South Carolina. She informed them that although her husband, Hyman, had earned the respect of their Gentile neighbors as a very successful clockmaker and silversmith, and although "one [i.e., a Jew] can live here peacefully," she and her family were "leaving this place because of [the lack of] Yehudishkeit," or Jewishness, which "is pushed aside here." She explained that the *shohet*, or ritual slaughterer, buys nonkosher meat, there is no Torah scroll in town, all Jewish-owned shops are open on the Sabbath, there are no educational opportunities available for her two children, and almost none of the worshippers on the High Holidays wore ritual prayer garments. "You can believe me that I crave to see a synagogue to which I can go. The way we live now is no life at all."[1]

The desire of Jews in America to be financially successful and respected by members of the community at large without sacrificing Jewish observance and communal cohesiveness has been a hallmark of Jewish life in this country from the very dawn of its existence. But those eighteenth-century Jews living in America were acutely aware that America was different than the countries from which they had emigrated and in which many of their family members and religious authorities still lived. In a letter written in 1785 to a rabbi in Amsterdam seeking guidance on a complex issue challenging their community, two lay leaders in Philadelphia noted that they were "anxiously awaiting" the rabbi's reply "because this matter touches the very essence of our faith, especially in this country where everyone does as he pleases [*asher kol ish ha-yashar bi-enav ya'aseh*]." They wrote that in America, "the Kahal has no authority" over those who live in its midst, unlike the situation in Amsterdam and in many of those countries and communities they had left behind.[2] In the old country, the community still had a hold, to a greater or lesser extent, on those who lived within its geographical boundaries. In America, by contrast, the ability of the community to exercise any power was severely limited, as its leaders were only too acutely aware. And, some half-century later, a note written to a couple leaving Bavaria for Cleveland began with the warning, "Friends! You are travelling to a land of freedom where the opportunity will be presented to live without compulsory religious education."[3]

Living in America, with its emphasis on freedom, democracy, and individualism, was—and continues to be—both a blessing and a challenge to perpetuating Jewish values and practice in this country. It is a blessing because Jews have been afforded an unprecedented opportunity to exercise their religion unhindered by external controls and constraints. At the same time it serves as a real challenge because in a world without any "compulsory" prerogatives, any choices—including those to define and reject Jewish practice and identity—are possible and even celebrated. And the more traditional the values and practice, the greater the challenge to its perpetuation.

In this American world that celebrates personal autonomy and individual choice, Orthodoxy has found a place. For more than a hundred years it lived in the lives of dispersed individuals committed to it who acted alone, bereft of any institutional infrastructure or support, and then somewhere in the second half of the nineteenth century, it found expression in robust communities that were beginning to be founded and developed. True, Orthodoxy's place in American Judaism was far from assured; even as late as the 1950s its "decay" was predicted and noted in respected circles.[4] But American Orthodoxy has resoundingly confounded these negative prognostications. The greatest sociological surprise (or miracle, depending upon one's perspective) of twentieth- and twenty-first-century American Judaism is not only the dogged continued presence of Orthodoxy in this country, defying all odds, but the extraordinary growth that it has experienced. With increasing confidence, institutional strength and extraordinary unselfconsciousness, Orthodoxy has achieved a presence and prominence in America simply and literally unimaginable even fifty years ago.

But one cannot speak of one religious group identified as American Orthodoxy. Sociologists generally divide that group into Ultra-Orthodox (including "Hasidic," "Yeshivish," and even "Heimish") and Modern Orthodox, each with its own set of assumptions, beliefs, and practices while sharing much in common. This book is devoted to exploring these categories in the Modern Orthodox community.

The fundamental point of departure of the Modern Orthodox perspective is generally described as combining a commitment to living a life shaped by Halakhah with an acknowledgment of the legitimacy, value, and, for some, even the necessity of "non-exclusively Torah" disciplines and cultures to enhance one's human personality and even one's spiritual religious persona. Of course, this combination certainly predates modern times.[5] However, it has been brought more sharply into focus in the last decades as Orthodoxy has confronted the ever growing diminution of religious authority, the values and demands of feminism, the task of identifying the theological significance of the State of Israel, the claims of a larger and vocal liberal community, secularism, academic Jewish studies including biblical criticism, claims for the primacy of individual conscience, and cultural relativism. Inherited truths and assumptions have been challenged by a range of contemporary values, and the effort to retain a commitment to both has led sometimes to creativity and original thinking and sometimes to frustration, inconsistency, and even conflict.

We are greatly indebted to Dr. Zev Eleff, already an outstanding scholar in the field of American Jewish life, for tracing the history and current state of this social and intellectual movement through a series of carefully chosen primary texts. Blessed with a prodigious intellect, wide-ranging knowledge, firsthand engagement with his specific subject matter, clarity of writing, richness and depth of religious commitment, indefatigable energy, and generosity of spirit, Dr. Eleff has produced a volume that enables its reader to grapple with the complex issues of identity and ideology, religious practice and social behavior, rootedness in tradition and openness to new ways of thinking and acting that define Modern Orthodoxy both in private as well as in public spaces. Dr. Eleff explores the inherent complexity in maintaining a commitment to both "Modern" and "Orthodox," and he does so with great nuance and sensitivity. This work will be invaluable to those interested in the challenges of living meaningful religious lives in our contemporary world, Jews and non-Jews alike.

In the second half of his poem entitled "Tourists," the late Israeli poet Yehuda Amichai, wrote:

> Once I sat on the stairs at the gate of David's Tower and put two heavy baskets next to me. A group of tourists stood there around their guide and I served as their orientation point. "You see that man with the baskets? A bit to the right of his head, there's an arch from the Roman period. A bit to the right of his head." But he moves, he moves!! I said to myself: redemption will come only when they are told: You see over there the arch from the Roman period? Never mind: but next to it, a bit to the left and lower, sits a man who bought fruit and vegetables for his home.[6]

There is much wisdom here, of course, but the worldview of Modern Orthodoxy argues that Amichai is wrong. At the end of the day, both the "arch from the Roman period" (the tradition) and the "man who bought fruit and vegetables for his home" (the contemporary) need to be in conversation, both celebrated and affirmed at the same time. Our thanks to Dr. Eleff for helping us appreciate the vital necessity—and complexity—of this most important effort.

Preface

In June 1869, a New York Jewish newspaper reported on what it observed to be a new spectacle in Europe. In Prague a number of Jews had identified as "Specific Orthodox." The abstruse term indicated a religious viewpoint that could be plotted somewhere in the wide gulf between "Strict Orthodox" and "Radical Reform."[1] In Berlin critics accused a congregation of a disingenuous posturing between these same two poles of Judaism. In response, a most ardent traditionalist commentator warned his readers against joining with the "miscreants."[2] Reformers in the United States noted all of this, dubbing both cases examples of "Modern Orthodoxy," which they judged to be a "most paradoxical phenomenon in Judaism."[3] They were not alone. Later, and in a much more strident tone, Rabbi Emanuel Schreiber of Chicago declared that "Modern Orthodoxy is a ridiculous farce."[4]

Others used the term to describe a specific segment of America's Jews, but in a more favorable fashion. In the 1860s, a leading spokesman for the Independent Order of B'nai B'rith used it to boast of his fraternal organization's diverse membership. The writer described how "the ancient Orthodox, the modern Orthodox, the Conservative Reformer, and the Radical Reformer sit side by side in the Lodge Room."[5] In 1883 a group of Jews in Rochester parted ways with a Reform congregation but could not find a comfortable place within the local Eastern European Orthodox enclave. Instead, they founded a "modern Orthodox" synagogue. The German Jewish extracts attempted to keep with the "spirit of the times" but desired a worship that was "not quite so radical as to be considered 'unqualified reform.'"[6] "Modern Orthodox," they decided, dutifully described that goal.

In this post–Civil War era, "Modern Orthodox" Judaism served as a marker of religious observance and ritual. Yet it was not always the most useful religious nomenclature; there was no consensus on what exactly the label represented. The same was true of the "Moderate Reform,""Radical Reform," and "Conservative" designations. Distinctive movements within American Judaism did not begin to emerge until the first decades of the twentieth century.[7] Meanwhile, "Modern Orthodoxy" remained a contested symbol of religious identity between leaders of the Orthodox Union (OU) and the Jewish Theological Seminary (JTS) in New York. The situation persisted until after World War II, when most abandoned the title since the earlier disputes rendered the term a hollow catchphrase without concrete meaning.

This is no longer the case. At present, 3 percent of about five million American Jews affiliate with Modern Orthodox Judaism despite the fact that there is no central institution that can claim ownership of the camp.[8] In New York, Yeshiva University competes with relative upstart Yeshivat Chovevei Torah for rabbinical students. The newer seminary preaches a more "Open" form of Orthodox Judaism.[9] It is not entirely clear that either school is interested in serving as a flagship for the Modern Orthodox movement.[10] Other institutions relate similarly equivocal attitudes. Long ago, an observer warned of the religious unevenness of the Rabbinical Council of America (RCA) and the Young Israel synagogue movement, a quality that continues to persist into the present.[11] Likewise, a concerned rabbi once charged that another and much larger synagogue organization, the Orthodox Union, was "completely under the influence of the extreme right."[12] The veracity of these claims is beside the point. That commentators have questioned the Modern Orthodox bona fides of these institutions bespeaks their religious fluidity and diversity. It also signifies the decentralized nature of Modern Orthodox Judaism.

Notwithstanding this latter matter, there exists an agreeable—although somewhat vague—description of this religious group's creed. In 2013 the Pew Research Center defined the Modern Orthodox movement as a religious group that "seeks to follow traditional Jewish law while simultaneously maintaining a relationship with modern society."[13] The pollsters separated this cohort from Hasidic and Yeshivish breeds of Orthodox Jews. Modern Orthodoxy's adherents can trace their movement to the late 1960s, when Rabbi Norman Lamm led a resurrection of Modern Orthodox Judaism from a depressed and fallow state.[14] He was not in the majority at first. Other leaders refused to wear the mantle. Some leading lights of Orthodox Judaism "detested" the Modern Orthodox marker.[15] In those days, no less a leading figure than Rabbi Emanuel Rackman pronounced that "one can hardly regard modern Orthodoxy as a movement." He insisted that it was "no more than a coterie of a score of rabbis in America and in Israel whose interpretations of the Tradition have won the approval of Orthodox intellectuals who are knowledgeable in both Judaism and Western civilization."[16]

Rackman was wrong. As its leading spokesman, Lamm reenergized a most lethargic community. In the 1960s, a Louisville rabbi "postulated that Orthodoxy has made far greater strides in the past fifteen years than it had made in the preceding fifty."[17] Lamm deserved much of the credit for this upswing.[18] The New York rabbi and future president of Yeshiva University championed an Orthodox Jew's ability to "maintain our undiminished loyalty to the Halakhah" (Jewish law) while completely engaged in the societal currents that flowed around him or her, leaving behind any and all "antagonistic attitudes."[19] Lamm was helped along by a cadre of committed young people who likewise proved Orthodox Judaism's compatibility with postwar American culture.[20] They exercised a spirit that broke from an emerging right-wing enclave. In contrast to the so-called Ultra-Orthodox Jews, the young Modern Orthodox supported Zionism, advanced education for women, and dialogue with leaders of other Jewish religious movements. Most of all, they convinced others to follow their lead.

Of course, the tenets of American Modern Orthodox Judaism were not without precedents. In the nineteenth century, Rabbis Samson Raphael Hirsch and Esriel Hildesheimer modeled a religious outlook that bridged the worlds of traditional Judaism and modern culture.[21] However, Hirsch's program did not support Zionism, nor did the Frankfurt ideologue approve of the critical Judaica scholarship known in Europe as Wissenschaft des Judentums. Hildesheimer departed with Hirsch on these two points, but his antagonism toward cooperation with non-Orthodox Jews also separates him from the later incubators of Modern Orthodox Judaism in the United States. Moreover, neither German rabbi embraced the designation of "Orthodox" (and certainly not "Modern Orthodox") to describe their religious missions. Hirsch much preferred "Gesetzestreuer Juden" (Torah-Faithful Jews).[22] In 1873 Hildesheimer founded a rabbinical school in Berlin that he called the Rabbiner-Seminar für das Orthodoxe Judentum. Yet he dropped the "Orthodox" moniker ten years later, as he no longer required it to distinguish his curriculum from Zacharias Frankel's more liberal rabbinical school in Breslau.[23] In fact, Hildesheimer favored Hirsch's formulation and made good use of it. In 1897 he established the Vereinigung traditionell-gesetzestreuer Rabbiner (Union of Traditional Torah-Faithful Rabbis) to provide German Jewish clergymen with a rabbinical organization that would be free from intradenominational mingling.

The Modern Orthodoxy conjured up by American Jews, then, divided itself from these earlier models in both name and motif. It drew its approach to traditional Jewish learning from the yeshivot in Eastern Europe. It borrowed its Zionist ideals from twentieth-century thinkers in Israel and the United States.[24] In addition, this American movement also differs from similar groups in present-day Israel. Unsurprisingly, the so-called Dati Le'umi Jews in the Holy Land emphasize Zionism more than their traditional coreligionists in the United States. Yet there exist even more profound differences. In Israel, wrote one sociologist, the religious Zionists desire to "leave nothing outside the boundaries of religion."[25] Perhaps something of an overstatement, it is certainly the case that Dati Le'umi Jews are prone to create an integrated religious culture in Israel that does its best to transform somewhat secular elements like politics and business into religious experiences.[26] In keeping with the teachings of Rabbi Avraham Yitzhak Kook and his son, Rabbi Zvi Yehudah, they do all this for the sake of a fervent messianic Zionist agenda.[27] Modern Orthodox Jews in the United States are comfortable with a far more "compartmentalized" lifestyle.[28] True, religiously observant Jews accept the dictates of Halakhah in all areas of life, but this hardly rivals the sort of religious pathos achieved in Israel. In the Holy Land, there is much and recurring discussion on Judaism's responsibility to govern public policy, legislation, and Sabbath bus schedules. In the United States, Orthodox Jews have preferred to abide by the separation of church and state, relegating Judaism to carefully circumscribed religious spheres (e.g., the synagogues and schools). To a large extent, American Modern Orthodoxy is indeed an amalgam of earlier incarnations. However, its complex makeup makes it unique to its time and place. To put it succinctly, Modern Orthodox Judaism is a movement indigenous to North America.

Today, hundreds of synagogues and day schools unite under the banner of Modern Orthodoxy.[29] In many instances, the leaders and followers of this religious community hold up Rabbi Joseph B. Soloveitchik as their "symbolic exemplar" rather than bother to articulate a well-formulated approach to their convictions.[30] Known endearingly as the "Rav," Soloveitchik ordained thousands of Orthodox rabbis at Yeshiva University. He was a master Talmudist and a brilliant Berlin-trained philosopher. In fact, the Rav eschewed designations that might narrow his reach, but there is little doubt of his utility in advocating the cause of Modern Orthodox Judaism.[31] In 2014, for instance, the Judaic studies principal of Maimonides School in Brookline, Massachusetts, averred that it was the Rav's "ideas and writings that helped shape Modern Orthodoxy."[32] While Soloveitchik may not have viewed it as his charge to cultivate Modern Orthodox Judaism, he remains the crucial figure and "human pillar" of the movement.[33]

Still, the Modern Orthodox community is far from coherent. Online dating websites offer users the choice to identify as "modern Orthodox-liberal" or "modern Orthodox-machmir" (stringent), among other categories.[34] Furthermore, supporters do not all agree on the extent that adherents can engage in secular and liberal realms. For example, recent commotion over an approved approach toward homosexuality proves the difficulty of achieving consensus.[35] What is more, proponents of Modern Orthodox Judaism part ways over the application of various areas of Halakhah to contemporary life. To be sure, most Modern Orthodox Jews observe the Sabbath and maintain high levels of kashrut observance. Yet many disagree on how to interpret Jewish law in both public and private spheres. To offer fiercely contested examples of each: rabbis and laypeople argue about the appropriate role of women in sacred spaces and the use of birth control.[36] The current condition of this tension-filled community can be understood by placing Modern Orthodox Judaism in its historical context. This collection of texts seeks to accomplish exactly that.

Time Period

The struggle to adhere to Halakhah and interact with "modern society" preceded Norman Lamm, as well as all varieties of Jewish life in the United States. It remains a difficult matter for scholars to decide the boundaries of the "premodern" and "modern" periods of Jewish history.[37] Yet we may pinpoint with precision the moment that "Orthodox" Jews began grappling with this problem in the United States. In 1825 a band of young Jews founded the Reformed Society of Israelites in Charleston, South Carolina.[38] The group produced a revised worship and altered the Maimonidean Articles of Faith to a religious system that better suited its progressive platform.[39] In the United States, the organization of this short-lived "heterodox" society pushed more traditional elements to designate themselves as adherents of "Orthodox" Judaism, especially once Reform congregations emerged in other areas like Albany, Baltimore, and New York. Before then, the term held no meaning for Jews in the New World.[40] Modes of worship were "traditional." Violators of Jewish law were deemed miscreants; they were hardly ideologically or steadfastly "reform."[41]

Subsequent to the Charleston affair, Orthodox Jews fought against a tide of religious reform that suggested that the old customs and rites were outdated and out of touch with modern American sensibilities. Some traditionalist enclaves withdrew from the debate altogether, choosing instead to sequester themselves in synagogues that retained the Old World customs and traditions.[42] Most, however, looked for some sort of balance between tradition and modernity, whether they realized it or not. Accordingly, the majority of Orthodox congregations in the United States tapped rabbis or ministers to deliver weekly English sermons and deleted some of the optional sections (piyutim) from their prayer books.[43] Neither change would have been countenanced earlier. Worshippers appeared in synagogue dressed in elegant modern attire, refusing to wear the outmoded outfits and styles worn by their coreligionists in Europe.[44] In increasing numbers, the leading exponents of Orthodox life were Jews who could present their cases with exceptional knowledge of Jewish and philosophical sources. Orthodoxy modernized, even as it repelled its Reform rivals.

Owing to this, I have selected documents and materials for this book that pertain to much more than the current, most solidified iteration of "Modern Orthodox Judaism." Part 1: "Orthodox Judaism and the Modern American Experience" reaches back to the nineteenth century. Then, self-identifying Orthodox Jews contended and defended their cause against a host of competing elements. Historians estimate that about 2,500 Jews lived in the United States in 1800. Sixty years later, the Jewish population increased to 150,000.[45] Most of these immigrants hailed from Central Europe, and they brought with them German practices that differed substantially from the rituals of Portuguese Jews (Sephardim) who had settled in British America.[46] Rather than clash with the old guard, the newcomers established their own communities and built synagogues to fit their German traditions. The new congregations were influenced by other currents as well. In the middle decades of the nineteenth century, Reform gained a sturdier foothold in Europe. In time, German émigrés transmitted this more liberal religious culture to American Judaism, as did reform-trained ministers. Also, homegrown American Protestant culture stressed values like decorum and domestic refinement.[47] Orthodox Jews did their very best to keep pace with these incoming trends, but also defended their creed as more authentic than other, more reformed incarnations.

Many of the sources in this first part explore the Orthodox reaction to reform. In particular, some of the most important polemics surrounded the immutability of the Oral Law (Torah she-Ba'al Peh) and proposed changes to the traditional prayer book. In addition, this collection includes texts that show how so-called Orthodox women and men behaved in their traditional Jewish lives. In other words, the texts demonstrate "lived religion" rather than statements of principles and declarations by the rabbinic elite. Further, these documents offer particular insight into the development of this community. This period was also marked by the transformation of religious authority that shifted power from the laity to the American rabbinate. While this change is more evident within Reform ranks, Orthodox congregations also raised the stature of their clergymen. The best example of this took place toward the end of the century. In 1886, traditional ministers led a movement to establish a rabbinical seminary in the United States. They insisted that the Jewish Theological Seminary of America was an "Orthodox" school.

Part 2 details the "Contest for Modern Orthodox Judaism." In large measure, the competition was started by the emergence of a new cohort on the American Jewish scene around the turn of the twentieth century.[48] Jews from Russia and Poland immigrated to the United States in droves. In 1880 the Jewish population totaled at most 300,000. Forty years later, when the mass migration was near an end, Jews numbered more than three million women and men in the United States.[49] Some of the new arrivals viewed the United States as a "Goldene Medine" (golden land) whereas others treated it rather gloomily as a "Treifene Medine" (unkosher land).[50] The latter group of greenhorns resisted entry into the existing religiously traditional congregations and institutions. They preferred to establish their own organizations, which claimed a more "authentic" form of Orthodox Judaism. In response, another legion of Jewish leaders vowed to protect the core of their faith and accommodate to American norms.[51]

Many who sided with this second group were also a part of the Orthodox Union and the Jewish Theological Seminary and branded themselves "Modern Orthodox."[52] Nationwide, young Americans started to describe themselves as "moderns," to separate themselves from their Victorian forebears.[53] Moreover, to all of these men, the term indicated a set of beliefs that fell somewhere in between Eastern European Orthodox and Reform Judaism. Still, the label lacked precise meaning, since it was employed by Jews of varying religious and ideological stripes. This was intentional, an attempt to appeal to Jews who considered themselves "traditional" yet "modern" and those whose "orthodoxy" served as the most important adjective in their religious identities. Accordingly, in 1920 a "prominent rabbi" in the South placed an advertisement in a New York newspaper to publicize that he "would consider a change of pulpit," so long as it was situated in a "conservative or modern orthodox congregation."[54] This circular shows, quite reasonably, that a broad branding scheme was a smart marketing strategy employed by traditional clergy. What is more, the "accommodators" did not all share the same beliefs.

Eventually, the Orthodox Union men turned to other descriptors that did not confuse their mission with those of JTS. The same held true of the Rabbi Isaac Elchanan Theological Seminary (RIETS). In the school's first concerted attempts to place rabbis in synagogues, the school's leaders tried to persuade congregations to use clearer terms. In 1928, for example, a RIETS administrator responded to a letter from a Nebraska synagogue with the following request: "Please advise by wire what you mean by Modern Orthodox congregation. Our graduates while American born modern in fullest sense of the word are however strictly orthodox."[55] Most JTS graduates at this time found greater comfort in affiliating with Conservative Judaism rather than any denominational subset such as "semi-Reformed" or "Modern Orthodox."[56] Orthodox and Conservative leaders started to truly move in separate directions.

Consequently, few rabbis or laypeople made use of "Modern Orthodox" in the 1930s and 1940s. Traditional Jews who did not seek refuge within Conservative Judaism shied away from it, since it was a relic of an earlier iteration of Conservative leaders. Consider the musings of a rabbi in Chicago:

One of the Thirteen Articles of Faith, which the orthodox Jew recites daily, says, "I believe with perfect faith that this Torah will not be changed, and that there will never be any other Torah from the Creator, blessed be His name."

Orthodoxy therefore maintains that basic Judaism is not subject to change. Thorndike's Senior Dictionary defines the word "modern" as "up-to-date, not old-fashioned," which plainly implies the principle of change. For this reason the expression "modern orthodoxy" is a contradiction in terms. It is employed by orthodox congregations which admit that they are bending toward conservatism.[57]

Others may have attempted to rescue "Modern Orthodox" from confusion but ultimately decided against that course of action because of the ambiguity that had surrounded the phrase for decades; one young person, no doubt with Conservative Judaism in mind, noted that it still carried "severe connotations."[58] The nomenclature was therefore simultaneously freighted with historical baggage and loaded with insufficient ideological meaning.

This changed in the late 1960s as Lamm and a crop of young Orthodox leaders breathed new life into the Modern Orthodox brand. Part 3 of this book investigates the development of this Modern Orthodox movement. One of the difficult matters is counting this population. In 1958 one expert estimated that the Orthodox population in the United States was just more than 500,000 women and men.[59] Since then, the reports issued by the National Jewish Population Survey indicate that the Orthodox community has numbered anywhere from 400,000 to nearly 600,000. Of course, only a portion of these figures represents the "Modern Orthodox" enclave. This section pays close attention to the social, intellectual, and cultural identifiers of the burgeoning religious group. In addition, Modern Orthodox leaders reacted to monumental events like the Holocaust and the founding of Israel. Modern Orthodox Judaism grappled with these subjects and, of course, feminism in the last decades of the twentieth century. The concluding sources in this volume indicate the internal tensions and external pressures on Modern Orthodox Jews.

שבת
Shenk Singles

קיץ
Shabbaton

Come join the Yeshiva Community Shul and YU Connects
for an inspiring and entertaining Shabbos

Join Community families for dinner with other great
singles, an Oneg and then a lunch with facilitators from the
Community and Rabbanim, Followed by the Motzei Shabbos
Shenk Saturday Night Live Comedy Evening
Shabbos Vayakhel 25th Feburary
22nd Adar I

A great Shabbos, with great friends, and even better food!

Members $35 Non-Members $45

For Modern Orthodox
Machmir Singles
Ages 21 - 31

RSVP to ycsshidduch@gmail·com
by February 15th
All profiles will be reviewed by Shadchanim
Who will help you meet that someone special!

In 2011 this flyer was distributed on Yeshiva University's men's campus in New York. While the YUConnects matchmaking program serves many different kinds of Orthodox Jews, this circular targeted singles who identified as "Modern Orthodox Machmir." Courtesy of Yeshiva University.

In this period, Modern Orthodox Judaism was not a contested title. At this historical juncture, other religious movements like Conservative Judaism and the Ultra-Orthodox possessed features and institutions that fully separated them from Modern Orthodoxy. In fact, Rabbi Shimon Schwab of the Ultra-Orthodox variety rarely missed a chance to point out "all the drivel and distortions spoken or written by some of the so-called 'modern-orthodox' spokesmen."[60] This does not mean that Modern Orthodox Judaism remained stagnant. To the contrary, its movement was indexical, sometimes sliding to the right and at other times to the left. The religious group was dynamic while also volatile. In some sense, Modern Orthodoxy's struggle to maintain cohesion is the historical narrative that links each document in this book. No doubt, the religious debates and dilemmas will ensure that Modern Orthodox Judaism remains both curious and provocative for many years to come.

Acknowledgments

In 2006 David Singer stated matter-of-factly that the "history of modern Orthodox in the United States is yet to be written." Its historians, continued Singer, will no doubt include the "Greenberg-Lichtenstein exchange of 1966" in the Modern Orthodox narrative. In fact, this book includes the confrontation between Rabbis Irving Greenberg and Aharon Lichtenstein, as well as 154 other important documents that help explore the developments and transformations of Modern Orthodox Judaism in the United States. I did not work alone in accumulating and preparing these primary sources for publication. To the contrary, I was helped along by colleagues, friends, and family. It is my pleasure to acknowledge them and express my boundless gratitude for their support.

First, I thank Barry Schwartz and Carol Hupping of the Jewish Publication Society for their invitation to work on this project and their invaluable help in seeing this book to completion. I am very grateful for their professional advice and encouragement throughout this process, as well as the entire staffs at JPS and the University of Nebraska Press. I also acknowledge the generous financial support of the Landes family, as well as their belief in the importance of this book. In addition, I benefited from the wonderful help of dedicated archivists and librarians. I obtained several foundational documents, photographs, and important information for this anthology with the help of Gary Zola, Kevin Proffitt, and Elise Ho of the American Jewish Archives, Arthur Kiron and Bruce Nielsen of the Herbert D. Katz Center for Advanced Jewish Studies at University of Pennsylvania, Melissa Simmons of Hebrew Union College, Jan Schein of the Chizuk Amuno Congregation Archives, Moshe Kolodny of the National Orthodox Jewish Archives, Jeremy Katz of the Cuba Family Archives for Southern Jewish History, Maggie McNeely of Brandeis's Robert D. Farber University

Archives, Ruth Wallasch of the Architecture and Fine Arts Library at USC, Simon Elliot of the Library and Special Collections at UCLA and the staff at the London Metropolitan Archives. Finally, I am always indebted to Shulamith Berger, Moshe Schapiro, and Deena Schwimmer of the Yeshiva University Archives and Gottesman Library. For a number of years, Deena, Shuli, and Moshe have happily supported my scholarship and guided me through the vast materials held in their facilities. In particular, I thank Shuli for her friendship and motivation to aid my work in American Jewish history.

I am very grateful to the historians and scholars who reviewed sections of this work and pushed me to think harder about the history of Modern Orthodox Judaism. Foremost, this documentary history is a credit to my teachers. Jeffrey Gurock of Yeshiva University has dedicated much of his career to the history of Orthodox Jews in the United States. The number of scholars reading and writing on American Orthodox Judaism has much to do with his pioneering efforts. This book was made possible because of his scholarship and mentorship. In addition, Jonathan Sarna trained me at Brandeis University to think broadly and critically about the history of American Judaism. As usual, he shared his knowledge and countless hours to improve this anthology. Similarly, I owe much to Jacob J. Schacter for his continued mentorship and devotion to my work. With sensitivity and rigor, Rabbi Schacter offered crucial insight throughout the production of this history. I extend my gratitude, as well, to Menachem Butler, Adam Ferziger, Sylvia Fishman, Eli Genauer, Bruce Ginsburg, Gil Graff, Eugene Sheppard, and David Starr for their criticisms, ideas, and suggestions that helped shape this work. Jonathan Engel read every page of this book and made it much better. In addition, I am grateful to David Ellenson, Yitzi Ehrenberg, Rachel Feingold, Hillel Goldberg, Meir Hildesheimer, Elie Hiller, Haskel Lookstein, Adam Mintz, Freda Rosenfeld, Jeffrey Saks, Barry Stiefel, Gil Student, Yair Sturm, Harvey Sukenic, Shimon Unterman, and David Wolkenfeld for their aid on specific sections of this volume. I also thank the juniors and seniors at Maimonides School who studied dozens of these documents in my classroom and offered wonderful comments that inform a number of the annotations in this book. I also acknowledge Alan Kadish and Brian Levinson of Touro College and Hebrew Theological College for believing in and tapping me to help lead their schools. I excitedly look forward to working with them in Chicago.

Finally, I offer boundless thanks to my family. Their love and support has in some respects transformed this project from a scholarly endeavor to a very personal project. No doubt, my grandparents Esther and the late Jack Moss were two Holocaust survivors among thousands who "overwhelmingly chose to re-create Jewish life." Morton and Annette Eleff, my paternal grandparents, are first-generation Americans who moved Orthodox Judaism to the suburbs and embraced the challenge of building schools and synagogues. My parents, Susan and Scott Eleff, were of a new breed of Orthodox Jews who benefited from the undertakings of their forebears and furthered those labors to enhance the Modern Orthodox cause. Similarly, my in-laws, Paul and Marcy Stieglitz, experienced and remain committed to much of the same work. My wife, Melissa, and I discuss these matters often. I love her more than I could have imagined, and her help and support of this book reminds me of my great fortune to share a life with her. Our wonderful daughter, Meital, has learned much about American Jewish history in her first three years of life. In return, she has taught me much more and given more profound purpose to life. Jack is our peppy one-year-old who arrived just after I completed the manuscript of this book. I dedicate this work to him. After all, he and his sister are the greatest treasures I can offer to the future of Modern Orthodox Judaism.

Modern Orthodox Judaism

PART 1 | Orthodox Judaism and the
Modern American Experience

1 | Engaging Reform

On November 21, 1824, a group of disenchanted Jews submitted a petition to the trustees of Congregation Beth Elohim in Charleston. The young, sizable cohort—forty-seven men signed the "memorial"—requested a truncated Sabbath and Hebrew-free worship.[1] The letter reflected concurrent sentiments in Europe, but was unprecedented in American Jewish life from the time Jews first moved to the New World in 1654. The trustees refused, explaining that their bid was out of line and in breach of the congregation's sacred constitution. Turned down, the "handful" of petitioners established the Reformed Society of Israelites. Led by playwright and journalist Isaac Harby (1788–1828), the Charleston circle drafted bylaws that vowed to uphold the Law and the Prophets and the Five Books of Moses but made no mention of the Talmud or any other Jewish sacred texts.[2] In 1825, on the first anniversary of the group's petition to the Charleston congregation, Harby made it clear that his friends embraced the "true legitimate authority of the Bible," but he also pledged to "throw away Rabbinical interpolations" of Judaism.[3] He compared his reformist efforts to Martin Luther (1483–1546), who "shook the papal supremacy to its foundation."[4] This, then, was the first organized Reform-styled Judaism in the United States.

Opposition followed. Jacob Mordecai (1762–1838) of Richmond, Virginia, penned a lengthy response to Harby's widely disseminated discourse. He accused the Charleston reformers of besieging the "fortress of Judaism" with their "banner of skepticism." In New York, traditional Jews happily received Mordecai's remarks in the hope that it might "steady the minds of the wavering amongst us."[5] In addition, Mordecai Noah (1785–1851) slammed the Charleston circle for their work to "retrograde" American Judaism. Perhaps the leading Jew in the United States at this time, Noah's opinion mattered, although he did not—nor could he, in all probability—refute the heterodox planks of the Reformed Society as Mordecai had tried to do in his discourse. Instead, Noah resorted to political jargon replete with rhetorical flare that had so well suited other American writers.

Neither Mordecai nor Noah stymied the reformers' labors. Something else did. In 1828 Harby moved from Charleston to New York. To be sure, the economic decline of Charleston had much to do with the religious drain. Yet Harby's departure deflated the society far more than his antagonists' attacks. Still, Charleston remained the cradle of American Reform Judaism.[6] In the 1840s, a number of the Reformed Society's leading men helped push Beth Elohim in this direction. Led by its minister, Gustavus Poznanski (1804–79), the congregation rid itself of a number of rabbinic dicta. Most notably, the Charleston clergyman removed the second festival day from the major Jewish holidays and installed an organ in the synagogue's sanctuary.[7] Once again, a number of self-appointed defenders of Orthodox Judaism denounced the new wave of Charleston reformers. These efforts slowed the tide of reform, but could not block it altogether.

Moving forward, protectors of traditional Judaism engaged reform, but not always under the banner of Orthodox Judaism. In 1845 Isaac Leeser (1806–68) of Philadelphia was unconvinced that he needed to identify squarely with an "orthodox party in Judaism."[8] In time, Leeser accepted this designation but not until the lines between him and Reform ministers solidified. The fluid barriers of affiliation bothered a number of the staunchly Orthodox Jews in America. The other critical matter in this period was the varieties of Orthodox religious life. In fact, an affiliation with an Orthodox enclave was not a predictor of adherence to Jewish law. Desperate to provide for their families—or to earn enough to pay for their voyages to the New World—Jewish men believed that they had no choice but to labor on the holy day. Some of their more fortunate coreligionists attended synagogue on the Sabbath, but flouted Halakhah in a different manner: they married non-Jews. In many instances, intermarried Jews would have claimed that their exogamous lifestyle was due to love or social status and had no bearing on their beliefs in Judaism.[9] Perhaps more than matters of Jewish belief, these everyday problems were the most vexing that these Orthodox Jews faced in the United States.

SECTION 1 | Charleston Clamorings and Other "Heresies"

"Retrograde Instead of Advancing"

Mordecai Noah | OCTOBER 18, 1825

Mordecai Manuel Noah was a politician, newspaper editor, and communal leader. In his lifetime, he served as consul to Tunis and chairman of the John Tyler Central Committee and Grand Sachem of Tammany Hall. Noah was a leading member of New York's Shearith Israel congregation and delivered the keynote discourse at the congregation's synagogue consecration ceremony in 1818. He also led a number of Jewish charitable organizations. In this editorial, Noah responded to a question he had received about an upstart Reform movement in Charleston, South Carolina.

A weekly religious journal printed in this neighborhood lately stated that a schism had taken place among the Jews in Charleston, S.C., one portion of which had determined to relinquish the Hebrew language and adopt entire new forms. The journal alluded to expresses an opinion that it is intended to lead to a conversion from their ancient faith.[10] To do away [with] such an impression, and to protect the fidelity of the pious, it is proper to state, that the reform contemplated, originated with a few persons, descended from Jewish parents, but who are unacquainted with the essential forms of the religion.[11]

One of the new-lights is now employing himself in attempting to ridicule any effort to make the U. States an asylum for his oppressed and unfortunate brethren; and in this work he is seconded by the Editors of the *National Gazette* and the *American*, who have never, we believe, felt disposed to aid any nation of the old world in enjoying the freedom and benefits of the new.[12]

If the works of charity and patriotism; if duty and inclination, could be checked by the sneers and ridicule of such men, we should retrograde instead of advancing, and those who were enemies to their country in time of war cannot wish to strengthen that country in time of peace.[13]

New Lights and Old Lights

A Member of the Reformed Society of Israelites | OCTOBER 28, 1825

The Charleston reformers responded to Mordecai Noah's unfavorable view of their operation. Historian Gary Zola suggested that the writer was probably David Nunes Carvalho (1784–1860) or Isaac Nunes Cardozo (1786–1855), both members of the Reformed Society of Israelites.

Mr. Editor.—I perceive that the essay, signed "Common Sense," which appeared in your paper a few weeks past on Mr. Noah's ridiculous proceedings at Grand Island, has excited the anger of that gentleman.[14] He has given way to some intemperate remarks in his Journal, on its being published in some of the leading papers at the north, with compliments on the beauties of the composition—on the discrimination and good taste it evinced—and its being one of the best communications on the subject of which it treats, that has been yet published. Mr. Noah, without attempting to overturn any of the positions in "Common Sense," sneers at the production, and attempts to ridicule it, because, forsooth, the author is what *he* calls one of the *"new lights"*—that is one of the large and respectable number of Israelites, who are only aiming at a few reforms in the present mode of worship in this city; whose chief object is to have a part of the service said in English (the Hebrew language being almost obsolete as a vehicle of communication, and but little understood) so that *all* may understand what is said and be able to appreciate it accordingly. They never did and never will attempt, as it is said by Mr. Noah, to strike at the fundamental principles of their faith; they consider them as of too ancient and sacred a character to be meddled with. The Editor of the *Advocate* may rest assured that all such paltry attempts to parry the successful blows that are aimed at his foolish plans and productions are totally unavailing—they show the scantiness of his material and display his impotence. It is of no avail, we assure him, to show his anger, because his title as Governor and Judge of Israel will not be acknowledged: It is of no use when he cannot rebut argument by argument, to *call names*—such conduct is splenetic and boyish. Before we part, however, we would whisper a wholesome truth in Mr. Noah's ear. He should know that public opinion has some virtue in it, and is of great force and influence in all countries and on all occasions:—when, therefore, Mr. Noah persists in standing on such a slender foundation as *his own* talents and influence (Heaven save the mark) in spite of the very general terms of reprobation and ridicule his late conduct has met throughout the country, he must expect to be overturned, as often as the ground on which he stands is weak and untenable.

This Happy Land

Isaac Harby | NOVEMBER 21, 1825

Isaac Harby was an educator, journalist, and playwright. The extent of his Jewish education is unclear, although he did possess a number of volumes of Judaica in his library. In 1825 he joined with other disenchanted Charleston Jews to found the Reformed Society of Israelites. Harby may not have been the architect of the movement, but due to his fame in the non-Jewish world, he quickly emerged as the spokesman of the group. He delivered a discourse on the first anniversary of the Reformed Society. The published edition of his talk, of which the first pages are reproduced here, circulated among Jews and very prominent non-Jews such as Thomas Jefferson (1743–1826) and John C. Calhoun (1782–1850). Elsewhere in his remarks, Harby blasted "Rabbinical interpolations." In his opening comments, though, he made it clear that his vision was to fit Judaism into the wider realm of American religion.

It is almost superfluous to inform you, my respected friends, of the purpose for which you are this day assembled. It is to celebrate the first Anniversary of a Society, whose existence—whose name alone—forms an era in the history of your race, gratifying to every Philanthropist. The great cause of Improvement in Government, in Religion, in Morals, in Literature, is the great cause of mankind. Bigotry and Despotism may rear their "miscreated fronts" to thwart your way, but the consuming beams of Truth must drive them back to their original darkness.[15] In this happy land, however, you have no such obstacles to oppose;—equality of laws and freedom of conscience leave you a wide and cheerful field to act upon.[16] You have no enemies then, but the inveteracy of habit, and the timidity of ignorance. Against these you have already struck a noble blow; be true to yourselves and the victory is your's. The man who meanly crouches to mental oppression is an object to be pitied by the good, contemned by the courageous; but he that nobly breaks the intellectual chain, and stands forth the champion of Reason and of Virtue, is a being honorable to the earth from which he sprung, and approved of by that heaven to which he aspires.

In the short revolution of a single year, what a spectacle does your Society present! You began your career with only a handful of men; some of them not yet determined how far their fears or their wishes might carry them. Your opponents falsely prophecied that this "handful" would soon melt away, and the "Reformed Society of Israelites" dissolve into air.[17] But the spirit of the constant among you has been diffused throughout the whole mass, and you can now enumerate a respectable number,—trifling indeed for the purpose of moving mere "brute matter"—but one of immense *moral force* in the cause in which we are embarked. The pen of Luther was the great intellectual lever which shook the papal supremacy to its foundation,—why may not the virtuous example of a few Israelites, then, shake off the bigotry of ages from their countrymen?—Your principles are rapidly pervading the whole mass of Hebrews throughout the United States. The progress of truth, however slow, is irresistible; and I should not wonder if the principles I speak of were to settle permanently among the Jews of Europe, even before the despotic governments of that portion of the globe extended to our countrymen the political privileges of their other subjects.

But the consideration of what may be effected abroad is but of minor importance to the great and *practical* objects we have in view. Our sphere of action is at present limited to *home*. It is in Charleston, and—in its more immediate consequences—in the United States, that we are to look for the experimental development of our system. What is it we seek? The establishment of a New Sect? No; never. Let other systems of religion split into a thousand schisms; let other modes of faith present to your eyes the motley scene at which Philosophy may smile, and true Piety must weep—brethren instructed in a religion of mercy warring against each other by the arm of flesh and the weapons of theological pride. Let these examples of human error be seen in other religions—but it is the glory and test of the Jewish faith that its followers worship one God—that when they raise their hands to veil their eyes, and repeat—"Hear O Israel, the Lord our God, the Lord is One" (Deut. 6:4)[18]—they regard only the God of their Fathers, the Lord of all creation, the Supreme Jehovah. This be your boast, this be your bond of union.

A Jewish Luther

Jacob Mordecai | 1826

One of the more learned Jews in early nineteenth-century America, Jacob Mordecai was an educator and communal leader in Virginia. Mordecai became well known for his polemics against Christian missionaries. He also prepared a handwritten twenty-five-page response to Isaac Harby's anniversary discourse delivered before the Reformed Society of Israelites in Charleston in 1825, copies of which reached Jews throughout America. Much of Mordecai's remarks consisted of detailed expositions of the Bible. This excerpt includes the first volley of Mordecai's attack on Harby, in which the author offers more general comments on Harby's "reform" program.

We have read the discourse delivered by Mr. Harby to an assemblage of persons calling themselves the Reformed Society of Israelites in Charleston transmitted to us by a member of that body. It was our first intention to let it pass unnoticed—but on further reflection the bold and unhesitating manner of the author seems to defy any explanation on the part of the congregationalists; we will nevertheless presume to examine the principles he advocated and test their solidity and their orthodoxy by the translations of Holy writ. The matter contained in the first pages of the address is a repetition of the remonstrances to the Junta, tho it is not everywhere in unison with it—this part of the subject has been already noticed in communications to the corresponding Society.[19] The impression we received in sending that remonstrance has been fully confirmed by the recent address, that the object of the master spirit was to destroy the ancient fabrick of Israelite worship and to gradually undermine all confidence in their religion under the pretext of divesting it of Rabbinical impurities and interpretations; the Seal of this gentleman (who presents himself to notice in the character of the reformer) is to us a little paradoxical, for if we are rightly informed he has not been a member of the Jewish congregation for the last Ten Years or subjected himself to any inconvenience by conforming to either the Mosaic or Rabbinical laws. We fear he knows too little of the customs, their origin, force or value &/or that little is indebted to Hebrew writers.

We shall continue to remark on some parts presented to our view in a style rather too familiar for the subject, and combining topicks totally irrelevant to it. Like Luther, he is desirous of being a pioneer whose pious zeal is to clear the paths and deliver his countrymen from the bigotry of ages. We are however disposed to doubt the affinity of their respective cases, as well as the correctness of the assertion that "the pen of Luther was the great intellectual lever which shook the papal supremacy to [its] foundation." Were we disposed to contest this position we have ample means at hand to prove the reformation cannot be solely credited to Luther, others had preceded him without success, but many power causes contributed at that precise period to promote a change—a combination not likely to occur in favour of the present champion of Jewish reform. We refer those inclined to pursue this unpromising subject to [Abraham] Ruchat's history of the reformation, to Homer, and to other historians.[20] We have no wish to examine a controversy which led to blow and slaughter, to the fire and the stakes, to every degree of atrocious persecution and spiritual intolerance—we take no interest in the variant faith of the hundreds of sects to which that reformation has given birth. They should serve however as lessons to our brethren and teach them to avoid the shoals and quicksands upon which others have been wrecked.

In discussing a subject interesting only to the Jews we should studiously avoid all contact with any of the prevailing sects of the popular religion,—professing equal respect for them all. We do not mean to insinuate that the intellectual powers of the author of the discourse are inferior to those of his great prototype or that they are incapable of moving the "mountains of bigotry from the foundation in which they have been imbedded since the days of Moses," could he exercise his powers on a less confirmed, less stubborn and less stiff necked sons? The reformation now proposed we believe has nothing to plead in common with that which is held out as an encouraging example to the disciples of his school. The synagogues possess no wealth, the Rabbis no immunities, they pretend to no vicarious authority to pardon sins, lay claim to no hereditary or miraculous powers, and wallow neither in Riches or Luxury. This ephemeral attempt may engender evil, spread divisions in families, encourage popular prejudices by diffusing erroneous statements, without producing a single benefit worth the struggle it is making to bring itself into notices. It may for a time weaken the pecuniary resources of the local synagogue, but it will add nothing to its own means. The one may fall, but the other cannot rise upon its ruins—like other reformers they will, if their views are ever realized by gaining the ascendancy over their brethren, become enthusiasts, subscribers of every established system, levellers of everything human, perverters of everything divine within the pales of the synagogue that opposes their fanciful system.

An Open Letter to Gustavus Poznanski

Isaac Leeser | 1843

Isaac Leeser was a minister and Jewish communal leader in Philadelphia. A native of Westphalia, he rose to prominence as the minister of Philadelphia's Mikveh Israel and as editor of the Occident, *America's first long-lasting Jewish newspaper. In his monthly, Leeser championed Orthodox Judaism against reformers like Charleston's Gustavus Poznanski and, later on, Rabbi Isaac Mayer Wise (1819– 1900) of Albany. In this open letter published in his newspaper, Leeser called on Poznanski of K. K. Beth Elohim to defend himself against charges of "heresy" and his supposed denunciation of the medieval philosopher Moses Maimonides's (1138–1204) Principles of Faith.*

Rev. Sir,

Were I to follow my own inclination, I would to a certainty not disturb you in the retirement which you have just now sought by your voluntary abdication of the office of minister, for which you had been elected during life by your late constituents.[21] But as I have a duty to perform to the religious community of Israelites in America, who have heard of your official conduct, and as your retirement took only place, as one may judge, in consequence of the commotion which your official acts have produced in a once united congregation:

I feel myself imperiously called upon to address you in this public manner, in order to obtain, if it meets your views, a full exposition of your ideas on religion, which I herewith promise to lay before the public in the same vehicle through which I address them now.

. . . There is yet one subject connected, with the received doctrines of our church, to which I must call your attention.[22] I alluded to your reputed opinion in the last number of the *Occident*, page 209, in the paragraph commencing "Several painful rumours"; then I could hardly credit it, though I could not doubt the veracity of my informants.[23] But since that passage was written, I received the *Charleston Observer*, a paper in the interest of the Presbyterian Society, and edited by the

Rev. B. Gildersleeve.[24] The number before me is that of June 17th, and contains among other things the following:

Among what we have been in the habit of regarding as the fundamental articles of the Jewish creed, are, 1st, the unity of God—2nd, the resurrection of the dead—and 3rd, the coming of Messiah. And we had always understood that the Jewish people generally interpreted the prophecies as teaching the literal return of their people to the promised land.

But if our correspondent were present at the dedication of the New Synagogue, he will probably recollect that the officiating Rabbi, in his eulogy upon this city and land, spoke of them as the only Jerusalem, and the only Palestine, which he and his people, who were enjoying our free institutions, either desired or sought.[25] We do not profess to give the words; but the substance of his address was reported in the *Courier*, to which reference can be had. From this we inferred that the officiating Rabbi and his people in the city did not believe in the literal return of the Jews to the promised land. And this opinion was confirmed by a subsequent interview with him less than a year since. And at the same time we received the impression that neither he, nor those attached to his peculiar views on this point, believed in the *personal* coming of Messiah. He seemed to us to take the same liberty in interpreting the prophecies of the Old Testament touching Messiah, that he had previously done touching the return of the Jews. It struck us that he regarded both not in a *literal* but in an *emblematical* point of view—and that free institutions—a cessation of hostilities—and the general prevalence of peace and good-will among men, constituted the only Messiah which he anticipated.[26]

I have learned since, from undoubted authority, that you should have expressed similar views to my friend the Rev. Wm. T. Brantley, D.D., of the Baptist connection, and the Rev. Mr. Barnwell, of the Episcopal church.[27] I might, perhaps, be inclined to doubt the correctness of the memory of all these three gentlemen (which I admit would be acting very unjustly to them,) were it not that the *creed*, as affixed to the walls of your late Synagogue, gave the amplest confirmation to the correctness of their recollection.[28] It seems your twelfth and thirteenth articles are in these words, the correctness of which I presume you will probably admit:

12. "We believe that the Messiah announced by the prophets is *not* come, the prophecies relating to his coming *not being fulfilled.*"
13. "We believe that the soul is *immortal,* and that we shall be accountable for our actions in the life to come."

Upon this I have to remark, that if you believed in the bodily coming of the Son of David, and did not view him merely as an ideality, some philosophical image: you would not have altered the words of the usual creed, which are, "I believe with a perfect faith in the coming of the Messiah; and although he tarry I will nevertheless look for him daily that he may come." In brief, I cannot understand how not believing in the accomplishment of any thing can be a matter of belief, or creed. The wording of your profession of faith is apparently merely antagonising to Christianity. This is the first time in my life that I have learned that it is the duty of Israelites to refer to the opinions of any set of men, however respectable for talents and numbers, as a part of their profession of faith. Our religion stands independently and maintains the same position as regards doctrines and duties, which it did from the beginning. Now before the alleged coming of the Messiah, it would certainly have been singular to asseverate "that he had not come," as a matter of faith; and I really do not understand how the ideas of Christians that he has come, can affect our creed so as to require the alteration of its words which you have either introduced or countenanced. But drop your concealment if you have any; do you believe or not that the Messiah will come? Or do you believe that he has neither appeared nor will appear? For your wording is so obscure that it may bear either interpretation. Do let us know, that we may be able to understand in what light you wish Judaism to be regarded, whether as a fabric, frail and changeable, or based on the Rock of Ages, unchangingly the same.

Lastly, with respect to your thirteenth article as quoted above, it certainly is not what we have a right to expect from a Jewish divine who professes to teach religion as he has received it. Our creed is: "I believe with a perfect faith that there will be a revival of the dead at the time it may be the pleasure of the Creator, whose name be blessed, and whose memorial be exalted for ever and unto all eternity." The immortality of the soul is included in the eleventh article, which speaks of rewards and punishments, and is, by the by, an idea which many of the heathens believed in; but the *resurrection* is a peculiar Jewish doctrine, and to this we must profess ourselves as sons of Israel. Do you believe in it? or think you that they who sleep in the dust of the earth will not arise to everlasting life?

I will not weary you any longer, my letter being already more extended than I could have wished; but it is much too short yet to express all my views on the important subjects herein embraced. But when I have your views, I shall add such remarks as I may deem necessary, and if you decline answering, it will then be time enough to enlarge upon points which I have now omitted.[29]

In conclusion, I beg leave to assure you, that though opposed to reform as carried on by yourself, I am not opposed to legitimate improvements in the manner of conducting our public worship; but I want the sanction of men who have made religion the business of their lives, whose piety is a warrant that they will do nothing to yield to public clamour which it would be wrong to yield upon grounds of law and solid reason. Yet so much has been done already without authority that I verily believe that it would be safer to retrench than to extend reform. Whatever can be done in a legal manner has or will be done by our ecclesiastical chiefs; and even their reforms I would look upon with suspicion, unless their necessity and practical usefulness were clearly established.

Probably I may be branded with the epithets "hyperorthodox, dark, rabbinist"; whilst in truth many others will believe me to be too free and bold in my opinions. Yet in the middle course there is always safety and not rarely the path of truth. Still, I shall not be terrified from that which

I consider the strict line of duty, and hope to be strengthened by that aid which we all stand in need of. I trust that you will agree with me in saying that we require no agitation. Persecution long terrified us in our houses and in the field; and now, when peace from abroad dawns upon us, let those who are the leaders endeavour to scatter peace also within the dwellings of Israel. What, are we so much wiser than our progenitors, to maintain that whatever they did was foolish and unsound? Must we for such reasons endeavour to break down the ancient landmarks and the fences of the law? May the Guardian of Israel forfend this, and may his blessing bring an increase and prosperity to the good cause of the law of his bestowal.

In the name, therefore, of our common faith, a religion dear to the heart of all Israel, I call upon you to pause, and to withdraw yourself from the dangerous course which you have, I hope thoughtlessly, been pursuing; join your efforts, Mr. Poznanski, to those of others to restore peace in the midst of your former congregation; yield the interest of a party for the good of the whole community; and receive the favour of your God, the approbation of your conscience, and the applause of thousands of honest hearts, as the reward for the sacrifice which such a step may for a moment require of you.

Yours respectfully,
Isaac Leeser
Philadelphia, Tamuz 27th, 5603.

"Some Wolves Clothed in Sheep's-Cover"
Abraham Rice | 1848

Rabbi Abraham Rice (1800–1862) migrated to the United States in 1840, making him the first ordained rabbi (conferred upon him by Rabbi Abraham Bing [1752–1841] in Würzburg) to settle in the United States. He accepted a position at the Lloyd Street Synagogue in Baltimore. By all accounts, the pious Rice endured a miserable ministerial career and retired from the rabbinate in 1849, although he continued to play a role in the Jewish community and returned to congrega-

tional work at the very end of his life. In 1848 Rice wrote to Isaac Leeser to ask that the Philadelphia minister cease his cooperation with "Reform" leaders in the United States. To make his point, Rice drew upon traditional texts as well as recent events in Europe. In the end, Leeser's efforts to convene a conference with more religiously liberal elements were squashed, more by lack of congregational interest than by Rice's stern warnings.

BALTIMORE, 15TH DEC. '48

My Dear friend,

I think, we are acquainted enough to talk with you freely, what my humble opinion is, about the convention of Rabbis, spoken of in your last Periodical.[30] I know very much, that you are sincere in religious matters and you are the last who wants to make any innovation, but let me tell you as a friend you have to consider also that in your early times you were mingled with the American life; many of your ideas will not do for true Judaism, though you may think it is no harm in it. The Kuzari says: "Your intention is pleasing [to God] but your actions are not pleasing."[31] Further you know that we have a certain class, which the word "Religion" is every moment in their mouth, but in the heart is nothing as selfishness and the true God fearer is wanting. What benefit shall arise from this "reunion"? If we all act according to our Shulhan Arukh, one Jew can live in one corner of the world and yet we have with him one rule and regulation.[32]

... Is the Convention of the German Rabbis lost from your memory?[33] Are our Rabbis better men? Have we not some wolves clothed in sheep's-cover? How is it possible to establish equal reform in our prayers? And if it were possible, what is done for true religion? These all are only form and not essential parts of religion. Would or can this convention establish rules for keeping the Sabbath strictly? That every married Jewish lady has to go to mikveh?[34] Or will come the question from them to abolish the second day of the holidays? I, for my part, can tell this prophecy, that the latter question will come sooner off. ... In the same manner, I consider such a Convention.

We like to be like other sects. They have their convention; we must have ours too. Our Shulhan Arukh is our Conference.

. . . My Dear, I hope you will not find yourself offended by my talking. You know me—for out of the abundance of my complaint and grief have I spoken hitherto. Take therefore the admonition of a true friend and consider well, before you go in for such a step; reflect seriously on the consequences of introducing such a Convention who will be attended with dangerous consequences.

I remain for ever
Your truly friend and humble servant
   A. Rice

N.B. You must not laugh about my language. I write in English only for that reason, to make me more acquainted with the words.

What Prevails among the Jewish People?
Mordecai Noah | 1850

In 1850 Rabbi Isaac Mayer Wise participated in a series of debates with Rabbi Morris J. Raphall at Charleston's Beth Elohim (Reform) and Shearit Israel (Orthodox) congregations. During this episode, Wise declared that he did not believe in the Resurrection of the Dead or the Coming of the Messiah. Maimonides had canonized both religious beliefs in his Principles of Faith, a widely accepted Jewish creed. This was the first major radical proclamation issued by Wise since he arrived in the United States in 1846. In turn, Mordecai Noah was asked to comment on this event and offered an incredulous response. He took the matter far less seriously than Leeser had in his letter to Gustavus Poznanski on the very same matter.

Question: "I read in one of our papers the startling fact that a learned Jewish rabbi had openly declared in Charleston that he had no belief in the resurrection of the dead or in the coming of the Messiah. Is this an isolated case with your people, or is it the prevailing belief?"

Answer: The rabbi did make that declaration, but played the hypocrite as to his own belief.[35] He was applying for the place of reader of a reformed Jewish congregation; but not understanding the extent of the reform, which was merely ceremonial and not doctrinal, he ventured upon this declaration and was of course rejected.[36] A belief in the resurrection of the dead and in the coming of the Messiah universally prevails among the Jewish people.

SECTION 2 | Living Orthodox Judaism

This Is Religious Liberty in America
Abraham Kohn | 1843

Abraham Kohn (1819–71) emigrated from Bavaria in 1842. The twenty-three-year-old began peddling, moving westward until he reached Chicago. In 1847 a now financially established Kohn served as a founding member of Kehillath Anshe Maariv. In the meantime, Kohn struggled to observe basic Jewish law. He recorded his religious failings and the guilt that came with that in his diary, a section of which is reproduced here.

God in Heaven, Father of our ancestors, Thou who hast protected the little band of Jews unto this day, Thou knowest my thoughts. Thou alone knowest of my grief when, on the Sabbath's eve, I must retire to my lodging and on Saturday morning carry my pack on my back, profaning the holy day, God's gift to His people, Israel. I can't live as a Jew. How should I go to church and pray to the "hanged" Jesus? Better that I be baptized at once, forswear the God of Israel, and go to Hell . . . by the God of Israel I swear that if I can't make my living in any other way in this blessed land of freedom and equality, I will return to my mother, brothers, and sisters, and God will help me and give me His aid and blessing in all my ways.

The open field is my temple where I pray. Our Father in heaven will hear me there. "In every place where thou shalt mention My name I shall come to thee and bless thee." This comforts me and lends me strength and courage and endurance for my sufferings. And in only two more weeks I shall find something different.

Millerism seems to be somewhat on the decline, and I don't hear as much of it as formerly.[37] Mormonism is another superstition which, in the progressive and enlightened nation, seems to make strides. A certain Joe Smith, now living and preaching to the people in the western states, claims to be the true prophet of God, a priest of Melchizedek.[38] He purports to have found the true Bible and rejects Jesus, Moses, and Mohammed alike. He proclaims a new religion to the credulous people and, absurd as it seems to me, it is reported to have more than thirty thousand disciples. Terrible!

For more than three months I have not been in the mood to continue my diary or to write anything at all: In the middle of March I had hoped to get rid of my peddler's existence. But I was forced to take up my pack again, and from February 26th to March 11th, I journeyed towards Worcester, where I was to meet my dear brothers. On March 1st, I came to Worthington, where I met a peddler named Marx, from Albany, married and an immigrant from Frankenthal in Württemberg. Wretched business! This unfortunate man has been driving himself in this miserable trade for three years to furnish a bare living for himself and his family. O God, our Father, consider Thy little band of the house of Israel. Behold how they are compelled to profane Thy holy Torah in pursuit of their daily bread. In three years this poor fellow could observe the Sabbath less than ten times. And he is a member of the Jewish congregation in Albany. This is religious liberty in America.

Our Holy Place

Trustees of the Congregation Shearith Israel | 1847

Intermarriage was a fact of life for the Portuguese Jews who constituted the first cluster of Jews to migrate to the New World. According to one scholar's tabulation, nearly 30 percent of American Jewish marriages from 1776 to 1840 involved a Christian partner. Many Jews married Christians because of their social status and close business dealings with non-Jewish communities. At first, most Jewish congregations tried to avoid punishing intermarried members. This document, therefore, reflects a change in tolerance and mind-set of New York's leading congregation. The first Jewish congregation founded in America (probably in the 1720s), K. K. Shearith Israel in New York, took public action against intermarriage by disseminating this message to its members.

NEW-YORK, 4TH NISSAN, 5607

Sir,

At a Meeting of the Trustees of the Congregation Shearith Israel, the following was adopted.—

Resolved, that no Seat in Our Holy Place of Worship, shall hereafter be leased to any person, married contrary to our religious laws; and no person married contrary to our religious laws, shall be entered in any of the Burying Grounds belonging to this Congregation.

Ordered, that the Clerk send a printed copy of the foregoing resolution, to each seat holder.

Extract from the Minutes.

N. Phillips, Clerk.

Strange Misbehavior
Max Lilienthal | 1854

Max Lilienthal (1815–82) arrived in the United States in 1845. His reputation as a traditionalist and university-trained scholar preceded him to the United States. In New York, he served as the rabbi of three German congregations but lost his position a few years later after a public disagreement with lay leaders. For a while, Lilienthal remained in New York, earning his living as a teacher. Shortly after he published this survey of Jewish life in a New York newspaper, Lilienthal accepted a call to lead a congregation in Cincinnati, where he began to openly explore reli-

gious reform. This excerpt of his observations offers a candid view of Orthodox Jewish life in New York in the mid-nineteenth century. It was published under Lilienthal's thinly veiled pseudonym, LD, the initials of "Dr. Lilienthal" reversed.

There is no doubt that a great disharmony, a great diversity of views and opinions, prevails in the camp of Israel. Instead of the former blissful peace and harmony, which was our shield and strength, there are now few points, upon which a unanimous verdict would be given. It is of no use to call upon the reformers with the accusations: you have proposed and introduced all kinds of innovations, and thereby estranged the hearts of the parents from the children, and the hearts of children from the parents. It is of no avail to exclaim, the orthodox party by their immovable stability have forced the opposition, to leave their doctrines and to try for themselves what they possibly could do. The disharmony exists for one cause or the other; the sickness shows itself with all its symptoms and the question arises, what remedy has to be applied in order to avoid the imminently dangerous consequences. Let us for this purpose review the different parties.

There is firstly: the large mass of the people that simply believe all and everything which has been transmitted to them from former ages. They do not inquire after the sublime doctrines of their religion; they do not investigate the difference of their creed from that of other denominations; they have no idea of the future destiny of their faith; they are satisfied that they are born as Jews; notwithstanding all kinds of persecutions they feel themselves happy as Jews; and they hope and wish and pray to die as Jews. No doubt arises in their minds; no comparison between the decayed condition of their nation and the flourishing state of other people suggests itself to their reasoning faculties; they are fully and entirely satisfied if they can live and observe the religious ceremonies as their blessed ancestors have done; and if they are enabled, to attend daily to the service in the morning, afternoon, and evening, if they can have a Kosher housekeeping, if they can observe the Sabbath and the holidays, then all their wishes are fulfilled, for they are as good Jews as their fathers of blessed memory ever have been. They like the mystic and mystery; they are fully convinced that by reading a chapter of the Mishnah they work for the best of their soul; that by strict observance of every Minhag [religious custom] they perform a duty towards God and win especial favor. They look around them, and seeing so many changes, they sigh and long for the good times gone by, but feel themselves not in the least affected by the most astonishing alterations. They believe—and belief and faith make them happy and contented.

There is a second party that has already come more in contact with the world and that with sagacious foresight understands very well that something must be done to satisfy the wants of the time. It is the party of external order and decorum. They know that the disorder that prevailed in the synagogues of old cannot be tolerated any more; that a choir and sermon can be introduced in the service without giving up an iota of Orthodoxy; that although even this is reform and may fairly be called Chukat Hagoyim [Ways of the Gentiles], some concessions have to be made if the service shall not be disserted by a large number of their coreligionists. They are willing to add something to the services and religious ceremonies, but will never agree that anything should be subtracted therefrom. They do not wear their beard any more in the nine days of Ab; they shave them themselves on Yom-tob, &c. but consider themselves anyhow as good Jews as the first class, who are willing to banish and excommunicate at any cost and any risk, reform and reformers.[39]

There is a third class who have made great concessions to life and its exigencies. For the sake of becoming wealthy and independent they have opened their stores and magazines and violated the Sabbath; for the sake of having a start and making their living, they went peddling in the country and ate at every farmer's table. Or there are others who have two kinds of Shulchan Aruch, one regulating them while they are at home, and the other when they are abroad. At home they keep strictly every minute ceremony, but abroad they indulge in the luxuries of the first-class hotels; they enjoy the delicacies of the watering places without feeling their religious conscience troubled or molested in the least. They do not give themselves any account of this strange misbehavior, they do not ask and do not answer who allowed or permitted them to do so; necessity in the beginning urged them so to act, &c., they got used and accustomed to it, and habits will become our second nature. Notwithstanding these misdemeanors, they consider themselves orthodox, firmly and fiercely opposing any reform. We have to live in this way, they will assert, we cannot help it, wife and children must be supported; but as soon as we shall have accumulated some fortune we shall again become pious and will convince you that we are no hypocrites. Well, this is the party of momentary exceptions [Hora'at Sha'ah] and privileges, and this party, especially in this country, is a very large one. They may indulge in all kinds of exceptions, but would combat it with all their might if any Rabbi legally would sanction these exceptions. Their motto is: I may be drunk, but my driver must be sober.

An Aunt's Admonishment

Anna Marks Allen | 1858

Anna Marks Allen (1800–1888) was a leader of Philadelphia's Jewish community. She was active in the Female Hebrew Benevolent Society (est. 1819), and served as its treasurer for four decades. Allen was one of the founders of the Philadelphia Jewish Foster Home and Orphan Asylum (est. 1855) and led the organization as its first directress. She also helped form the Jewish Sunday school in Philadelphia (est. 1838) led by Rebecca Gratz (1781–1869). This document sheds light on the responsibility of Jewish women to uphold their faith and to encourage men and boys to do the same.

PHILA., JUNE 28, 1858

My dear Lewis,

Accompanying these few lines, you will receive articles suitable for a Boy soon to become *bar mitzvah,* and with them accept the love and Blessing of your aunt who sincerely congratulates you on your attaining so important an Epoch in your life.

May you live to be a credit to yourself, a comfort and Blessing to your dear parents, and the Pride and protector of your sisters. As your God Mother, my dear Lewis, I may be allowed the privilege, perhaps, of speaking to you of the Many *Duties* and *Responsibilities* which every *Day* and *Hour* of your life increases and assumes a more important character.

In the first place, my dear Boy, let the duties you owe your *Maker ever* predominate over every other. Diligently study our *Holy* laws and Ordinances, so that when you look upon the Sacred Emblem of *Faith* (The Tzitzith) you may be reminded that *no Tem[p]tation* that the world can offer may induce you to forsake your God. And when you Bind upon your Body the *Tephillin*, you Must remember that it is not *only* intended to Commemmorate the Chief Commandment of the Mosaic Religion, but that we Must *Obey* and *do* them, so that the Mantle that Envelops you when in the House of God may not prove a Covering for *vain thoughts* and Evil *Imaginations*.[40]

Next comes, my dear Lewis, your *duty* to your parents. I cannot point out a more impressive and beautifull passage by which to Govern your actions than that contained in the fifth Commandment: "Honor thy Father and Mother" (Ex. 20:12). What a vast amount of Duties do these Emphatic words contain! To Define them, my dear Nephew, would take a more able pen than mine, but let us hope as you advance in Youth and Manhood that the Instruction you Receive from your dear parents and Teachers, and your own good sense, may develop them. And may the *Holy One* of *Israel Enlighten* your *Eyes* and impress them on your *Heart* that you may "do *always* that which is Right in *His* Sight"

   Is the prayer of your
     Aunt Ann

CONCLUSION

In 1848 Rabbi Abraham Rice of Baltimore complained in rather broken English about Isaac Leeser's partnership with reformists. He pleaded with Leeser to narrow his circle of religious leaders, but Leeser would not relent. Instead, the Philadelphia minister labored to convene a meeting of congregational leaders for the purpose of unifying American Judaism. That the convention did not take place is beside the point. In the earliest incarnations of Reform, the leading defenders of the "old ways" eschewed the mantle of a separatist Orthodox Judaism, even as others viewed them in that theological costume. Fluidity, then, was the dominant feature of religious discourse in this period.

Rabbi Rice's losing battle over religious observance highlights another area of religious fluidity. Earlier, in 1840, Rice arrived in New York, the first ordained rabbi to migrate to the United States. In Gotham, the Orthodox scholar was invited to deliver a Sabbath sermon at Congregation Anshi Chesed. Of that discourse, one layman recalled much later that Rice declared "that his mission in coming to America was to establish the true orthodox faith in this country."[41] In all probability, the Bohemian preacher had in mind that his "true" form of Orthodox faith would conquer the non-observant rather than the nascent reform culture within American Judaism. Of course, many Jews remained punctilious in their religious observance and faced the consequences of their resultant social and economic limitations. These women and men insisted that God would assist them. If not, they vowed to return to Europe where they would suffer hardship, but at least they could do this together with a larger cohort of uncompromisingly vigilant Jews. Finally, probably the largest group of Jews in the United States found a middle ground. These Jews strictly abided by the cardinal obligations of Jewish law but opted out of other, more "flexible" areas of religious life, as described by Max Lilienthal. Most important, all of these types worshipped in Orthodox congregations while they frowned upon the minority of the Jewish population that wandered off to the growing number of Reform synagogues. In a real sense, Orthodox and observance had little correlation, if any at all.

2 | The Traditional Talmud and Response to Reform Prayer Books

In October 1843 a New York Jew took particular notice of a letter printed in Isaac Leeser's monthly journal. The correspondence derived from the pen of Benjamin Cohen Carillon (b. 1810) of the Danish West Indies, who proffered his beliefs on the sacredness of the Talmud. It was, to the Manhattan reader, a "source of gratification" that the Philadelphia minister published an essay that "at last broached the subject of rabbinical authority."[1] The matter had elicited much attention in Europe, as Orthodox and Reform leaders debated the flexibility of the Jewish laws decided in the Talmud's oral tradition rather than being explicitly stipulated in the Bible. Long ago, Maimonides had challenged earlier sages who had assumed that Moses received the entire Oral Law at Sinai.[2] Maimonides cursed this "bizarre" suggestion. He insisted that while the methods for interpolation were divinely transmitted, the laws themselves were man-made.[3] The Maimonidean position remained the dominant view until the nineteenth century, when Orthodox defenders like Rabbi Samson Raphael Hirsch (1808–88) found it insufficient in their debates with reformers.[4] To them, Maimonides offered too much power to men, especially those who sought to augment or alter rituals and religious behaviors. Instead, Hirsch and others claimed that each word of the Oral Law was derived from Heaven; Reform Judaism, therefore, was heretical for attempting to modify any part of the Talmud's statutes and ordinances. In time, the Talmud debate migrated to the New World and further loosened the ties between traditional and liberal Jewish leaders.

Theology was certainly not the only point of controversy. More obvious ritual changes also occupied the minds of religiously conservative

Jews. The Orthodox vociferously opposed a number of reforms introduced in American synagogues. They took exception to the removal of the *mehitzah*, the partition that separated women and men during prayers, as well as the deletion of the second festival day of major holidays from the Jewish calendar.[5] But traditionalists deemed the transformation of Jewish worship the most egregious offense of all. In the 1850s, Reform rabbis published revised prayer books. In 1855 Rev. Leo Merzbacher (1809–56) of New York's Temple Emanu-El edited a modified prayer book.[6] One year later, Rabbi David Einhorn (1809–79) published his much more radical *Olat Tamid* for the use of his congregation in Baltimore.[7] In 1857 Isaac Mayer Wise's *Minhag America* appeared in Cincinnati.[8] Orthodox Jews viewed the reformers' emendations of the traditional prayer book as a direct affront to Jewish life. For them, the form of worship was more than just a theological statement; it stood for the memories and traditions that had passed through generations of Jewish women and men. In a sense, the prayer book symbolized Orthodox Jews' connection to the Old World and provided them with the strength to carry that link forward to their children and grandchildren.

SECTION 1 | Talking Talmud

"The Talmud Is Not Divine"

Benjamin Cohen Carillon | AUGUST 10, 1843

In 1842 Benjamin Cohen Carillon was appointed minister of a large congregation (five hundred members) on St. Thomas in the Danish West Indies. The congregation had looked for someone of "gentlemanly deportment, possessing a thorough knowledge of the English language, a strict Mosaic believer, a liberal man who does not place rabbinical writings on a level with the Pentateuch." Carillon's letter to Leeser certainly proved him at least partially qualified to fit this profile, although his overall stormy tenure on St. Thomas ended in 1846. The

remainder of Carillon's biography is sparse after this point. In any case, Leeser
published Carillon's letter on Reform and the Talmud in his Philadelphia news-
paper, the Occident. *It set off a lively discussion on the nature of the Talmud*
and its role in Jewish life.

Rev. Isaac Leeser,

Respected Friend,—As I know how much you are interested in the welfare of our people, and above all, in their religious development, I believe it will give you satisfaction to be acquainted with the situation of my congregation, and with the improvements I have introduced there. When I arrived here, I found the congregation number about five hundred souls, and it increases with every day. We have here Jews from all parts of the world, Frenchmen, Englishmen, Dutchmen, &c. In former years the religious spirit had almost died away; but thank God, there is now a revival. Many who before did not keep the Sabbath now do so, and every week the Synagogue is better attended.

I cannot sufficiently praise Mr. Aaron Wolff, the president of the community.[9] He has established a Sunday-school, where all the children of the congregation are taught our blessed religion. Your "Catechism for Younger Children" is used, as being the best existing in the English language.[10] We moreover have made a law, sanctioned by the king, "that all the children have to be confirmed when they have entered their fourteenth year;" and for the purpose I have composed a confirmation, which ere long I will take the liberty of sending to you, to have it printed under your care.[11] All offerings except one, when called to [the] Sepher, are abolished, and the greatest order reigns in the Synagogue during divine service.[12] As very few of the children could read the sacred tongue, I established a school where I teach the Hebrew gratis, and in one year I hope, under the blessing of Israel's God, to see all the children able to join in the worship.

On my arrival, I found the congregation disposed to adopt the prayer book of the "Reformed London Jews."[13] Almost every one was provided with a set, and they had only waited for me to approve it. To the amazement of many, I rejected that book entirely, and I will give you my reasons. 1st. The most beautiful hymns of the Portuguese liturgy were left out. 2nd. Why should I sanction a prayer-book adopted by a few laymen having no Rabbi among them? My greatest reason, however, was that the Rev. Mr. Marks had dared to deny all Talmudic authority.[14] Now, denying the divine claim of the Talmud, or its authority, are two different cases. Mr. Hurwitz, who certainly knows more of the Talmud than Mr. Marks, has said that "The Talmud is not divine"; and so do I say.[15] But I agree with Mr. Hurwitz, that the Talmud is the satellite of Holy Writ; that it contains those illustrations and interpretations of Scripture which were given by our blessed teacher, Moses himself; and that by denying the authority of these illustrations and interpretations, we deny Holy Writ itself; because without them, Scripture would be unto us as a sealed book. The presumption of Mr. Marks is the greater, as even the Christians acknowledge the authority of the Rabbis, in whatever concerns the rules of grammar. Nay, dear friend and fellow-labourer in the vineyard of the Lord, I would not approve a rite established by men who speak so lightly of those noble Rabbis, the pillars of the Synagogue, the spiritual fathers of Israel, and, under God, the cause of our existence as a peculiar people. I confess that we are at liberty to alter customs, to substitute prayers; but we must not touch the essential points of our religion. I would like to know whether Mr. Marks lays Tephillin [phylacteries] or how he wears the Tsitsit [fringes]? If he does, then he contradicts himself, as it is only by Rabbinic authority that we know how to obey those and most other commandments.

Nevertheless, I have granted several alterations which I shall communicate to you at another opportunity. Suffice it to say, that this congregation gradually increases in piety and faithfulness, and that the Eternal Unity is worshipped in this Island by the children of that people which "He hath given for a light to the gentiles," and chosen to be "the witnesses of his Unity."

Hoping that the God of our fathers may spare you many years, for the spiritual well-being of his chosen ones, I remain most respectfully yours,

B. C. Carillon

At the Risk of Being Considered Hyper-orthodox
Henry Goldsmith | OCTOBER 6, 1843

Henry Goldsmith was a founding member of Congregation B'nai Jeshurun and a Hebrew teacher in the congregation's school. He was also a leading figure in the Hebrew Benevolent Society of New York. In this letter to Leeser, Goldsmith defended his "Orthodox" position on the Talmud's "divinity" against the prior statements issued by Benjamin Carillon.

NEW YORK, TISHRY THE 12TH, 5604

To the Editor of the *Occident*,
It was a source of gratification to me to see in the last number of the *Occident* that some one has at last broached the subject of rabbinical authority. I am alluding to the Rev. B. C. Carillon's communication, without, however, sharing his sentiments, as you will perceive from the remarks which I beg to submit to your consideration. It appears to me that persons the most capable of handling the subject have hitherto been the most backward in doing so. The only reason I can assign for their silence is, that those denying or doubting the divine authority of the sages are not willing to avow their principles openly, for fear of subverting our from-time-immemorial-adopted system of worship and ceremonial observances. Others, who have implicit faith in what the rabbins taught us, prefer their inward belief to remain unknown, to incurring the risk of being considered hyper-orthodox. The time has now, however, arrived, that one ought to take a bold stand, and defend our long-cherished traditional faith

against the invaders of our most sacred territory. Since the publication of the first number of your periodical, I anxiously watched to see if any one would undertake to argue the point. I was silent, for I said, "Let days speak, and multitude of years should teach wisdom" (Job 32:7). Besides, I feel my inability to do ample justice to such an important question. But as the Rev. B. C. Carillon has assumed a position which requires and demands refutation, I will exert my utmost endeavours to do so.

The reverend gentleman wishes to draw a line between the divine authority of the sages and that ceded to them by mankind on account of their superior wisdom and grammatical knowledge. Now, I am of the opinion that no such distinction can be made. No law is binding to us unless it be divine; therefore, if the Talmud be not divine, it is not binding. If the question be asked, "Were the rabbins inspired or not?" I would unhesitatingly answer in the negative. Since after the destruction of the holy temple, prophecy and the divine spirit [Ruah ha-Kodesh] have been taken away from Israel; but as regards traditional laws, they are most unquestionably divine, having been transmitted to our sages from Moses by the hands of Joshua, the elders, the prophets, &c., as we find in Aboth (1:1). Nor is it possible that the law of Moses should have been given to the Israelites without subsequent or simultaneous explanation. Since, to the majority of those blessed with the divine gift, it must have been wholly or partly unintelligible on account of their ignorance (having just emerged from bondage, it is not to be supposed that they could have been sufficiently enlightened to understand the Word of God), in consequence of which, when he commanded them, "And you shall recite it day and night" (Joshua 1:8), it would have been unreasonable to exact it from them, had he not provided them with a tradition, or oral law, which was ready to explain and interpret every item of that law, and which was only compiled and committed to writing at a time when the Jews began to be dispersed, and fears were entertained of its being entirely forgotten, or at least of its becoming corrupted. I could quote many an authority to substantiate what I here assert, but think it unnecessary, as these facts must be known to the majority of your readers. . . .

Nevertheless, I do not wish to advance that every word contained in the Talmud is of divine origin. Nay, far from it. Such as the rabbinic lore [Midrashei Haggadot], and interpretations of passages in Scripture where no point of law is at issue, I do not consider to be authority. You will find Aben Ezra, Kimchi, Rashi, Maimonides, and many more of our principal commentators to interpret passages in diametrical opposition to the Rabbis.[16] I am alluding only to Halakhah, and that is all which is claimed by them or for them.

Should my opinions be attacked, you will always find me prepared to defend them to the best of my poor ability. I am yours very respectfully,

Henry Goldsmith

A Return to the Maimonidean View?

Abraham Rice | 1844

Rabbi Abraham Rice was the most learned Jew to enter into the Talmud debate held in Leeser's monthly newspaper. Whereas Goldsmith argued from a commonsense perspective, Rice disagreed with his fellow Orthodox religionist based on biblical and rabbinic sources.

Mr. Editor,
The kind indulgence with which you were pleased to notice my first attempt to write in the English language induces me again to speak freely concerning the letter of Mr. H. Goldsmith, and to offer at the same time some remarks upon the course of the Rev. Mr. Marks towards the Talmud.[17]

The endeavours of Mr. Goldsmith, to prove the divine authority of the Talmud, are in so far praiseworthy as they show his adherence to that compendium of laws; but in my humble opinion, it is as dangerous to enlarge the limits of talmudic authority as infidelity itself. The reason for this opinion cannot be better supported than from the letter of Mr. G. itself. He says, "There is no *juste milieu*; the Talmud is divine, or it is not entitled to authority."[18] This conclusion must appear erroneous to every man who has studied the Talmud in a proper manner.

On the contrary, the Talmud is entitled to authority, though every part of it is not divine. But the question "Who gives the Rabbins the right to make laws?" is answered in the Talmud itself. The Talmud takes up the question "How can we say in our blessings when performing a Rabbinical ordinance 'who hath sanctified with his commandments and commanded us,' when in no place in the law is such an ordinance as the talmudical law (Shabbat 23a) of lighting the lamps on the festival of dedication or the reading of the book of Esther on Purim enjoined by the Almighty?"[19] To which it is answered, that we are specially commanded in Deut. xvii.11: "According to the law which they (the teachers) shall teach thee, and according to the judgment which they will say unto thee shalt thou do, thou shalt not depart from the thing which they will tell thee to the right or to the left." Here the Lord requires of us to follow the laws which our Rabbins may make, and all Rabbinical ordinances possess divine authority only in so far as the injunction "Thou shall not depart" extends. This is the true *juste milieu* which Mr. G. has, perhaps from inexperience in the correct talmudical exegesis, denied to the Talmud.

The same is maintained by Maimonides, in his preface to his Yad Hachasaka: "All institutions and ordinances of the Rabbins are enjoined by the Lord, so that we may not depart from them, by his holy word which maintains, Thou shalt not depart, &c."[20]

This authority to make ordinances has ceased with the close of the Talmud, when the Israelites became more scattered in small numbers all over the world, and there lived no longer masses of a thousand learned men in one place, as it was in the earlier times, when all the doctors who taught in the spirit of the Talmud lived in the Holy Land or its vicinity. Maimonides says, therefore that "Institutions and ordinances since then adopted by any ecclesiastical tribunal have never been able to receive the universal sanction in Israel, as was the case with the enactments recorded in the Talmud."

Upon the whole, I cannot understand Mr. G's views, that either "the Talmud is divine or is not entitled to authority." Such an assertion would bring us upon absurdities, or lead us to reject all obligation of its contents. Is the second day of festivals a divine law? Surely not; still we claim that the Talmud had the right to make such a law and that the people could not reject it from the principle "Thou shalt not depart," and there are many hundred ordinances where the Talmud proceeds upon the same authority.

The Cleveland Conference

Isaac Leeser | 1855

In 1855 Isaac Mayer Wise, then of Cincinnati, convened a conference in Cleveland to unite American Jewish congregations. At the outset Wise hoped that he and the other rabbinic delegates could agree upon a set of Jewish dogma and a prayer book that would be acceptable to all Jews in the United States. Despite earlier proclamations to the contrary, Wise surprised many, including Isaac Leeser, with a very favorable position on the Talmud's authority in dictating Jewish observance. Afterward, however, Reform and Orthodox ministers debated how best to formulate a platform on the Talmud that would be amenable to all parties. Below are some of Leeser's reflections on the conference's proceedings.

Dr. Wise requested permission to offer some remarks . . . he produced a paper, which he read, and much to my gratification the first clause of the platform which he proposed was about in these words: "The first conference of American Rabbins acknowledge[s] the Bible which we have received from our fathers as the revealed word of God, given to us by divine inspiration."[21] The second then affirmed that the Talmud contains the logical and legal development of the Holy Scripture and that its decisions must guide us in all matters of practice and duty."[22] The third clause asserts that "this conference and all future Synods will act according to these principles." The fourth maintains that "the illiberal assertions contained in the Talmud are not of the kind referred to and have no binding force on us." I took no notes; consequently I cannot say that I have conveyed, especially in the latter, the precise words used; but the reader may depend on the general accuracy of this statement.

When Dr. Wise had resumed his seat, Dr. [Max] Lilienthal arose and spoke feelingly of the deplorable state of confusion, disunion, and absence of religion observable among us, and that every effort ought to be made to counteract such an unfortunate condition of things, and that the platform just read would contribute to produce a unity of action among congregations, and lead ultimately to an improvement of the evils which we all had to deplore.—A motion having been made that the resolutions offered by Dr. Wise be read by sections and separately acted on, I deemed it my duty to offer my views, as there was now something before the meeting to which I could assent. I then said, "that had the orthodox ministers and congregations known on what principles those who had called the conference meant to act, no doubt many more would have been present.[23] But the people had feared them and dreaded that they might propose measures subversive to our religion. I myself dreaded them, wherefore I had hitherto kept aloof. But the platform read by the President was, taking it altogether, such as would demand my approbation; and it would therefore be well to let the world know what sentiments influenced the conference, in case the platform be adopted, and then adjourn at once till next summer, to some central eastern city; and there expect the cooperation of those who had been kept away now by the uncertainty which had been referred to. For my part, I would consider the 17th of October a day of joy for Israel, if all Jews would adopt in sincerity the Bible as the inspired word of God and the Talmud as indicating the rule of life by which they would be governed." Dr. Lilienthal replied in a friendly manner, to which I rejoined similarly, after which the first clause of the platform was of course unanimously adopted. The second clause having been read again, Rabbi Joseph Levy, not deeming the wording explicit enough, moved that a farther consideration be postponed till the following morning, which was done, and the conference adjourned. . . .

Pursuant to adjournment the members met again at the time appointed, when the Rev. Dr. [Leo] Merzbacher, of New York, also appeared and took his seat.[24] After the journal of the first day had been read, together with several letters regretting the inability of the writers to attend, and some other unimportant matters having been discussed, the unfinished business of the preceding day was called up, and all the progress made during the session was to strike out the word "development" and insert "exposition," so as to read "logical and legal exposition of the sacred Scriptures." Still several members did not think the phrase definite enough, as not expressing the binding authority of the traditions embraced in the Talmud.

The conference therefore adjourned till 3 p.m., at which time the discussion having been resumed, Dr. Wise moved the appointment of a committee to whom the matter should be referred. I moved a postponement of Dr. Wise's resolution, that I might offer one of my own. This was carried upon division, when I offered the following: "That it is the opinion and conviction of this conference, that the Talmud contains the divine tradition given to Moses, and that all Israelites must decide all questions according to its decisions." In explanation I urged "that, however unpleasant the words *orthodox* and *reformers* might sound, and to no ears harsher than to mine, it was a deplorable fact that we were divided into two parties; and that unless something were done, and that speedily, it was to be dreaded that we should be hopelessly alienated from each other, and that we should then present *catholic* and *reformed* Israelites. . . . It would therefore be only proper to acknowledge at once that, if we are to seek for the traditions of God anywhere, it must be in the Talmud; and with this all Israelites would be satisfied and have a common ground for elucidating our religion in all future conferences in which, as I had said the preceding day, many more congregations than now represented would hereafter take part, when they see that the principles on which all our actions must be based are such as to challenge their hearty approbation." After a long discussion in which Mr. F. I. Cohn, Mr. Levi, Mr. Adler, Dr. Wise, Dr. Cohn, Dr. Lilienthal, and Dr. Merzbacher took part, a compromise was at length adopted, asserting "the Talmud to contain the traditional, logical, and legal exposition of the sacred Scriptures," &c., with which, I think, all the members were satisfied, as the *word traditional necessarily embraced a divine communication*, which having been preserved as the Talmud, has come down to our own time.[25]

It Is Decidedly Heretical
Morris J. Raphall | 1856

Upon departing from the meetings in Cleveland, Isaac Leeser believed that he had negotiated an authentically "Orthodox" position on the authority of the Talmud and its relationship to the Bible. Rev. Morris J. Raphall of New York's influential B'nai Jeshurun disagreed, however. In the end, both Reform and Orthodox leaders opposed the dogma established in Cleveland, to the chagrin of both Leeser and Isaac Mayer Wise. Here is an excerpt from Raphall's published thoughts on the Cleveland meetings.

Though the "Platform" is collapsed, "dead as Julius Caesar," and no effort can galvanize it into life I respond to the call, and when the Editor of the *Israelite* emphatically asks: Does M.J.R. reject the 'articles of Union' as heretical?"[26] I answer with equal emphasis: "Yes! I do reject the 2d article as decidedly heretical." And it is not merely heretical but it is "a snare, and a delusion!" As such it has been rejected, repudiated, and condemned by every reforming body in the United States beyond the immediate and personal influence of the Editor of the *Israelite*, while every true Jew scorns to barter away the "divine authority" of the "oral law," which "Moses received from Sinai and transmitted," to barter that away for the vapid formula—devoid of all spiritual

authority—concocted at Cleveland: A formula too wire-drawn to satisfy the practical innovator, too unreal and newfangled to deserve one
minute's attention from the pious Israelite—Judaism has no room for
Schleiermacher-Protestant ideas: the Oral Law is something very different from a mere historical tradition.

SECTION 2 | The Modified Mahzor

An Ornament for Parlor-Tables
Bernard Illowy | 1855

*Rabbi Bernard Illowy was one of the most decorated rabbis in America. The
Bohemian scholar had studied with Rabbi Moshe Sofer (Hatam Sofer) in Press-
burg (1762–1839) and earned a doctoral degree from the University of Budapest.
Despite these credentials, Illowy never gained a solid foothold in the United States,
itinerantly moving from pulpit to pulpit throughout his career. At the time of this
letter, Illowy lived in St. Louis. In this notice, he publicly issued a stern warning
against congregations that might consider adopting a prayer book recently published in New York. In 1855 Temple Emanu-El, a leading Reform congregation
in Manhattan, had produced a form of Sabbath worship that retained most of
the traditional text in the original Hebrew. Still, the prayer book omitted some
important sections, most notably the Mussaf service. This was unacceptable to
Orthodox men like Illowy.*

To the Rev. Dr. Wise,
Editor of the Israelite:[27]

Dear Sir
Several members of both the congregations of this city (St. Louis)
found themselves induced, partly perhaps by the beauty of the binding and the fineness of the paper of a prayer-book recently published in New York and adopted in the Temple Emanuel, and partly

perhaps by the brevity of its contents, to endeavor to procure its adoption in their respective Synagogues;[28] but when these gentlemen asked me for my consent to this measure, I told them in plain terms that I could not acknowledge the work as a Jewish prayer-book, that it might be good enough for those Israelites who have no other use for their prayer-books than to keep them as an ornament for their parlor-tables, but no true Israelite could use it as a prayer-book proper, those I mean who yet believe in the revelation of God and His promises through His prophets, who keep and observe the statutes of the oral law (Talmud) and consider the Shulchan Aruch as the guide of their religious life, and its decisions as obligatory in all matters concerning their daily life, their conduct in the house of God, and their worship. For this book regards the words of revelation, the sayings of the prophets, and those sublime truths which made our fathers happy, which consoled them in their hours of trouble—those truths which upheld and sustained them amidst the incongruous mass of nations they were among—those truths for which they sacrificed all early happiness, all for which strives in this world, so as to keep and bequeath them as an heirloom to us their children; for which they encountered the most terrible death, and for which they shed their precious blood,—as mere fictions, and repudiates what has been regarded by us as fundamental doctrines for thousands of years in Israel; and it departs completely from the statutes of the Talmud and the teaching of the Shulchan Aruch.

I furthermore announced to them that any Israelite who uses this book in his house for the purpose of prayer is entirely excluded from all religious communion by the decision of the Jewish canon law. Those gentlemen then asked me to make this announcement public, and to sustain it with sufficient arguments and proofs. To satisfy, therefore, this just demand, I must ask you to grant me a small space for the purpose in the columns of your paper; and as I am fully convinced of your partiality, and your thorough theological knowledge, I not only expect that you will grant my request, but also that you will not withhold from us your own opinion on the subject.

A Letter from an "Enlightened Orthodox" Jew

Benjamin Franklin Peixotto | 1859

Benjamin Franklin Peixotto (1834–90) was a descendant of one of the early Portuguese families in the United States. He was a political editor of the Plain Dealer *in Cleveland and a former protégé of Stephen A. Douglas (1813–61). Peixotto was also a merchant and superintendent of the local Jewish Sunday school. In this private letter to Isaac Leeser of Philadelphia, the Cleveland traditionalist asks his correspondent to help him defend Orthodox observance against religious reform and all of the modern sensibilities that its champions attached to it.*

CLEVELAND, NOV. 16, 1859

Rev & Dear Friend,

In my last letter I informed you of a contemplated movement among our people having in view the union of the two congregations in order to secure better religious and educational advantages for both adults & children.[29]

I was unable to give you then the real objects entertained by those most zealous for the proposed consolidation. Since this meeting of the committees and their preliminary reports to both Kahals, the real intentions have become manifest and these I propose to make known to you.

Let me premise by saying the present condition of both Kahals educationally considered is deplorable, at least in the light of the advanced progress of this age.

Now it is proposed by the zealots to build a new synagogue, first disposing of one or both of the existing structures and have its interior constructed for family pews for male and female, to adopt a new minhag, engage a reform preacher, and in a word go the whole figure *a la Dr. Wise.*[30]

In the limits of a letter I cannot give you an adequate idea of the wishes and intentions of the so called reformers. Let me say that a very large number if not quite a majority of the members of both societies are ready and anxious to adopt these views and prayers unless speedily enlightened as to their apostasy. The only saving clause to us, for I class myself among those who will resist to the utmost this wholesale system of innovation to use no harsher term, is that if a majority of both societies determine to adopt these doctrines we can restrain them from selling the property as we own and possess in good title seats forever in the respective buildings and they do not propose to allow us for these any compensation or return either whole or in part in their new edifice.

I have looked up the legal authority on this point besides taking the benefit of counsel. Now I am willing and ready to surrender all real and personal interest I own in the synagogue and unite with the society provided there shall be no overreacting and departure from the limits of enlightened orthodoxy.

I am in favor of a practice of enlightened views, a school of doing away with certain customs (mere forms) of repetition of prayers and of other sensible modifications, but I decline to reject the belief in a personal Messiah and the resurrection of the body, these I hold as fundamental principles of our faith that cannot be abolished or abandoned.

Now with reference to pews. I believe neither the Pentateuch nor Prophets speak advisedly on this point, the only reason for the separation of the sexes I have ever heard advanced and have entertained myself have been with reference to cleanliness and the reverse at certain periods in the other sex.[31] Understand me though that while I say this to you privately, I maintain publicly an observance of the old custom that I have already done so in more than one speech on the subject. Now I want your advice on this point and argument to sustain my public position, for my private conviction rather favors the mingling of both sexes in the synagogue on an equality. It is true, it assimilates in form to Christian mode of worship, but certain devotion if only apparent, is not wanting in the appearance of their congregations. Give me some good solid reason or law why they should not sit together. I wish it was in my power to have the benefit of your society for at least two hours that we might go over all these points.

I stand in need of confirmation of assistance of counsel of authorities etc., etc. My mind misgives on many points advanced in favor of changes. I see much that might be adopted with benefit, much that would cause Israel to depart eventually from its ancient faith. . . .

Will you break away from your numerous duties for an hour to give me the benefit of your counsel and experience? Oh would it were I could see you. I study the law constantly, but my duties will not allow me time to grasp hold of all I could wish to explore and examine and determine and then being all alone I fear to reply singly on my own judgment lest it lead me astray. A few years more study will determine my mind, but these years must be directed in a measure by better wisdom than that which now falls to my share.

Please write me speedily.

Greatly obliged
Your very true and sincere friend
    B. F. Peixotto

On Burning Reform Prayer Books
Eliyahu M. Holzman | 1865

Little is known about Eliyahu Holzman, a scribe and shohet (ritual slaughterer) from Courland, Russia. In 1865 he published a twenty-five-page tract titled Emek Refa'im *(Valley of Ghosts). The polemical work mainly attacked Isaac Mayer Wise for his prayer book and other reforms associated with him, such as the introduction of females into synagogue choirs. The short work was uneven and written in an awkward mix of biblical and rabbinic Hebrew. In this reproduced section of Holzman's pamphlet, the author suggested that Jews burn Wise's* Minhag America *and justified the action based on rabbinic texts.*

I composed this small tract in honor of my great teacher who is wise and clever, Rabbi Schachne the son of Yitzhak who is called Isaacs, on whom the spirit of God encourages to sanctify His Name in public [Kiddush Hashem].[32] Let God be with him as He was with Elijah on

To the Jewish Public.

M. E. HOLZMAN, *Scribe, of Courland, Russia,* begs to inform the Jewish people of the United States, that he has now in Press, and will shortly appear, a translation of this work, which has for its object arguments, demonstrating the sinfulness of those who attach themselves to the new system now attempted to supersede the rituals and customs of Israel, established from time immemorial. It is unfortunately too well known that a sect has arisen in Israel who attempt to form a new code for public worship, embracing instrumental and vocal music. Choristers composed of male and female voices. Israelites and non Israelites, erasing the name of Synagogue and substituting the term Temple. The whole of these charges emanating from men who call themselves Doctors, and who are in fact destroyers of all that is sacred; their lips move in sanctity, and deception is in their hearts. The author, desiring to preserve in fact, the prayers compiled by *"the men of the great Assembly,"* has issued this work to prevent further encroachments in our holy ritual, and to prove that the course pursued by these innovators tends to uproot the "Scion of God's planting," and to sow seeds of discord detrimental to the welfare of Israel and opposed to the conservative course which tends to keep Israel distinct and holy.

I strongly recommend the within meritorious production.

 { L. S. }

M. J. Raphall, Dr.

I most readily endorse the remarks of the Rev. Dr. Raphall.

S. M. Isaacs.

In 1865 Eliyahu Holzman published a thin pamphlet designed to attack the liturgical changes issued by Jewish reformers in the United States. In a section that preceded his polemic, Holzman included approbations by leading traditionalist Jewish ministers in New York. Courtesy of Klau Library, Hebrew Union College–Jewish Institute of Religion, Cincinnati.

Mount Carmel to remove the prophets of Ba'al who falsely prophesized.[33] So shall God blessed be He remove this obstacle and stumbling block from the midst of the people of God, on which a great many have fallen. . . .

This is the general principle, as well as the details therein: all sacred books written by a heretic do not require burial. They may only be purified through incineration. This is a commandment incumbent upon all sons of Israel.[34]

Anyone who calls himself a member of Israel, when he sees this wayward book that has engraved on it "The Prayers of B'nai Yeshurun" and "Minhag America" must immediately burn it.[35] No one in the United States of America is capable of amending the prayers or piyutim that were established by the ancients. Anyone who dares to embark on this is labeled a heretic.

Minhag Ashkenaz and Minhag Reform

Samuel Myer Isaacs | 1866

Samuel Myer Isaacs (1804–78) was the minister of B'nai Jeshurun and later Shaaray Tefila in New York. In 1857 he founded the Jewish Messenger, *a weekly newspaper that, along with Isaac Leeser's* Occident, *publicly supported the Orthodox cause against Reform periodicals. Isaacs was also one of the founders of the Board of Delegates of American Israelites, established in 1859. This document is a section from an affidavit submitted by Isaacs on behalf of plaintiffs who halted reforms at Congregation Anshi Chesed in New York. The author of this testimony responded to the charge of reformers that the German worship known as "Minhag Ashkenaz" was not a fixed and unalterable rite.*

145 WEST 46TH STREET,

NEW YORK, JANUARY 25, 5626

Dear Sir,

The question as to the true meaning of the "Minhag Ashkenaz," which is now agitating the Congregation Anshi Chesed, may be readily defined as the "custom of Germany," to distinguish it from the customs of Israelites in other parts of the world,—although it often occurs that German Jews emigrating to other quarters retain their own "customs" or "minhag," as more in accordance with their early training and more congenial to their spiritual feeling.[36]

When a congregation is established, it is usual to fix and determine its "Minhag," and this becomes, from the moment of its adoption, sacred and unmovable.

Besides the "Minhag Ashkenaz," there are the "Portuguese" and the "Polish," which are of general acceptation in Europe and America, and the "Minhag Amsterdam" which, operating in Holland, is adopted also in the Dutch colonies. All these Minhagim are represented in America, the "Minhag Ashkenaz" most extensively, perhaps. This same Minhag has been adopted by one congregation in Jerusalem. The "Minhag" includes the ritual, the form of Synagogue services, and other ceremonies. Israelites differing in Minhag are nevertheless to all intents and purposes brethren in faith.

A congregation having adopted a "Minhag" is not authorized to depart from it, nor is the Rabbi warranted in abridging, obliterating, or holding in abeyance any of the prescribed lessons or portions of the ritual.

Within the past half century, great efforts have been made, especially in Germany, to "modernize" the Synagogue service and in some instances, with effect; but such congregations have then ceased to be considered as retaining the minhag previously adopted and have been regarded and designated as "reformers." Among these, for example, are the congregations to which Drs. [David] Einhorn, [Isaac M.] Wise, and [Samuel] Adler are attached.[37] But even these three have not adopted a uniform ritual, their "customs" differing materially. While as you know, I am the spiritual guide of a congregation which adopted the "Polish Minhag," that does not prevent me from worshipping in a synagogue where they retain a different "Minhag," except that I never did or could worship in a so-called reform temple.

In 1855 American Jews moved the Talmud to the center of religious discourse. Isaac Mayer Wise of Cincinnati's B'nai Yeshurun convened the so-called Cleveland Conference to unite Jewish congregations under a set of religious planks.[38] His second and most contested platform called for the belief "that the Talmud is acknowledged by all as the legal and obligatory commentary of the Bible."[39] The statement's vagueness hardly helped achieve a consensus. To the contrary, the Orthodox and Reform rabbinical delegates in Cleveland argued over the language and its implications, much to the excitement of American Jews, who noticed "lively" and "increasing" discussions on the Cleveland meetings in major Jewish centers and "even in the smallest congregations."[40] In the end, the Cleveland convention failed to unite American Judaism. Rather, it moved traditional Jews toward the viewpoint of Samson Raphael Hirsch and the more militant anti-Reform school. In fact, one Orthodox rabbi charged that anyone who deviates from the "sages of the Talmud" could not be "considered a Jew." The lines between Orthodox and Reform were still not fully formed, but the Talmud discussions directed American Judaism toward these firmer barriers.

Yet for many American Jews, the Talmud, written in terse Judeo-Aramaic, was a closed book. Accordingly, many more staunchly Orthodox Jews were far more taken aback by the changes that reformers made to the traditional prayer book. Far better versed in its language, Orthodox-leaning Jews were discomfited by the deletions and emendations to the worship that had been taught to them by their parents and grandparents in Europe. In subsequent years, these religionists refused to pray in what would soon be called "Minhag America congregations," a reference to Wise's Reform prayer book.[41] Instead, they filled the seats of Orthodox synagogues and grew more comfortable with that religious designation.

3 | An Orthodox Ministry

In September 1851 Rev. Henry A. Henry (d. 1879) delivered a sermon at Temple Emanu-El in New York. The minister was known as a staunch defender of "old country" Judaism and was therefore out of place at the Reform-minded temple.[1] Still, a chance to address a large forum like the kind offered to him at Emanu-El was too much for the out-of-work clergyman to turn down. Soon afterward, leading members of Shaaray Tefila invited Henry to deliver a discourse at their Orthodox congregation. However, Shaaray Tefila's president ultimately turned Henry away, banning him on the grounds that the so-called Orthodox rabbi "made an acquaintance with the radicals at the reform Temple" and consequently "unfitted himself by this act, from ever preaching again in an Orthodox congregation."[2]

The brief episode reflects a rigidly divided American Jewish community. It also bespeaks the laity's control of the religious sphere in the mid-nineteenth century. The itinerant Henry could attest to this point firsthand. Directly before his trip to New York, the unordained clergyman was fired by his Cincinnati congregation on the grounds that "his Conduct has not been such as becoming a Minister of a [*sic*] Honourable Congregation."[3] Most Jewish ministers suffered domineering trustees, but the more traditional class of rabbis endured the worst of it. The reforms to worship initiated by liberal ministers raised the minister's role in the service while it pushed out the liturgy and customs that laypeople were most comfortable observing. On the other hand, congregations that remained in line with traditional practices upheld forms of ritual that could be officiated by a layperson. Exceptional men like Morris Raphall of New York and Rev. Sabato Morais (1823–97) of Philadelphia attained high status in their congregations. In most instances, however, the rabbi was an expendable commodity in this American religious setting. In time, though, the stature of the Orthodox rabbi started to change.

For all American religions and denominations, the Civil War served as a reminder of the importance of an "authority" to maintain order in all public spheres.[4] The Orthodox clergyman—no matter his idiosyncratic designation of hazzan, minister, reverend, or rabbi—benefited from this change as well. The shift was most evident in two events in the 1880s. In 1885 Rabbis Alexander Kohut (1842–94) and Kaufmann Kohler (1843–1926) of New York debated each other on the matter of religious reform. Their sermons attracted hundreds of listeners and provoked much conversation in other congregations and in the editorial pages of Jewish newspapers. One year later, a group of traditional clergymen established the Jewish Theological Seminary Association in New York. In the past, others had formed rabbinical schools in the United States. In 1875, for example, Isaac Mayer Wise established the reform-minded Hebrew Union College in Cincinnati. Yet the New York seminary was the first long-lasting rabbinical school established as an "Orthodox" rabbinical school.

SECTION 1 | The Impaired and Itinerant "Rabbi"

Rabbinic Tenure
Max Lilienthal | 1854

Rabbi Max Lilienthal wrote this article shortly before he reentered the rabbinate in Cincinnati. Earlier he had left his position as rabbi of three New York congregations after a bitter dispute with the laity of those communities. In this open letter, the author intended to show the consequences of the poor financial and itinerant state of Jewish ministers in the United States.

It is a remarkable fact that all the minor congregations appoint their ministers for the short term of one year, while almost all the larger

Jewish congregations have elected them for a much longer period and many of them for life.

The Rev. Dr. Raphael, Rev. Dr. Merzbacher, Rev. S. M. Isaacs, Rev. J. Lyons in New York; Rev. Dr. I. M. Wise in Cincinnati; Rev. J. K. Gutheim in New Orleans are all elected and appointed for life.[5] The Portuguese congregations gave the impulse to that laudable mode of appointment and were readily followed by all those congregations distinguished by wealth, intelligence, and love of order and decorum.[6]

The minor ones yet resist, insisting upon having the ministry in their hands, that, by their annual elections, they wish to control the behaviour of their ministers, that besides they wish to show the might and influence of every single and individual vote; they say, as no officer of the congregation is elected for life, the ministers neither shall enjoy such a privilege.[7]

Well, what are the consequences? That, with a very few exceptions, they have no ministers of talent and eminence! That respectable men who hold an office are tired and try to get rid of it as soon as possible; that men who by their education think themselves unfit to make their living otherwise but in such an office are applying for it; and the office itself becomes void of all influence, the incumbent fearing to exercise any as the apprehension of being discharged continually hovers about him.

Do not say, if we could get the right kind of men, we would appoint them for life. America has not yet raised any; for the present generation at least, they have all to be called from Europe; and what Rabbi, holding office there for life, would resign his firm position in Europe for such an uncertain and dependent one as those in America? Or who would be so void of conscience to entice by glittering representations a man, a father of a large family, to quit his office in Europe for such precarious positions, as the majority of congregations offer in America?

No, brethren, there a remedy should be applied too, and this very speedily. I do not say that you should give up the control over the conduct of your ministers; no, we want no clerical, hierarchal, or absolute power vested in one person, may he be called Rabbi or Bishop; but appoint them at least during good behavior, and you do not lose any of your influence.[8] Or appoint them under condition that they can only be discharged if two-thirds of the members of the congregation vote for it; well, then the rights of the congregation as well as the ministers are secured; the office becomes an honorable, a respectable one, while at present it is worse than that of a maid servant; for she has to please but one mistress while the Jewish minister has to creep and to play the hypocrite in order to offend nobody and to please everybody.

Perhaps you will object it is of no consequence, what position our ministers occupy; for our money we can always get one or the other, and this is all we care for. No, gentlemen, if this abuse be not redressed in a very short time you will be unable to get ministers at all; for who would educate his child for such a precarious station of life? You all will certainly reply: "my child shall neither become a Rabbi, nor a Chasan [cantor]; I do not want this bread for him; I prefer any other trade or position." Well, every father feels and thinks for his children as anxiously and earnestly as you do; no one then will run such a risk with the future existence of his sons; and from whence will you then get your ministers? The present want is supplied from Europe, where men, educated by their parents for these vocations and that for the sake of Heaven [Shem Shamayim] are coming over and destitute of all means and ability of supporting themselves apply with repugnance for the vacant offices; but what afterwards?

Three different reasons in times gone by induced parents to dedicate their boys for the Jewish ministry. Firstly, it was an appointment for life and was fairly to be brought into account; secondly, the parents did it for the sake of God and religion, hoping thereby to attain a higher reward in the future life; thirdly, the Jewish ministry was an office of personal honor and distinction as well as a securing respect and esteem towards the whole family of the Rabbi; and these three reasons combined induced parents to educate their sons for the Jewish ministry and their sons to devote themselves to this holy vocation. In this country, however, and especially among the Polish and German congregations, it is just the reverse. An appointment for life is an exception; piety and the so-called sake of Heaven is not among the stirring agencies of our age; and a place of honor—well, we prefer to keep silent in this respect. The old name of "subjugation" [meshubad] is still too much the order of the day, to bring honor and distinction into question. But all this prevents young tolerated Jews from devoting themselves to clerical offices, the law necessarily will be forgotten, and a want of really proper men will soon be felt. And who then will be blamed, the congregations or the ministers, if the pulpits will be without able preachers, the schools without well instructed superintendents, and all our clerical offices without judicious ministers?

Dr. L.

A New Calling
Palestine | 1862

The writer who used the pseudonym "Palestine" contributed frequently to Isaac Mayer Wise's Cincinnati newspaper. The author was careful not to reveal too much personal information. Yet, judging from his detailed letters on various New York synagogue happenings, we might speculate that he did not affiliate with any one particular congregation. His columns also do not offer whether he considered himself Orthodox or Reform, but he was probably inclined toward the latter. In this installment, Palestine shared more positive views of the American rabbinate that were not limited to Orthodox or Reform ministers.

NEW YORK, JUNE 16, 1862.

Editor of the *Israelite*:
No news! No gossip!—nothing startling and I fear nothing that will have interested your readers, when he or she shall have perused this epistle, nevertheless I venture to describe a conversation I had the pleasure to listen to the other evening.

The topic was on the necessity to instruct and raise some of our youth to the study of theology. I had the satisfaction to perceive that it was created out of the *Israelite* where your correspondent lamented the scarcity of ministers or Rabbis.

The group consisted of four gentlemen and one lady, and whilst the men were smoking some of Simonfeld's best, and the lady plying her needle as if life would depend on it, or character to be established, one of the gentlemen commenced by remarking that he was struck very forcibly with an observation in the *Israelite*, concerning what should be done so as to uphold and keep intact our cherished religion.

"Well," remarked another, "the first and only remedy lies with the ministers, and there we are rather deficient; I remember well that some 4 or 5 years ago, a member of the finance committee to the Temple Emanuel recommended that an annual stipend should be offered to any youth that would study Jewish theology, but it was ignored, as it is with all and everything, where no tangible or perceivable interest is offered at once to the masses, matters of the utmost vitality will never grow in favor; they will lie dormant and decay.[9] If at that time, this recommendation had been adopted, who knows if it would not have given an impetus to some youth, who, by this time, might be a shining star among the theologians, and a sparkling jewel to the Israelites."

"Yes! Yes!" said a third, "you can not get a father to educate his son for the pulpit, or suffer him to become a minister; to be dependent on Jews is a severe, a difficult calling, hardly ever appreciated, and to say the least of it is a hard lot."

"I don't think so," said the lady, dropping her needle, erecting her head, her eyes flashing with animated intelligence. "My son, should he have the natural capacity to become a learned man, I would not hesitate to educate him to the sacred calling of a minister; do we not see, almost every day, that ministers of the Christian denomination do actually represent their community, as well in spiritual as in worldly affairs?[10] Is he not respected and honored? Does he not wield great power in his congregation? He is at the head of everything; he distributes their charity, in benevolence and kindness! He gathers funds for that purpose, when needed! He looks to the instruction of the rising generation; he is endeared to his flock by a thousand ties! He blesses the infant, when yet in its cradle! He binds into wedlock the husband and wife! He is jovial and kind at our festivals; in our afflictions, sympathizing and consoling; thus, by all these circumstances combined, he is looked upon with love, with veneration and with reverential fear,—this alone is sufficient to satisfy a laudable ambition, and then again, a learned man is always rich, he never needs to have cares, nor worldly sorrows; his capital in learning, sagacity and wisdom is not subjected to depreciation, and so if a minister is a good-hearted man, what he first of all should be, then indeed he must be happy and contented."

Thus ended a conversation which gave rise to a series of themes; one on the ten commandments; another on the Sabbath, which I may resume in my next.[11]

    Palestine.

Isaac Leeser's Successor
Alfred T. Jones | 1869

Descended from the earlier Jewish settlers in the United States, Alfred Jones (1822–88) was a printer and communal worker. In 1875 he founded the Jewish Record in Philadelphia, a weekly newspaper that championed a moderate Orthodox viewpoint. This text is an excerpt of a sermon that Jones, as president of the congregation, delivered on the occasion of Rev. George Jacobs's (1834–84) appointment as minister of Beth El Emeth in Philadelphia. It reflected the high esteem with which he and other Philadelphians viewed the rabbinate in the post–Civil War era.

The electors of the Congregation wishing to act with one deliberation, and to avoid any charge of hasty or inconsiderate action, have carefully and respectfully considered all applications for the office of Minister, which they had invited, and I have now the pleasure formally to announce that they have concluded by the unanimous and unsolicited call, to invite hither the Rev. George Jacobs (1934–84) of Richmond.[12]

There is a coincidence here which I cannot refrain from noticing and which I hail as one of happy augury. When, years ago, vile aspersions from abroad against the Jewish race and faith reached the city of Richmond, the latent powers of an unknown Jewish youth were aroused, and Isaac Leeser sprang suddenly forth as the champion of his people.[13] In Richmond he first seized the pen, rendered by him immortal, and electrified the American Hebrews with its wonderful force, leading them forward in the path of enlightenment, in resistance to oppression, in vindication of their rights, and in reliance on their own innate power.[14]

In Richmond, likewise, George Jacobs commenced his career as a Jewish divine and writer, and by his piety and zeal not alone became endeared to his flock, and secured the respect of the community in which he lived, but his reputation spread abroad among his people, and his flattering record directed our attention towards him.

From Richmond Isaac Leeser was summoned to Philadelphia, to commence his brilliant career of usefulness.[15] From thence, also, have we invited his successor in the pulpit, who has before him for emulation and encouragement, the bright example, the great success, and imperishable renown achieved by his lamented predecessor.

The ordeal through which your new Minister has to pass will necessarily be a trying one. Apart from the fact of being a stranger among us, and the necessity for assimilating himself to the various peculiarities and dispositions with which he will come in contract, he is likely to be judged by the standard of the ablest Jewish divine of our age.

I believe him to be equal to the emergency. The high esteem in which he has been held by his former congregation is a sure evidence of his merit, and the fact that he possessed the respect and confidence of Isaac Leeser speaks volumes in his praise. I am satisfied he will bring the discharge of his duties, abilities of a high order, ardent zeal to labor in his holy calling, and fervent devotion to that ancient faith, which has been the life and preservation of Israel, since the memorable day our ancestors assembled at the foot of Horeb. Your new spiritual guide will direct you with the might of love, the control of mildness, and the commanding majesty of character. Let his good qualities cause your hearts to expand towards him, as the tender flower opens to the genial sunshine; for henceforth, to him our youth, in whom our hopes and joys are centered, will look for instruction, example, and advice—those of mature years for counsel or support in the hour of trial, seeking for him to pour the balm of consolation into wounds that sickness or sorrow may rend into the soul—while the heart of the aged will glow with hope and with him drink invigorated draughts at the perennial spring of God's divine love.

I earnestly bespeak for him, your punctual and constant attendance at the House of worship, it will strengthen his efforts. Give him your undivided attention during the recitation of the prayers, it will lighten his task and render it more pleasant. Especially avoid all conversation and audible whisperings, it will enable him to concentrate his attention on the service. Listen earnestly to the words of admonition or advice he may address to you, it will inspire the preacher and give him confidence. Let our wives, our sons, our daughters, our aged, and our young gather round him and harken to his voice; let the warm sympathies of our hearts go forth towards him and transfer, if possible, all the high esteem and abiding love entertained for his illustrious predecessor. More, he will not ask—more, you cannot give.

Do not let these entreaties fall on listless ears—do not, I implore you—even though you may not regard the source from whence they emanate as entitled to advise or instruct. Only ask yourselves, are my words just? Am I right? Then if so, I beg you act accordingly.

SECTION 2 | Defenders of Tradition

The Ethics
Alexander Kohut | MAY 30, 1885

Rabbi Alexander Kohut settled in the United States in 1885 after establishing himself as a distinguished Talmud scholar in Hungary. He accepted the call of New York's Ahawath Chesed, despite the congregation's Reform orientation. In truth, Kohut's "middle of the road" Neolog religious views placed him in between most Reform and Orthodox American rabbis. Still, he quickly emerged as a champion for "Orthodox" and "Conservative" Jews. Shortly after his arrival, Kohut commenced a series of German-language lectures that attacked Jewish reform. This is an excerpt from his inaugural presentation on "The Ethics of the Fathers" at Ahawath Chesed.

This digression suggests to us that not everyone should be condemned who cannot observe all the laws with equal fidelity—taking for granted, however, that he acknowledges the binding character of the Law. Only he who denies this, who rejects on principle the validity of the Mosaic-rabbinical tradition, thereby banishes himself from the camp of Israel, writes his own epitaph: "I am no Jew, no adherent to the faith of my fathers." He denies that Moses received the Torah on Sinai and handed it down to Joshua, he to the Elders, these to the Prophets, they to the Men of the Great Synagogue; and so on to the Soferim, the teachers of the Mishnah, and the writers of the Talmud (Avot 1:1). He who breaks down the truth of tradition ceases to be a Jew—he is a Karaite.

This Jewish sect, which arose in the ninth century, recognised only the validity of the Written Law and rejected the Oral Law. What did it accomplish? Nothing. It decayed and disappeared. We cannot maintain Judaism without tradition. Without the oral teaching we cannot comprehend the written, out of which it is developed. This oral teaching served to guide the infant steps of Judaism, and when Israel grew to man's estate, it proved a safe path on which his religion historically unfolded. This path we do not wish, nay, we never shall leave.

A Reform which seeks to progress without the Mosaic-rabbinical tradition is a deformity—a skeleton without flesh and sinew, without spirit and heart. It is suicide; and suicide is not reform. We desire a Judaism full of life. We desire to worship the living God in forms full of life and beauty; Jewish, yet breathing the modern spirit. Only a Judaism true to itself and its past, yet receptive to the ideas of the present, accepting the good and the beautiful from whatever source it may come, can command respect and recognition.

But let us guard carefully against heresy-hunting. It is worthy of note that the first moral truth enunciated in the Ethics is this: "Be circumspect in judgment." We believe that we represent true Judaism. Let us not excommunicate the leaders and members of other congregations who maintain a different standard. While we may deplore the fact that each swings his censer of separate religious views, let us realise that everyone must strive after truth in his own manner. Let us learn tolerance from the Rabbis of old, so often and so unjustly decried as intolerant, who said: "Israel is to be likened unto the pomegranate; even the seemingly insignificant among him is full of virtue and humanity, as the pomegranate is full of seed."

How much that is good and humane is practised by the Reformers. Our *false* Orthodox—(sincere and honest Orthodoxy is tolerant)—who are so ready to use harsh words and who would deny the Jewish name to everyone who differs from them in opinion, should judge with greater leniency the Jewish heart that dispenses charity. Where the Jewish heart still beats, Judaism and Jewish piety are not extinct. Therefore, "Be circumspect in judgment."

On the other hand, we call to those of more liberal tendencies, in the words of the same ethical maxim: "Raise up many disciples and make a fence around the Torah." How glorious would be the outlook of American Judaism if these two precepts were fulfilled!

I know but little as yet of the Jewish statistics of this great country. I do not know whether New York has 90,000 or 100,000 or 120,000 Jews.[16] Be their number what it may, I say: "May the Almighty multiply and bless them!" But I am sure that they are not all members of Jewish congregations. I would be satisfied with a third or a fourth part. This is an anomaly that should not continue.

I do not know whether it will be my good fortune to have your sympathy in my religious attitude—that of Mosaic-rabbinical Judaism, freshened with the spirit of progress, a Judaism of the healthy golden mean. I hope I shall. For such a Judaism I plead. Unfurl, then, your banner of REASONABLE PROGRESS. You must. I know you will.

Backward or Forward?

Kaufmann Kohler | JUNE 6, 1885

Rabbi Kaufmann Kohler was a Reform rabbi and later president of Hebrew Union College (1903–21) in Cincinnati. In the summer of 1885, Kohler took on the challenge to respond to the anti-Reform lectures delivered by Alexander Kohut at New York's Ahawath Chesed. In response, Kohler launched a series of discourses of his own that defended his Reform principles. The back- and-forth between the two rabbinic orators caused a sensation among American Jews, one of whom described the episode as a "red hot" debate. This text is the beginning of Kohler's first lecture.

The confirmation solemnities being over, and the Sabbath schools having finished their work for the season, what attraction can the pulpit offer to a fastidious audience that craves for dainties in place of wholesome food?[17] Shall I speak on the new Bible translation?[18] How many Jews to-day care to read the Bible, or take interest in that piece of antiquity? There is a novelty offered to our New York Jews in the appearance of a new rabbi of renown who, with laudable courage and independence, gives free utterance to his rigid conservatism, boldly challenging Reform Judaism by the open declaration that he who disavows the statutes and ordinances of Mosaico-Rabbinical Judaism on principle has forfeited the name of Jew. Of course, the novelty of the learned speaker's notions and attitude creates a stir and a welcome sensation throughout the Jewish circles of New York, and an opinion about the influence to be exercised by the new rabbi, for whom I cherish the highest regard, both as an eminent scholar and as a most sincere and earnest advocate of conservative Judaism, would be rather premature. Personally, I gladly and heartily wish him the greatest success, and I have little doubt that, being supported and encouraged by our *exclusively* conservative local press, he will exercise a wholesome influence upon the consolidation and the right coalition of the different elements of our congregations which are at present too often brought together without unity of purpose and principle.[19]

But the gauntlet thrown into our face must be taken up at once, and I to-day simply propose to ask the question: Are we progressing, or ought we to retrograde? Has Reform Judaism come upon a sand bank, so that we require Talmudical orthodoxy to set us afloat again, or are we still strong enough to stand at the helm and steer American Judaism towards its lofty goal?

Mark well. Mere cant and bombastic phraseology will do us no good. Gibes and sneers cast at orthodoxy or at reform by opponents will not solve the question. Even our much-vaunted progress is far from being an undisputable fact. History has its constant ups and downs, its luminous and its dark epochs. Upon every exertion and exhaustion of the intellect follows a reaction of the heart. Periods of rationalism give way to periods of mysticism and dark superstition. Upon the sunny days of Jewish learning and independent research in Spain came the frantic vagaries of the Cabbala. Maimonides' name was beclouded by the holy Zohar and Rabbi Isaac Luria.[20] And, indeed, he who knows how to read the signs of the time may, without being a Daniel, well foretell the coming reaction, which may render the twentieth century less intellectual than ours. There is even in our midst an increasing shallowness of thought visible everywhere, whilst the emotional is pressing forward to take the lead. Still the question of the hour is: Retrogression or progress? Must we, after having dropped the obsolete observances of by-gone days, after having worked for thirty-five years in this country for emancipation from the yoke of Mosaico-Talmudical Judaism, again bend our neck to wear it in order to be complete Jews in the sense of orthodoxy, or may we persist in claiming, as we did thus far, to stand on a far higher ground, whilst discarding a great many of the ceremonial laws of the Bible and tradition, and placing ourselves on the standpoint of prophetical Judaism, with the Messianic aim as its world-embracing goal?

Mosaico-Rabbinical Judaism is retrospective. It has not the courage to stand on its feet. It subsists on the merits of the forefathers. Its very ritual, its whole mode of worship, it considers only as a feeble substitute for the temple sacrifice. It longs for the restoration of temple and state in Judea, hoping for the restitution of the entire Mosaic system of social, political, and religious life. It clings to the maxim: "If we are common men, our ancestors were angels; and if they were but common men, we must rank among the brutes" (Shabbat 112b). Reform Judaism, on the contrary, looks forward with hope for a far brighter future, beholding in the Messiah the ideal of mankind to be realized by the Jewish people through all the factors and agencies of civilization and progress, and in the temple of Zion's hills the house of prayer to be opened on all spots of the globe for all nations to worship the Most High as the Father of all men. Its golden era lies not behind, but before us. Which of the two views then is more in congruity with the drift and spirit of our age and of all ages of human history? Which are we to espouse? The one that turns the dials of the time backward, or the one that proudly points to the forward move of history? The one that wails over the ruins of the past, over the decay of ritualistic religion, over the downfall of creeds and blind authority-worship, or the one that hails the rising faith in all that is divine in man, the building up of a religion which already our prophets of yore proclaimed to be as broad as man and as wide as the globe?

What Is Progress?

Alexander Kohut | AUGUST 15, 1885

Rabbi Alexander Kohut delivered his Avot lecture on successive summertime Sabbaths. On some occasions, he only alluded to Kaufmann Kohler's weekly rebuttals. On others, he was more forthcoming in retaliation. This is an excerpt of one of Kohut's more explicit responses to his Reform rival.

As long as man lives, he must be active, and only as he is active does he live. Progress is the law of life. "If you leave me for a single day," says the Torah, "I will leave you for two" (JT Berakhot 9:5)—which is to say, in other words: You move and I move; if you go backward one day and I go forward, we shall be two days apart. No to progress means retrogression. "The disciples of learning have no rest either in this life or in the next. As it is said: 'They go from strength to strength'" (Berakhot 64a).

The question for us is, what shall we call Progress in Religion and how can we best conserve our energies? If "Progress" is to be evidenced by destruction and not by construction; if it merely means the giving up of ancient and venerable customs that have been honored by long usage and which bring comfort to the soul, and offers nothing in their place, then every well-meaning Jew will call such "progress" retrogression. It was a keen observation of the Rabbis, when they remarked: "A broad stride robs a man of the five-hundredth part of his vision" (Berakhot 43b)—that is to say, our vision is apt to be beclouded when we take too great paces.

In the impetuous haste to abolish time-honored Jewish customs, our historical vision becomes blurred, and we are apt to lose sight of the distinction between the significant and the insignificant, the more and the less important. Hence Hillel teaches: "He who does not study is deserving death" (Avot 1:13). He who learns nothing from Israel's rich historic past, who does not distinguish between that which is eternally binding and unchangeable and that which is of secondary importance and subject to the circumstances of time and place,—such a one condemns Judaism to stagnation and death. . . .

Only when the Rabbis of this country shall be moved by a common endeavor for wise moderation, unaffrighted at the "Backwards" cry—which may, after all, be beneficent progress; only when Religion shall again have been restored to the home, where it now lies, sadly neglected; and, speaking generally, only when conservative progress rather than ungovernable speed shall characterize our religious movement, can the outlook for Judaism be hopeful.

The time has come. It is NOW. "If not now, when?" Never were conditions so opportune as here and to-day. In all civilized countries the Jews are held in honor, regardless of their creed. Orthodox Jews stand in as high esteem as those of Reform tendencies. A Sir Moses Montefiore enjoyed the friendship of royalty.[21] Sir Nathaniel Rothschild is a Conservative in Religion. Yet on taking the Oath, kept his head covered.[22] Is he less respected than our Reformers, who, during divine service, worship with uncovered heads?

The times are calling to us: "Bring order out of this chaos" "And if not now, when?" Ye Rabbis, be heedful of the old Talmudic saying: "He who would force the hour, *i.e.*, who would bring things to pass before the time is ready for them, will in all probability fail. He, however, who— recognizing that the opportune time has come, takes advantage of it, will undoubtedly succeed" (Berakhot 64a).

The opportune moment cannot be created. It cannot be brought about by violent means; but when it has come, it behooves us to take advantage of it—it may not pass our way again. Let us, then, be up and doing!

SECTION 3 | An Orthodox Seminary?

To the Hebrews of America
Henry Pereira Mendes | 1886

Rev. Henry Pereira Mendes (1852–1937) was the minister of Shearith Israel in New York and a Jewish communal leader. In 1886, his congregation hosted a meeting of the founding members of the Jewish Theological Seminary Association. After much festering and politicking, Mendes and other clergymen established the rabbinical school as a more traditional alternative to the Reform Hebrew Union College. This document is derived from a fund-raising circular that Mendes sent to congregations in the United States and overseas. In it, Mendes stressed the need for a seminary to help acculturate Eastern European migrants, but he omitted any mention of the seminary's religious orientation or anti-Reform foundation.

Throughout the Country Jewish Communities are growing up in all directions. It is due not only to the natural increase in our numbers, but also and especially to the enormous influx of immigrants in the last few years.[23]

Honor or shame will be attached to the Jewish name, according as these communities develop. It will be our fault if they do not become a source of honor, and of strength by forwarding the true interests of our faith, and gaining the esteem of the world for its followers.

To secure these ends our congregations throughout the States must be provided with Rabbis and Teachers who will enjoy the confidence of the flock entrusted to their care, and at the same time will be able to command the respect of Jew and Christian for our religion, by respecting it themselves.

In both congregational and communal work the influence of cultured ministers, faithful to our religion, learned in our law, and endowed with University education, cannot be overestimated. By their intelligent efforts they will raise the standard of their congregation; by their educational labors with the young people and children they will foster love and respect for Judaism in the next generation, and by their own consistent and religious life they will set a proper example of devotion to the faith for which our ancestors labored and died.

To train such ministers, the Jewish Theological Seminary Association has been established in New York. Combined with the education necessary for a Rabbi will be a University Course at Columbia College or the University of the City of New York.

The movement has become popular, for all true Hebrews understand the importance of the undertaking.

Many Congregations in different States have already joined. Many ladies and gentlemen have contributed. While one gives five dollars [today, $130] as a humble offering, another has given $250 [today, $6,385] with a hint that he may give more. This one gives $10 [today, $255] as a patron, another has given $500 [today, $12,770] for the sacred cause. One gives $25 [today, $640] annual subscription for a certain number of years, another has given $1,000 [today, $25,540] in memory of her beloved dead, and so on.

Members of a family, or lodge, or society can combine with small sums or can endow a scholarship ($2,500) [today, $63,850] to be named in memory of the dead or after the donor.

You are most earnestly requested to obtain subscribers, patrons and donors for the sacred duty of perpetuating Judaism and securing honor to the Jewish name.

It is hoped you will fill with as many names as possible the appended blank and forward it by May 7th to

H. Pereira Mendes,
Honorary Secretary and Treasurer,
Pro tem.

A School for the Intelligent Orthodox

Sabato Morais | 1887

The Italian-born Rev. Sabato Morais was Isaac Leeser's successor and longtime minister of Mikveh Israel in Philadelphia. Morais was particularly active at the end of his life as an advocate for Russian Jewish immigrants in the United States and as the founding president of the Jewish Theological Seminary Association. In this letter to the American Hebrew, *the Philadelphia minister defended his rabbinical seminary on religious grounds against attacks from both Reform and Orthodox elements. Morais was unable to articulate a pithy description of the seminary's religious viewpoint. Instead, he described it as "cultured conservativism, or intelligent orthodoxy."*

With all my heart I had hoped that at no time I should feel morally bound to notice aspersions against an institution created in the interest of Judaism, as transmitted by the fathers. I greatly deplore the necessity now arisen, which compels me to show cause for grievance.[24] But though wounded to the core, I will suppress painful emotions, and hold my pen under absolute control. Nothing that I shall write shall betray anger, nor the absence of good breeding. The cause which I fondly cherish is pure; far be it from me to sully it with the fumes.

Admit: the "Jewish Theological Seminary" cannot lay claim to universal applause through its achievements. It is yet in its incipiency. I shall leave it to the near future, under the guidance of a benign God, to prove that it does deserve the countenance and material support of Israel in America. But not because the Seminary is in its infancy can I see it exposed to contumely and keep silent. I would commit an unpardonable sin were I not to try to vindicate it, so as to roll away the shame unwarrantably fastened upon an institution designed to do my faith honor.

Exaggerations in praising men or things are not distasteful to my nature; but I feel that I simply pay obedience to Truth, when I declare that the seminary is consecrated to cultured conservativism, or intelligent orthodoxy, if the expression be thus better understood.[25] To call the object of my pleading "the hot-bed of exclusiveness and downright bigotry" is to woefully misapprehend its aim—I will not say, to malign it most cruelly. When the students who must be trained how spiritually to minister to God's chosen people will be taught to shrink within themselves, and with pretentious piety shun the association of men who cannot share their views, I shall pray that Divine displeasure may fall upon a proscribing institution of learning. But never will hatred blend with our preceptors' tuition.

No! in very deed, love for the religion saved at the price of ages of sufferings; a longing for a union under the standard of Sinai—the ensign held high by prophets and sages—gave origin to the Theological Seminary. Ushered into life by such sentiments, it must continue to exist and command public regard. It were its death and disgrace to adopt for its government prescriptions suggested by the avowed adversaries of that nursery of Hebrew lore.

To the question asked, whether the pupils will *impartially* receive instruction in Wellhausen as well as Rashi, and be reasoned with against believing in the genuineness of the law and traditions, every fibre of my being forcibly answers NO.[26] Is this deception? Is it "sailing under false colors"? Or, imposing on the community of my brethren, "seeking to create the impression that the seminary has no color"? I repeat it most emphatically. The object whose progress I wish to promote has an undisguisedly defined purpose. It must tend to conserve that which is threatened with total extinction.

Its mission is to rebuild what has been inconsiderately pulled down. The attendants at the theological seminary must listen to dispassionate arguments proving that the books prized by our ancestors are more than life, to bear internal evidences of their authenticity, that ordinances compatible with our present denationalized state possess a validity recognized by the vast majority of our scattered race. For to this patent fact we owe the erection of synagogues everywhere, holy convocations, and the regulations which distinguish our home life.

After the scholars shall have become throughout imbued with the verities entrusted to their guardianship for an honest dissemination, after years of conscientious teachings shall have filled them with a spirit of unswerving devotion to the Torah, they may, without fear of harm, read modern thoughts as advanced by German and Dutch theorists.

And here I may be allowed to add that an assertion I made at the opening of the Seminary, and which perhaps I did not lucidly set forth, was meant to convey precisely what I have now stated.[27] A learned colleague at one time, and an estimable Israelite at another, took me to task for having said what they interpreted as exclusiveness and bigotry.[28] Surely they will concede that it is neither consistent nor wise to let youths destined for the office of Rabbis alternately read radically opposite views. Now, for instance, be shown God's hallowing of the seventh day, anon the extravagant opinion that the Sabbath was borrowed from astrological superstition of ancient heathens; now, teach them a treatise of the Talmud concerning prohibited viands, and shortly after present for their perusal essays on the advisability of abolishing all dietary laws. That system may commend itself to the minds of some as *impartial*, but truly if it does not succeed in throwing the students into a state of indescribable perplexity, it will never enable them to become faithful exponents of Rabbinism or of Mosaism.

That the scholars now in the Jewish Theological Seminary of New York, and those who shall enter it hereafter, may represent the ancient faith honestly is the earnest endeavor of a number of well-meaning Israelites.

Venturing to speak of myself individually as an official deeply interested in the institution, I solemnly declare, once for all—to eschew distasteful polemics—that my controlling thought is to help in raising preachers who believe in the sanctity of traditional Judaism, and who shall proclaim it fearlessly, and yet with freedom from ill-will and animosities; preachers whose characters will challenge respect, and suasively win many a waverer over to intelligent conservativism; preachers widely acquainted with the literature of the past and of the age in which we live, and therefore fit to associate with the highest and the best in the enlightened country which it is their happiness to dwell in.

"Jesuitical, narrow-minded, fanatical teachers of religion" shall not proceed from the Jewish Theological Seminary. That ominous prediction chronicled in the last issue of THE AMERICAN HEBREW will not come to pass. "Commit thy works unto the Lord, and thy purposes shall be established" (Prov. 16:3). Such is the conviction and ardent prayer of

S. Morais.
Philadelphia, Ab 11th, 5647 [August 1, 1887]

To Preserve Judaism Above All Else

Jacob H. Schiff | 1900

Jacob Schiff (1847–1920) was a German-born banker and Wall Street financial titan. His influence and money touched many sectors of American Jewry, particularly in efforts to assist Russian immigrants to the United States and the fight against antisemitism. As this document attests, Schiff was a force in the religious sphere as well. He was a member of the Reform Temple Emanu-El in New York but harbored sympathies and exhibited traditional behavior that did not fit so neatly into that more religiously progressive Jewish camp. In 1900 New York's leading Jewish newspaper, American Hebrew, *asked Schiff to comment on a proposal to merge the Orthodox Jewish Theological Seminary in New York and the Reform Hebrew Union College of Cincinnati. The philanthropist's response indicated his (and other American Jews') belief that rabbis affiliated with Ortho-*

doxy and Reform Judaism were not yet so divided and could still cooperate with each other.

Dear Sir:

There are in this country two institutions for the training of Rabbis. The Hebrew Union College was established twenty-five years ago for this purpose.[29] The parent body, the Union of American Hebrew Congregations, had for its main object the support of this institution.[30]

Circumstances, that we need not enumerate here, led to the withdrawal from the parent organization, and hence from the college, of those constituent members belonging to the orthodox or conservative section, and later to the establishment, under the presidency of the late Sabato Morais, of the Jewish Theological Seminary in New York.

Since the death of Dr. [Sabato] Morais the New York institution has been entertaining the idea of calling to its leadership some man who, by his learning and by his talents, would command the respect of the Jewish world, regardless of doctrinal lines. Lack of sufficient means has prevented, as yet, the accomplishment of this purpose.[31]

The Hebrew Union College, though in its twenty-fifth year, and having its representatives in the most prominent congregations in the land, is sorely in lack of funds, and the death of its founder, the late lamented Isaac M. Wise, has given fresh impetus to the movement for an endowment commensurate with the needs of the institution.[32]

Both of these institutions are seriously hampered in their usefulness by lack of financial support; both, at the present time, are without permanent heads.

It has been suggested that this is a good time to take into consideration the advisability of forming one strong institution for the training of Rabbis by the union of the two existing ones.

The position that you occupy in the community will give weight to your views upon this most important subject, whether you favor or oppose the idea, and we therefore will be pleased to have you take part in a symposium in THE AMERICAN HEBREW, dealing with the matter. Your reply by return of mail will greatly oblige,[33]

Yours very truly,
THE AMERICAN HEBREW

To the *American Hebrew*:

I am in receipt of your communication of the 26th inst. In which you ask for an expression of views on my part, whether I favor or oppose the suggestion which has been made, that this is an appropriate time to take into consideration the advisability of forming one strong institution for the training of Rabbis through a union of the Hebrew Union College at Cincinnati and the Jewish Theological Seminary of New York.

At the very moment of the recent home-going of the sainted Rev. Dr. Isaac M. Wise, it occurred to me that the moment had arrived when efforts should be made to unite the two struggling existing institutions, which each in its present condition could not and does not do justice to the great cause which both institutions should serve.[34] It does not appear to me that a seminary for the education of Jewish Rabbis need necessarily to be either under orthodox influence or reform management, especially not in this country, with its constant shifting movements, and where the orthodox Jew of to-day is to-morrow found in the reform camp. To me it is not a question of whether orthodoxy or reform should be sustained and perpetuated; the question much nearer to me is, how can Judaism be maintained as an active force in the daily life of our people, so that they may not become swamped by materialism and indifference, as is seriously threatened. In a serious effort for this maintenance of Judaism, the orthodox and reform Jew can, should, and must join hands, and in no way can they better do this than by joining in the creation of a strong institution, from which sincere, earnest, and capable men shall become graduated—true Jews, who shall be able to be teachers, leaders, and missionaries among our people. Perhaps I can do no better than to quote in full from a letter I have written on this subject some two weeks ago to one of the leading men in the management of the Hebrew Union College in Cincinnati as follows:[35]

> With characteristic and entirely justified promptness those in charge of the Hebrew Union College have, as I learn, taken steps to perpetuate Dr. Wise's memory in a manner in which its becoming a blessing shall be appropriately assured. There can not be any doubt that Dr. Wise, having lived for the College, would have wished for nothing better and higher, than that through his death the future of the College might become assured. And we need a strong Hebrew College so greatly! Not one which vegetates, maintained in a half-way manner, and which, being entirely dependent upon the support of the few, often grudgingly given, cannot expect to create the apparatus and furnish the facilities, with which a high seat of learning needs to be equipped, if it is to fulfill the mission of educating and graduating men, who shall truly become teachers, ministers, and leaders in American Israel.
>
> That the Hebrew Union College has been able to fulfill this mission, I trust you will pardon me for saying, is, in my opinion, not the case. For this the men, who with the late Dr. Wise, have actively guided the fortunes of the College are indeed not to blame. Indeed their zeal, energy, and intelligence has, under trying conditions, done all and more than could be expected. But the fact remains that in its career of, I believe, more than a quarter of a century the College has, with the exception of a handful, not produced any ministers of real prominence, certainly none equal of the Rabbis, such as you and I have been wont to look up to as Jewish teachers and leaders; men of the stamp of Jellneck, Holdheim, Geiger, Stein, Adler, Einhorn, Huebsch, Lilienthal, Samuel Hirsch, Wise, and others who have passed away during our generation.[36] And at no period perhaps has Israel, especially American Israel, been more in urgent need of great

teachers and influential leaders than at the present time. In this, I believe, you will heartily agree with me, for I am very certain you recognize as fully as I do, without entering into arguments, the grave dangers which threaten the spiritual life of the present and the rising generation of our co-religionists.

And this at once brings to me the purpose which has prompted me to write to you. If the College is to have a greater future, it needs to be placed upon an entirely different basis and footing than it now has, but whether this can be efficiently done, in its present surroundings, appears to me rather doubtful. Cincinnati, in the first instance, does not possess, I believe, an academic atmosphere. Its College, valuable local importance though it may possess, is hardly recognized among the leading universities and scientific schools of our country, and aside from this, even this local college has, I have been informed, closed its doors to the free admission for the students from the Hebrew Union College, such as is generally granted by the larger universities and colleges throughout the country to students in Theological Seminaries. Nor is it necessary that I dwell here at length upon the importance and desirability of locating a College where large local resources and wealth can be utilized in its favor, nor emphasize the fact that a seat of learning should be there situated where men of knowledge and science will come for other reasons than alone for the professional emoluments which can be offered them.[37]

I am writing you so unreservedly because I know you to be above small considerations, because I feel assured that in a manner of such grave importance to American Judaism, you will not let local pride alone influence you. Without therefore wishing to advance the statements made as undoubtedly correct, I should like you to carefully consider for yourself, and with others if you so desire, whether the weal of the Hebrew Union College in the first instance and that of American Judaism in consequence would not be better promoted if at the present junction proper ways and means could be devised to remove the College to New York or any place where conditions exist and can be created, destined to secure to it the attainment of the high position it should occupy, if it is to become the seat of Jewish learning from which American Israel shall be able to draw teachers who shall be leaders and ministers who shall be missionaries in the highest sense of the word.

Jacob H. Schiff

May 1st, 1900

CONCLUSION

The 1880s were a crucial decade for the traditional American rabbinate. The Orthodox ministry gained unprecedented confidence in its fight against reformers. In 1883 the more-or-less Reform Hebrew Union College celebrated its inaugural graduating class with a banquet. Its menu included littleneck clams, soft-shelled crabs, shrimp salad, potatoes in lobster bisque sauce, and frog legs in cream sauce.[38] The egregious violation of Jewish dietary law at the so-called Trefa Banquet infuriated Orthodox guests, some of whom walked out of the dinner reception and launched a public campaign against their Reform hosts. Two years later, the newly arrived Alexander Kohut enchanted his New York congregation with learned dissertations on "Mosaic-rabbinical Judaism" and censure of the radical Reform he observed in Manhattan. The scholar's proclamation encouraged thousands of "Orthodox" listeners and readers and inspired a "red hot" debate with his Reform rabbinic neighbor, Kaufmann Kohler.[39]

As a result, a more empowered rabbinate asserted itself in the United States. On the liberal end, the Kohut-Kohler exchange moved its leading exponents to convene a rabbinical conference at Pittsburgh that would attempt to "consolidate" and outline "platforms" to stand for the official creed of Reform Judaism.[40] On the other end, the traditional rabbinate sought to establish a rabbinical school that would most appropriately serve its American constituencies. In 1886 a group of anti-Reform rabbis founded the Jewish Theological Seminary Association. Its opponents were quick and adamant to label it an "Orthodox" school.[41] Yet the leaders of the seminary, like Sabato Morais, qualified the seminary's "Orthodoxy" in broad and enlightened terms. No doubt, that reluctance to confirm a bold Orthodox stance appeased some but infuriated others who wished to firm up their Orthodox brand. In the end, vagueness kept alive the debate over what could and could not count for Orthodox Judaism in the United States and opened up a pathway for a new movement in American Judaism.

PART 2 | The Contest for Modern Orthodox Judaism

4 | The Arrival of Eastern European Immigrants

INTRODUCTION

In 1893 Rabbi Yisrael Meir Kagan (1838–1933) published a thin tract that warned coreligionists living in Eastern Europe not to migrate to "far off lands." Beginning in earnest in the 1880s, hundreds of thousands of Jews departed Europe for "better futures" in the United States, increasing the Jewish population from 250,000 in 1880 to about 3.5 million in 1924, when officials closed off most migration to America's shores.[1] Many of these migrants began their American sojourns as traditional Jews accustomed to the Orthodox regimens of Judaism. The famed rabbi known as the Hafetz Hayyim urged "God-fearing" Jews to resist the urge to settle in Africa and England as well. Yet he was particularly fearful of Jewish life in America, where it is "impossible to act as a faithful Jew in accordance with Sabbath observance and other similar matters in a proper fashion."[2] In time, a number of Jews concurred with the Hafetz Hayyim's assessment, but not before they set foot on American soil.[3] A popular folksong among Jews in St. Louis mocked the supposition that "America is a goldene medina," a golden country. "Woe to Columbus," the song continued, since it was so difficult to find employment and "there is no family pride in America."[4]

The first group of documents in this chapter expresses these grave concerns. Some of the best writings that explore the incongruity of religious life in America compared with conditions in Europe deal with the female experience. Two such selections drawn from memoiristic literature are provided below. Traditionalist Jews did not simply give up. Rather, "resisters" of American acculturation founded institutions that they believed might help retain the religious culture as they remembered it, however romantically, in Eastern Europe.[5] In 1888 Lower East Side Jews arranged for the appointment of Vilna's Jacob Joseph (1840–1902) as chief rabbi of New York. To be sure, the so-called chief rabbi held some progressive views, but he was nothing like the more "enlightened" and "Orthodox" men who led the Jewish Theological Seminary in New York. On the day of Rabbi Joseph's funeral, a large group of "resister" rabbis met to establish the Agudath Ha-Rabbonim, another institution that hoped to preserve the old ways of Judaism.

Not everyone agreed with this strategy, even as Jews faced the hardships of immigrant life in the United States. In Europe, many Jewish leaders pointed to disastrous social conditions there and pleaded with their followers to settle in the United States.[6] In New York, immigrants also encountered "accommodators" who sought to facilitate Orthodox life in its new American surroundings. The leaders of these efforts founded the Union of Orthodox Jewish Congregations (Orthodox Union) and, in time, spearheaded the Young Israel movement. There was no consensus on how traditional Jewish life might be synthesized with Americanism, nor did all of the earliest proponents of these organizations wish to define themselves as Orthodox. Rather, they followed the lead of philanthropist Harry Fischel (1865–1948), who often used his own rags-to-riches story to prove that Orthodox Jews could "make it" without disobeying the strictures of the Sabbath and other areas of Jewish law.[7] In other words, they wished to present the United States as a viable option for religiously conscientious traditional Jews. The final documents in this chapter explore the innovative creations concocted by these accommodators—usually German-trained Orthodox rabbis—and the philosophies that underpinned their efforts. In their work we find renewed attempts to foster a modern and Orthodox movement.

Sabbath at the Polish Shul

William M. Rosenblatt | 1872

This report of a Sabbath prayer service in a makeshift synagogue reveals much about the Eastern European Jewish culture that took hold of Manhattan's Lower East Side at the end of the nineteenth century. Not much is known about the writer's life. To be sure, this account precedes the mass migration of Russian and Polish Jews to the United States that began in earnest in the 1880s. Still, it conveys a vivid (and cynical) impression of a new brand of Orthodox Judaism that did not blend in easily with the American- and German-style congregations that Jews had established for themselves in the United States in the prior decades. Rosenblatt's essay also includes a description of the toned-down bar mitzvah ceremony that Eastern European Jews brought with them to America. In time, leading members of the German Jewish community in the United States organized efforts to acculturate these Russian Jews to New World norms.

But to return to the synagogue in Baxter street. They went through all the well-known prayers which precede the reading of the Pentateuch—through the Psalms, the extracts from the Bible, and the touching entreaties for deliverance from their exile. I picked up a prayer-book which lay at my side, and turned over its leaves. It was the standard edition which among all the Orthodox is still in use, as well as among some of the Reformed Jews, although the latter have weeded out many inappropriate and objectionable passages. There was no translation to the book. Many Russian-Polish Jews would think a translation an outrage. Fortunately, I understood Hebrew—better, perhaps, than the majority of the worshippers in the synagogue, who, like the majority of all the Jews of to-day, have acquired the ability to read the mere words with tremendous rapidity, but without knowing the meaning of any except the most frequently recurring.

Presently we reached the silent prayer, during which all stand with their faces to the east.[8] That concluded, the doors of the ark were rolled back, and the parchment scroll of the Pentateuch, on which every letter has been formed by hand, was taken out and deposited by the reader on the desk. The president of the congregation, the sexton, and another officer then stationed themselves about the scroll, and the reader began to recite to the peculiar, monotonous tune which is customary among the Orthodox. The passage read is always cut up into parts, and at the beginning of each a member of the congregation is called to the desk by the reader, who addresses him by his Hebrew name (every Orthodox Jew has that) and tells him in Hebrew to arise. He steps forward, recites the customary short prayer, looks on the scroll while the reader goes over it, and when the end of the part is reached makes a small donation to the congregation and gives place to another. Strangers who are Jews are usually given the preference in this, which is considered an honor.

I knew this, and did not expect to escape on this occasion. I presently saw that the reader, the sexton, and the president were whispering together, and I felt that my fate had been sealed. But they were evidently in doubt. They appeared uncertain what to think of me. Was I a Jew like themselves, but changed in expression and softened in feature by profane education and intercourse with the outside world; or was I simply a Christian, a Mormon, or a Pagan? The sexton seemed determined to dissipate the doubt. He approached me and asked me if I desired the honor of being called to the desk. Knowing it would be considered discourteous if I admitted my extraction and still refused the distinction which was tendered me, I replied in the affirmative. Upon that he asked me for my Hebrew name, and I gave him Moses bar Samuel—Moses, the son of Samuel. A thalith was taken from the ark and given me. I wrapped it about me and awaited my turn, endeavoring meanwhile to recall the words of the prayer which I would be expected to recite.

Moses bar Samuel was presently called. Arising from my seat, I stepped to the desk, and grasping the peculiar tassel at one corner of my thalith, pressed upon the parchment scroll and then brought it to my lips, uttering aloud at the same time the customary benediction. As I concluded, the whole congregation chimed in, and then the reader began. For five minutes or more he rattled away without a single pause for breath, and then finished with an extra flourish and an original note or two in his tune, to do me especial honor. I made a second benediction, like the first, in Hebrew, and after informing the reader that I wished to donate the sum of one dollar [today, $17] to the Chebrah Bnai Jisrael Adath Kodesh (the Holy Congregation of the Sons of Israel)—a fact which he immediately announced to the congregation in the course of his erratic Hebrew melodies—I made way for the next name and retired to my seat.

The next man happened to be a newly made one; that is, he was a lad who had just reached the age of thirteen, and was therefore entitled to be classed among the adults. The thalith which he wore had been made expressly for him, and he had never worn it before. He uttered a benediction in the same way as the others had done it, but on concluding it he began to read the scroll himself instead of allowing the reader to do it, and did it to the same tune and in the same measure. He had probably spent a month in preparing himself for this task, under the guidance of the reader. It is an old custom, and one which the most Orthodox Jews cling to determinedly, while vestiges of it are found in almost every synagogue of the United States, however advanced the congregation may be. Connected with the ceremony is a noble idea. Every error that a boy may commit before his thirteenth year his parents are held responsible for; but after reaching that age he must bear upon his own shoulders the consequences of all his acts, and in order to bring the truth of this more strongly before him, and to invest him with a certain degree of self-respect and self-reliance, he is formally admitted to the congregation on the Saturday following his thirteenth birthday, with the ceremonies which I have just described.

The boy's performance over, the scroll was rolled up and covered with its silken gown, amid a universal uprising and the confused murmuring of fifty praying voices. The scroll was then replaced in the ark, the doors were closed, and the concluding services were commenced. I was somewhat lost in thought when the sexton again approached me. His question was rather embarrassing. Would I like to say the *mussaph* prayer? In other words, would I like to rise before the congregation and sing this prayer to the customary tune? They seemed to have formed a high opinion of my ability after my creditable performance at the desk; but notwithstanding that, I now had to confess, humiliating though it was, that to do this second thing was utterly beyond my powers. I told the sexton as much, and with a look of kindly pity he left me once more in peace.

The Chief Rabbi's Sermon
Abraham Cahan | 1888

In 1888 the Association of American Orthodox Congregations invited Rabbi Jacob Joseph (1840–1902) of Vilna to serve as chief rabbi for New York. The election followed the death of Rabbi Abraham Ash (1813–87) of the Beth Hamidrash Hagadol on New York's Lower East Side, who had played a prominent role among Eastern European Jewish immigrants in Manhattan. The association represented a number of leading Orthodox congregations but could not achieve a consensus among all traditional Jews in New York. Upon arrival, Joseph suffered political turmoil and illness. A leading Jewish socialist, the Belarusian-born Abraham Cahan (1860–1951), best known as editor of the Yiddish-language Jewish Daily Forward, *wrote his impressions of one of Chief Rabbi Joseph's first sermons in New York. In his view, the talents that made Joseph successful in Europe were not in concert with the expectations that New York Jews had for their rabbi in America.*

The orthodox Russian Jews now decided to bring over a famous rabbi. There was among them in New York no outstanding rabbi.

Among the leaders of those who wanted to import a great rabbi was the cap manufacturer Joshua Rothstein, the president of the Yeshiva Etz Chaim who had tried to help me get the English books. The plan was to bring over a rabbi from a large Russian city who would command the respect of both Jews and gentiles. No single community was able to do this on its own, and so it became necessary to combine resources.

For this purpose, eighteen synagogues finally joined in an alliance. They resolved that the new rabbi would carry the title of Chief Rabbi. After many meetings and much letter writing it was announced that Rabbi Jacob Joseph, the leading preacher of Vilna, would be brought over to become the Chief Rabbi.

In the old country the rabbi is not always a preacher. But in America a main role of the clergy is to conduct services and deliver sermons. American practice influenced the decision that the Chief Rabbi must also be an outstanding preacher. The sermons would become a strong bond holding the alliance of the eighteen synagogues together in support of the Chief Rabbi.

I had an uncle, Michael Beirack, in Vilna. He wrote me a letter in which he said:

> Rab Yankev Yoisef is very dear to us. He is a sagacious scholar and a rare, God-fearing man. Our hearts are heavy with pain because we have had to part with him. One does not want to lose such a precious treasure.
>
> See to it, Alter, that the Jews in New York know what a diamond they have taken from us. See that he is properly appreciated. I know that you don't attend a synagogue, but you have a Jewish heart. So tell everyone that Vilna was proud of him and that New York should appreciate the precious crown it has now acquired.

Now it was the turn of the orthodox Jews to buzz with excitement.[9] The Chief Rabbi arrived in July 1888 and was received with much pomp and ceremony. [Pinchas] Minkowsky, too, had been enthusiastically received.[10] But this was the new Chief Rabbi, not the cantor of a single community but the leader of eighteen synagogues.

The English-language press, still without photography, presented vividly written descriptions of the Chief Rabbi and quoted him at length on a variety of subjects.

Although I had no connection with the world of orthodox Jews, as an observer of Jewish life I was interested in the role of the Chief Rabbi. I was most interested in hearing his sermons; but not for the purpose of writing an article about them. I was reluctant to be critical, even if my judgment required me to be so. On the other hand, as a socialist it was impossible for me to write in a friendly manner about a religious subject.

Progressive persons among us were convinced that in America a rabbi could not escape hypocrisy. Often I said, publicly as well as privately, that there were genuinely admirable and honest rabbis in the old country. But the new world was hostile to the orthodox spirit that flourished in the old-world Jewish centers.

In the old world a synagogue elder was more or less learned, was shy and humble before God and man. How could the Old World purity and honesty persist in the new environment where an ignoramus could become president of a synagogue only because he had "worked his way up?"

I went to hear a sermon by the new Chief Rabbi. He impressed me as being a scholar and an honest man of simple faith. But I could see also that he was not a happy man, that neither the honor, nor the fuss, nor even the large salary were of primary importance as far as he was concerned.

It was only his second or third sermon since his arrival and already he was making a clumsy attempt to accommodate himself to his audience by using American Yiddish. Once he used the word "clean" for "rein," and it was easy to see this was purposely done to show he was not a greenhorn. His efforts to acquire social polish failed.

At one point he reached for a handkerchief in his pocket. It began to come out, long and blue. He was suddenly embarrassed and struggled to put the handkerchief back into his rear pocket. It twisted around his hand. In desperation, he put the handkerchief on the lectern and soon had both his hands entangled in it. His American words sounded unnatural. It was a pity.

I surveyed the congregation. Almost all around were men dressed in a fine American style: pressed suits, starched collars, neckties, and cuffs, clean-shaven and spruced up. The rough edges of a small East European congregation had been replaced with American polish and sophistication. They looked upon their Chief Rabbi and decided he was a greenhorn.

Rab Yankev Yoisef was like a plant torn out of the soil and transplanted into a hothouse. His health deteriorated. He suffered a paralytic stroke.

The Charleston Responsum
Naftali Zvi Yehudah Berlin | 1894

In 1894 the descendants of Rabbi Naftali Zvi Yehudah Berlin (1817–93) published a collection of their father's halakhic treatises (responsa). In one undated responsum, the famed head of the Volozhin Yeshiva (commonly known by the acronym Neziv) in Lithuania answered a query posed to him by an anonymous member of Charleston's Orthodox community. In all likelihood, the Charleston Jew asked about the advisability of Congregation Shari Emouna rejoining with Brith Shalom. Members of the former congregation had broken away from Brith Shalom and its congregants, who allegedly violated the Sabbath and other areas of Jewish law. Berlin's negative response, a portion of which is reproduced below, bespoke Eastern European leaders' intolerance for halakhic miscreants and American Orthodoxy's reliance on a transatlantic line of communication with rabbinic scholars in Europe.

With regard to joining with the organization (synagogue) called Beth Jacob, which includes those who publicly desecrate the Sabbath: God forbid that one should associate with them in any matter related to the service of God.[11] It is stated in *Shulhan Arukh* (Orah Hayyim 55:11) that sinners or those who [occasionally] commit transgressions are counted toward a religious quorum. Yet this is only meant for those who violate one area [of Jewish law]. Even though it is written (Prov. 21:27) that the "[Temple] sacrifices of the wicked is an abomination," nevertheless, we accept the sacrifices of sinners of Israel, as it is stated in [Talmud Bavli] Hulin 5a, this is the law so that they will return in repentance, and for the honor of Heaven we rule leniently for prayer.[12] However, we do not accept the Temple offerings of one who worships idolatry or violates the Sabbath in a public manner, since such a person is in a fixed position and will not repent in the future.[13] Therefore, his prayer is also an abomination—so how may one join with such a person? Behold, in an instance where one's prayers are an abomination, he is not in fulfillment of his requirement to pray on any level, as it is stated in [Talmud Bavli] Berakhot (22b.).[14]

Father and Mother

Anzia Yezierska | 1890

Anzia Yezierska (1885–1970) was an immigrant American novelist. Her stories often depicted the immigrant's (not always Jewish) struggle to acculturate in America. Her writings also throw light on the experiences of female émigrés to the United States. In particular, this portion from her acclaimed novel Bread Givers *underscored the incongruity between Old World Jewish gender expectations and the changing opportunities for young women at the turn of the twentieth century.*

It was now time for dinner. I was throwing the rags and things from the table to the window, on the bed, over the chairs, or any place where there was room for them. So much junk we had in our house that everybody put everything on the table. It was either to eat on the floor, or for me the job of cleaning off the junk pile three times a day. The school teacher's rule, "A place for everything, and everything in its place," was no good for us, because there weren't enough places.

As the kitchen was packed with furniture, so the front room was packed with Father's books. They were on the shelf, on the table, on the window sill, and in soapboxes lined up against the wall.

When we came to America, instead of taking along feather beds, and the samovar, and the brass pots and pans, like other people, Father made us carry his books. When Mother begged only to take along her pot for *gefülte* fish, and the feather beds that were handed down to her from her grandmother for her wedding presents, Father wouldn't let her.

"Woman!" Father said, laughing into her eyes. "What for will you need old feather beds? Don't you know it's always summer in America? And in the new golden country, where milk and honey flows free in the streets, you'll have new golden dishes to cook in, and not weigh yourself down with your old pots and pans. But my books, my holy books always were, and always will be, the light of the world. You'll see yet how all America will come to my feet to learn.

No one was allowed to put their things in Father's room, any more than they were allowed to use Masha's hanger.

Of course, we all knew that if God had given Mother a son, Father would have permitted a man child to share with him his best room in the house. A boy could say prayers after his father's death—that kept the father's soul alive for ever. Always Father was throwing up to Mother that she had borne him no sons to be an honour to his days and to say prayers for him when he died.

The prayers of his daughters didn't count because God didn't listen to women. Heaven and the next world were only for men. Women could get into Heaven because they were wives and daughters of men. Women had no brains for the study of God's Torah, but they could be servants of men who studied Torah. Only if they cooked for the men, and washed for the men, and didn't nag or curse the men out of their homes; only if they let the men study the Torah in peace, then, maybe, they could push themselves into Heaven with the men, to wait on them there.

And so, since men were the only people who counted with God, Father not only had the best room for himself, for his study and prayers, but also the best eating of the house. The fat from the soup and the top from the milk went always to him.

Mother had just put the soup pot and plates for dinner on the table, when Father came in.

At the first look on Mother's face he saw how she was boiling, ready to burst, so instead of waiting for her to begin her hollering, he started:

"Woman! when will you stop darkening the house with your worries?"

"When I'll have a man who does the worrying. Does it ever enter your head that the rent was not paid the second month? That to-day we're eating the last loaf of bread that the grocer trusted me?" Mother tried to squeeze the hard, stale loaf that nobody would buy for cash. "You're so busy working for Heaven that I have to suffer here such bitter hell."

We sat down to the table. With watering mouths and glistening eyes we watched Mother skimming off every bit of fat from the top soup into Father's big plate, leaving for us only the thin, watery part. We watched Father bite into the sour pickle which was special for him only; and waited, trembling with hunger, for our portion.

Father made his prayer, thanking God for the food. Then he said to Mother:

"What is there to worry about, as long as we have enough to keep the breath in our bodies? But the real food is God's Holy Torah." He shook her gently by the shoulder, and smiled down at her.

At Father's touch Mother's sad face turned into smiles. His kind look was like the sun shining on her.

Daughter of the Ramaz
S. N. Behrman | 1893

The son of Eastern European immigrants, Samuel Nathaniel Behrman (1893–1973) was a playwright and frequent contributor to the New Yorker. In an essay published in that magazine, the writer related his memories of his uncle's wife, Ida. This excerpt from Behrman's short story describes the arduous transition of a young woman from traditional Jewish life to American social norms.

About the time I was born, a radiant event took place in my family. The details were impressed on me early. While my parents and my two older brothers were living a quiet and uneventful life on Providence Street, in Worcester, there suddenly fell into my family's collective lap an unbelievable and breathtaking bounty.[15] It had the quality of a miracle because it was so easy and instantaneous and transforming. It lifted my parents to the Providence Street skies, distinguished them. It was as if there had suddenly been conferred on my family—without any of its members doing anything at all to deserve it—the award of the

Légion d'Honneur. From that moment, they were set apart, revered, envied. My father was highly thought of as a Talmudic scholar, but the rest of us were ordinary enough. Why were we singled out for this extraordinary blessing? There were other Talmudists on the street, and *they* had families, too. Nevertheless, it was to us that it happened—the sudden arrival of a tremendous, unearned social increment—and nothing could be done about it by those who envied us. There was compensation even for them, because the lustre of our new distinction was great enough to shed its glow over the whole community. Had it been aware, all of Worcester might have reveled in it. But Providence Street knew, even if the rest of Worcester didn't. What happened was the totally unexpected engagement, in 1893, of my Uncle Harry, who lived a couple of blocks away on Providence Street, to a Boston girl named Ida, the daughter of the Ramaz.[16]

There is an enchanting, almost untranslatable Yiddish play by Peretz Hirschbein called "Green Fields."[17] It is laid in an impoverished ghetto village in Russia toward the end of the last century, and it tells of a wandering Talmudic scholar who is travelling on foot from a small Yeshiva, or rabbinical school, to a large, famous one in a big town hundreds of miles distant. He spends the night in the poor little hamlet. The illiterate Jewish peasant into whose yard he wanders is dazzled by the appearance of a man of the written word, and runs in to tell his family of the incredible stroke of good fortune. He is hysterical with gratitude to God. When the rich man of the village hears that the Talmudic scholar is staying in the poor man's house, he is angry. If this man of God is staying in the village, naturally he must stay with him. The play is concerned with the fierce social rivalry in the village over entertaining the poor scholar, over having as a guest, if only for a few hours, a man who can read. When I saw this play in Los Angeles some years ago, performed with remarkable delicacy by Jacob Ben-Ami, I understood better the sensation on Providence Street when my Uncle Harry's engagement to Ida was announced.[18] For Ida's father, the Ramaz, was one of the most famous rabbis in the world. He was so famous that he was called not by his real name—Rabbi Moshe Zevulun Margolies—

but by a name coined from gold-rimmed spectacles. My family knew his face even before the windfall, because his photograph hung in the living room of our tenement, as it did in the living room of most other Providence Street tenements.

The Ramaz, who was then presiding over the Baldwin Place Synagogue, in Boston, to which he had been summoned from Lithuania seven years before, traced his descent from a celebrated rabbi known as the Rashi, one of the greatest of Talmudic commentators, who lived in France in the eleventh century. "Rashi" is also a name coined from initials; his true name was Rabbi Shlomo Yitzhaki. (The renowned Maimonides, whose full name was Rabbi Moshe ben Maimon, was called Rambam.)[19] The Rashi wrote one of the books of commentary—the book, too, is known as the Rashi—that orthodox Jews labor over endlessly in their Talmudic studies. Modern French philologists, the encyclopedias say, still go to the Rashi for examples of French literary usage in the Middle Ages. Some notions of the Ramaz's vast influence may be gleaned from the fact that in 1906, when he was presiding over the Congregation Kehilath Jeshurun, on West Eighty-fifth Street, in New York—and he was still presiding over it when he died in 1936, at the age of eighty-five—a delegation of seventeen members of the Providence Street synagogue, after visiting him to ask his advice on some synagogue question, decided to pay him an architectural tribute by rebuilding the house of worship on Providence Street in exact, if scaled-down, imitation of the Ramaz's synagogue.

The addition to the family of this illustrious aunt was a blessing far beyond what anyone could have imagined when the first breathless rumor of my Uncle Harry's engagement reached Worcester. Ida brought into our rather lugubrious, God-obsessed circle an exhilarating earthy gusto, strongly flavored with an almost ribald skepticism. The descendant of the Rashi bore her immense heritage lightly. Her gaiety was more than merely paradoxical; it was downright shocking. Whispers about Ida began to trickle along Providence Street soon after she settled down to housekeeping there with my Uncle Harry. In Worcester, Ida's attitude was always that of a worldling forced by awkward circumstances to reside briefly in the provinces, and she sailed serenely above the invidious rumors. When Ida, who was then seventeen, married my Uncle Harry, who was ten years older, she was a beautiful girl, with large, clear blue eyes and abundant light hair; she looked like a Holbein.[20] Men stopped to chat with her on a sidewalk. On Providence Street, this was not considered proper for a married woman. For a married woman whose father was the Ramaz, it was considered blasphemous. Uncle Harry's sister, a strict doctrinaire, complained to him that Ida's promiscuous sidewalk conversations were becoming a scandal. My uncle, still incredulous at the acquisition of such a bride, told his sister that it was none of her business and that the daughter of the Ramaz could do no wrong, and suggested that the reason she herself never became involved in sidewalk conversations was that she was aggressively homely. There were other charges against Ida. One was that she brought home too many bundles, by which people meant that she was extravagant and wasted her husband's substance. As my Uncle Harry was a peddler of notions—pins, needles, and other small household accommodations, which he sold from house to house in such outlying communities as Ware, Fitchburg, Auburn, Webster, and Shrewsbury— there couldn't have been too much substance to waste, but the charge persisted. Later on, Ida bought an upright piano, on time. This was a nine days' wonder. It wasn't that Ida was musical; she had discovered that her husband had a tendency to throw things around when he was irritated, and the solidity of a piano appealed to her. A more serious charge was that she attended the matinees at Poli's vaudeville theatre on Saturdays. Such a violation of the Sabbath was unthinkable. Harry fiercely denied the charge, but one Saturday when a telegram arrived saying that Ida's mother was seriously ill, Harry went at once to Poli's and had Ida paged. When she was found, she pointed out that she had bought the ticket in advance, so that no money had changed hands on the sacred day.

Ida always said that she was not a "private woman." Aware of the gossip about her, she explained that she simply had to talk to men on the sidewalk. By not being a "private woman" she meant that she was the helpless victim of a passionate avocation, which she lovingly called a disease: This was her consuming interest in matchmaking. It colored her entire life. When it had begun she couldn't remember. She looked down on professional matchmakers, although she often had to come into contact with them, and, being proud of her amateur standing, she never took out a license. Ida had the true amateur's love, a devotion untainted by the profit motive. No one was safe from Ida—not even her own children, or any widowed in-laws, or her father. The feeling among orthodox Jews that a rabbi should not remain unmarried was a help to Ida, for the Ramaz outlived three wives and gave her talents a lot of play.

The Bylaws of the Agudath Ha-Rabbonim

The Union of Orthodox Rabbis of America | 1902

On July 29, 1902, the day of Chief Rabbi Jacob Joseph's funeral, sixty North American rabbis met at the Machzike Talmud Torah on the Lower East Side to form the Agudath Ha-Rabbonim (Union of Orthodox Rabbis of the United States and Canada). At the start, the organization was led by Rabbi Bernard Levinthal (1864–1952) of Philadelphia. Members of the Agudath Ha-Rabbonim had earlier voiced concern over the "constant desecration of the Torah" in the United States. Accordingly, the rabbinical group was established to help retain the older ways of Orthodox Judaism in the United States. This first section of the Agudath Ha-Rabbonim's bylaws concerns the highly restrictive qualifications for membership, thereby ruling out more accommodating rabbis ordained at the Jewish Theological Seminary in New York.

MEMBERS OF THE UNION

1. For membership to the Union, only the following may be selected: a) someone who was ordained to rule on Jewish law by the great and sagacious rabbis of Europe. b) and also holds a rabbinic position within an Orthodox congregation and guides his people in the path of God and proper actions.

2. A candidate may not receive membership until one member shall nominate him as a worthy and exceptional rabbi before the

Executive Committee. Afterward, the Executive Committee shall designate three members of the Union who are familiar with the candidate and shall inquire into the rabbinical ordination and the character of the candidate. The Executive Committee shall receive the information and deliberate. If each member of the Executive is in complete agreement then the candidate shall be accepted as a member. However, if the Executive Committee is not in complete agreement then the matter shall be put forward to the annual convention and membership shall be determined based on a majority vote.

PAYMENTS

1. It is incumbent upon every member to pay six dollars [annually] [today, $160] for the maintenance of the Union. Payments shall be made at the beginning of each half-year cycle, specifically: in Tamuz—three dollars, and in Tevet—three dollars shall also be given.[21]

2. If six months pass and a member has not paid his designated dues, the Secretary shall send a bill of notice that shall indicate that if payment is not sent within a week all benefits of membership shall be suspended by the Union's board. The Secretary shall read the names of all members with outstanding payments at the annual convention and shall put to a general vote to decide how to handle the matters of these members.

THE ORGANIZATION OF THE UNION

1. The following officers shall be elected at each annual convention: one Chairman, one Secretary, one deputy, and six committees:
   1) Executive Committee to manage all affairs of the Union.
   2) Education Committee to oversee the general and particular curricula matters in Talmud Torahs and schools.
   3) Yeshiva Committee to oversee curricular matters and divisions within the yeshivot and to assist in the establishment of new yeshivot in capable locations.

4) Sabbath Committee to find ways to strengthen Sabbath observance among our brethren and render it appealing to them.

5) Kashrut Committee to supervise on all matters and elements that require kashrut and standards that will prevent concerns of wrongdoing, and so that it shall be clear to all that there are valid kashrut standards that are trusted by the members of the Union and sufficient in every locale.

6) Peace and Benevolence Committee to mediate equanimity between rabbis [Hakhamim] and the laity [Am], and to offer material and spiritual support to the rabbinic members of the Union as much as possible, according to the time and place.

At the annual convention an Ordination Committee shall also be selected to ordain the best and worthy scholars and to crown them masters of Torah, sages, pure of character, and God fearing.

SECTION 2 | Accommodating to a Goldene Medine

The Orthodox Convention

Orthodox Jewish Congregational Union of America | JUNE 8, 1898

In 1898 a group of traditional-minded laymen and rabbis representing fifty congregations met at Shearith Israel in New York. After much debate, the delegates established the Orthodox Jewish Congregational Union of America, later renamed the Union of Orthodox Jewish Congregations of America (also known as the Orthodox Union). The proceedings of the New York convention revealed a widely held consensus on the organization's position on Zionism but a divide on the use of "Orthodox" to describe the new institution.

Rev. Dr. [Henry Pereira] Mendes was called to the chair. He spoke briefly, saying that he had wished to address them on "The Judaism we love so well," and hoped to during the convention. Mistakes had been made, no doubt, in the calling of the convention and arrangements for its conduct, but it was the first of its kind and it was hoped that a satisfactory plan would be devised for calling a larger and more representative convention.

A statement of principles was then read.[22] Mr. [Lewis] Dembitz objected to the use of the word "orthodox."[23] It did not sufficiently indicate the purpose of the organization. Orthodox was used to cover one's belief; persons who did not live a Jewish life but read the olden prayers were, according to the generally accepted view, Orthodox. He preferred a title like Shomre Hadath, "Observers of the Law."

Dr. [Bernard] Drachman favored the name "Orthodox" because it stood for something in the community.[24] Orthodoxy has been identified in the popular mind with strict observance of the law, and we should cling to it. Revs. [Henry] Schneeberger and [Meldola] De Sola spoke in the same strain.[25] The latter said that he would like to see the word "Orthodoxy" written across the clock upon the platform. The chair, Dr. Mendes, protested against this use of the name, as Orthodoxy should never be time-serving.

Objection was made by some of the speakers to some of the phraseology of the statements of principles and on motion of Max Cohen it was referred back to the committee.[26]

A report of the Committee on Zionism was then submitted by Mr. Cohen, after which the convention adjourned till the afternoon.

From the report of the Committee on Zionism we take the following brief extracts:

"The desirability and the necessity of offering to those of our brethren dwelling under the rigor of oppressive laws a refuge legally assured to them cannot be questioned. The logic of events points again to Palestine and the surrounding fertile districts as the land of promise.

"Historical associations and prophetic promises invest the land of Israel with an attraction for the Jew, and awaken among the Gentiles a recognition of fitness for this purpose not possessed by any other region.

"The elimination of the idea of the political State from the present programme of Zionism averts the possibility of opposition from the Turkish government or from those European powers that have special interest in the holy places of the cradle of Christianity.[27]

"The proposal to assist existing colonies by the addition to them of desirable members and by opening depots for the reception and sale of their products in the commercial centers of Europe and America is so eminently feasible and promising that merely to state it is to secure its approval.

"We unhesitatingly affirm that there is nothing incompatible between enthusiastic adherence to Zionism and the most ardent American patriotism, and what we can affirm for American, our English brethren can affirm for British patriotism, and our European brethren as to their respective countries.

"The Jew, believing in promises of the prophets, looks forward to the time when all men shall dwell unitedly and in peace, inquiring not of one another as to race or birthplace, but while waiting for the fulfillment of his ideal of the perfect brotherhood of man he remains a faithful and law-abiding citizen of the nation wherein his lot is cast.

"The situation need only to be looked at from the common-sense point of view to see what an idle chimera our good friends have conjured up to frighten themselves with.

"Should a Jewish State independent or subject to the Sultan be established in Palestine, Jews all over the world would take a peculiar interest in it from a motive identical with that which inspires their patriotism towards their own country."

What Is Orthodoxy?

Henry Pereira Mendes | 1898

Henry Pereira Mendes served as minister of Shearith Israel in New York and was the founding president of the Union of Orthodox Jewish Congregations of America. He published this response to news coverage of the founding meeting of the Union, held at his congregation. In this essay, Mendes describes his organization as part of a "Modern Orthodox" movement in the United States.

The reports of the recent Orthodox Convention are strangely incorrect. What Orthodox Convention would propose to change seventh-day Sabbath to Sunday as was reported in one paper? And the charge that "Reform had destroyed the Sabbath and had put Sunday service in its stead, had destroyed Judaism in the home, had spread infidelity far and wide, and paved the road to apostasy," was put in my mouth, when my constant effort has been not to permit Reform Judaism to be blamed as a whole for vagaries of individual Reform ministers, whom the more prominent Reform ministers themselves condemn. Wherein Reform Judaism is as a whole blameworthy, and very blameworthy, I shall presently state.

To introduce my subject, what is Orthodoxy, I need not remark that Orthodoxy does not consist of changing Sabbath to Sunday, and it does not consist of blaming a whole body for the sins of a few.

Our religion originates in the Bible.

Whatever in the Bible conduces to a higher standard of conduct, constitutes our religion, or Orthodox Judaism, as I understand it.

The word "orthodox" is misleading. Philologically it means "right opinion." Every one is apt to believe his own opinion to be the right one, and therefore is, in his own eyes, Orthodox. Ordinarily, however, the term is applied to those who are strict observers of forms as well as the rules of conduct.

Inasmuch as the Bible, the source of our religion, exalts conduct over ceremony and condemns forms where he who performs them is himself impure or sin-stained, the injustice of applying the term "orthodox" to those who perform ceremonies but who break laws of conduct, becomes at once apparent. The truly Orthodox man is not only an observer of forms. He is even more than a religious man, for a religious man may scrupulously perform merely religious duties and charitable duties. He is a spiritual man whose whole life is a constant reaching out to God, a constant effort to be at peace with himself, at peace with his fellow-creature, and at peace with his God.

True Orthodox Judaism, therefore, is spirituality of life. It is not simply religious life or outward conformity, and still less is it ceremonialism. The religion of the Bible shows us the three guiding principles which I try to make household words. They are loving-kindness, justice, and purity; or as a later Prophet changed them, "loving-kindness, justice, and modesty."

... To the smallest minutiae [the] Talmud lent its attention, but in the mass of ceremonial law, I repeat the Rabbis never lost sight of the importance of moral law.

We may not blame modern Orthodox Judaism if any of its disciples are guilty of breaking moral law while presumably observant of ceremonial law, any more than we can blame Christianity as a religion because the *Maine* was blown up by a nation professing it; or that we may blame Reform Judaism, as I have said, for any of the vagaries of which the younger leaders are guilty, but which the older leaders condemn.[28]

But we blame the individual, and we say that he who is ever so observant of Rabbinical, of Biblical ceremonial law, but who does not live up to the high ideals of conduct as proclaimed by the Prophet, Psalmist, and Rabbi is not an Orthodox Jew.

Modern Orthodoxy in the Light of Orthodox Authorities
Gotthard Deutsch | 1898

Rabbi Gotthard Deutsch (1859–1921) was a scholar and professor of history at the Reform Hebrew Union College in Cincinnati. At the turn of the twentieth century, Deutsch was particularly active in the American Jewish press as a staunch critic of Orthodox Judaism and Zionism. This source is an excerpt from a series of articles originally published in the Reform Advocate *and soon after published as a pamphlet by that Chicago-based newspaper. In this essay, Deutsch argued for the incompatibility of "Modernity" and "Orthodoxy."*

My queries as to what constitutes the principles of our American orthodox brethren, published in the *American Hebrew* of July 15, have remained unanswered.[29] I therefore would have a perfect right to adopt the view of Rabbi [Tobias] Shanfarber, expressed in an editorial of the *Jewish Comment*, that these queries are unanswerable.[30] However, I shall be more modest and presume that they were not deemed sufficiently precise, serious, or scientific to deserve consideration on the part of the proper authorities, and therefore, following the good old injunction, I shall "try, try again."

The first question that presents itself when we wish to know the boundary-line between orthodoxy and heterodoxy in Judaism is: *Who is to define what orthodoxy really is?*

It is only in Roman Catholicism that this question is answered with sufficient clearness by the dogma of papal infallibility. Should any question of religious import arise, the pope will settle it, for speaking *ex-cathedra*, he is the mouthpiece of the Holy Ghost. One may disagree with the pope, but then he places himself outside of the church. It is less probable for any of the Protestant churches to give the proper definition of orthodoxy. Let us take as an illustration the rigid Presbyterian church. Her official creed is the Westminster confession, but the body of men who drew up this creed were not inspired by the Holy Ghost; they were only learned theologians and sincere Christians but subject to human fallibility.[31] Besides, one might accept the confession and still differ from the body of the church on some important point in dogma. The heresy trials of Professor [Charles] Briggs and Henry Preserved Smith were based on the interpretation of some words in the Westminster confession.[32] Briggs and Smith claimed that the words "The word of God as contained in Holy Scripture is our infallible guide" left room for Biblical criticism because the Bible is not the word of God, but the word of God is contained in the Bible, which, besides, contains the word of men. Their opponents, however, insisted that every word of the Bible is infallible. From a strictly ecclesiastical point of view the two heretical professors had exactly the same right to define what orthodox Presbyterianism is, as had the opponents.

Judaism allows to its professors a still greater latitude. *Who gave the Shul'han Arukh any authority?* There was never any convention held which adopted the Shul'han Arukh as an authentic codification of the Law.[33] The work is a private attempt of no more doctrinal authority than [Kaufmann] Kohler's "Guide for Instruction in Judaism."[34] I have to be explicit on that point, so that my words may not be misconstrued. I do not intend to belittle Joseph Karo nor do I wish to flatter Kohler. My idea is simply this: In Roman Catholicism, as it was defined at the Vatican council, Pope Pius IX is a religious authority, because he is the mouthpiece of the Holy Ghost, although he may have been a perfect ignoramus.[35] On the other hand Ignaz von Doellinger, after the church declared him a heretic, is no authority whatever, although he was one of the greatest Catholic theologians.[36] In Judaism, however, there is no way of settling the question of authority and in the sense of the canonical law. Wise, Gottheil, Kohler, Hirsch, and even my humble self have the same right to consider our views as authentic interpretation of Jewish doctrine as have Mendes, Klein, Jacob Joseph, or Israel Salant of Jerusalem.[37]

. . . The question is therefore in order, and the honest orthodox will not dodge it but answer it fairly and squarely: Will you teach in your Sabbath-schools that there is, in spite of Galileo and Newton, an immense cavity under our feet in which a terrible fire is kept burning, where sinners will suffer eternal or limited torments (Baba Metzia 58b)?[38] Will you teach that the sufferers may be relieved and delivered when their children recite prayers and especially when they say Kaddish?[39] If you do not, you dodge the doctrines of good old orthodoxy.

If you allow the Shul'han Arukh to be a source from which dogmas may be derived, you will find yourself face to face with views that will inconvenience you just as they always were highly inconvenient for educated people of orthodox inclinations. Zacharias Frankel, in his recently published correspondence, advises a friend against the compilation of a text-book of Jewish religion, for a compendium containing all dogmas of the Jewish religion would only have the effect of frightening the young people or would create bigots.[40]

There is an important point in Jewish dogma which in modern times is also frequently dodged, and this is the superiority over the secular of our rabbinical literature or the infallibility of the Talmud in scientific matters. I do not imply that Dr. H. P. Mendes or even Dr. Klein believes the Copernican system to be a fallacy because the Talmud teaches that the sun revolves around the earth.[41] But I say that as soon as they accepted the Copernican system, they are not orthodox in the sense in which this term was generally understood in the sixteenth and even at the close of the eighteenth century.

Pictures of Jewish Home Life
Esther J. Ruskay | 1902

Esther Ruskay (1857–1910) was a prominent Jewish writer and activist. She held senior roles in the National Council of Jewish Women and the Young Women's Hebrew Association. She also helped lead the Educational Alliance on Manhattan's Lower East Side. Established in 1889, the Educational Alliance helped acculturate Jewish immigrants from Eastern Europe. In addition, Ruskay published a collection of essays, some of which were intended to prove to both her fellow second-generation American Jews and immigrants that traditional Jewish life was a viable lifestyle in the United States. This is evident from the excerpted essay below.

There are Jewish boys and girls who, besides the advantage of a thorough education in the schools of our city, are unconsciously being put through another and more important training at home. The boys are bright and modern—all American boys are that—and the girls are ambitious and fond of pretty things. There are few American girls who are not ambitious to improve and who are not dainty in their tastes. These boys and girls are well housed and well cared for—are, in fact, surrounded by all the signs of wealth and ease.

The father is a busy man, engrossed in the problem of providing for his large family, and the mother is employed from early morning until night attending to the management of her house and the wants of her large brood of children. Notwithstanding these cares, the father still finds time to interest himself in politics, in the amusements of the day, and in the synagogue of which he is a member and a regular attendant, and the mother sews for the poor once a week and finds time to look after the wants of one or two families in need.

But on Friday, the day preceding the Sabbath day of rest, it is a perfect hive of busy bees. Last polish to the silver and door knobs, last finishing of school tasks and putting away of music—for no one writes or studies or practices scales on the Sabbath—and last stitches put in bows and finery, for even the servants are not allowed to do anything save the most necessary labor. An extra scrubbing and brushing makes the faces of the younger members of the family as polished almost as the silver on the sideboard. The older ones are trusted to look after themselves.

... What a bustling day! It needs must be, for nothing so upsets the head of the house like getting late for the synagogue service, and it is his express desire that when he leaves the house he shall carry with him the impression of work done and a picture of the mother-bee with wings folded and at rest. Therefore, everything is done in good time and season.

Somewhere around sunset, the father, dressed in his best, accompanied by his boys—and they are of all ages and sizes—issues from the house to attend the Sabbath eve services. Nor does he forget, on going out, to touch reverently the tiny enclosed scroll, wherein are contained the "Hear, O Israel," and a paragraph declaring the duty of our nation to obey the laws of God, which is attached to the jamb of the doorway. The words "Thou shalt nail them upon the doorposts of thy house" are not only heeded in this household but their meaning is fully understood and appreciated.

While they are away, the good mother, very beautiful and dignified in her carefully donned attire, lights the Sabbath candles. She is careful to light them a little earlier, because she has heard in her girlhood—listening at the knee of a serene-faced old grandmother—that the unquiet souls of the dead, who may be suffering in another world, are blessed with rest on the sacred Sabbath. This same mother, when the Sabbath day is over and the new week about to begin, delays the lighting of the lamps, that the day of rest may be lengthened for these sufferers in spirit.

Around the mother lighting her Sabbath lights cluster the little ones, patiently waiting for the completion of the blessing, for sometimes this moment of uplifting is the only one in a busy, anxious week that she can give to calm thought and meditation.

The maids move softly about, putting the last touches to the table; and when each little face receives its Sabbath kiss, the help proffered by the children in placing the chairs and drawing down the shades is not despised.... The beauty and value of it all does not strike one during the years when it is gone through with as a matter of course and as a habit, but later on in life, the memory of it and its effect in softening character are inestimable. No need to tell of the meal that follows, when platters that have come in filled are taken away empty, and cake after cake disappears as if by magic; nor shall I tell of the next day, which, after the synagogue service, is taken up in visits to grandma and relatives, pleasant walks in the park, and the reading of books. It is a thoroughly enjoyable day, full of rest and easy conscience, with few thoughts of the workaday world to mar its pleasure or disturb its peace.

Young Israel
Hebrew Standard | 1913

In 1913 the Young Israel movement was established by college students and other young Jews. The group hosted lectures delivered by prominent rabbinic leaders like Rabbis Joseph Hertz (1872–1946), Mordecai Kaplan (1881–1983), and Judah Magnes (1877–1948). The first two men were leading graduates of the Jewish Theological Seminary, a school that had close ties with Young Israel in its earliest years. The founders, who tried their best to remain anonymous, routinely published short statements in the Jewish press that argued for Judaism's compatibility with American culture while eschewing labels such as "Orthodox" or "Traditional." Young Israel was a major agent of Americanization for immigrant Jews.

This is an organization composed of a number of young Jews and Jewesses living on the Lower East Side of New York. There are thousands of young Jews and Jewesses in this city unaffiliated with any Jewish organization. The name "Young Israel" expresses the object of the movement.[42] It is an appeal to the young men and women of the House of Israel to strengthen their Judaism. It is an attempt to bring about a revival of Judaism among the thousands of young Jews and Jewesses of this city whose Judaism is at the present time dormant. The appeal is to all Jewish young men and women, whatever be their views of Judaism, whatever be their social or economic status. The movement is not Orthodox or Reform. It is not Zionistic or Socialistic. It intends to awaken Jewish young men and women to their responsibilities as Jews in whatever form these responsibilities are conceived. Young Israel believes in the old Jewish doctrine: all Israel are brothers. We are convinced that through a broad earnest appeal to the Jewish spirit of our young men and women, the Jewish people will be strengthened and Judaism made a living force.

Proposal for a Five-Day Work Week
Bernard Drachman | 1915

In his attempt to revive Orthodox Judaism in America, Rabbi Bernard Drachman focused a great deal on Sabbath observance and served as president of the Jewish Sabbath Alliance of America. In this role, Drachman tried to persuade Jews to close their businesses on Saturdays and lobbied for state legislatures to repeal blue laws that prevented shopkeepers and workers from operating their stores on Sundays (and compelling them to work on Saturday). In this excerpt from an appeal delivered before Protestant leaders in California, Drachman argued that as citizens of a "free country," Jews and Christians ought to support a five-day workweek that would enable all devout religionists to properly worship and observe their respective Sabbath days. This initiative, figured Drachman, would help financially fortify the large numbers of immigrant and first-generation American Orthodox Jews and permit them to more easily observe traditional Judaism.

The proper observance of the Sabbath is equally dear to all true religionists, Jews and Christians alike. All who believe that religion is of vital import, spiritual and ethical, in the life of men, recognize the indispensable need of a weekly interruption of the whirl and grind of material things, of the business and labor which are so hard and exacting in this age of intense economic pressure, and of the observance of a peaceful, restful, and holy day, free from all thought of secular activity and devoted exclusively to higher things, to spiritual uplift and communion with the Divine.

The Sabbath, with the opportunity which it affords of attendance at public worship and listening to words of wisdom and moral instruction and with the suggestion of spiritual mediation and introspection which its sacred quietude naturally produces, is most admirably adapted for arousing and strengthening the religious sentiment, for developing the religious frame of mind.

It is, therefore, of the highest importance to the cause of religion to promote Sabbath observance, to assure to every man, woman, and child in the community the enjoyment of the Sabbath of twenty-four consecutive hours of freedom from secular cares and of opportunity to lead a spiritual life. Unfortunately, the Sabbath problem in the modern world is attended with obstacles which render its proper solution a matter of the utmost difficulty.

First, there is the difference of opinion as to the day upon which the Sabbath is to be observed. The Jewish tradition, going back to dim antiquity, to the period of the world's history in which the Sabbath originated and expressed an explicit Biblical precept, tells us that the term "Sabbath" applies to the twenty-four hours from sun-down on Friday to sun-down on Saturday.

Accordingly, the Jews and those Christian sects who agree with the Jews on this point observe that weekly period as the Sabbath.[43] The bulk of Christendom, of course, for theological reasons satisfactory to it, holds a different view and observes the first day of the week or Sunday as Sabbath. It is idle to expect either of the opposing parties to give up their views on this point. Each party looks upon its stand on the Sabbath question as fundamental to its faith and adheres tenaciously thereto, without thought of surrender.

The observance, therefore, by all of the one day as Sabbath is out of the question. Any attempt to enforce such universal observance by legislation would mean a serious wrong to a large part of the community and would be resented as religious persecution and tyranny.

There is another very serious difficulty in the fact that the need of a large portion of the community for a day of recreation and recuperation interferes very greatly with the observance of the one weekly day of rest as a time of worship and religious quietude. The young men and young women who have been tied down for six weary days to hard and exacting toil, who have been confined to the shop and the factory with no opportunity for the bright outdoor life which their young blood demands, are in no mood for church-going on Sunday or Saturday. They want to be out in the open, indulging in the active physical exercise for which, after six days of cramped confinement, their young bodies crave. They want to dance and romp, to play baseball, to row and to ride. They resent the attendance at worship as another form of irksome confinement, and if compelled against their will to abstain from the physical activity which they crave and to attend services which they are in no mood to appreciate, they are only too apt to turn against religion altogether.

This craving for exercise and recuperation is quite natural and justifiable, yet it is impossible for religious authorities to consent to its unrestricted gratification on the Sabbath. To do so would be to deprive the holy day of its devotional character and would reduce it to a day of merely secular recuperation. There seems to be but one way to overcome the difficulty. That would be to have two days of rest in the week, one to be purely secular in character and devoted to physical recuperation, the other to be purely religious and devotional.

I suggest that the Sunday and Saturday be selected as the days, as they already possess in great measure the required characteristics. The Christian would observe the Sunday as holy time and the Saturday as a secular holiday; the Jew would naturally reverse the process and observe the Saturday as Sabbath and the Sunday for secular recreation. Business and industry would, in this event, be discontinued on both days, except as regards the period from sundown on Saturday until midnight which is not regarded as Sabbath by either religion and which could be usefully employed in providing the necessaries of household and personal use on Sunday.

This, it appears to the writer, would be an ideal solution to the Sabbath problem. It would give ample opportunity for satisfying the needs of both the soul and the body, of doing justice alike to the claims of religion and the sanitary requirements of physical recreation. It would also make an end of the constant strife between observant Christians and Jews as regards the effect of Sunday laws on the latter.

What the Sabbath-keeping Jew resents in the Sunday laws is not the rest-day idea—that is a doctrine of his own faith—but the fact that the selection of the Sunday for general observance puts him in a position of inequality over against the Christian, compels him to restrict himself to five days' business, while his non-Jewish competitor enjoys the full privilege of six. The institution of two days of rest would put all citizens on a plane of equality and remove this long-standing grievance. The idea does not seem impractical.

The Saturday is already observed to a great extent as a half-holiday in both mercantile and industrial establishments and is found entirely feasible, indeed, very satisfactory and beneficial.

It would not seem to be a matter of great difficulty to add the few morning hours to the holiday and to spread the observance to those sections of the community which have not yet taken it up.

What is needed is a vigorous campaign of education to show the community the eminent desirability of the double weekly holiday from every point of view, sanitary, social, and religious. The writer for one is convinced that if the custom of observing two weekly rest-days is ever definitely accepted by the community it will speedily demonstrate its usefulness and desirability and will remain a permanent and cherished institution of our people.[44]

The Synagogue Council of America

Abraham Burstein | 1927

Rabbi Abraham Burstein (1893–1966) was a graduate of Columbia College and one of the first American-born ordainees of the Jewish Theological Seminary. He served in a number of Jewish organizations, including the Synagogue Council of America, and represented the more "Orthodox" wing of Solomon Schechter's *(1847–1915)* growing circle. The literary editor of the Orthodox-leaning Jewish Forum, Burstein's positive stance toward the Synagogue Council was adopted as the organ's official view of Orthodox participation. Founded in 1926, the Synagogue Council served for many decades as an umbrella organization for the major American rabbinical and synagogue institutions. Later on, membership in this interdenominational body emerged as a source of controversy for Orthodox Jews.

Every small town has its mark of cleavage—sometimes a railroad track, sometimes a river—which divides off one class of its citizenry from another. There are differences between rich and poor, black and white, the American and the foreign born. The same type of cleavage, a score of years ago, still existed among American Jews. Reform and orthodox elements not only worshipped in different edifices, but they lived in different parts of the city and were altogether apart in their social and communal life. The differences arose largely out of national origins and the ability, or lack of ability, to speak the English language.

The remarkable changes in past years in the status of various classes of American Jewry have been made evident in the newly formed Synagogue Council of America. Representatives of reform, orthodox, and "conservative" national groups now meet at regular intervals during the year, in all amity, and decide on such matters of policy as all the groups can concur in.[45] It has been the pleasure of the delegates to discover that the number of matters in which all classes can find agreement comprises almost everything in the general life of Jewry. Observance of the Sabbath, the five-day working week, relief of suffering, resuscitation of scattered Jewish communities, defense of Jewish rights, and a host of other subjects of importance are presented to their meetings. A provision of the constitution declares that all delegations must favor any proposal finally passed by the Council. And to date, the differences that have come out in discussion have been altogether trivial.

No matter how closely the observant Jew clings to his traditions, and how earnest his desire to bring back the wanderers to the fold of his ancient faith, he still recognizes that in a world constituted as the present one there must be unity, in many particulars, in the religious life of American Jews. We welcome the advent of the Council and are sanguine that it will perform incalculably great service for our people and our faith on this continent.

CONCLUSION

In 1908 Rabbi Bernard Drachman delivered a discourse on Judaism and "Modern Science" at Philadelphia's Mikveh Israel.[46] A graduate of Columbia College and the University of Heidelberg, Drachman was one of the best academic trained Orthodox rabbis in the United States. He was also a founding member of the Union of Orthodox Jewish Congregations. As the president of the Jewish Sabbath Alliance of America, Drachman tried to ensure that the New World could facilitate the economic and religious needs of Sabbath-observing Jews. He was part of an initiative conducted by German Jewish extracts to assist Russian and Polish newcomers acclimate to America. Moreover, this sort of work, as well as Drachman's Philadelphia lecture, captures the American Orthodox leadership's attempt to prove that the United States was in fact a "Goldene Medina" for Orthodox Jews.

Others shared a grimmer depiction of Orthodox Judaism's viability in the United States. To some, Orthodox Jews were not just unable to cope with an unfavorable immigrant economic climate; in fact, they contributed to an immoral situation noticed by many non-orthodox and non-Jews. In 1925 Rabbi Simon Glazer of the Hebrew Orthodox Rabbis of America testified to the assistant Secretary of the United States Treasury that only a handful of American rabbis could be trusted to handle sacramental wine during the Prohibition Era. The rest, attested Glazer, held untrustworthy credentials and were suspected of abusing their rabbinical station and selling alcohol on the black market.[47] In the final analysis, both perspectives are correct. Many traditional-minded Eastern European Jewish émigrés adapted to American norms and thrived along with their Orthodoxy in their new environs. Others—the majority, likely—did not. The Agudath Ha-Rabbonim focused on the former treifene ('unkosher") viewpoint and saw the poor economic, social, and religious conditions in the United States. These Orthodox Jews resisted cooperation with Orthodox accommodators. Instead, they took measures to protect themselves and other Jews from the "perils" of American life.

5 | Trailblazers

In December 1840 Rabbi Herbert Goldstein (1890–1970) mourned the untimely death of Rabbi Bernard Revel (1885–1940). "He had no peer," extolled the spiritual head of New York's Institutional Synagogue. "He was at home everywhere, in both religious and secular cultures."[1] Many others joined in eulogizing Revel, the president of the Rabbi Isaac Elchanan Theological Seminary in New York. He was an uncommon individual, able to appease the religious proclivities of the strictest and the most enlightened Orthodox Jews. In 1915 Revel was appointed president of the rabbinical seminary. His presence instantly elevated the stature of the school, which could now compete with the Jewish Theological Seminary to place rabbis in traditional pulpits.[2] One year later, Revel founded the Talmudical Academy, a Jewish high school that, he believed, would be up to the task of "coordinating and unifying the forces of education of our spiritually endowed youth, ... bringing harmony and light into their spiritual lives, ... [and] quickening their Jewish consciousness and widening their moral and mental horizons."[3] In 1928 Revel established Yeshiva College to foster a "harmonious growth in which the bases of modern knowledge and culture in the fields of art, science, and service, are blended with the bases of Jewish culture."[4]

The excitement over Revel's work was widespread. In 1921 a group of Chicago rabbis opened the doors of the Hebrew Theological College. An observer at the dedication ceremonies described the moment as a "red letter day in the annals of Orthodox Judaism."[5] Another commentator celebrated the Chicago school in tandem with Revel's seminary. "In both locations sit boys who were born in America and are excelling in Torah study," extolled this Chicago Jew.[6] Non-Jews also appreciated Revel's modern Orthodox trailblazing efforts. The president of

Stanford University hailed Revel's entire educational constellation as the new center of "Torah, Talmud, Jewish philosophy, theology, history, and literature."[7]

Not everyone agreed, however. As one Jewish intellectual, Henry Hurwitz, asked, "How indeed could an honest man see eye to eye with [Rabbi Leo] Jung—or even Revel?"[8] He was far more flattering to Solomon Schechter of the Jewish Theological Seminary. Upon Schechter's death in 1915, Hurwitz published someone else's words about the "scholar and humanist" whose "death was the greatest loss that American Jewry has sustained in years."[9] Schechter was also a pathbreaker, who more than held his own as a master of both rabbinic and western canons. In 1902 he arrived in New York to assume the presidency of the reorganized Jewish Theological Seminary. Schechter shuffled the faculty and vowed to produce better scholars and rabbis than the school had yielded in its earlier incarnation. His bona fides impressed a wide spectrum of American Jews. In fact, upon reviewing Schechter's inaugural address, a Reform commentator mused that the speech "would not have sounded out of place in the halls of the muchly criticized Hebrew Union College of Cincinnati!"[10] Yet Schechter did not approve of Reform Judaism, and he sided with Orthodox Judaism when pressed to profess it. Consequently, both Revel and Schechter offered their students and adherents powerful attempts to fortify a "Traditional" or "Orthodox" Judaism in the first decades of the twentieth century.

SECTION 1 | The Revel Revolution

An Orthodox High School
Solomon T. H. Hurwitz | 1916

Solomon T. H. Hurwitz (1885–1920) immigrated with his family to New York in 1894. He graduated from public school and subsequently earned an undergraduate degree from New York University and a doctorate from Columbia Univer-

sity. In 1916 Bernard Revel of the Rabbi Isaac Elchanan Theological Seminary hired Hurwitz to serve as the founding principal of the Talmudical Academy. Located on the Lower East Side, the Talmudical Academy was one of the first (all boys) Orthodox Jewish high schools in the United States. In 1920 Hurwitz died, a victim of the devastating worldwide Spanish flu pandemic. In this essay, Hurwitz defended the Jewish day school against charges of parochialism (like the Catholic schools) and of being an unnecessary institution; most American Jews advocated public schools, the "temples of liberty" that helped acculturate immigrants in the United States.

During the past week the Committee on Education of the Union of Orthodox Rabbis, of which Dr. Bernard Revel is the chairman, has carefully considered the plan recommended by the committee at the last convention of the rabbis and of the Mizrachi to promote the establishment of at least one parochial school in every large Jewish community and to urge upon the directors of Talmud Torahs to establish Jewish day schools in the present Talmud Torah buildings which are unoccupied the greater part of the day.[11] The term "parochial school" is a late importation in the orthodox Jewish camp and despite all prejudice on the part of the so-called liberals appears to have acclimatized itself very rapidly in the Jewish world. In reality, recent though the introduction of the term may be, the institution which it connotes boasts of a hoary antiquity. What is the Jewish parochial school? What is its importance in Jewish life? How does it differ from other parochial schools?

The Jewish parochial school carries forward into this country the traditions of the Jewish cheder of Eastern Europe. In Russia, Poland, and Galicia, the cheder is the Jewish educational unit. Its purpose is to give the Jew that amount of elementary education which will suffice to carry him through life. Not only are the Jewish studies taught in the cheder, but whatever secular studies are deemed necessary are given a place on its curriculum. The language of the country and the three r's are taught in the best cheders of Europe. But what is most important is the fact that the Jew who has imbibed his Judaism in the cheder clings tenaciously to his religion at whatever costs. And the secret of the magical power lies in the fact that in the cheder only Jewish influences are brought to bear on the life of the growing child who emerges from his Jewish environment at the period of maturity with a complete Jewish Weltanschauung and is prepared to battle for his religious convictions against all odds.

The charge constantly hurled against the parochial school is its narrowing mental influence. Our liberal Jews often repeat that the Catholic parochial schools are a great menace to the safety of our country. We shall not stop to rebuke the serious indictment pronounced against twelve millions of American citizens by a minority not any too popular, but we are ready to assert, from a close study of the actual facts in the case, that the patriotic loyalty of the graduates of such schools is on a par with the patriotic loyalty of the average public school graduate. If by narrowing influences the liberals mean loyalty to a three thousand year tradition, the Jewish parochial school system prides itself on preserving just such loyalty. The great success of the Jewish parochial school lies in the fact that it smoothes out the path of readjustment to American conditions, for the immigrant child, and, at the same time, preserves a harmony between his Jewishness and his Americanism. The mental agony of the Jewish public school pupil when he is suddenly thrust into an environment so different from his home environment, the dualism which enters into his life and divides his sympathies alternately between school and home, the clash between parent and child which is bound to appear sooner or later, is entirely avoided by the parochial school.

Here the Jewish child feels himself at home. His freedom of expression is not stunted by a constantly present, unhealthy fear of the attitude of his Gentile neighbor towards him. He cultivates early a healthy communal spirit and his Judaism becomes an integral part of his spiritual life through a natural course and not through artificial stimuli.

There are several parochial schools on the Lower East Side and one in Brownsville. The largest of these is the Rabbi Jacob Joseph School and the oldest is the Etz Chaim Talmudical Academy, now the preparatory department of the Rabbinical College.[12] In all of these there is a complete harmony between Jewish and secular study. The Jewish studies are naturally given first place on the curriculum and the five best hours of each day, from 9 to 3, are devoted to them. The English studies are from 4 to 7 in the afternoon. The charge that the children of these schools are overworked falls to the ground when it is remembered that the school day of the average Jewish child who receives some Jewish education is usually until 6 or 7 o'clock. Moreover, by interspersing play periods during the school hours the children are given healthy exercise and are kept away from the baneful influences of the street to which they would otherwise be addicted.

The secular instruction is of the first order in the opinion of the different district superintendents of the Board of Education to whose careful supervision the schools are subject. The reason for this is quite evident. The Jewish child, naturally bright, competes here with other children of equal or greater ability, whereas in the public school he has to contend with his less capable, non-Jewish fellow students. Moreover, the Talmudic discipline sharpens his mind to a high degree and very early develops his keen reasoning powers. This is a truth that none will gainsay. The present writer has been told repeatedly by different school superintendents that the boys of the Jewish parochial school take highest honors in the high schools of the city.

We must bear in mind that the Jewish parochial schools have not been founded from the same point of view as the Catholic schools. As we said, the Jewish parochial schools are carrying forward the tradition of the Jewish cheder—an institution which carries with it a pedagogical tradition of at least 2,500 years, and which has been tried out by the Jewish people in every clime and in every period. They start with the hypothesis that Jewish learning is as important to life as any other form of education, that moral development must be given first place and purely intellectual development second place. And this can only be done by devoting the best part of the day for the development of Jewish ideals. The Catholic schools, on the contrary, have a purely preservative function. They attempt to keep the mind of the Catholic child free from certain pernicious influences which would be likely to pervert his beliefs. They have little of constructive knowledge to give the child in addition to what any other Christian boy or girl receives.

This essential difference must be borne in mind when speaking of the Jewish parochial school and herein lies the answer to the oft-repeated charge of the narrowing influences of the system. Quite the reverse, the facts in the case prove that the life of the Jewish child is made richer and fuller by a systematic and thorough study of Judaism in addition to the regular routine demanded by the public school curriculum.

The Question of the Time
Eliezer Ladizinsky | 1926

In the 1920s, America's Orthodox Jews recognized that they could no longer rely on Europe for their religious sustenance. New legislation rendered it nearly impossible for Jews on the Continent to settle in the United States. In 1926 a young rabbinical pupil in RIETS reflected on the current conditions and isolation of his coreligionists in America. Eliezer Ladizinsky penned a column in a student publication that identified a number of grave weaknesses within his Orthodox community but also offered hope for his emerging generation to steer it back on course. Little is known about Ladizinsky, but his attitude bespeaks the self-awareness and growing self-confidence of the students who enrolled in Bernard Revel's Orthodox rabbinical seminary.

The future of American Judaism has been written about frequently in newspapers and discussed from pulpits. Of late, the closing of the gates of the United States to our brethren who wish to emigrate from Eastern Europe has occasioned much debate over the fate of Judaism in the not too distant future.[13] Some say that now, as the source of our religious vitality has been halted, American Jews must, with all their power, generate the courage to fortify Judaism in its new environs; others reason that the foundations of this American Jew are not at all solidified and therefore first need to be strengthened.

Either way, whether the truth lies with the first group or the second, the fact that this question is on the agenda is critically important.

The question, as I see it, is whether "an American Jew" has any merit to its name.

We are accustomed to call ourselves in name and conceive ourselves as part of distinct communities. When we speak of Polish Jews, a specific image passes before our eyes of this Jew—of both his superficial and inner qualities, his physical and spiritual attributes. The Polish Jew appears before us in stark contrast to the Lithuanian Jew or the Bessarabian Jew. He has a particular form and a particular coloring, a condition of his ethnic background.

Let us now recall the so-called American Jew and what kind of image this invokes in our mind. No doubt, it will conjure up a formless creature, consisting of many parts and many hues. It has no great splendor, nor does it possess defined features. This creature is left to scream out: "It is I for whom you call out!"

In truth, in America there are clusters of different types of Jews, members of the Diaspora settled in one country; not one united community cut from a single cloth. In New York, for example, there are geographical areas that mark the borders of our different enclaves. The Galician extracts are settled in this part of the city, from this street until that one; from this street until that street live the Lithuanian Jews. Our brethren have also brought with them their various levels of "status" [yihus] and polemics from their native lands. The Lithuanian Jews think of themselves as the "yeast in the dough" (Berakhot 17a) and look at the Galician Jews with contempt.

In light of this—after such divisiveness—are we capable of uniting together as American Jews?

The foregoing is intended to deny the present formation of an American Jewry. However, it is not meant to suggest that such a notion would be impossible to establish in the next generation. There is "clay" and "spirit" in this country.[14] From this, we can build an American Jewry.

Yet this recognition—the recognition that it is possible to construct such a building—places upon us great historical responsibility.

Spirit without a form can potentially destroy what we have already built. [The spirit] blasts through our streets and renders it impossible to safely access our buildings and prevents us from further construction. We must recognize the good in the "clay" as we do in the "spirit" that is in our hands and to know with absolute clarity what we intend to build. The value of this moment is great, and the historical charge is immense. I will write more on this for another occasion.

Yeshiva College
Bernard Revel | 1928

In 1915 Bernard Revel was elected president of the Rabbi Isaac Elchanan Theological Seminary (RIETS). Perhaps his greatest achievement as the school's leader was the founding of Yeshiva College. In 1945, after Revel's death, the college evolved into Yeshiva University. Revel published this "statement of aims" shortly before the college opened in 1928. The essay offered a very particular view of Revel's school, which did not seek to become just like any other American college.

The aim of the Yeshivah College is to afford a harmonious union of culture and spirituality, to bring into the field of American education the contribution of the spiritual values of Judaism, of the Jewish ideals of education, of the Jewish perspective upon learning and knowledge. It will be neither a general college nor a mere professional school but an institution of learning for Jewish youth who consider Jewish learning part of the mental and moral equipment they wish to obtain through a college education, where Jewish studies are an integral part of the course in the humanities, and general culture included in the curriculum of those who prepare themselves for the rabbinate and for teaching. Without an education that is harmonious and adequate, that trains the Jewish heart and will as well as the mind, Judaism cannot maintain itself. Through virile and circumspect education Israel has preserved his faith and identity, and only through education that is in close keeping with the forward movement of life will the teachings and ideals that are Judaism be transmitted to the American generations of Jewish youth.

American Israel must aim at a system of education which shall be true to the Torah and the traditions of Universal Israel, yet equally American, rich with the best of Israel's concepts of life and conduct and moral idealism, wrought with the best of his new heritage and achievement.

The Yeshivah College will dedicate its energies to the education of a small number of American Jewish young men of promise, introducing them to the cultural attainments of all of mankind in the fields of art, physical science, and social science. On the foundation that has been laid in the several Hebrew day schools in New York and in the rest of the country, particularly in the Yeshiva High School, which numbers over 400 students, the Yeshivah College is reared with the aim of educating, both liberally and Jewishly, a select number of Jewish young men who have already been imbued with the spirit and the sanctity of Judaism and its teachings. It will be the aim of this college to educate and prepare these young men for their allegiance to their family and to God as well as to their country. Only as we understand our manifold relations are we really prepared for complete and right living. Allegiance to country without allegiance to God is distorted loyalty that impoverishes rather than enriches a nation.

A great American educator, in a letter to the Yeshivah, said: "There are minds that can attain their highest development only in an environment that is spiritually sympathetic." There are still, among American Jewish youths, natures that are religious and sensitive to matters spiritual—their birthright and heritage. Thrust into an environment that is not altogether sympathetic, these students fail to respond. An understanding of the backgrounds of Judaism, its teachings and ideals, will quicken the student's insight into his liberal and social studies. In existing colleges and universities most of our student youth are either lost sight of, or, in mistaken efforts at adjustment, are led to efface, or even deny, their Jewishness. In either case Israel suffers a serious loss. Nor is America enriched by this unnecessary abandonment of the religious, cultural, and spiritual ideals and values of Judaism that have helped shape the course of humanity.

While it is not expected that the Yeshivah College will take its place in the near future in the forefront of our higher institutions of secular learning, it will aim to attain and maintain high academic standards.

There have existed in this country, since its beginning, schools for higher learning, founded and maintained by various religious groups.

The true exponents of American culture agree that the enrichment of America will not be furthered by the submerging of all the cultural and spiritual phases and heritages of its constituent elements, but that an American educational and spiritual Renaissance will best be advanced by an equable cultural "give and take" among its various groups. The contact of our student youth with the sources of our culture can but stimulate the Jewish creative faculties in all fields of cultural endeavor. We can serve our country and humanity best by training our youth in the knowledge and in the spirit of Israel's moral standards and spiritual values. The strengthening of Judaism—a vital force in the humanizing of mankind—through the establishment of institutions of higher learning such as the Yeshivah College can mean but added strength to American spiritual progress and make but for the enrichment of American culture and thought.

Some of our talented young men, seeking knowledge and ideally inclined, will find a College of Liberal Arts and Science under Jewish auspices, a home where they will realize their mental endowments for the enrichment of general and Jewish culture. The Yeshivah College will, as it grows and advances, constitute a contribution to American Jewish life and help perpetuate and advance Jewish ideals and culture, together with the dissemination and increase of general knowledge. It is expected that the Yeshivah College will attract a group of creative personalities to its faculty and will create and, in time, help supply the demand for constructive Jewish academic forces with a Jewish perspective and trend of mind, to whom nothing Jewish is alien. The Yeshivah College thus carries a message of hope to the spiritually languishing student youth.

The Yeshivah College aims to foster this harmonious growth, in which the bases of modern knowledge and culture in the fields of art, science, and service will be blended with the bases of Jewish culture, to develop informed and devoted sons in the undying spirit and faith of Israel. The College aims at the inculcation of an abiding consciousness of the high ideals and the spiritual heritage of the Jewish people and at the development of intellect and character, through the pursuit of those humanizing studies by which life as a whole may be elevated and enriched, conducted in an environment that is spiritually sympathetic, producing a mind consistent in its outlook and capable of seeing the harmony of life.

The Yeshivah College aims to make real the true Yeshivah ideal, the development of a select body of young men who, in the rabbinate or in Jewish scholarship, in teaching or in social service, or in whatsoever field of work, shall be the standard-bearers of a true Jewish life, the moral and spiritual leaders of their communities, because they have carried with them from the Yeshivah and its college the ideals of scholarship, spirituality, and service, because they are most nearly making actual in their daily living the ideal of a life of service based upon learning, loyalty, and love of the eternal truths of the Torah and understanding and love of their fellowmen.

It will be the aim of the Yeshivah College to spread a knowledge of Judaism in its wider sense, together with general culture in the harmony between Shem and Jephet spoken of by our sages (Megillah 9b): to train its students in full appreciation of the Jewish contribution to the spiritual and intellectual progress of mankind, to inspire them to the conservation and application of this contribution, and to imbue them with a spirituality that flows from the deeply dug Jewish wells of spirit undefiled. In this institution Jewish culture will be on the same plane of opportunity and dignity as the classical studies and modern culture. We believe that the more unified and interrelated the forces of education, the more potent they become. Under the same auspices to give both general and Hebrew training, to develop character through a single agency by both personal and religious appeal, gives greater promise of quickening moral consciousness and of a mind that is spiritually integrated.

The graduates of the Yeshivah College will be imbued with the Jewish spirit and the Jewish philosophy of life. Such a Jewishly educated and inspired laity will qualify for that leadership which we now lack and the absence of which is the greatest drawback to American Jewry. It will give Jewish life new vigor and meaning, will aid in the spiritualization of our lives and the synthesis of the Jewish personality, bringing into harmonious relation the mind of the Torah—true student youth and the modern mind.

A photograph of the "pioneering" undergraduates of Yeshiva College, as depicted in the 1929 edition of *Masmid*, the longtime student yearbook. Bernard Revel is pictured in the middle row, third from the left. Courtesy of Yeshiva University Archives.

The Hebrew Theological College of Chicago
Hyman L. Meites | 1924

Hyman L. Meites (1879–1944) was a newspaper editor and publisher in Chicago and an active Zionist and founder of the Jewish Historical Society of Illinois. The pioneers of the Chicago-based rabbinical school did not work in tandem with Revel and the New York rabbis. However, the Chicago men patterned their work after Revel and saw their mission on behalf of traditional Judaism as complementary to his in New York. Meites offered this overview of the Chicago seminary in the early stages of its history.

About three years ago, three Chicago rabbis, Ephraim Epstein, H. Rubenstein, and A. I. Cardon, working in unison, succeeded in forming a rabbinical school intended, at the time, to offer a continuation of the course given in the Yeshivath Etz Chaim.[15]

From a class of five students studying at Rabbi Rubenstein's home, the organization in 1921 had grown to forty students and three teachers and was housed in the Grenshaw Street Talmud Torah. At this point the needs of the school outgrew the means of its instigators and consequently a reorganization occurred which placed Ben Zion Lazar at the head of the project, which now took on a community aspect....[16]

Under the guidance of its new leaders the progress of the institution was given new impetus, culminating in the erection of a new college building, which was formally opened December 27, 1922.

The building, a monument to Jewish learning in Chicago, is a beautiful structure standing on a lot 125 by 188 feet on the northeast corner of Douglas Boulevard and St. Louis Avenue and represents a $200,000 [today, $2,750,000] investment by the Jewish community.[17] It houses a library of four thousand volumes of Hebraica. Its classes and study rooms are spacious and beautifully furnished, and its large assembly hall artistically laid out. In addition, it contains a kitchen and lunchroom, shower baths, beautiful grounds, and all conveniences that make for an atmosphere conducive to study. At present the guidance of the institution is entrusted to Rabbi Saul Silber....[18]

The purpose of the college is twofold. First, it aims to serve as an institution for higher learning and to provide a center for the very highest expression of Jewish culture. Second, it offers a complete course of study for those students who wish to prepare themselves for the rabbinate or for Jewish teachers.[19]

With these purposes in view the school is divided into three departments: (1) the preparatory, (2) the collegiate or rabbinical, (3) the normal or teachers' college. The curriculum includes the study of biblical, rabbinic, medieval, and modern Jewish literature, Jewish philosophy, history, and ethics. In addition, the rabbinic students are given courses in homiletics, public speaking, and other subjects; and the candidates for teaching positions are given courses in pedagogic methods. All courses are presented in a modern and Jewish manner by a faculty of capable teachers. Classes meet twenty hours a week, except for two weeks during the summer and holiday vacations.

The preparatory school is attended by 180 students, the collegiate by 85, and the teachers' college started with an enrollment of about 35. All of these students attend (or are graduates of) Chicago high schools or colleges. There are 32 of those that attend the latter. The student body is by no means a local aggregation, but numbers representatives from every section of the country, as well as from other lands.

The men at the head of the Beth Hamedrash L'Torah are planning upon the addition of several European scholars to the faculty, upon important additions to the library, and upon an extension to the present building to provide the greater facilities already needed.[20]

SECTION 2 | Solomon Schechter and the Orthodox

Is Schechter Orthodox?

Emanuel Schreiber | 1902

Rabbi Emanuel Schreiber (1852–1932) held Reform rabbinic posts in a number of American communities, including Congregation Emanu-El in Chicago. He spearheaded a number of literary endeavors in his lifetime and was an outspoken advocate of radical reform. His critique of Solomon Schechter appeared as the Hebrew Union College was finalizing plans to appoint the rabbi and scholar Kaufmann Kohler as its second president. The renowned Schechter posed a threat to Reform Judaism's grip on Jewish scholarship. This is an excerpt from the first in a series of articles authored by Schreiber to discredit the so-called Orthodox victory in uniting the New York seminary with Solomon Schechter.

When Moses came down from the mountain, angry with his people who worshipped the golden calf, Joshua, hearing the wild voice of the people shouting, said to Moses, "The noise of the battle is heard in the camp." But Moses answered, "It is not the cry of men encouraging to fight, nor the shout of men compelling to flee, but I hear simply the voice of shouting" (Ex. 32:17–18).

Since the coming of Prof. [Solomon] Schechter to this country we have heard a noise from both sides of the Jewish camp, the so-called Orthodox cry "Victory" seeing in him the David who will lay low the Goliath of Reform.[21] A certain class of Reformers takes up the same cry, shouting and vociferating. "To thy tents, O Israel, Reform is in danger, and something must be done to save it." We do not know whether this fear is serious or manufactured. But, be this as it may, it is utterly unjustifiable. All this noise is neither the voice of victory for Orthodoxy nor the voice of defeat for Reform. The first has no cause for jubilation, the latter has no cause for fear. At present we can judge Schechter only by his past, i.e., by his writings, and as he is entitled to be considered an honest man, who will not belie his past, all apprehensions concerning his attitude toward Reform are groundless. But before entering into this subject, we may mention that Jacob Schiff, who has always been identified with Reform Congregations, is not likely to give support to any movement which might injure the cause of Reform Judaism.[22] We also are aware of the fact that Schechter, while in Vienna and Berlin, had intimate relations with men who were known as opposed to Orthodoxy.[23] In England he belonged to a coterie of men who stand for Progress and Reform. But, inasmuch as the man's religious views and opinions can best be learned from his publications, we intend to show by his own words where he stands. For, in the end, not the fact whether a man eats Kosher or prays with his hat on, but what he teaches, is decisive for his position to Judaism.

In the introduction to his "Studies in Judaism" we read as follows: "Some years ago when the waves of the Higher Criticism of the Old Testament reached the shores of this country, and such questions as the heterogeneous composition of the Pentateuch, the comparatively late date of the Levitical legislation, and the post-exilic origin of certain Prophecies as well as of the Psalms began to be freely discussed by the press and even in the pulpit, the invidious remark was often made: What will now become of Judaism, when its last stronghold, the Law, is being shaken to its very foundations? Such a remark shows a very superficial acquaintance with the nature of an old historical religion like Judaism and the riches it has to fall back upon in cases of emergency."[24]

According to this, Judaism can lose nothing of its vitality if the so-called third book of Moses was not written by Moses at the dictation of God. Now, this doctrine is certainly not compatible with what is generally considered "Orthodox Judaism." For, if the Levitical legislation is not of Mosaic origin, the dietary laws and the laws concerning Yom Kippur lose their authority. We cannot see the difference between this theory and the Radicalism of Dr. [Emil] Hirsch and others.[25] A great deal of noise is made by the Cincinnati School of Reform that the coming of Schechter to this country and the rich endowment of the New York Seminary by men known as sympathizers with Reform means a reaction against Reform. No such a thing. The placing of Schechter at the head of the New York School over which [Sabato] Morais presided means a great victory for progressive, liberal Judaism.[26] For Schechter's position regarding the Bible,—and this, it can not be too often repeated, is the only criterion by which a Jewish or Christian Theologian's liberalism can be gauged—is more advanced and more modern than that of the late President of the Cincinnati College, Dr. [Isaac M.] Wise. Here is the proof. In his last book, "Pronaos to Holy Writ," which, as he himself told us, he considered his most important publication, he takes a strictly Orthodox position on the Bible. As *unum pro multis* the following passage of the "Preface" may find place here: "The science commonly called Modern Biblical Criticism, actually Negative Criticism, which maintains, on the strength of unscientific methods, that the Pentateuch is not composed of original Mosaic material, no Psalms are Davidian, no Proverbs Solomonic, the historical books are unhistorical, the Prophecies were written post-festum, there was no revelation, inspiration, or prophecy, must also maintain that the Bible is a compendium of pious or impious frauds, willful deceptions, unscrupulous misrepresentations."[27] "The authenticity of the Mosaic records is the foundation of all Bible truth. The whole system of righteousness, justice, and equity depends for evidence of the authenticity and veracity of the Pentateuchal records."[28] Thus argues the "Reformer" Wise.

On the other hand is this argument refuted by the "Orthodox" Schechter, who meets such old-fashioned arguments with the following answer: "Such a remark shows a very superficial acquaintance with the nature of an old historical religion like Judaism and the resources it has to fall back upon in cases of emergency." This means, if it means anything, that no matter how radical and destructive the results of Higher Criticism might prove, so far as the authenticity of the Pentateuch is considered, Judaism with its rich resources cannot be unfavorably affected, because the Bible like any other literature is the self-revelation of the national soul and genius of the Jewish nation, because the Bible is the product of Judaism, but Judaism is not the product of the Bible. Who, then, is here the "Orthodox," the late President of the Reform College, or the new President of the New York Institution? And who please has the right to say that Prof. Schechter has, since his acceptance of the position in New York, changed his opinions, uttered in 1896? On the contrary. When a few months ago a reporter of an Orthodox paper in New York interviewed the Doctor and asked him regarding his views or "Richtung" [direction], like a man he answered, "I shall not belie my past." What more could he say?

The "General Religious Tendency" of the Seminary

Solomon Schechter | 1902

Solomon Schechter arrived in New York on April 17, 1902, to assume the leadership of JTS. This is an excerpt from his inaugural address, "The Meaning and Scope of the Jewish Theological Seminary." Delivered on November 20, 1902, the content of the speech was traditional, but Schechter stopped short of describing the rebooted school as Orthodox. Although, when pressed, Schechter accepted the "Orthodox" designation for himself, he preferred to align with "Catholic Israel," a broad and vague term that he hoped could attract a wide swatch of America's Jews.

It is hardly necessary to remark that the Jewish ministry and Jewish scholarship are not irreconcilable. The usefulness of the minister does not increase in the inverse ratio to his knowledge—as little as bad grammar is especially conducive to morality and holiness. [Leopold] Zunz's motto was "Real knowledge creates action" and the existence of such men as R. Saadya Gaon and R. Hai Gaon, Maimonides and Nachmanides, R. Joseph Caro and R. Isaac Abarbanel, Samson Raphael Hirsch, Abraham Geiger, and an innumerable host of other spiritual kings in Israel, all "mighty in the battles of the Torah," and voluminous authors, and at the same time living among their people and for their people and influencing their contemporaries, and still at this very moment swaying the actions and opinions of men; all these bear ample testimony to the truth of Zunz's maxim.[29] No, ignorance is not such bliss as to make special efforts to acquire it. There is no cause to be afraid of much learning or, rather, of much teaching. The difficulty under which we labor is rather that there are subjects which cannot be taught and yet do form an essential part of the equipment of a Jewish minister.

But first let me say a few words about the general religious tendency this Seminary will follow. I am not unaware that this is a very delicate point, and prudence would dictate silence or evasion. But life would hardly be worth living without occasional blundering, "the only relief from dull correctness." Besides, if there be in American history one fact more clearly proved than any other, it is that "know-nothingism" was an absolute and miserable failure.[30] I must not fall into the same error. And thus, sincerely asking forgiveness from all my dearest friends and dearest enemies with whom it may be my misfortune to differ, I declare, in all humility, but most emphatically, that I do know something. And this is that the religion in which the Jewish ministry should be trained must be specifically and purely Jewish, without any alloy or adulteration. Judaism must stand and fall by that which distinguishes it from other religions as well as by that which it has in common with them. *Judaism is not* a religion which does not oppose itself to anything in particular. Judaism is opposed to any number of things, and says distinctly "thou shalt not." It permeates the whole of your life. It demands control over all your actions, and interferes even with your menu. It sanctifies the seasons, and regulates your history, both in the past and in the future. Above all, it teaches that disobedience is the strength of sin. It insists upon the observance both of the spirit and of the letter; spirit without letter belongs to the species known to the mystics as "nude souls" [nishamtin armelin] wandering about in the universe without balance and without consistency, the play of all possible currents and changes in the atmosphere. In a word Judaism is absolutely incompatible with the abandonment of the Torah. Nay, the very prophet or seer must bring his imprimatur from the Torah. The assertion that the destruction of the law is its fulfillment is a mere paradox, and reminds strongly of the doctrines of Sir Boyle Roche, the inimitable maker of Irish bulls.[31] He declared emphatically that he would give up a part and, if necessary, the *whole* of the constitution *to preserve the remainder!*

President Abraham Lincoln, the wisest and greatest of rulers, addressed Congress on some occasion of great emergency with the words: "Fellow citizens, we cannot escape history."[32] Nor can we, my friends. The past, with its long chain of events, with its woes and joys, with its tragedies and romances, with its customs and usages, and above all with its bequest of the Torah, the great entail of the children of Israel has become an integral and inalienable part of ourselves, bone of our bone and flesh of our flesh. We must make an end to these constant amputations if we do not wish to see the body of "Israel" bleed to death before our very eyes. We must leave off talking about Occidentalizing our religion—as if the Occident has ever shown the least genius for religion—or freeing the conscience by abolishing various laws. These, and similar platitudes and stock phrases borrowed from Christian apologetics, must be abandoned entirely if we do not want to drift slowly but surely into Paulinism, which entered the world as the deadliest enemy of Judaism, pursued it through all its course and is still finding its abettors among us, working for their own destruction. Lord, forgive them, for they know not. Those who are entrusted with carrying out the purpose of this institution, which as you have seen aims at the perpetuation of the tenets of the Jewish religion, both pupils and masters, must faithfully and manfully maintain their loyalty to the Torah. There is no other Jewish religion but that taught by the Torah and confirmed by history and tradition, and sunk into the conscience of catholic Israel.[33]

I have just hinted at the desirability of masters and pupils working for one common end. You must not think that our intention is to convert this school of learning into a drill ground where young men will be forced into a certain groove of thinking or, rather, not thinking; and after being equipped with a few devotional texts, and supplied with certain catch-words, will be let loose upon an unsuspecting public to proclaim their own virtues and the infallibility of their masters. Nothing is further from our thoughts. I heard once a friend of mine exclaim angrily to a pupil: "Sir, how dare you always agree with me!" I do not even profess to agree with myself always, and I would consider my work, to which with the help of God I am going to devote the rest of my life, a complete failure if this institution would not in the future produce such extremes, as on the one side a raving mystic who would denounce me as a sober Philistine; on the other side, an advanced critic, who would rail at me as a narrow-minded fanatic, whilst a third devotee of strict orthodoxy would raise protest against any critical views I may entertain. "We take," says Montaigne, "other men's knowledge on trust, which is idle and superficial learning. We must make it our own."[34]

A Dangerous Situation

American Hebrew | JUNE 17, 1904

The traditionalist editors of the American Hebrew *were well-known supporters of the Jewish Theological Seminary and critical of the Agudath Ha-Rabbonim (Union of Orthodox Rabbis of the United States and Canada), ever since the organization's inception in 1902. Called to act in defense of Schechter and the Seminary, this editorial was the newspaper's first large-scale attack on that rabbinical group.*

In a recent issue of the *American Hebrew* we called attention to a resolution passed by a number of Orthodox rabbis, who have formed themselves into a union, condemning any of their colleagues preaching in English or countenancing the teaching of the Jewish religion in any other language but Yiddish.[35] It is evident that these rabbis did not consider this sufficient, for they have now gone a step further, and have issued a circular in which they say that the graduates of the Jewish Theological Seminary, "who call themselves rabbis," have no right to act as rabbis and teachers, "according to the law of the Scripture and the Talmud," and warning any Orthodox congregation against appointing seminary graduates as their spiritual guides. One of the most prominent congregations in this city recently appointed a former seminary student as its religious head, and all the fury of these Orthodox rabbis has been directed against this synagogue and its leaders.

Before discussing whether the needs of the country require rabbis of the old-fashioned school or spiritual leaders who shall be imbued with a spirit of the time, we would like to know who appointed the members of the Union of Orthodox Rabbis (composed exclusively, it is well to say, of Russians) as authorities to lay down the law in regard to the appointment of rabbis? Has the individual who signs this circular as president of the union any special dispensation to pronounce what cannot be regarded in any other light but in that of a Herem [excommunication]?[36] We are sure that the great Orthodox rabbis of Russia would not have sanctioned the issue of such a disgraceful circular.

These men desire to transplant here conditions which, even for one moment, cannot be allowed to exist. Are these rabbis so senseless as to believe that their methods and ideas can possibly have any weight or influence with the growing generation of Jews in this country?

If it be their desire to raise the standard of the Orthodox rabbinate in this country, they will receive the fullest support of the whole of the Jewish community, but when they presume to denounce those who honestly and sincerely preach and teach Judaism, then their denunciation will meet with the condemnation it so richly deserves.

The rabbinate needs uplifting, but it is the rabbinate to which the members of the Union of Orthodox Rabbis belong. The Yiddish-speaking rabbis will only then have the right to speak with authority when they will have evinced a desire to serve the best interest of Judaism. Meanwhile, they had better set their own house in order. Their continual tendency to quarrel, their bickering and denouncing of each other, as was recently the case on the Lower East Side of New York, is a disgrace to our religion, and tends to lower us in the eyes of our fellow-citizens of other faiths.

In sending out the Herem, Rabbi [Bernard] Leventhal and his colleagues have been guilty of a Hillul Hashem, a profanation of our Holy Faith.

The conduct is calculated to prejudice the well-being of their coreligionists here, and to produce a condition that may seriously react upon their brethren in Russia, who look longingly towards America.

The Orthodox Rabbis and the Seminary

Judah David Eisenstein | JULY 1, 1904

In 1872 Judah David Eisenstein (1854–1956) migrated to the United States from Poland. A longtime member of the Beth Hamedrash Hagodol on New York's Lower East Side, Eisenstein was a bibliophile and encyclopedist. He was also a communal activist, typically taking the side of his Eastern European coreligionists. He did exactly that in his defense of the Agudath Ha-Rabbonim's attack on Solomon Schechter and his circle.

Your editorial, "A Dangerous Situation," calls attention to a resolution which you claim was passed by the Union of the American Orthodox Rabbis, condemning the preaching and teaching in English except in Yiddish. I must say that you are misinformed, as their by-laws expressly stipulate teaching in English when that language is spoken best by the pupil. As to preaching, several of their own members often preach in English.

Regarding their other resolution, in condemning the New York Theological Seminary and branding it as non-Orthodox, this is true. But you cannot blame the rabbis for their action, since Professors [Solomon] Schechter and [Louis] Ginzberg, the leaders of that institution, are expounders of High Criticism, which is anything but Orthodoxy.[37]

In the seventh volume of the *Jewish Encyclopedia*, article Law, Codification of, signed by Professor Ginzberg and approved by Professor

Schechter, says: "Israel was a 'People of the World' long before it was a 'People of the Book,' and the law of the Hebrews, like those of most other nations, were written down only after they had been in force for a long time." "Deuteronomy xv.12, in contradiction to Exodus xxi.7, orders that a daughter sold into slavery by her father shall be free in the seventh year, and that during her time of service she cannot be forced by her master to become his wife."[38]

According to the Professor, Deuteronomy was compiled after "the ruling party in Judea supported the authority of the Godless King Manasseh." Part of Leviticus, the Professor says, originated in the period of Ezekiel. He doubts whether at the end of the Babylonian exile, 400 BC, "the various parts of the Pentateuch were already combined into a book, but the definite codification of Biblical law in any case did not take place later than 350 BC."[39]

If anyone can claim such views as orthodox, then Isaac M. Wise, the founder of Reform in America, who to his credit be said, strenuously opposed High Criticism, may truly be called a pious Jew, a Hasid.[40]

Or, perhaps, this new High Critical Judaism is what Professor Schechter styles "Catholic Israel." If so, it is high time to organize a "Protestant Israel" to protest against such rot and decay in Judaism.

The position of the Orthodox Jews or Jewish Judaism is very clear on this point. The Mishna says that all Jews have a share in the world to come, except one who disclaims the Revelation of the Torah (m. Sanhedrin 10:1). Maimonides defines a "Kofer ba Torah": One who says the Torah was not revealed by the Almighty through Moses, or disputes the traditional interpretation, or that any command of the Torah is obsolete or has been changed. One who proclaims such doctrine is classed with the apostate and a deserter of Judaism (Hil. Teshuvah 3:8).

I sincerely trust that the Professors will have the manliness to publicly deny or admit this charge.

J. D. Eisenstein
New York, June 26, 1904

A Reaffirmation of Traditional Judaism

Max Drob | 1929

In July 1929 Rabbi Max Drob (1887–1959) delivered an important lecture at the Rabbinical Assembly of the Jewish Theological Seminary's annual convention. He was one of the first graduates of the reorganized JTS under Schechter's leadership and the rabbi of a large congregation in the Bronx. Drob was also a prominent spokesman of the more traditional elements within Schechter's circle and fought vigorously to prevent the emergence of a "Conservative Judaism" that was separate from what Drob described as "Traditional" or "Orthodox" Judaism. His conference presentation alienated him from more radical JTS men but garnered the attention of the Jewish Forum. *The editors of the Orthodox-leaning periodical commented favorably on Drob's discourse and republished the lecture in their magazine. A large section of Drob's speech is reproduced below.*

When I decided to enter the ministry, I chose the Jewish Theological Seminary because I believed it to be an institution for the promulgation of Traditional Judaism. Reading its history, I learned that Sabato Morais of blessed memory founded it because the older institution at Cincinnati had definitely broken with tradition. At first he had believed that Torah was non-sectarian and that it was possible for one institution to prepare men for both the traditional and the then less traditional congregations. When, however, in 1885, the leaders of the Hebrew Union College met at Pittsburgh and adopted a radical platform, Dr. Morais realized his error and set about to found a separate institution for the training of Rabbis pledged to Traditional Judaism.[41] Thus the Jewish Theological Seminary from its very inception was committed to Traditional Judaism. Many have been the detractors of the Seminary, but I challenge them to point to any instance wherein it has deviated from its avowed loyalty to tradition.

Dr. [Solomon] Schechter of blessed memory repeatedly stated that the Seminary is not the center nor even the nucleus of a third party in Judaism. The Seminary, he insisted, has no desire to promulgate a new Schulchan Aruch or even to amend the old one, and it certainly presents no new theology. Higher criticism he decried as "higher anti-Semitism" and he cautioned us against adopting its conclusions. He required the professors and the students to observe Traditional Judaism, a requirement which can be found in every Register of the institution. He saw to it that the model synagogue at the Seminary was conducted in strict accordance with tradition, and its beautiful service reflected the spirit of loyalty that animates the institution. When the United Synagogue was founded, its constitution distinctly stated that it did not sanction the innovations made by some of its constituent synagogues.[42] If there has ever been a change of front, no statement to that effect has ever been made. I look in vain for a record that the United Synagogue ever amended that clause in its constitution or that the Jewish Theological Seminary ever ceased to be loyal to the avowed purpose of the founder. In preaching and teaching Traditional Judaism, I therefore feel that I am loyal to the charge given me at my ordination eighteen years ago.

Since that time, I have received no revelation from God urging me to reform Judaism, nor have I been conceited enough to feel divinely ordained to reconstruct Traditional Judaism. Had I been asked to recast Judaism, I might have been tempted to create a Judaism different in many respects from tradition. Yet, on second thought, seeing the mess our Reform colleagues have made of their task, I believe that I would still prefer the cumulative wisdom of the ages to the snap judgment of the day. Had I, during these eighteen years, come to the conclusion that I could no longer preach and teach Traditional Judaism, I would have been honest enough to part company with the Seminary, the Rabbinical Assembly, and the United Synagogue.[43] Likewise, had these institutions, God forbid, departed from Traditional Judaism, I would have felt it my duty to break with them, painful as the process might have been.

Traditional Judaism, as it was taught in the Seminary, differs from the so-called Orthodox Judaism as practiced in Eastern Europe only in method. Without casting any reflections on our East European brethren, we believe that Traditional Judaism in this land can be promulgated only in synagogues that are outwardly as well as inwardly beautiful and at services where decorum and order prevail. We believe that

Traditional Judaism must be preached in English, a language which the people understand, and by men who are the masters of their congregation by virtue of their secular as well as their religious education. The Hebrew School, we insist, must be as beautiful as, if not more beautiful than, the secular school and must employ the latest pedagogic methods, as only in that way can the old truths of Judaism be imparted to the young. With orthodoxy as it is practiced by the United Synagogue in England or by the enlightened orthodox congregations of Germany, we are heartily in accord. For real Orthodox Judaism has never been opposed to beautiful synagogues, to orderly services, or to modern methods of teaching and preaching. The "beauty of holiness" was not discovered by Reform Judaism; it was always the possession of Traditional Judaism. Only the pitiable economic conditions and the lack of order characteristic of Slavonic lands weaned the Jew from his love for the beautiful. As the Jew in America rises culturally, he sees to it that his synagogues reflect the higher cultural standards prevailing in his home life.

As to the content of Judaism, there is really no difference between the Traditional Judaism as it was taught at the Seminary and Orthodox Judaism. We believe in the divine revelation of the Torah, in the binding character of tradition, and the duty to practice the laws of Judaism as promulgated in the Torah, as interpreted by the Talmud, and as codified by the sages of Israel.

We realize that life has not stood still since the Torah was promulgated. In every age and in every clime, conditions have arisen calling for the readjustment of the old to the demands of the changed times and the changed environment. Judaism has not been deaf to these demands for the readjustment and change, but it has insisted that they be made in the prescribed manner either through interpretation by the competent scholars or through legislation by a duly constituted Sanhedrin.[44] It is a libel to state that Judaism in post-Talmudic times became petrified and set its face against the demands of life. What really happened was that Judaism opposed wanton or unlicensed change either by individuals or by groups. Rabbi Joshua and Rabbi Eliezer, for example, were taught the lesson that Judaism as a religion of "law and order" demands the subordination of one's individual opinion, sound as it may seem, to the will of the constituted authority (m. Rosh Hashanah 2:8–9, and Bava Metzia 59b).[45] Otherwise, chaos and anarchy may result. If therefore we feel that certain laws like that regarding the Agunah, for example, require revision, we are at liberty to do so if, by examining the laws in question and by the accepted rules of interpretation, we find them amenable to revision.[46] Failing to find such justification, we should be loyal enough to tradition to obey these laws, difficult as they may be, until "Catholic Israel" shall have legislated their revision. In asking this, Traditional Judaism makes no greater demand than our government, which has always insisted that as citizens we obey the laws of the land until they are amended or repealed.

CONCLUSION

In April 1916 the editors of the *American Hebrew* congratulated "Modern Orthodox" leaders for reviving religious life in American Judaism. The journalists were referring to the rabbis ordained at Solomon Schechter's seminary. "With the reorganization of the Jewish Theological Seminary and the coming to this country of the late Dr. Schechter," wrote the editors, "a different situation developed."[47] In contrast, the editorial issued no commendation to the leaders of the Orthodox Union or the relative upstart Bernard Revel. Yet Schechter's popularity had its limitations. The Agudath Ha-Rabbonim was quick to strike Schechter and his rabbinical school out of the Orthodox camp. This disappointed Schechter, who abided by the strictures of Jewish law and eschewed any "Reform" or "Conservative" designation directed at him. In 1905 Schechter announced, "It is not necessary to emphasize that this is an orthodox seminary; it is a Jewish seminary. Of course it is orthodox also. I never knew that I am orthodox till I came to this country. In my father's home we used to speak more of Judaism than of orthodoxy."[48]

The Agudath Ha-Rabbonim also harbored concerns for Revel's programs. As the self-professed "spiritual guardians" of Revel's school, the right-wing rabbis appointed a Rabbinical Advisory Board to work with the young president and ensure that Revel would not "make changes in the Yeshiva" on his own "initiative."[49] That the rabbinical group deigned to take issue with both men and their institutions indicated the inroads that they had paved in traditional Jewish life. Owing to the importance of both, then, the American adventures and visions of Bernard Revel and Solomon Schechter helped shape the borderlines of Orthodox Judaism in America.

6 | The Parting of the Ways
Orthodox and Conservative Judaism

INTRODUCTION

In 1913 the Los Angeles Jewish press announced the formation of the Modern Orthodox Congregation Shaarey Tefila. The new synagogue was to be led by an Orthodox rabbi and house a traditional-minded Talmud Torah, but left much else open to speculation.[1] Likewise, a Chicago congregation claimed that it met "all the demands of a modern orthodox synagogue" but failed to enumerate those qualifications.[2] Seven years later, a "Prominent Rabbi" of a "large congregation in the South" placed an advertisement in a New York newspaper to announce his consideration for a "change of pulpit." The anonymous rabbi stressed that only Conservative or Modern Orthodox congregations were desired.[3]

In the first decades of the twentieth century, it was not at all clear how to define a "Modern Orthodox rabbi or congregation. A Jew in Brooklyn warned his coreligionists sitting in Modern Orthodox congregations "not to allow their modernity to carry them into the camp of Reform."[4] Accordingly, some tried to get rid of the "Orthodox" designation altogether. Rabbis like Leo Jung and Joseph Lookstein (1902–79) of New York preferred—albeit with some reluctance—"Torah-True" or "Traditional" to describe their religious beliefs. On the other side, Conservative leaders also struggled to gain traction for their theological brand. In 1930, for instance, Rabbi Louis Finkelstein (1895–1991) admitted in his presidential address to the Rabbinical Assembly that "Conservatism" was a term that he "disliked" due to "its implication of further schismatism."[5] Yet at least one other JTS man was unsympathetic. He called on like-minded clergymen and congregations to banish equivocal names like "semi-Reformed" and "Modern Orthodox" and instead ally with Conservative Judaism, a label that had more potential to garner more "affirmative principles."[6]

The trouble for all of these clerics was that "affirmative principles" were rare commodities at that time in the American Jewish marketplace. For instance, well into the post–World War II era, mixed seating could not differentiate Orthodox and Conservative congregations; many of both featured it. In the 1940s the rabbi of K.I.N.S. in Chicago—which identified as Orthodox and sat women and men together—argued that the two most important features of an "Orthodox" congregation were that it conducted its worship with the traditional prayers and that its pulpit was assigned to an Orthodox seminary-trained rabbi: "It is my opinion that while Orthodoxy must strive to retain the tradition of separate pews wherever possible, a synagogue may still be labeled Orthodox if this is lacking, provided the other factors I outlined are present."[7] In 1950 Conservative leaders permitted driving to synagogue on the Sabbath under certain conditions. Orthodox rabbis certainly did not approve, but they were also aware that many of their congregants traveled by automobile to their synagogues as well.[8] On occasion, Orthodox proponents—typically the more right-wing variety—singled out acts of "heresy" that separated their camp from Conservative Judaism. Participation in the interdenominational Synagogue Council of America and the "reconstructionist" philosophies of Rabbi Mordecai Kaplan were two important flashpoints that bore out this point. Eventually, and however reluctantly, these episodes helped define Orthodox and Conservative Judaism.

SECTION 1 | What's in a Name?

A Definition of Modern Orthodox

Henry Pereira Mendes | 1913

Reverend Henry Pereira Mendes was the founding president of the Union of Orthodox Jewish Congregations (Orthodox Union) and rabbi of Shearith Israel in New York. Always a traditional Jew, Mendes at first vacillated on his religious self-definition. Earlier in his career, he described himself as part of "Historical Judaism" and eschewed an "Orthodox" designation, even as he took the helm of the Orthodox Union. In 1913 he wrote to Dr. Cyrus Adler (1863–1940) about the possibility of incorporating the Orthodox Union into a larger synagogue body led by Solomon Schechter and others within the Jewish Theological Seminary. In this letter, Mendes proposed a merger but only on condition that the new institution embraced his brand of "Modern Orthodox Judaism."

NEW YORK, FEBRUARY 14TH, 1913.

My dear Dr. Adler,[9]

Dr. [Solomon] Schechter and Rabbi [Jacob] Cohn have both had several interviews with me concerning the proposed Agudath Jeshurun or Union for Promoting Traditional Judaism in America.[10] I have carefully examined the Preamble to the Constitution and the sketch of the Constitution sent to me. I understand that you are Chairman of the Constitution Committee and I therefore write to you.

In order to explain my views to you let us for the moment agree to the following definitions, even if they are not exactly correct:

First: Russian Orthodoxy. This is the Orthodoxy which insists upon a certain ritual and certain forms, but objects to English Sermons, has little or no decorum, fails to hold its young men and young women, refuses in its schools Hebrew and religious education to girls, and cares little whether women and girls attend religious service or not. It also insists upon such customs as the Shaitel and, in a word, degrades womanhood as you and I understand it.[11]

Second: Modern Orthodoxy, as represented by, for example, your and my Congregation and several Ashkenaz Congregations such as those in Baltimore, Philadelphia, and Montreal. This Orthodoxy resists innovations such as organs, pews, disuse of Taleth, female voices in the choir, Christians in the choir, etc.

Third: Conservative Judaism. Let this term mean the Judaism which permits some of the innovations named.

Fourth: Reform Judaism, which in addition to such innovations, rejects certain historical beliefs and aspirations, such as Restoration, etc.

Fifth: Radical Reform, which publishes a Pittsburgh Platform, or a Programme of the Cincinnati Teachers Association, which presents the Bible as myth and folklore, an epic like an Iliad.

Which of these Judaisms will the proposed Union countenance? Can a scheme be adopted which by the moral force of its reasonableness shall attract Orthodox Congregations, shall appeal to Russian Orthodox Congregations, and shall strengthen and increase the Jewish loyalty of the Conservative Congregations? That will depend upon how you frame the Constitution.

The "Modern Orthodox" Rabbi

Solomon Zucrow | 1928

Solomon Zucrow (1870–1932) was professor of Talmud at Hebrew Teachers College in Boston. Much of his work concentrated on the flexibility of Jewish law, a point that he encouraged rabbis in his own time to consider. In particular, Zucrow was frustrated that traditional leaders refused to take action and retroactively absolve the marriages of women who were deserted by their husbands and unable to receive the requisite bill of divorce to remarry. In this postscript to his work on change in Halakhah, the writer expressed hope that the new crop of "Modern Orthodox" rabbis, presumably graduates of the Jewish Theological Seminary in New York, would rise up to his challenge.

I am convinced that the future of Judaism lies in the hands of the modern orthodox rabbi.[12] He is the only man who can once again make of our religion a "Law of Life." Possessing a secular as well as a rabbinic education, he can appeal to both the old and the new generation. It is for this rabbi to set up a standard of Jewish religious observance for the present day. He must clearly discriminate between those laws and observances that are important for the spiritual welfare of our people, but which are no longer kept because of the indifference and ignorance of the Jewish masses, and those laws which we need no longer obey, because they have become meaningless for us, or are averse to our conception of life and the value of right and wrong. With reference to the first category, the rabbi must make the people understand that Judaism is not merely composed of a few abstract dogmas, such as the unity of God and the brotherhood of man, but that it seeks to influence the conduct of men and women at every point. This it can do only by means of a system of laws and observances which shall enter into the daily lives of the people. To discard in summary fashion the entire body of ritualistic and social laws handed down to us by our forefathers must lead inevitably to the elimination of Judaism as a force in human life. With regard to the second category of laws, i.e., those which are out of date and have been rendered useless for the very purpose for which they were originally enacted, the rabbis must not allow them to stand and so impede the development of religion. Prolonged insistence upon the validity of such laws leads people to think that our religion in its entirety is a matter of the past, a glorious past indeed, but nevertheless a dead past.

Our spiritual leaders of today must avail themselves of the prerogative to which they are entitled. Perhaps the greatest factor in the historical development of Jewish law was the very prerogative with which, according to the Talmud, Scripture invested the rabbis of every generation. It is their right, and even their duty, according to talmudic teaching, to abrogate even biblical laws when some cogent reason therefore exists, and especially if the cause of religion would be strengthened by such an act (Yevamot 89b).

Why should not our spiritual leaders, assembled in council, make use of their prerogative, and harmonize the conflicting claims of religion and life? I am fully aware of the fact that those rabbis who would agree to act on this suggestion would be confronted with the statement found in the Talmud: "One rabbinical court cannot repeal any law established by another court unless the former outnumbers the latter and surpasses it in the scholarly attainments of its members" (Megillah 2a). This principle actually has deprived the rabbis of recent times of freedom of action, since it has become an axiom among our people that the scholarship of the ancient rabbis can never be attained by any rabbi of these later ages. We must once and for all break with this

אן אפּעל צו אטלאנטער אידען פאר
די הייליקייט פון שבת און כשרות

מיר די רבנים פון אטלאנטא גיבען צו וויסען אז די בעל"ב בוטשערים און
דעליקאטעסען סטאורס פון אטלאנטא האבען זיך פאַרפליכטעט צו היטען די היילאייצו
פון דעם שבת אין דעם כדין, און האבען פאַריכטעט זיך צו עפענען שבת אז סמאורס
פאר דער צייט וואס איז קרוליכם נאך דעם איידישען דין.

די רבנים זעלען אנאנסירען די צייט יעדע וואך.

ראיתם אפעליגן מיר צו די אידען פון אטלאנטא — העלפט דורכפירין די
די שמירת שבת ! קומם נים קויפען בעפאר דער שבת איז אריבער !

קויפט נאר אין די סטאורס זעלכע האלמען פאַרמאכט דעם שבת
שבת'דיגען טאג. ערמיס זעם איר זין זינער אז די כשר'ע ארטיקלען
זיינען ריכטיג כשר.

נאר דער זעלכער וואָס זיין סטאר פאַרמאכט שבת איז באלויבם
אויף כשרות !

הרב טוביה געפן
הרב צבי חיים עפשטיין

An Appeal to Atlanta Jewry for the Sanctity of the Sabbath and Kashruth

We take this opportunity to announce that all Jewish owners of Kosher Butcher Shops and Delicatessen Stores have pledged themselves to keep their stores closed on the Sabbath according to Jewish Laws.

One of the essential requirements of the Law of Kashruth is that stores selling Kosher products be closed on the Sabbath Day.

ONLY HE WHO KEEPS HIS STORE CLOSED ON THE SABBATH CAN HAVE THE CONFIDENCE OF THOSE WHO SEEK KOSHER PRODUCTS!

Our appeal to the members of our Orthodox community is:

Help us assure Kashruth in Atlanta by refraining to buy on the Sabbath. Cooperate with us by encouraging your Jewish Storekeeper to keep closed on the Sabbath Day, refusing to buy on that day. BY SO DOING YOU WILL AID US IN OUR EFFORT TO ESTABLISH THE INTEGRITY OF KOSHER PRODUCTS SOLD IN ATLANTA.

The laws of Kashruth are a distinguishing mark of the Jew. By strict observance of the practice of the Dietary Laws we strengthen ourselves against enervation of Jewish life and attacks upon Jewish sincerity.

RABBI TOBIAS GEFFEN
RABBI HARRY H. EPSTEIN

In Atlanta, "Conservative" and "Orthodox" rabbis worked together to uphold religious observance and blurred the lines of denominational distinctions. In this broadside, Rabbi Tobias Geffen (1870–1970), a staunch advocate of European-style Orthodox Judaism, and Rabbi Harry Epstein (1903–2003), the head of a mixed-seating congregation who most often described himself as part of the Conservative camp, announced their efforts to promote Sabbath compliance within the city's traditional community. To reach as many people as they could, the rabbis notified their readers in both Yiddish (for the staunchly European Orthodox) and English (for the Americanized traditionalists). Courtesy of the Cuba Family Archives for Southern Jewish History of the Breman Museum.

principle, for it runs counter to the facts of Jewish history and to the historical development of Jewish law and is, moreover, quite illogical.

What Is Orthodox Judaism?

Leo Jung | 1930

Rabbi Leo Jung was the longtime rabbi of the well-heeled Jewish Center on New York's Upper West Side. Ordained by Rabbi David Hoffman (1843–1921) in Ber-

lin and holder of a doctorate from the University of London, Jung was a public intellectual and a leader in a number of Orthodox organizations. This excerpt is derived from an essay in the Jewish Library, *a series of popular books edited by Jung and intended to defend and teach the "principles" of traditional Judaism. This selection revealed Jung's reluctance to self-define as "Orthodox." Owing to the vagueness of the label and the disparate religious communities that designated themselves by it, Jung believed that "Orthodox" was insufficient.*

What is Orthodox Judaism? Rather let me state what it is not. By a process of elimination we may arrive at a right definition. The word "orthodox" in itself is insufficient. It expresses nothing positive about the Jewish faith. I would suggest "Torah-true" as more appropriate, were this Germanic compound acceptable as an English term. However, for our present purpose, we may use the term "orthodox" to designate the man or woman who lives in accord with Jewish faith and practice.

Orthodox Jews have been called fundamentalists. The inference here is that the Jew puts a single interpretation on Biblical accounts, holds such exclusively true, and rejects as blasphemy every effort at reinterpretation. This charge is not half as amusing as it is untrue. Interpretation in Judaism has been not only a privilege but a duty. It is through interpretation and reinterpretation that the Bible has remained a book of life. From the first Midrash, through the philosophical works of the Middle Ages down to the commentaries of our own time, from Midrash Rabbah to Samson Raphael Hirsch and Malbim, a thousand interpretations have been offered, each striking a new note, each offering a new nuance, each welcomed as a new contribution to the Torah.[13] We never hear of any Jew being read out of the synagogue because of such interpretation. On the basis of the acceptance of Revelation, freedom has been allowed to individual ingenuity. Fundamentalism among the Protestant non-Jewish friends of the Bible rests on the Authorized Version or some other translation of the original Hebrew text and of the so-called New Testament, every letter of which translation or mistranslation they consider divine truth.[14] Such fundamentalism is un-Jewish. But if Jewish Fundamentalism implies loyalty to such Jewish fundamentals as faith in God, in Revelation, in the binding character of Jewish Law, then every good Jew is a Fundamentalist.

Even among Jews we find some who consider Orthodox Judaism as out of touch with modern times. Never did they err more profoundly. Jewish law develops through application of precedent to new conditions, exactly as English or American law does. The Responsa of the rabbis, dealing with modern questions, keep the Jew in rapport with changes in his environment, and with the problems of today and tomorrow. These Responsa accompany Jewish life all through history and help the Jew to live with the Torah as with a law which is ever alive, fresh, and clear with every new question and answer. Just as reinterpretation has given Jewish literature the best of Greek thought and the essence of Hegel and Kant, so, through application of precedent to new conditions, has Jewish practice remained vital and creative.[15]

Judaism is in advance of our time, not only in its prophetic dream of the days when nation will not lift up sword against nation, but especially also in its social and marriage legislation. "Torah im Derech Eretz," the combination of the Judaic ideal with modern methods of transmission, has been a time hallowed postulate of Judaism.[16]

The main disability of Orthodox Judaism lies in the fact that it is—in this country at least—largely unknown in theory, and rarely seen in fair operation. Orthodox Judaism is not to be identified with Ghetto conditions. It claims no inherent kinship with inefficiency or lack of articulation. It does not deny or reject anything that is good and beautiful in modern culture. Its greatest handicap is the profound ignorance as to its character, function, and destiny prevailing in the mind of the American Jewish youth. To the majority of American Israel, Orthodoxy is associated with unsightly mass habitation on the Lower East Side. Torah-true synagogues are associated with a lack of decorum, a pulpit empty of a message for the youth, and profound disability to understand or to deal with the problems facing Jewry in this country.

Such weakness are due not to Orthodoxy but to the orthodox Jew. They are the results not of orthodox Jewish teaching or living, but of czarist oppression, sweatshop conditions, and the average plight of the immigrant. Fundamentally and enduringly let us distinguish between Orthodoxy as a system of life and the present panorama of orthodox Jews in America. That conditions have been improving is well known. That the orthodox Jew is arousing himself is becoming increasingly felt. But Orthodoxy is neither responsible for, nor to be associated with, the disabilities or faults of the American orthodox Jew.

What then is Jewish Orthodoxy? Orthodoxy is the expression of the genuine historical faith of Israel, based upon the revelation of Sinai, the Torah, the Bible, the teaching of the rabbis. Orthodoxy is the Jewish expression of Judaism. Orthodoxy embraces worship and charity, public righteousness and private devotion, social service and individual purity. Judaism is based on the assumption that ideas must be made tangible for man to realize them. Hence Revelation is followed (Ex. xx) by Legislation (Ex. xxi).[17] The great ideals taught in the Torah cannot be translated into life, unless their message is brought home. The religious idealism of the Torah would remain vague and remote, unless the people were trained to consult their ideal interests as of essential importance.

Ceremonies, symbolizing profound spiritual truth, are part of the method of Judaism. What to the uninitiated seems to be a maze of legalistic devices is but the blessing of a system of life, so arranged as to attune us to the highest ideals of man, to accustom us, by the humanitarian exercises of Mitzvah, to look for the ideal rather than the material, to look upon all humanity rather than upon a single clan, and upon the whole of Jewish history rather than upon a narrow local scene.

The Rabbinical Council of America

Solomon Reichman | JUNE 20, 1935

In 1935 a group of rabbis invited their Orthodox colleagues to attend the first meeting of the Rabbinical Council of America. Below is the letter sent by the organization's secretary, Rabbi Solomon Reichman (1898–1984). Eight years earlier, Rabbi Leo Jung had established the Rabbinical Council of the Union of

Orthodox Jewish Congregations of America, but the clerical body never amounted to much. In 1935 the RCA was relaunched and composed mainly of the graduates of the Rabbi Isaac Elchanan Theological Seminary (RIETS). In 1942 the RCA invited graduates of the Hebrew Theological College in Chicago to join its ranks.

19 Sivan 5695

Dear Colleague:
The first National Convention of the reorganized Rabbinical Council of the UOJC and the Rabbinical Association of the Yeshiva will take place, please G-d, July 1st and 2nd, at Belmar, N.J., at the Hotel Carlton, 9th Street and Ocean Avenue.

Through the Convention we hope to make at last a definite forward step toward the creation of a united front in the Orthodox Rabbinate in this country, so sorely needed in this age of irresponsible and confusing leadership.

Fully aware of the seriousness of the problems confronting us as Orthodox Rabbis, we have prepared a program of vital interest to all of us.

Is it necessary to emphasize the hardships, both spiritual and material, wrought upon every one of us by the lack of unity within our ranks?

Don't you feel that it is high time for us to strengthen our organization, so that it will in turn help us to cope with the many problems facing us in our work?

We, therefore, hope that you will immediately fill out the enclosed card and return it at once. This will enable us to make the necessary arrangements at the hotel. There is a special rate of $7.00 [today, $120] for the two days, including room and board, for the Rabbis and their guests.

With Torah Greetings,
Solomon Reichman
Secretary

Orthodox–Traditional–Torah-True Judaism

Joseph Lookstein | 1940

Rabbi Joseph Lookstein was the spiritual leader of the affluent Congregation Kehilath Jeshurun on Manhattan's Upper East Side. He founded a day school (Ramaz, est. 1937) and served as president of the Rabbinical Council of America as well as the interdenominational Synagogue Council of America. Like Leo Jung, Lookstein was hesitant to describe himself as "Orthodox."

It is singularly strange that the oldest branch of Judaism and the one nearest to its ancient source bears a name which is not of Jewish connotation. The term "orthodox" is generally used in Christian theology to designate the original Church as distinct from its various and eventual reformations.

Strange as that may be, it is, nevertheless, comprehensible. For the descriptive "orthodox" was appended to Judaism not by the adherents of Orthodoxy but by the deserters from its ranks. They, of course, never intended that the word "orthodox" which means "right opinion" would be taken in its literal sense. They intended rather to label that branch of Judaism as static, ancient, and unprogressive. In America, for example, Orthodox Judaism came to be associated in the minds of some with Fundamentalism, which is again a non-Jewish category.

Because of these reasons it is understandable why Samson Raphael Hirsch used the name "Torah-true" Judaism as a better and more correct designation.[18] Frequently, too, we will hear of it as "traditional" Judaism, which is, to say the least, a more flattering name. Recently the name "Neo-orthodox" was suggested, implying a distinction between the contemporary adherents of this form of Judaism and those of a century ago. Though the term is academically attractive, it is not warranted by fact.

Whether the adjective "Orthodox," "Traditional," or "Torah-true" is used, the intention is to describe a philosophy of Judaism which represents a faithful retention of the beliefs, the principles and observances of the Jewish people as handed down from generation to generation, from the day of Moses to our very own.

This philosophy of Judaism, therefore, does not bear the label "made in Germany," as does Reform Judaism, nor "imported from England and improved in America," as does Conservative Judaism.[19] Its ancient pedigree is recorded in the opening paragraph of the tractate Aboth. "Moses received the Torah from Sinai and delivered it to Joshua, and Joshua to the Elders, and the Elders to the Prophets, and the Prophets delivered it to the men of the Great Synagogue" (1:1). The inspired genius of our sages in Palestine and Babylonia wrought its impression upon it. Maimonides and the codifiers gave order and system to it. Rashi and the Tosafists interpreted it.[20] The academies in eastern Europe preserved it and the Rabbis through the ages in their response gave vitality to it by reconciling the situation of life with its ancient teachings. This entire process is called "Tradition" and represents the inner dynamics of Jewish Law as Orthodox Judaism understands it.

... From the point of view of numerical strength, Orthodox Judaism very probably has the largest constituency in American Jewish religious life. That it does not exert an influence commensurate with its numbers is due to several factors. For one thing, it was late in learning the importance of organization; for another, its principal spokesmen in the past were Rabbis from Eastern Europe who, while possessing great learning and scholarship, could not, unfortunately speak the language of America. As a result, Orthodoxy came to be regarded by many as a sort of ghetto Judaism. Fortunately all of that is rapidly being overcome. The Union of Orthodox Jewish Congregations of America now has more than five hundred Orthodox synagogues affiliated with it. The Rabbi Isaac Elchanan Theological Seminary and Yeshiva College, under the distinguished leadership of Dr. Bernard Revel, a world renowned scholar, has been training hundreds of gifted young men for the American Rabbinate and for the role of intelligent lay leadership. Already over two hundred of the graduates from this institution are occupying positions of prominence in leading Orthodox congregations. They are united in the Rabbinical [Council] of America and, together with their older colleagues in the Union of Orthodox Rabbis of America, constitute the supreme religious authority for American Orthodoxy.

The Yeshiva College, the only college of liberal arts and sciences under Jewish auspices, has successfully performed the experiment of integrating Judaism and Americanism and gives to the Yeshiva students, in addition to their great Rabbinic learning, the added advantages of secular knowledge. The Teachers' Institute of the Yeshiva College, under the outstanding scholar and educator Dr. Pinkhos Churgin, has been sending forth well-trained Hebrew teachers for the schools of the country.[21] Some of them are principals of leading schools and a few have won distinction in the wider areas of community educational systems. The College maintains also a graduate school for advanced study and Jewish research. It issues two scholarly journals: one *Horeb* in Hebrew, and the other *Scripta Mathematica* in English. Several other institutions for the training of Rabbis exist and one of them, the Rabbinical College of Chicago, is gaining rapid recognition.[22]

A valuable asset to Orthodoxy and essential to its viewpoint is the chain of parochial schools that it supports throughout the country. In New York, Baltimore, Chicago, Philadelphia, and other large cities, such schools are growing in number. It is estimated that some five thousand children are educated in these schools alone, besides those in the numerous afternoon schools that are under the aegis of Orthodoxy. Indeed America has become the scene of major operation and achievement for Orthodox Judaism.

Orthodox Judaism undoubtedly makes the severest demands upon its adherents. It does not countenance concession for the sake of convenience. It does not approve of compromise for the sake of comfort. It will not surrender eternity for the sake of modernity. But it does offer the greatest possibility for Jewish fulfillment and the surest promise for Jewish survival.

"A Modern Orthodox Congregation"
Joseph Rudnick | 1925

Joseph Rudnick (1869–1936) was a prominent businessman and banker. He was simultaneously president of the traditional-leaning Kehillath Israel in Brookline and the Orthodox Temple Israel in Nantucket and a vice president of Beth Israel Hospital. In 1925 Kehillath Israel's membership voted on whether to introduce mixed seating into the synagogue. The final tally decided in favor of family pews. Most interesting in this article is Rudnick's use of "strict orthodox" and "modern orthodox" to describe the religious transition of his congregation.

The problem of the seating arrangement at our Temple was thoroughly debated at the meeting of February 25 and fought out with an Australian Ballot in accordance with a petition signed by seven members of good standing who demanded that such a vote be taken.[23] The result of the vote is known to all.

At first, when the question came up before the Board Meeting and members at large, I expressed my opinion and hoped that Kehillath Israel would remain in every way an orthodox congregation, and I had hoped that we would have a sufficient number of Jews in Brookline of the type that would support a strictly orthodox synagogue. There were, however, an overwhelming majority of people who had given money toward the erection of the Temple and who felt that this Congregation should be what is called "A Modern Orthodox Congregation."[24]

It is my hope and feeling that those who have not carried out their point will not take the matter too seriously and cause a break in the congregation for which so many of us worked. While they may feel that we have parted from an ancient custom, let them find consolation in the fact that they will have the opportunity to have their sons and daughters with them at our service instead of having them in any other temple, which may be entirely reformed. Why not make an effort to have the young men and women with us, rather than letting them go where they see fit?

Under the proper supervision, with a sincere spiritual leader, we hope to be able to set an example that will benefit the entire Jewish community, particularly the younger generation.[25]

I wish to plead with the small minority who feel that they have to leave us on account of our transgression that we need them in our midst to promote a stronger Judaism.[26] We need them for the sake of peace and harmony and we need them for the sake of the young people. I hope that all the young and old will go together and nothing will be done to hurt the interest of the struggling community, at this time when we are in the extreme need of every cent that can be obtained to meet our obligations.

I want to appeal to the young men and women of this community, the so called "victors," that they must at once show their interest as they have promised that they would do so if this congregation would fulfill their wish. There is no excuse now for anyone to stay away, or refuse to give their support to the Temple, or not to pay their contributions which have been pledged. The issue was settled in your favor and it is your duty to do your utmost to put this congregation on a high standard in every way.

I plead with the ladies of this community, who were so eager to sit with their husbands and children, that they show their appreciation by giving us their full support and assist us in raising funds for the Congregation and also to help us spiritually to make this Temple a real House of God.

The President alone cannot do all the work.[27] The task is too hard for one man and it is the sacred duty of every one of you, young and old, to work in harmony and peace for your Temple and for your God.

Joseph Rudnick, President.

May Men and Women Sit Together in Shul?

Joseph B. Soloveitchik | 1954

In 1954 the editors of the Yiddish-language Der Tog *submitted three questions on "American Orthodox life" to Rabbi Joseph B. Soloveitchik (1903–93). Soloveitchik had just emerged as a public figure, but was not yet well known beyond his hometown of Boston and in New York, where he taught Talmud at Yeshiva University and was known reverentially as the "Rav." One year prior, he was appointed chairman of the RCA's Halachah Committee. He responded to two queries on the permissibility of Orthodox Jews to participate in interdenominational organizations and the propriety of assuming non-Jewish names in private and public domains. In this third (and oft-republished) responsum below, Soloveitchik stressed the importance of separate seating in Orthodox congregations. He refused to permit his followers to pray in a mixed-pew synagogue—a configuration of worship that Soloveitchik contended was foreign to Judaism.*

To make absolutely clear my position on this laden question, I would like to relate this incident:

A young man moved into a suburb of Boston, where the only existent synagogue had men and women sitting together. He asked me what he should do on the High Holy Days, Rosh Hashanah and Yom Kippur; until then, on account of the mixed seating, he had not entered the synagogue; but on the Days of Awe he was very reluctant to remain at home. I answered him that it were better for him to pray at home both Rosh Hashanah and Yom Kippur, and not cross the threshold of that synagogue. A few days later he telephoned me again: he had met the man who was to sound the shofar in that synagogue, and this man had warned him that if he did not come to the synagogue he simply would not hear the shofar at all, for the man would not sound the shofar again, privately, for his benefit. The young man practically implored me that I grant him permission to enter the edifice, at least for a half hour, that he might hear the shofar blasts. I hesitated not for a moment, but directed him to remain at home. It would be better not to hear the shofar than to enter a synagogue whose sanctity has been profaned.

My stringent position regarding the mingling of men and women arises from several reasons.

First of all, such mingling is forbidden according to the halachah. In certain instances Biblical law prohibits praying in a synagogue where men and women are seated together. Such a locale has none of the sanctity of a synagogue; any prayers offered there are worthless in the eyes of the Jewish Law.

Secondly, the separation of the sexes in the synagogue derives historically from the Sanctuary, where there were both a Court of Women and a Court of Israelites. In its martyr's history of a thousand years, the people of Israel have never violated this sacred principle. Moreover, when primitive Christianity arose as a sect in the Holy Land and began to slowly introduce reforms, one of the innovations which the sect established at once in the externals of synagogue practice was to have men and women sit together. In many instances mixed seating was the unmistakable sign by which a Jew could recognize that he had found not a place of sanctity for Jews to pray but rather a prayer-house for a deviating sect; for in those times the Christians had not yet formally differentiated themselves from traditional Jewry. As a secret sect they endeavored to hide their identity, and only through certain definite signs could they be recognized.

It would seem to me that our remembrance of history alone should keep us from imitating today the practice of primitive Christianity almost 1,900 years ago.

Thirdly, the entire concept of "family pews" is in contradiction to the Jewish spirit of prayer. Prayer means communication, with the Master of the World, and therefore withdrawal from all and everything. During prayer man must feel alone, removed, isolated. He must then regard the Creator as an old Friend, from whom alone he can hope for support and consolation. Behold, as the eyes of servants look unto the hand of their master, as the eyes of a maiden unto the hand of her mistress, so our eyes look unto the Lord our God, until He be gracious unto us (Ps. 123:2).

Clearly, the presence of women among men, or of men among women, which often evokes a certain frivolity in the group, either in spirit or in behavior, can contribute little to sanctification or to the deepening of religious feeling; nor can it help instill that mood in which a man must be immersed when he would communicate with the Almighty. Out of the depths have I called Thee, O Lord (Ps. 130:1), says the Psalmist. Such a state of being will not be realized amid "family pews."

In my opinion, Orthodoxy must mobilize all its forces and wage an indefatigable battle against the "christianization" (I have no other name for it) of the synagogue—a process which is being accomplished by people who possess no sense of halachah and no historical-philosophical concept of the nature of prayer; but they do have the arrogance to wreck principles and traditions which have become hallowed through blood and tears.

And I do not believe this battle will be a lost one.

In the mingled seating of women and men I see no progressive idea which should appeal to the person of culture. The American Jew, though he is ignorant in matters of Jewish law, has a great amount of common sense and a certain intellectual honesty. I am convinced that if the Jewish public were to be truly enlightened on this matter, it would react quite differently to this reprehensible reform. It would understand that the separation of men and women implies not disrespect or contempt for woman, as the representatives of the half-reformed camp would interpret. On the contrary, it is based on the Jewish sense of modesty, a sense identical with the attitude of reverence for Deity, a sense which the Judaism of Abraham and Sarah has shown toward woman as the mother and builder of the people Israel. When they, the angels, said unto him: Where is Sarah thy wife? Abraham simply replied, Behold, in the tent (Gen. 18:9).

In practical terms, Orthodoxy has three tasks: (1) to conduct a program of education through the oral and the written word; (2) to morally support those individual laymen and rabbis who often give themselves in self-sacrifice to a battle for the sanctity of the synagogue. Mostly an action for reform will begin with the obstinacy of one despot in the brotherhood or sisterhood. Were the observant Jews well organized, and if they but had a more aggressive attitude, the reform could, in many instances, be averted. (3) Orthodox organizations should undertake to build synagogues in the suburbs and new communities where Jews are settling. If the various synagogue organizations ... would concentrate on organizing new synagogues and Jewish communities in America, they could accomplish much.

We have not yet lost the battle, for we have not yet begun to fight. We have but abandoned the synagogue, much as the French abandoned Paris before the Germans fired the very first shot. Even today, however, we can yet defend our positions—if we will but have the determination. We must have the will to give battle, for the synagogue is the center of Jewish communal life in this country. No movement or organization is as strong as the synagogue. When we lose a House of Prayer, we lose a strategic position. A right battle for principles is always a worthy and honorable endeavor.

Gird thy sword upon thy thigh ... prosper, ride on, in behalf of truth (Ps. 45:4–5).

A "Family Seated" Orthodox Synagogue
Julius Katz | 1956

Julius Katz was a leading member of Congregation Chevra Thilim in New Orleans. He was also a plaintiff in Katz v. Singerman. His was the minority group that appealed to the Louisiana courts to block the congregation's move to family pews. In fact, there were three high-profile court cases that all centered on this religious matter. In the New Orleans case, the lower courts ruled in favor of the plaintiffs. In 1961 the Louisiana Supreme Court overturned the ruling, largely on the belief that courts should not interfere with ecclesiastical matters and on the basis that the congregation's rabbi supported mixed seating. This letter to Rabbi Morris Finer (1912–85) of Yeshiva University indicated the confusion among American Jews on how to distinguish Orthodox from Conservative Judaism.

Dear Rabbi Finer:
A Mr. Gus Singerman, leader of the opposition and candidate for

president under the mixed pew seating plan, issued a letter this date, excerpt of which is below:[28]

> Many more than half of all the Orthodox Synagogues throughout our country are family seated and have Rabbis in their pulpits who have been placed there by the largest Orthodox Yeshivas of our country, including the Hebrew Theological College of Chicago and the Yeshiva University of New York.
>
> Rabbi Isadore Goodman, who recently visited with us and whom you may or may not have heard in his address on Orthodox versus conservatism, is a graduate of and ordained Rabbi by the Yeshiva University of New York.[29]
>
> The Yeshiva University of New York has 380 Rabbis in Orthodox Synagogues throughout the nation. More than half of these are family seated.
>
> The Hebrew Theological College of Chicago, the second largest Yeshiva in our country, has several hundred of their ordained Rabbis placed in Orthodox Synagogues throughout the nation; more than two-thirds of these Synagogues are family seated.
>
> Family seating is therefore *not conservatism,* as some would like you to believe, in order to confuse the issue. Family seating in an Orthodox Synagogue is a family seated Orthodox Synagogue and *nothing else.*

This is being forwarded to you for immediate consideration and if possible repudiation by you. . . . Inasmuch as the election is this coming Sunday, it is highly important that I receive from you a letter in detail concerning the statements made by Mr. Singerman as to their truth or untruth in order that ample publicity can be made of this fact to our membership.

I shall expect to hear from you immediately by return air mail special delivery for which I thank you in advance.

Very truly yours,
    Julius Katz
    500 Canal

A New Religious Group in American Judaism?

S. Felix Mendelsohn | 1943

In 1919 Samuel Felix Mendelsohn (1889–1953) was appointed rabbi of the Reform Beth Israel in Chicago. He was a regular contributor to the Chicago Jewish press and a keen observer of the Orthodox community in that city. In this column, Mendelsohn reacted sharply to a "new" phenomenon described as "Modern Orthodoxy."

Question: Your definition of conservatism in the *Sentinel* of January 21 is enlightening. Recently it has come to my notice that some congregations style themselves "modern orthodox." Will you please explain this term also? Does that mean that we have a fourth religious group in American Judaism?

—Mrs. L.R.G.

Answer: Rabbi Leo Jung, a recognized leader of orthodoxy, says in the *Universal Jewish Encyclopedia*, "Orthodox Judaism holds to one principal doctrine, the doctrine of revelation, which means that the Torah contains absolute truth, that it is not the work of Moses, but the word of God."[30]

One of the Thirteen Articles of Faith, which the orthodox Jew recites daily, says, "I believe with perfect faith that this Torah will not be changed, and that there will never be any other Torah from the Creator, blessed be His name."[31]

Orthodoxy therefore maintains that basic Judaism is not subject to change. *Thorndike's Senior Dictionary* defines the word "modern" as "up-to-date, not old-fashioned," which plainly implies the principle of change. For this reason the expression "modern orthodoxy" is a contradiction in terms. It is employed by orthodox congregations which admit that they are bending toward conservatism.

It is our opinion that the use of the term "modern orthodoxy" is highly objectionable. It is misleading, and it increases the spiritual confusion already prevalent in American Judaism.

The Excommunication of Mordecai Kaplan
Agudath Ha-Rabbonim | 1945

Founded in 1902, the Agudath Ha-Rabbonim had always taken a very critical stance against the Jewish Theological Seminary and its exponents. In 1945 Rabbi Mordecai Kaplan published his Sabbath Prayer Book, a worship that featured radical revisions to the traditional liturgy. On June 12, 1945, the Orthodox rabbinical group met at the Hotel McAlpin in New York and conducted a ceremonial book burning of Kaplan's work. Some of the more traditional members of the Jewish Theological Seminary defended the Agudath Ha-Rabbonim's actions, as Kaplan was part of the most liberal branch of Conservative Judaism. This is an English rendering of the full text of the Agudath Ha-Rabbonim's official excommunication of Kaplan and his work.

In a meeting of the leaders of our people, rabbis of New York and its neighboring communities—roshei yeshiva [yeshiva deans], hassidic masters, Talmud scholars of large and small yeshivot—on Tuesday of the week corresponding to the reading of "Separate Yourselves from among this congregation," on Rosh Hodesh Tamuz, 5705 convened at the behest of the leadership of the Agudath Ha-Rabbonim of the United States and Canada and the Va'ad Ha-Rabbonim of Greater New York. They assembled to address the terrible scandal conducted with high-handedness and great brazenness, by the one known as Dr. Mordecai Kaplan, who has published a new monstrosity known as "Seder Tefilot." This has introduced heresy and total apostasy to the God of Israel and the foundations of faith of Israel's Torah—as to the final destination of this heresy you can tell—and therefore we have decided here as one, unified congregation to excommunicate and ban him, and to separate him from the community of Israel, until he returns in full repentance, per the law and the religion.

This we publicize and declare, before the King of the Universe and with the power vested in His Holy Torah, and with all the force and strength of the Law. It is completely forbidden to use, and there is a full ban on the prayer book mentioned above wherever it is seen or found within the borders of Israel. It is a snakebite for which there is no cure for anyone who handles this aforementioned prayer book or places his eyes upon it, whether this may be an individual or a congregation. And all who listen to this pronouncement shall be blessed by the Source of all blessings.

The Conservative Beth Din

Fabian Schoenfeld | 1954

Fabian Schoenfeld (b. 1924) was rabbi of the Young Israel of Kew Garden Hills, New York, and chairman of the Council of Young Israel Rabbis. The Young Israel resolution and Schoenfeld's article responded to renewed attempts within the more-fortified Conservative Movement to aid Jewish wives who could not obtain a get, a ritual divorce, from their husbands. According to Jewish law, a husband must issue his wife a bill of divorce. Therefore, a recalcitrant husband or a situation in which the husband is lost and his death cannot be confirmed can prevent a woman from remarrying. In December 1952, the faculty of the Jewish Theological Seminary (JTS) and the Rabbinical Assembly convened a conference to "explore the possibilities of strengthening family life in accordance with the principles of Jewish law and tradition." The end result was the founding of the National Beth Din and a revised marriage contract (ketubah) authored by a renowned Talmudist, Rabbi Saul Lieberman (1898–1983) of JTS. As this opening section of his statement made clear, Schoenfeld and other Orthodox rabbis found this innovation fully unacceptable.

A resolution [was] submitted to and passed by the delegates to the proposed establishment of a National Beth Din by the Rabbinical Assembly of America and the faculty of the Jewish Theological Seminary, the official representatives of Conservative Judaism in America. We do not propose herewith to enter into a discussion of the theological differences that divide our movement and orthodoxy in general on the one hand and the adherents of Conservative principles—if such, indeed, exist—on the other. It is our intention, however, to explain to the Jewish public the reasons which have prompted us to state in no uncertain terms our inflexible opposition to the latest religious escapades of our misguided brethren who seem to wander aimlessly in the strangling labyrinth of Conservative innovations.

The alleged purpose of the projected Beth Din is "to preserve the integrity and advance the welfare of the Jewish family in accordance with Jewish law and Tradition, and further the dynamic process inherent in the Jewish Tradition."[32] This Beth Din specifically is "to deal with all matters concerning the Jewish law of marriage" and also to seek solutions for cases "where a civil divorce has been granted and no *get* has been issued." The *United Synagogue Review*, September 1953, from the pages of which these quotations are cited, further states that a period of six months was to be devoted to obtain the cooperation of the Orthodox and Reform Rabbinical bodies, and that if such cooperation was not in sight the Beth Din would be established forthwith. Finally it is said that this "historic step symbolizes the determination of the Conservative movement to demonstrate the flexibility and the developmental character of Jewish law."

Let us now examine and analyze these statements and the ideas put forth by the Conservative movement which is about to father this latest of deceptive measures taken by their spiritual heads. Let us do so, calmly if we can—a difficult assignment, when the ire of thousands of years of Jewish learning and Jewish tradition as embodied by the Written Law and the Oral is roused by the spectacle of spiritual leaders who have flouted every sacred concept of Jewish Law and Tradition now claiming to solve the admittedly stern problems of Marriage and Divorce "in accordance with Jewish Law and Tradition."

It has always been the policy of the Conservative leadership to garb their pronouncements in a cloak of traditional quarters. The public announcement of their intention to create this Beth Din is another perfect example of this clever but dishonest strategy. The wording and phrasing of the text which informs us of the proposed establishment of the

Beth Din is such that on the surface there is little that could be subjected to severe criticism. Were this text placed in front of the average Jewish layman without any indication as to its origin, he would have to be possessed of a very suspicious character to discover a Conservative background.

But beneath this carefully and correctly phrased statement lies spiritual malice which intends to break the ageless chain of Torah-tradition which alone has preserved the welfare of the Jewish family; which alone has made the Jewish household the impregnable stronghold of Jewish history. It is at this fortress of our people that the poison of Conservative ideology is now directed. The fact that this act may be the result rather of ignorance than of malice aforethought does nothing to mitigate this ill-intentioned deed.[33]

The Synagogue Council Ban

Eleven Roshei Yeshiva | 1956

In 1956 President David Hollander (1913–2009) of the Rabbinical Council of America submitted a query about the acceptability of his rabbinical organization's participation in interdenominational bodies. A group of eleven leading scholars and heads of Orthodox yeshivot that included Rabbis Moshe Feinstein (1895–1986), Yitzchak Hutner (1906–80), Yaakov Kamenetsky (1891–1986), Aharon Kotler (1891–1962), and Yaakov Ruderman (1900–87) issued a response forbidding such cooperation. The letter reflected a turn toward a more insular Orthodox community in the 1950s. The document also signaled a more crystalized understanding of the barriers between Orthodox and Conservative Judaism. Noteworthy, Rabbi Eliezer Silver (1882–1968) and Rabbi Joseph Soloveitchik refused to add their signatures to this proclamation.

We have been asked by a number of rabbis in this country and by a number of teachers and ordained rabbis of our yeshivot if it is permissible to participate with and be a member of the New York Board of Rabbis and similar groups in other communities, which are composed of Reform and Conservative "rabbis."[34]

Having gathered together to clarify this matter, it has been ruled by the undersigned that it is forbidden by the law of our sacred Torah to be a member of and to participate in such an organization.

We have also been asked if it is permissible to participate with and to be a member of the Synagogue Council of America, which is also composed of Reform and Conservative organizations.

We have ruled that it is forbidden by the law of our sacred Torah to participate with them either as an individual or as an organized communal body.

May God, may He be blessed, have mercy on His people and seal the breaches and we be worthy of the elevation of the glory of our sacred Torah and our people, Israel.[35]

A Conservative Converts to Orthodox Judaism
C. E. Hillel Kauvar | MARCH 21, 1958

Charles Eliezer Hillel Kauvar (1879–1971) was the rabbi of Beth HaMedrosh Hagadol Congregation in Denver. In 1957 the congregation left the United Synagogue amid scandal. Earlier the Denver Jews dismissed two Conservative rabbis from their pulpits, at the behest of Kauvar, on the grounds that they had violated kashruth and other cardinal Jewish practices. In 1958 Kauvar resigned from the Conservative rabbinical organization, a move that Rabbi Louis Finkelstein, the president of the Jewish Theological Seminary, later called "not wise and not helpful to traditional Judaism."

MARCH 21ST, 1958
Rabbi Aaron Blumenthal, President, Rabbinical Assembly of America, 3080 Broadway NY

Dear Rabbi Blumenthal,[36]
After long consideration, I have reached the decision regretfully to tender herewith my resignation from the Rabbinical Assembly of America for the following reasons:

Having been one of the organizers of the Rabbinical Assembly, I know that it was the intention of the founders that the Rabbinical Assembly be an instrument to cherish and promote Traditional Judaism in an ideal American setting without deviating in any way from Torah-true Judaism. Unfortunately in the past fifteen or twenty years, the leaders of the Rabbinical Assembly have chosen to introduce a new "philosophy" of Judaism, and have condoned changes and innovations and interpretations which in my judgment are contrary to the spirit and the letter of the Torah, and which are not consistent with the principles upon which the Jewish Theological Seminary, the Rabbinical Assembly, and the United Synagogue were founded.[37] The protests of these members of the Rabbinical Assembly who have remained true to the original pattern have been ignored and at times even ridiculed.

For these reasons I find that I can no longer remain a member of a Rabbinical Organization which has rejected many of the religious principles and precepts upon which I have based my personal life and my ministry as a rabbi.

I therefore wish to sever my affiliation with the Rabbinical Assembly of America, effective immediately.

I trust that you will read my letter in its entirety to the Membership Committee.

Wishing you a happy Pesach, I am,

Very truly yours,
    Rabbi C. E. Hillel Kauvar
    Denver, Colorado

A Convert within Your Gates

Samson R. Weiss | APRIL 3, 1958

The German-born Rabbi Samson Raphael Weiss (1910–90) was a lifetime organizational leader within American Orthodox Judaism. In 1945 he founded the Young Israel Institute for Jewish Studies in New York and later served as the executive vice president of the Orthodox Union. He interpreted Rabbi Kauvar's and his Denver congregation's rejection of Conservative Judaism as a major victory for Orthodoxy.

13 Nissan 5718 / April 3, 1958
Rabbi C. E. Hillel Kauvar
King David Hotel, Jerusalem, Israel

Dear Rabbi Kauvar,

Thank you very much for your letter of Nisan 2 [March 23, 1958]
which I received on Monday. Due to a trip to Chicago from which I
returned this morning, I could not reply earlier.

Please let me tell you how deeply moved I was to receive the copy
of your letter to the Rabbinical Assembly. Your resignation is a statement which should be widely publicized so that its impact may be
felt upon the entire Jewish community, major parts of which are
groping in the darkness of confusion and uncertainty. If you give me
the permission, I shall make copies available to the proper channels.

So far, only Mr. Ivan Salomon and Rabbi [Solomon] Sharfman,
the President of the Rabbinical Council, have been notified by me
of your letter to the Rabbinical Assembly. I am sure you will hear, in
the near future, from the Rabbinical Council.[38]

Once more, many thanks for taking me into your confidence
and my warmest wishes for a Chag Kosher Vesomeach [kosher and
happy holiday] in the Holy Land.

Very sincerely yours,
    Dr. Samson R. Weiss,
    Executive Vice President

CONCLUSION

In July 1961 Rabbi Simon Dolgin (1915–2004) of Los Angeles published
an open letter that compared Conservative Jews to gentiles.[39] Two
years earlier, Dolgin's Beth Jacob Congregation had voted to install a
mehitzah in all of its prayer services.[40] Before this, perhaps, the religious leader of the up-and-coming Beverly Hills congregation could
not have offered so sharp a distinction between his own Orthodox

community and his Conservative counterparts. More visible distinctions between Conservative Judaism and Orthodoxy around midcentury allowed leaders of both communities to embrace their respective religious nomenclature and, in some instances, denigrate one another.

The parting of the ways between Orthodox and Conservative Judaism carried lasting effects. By the end of the 1940s, under the crush of its religious and political ambiguity, few rabbis and laypeople identified as Modern Orthodox Jews. From the vantage point of Orthodox Judaism, the sources in this chapter document these developments. The implications of these changes forced "Modern Orthodox Judaism" to lie fallow. Earlier, the designation had proven valuable as a flexible label that could attract a wide swath of traditional Jews. Later on, though, rabbis and lay leaders feared "Modern Orthodox" as a vague term that could too easily be mistaken for another Jewish group. In the end, this situation provided for the terminological respite needed for later Orthodox leaders to reclaim "Modern Orthodoxy" as its banner.

PART 3 | A Modern Orthodox Movement

7 | Becoming Modern Orthodox Jews

In 1962 Milton Himmelfarb (1918–2006) introduced American Jews to an "unknown Jewish sect" that he described as "Modern Orthodox."[1] This group, alleged the writer, was led by the Yeshiva University–trained rabbis who identified with the Rabbinical Council of America. This emphasis placed on Orthodox Jews was probably a startling inclusion to observers who had recently predicted the group's demise.[2] Soon thereafter, Rabbi Joseph Soloveitchik glibly adopted the label as his own but quickly distanced himself from the "Modern Orthodox" designation.[3] In the early 1960s, then, the term had gained some traction in Orthodox circles, but many feared that it still carried "severe connotations" and was too closely connected to the exponents of Conservative Judaism.[4]

The term was suitable for a crop of young Orthodox ideologues who had gained much attention in the 1960s. In 1965 historian Jacob Neusner (b. 1932) identified the burgeoning movement in American Judaism that he labeled the "New Orthodox Left." In this group Neusner included Yeshiva College faculty members Rabbi Irving "Yitz" Greenberg (b. 1933) and Dr. Charles Liebman (1934–2003).[5] Others might have added another Yeshiva man, Rabbi Emanuel Rackman (1910–2008). In all probability, the editors of *Tradition* would have suggested the insertion of Rabbi Eliezer Berkovits (1908–92) of Chicago's Hebrew Theological College into this group as its elder statesman. The Rabbinical Council of America's journal had just published Berkovits's criticisms of American Orthodoxy and felt compelled to warn readers that "most of our Editorial Board disagrees with the views expressed in this essay."[6] Others described this group as the new leaders of Modern Orthodoxy. This worried some observers who feared the flexibility with which these men viewed Jewish law. Accordingly, one writer drew a line between Modern Orthodox Judaism and "Orthodox Modernism." The latter, he felt, adopted a "modernism couched in Orthodox forms" and reflected the "radical" views of Greenberg and other liberal Orthodox thinkers.[7]

However, this group rejected the chance to steer a Modern Orthodox Movement that might function as a subdivision within American Orthodox Judaism. Irving Greenberg described the title as a "term which I detest."[8] Likewise, Emanuel Rackman denied that anyone could "regard modern Orthodoxy as a movement."[9] In the end, it was Rabbi Norman Lamm (b. 1927) who emerged as Modern Orthodoxy's leading light. He did not do it alone. In 1968 prominent lay leader Moses Feuerstein (1916–2009) credited young people with inspiring a "religious revival."[10] Lamm and others were greatly encouraged to lead a coterie of day school–educated youngsters in this new epoch of Modern Orthodox Judaism. Elsewhere, modern and Orthodox men like Rabbi Hershel Schachter (1917–2013), who was elected chairman of the Conference of Presidents of Major American Jewish Organizations in the late 1960s, reached beyond the Orthodox community to emerge as leaders of important Jewish institutions. Nevertheless, Lamm accepted the mantle with a degree of hesitation. Yet, as a scholar and halakhist positioned at the center of American Orthodoxy, Lamm and his Modern Orthodox Movement received a far better reception than the members of the "New Orthodox Left" could have garnered.

SECTION 1 | The New Orthodox Left

The Search for a Modern Orthodox "Ideologist"

Charles S. Liebman | 1965

In 1965 sociologist Charles Liebman published a study on "Orthodoxy in American Jewish Life." His influential scholarly and popular articles on Orthodox Jews in the United States were read by many of the group's rabbis and lay leaders and earned Liebman a place as one of the leading lights of the so-called New Orthodox Left. In this excerpt from his seventy-two-page article in the American Jewish Year Book, *Liebman identified, with some reservations, a burgeoning Modern Orthodox movement and labeled Rabbi Emanuel Rackman of Long Island as its ideologue and leader. In addition to his work on Orthodox Judaism, Liebman wrote extensively on Israeli Jews and Zionism.*

By modern Orthodox we mean those individuals and institutions among the committed Orthodox who tend toward the church end of the church-sect continuum.[11] On the one hand, they seek to demonstrate the viability of the *halakhah* for contemporary life; on the other, they emphasize what they have in common with all other Jews rather than what separates them. Until recently they composed almost the entire upper-income, well-educated strata of the committed Orthodox. Many of the best-known Orthodox congregations in the United States, and most of the wealthy ones, are led by modern Orthodox rabbis.

Like the other groups within American Orthodoxy, the modern Orthodox have not produced any systematic statement of their ideology, in part, perhaps, because they shun the practical consequence of their philosophical or theological position, and in part because none has been sanctioned by eminent talmudic scholars, still acknowledged as the arbiters of ideology. To the extent, however, that the modern Orthodox have produced an ideologist, it is probably Rabbi Emanuel Rackman, although his position is not representative of all modern Orthodox Jews. He is certainly the favorite target of the Orthodox right wing, notwithstanding the private concession of at least some of its members that he has brought more people into the Orthodox fold than any other person. Rackman has published widely on *halakhah*, Jewish values, and contemporary life.[12] His concern is with understanding the meaning of the halakhic injunctions in order to find contemporary applications. In the course of his efforts he has suggested what many feel to be a radical reinterpretation of the *halakhah*:

The Halakhah is more than text. It is life and experience. What made the Babylonian and not the Palestinian Talmud the great guide of Jewish life in the Diaspora was not a decree or a decision but *vox populi*. From Maimonides it would appear that it was the acceptance of the people who by custom and popular will constituted the authority. Can a Halakhic scholar lose himself in text exclusively when the texts themselves bid him to see what practice "has become widespread among Jews," what is required socially "because of the precepts of peace," what will "keep the world aright," and many other social criteria? These standards are as much a part of the Torah as the text themselves.[13]

Rackman is also prominently associated with the idea that Orthodox Jews, both individually and institutionally, must cooperate with the non-orthodox. He is outspoken in his conviction that Orthodox rabbis should be free to associate with such groups as the New York Board of Rabbis and that Orthodox groups should remain affiliated with the umbrella organization for all religious groups, the Synagogue Council of America.

Making Orthodoxy Relevant in America
Irving "Yitz" Greenberg | APRIL 28, 1966

In 1966 Rabbi Irving Greenberg served as associate professor of history at Yeshiva College. That year the popular Greenberg agreed to an interview with freshman Harold "Hillel" Goldberg (b. 1946) that was published in the student newspaper. The editors recognized the import and innovative nature of Greenberg's views, as well as his openness to a broad range of ideas and people. Accordingly, the newspaper billed the publication as a "crucial article for all to consider." Greenberg also realized the significance of his ideas and was careful to review the content of the article with his student interviewer. In addition to the excerpt below, Greenberg also shared his belief that rabbis "should recognize that there is nothing wrong with sex per se and should promulgate a new value system and corresponding new halachot about sex."

What do you believe is the essential element in Jewish theology?

The covenant idea, the belief that an infinite G-d is concerned for man and will enter into a personal relationship with him.

The Noahic covenant implies that instead of destroying man each time that he sins, G-d will work with man, whatever his actions. G-d seems to have sanctioned man's freedom and accepted the fact that he tends to sin. Man's evil tendency suggests the need for at least one group to continually fulfill man's potential for living according to G-d's will, to continually testify that G-d exists. Ideally, the Jews perform this function by accepting the covenants of Abraham and Moses—by fulfilling their *halachic* obligations to man and G-d. We must testify to ourselves, to non-religious Jews, and to gentiles.

I believe that the definition of a Jew is one who takes the covenant idea seriously, who struggles to find its validity in his own life. It doesn't matter to me whether one calls himself Reform, Conservative, or Orthodox. However, I identify with Orthodoxy. Although too many Orthodox Jews merely accept the covenant doctrines and do not attempt to find their relevance to modern life, I still think that Orthodoxy has the largest number of people who do take the covenant idea seriously.

Do you feel that the categories "Reform," "Conservative," and "Orthodox" have any meaning?

The main reality in these categories is an institutional one. But too often the three classifications only blind one's vision. Today Judaism intellectually is shattered in a thousand different directions, and when we admit this, we'll be able to begin struggling with the real problems facing the American Jewish community. These classifications make it seem that any problem which arises can be neatly fit into three boxes, each one representing a denominational view. But this is just not true.

What is the primary problem facing today's Orthodox community?

Orthodoxy refuses to come out of the East European ghetto psychologically. In the ghetto, Orthodoxy floated off into its own world and it is still living there. Furthermore, Orthodoxy refuses to show sympathy to those who respond authentically to the fact that Orthodoxy has lost all connection with modern life. Conservative and Reform have taken the risk and dealt seriously with the problem of Judaism's relevancy to modern life, but I believe that they came up with the wrong answers.

Orthodox Jews inherit the notion that Judaism entirely transcends the temporal, that Judaism should be independent of local culture. We've come to think that a relationship with the Divine means separation from current or everyday life.

But on the contrary, our acceptance of the Mosaic covenant and the Jewish law is tantamount to the belief that G-d intervenes in the temporal and that we can experience infinite values in a concrete, worldly experience. Thus Jewish history is a history of human responses to the Divine approach—to Torah, Prophetic, and Talmudic values and *mitzvot*. Some of these human responses have led Jews to experience their *Zelem Elokim* [Image of God], and some have not.

The central issue in Judaism today is this: What are the concrete experiences that can lead us to an experience with G-d?

Ideally, how does Orthodox Judaism believe that Jews can experience the Divine?

Orthodoxy believes that the Divine can be experienced through the observance of every *halachah*. Yet Orthodox has escaped into the purely ritualistic realm of *halachah*, has homogenized *halachah*, and has made a routine out of it. I think that the basis of Orthodoxy's escape is the belief that Torah cannot stand up to the challenge of contemporary civilization. Thus our withdrawal from society is a means of "saving" G-d or covering up his "weakness." This attitude reflects our cowardice, for G-d and His Torah have enough vitality to live in any situation.

Our desire to withdraw is an indication of our unwillingness to admit that our beliefs are shallow. One with a religious attitude would not ignore America, but would question why we were brought here and how we can utilize America for the realization of Jewish personal and social ideas.

Orthodoxy should not unrealistically deny that conditions have changed, but should explore what meaning many of the *mitzvot* can have for us today. The willingness to explore is the valid component of certain Conservative approaches, but I often disagree with the Conservative application of this principle. Too many times the Conservative movement changes *halachah* because popular opinion demands the change. I believe that changes in *halachah* should not be the result of popular opinion, but the result of deliberate consideration by the *gedolim* [great Torah scholars].

How can Orthodox—*halachic* Judaism—become relevant
in America?

Orthodoxy must undertake three tasks. First, we must recognize that a democratic society not only liberates us from persecution, but can also energize us. In the past, we had to survive among barbarians. The premium that we paid for survival was the perversion of the idea of the Chosen People; we came to think of ourselves as inherently better than others. But our only unique characteristic is an obligation to live in a holy manner by observing commandments, to set an example.

The pressure of the ghetto is now removed, and democratic America can eliminate our superiority complex and return us to our ideals of human equality and social justice. We should not necessarily accept all of America, but at least we should exploit its attitudes and integrate those that illuminate and deepen our traditional Jewish framework. For example, we should recognize that it is our religious responsibility to participate in the current civil rights struggle.

Secondly, Orthodoxy must train a body of scholars in the new fields of study, especially in Biblical criticism.

We should acknowledge a debt to Bible critics. They have shown that the Torah is not toneless, but has elements in common with the temporal experience of the ancient Near East. This does not undermine our faith because the Jewish idea of a holy life is the proper utilization of the temporal. However, contemporary scholarship denies G-d and sees *only* the temporal qualities of the ancient Jews. We need Jewish scholars who assume that man can relate to G-d. This type of Jewish scholarship would illuminate our understanding of the ancient Jew; it would enable us to understand the exact point of meeting between the Divine and the temporal. We would be able to see how the ancient Jew utilized the temporal in a Divine manner.

Denying either the Divine or the temporal is no answer to the question raised by Biblical scholarship. We need to undertake Biblical scholarship in order to more fully understand our own revelation. We should be committed by faith to the Torah as Divine revelation, but what we mean by "Divine revelation" may be less external or mechanical than many Jews now think.

The third main task confronting Orthodoxy is a thorough re-examination of the *Shulchan Orach*. The purpose of *halachah* is to transform the mundane into the holy by the utilization of the *halachah* which applies to any given experience. But today, there are some experiences which *halachah* doesn't cover adequately, and we are unwilling to apply many *halachot* that deal with contemporary problems. The *Poskim* aren't meeting their responsibility in updating and fully applying our law codes. This inaction represents a denial of one of the basic tenets of Judaism: that our tradition may be applied to any situation. In short, the *halachah* has broken down.

Dear Yitzchak

Aharon Lichtenstein | JUNE 2, 1966

The Greenberg interview stirred much controversy within the American Ortho-dox community. A writer for the Agudath Israel published a harsh critique in the right-wing organization's monthly magazine. Inside Yeshiva University, Rabbi

Ahron Soloveichik (1917–2001) rebuked Greenberg, particularly for the latter's welcoming stance on biblical criticism. Most notably, Rabbi Aharon Lichtenstein (1933–2015) penned a lengthy open letter in the Yeshiva College newspaper. Like Greenberg, Lichtenstein was a young and esteemed member of the Yeshvia faculty and a Harvard PhD. He therefore saw it as his duty to publicly respond to the content and tone of his colleague's interview.

Dear Yitzchak,

It really wasn't very cricket of you to have written and/or superintended your article—text and commentary—for some eight months while leaving barely eight days at year's end for any reply.[14] There is obviously no time now for a fully proper response. So please consider this as just an expression of personal reaction rather than a thorough reply, much less the formulation of an alternative position.

Given the gravity of the issues involved, my opening complaint may seem a bit trivial. In a sense, it is. I mention it, however, because it is peripherally related to a genuinely basic issue. I do not refer to any of the substantive points you've raised but rather to the fundamental posture implicitly assumed throughout the article and explicitly described in its exegesis. As I understand it, you sought, perhaps primarily, not so much to present your own views on a number of issues, but simply to stir up discussion of them, to rescue them from the tundra of obscurity to which a conspiracy of apathy and silence had consigned them. And unless I sorely miss the mark, I very much suspect that, despite the furor and attendant unpleasantness, you think that you've succeeded and that you therefore feel both vindicated and content.

Well, I agree wholeheartedly with the aim—but I take issue with your mode of pursuing it. Basic problems should be discussed. A Torah-*Halachic Weltanschauung* vis-à-vis contemporary problems does need to be formulated and expressed. The need for such a formulation is great at any yeshiva, simply because *bnei Torah* must learn, at the personal level, to integrate their total experience within a *Halachic* framework and, at a more general plane, to develop genuine *Hala-*

chic solutions for problems confronting the community at large. At our *yeshiva*, however, it is paramount. Inasmuch as we do, albeit with varying degrees of enthusiasm, include general culture as part of our students' education, we incur a collective debt to them and to ourselves to help them grasp the relation—be it one of complement, irreconcilable conflict, or fruitless tension—between Torah and the given aspect of *Madah* [science or secular studies]. To place the full burden of integrating two worlds upon the individual student is neither fair to him nor in the best general interest of *Halachic* Judaism. For the simple fact is that in most cases, the student either cannot or will not do it, with the result that, assuming that he remains Orthodox, he either withdraws into a sort of observant secularism—a life largely motivated by secular values although regulated by religious norms—or retreats into a traditional bastion in order to avoid confronting the contemporary world altogether. These alternatives are by no means of equal merit. The first, even if sincere, is a shallow formalism while the second constitutes a genuine path to *avodat hashem* [service to God], which despite its lack of sophistication, I prize most highly. Simple piety and naïve faith may lack a certain dimension, but whether or not they take cognizance of contemporary trends, they are of infinite moment. However, as far as meeting the overall challenge of imposing *malchut Shamayim* [Kingdom of Heaven] upon society and history, both are clearly deficient. Of course, I oversimplify—there are all sorts of intermediate shadings—but I'm sure you'll recognize these as two directions which a rather substantial number of students are inclined to take.

The need for some authoritative *Halachic* and philosophic guidance is therefore clear and present. However, precisely because this is so vital and so sensitive an area, handling it requires the greatest possible care. And here I must take issue with both your precept and your practice. You contend that "there must be leeway to make statements wide of the mark if we are to develop the precise formulation. There must be leeway for exploring views which may ultimately be rejected." This is a nice nineteenth-century notion, and it has a pleasant liberal ring about it. Moreover, within certain limits, it is perfectly valid and thoroughly Jewish. But is it relevant to the present situation, and is its supposed manifestation in your article consonant with the proper discharge of our responsibility? Anyone who undertakes to discuss an issue publicly, he takes that issue seriously, assumes a double obligation: of inquiry and expression. He is morally bound both to come as close as possible to the truth and to be as accurate as possible in communicating that truth. Not just as possible for *him*. As possible for persons who, given the difficulty or the gravity of the issue, can genuinely be said to be reasonably competent to discuss it. With all due respect, there are matters about which you and I have no business issuing manifestos altogether. And of course the more serious the problem, the greater the responsibility to be precise—or, if need be, to remain silent. Whether the reality of error is genuinely regarded as a disaster, its possibility will be neither lightly regarded nor easily dismissed. How much margin for error is allowed on the Gemini flights?

... What are we to understand by "the fact that Orthodoxy has lost *all* connection with modern life"? I don't ask whether this is true or false. I simply ask what does it mean. Is there, then, no remaining link between ourselves—you and I are Orthodox, too—and modern life? The overall position you advocate is itself open to question. We might ponder the wisdom of Fulton Sheen's remarks that "he who marries his own age will find himself a widower in the next."[15] Be this as it may, however—I do agree with you to a point—can your statement of presumed fact stand scrutiny?

Or, to take another example, doesn't a statement like "democratic America can eliminate our superiority complex and return us to our ideals of human equality and social justice" require—both as an explicitly normative and implicitly historical dictum—a great deal of clarifying amplification? And, when you contend that "in short, the *halachah* has broken down," are you referring to *halachah* itself or to its scholars and interpreters? Or, as you would contend that the two are identical, doesn't this need to be elucidated? And isn't any breakdown partly a problem of communication?

... Finally, I must really object to the strident tone of much of the critique of contemporary Orthodoxy and some of its *Halachic* leaders. In this respect, the article—as well as other Cassandra-like public denunciations you've made on other occasions—seems strangely out of keeping with your citing Rav Yisrael Salanter [1810–1883] about justifying the world and criticizing oneself. Aren't one's fellow Orthodox Jews part of the world?

But all this requires full discussion, and I must come back to my original plaint. I can't really be done in a working week. I've merely ticked off areas of agreement or disagreement, rather than defined attitudes. Perhaps when time permits and my thinking on some of these problems has ripened, *od Chazon lamoed* [the vision is yet for the appointed time] (Hab. 2:3). In the meantime, I hope that you'll read this as it was written—not as an attempt to castigate or excoriate but as a plea, albeit at times a pungent plea, for a more careful and more responsible approach to the public discussion of basic *Halachic* and theological issues.

With best personal wishes,

Sincerely,
Aharon

The Radicals
Walter Wurzburger | 1967

Rabbi Walter Wurzburger (1920–2002) was a leading intellectual and leader within American Judaism. He held a number of pulpits and was the longtime editor of Tradition, *the journal of the Rabbinical Council of America. In this syndicated editorial, Wurzburger expressed his reservations about an emerging "radical" Orthodox atmosphere that some called the "New Orthodox Left" or "Modern Orthodox Judaism."*

Of late, there has been considerable speculation about the imminence of a schism within Orthodox Judaism in America. At the moment, most of the controversy still revolves around rather peripheral matters such as the propriety of participating in "interdenominational" synagogue or rabbinic bodies. But gradually there come to the fore manifestations of a more serious split that goes far deeper and is by no means co-extensive with the touchy integration-versus-separation issue.

The emergence of a "radical" movement that has been labelled the "new Orthodox Left" or "modern Orthodoxy" (if not "Orthodox modernism") has aroused strong opposition not only from the so-called right-wing extremist but even more "moderate" quarters.[16]

The "movement" is so amorphous that it cannot boast of an identifiable membership or of any kind of platform. Perhaps the best way to characterize it is to paraphrase Cardinal Newman's famous definition of a university. What has been labelled the "new Orthodox Left" or "modern Orthodoxy" is an atmosphere.[17]

One can hardly do more than point to an overall atmosphere that seems to permeate the "movement": a feeling of disenchantment with policies that have prevented Orthodoxy from developing its full potential in the modern world. It is widely felt that in spite of the phenomenal resurgence of Orthodox strength in recent years, far more inroads into the secular world could have been made if Orthodoxy had embarked on a concerted effort to demonstrate its relevance to modern conditions by coming to grips with the intellectual, moral, and social challenges of the time.

It is in this respect that "radical Orthodoxy" differs most sharply from the right wing, which regards "splendid isolation" as the ideal type of Jewish existence. In the opinion of the latter, confrontation with the world is an extremely hazardous enterprise which is bound to erode the authentic faith of the Jew.

"Radical Orthodoxy" fully recognizes the risks connected with "openness" to the modern world. But it maintains that in the free and open society of a democratic world, Judaism is religiously obligated to involve itself in the problems of contemporary society. Such an involvement is not only necessary on pragmatic grounds, lest charges of "moral isolation" or irrelevancy be raised against the Orthodox position.

There are compelling *religious* reasons for the overhauling of traditional policies towards the non-Jewish world, for under present conditions the application of Torah values could make a vital and constructive contribution to the solution of many social, economic, and moral
problems. The fulfillment of our religious mandate does not call for
retreat into a spiritual ghetto where we barricade ourselves behind the
ramparts of isolation and shun all contact with the social and political
issues that agitate modern man.

It is most important to stress in this context that HaRav J. B.
Soloveitchik—although he naturally would disassociate himself from
many proposals and policies advocated by some of his "followers"—
heartily endorses the responsibility of the Jew to involve himself with
the rest of the world in the "great universal confrontation between man
and cosmic order."[18]

It must be made clear, however, that even those within the Orthodox community who are most insistent in their demands for maximum
confrontation with the contemporary scene have no desire to "modernize" Judaism with a view to reducing or eliminating religious obligations that conflict with the pressures of modernity. There is no suggestion of easing the burden of the law by making compromises and
concessions to the temper of the times. The objective is *not* to reform
Judaism but to relate it to the contemporary world.

There is by no means any unanimity as to what constitutes the
most pressing challenge. There are those who deplore most the failure to develop a systematic philosophy of Judaism that expounds
Torah and halachic values in modern categories. Others are perturbed
at the failure to confront the challenge of Bible criticism and historic scholarship which as yet are largely ignored in many Orthodox
circles.

Still others echo Rabbi Emanuel Rackman's pleas for halachic creativity to take cognizance of the profound changes in historic realities,
which obviously affect the application of Jewish law. There is a general
feeling that a sense of insecurity born of a "stage of siege" mentality

makes it difficult at times for Orthodox Judaism to respond effectively to new situations (e.g., the Holocaust experience and the emergence of the State of Israel).

For example, the all-out opposition of many Orthodox organizations in the United States to proposed legislation outlawing not Shechita [ritual slaughter] itself but certain methods such as pre-Shechita hoisting and hackling widely used by the slaughter houses, seems also to betray a lack of adequate concern for such genuine religious values as the prevention of cruelty to animals.[19]

Some adherents of the so-called radical Orthodoxy are not so much agitated over problems involving strictly halachic matters encountered in the contemporary world, but by the embarrassing silence of responsible Judaism on many of the delicate and agonizing moral problems of the age.

Since Judaism demands total surrender to the sovereignty of God, it is religiously intolerable when Jews react to such issues as Vietnam, civil rights, anti-poverty programs, Medicare, etc., not on the basis of Jewish religious values but solely on the basis of secular considerations.

Judaism, in the opinion of many of the so-called radical Orthodox, would regain much of its vitality and zest if, instead of concentrating on what has been narrowly defined as the area of Orthodox concern (kashrut, Sabbath, family purity, etc.), it would address itself to all the facets of modern living.

Notwithstanding public pressure to the contrary, the primary objective of rabbis should not be the search for ingenious *heterim* [permissive positions] allowing us to evade the rigorous demands of the law, but rather to derive from the halachah applications and guidelines that will enable man to respond more fully to the challenge of sanctifying the totality of his life. In the final analysis, it is this "radical" demand for such uncompromising commitments that "radical Orthodoxy" holds out for those who seek not comfortable religious status symbols but the challenge of a viable and relevant religious life.

The College Bowl *Sensation*

Yeshivah of Flatbush Student Government | MAY 13, 1963

In the spring of 1963, a team of Yeshiva University undergraduates appeared on CBS's College Bowl *game show. For a few weeks, three yarmulke-clad young men and a "brilliant, mercury-like, and vivacious" but modestly dressed female team captain captured the attention of thousands of Orthodox Jews in the United States. The underdog Yeshiva team trounced the undefeated University of Louisville squad with its vast knowledge of trivia. The Orthodox youngsters soundly defeated the University of Nevada before losing a very close bout to the eventual champion, Temple University. The event was emblematic of a "youth revival" within American Orthodoxy. Young and old celebrated the YU* College Bowlers *for personifying the rebirth of Modern Orthodox intellectualism being generated through the community's youth. These sentiments are encased in this letter sent to the YU squad from student leaders of an Orthodox high school in Brooklyn.*

Dear Students:

The students of the Yeshivah of Flatbush would like to extend their heartiest congratulations on your decisive victory in yesterday's *College Bowl*.[20] Your fine effort will enhance the image of not only Yeshiva University, but also the entire Yeshiva movement and Jewish Community. You have made all of us proud to be Yeshiva students.

We wish you success in future *College Bowl* competition and in your effort to further the ideals and values of Torah-true Judaism.

Sincerely,
    Student Government Organization
    Yeshivah of Flatbush H. S.

The yarmulke-clad Yeshiva University team competing in 1963 on the nationally televised quiz show *College Bowl*. Courtesy of Shifrah Jungreis.

Watching with Great Enthusiasm and Excitement

Fifth Graders of Hillel Day School | MAY 22, 1963

In their first appearance as returning champions on the College Bowl, *the Yeshiva University "Mighty Mites" handled the University of Nevada by a margin of 285–185. Afterward Orthodox day school students in Detroit wrote to the YU team to relay their excitement to view fellow Orthodox young people compete on a popular nationally televised program.*

Dear Mrs. [Shifrah] Jungreis and Gentlemen:

We are students in the fifth grade of Hillel Day School in Metropolitan Detroit.

We have been watching you on *College Bowl* with great enthusiasm and excitement. We are writing to tell you we are all rooting for you and that we want to convey our best wishes and encouragement.

We would like to see you continue for the full five weeks and bring victory to Yeshiva University.[21]

Keep up the good work!

Mazal Tov!

Very sincerely,
    Grade 5 students

Modern Orthodoxy Is Not a Movement
Emanuel Rackman | 1969

On several occasions in the 1960s, sociologist Charles Liebman predicted that Rabbi Emanuel Rackman would lead a Modern Orthodox movement in the United States. Rackman was part of a "New Orthodox Left" that had gained wide popularity among young people but also much criticism. In 1969, he wrote an essay in which he turned down the reins of this nascent movement.

Rightly or wrongly, one Jewish sociologist has named me as an ideologist of "modern Orthodoxy." However, one can hardly regard modern Orthodoxy as a movement: it is no more than a coterie of a score of rabbis in America and in Israel whose interpretations of the Tradition have won the approval of Orthodox intellectuals who are knowledgeable in both Judaism and Western civilization. None of the rabbis feels that he is articulating any position that cannot be supported by reference to authentic Jewish sources. None wants to organize a separate rabbinic body, and several have rejected an attempt to publish an independent periodical, because they did not want the remotest possibility that this form of separatism [would] be interpreted as a schism in Orthodoxy. I, no less than they, deny any claim to innovation. Our choice of methods and values in the Tradition, our emphases, and our concerns may be different. But the creation or articulation of shades and hues hardly warrants dignifying our effort with the terms "ideology" or "sect." We know that the overwhelming majority of Orthodox rabbis differ with us and that the faculties of most Orthodox day schools and rabbinical seminaries disapprove of some of our views and so instruct their pupils. It is not our mission to have them join our ranks. Rather do we seek to help Jewish intellectuals who are being alienated from the Tradition to realize that they can share a commitment to the faith which is acceptable to them and at least as authentic as the one they have received from their teachers but which they feel impelled to renounce. We reject the multiplication of dogmas and their precise formulation.[22]

A Modern Orthodox Movement
Norman Lamm | 1969

Rabbi Norman Lamm was not part of the so-called New Orthodox Left. He held a highly influential position as rabbi of the Jewish Center in Manhattan and served as the leading rabbinic voice of the Orthodox Union. In his sermons, but with some reluctance, Lamm had identified himself as part of a "Modern Orthodox Movement." In this essay, Lamm acknowledged his hesitations but also embraced his role as a leader of this religious cause.

The facts about our community, as represented by the Orthodox Union, are rather encouraging. Numerically and institutionally, in terms of youth and influence, we are a significant group in this country. But we are beset by many problems. And our thorniest and most disabling problem is, curiously, an "identity crisis"—perhaps a sign of our youthfulness as an ideological movement.

Objectively examined, what binds us together as a separate entity is our full commitment to the Torah tradition and our openness, at the same time, to the wider culture of the world about us. To use two dreadfully inadequate words which normally describe us as a distinct group, we are both "modern" and "orthodox." I shall be using these terms only with the greatest hesitation. "Orthodox" is almost pejorative; it implies a stifling and unthinking narrow-mindedness. And "modern" is amusingly pretentious; it adds nothing to the validity or invalidity of a proposition. Jacques Maritain recently referred to this as "chrono-latry," the idolatry of what is newest or latest in time.[23]

But while this observation is true enough as it goes, it does not go nearly far enough. Merely to describe what we are is not a sufficiently convincing reason for being what we are or for persuading others to acknowledge our rightness and join our ranks. The greatest problem of modern American Orthodoxy is that it has failed to interpret itself to itself. This failure, which reveals itself in many ways, derives from a remarkable intellectual timidity which we should have long outgrown.

One should not be too harsh in judging the past. There were reasons—good reasons—for our apologetic posture. But it was humiliating. In confronting the outside world and those to the left of us, we seemed to be saying that while we hold on to the practices and doctrines of Jewish tradition, we are really just like everybody else, perhaps even more so. We appeared to be whispering, in unbecoming shyness, that we were not really foreign or dirty.

At the same time, we were and still are apologetic—almost masochistically—towards those to the right of us. We send our children to the universities. And we are going to continue to do so despite the campus's recent notoriety. The far right does not approve of our educational policy, which touches the heart of our distinctiveness, or our educational and congregational institutions. How do we justify ourselves? Neither by scholarship, nor by Halachic reasoning, nor by pointing to historical antecedents, nor by the philosophic validity of our stand. Instead, we present the lament of all apologies: vocational necessity! Our whole existence is thus based on a practical economic concession—the need of a college degree in order to get a better job.

Our problem, then, is that we have yet to accept ourselves openly and directly on the basis of our major contribution to Jewish life in this century: that it is our *religious* duty, our *sacred* responsibility, to live the whole Torah tradition in the world, instead of retreating from a world in which there is literally no longer any place left to retreat to. As long as this condition of spiritual timidity and intellectual diffidence prevails, we can hardly blame the non-orthodox world for accusing us of temporizing, the Chasidic world for ignoring us, and the Yeshivah world for disdaining us.

The challenge to our intellectual leadership is clear: to formulate the worldview of "modern Orthodoxy" in a manner that is Halachically legitimate, philosophically persuasive, religiously inspiring, and personally convincing. It is a tall order, admittedly, but one which we must fill if the great centrist mass of American Orthodox Jews is not to be pulled apart in all directions, as they stagnate in importance and inarticulateness for want of a clear worldview to which they can feel fully committed in good conscience.

In its encounter with the "outside world" of non-observant Jewry and the rest of mankind, Modern Orthodoxy must offer neither "more of the same" nor the illusory advantages of escape and withdrawal. It must present viable options to the prevalent doctrines of the culture of the West, in terms that men and women born into this culture can understand and appreciate. We must make available attractive Jewish alternatives to the nihilism and permissiveness and meaninglessness and Godlessness of secular life. These alternatives must be neither distorted nor compromised, but they must be expressed and elaborated in the cultural and psychological idioms of the contemporary world.

Judaism was born in protest against the idolatries of a simpler age and must not fail to reject those of our own, far more complicated day. Our message must always be critical and restless with the complacent dogma of a society content with the correctness of its spiritual paralysis.

I cannot accept the idea that Orthodoxy must defensively retreat and wait for Messiah until it speaks to mankind. We must engage the world right now and, speaking in a cultural idiom it understands, say that we are dissatisfied with it. We must declare forthrightly that its "sexual revolution" is atavistic, a throwback to pagan debauchery; that its conception of man is depressingly shallow; that its prescription for happiness is vulgar and dangerous; that its conception of education is trivial and dehumanizing.

We must, then, learn to speak persuasively and intelligibly to the man of today about transcendent purpose, about the meaning of the Covenant, about the significance of Halachic living both for personal meaningfulness and for the fulfillment of our conventional obligations.

Never again must we stoop to the kind of inane religious propaganda which we once considered so very "modern," which led us to offer as proof of the correctness of our commitment the avoidance of cancer of trichinosis by virtue of the practice of certain observances.

It is equally important that we interpret ourselves clearly, forthrightly, and unapologetically to those of our orthodox Jewish brethren who do not accept our involvement in the wider culture as an integral part of our world outlook. We must make it explicit and clear that we are committed to secular studies, including our willingness to embrace all the risks that this implies, not alone because of vocational or social reasons, but because we consider that it is the will of G-d that there be a world in which Torah be effective; that all wisdom issues ultimately from the wisdom of the Creator, and therefore it is the Almighty who legitimates *all* knowledge; that a world cannot exist, and that certainly an independent Jewish state cannot exist in the contemporary world, in which some of the best of its brains and the most sensitive of its religious spirits will condemn as sinful and dangerous those profane disciplines which alone can keep it alive and prosperous. Our *religious* commitment to such principles must be as passionate and as faithful and as *Jewish* as was that of the Hirschian movement, especially in the first two generations of its history, in the context of conditions that prevail in this second third of the twentieth century.[24]

For our own times, if we are to make any headway in the "contest for the Jewish mind," we must resolve the central dilemma of the tension between our "two worlds." A transcendental theological schizophrenia is no virtue. We must, in terms of our own tradition, formulate the method whereby we can accord religious significance to the "other"—the so-called profane or modern—world. But which branches of general knowledge are legitimate for the loyal Jew—the one who is not concerned with vocational dispensations but with a religious worldview? May we ever accord the status of Mitzvah to a secular discipline? Can we consider it technically as the performance of *talmud torah*—remembering that Maimonides himself felt so inclined? As a minimum, we may grant that scientific, especially medical, studies possess religious significance. As a maximum, they will never attain the rank of Torah and Talmud. But where do they stand in between these two poles?

Rav [Abraham Isaac] Kook, of blessed memory, spoke of harmony as the great Jewish ideal, and he comprehended within it the polarities of physicality and spirituality, of the sacred and the profane, even of faith and doubt as part of cosmic unity.[25] It remains for us to elaborate the metaphysical framework and, even more, fill in the practical details.

This does not at all mean that we reject or condemn or do not wish to cooperate intensively at all levels with those groupings within orthodox Jewry which do not accept these premises. On the contrary, with more confidence in the religious rightness of our stand, we will be less subject to intimidation by those who feel sure of their different commitments within the context of the Halachic discipline. Perhaps then we shall come to understand that the rabbinic dictum that "there are seventy facets to Torah" refers to social and cultural patterns and to intellectual formulations and attitudes as well as to exegetical approaches. We shall then realize that the Lithuanian yeshivah world was different from the Spanish world of Maimonides, and the Chasidic world different from that of Rashi, and all of them different from each other and from us and from the world of Rabbi Akiva.[26] All were different—and yet all essentially the same because all are aspects of one Torah, bound by one common Halachic commitment. This firmly and unequivocally excludes the non-orthodox movements. But it also means that Judaism need not always develop in one mold, whether that of Brisk or Satmar or Yeshiva University.[27] We have our own contribution to make to these "seventy facets of Torah," and it is not tergiversation or betrayal to state positively those emphases and issues wherein we differ.

I have the feeling that if Jewry and Judaism are to survive in the Diaspora, it will be indebted largely to our group. I do not mean this as a boast—I think it is frightening. If Israel is not to reduce to another Levantine mini-state, but is to become the political expression of the *am segulah* [treasured people], then it will be the result of the work and inspiration and self-sacrifice of like-minded groups in Israel, presently inarticulate and inchoate, with whom we must work in tandem. But this requires of us a keen awareness of our own responsibility, a refusal to remain weak-willed and apologetic, and the courage of our convictions that our approach is a legitimate expression of *avodath ha-Shem* [service of God].

The intellectual leaders of modern American Orthodoxy have a Herculean but exciting, vital task before them. Unless it is discharged properly and sensitively, we shall continue to bear the progressively heavy burden of a collective inferiority feeling which will earn us disdain from without and engender for us confusion from within.

"... Ye shall turn aside neither to the right nor to the left—but you shall walk in the way which the Lord your G-d has commanded you, that you may live and that it might be well with you, and that you may prolong your days in the land which you shall possess" (Deut. 5:29–30).

CONCLUSION

Rabbi Chaim Dov Keller (b. 1930) of Telshe Yeshiva in Chicago was one of the first to notice Norman Lamm's emergence as the leader of a Modern Orthodox movement. The right-wing Orthodox writer was quite pleased that it was Lamm who "stand[s] very much on the right" rather than a "man like Rabbi Rackman [who] represents what one might call the left wing of Modern Orthodoxy."[28] Lamm's position within the nascent Modern Orthodox initiative was rather sudden and hardly predictable. He had eschewed identification with it throughout the 1960s. No doubt, he was encouraged by the efforts of better Jewishly educated and proudly Orthodox young people like the students who appeared on the *College Bowl*.

It took some time before Lamm could fully embrace his role at the forefront of a community within American Orthodox Judaism.[29] Throughout the decade, his notions of a Modern Orthodox movement were limited to the somewhat more intimate confines of his pulpit and congregation. When placed on a broader stage, Lamm was more careful about nomenclature that might call into question his own affiliations and associations. In 1966, for example, he delivered the keynote address at the Orthodox Union's national convention in Washington DC. In the much publicized discourse that outlined the orator's detailed "program" for his traditional coreligionists, Lamm withheld any mention of Modern Orthodoxy.[30] And in May 1969 Lamm confessed to his congregation that he was "uncomfortable with the title Modern Orthodox," that "there is an arrogance about this assertion of modernity which should give offense to any intelligent and sensitive man."[31] Nevertheless, Lamm kept the label. The 1969 essay, then, was the future president of Yeshiva University's first public and pronounced articulation of his Modern Orthodox vision. Observers took notice. The right-wing commentators, in particular, took comfort that the leader of Modern Orthodox Judaism was a centrist rather than a member of the so-called Orthodox Left.

8 | Orthodox, Inc.

In 1966 Rabbi Arthur Hertzberg (1921–2006) compared rabbis and their denominations to "corporate enterprises."[1] By this, Hertzberg meant that "industrialized" Jewish enclaves in the United States manufactured robust educational programs and religious resources for their constituents in a period in which "there are no great, individual rabbinic careers." This did not necessarily redound negatively on American Judaism. To the contrary, particularly the Conservative and Reform communities featured vigorous synagogue and rabbinical organizations that permitted their rabbis and lay leaders to function as extensions of the movement. In the 1960s, Orthodox Jews also attempted to "incorporate" their constituent bodies.

The Orthodox day school movement emerged as the community's best brand. Between 1940 and 1950, Jewish day schools soared from 35 to 139 educational institutions, most of them Orthodox. In fact, while Jewish day schools situated in urban areas doubled in size between 1951 and 1964, suburban day school enrollment multiplied sevenfold in the same period.[2] The writings in this section indicate that this was a major source of pride and even encouraged a wave of triumphalism. Yeshiva University also flourished under President Samuel Belkin (1911–76). In the 1950s, Belkin had established a medical school and a women's college to complement the all-male Yeshiva College.[3] Eventually Stern College for Women, with the imprimatur of Rabbi Joseph Soloveitchik, emerged as a pathbreaking school for the advanced study of Talmud for women. The Modern Orthodox community absorbed all of these advances as part of its denominational portfolio.

But success varied. In 1960 the Rabbinical Council of America tried to standardize the prayer book in Orthodox congregations. They billed

theirs as an "old-new prayer book" that retained the ritual that all Orthodox Jews used but also "corrected" some minor points on which the
traditional worships sometimes differed. It also offered an English
translation that boasted to present the "original thought of the Hebrew
phrase."[4] A number of Orthodox Jews—on the left and the right—
viewed the publication of the RCA prayer book as an encroachment
on their particular traditions.[5] In the end, Rabbi Soloveitchik insisted
that his name be removed from the project, and the prayer book failed
miserably.[6] Other operations like the Orthodox Union's supervision
of kosher food fared better. In 1963, for instance, the *Wall Street Journal*
noted the rise of the OU's Kashruth Division and the familiar symbol
of a U inside a circle found on an increasing number of food products.[7]
Still, kosher certification also endured religious politics. This chapter
explores these and other matters that were part of an attempt to forge
an "Orthodox" brand.

SECTION 1 | The Day School

Maimonides School

Shulamith Meiselman | 1941

*Born into a celebrated rabbinic family, Shulamith Soloveitchik Meiselman (1912–
2009) was a very active member of her local Boston Jewish community. In this
letter written to a Boston newspaper, Meiselman applauded the early success of
the Maimonides School (est. 1937), founded by her brother, Rabbi Joseph Soloveitchik, and sister-in-law, Dr. Tonya Soloveitchik (1904–67). The writer was confident that day school education would revive interest in traditional Jewish life
and foster generations of Jewishly literate Orthodox Jews.*

It is with a heart full of pride that I, as a young Jewish mother, witness
the transformation of Jewish orthodoxy in Boston. For years, our highest ideals were crumbling away. Our religious education amounted to

a Bar Mitzvah training, a speech, a party, and then what? The boy forgot whatever he learned and grew perfectly indifferent to the call of the orthodox synagogue and other religious institutions. These existing conditions were quite unbearable to me and became more so after I had a child of my own. It has always been my worry that when my child grows up there would be no place in this community to provide her with a thorough Jewish education such as many of my friends in New York are offering their children. I spent many hours discussing this problem with my relatives and friends, and it seemed almost an impossibility to dream about establishing a parochial school of a yeshiva in Boston.

However, I was wrong. A few years ago, Rabbi Joseph B. Soloveitchik, with a handful of people, organized a small parochial school, the Maimonides Educational Institute. Hard was the task, particularly the rabbi's. Not only did they have financial trouble, but they had to persuade an indifferent community that the Jewish educational path that they were following would lead to a sterile religious consciousness. The founders of the school were not satisfied to view complacently Jewish youth drifting away from religious observance right after the Bar Mitzvah ceremony. They felt that the spiritual content of Jewish education should be so emphasized that it would become an integral part of the individual and would remain with him permanently. The school is recommended by the Boston School Committee, and the teachers are under their jurisdiction and supervision. The school is so organized that both English and Hebrew classes are over at 3:30. The child is free to play and enjoy sunshine and fresh air which his development requires. The problem of the child refusing to concentrate on his Hebrew studies because of long, tiresome hours is thereby eliminated. Skilled educators have fashioned the curriculum in such a way that no subject, Hebrew or English, is neglected or curtailed.

The community is beginning to realize the benefits of the Maimonides Educational Institute. The enrollment has increased to such an extent that it has outgrown the original location at the Young Israel Center of Ruthven Street and will be more spaciously and conveniently located at the new headquarters of the Yeshiva Rabenu Hayim Halevi at the corner of Washington Street and Columbia Road.[8]

The Yeshiva was organized two years ago by Rabbi Joseph B. Soloveitchik with the help of his great father, Rabbi Moses Soloveitchik, of sainted memory, in order to establish a new center of Torah which will bring light and comfort to suffering world Jewry.[9]

The Yeshiva Rabenu Hayim Halevi and the Maimonides Educational Institute are conducting a huge drive for the new building with Mr. Hyman Cline as chairman.[10] The campaign, in my opinion, is a beginning of a new page in the history of Boston Jewry. Let us hope and pray that the Jews of this city will respond liberally to the call of our Torah.

A Rabbinical Supervisory Council for Day Schools
Torah Umesorah | 1944

In 1944 Rabbi Shraga Feivel Mendlowitz (1886–1948) founded Torah Umesorah (National Society for Hebrew Day Schools). At that time, there existed about 70 Jewish day schools in North America. One decade later, that number increased to about 180 day schools, most of which identified as Orthodox. Torah Umesorah offered aid and organizational support to most of these schools. Perhaps the most interesting aspect of the organization was its ability to pair modern-leaning laypeople with a religiously right-wing Rabbinical Supervisory Council led by Rabbi Aharon Kotler. The structure of this partnership was outlined at Torah Umesorah's first national convention, held in New York on June 20, 1944. Below is an excerpt from the Certificate of Incorporation, accepted on September 6, 1944.

We, the undersigned, all being persons of full age, of whom at least two-thirds are citizens of the United States and at least one a resident of the State of New York, for the purposes of incorporating an unincorporated Jewish Congregation, pursuant to Article 10 of the Religious Corporations Law, hereby certify as follows:

First: A meeting of Torah Umesorah Society for Establishment of Torah Schools, an unincorporated Jewish Congregation, was duly called and held in conformity with the aforesaid Article of the Religious

Corporations Law at 132 Nassau Street, Borough of Manhattan, City and County of New York, on the 6th day of September 1944, at which meeting a majority of the duly qualified voters of said congregation, being at least six in number, were present. . . .

Ninth: There shall be an ecclesiastical governing body, to be known as the Rabbinical Supervisory Council, consisting of fifteen duly ordained Rabbis of Orthodox Hebrew Faith, who shall have supervisory control and direction of all matters concerning and relating to (a) religious problems and questions, and to (b) the religious functions, purpose, and objects of the corporation—and such other powers not in derogation of those specifically provided herein as may be provided by the By-Laws. All acts of the trustees in their administration of the affairs of the corporation, or respecting the control and administration of the temporalities and property, real and personal, belonging to the corporation, and to revenues, insofar as such acts concern or relate to (a) any matter constituting, affecting, or bearing upon any religious problem or question, or to (b) religious functions, purposes, or objects of the corporation, shall be subject to the discipline, rules, usages, control, and approval of said Rabbinical Supervisory Council, to which this corporation is hereby declared subject. The Rabbinical Supervisory Council shall have sole right to determine what act involves a matter constituting, affecting, or bearing upon any religious problem or question, or the religious functions, purposes, or objects of the corporation.

Orthodox Student Pride

Gwendolyn R. Buttnick | 1967

This essay, written by Gwen Buttnick (b. 1949), a day school graduate in Seattle WA, reflected the triumphalism with which Orthodox Jews viewed their day schools.

Not everyone sends his children to day school; some fear an inferior secular education. This is countered by the fact that first graders learn to read months before their gentile neighbors. Hebrew school graduates consistently make honor roll status in the public high schools. In

1965 when I graduated from public high school (there is no Jewish high school in Seattle), six of the top ranking ten graduates had attended the Seattle Hebrew Day School. This in a school of 2,800! A regional statistic, to be sure, but nevertheless typical of the success of Hebrew school students throughout the country.

Some parents do not send their children to day school because they feel that with only Jewish classmates they will suffer later from the effects of such segregation. This is not true. For 10 years practically all my friends were Jewish and I came in contact almost solely with Jews at Jewish functions. We needed those 10 concentrated, intensified years of training and education. It did take a short time to adjust to the bustling, unsheltered life of the public high school, but it certainly was not an impossibility.

The courses at high school seem easier and the teachers far less demanding than those of the day school years. The students are friendly, and in no way does the day school graduate feel he is an outcast. However, it would be untrue to say that he can completely identify with his new-found peers. He has for many years been exposed to great ideas and thoughts. His has been the world of *chumash* [Pentateuch], *dikduk* [Hebrew grammar], *Rashi, neviim* [books of the Prophets], and Jewish history, in addition to science, literature, and algebra. His young mind has been constantly filled with provocative and soul-searching questions: Why does God punish so harshly those who serve Him completely and totally? Or—who is greater, Noah in his day or Avraham in his? His mind is trained to meditate upon the value and importance of all he is taught. This concept, first used in religious studies, quite naturally follows into the student's secular learning, greatly increasing his awareness of all issues he faces.

All this points to the fact that it is not an easy program. And, in truth, it is suitable only for those with above-average gifts of curiosity and strength of purpose. Some children do drop out because they are unable to carry the load, but usually not before every effort is made to help them gain a grasp of the material. However, the school is definitely not composed of quiz kids—rather, of children who study hard and with zest, and who are coached by a patient, understanding, and helpful staff of dedicated individuals.

On the occasion of my graduation from day school, I remember something one of my teachers told us. He urged us to continue our Jewish education because it was impossible at age 15 to build within ourselves a tower of education that could last all our lives. I entered the school as a little girl of 5 who already knew much about the religion because of my environment. However, there were children in my class who knew nothing about Judaism. As the years passed we all gradually acquired something most abstract and intangible. We learned the feeling of Judaism—not merely the *mitzvoth aseh* and the prohibitions. Together we learned something that would remain with us for the duration of our lives, even if we were never to see a fellow Jew again. Somewhere, deep within our personalities, the school had set a spark burning. Whether this spark was to become a great flame or remain a tiny flicker would depend on ourselves and on our futures. Nevertheless, somewhere in the course of our ten-year study, the foundation stones of the tower of education which my teacher urged us to build were placed within the intellect and heart of each and every student.

SECTION 2 | Beyond the School

Camp Moshava

Lillian X. Frost | 1945

In 1939 Camp Moshava in Rolling Prairie, Indiana, was established to serve "religious youth" in the Midwest. The 1940s was a "crucial decade" in Jewish camping in the United States. Leaders of the Conservative and Reform movements as well as Zionist educators founded summer camps that drew children and young people and introduced them to their specific missions and values. While most of these camps did not espouse Orthodoxy, some maintained kosher kitchens and therefore appealed to Orthodox Jews. Camp Moshava was unique for its commit-

ment to both Religious Zionism and Orthodox Judaism. A frequent contributor in the Chicago Jewish press, Lillian Frost's (b. 1921) article below demonstrated the dual mission of Camp Moshava.

We have just had a most refreshing experience which has strengthened our respect for the "younger" generation and our conviction that our youth organizations must become more truly Jewish in nature. Their programs must be dynamic, and their approach to youth must be imaginative. Otherwise, we shall see the sorry spectacle of our youth becoming a catch-all for "young" people who won't grow up while the young people have no vehicle for expression. We have just spoken to Sallie Rubin, a 16-year-old young lady, and we'd like to tell you a little story. Sallie comes from an orthodox home, but most of her friends are not observant.[11] More and more she was being subjected to the pressures of her out-of-home environment, and she was being made to feel that she was "different." She began to wonder if perhaps the things which she had been taught were right or wrong. And then someone she knew was going to Camp Moshava, sponsored by the Hapoel Hamizrachi, and Sallie went, too.[12] She saw Jewish youth her age WORK TOGETHER, PLAY TOGETHER, LIVE TOGETHER in an atmosphere of positive Judaism. Being a young Jewess took on fresh meaning. She discovered a vitality, a lustiness she hadn't been aware of, and it was fun being Jewish! And she discovered Zionism, too, although she had been a member of a Zionist youth group for 2 years. ("Zionism was seldom presented at the meetings.") She returned from Camp determined to help other young Jews discover the richness of Jewish life and the role that Zionism plays in it. Together with some friends, she organized a club for this purpose. Already over 70 young people have joined! Does that have any significance?[13]

National Conference of Synagogue Youth
Abraham I. Rosenberg | 1956

Abraham I. Rosenberg (1913–85) was rabbi of Congregation B'nai B'rith Jacob in Savannah, Georgia. In 1956 Rosenberg wrote to Yeshiva University president

A "mifkad" flag ceremony in 1953 at Camp Moshava in Gelatt, Pennsylvania. Courtesy of Eric and Ora Zimmer.

Samuel Belkin about the struggles of maintaining a national Orthodox youth organization. Founded in 1954, the Orthodox Union's National Conference of Synagogue Youth underwent several false starts before solidifying itself in 1959. Unsure of NCSY's stability and in a desperate tone, Rosenberg suggested to Belkin that Yeshiva University expand its Youth Bureau to ensure that Orthodox youth continue to benefit from a national movement.

My dear Dr. Belkin,

May I ask your indulgence to seriously consider the following problem which has arisen in national Jewish Orthodox life and which we of the southeast deem extremely serious.

You may have heard that I spearheaded the movement within the Union of Orthodox Jewish Congregations to establish a national Orthodox youth organization.[14] I would like to add that I did this after I discussed the possibility of Yeshiva Community Service Division handling such an organization and was informed that at the time it would not be possible. I was successful in having the National Conference of Synagogue Youth come into being. Since that movement our own youth groups were completely and satisfactorily diverted from joining the Conservative movement's USY.[15] They found new interest in the synagogue youth activities, which satisfied their search for a sense of belonging.

Yesterday I received a letter from Rabbi Harold Cohen, the national director of NCSY, to the effect that the Union was disbanding all of their youth activities. There is no need, I am sure, for me to describe to you the deep sense of disappointment that such a decision engendered. I feel that this is almost like a death knell to our efforts for our youth.[16] What is true for Torah is also true for Avodah [religious work]. Therefore, "Im ein G'doyim ein T'yoshim."[17]

In the southeast the Orthodox synagogues have long been united under the name of Southeastern Synagogue Conference. Several years ago this group voted to affiliate itself with the Union and become one of their regions. This group is to meet in convention in Atlanta this coming January 25–27. On the 28th there will be a regional meeting of the RCA members, of which region I am chairman. At these conferences the question of the national youth organization will be discussed. May I therefore propose to you that should the Union decide to disregard our appeal for maintaining their youth activities, that Yeshiva, under the sponsorship of the Yeshiva Synagogue Council, embark upon an intensified national program for Orthodox youth.[18] I feel certain that all of our synagogues in the southeast would be most anxious to align themselves with that kind of a national synagogue body that will service our youth.

Please let me hear from you what you can do for us and what you might further suggest in this most serious dilemma.

With kindest personal regards, I am
Sincerely yours,
    Rabbi Abraham I. Rosenberg

Drisha Institute for Jewish Education

Soshea Leibler | 1980

In 1979 RIETS-trained Rabbi David Silber (b. 1948) established Drisha as one of the first programs to offer women advanced study in traditional Jewish texts. Shortly after it was founded, Soshea Leibler (b. 1955) visited the school on New York's Upper West Side. She discovered the socially and religiously Orthodox nature of the new organization and its female students.

In a stiflingly hot room, the six students sit hunched over their Talmudic tomes listening to one of their colleagues, who in a singsong voice is interpreting a troublesome passage. It is 12:40 Thursday afternoon, and class officially ended ten minutes ago.

What makes this class unique is that the students are women, all married and ranging in age from 20 to more than 30. They will soon be picking up their little ones from nursery school and heading home to tend to their households and families. But for the next few minutes they remain immersed in their studies, as they have been for the past three hours.

That evening, eighteen young women, mostly college and graduate students, straggle into the makeshift classroom of Drisha Institute for Jewish Education, located in the West Side Institutional Synagogue on Manhattan's Upper West Side. They chat amongst themselves as they settle into the brown scratched desks and take out their books and notebooks.

Upon a portable wooden blackboard in the front of the room a boyish looking Rabbi, David Silber, writes instructions for his class while taking care to greet each student as she enters the room.

When 7 p.m. approaches and class officially begins, Rabbi Silber steps aside. During the next hour the women, following blackboard instructions, read certain passages in the book of Genesis and study assigned commentaries. They study alone or in small groups. Their Rabbi sits nearby, also studying.

This hour, referred to as *hachana*, or "preparation time," is just one of the unique features of Drisha, a new school for women, which in its first year has attracted more than 100 students.

Miriam Alter, a West Side mother of three, spends two and a half hours every Tuesday morning at Drisha. Classes begin at 9:30 so that she and other mothers have time to accompany their older children to school before themselves coming to class.

On the few occasions when babysitter arrangements fall through, Miriam brings her infant with her. While she listens to Rabbi Silber, her baby sleeps in the adjacent corridor along with other infants. When an infant awakes—an inevitable occurrence—the mother normally takes up a position in the doorway, rocking her child while listening to the class.

"Going to class," says Miriam, "is total relaxation for me. Intellectually I don't have many outlets and here I find the release I need." Her husband, himself a Talmudic scholar, is supportive of her learning and tries to accommodate her study schedule in every way possible. Both parents feel Miriam's studies at Drisha will help in bringing up their children as Torah Jews.

SECTION 3 | Yeshiva University

Synthesis
Samuel Belkin | 1944

In 1943 Rabbi Samuel Belkin succeeded Rabbi Bernard Revel as president of Yeshiva College and RIETS (the school was renamed Yeshiva University in 1945). Under Belkin's leadership, Yeshiva expanded, establishing, among other programs, medical and law schools and a women's undergraduate college. Below is the vision of "Synthesis" for Yeshiva College that Belkin articulated in his inaugural addresses delivered on May 23, 1944. He favored a form of Jewish higher education that did not permit religious and secular matters to engage and conflict with one another.

Perhaps now the significance of Yeshiva College may become more apparent. The Yeshiva College was established, not for the sake of adding another college to the many excellent institutions of higher learning already in existence in this blessed land. Yeshiva College has endeavored to blaze a new trail of its own in conformity with the great American democratic traditions of education and in harmony with the spiritual heritage of Israel. It is a true college of liberal arts and science. It is not our intention to make science the handmaiden of religion nor religion the handmaiden of science. We do not believe in a scientific religion nor in a pseudo-science. We prefer to look upon science and religion as separate domains which need not be in serious conflict and therefore need no reconciliation. If we seek the blending of science and religion and the integration of secular knowledge with sacred wisdom, then it is not in the subject matter represented by these fields but rather within the personality of the individual that we hope to achieve the synthesis.

The Yeshiva is the living incarnation of divine wisdom of the Torah which sends out rays of spiritual and moral light to thousands of Jewish souls. The Yeshiva endeavors to perpetuate the Jewish spiritual philosophy of education. It seeks to implant in its students a spiritual and moral concept of life based upon the Torah, the prophets, and the endless traditions of Israel. The Yeshiva considers its primary function to be the training of spiritually minded men into a collective force for the perpetuation of the spiritual and moral essence of historic Judaism and for the benefit of our great American democracy. The college of the Yeshiva, like any other American college, endeavors to acquaint its student body with the mysteries of the universe, with the researches and discoveries of the human intellect, with the theories and speculations of the human mind.

We shall always look upon the Yeshiva College with its curriculum of liberal arts and sciences as indispensable for the intellectual development of our student body. We shall consider, however, the Yeshiva with its spiritual and moral teachings as the end, for a moral and spiritual way of life must be the aim and striving of every society. It is our intention to give to secular education a higher purpose and make the Yeshiva and Yeshiva College a living symbol of intellectual progress and moral activity. We believe that by reintegrating our lives with the ideals of the Torah and with our search after G-d's knowledge we may succeed in establishing a medium of unification for human knowledge.

A New Beginning

Yeshiva University Office of Admissions | 1978

In 1977 Yeshiva University launched its Beit Midrash Program at Stern College. Rabbi Joseph Soloveitchik delivered the inaugural Talmud lecture to sixty-five female collegians. Opened in 1954, Stern College for Women taught advanced Jewish studies to its female students, but this was the first time that it offered intensive undergraduate study in this typically male-oriented study. Student leaders described it as part of a "revolutionary spirit" that sought to "extend boundaries" and "disintegrate limitations."

A new era in Jewish education for women began in October 1977 when Stern College for Women inaugurated its Beit Midrash Program. As an innovator in women's education, Stern College has always been sensitive to the desires of young women of all backgrounds to actively participate in Judaism's tradition of learning. As an integral part of Yeshiva University, it has pioneered the advancement of college-level Jewish studies. Now, as educational opportunities for women are rapidly expanding, Stern College, the nation's only institution of higher education for women under Jewish auspices, has developed a setting and structure for learning that has been unavailable for women until the present.

While the study of Talmud has long been an option in its course offerings, with the initiation of the Beit Midrash Program, Stern College for Women has revitalized its Judaic studies curricula. The Beit Midrash Program is unique in several ways. It changes the intensity and format of women's learning through its use of the traditional combina-

Rabbi Joseph B. Soloveitchik delivering the inaugural Talmud class at Stern College's Beit Midrash Program. To the lecturer's right are rabbis Norman Lamm and Saul Berman. Rabbi Mordechai Willig also attended the lecture, though he is not pictured in this image. Courtesy of Yeshiva University Archives, Public Relations Photo Events Collection.

tion of *shiurim* (lectures) and its individualized group method of study (*chavruta*). The classes in Bible, Talmud, and Halakhah are available on three levels—elementary, intermediate, and advanced—so that any student, regardless of her previous preparation, is eligible for the program. It is the only program of its kind in the United States designed to allow women who have learned intensively in Israel or in a yeshiva high school to continue their studies on an equally comprehensive and advanced level. The Beit Midrash Program emphasizes learning from the original texts in order that students will master the necessary skills of learning. The broad scope of the Beit Midrash enables a student from any educational background to improve her level of learning so that she may continue to pursue satisfying study, even on her own, for the rest of her life.

The "ou" Symbol

Herbert S. Goldstein | 1933

In 1924, the Orthodox Union (ou) established the Kosher Certification Service (kcs). A project conceived by the Women's Branch, the kcs evolved into a highly sophisticated and profitable organization. In the early 1930s, the ou partnered with riets to expand its operation. All this was addressed by Rabbi Herbert Goldstein, who was the spiritual leader of the Institutional Synagogue in New York and chairman of the ou's Rabbinical Council. He also emphasized the importance of institutionalizing kosher certification to rid the community of long-standing professional and rabbinic abuse of this area of Jewish life.

The Union of Orthodox Jewish Congregations of America, through the ideal policy of Kashruth supervision, is slowly but surely gaining the complete confidence of the Jewish community. Up to about nine years ago, the Kashruth of articles labeled as "Kosher" were frequently questioned because many a "Hechsher" [certification] was obtained merely for a financial consideration.

Our Union, however, makes it unmistakably clear to each and every firm seeking a "Hechsher" that our endorsement is NOT FOR SALE. The only finances involved are those for the salary of the Mashgiach [kashrut supervisor], who is paid for his work for supervision. Furthermore, the Mashgiach does not become the employee of the firm involved. The exact amount of his remuneration is sent by the firm to the office of the Union, so that the Mashgiach must look to the Union as his employer.

It may interest our readers to know the procedure in granting a Hechsher. When a firm seeks our endorsement it is told, first of all, to send a written application to the office of the Union. At a subsequent meeting of the Executive Committee of the Union, the application is read. The committee then decides whether as a matter of policy a Hechsher for the product in question should be granted. If the committee acts favorably upon the application, it is then sent to our Rabbinical Council. The Rabbinical Council, as a rule, calls upon Mr. Abraham Goldstein of our Executive Committee, who is a leading Jewish chemist and an expert authority of Kashruth, for a complete analysis of the ingredients of the product.[19] After investigation by the Committee on Kashruth, a report is rendered to the Rabbinical Council for final action. If the product is found to be Kosher, and the proper supervision can be arranged, the firm is granted a Hechsher, and the President of the Rabbinical Council appoints the Mashgiach.

I know of no individual Rabbi, body of Rabbis, or Kashruth organization of any kind that handles Kashruth in such an ideal manner as is employed by the Union. Our method is approved by Jewish communities from coast to coast and has made the Union's Hechsher a universally recognized seal for genuine Kashruth.

How Kosher Is ou?

Alexander Rosenberg | 1958

Rabbi Alexander Rosenberg (1903–72) was the rabbinic administrator of the ou Kashruth Division from 1950 to 1972. Previously Rosenberg had helped establish the RCA's Kashruth Committee. By the end of the 1950s, the ou endorsed about a thousand food products. This interview with Rabbi Saul C. Framowitz, published in the Young Israel magazine, Viewpoint, *reveals the "politics" of kashruth supervision and its relationship to other Orthodox matters. Note that at this time the Orthodox Union's label was known as* uo, *shorthand for the organization's official name, the Union of Orthodox Jewish Congregations of America.*

Question: Rabbi Rosenberg, the Union of Orthodox [Jewish] Congregations of America would no doubt want the American Jewish public to regard the UO insignia as axiomatic and self-evident of certified Kashruth. However, inasmuch as your organization is composed of laymen rather than ordained Rabbis, what possesses you with the right of jurisdiction to exercise authority over matters of Kashruth?

Answer: While it is true that the Union is composed of a non-clerical constituency, the overall management of its Kashruth division is under the jurisdiction of the Joint Kashruth Commission of the Union consisting of 9 men, 5 laymen and 4 rabbis. These men are approved by the president of the Union upon the recommendation and authorization of the Rabbinical Council of America. All matters pertaining to religious or Halachic policy are governed by the Rabbinic Kashruth Commission in conjunction with the Kashruth Commission of the Rabbinical Council of America.

Question: By what standards is a company adjudged qualifiable for UO endorsement?

Answer: UO endorsement is granted only after an application submitted by the interested [company] has been exhaustively investigated and passed upon and the stipulated requirements in the form of a written contract agreed to. Each plant is constantly inspected by Rabbinic representatives who are generally Rabbis of congregations in the same or nearest accessible community. The supervising personnel are required to report regularly to the Kashruth Commission through the Rabbinic Kashruth Administrator of the Union.

Question: What, exactly, are these requirements?

Answer: The company must list all the approved ingredients and sources of supply. A clause in the contract between the company and the Union holds the company bound to notify the Union 30 days in advance of any intended change in method of production or equipment or any plan for adding new products. The Union has the right to inspect the plant without forewarning any time it desires during business hours. All labels of the company are submitted to the Union

In the 1930s and 1940s, a number of food companies advertised their Orthodox Union–approved kosher bona fides in the Jewish press. The Sunshine Company produced some of the most elaborate campaigns to encourage traditional Jews to trust and purchase its products. Reprinted with permission from *Jewish Life*.

for advance approval, and the Union is authorized to stop production of the products any time it chooses.

Question: How is the extent of remuneration to the Union by each company determined or apportioned for each issued endorsement? Does this fee in any way affect the prices of kosher commodities?

Answer: Fees are paid by the companies for given service on the basis of the over-all costs involved to the Union. As a result, while the operation is thus self-sustaining, no additional costs are incurred by the Jewish consumer, the products being distributed identically to Jewish and non-Jewish consumers.

Question: What measures does the Union employ in appointing or designating Rabbis or mashgichim to superintend the more than 900 products it endorses? And what standards must these applicants meet to qualify for designation?

Answer: This entails several steps. A primary factor in establishing an applicant's qualifications is a) A bona fide smicha bearing testimony to the individual's familiarity with the laws of Kashruth. b) The applicant's character and reliability are ascertained. He is judged on the basis of religious orientation. If he is deemed a worthy, G-d fearing man who would not falter on the job—who would not countenance mismanagement or any form of malfeasance, then he would be considered favorably. c) Another necessary attribute considered is experience and competence in dealing with the particular process. d) If two applicants appear equally qualifiable for supervisory engagement, proximity will play the decisive role. The one stationed nearest the firm will be appointed, for distance is often a great hindrance, impeding one's effectiveness and limiting promptness in discharging one's duties. e) The financial status of an individual is an additional matter of consideration. The one in most dire straits will be engaged.

Question: Does this unfavorable financial condition expose the supervisor to dangerous temptation?

Answer: Such fear is unfounded. It is a fact that the Union's supervisory personnel function under the direct jurisdiction of the Rabbinic Kashruth Commission and have no relationship with the company itself. The company neither hires, fires, nor compensates the supervisory personnel. In fact, the company may not even present them with a small gift without the Union's permission. Furthermore, the initial inspection of a plant is never made by the Rabbi or Rabbis who afterward become the plant's supervisors. Contractual agreement between the Union and the firm provides that inspections may be made as often as the Union may deem necessary to guard against inadvertent mishandling even after the supervisor has been assigned to the firm.

Question: How does the Union determine the exact fees that mashgichim are to be paid for their services?

Answer: Here again the determining factor is the amount of time, effort, skill, and toil expended during one's assignment.

Question: Is it not true that at least 90% of your Rabbinic supervisory personnel is selected from RCA members?

Answer: That might be so, but this is not for reasons of bias but more so for reasons of closer cordial ties with the RCA's Kashruth department. The RCA is also recognized as the largest representative Rabbinic organization in the country. We, however, also have in our midst rabbis from the Agudas Harabonim such as Rabbi [Eliezer] Silver and others from the Igud Harabonim who are well known to you.[20]

Question: Does the UO ratify the endorsement of rabbis whose Synagogues have mixed pews?

Answer: The problem of mixed pews, if regarded as incompatible to orthodox doctrine, first knocks upon the doors of our Roshei Yeshivah, some of which advocate commissioning their graduates to mixed-pew communities in the hope of improving religious standards there, by their trusted disciples. If these Roshei Yeshivah find these hazardous assignments consistent with their convictions without fear of jeopardizing the very lofty goals for which they aim, then we surely must acquiesce. It is needless, however, to say that we don't look favorably at the adverse conditions prompting such procedures by our esteemed Roshei Yeshivah.

SECTION 5 | Interfaith Dialogue

The Self-Appointed Spokesman

National Council of Young Israel | 1964

On September 14, 1964, the tradition-observing Rabbi Abraham Joshua Heschel (1907–72) of the Jewish Theological Seminary met with Pope Paul VI (1897–1978) to persuade the pontiff to strike out conversion of Jews and the charge of deicide against Jews from Catholic dogma. Two years earlier, the pope's predecessor had convened the Second Vatican Council to consider the Church's relationship with outsiders and the modern world. One of the landmark decisions of the council was to absolve Jews of the crucifixion of Jesus: "It cannot be charged against all the Jews, without distinction, then alive, nor against the Jews of today." Before this announcement, Heschel traveled to Rome to engage the pope. In response, Young Israel condemned Heschel's interfaith dialogue as a breach of Jewish tradition.

Professor Abraham Heschel of the Theological Seminary visited the pope to discuss the issue of a favorable resolution towards Jews from the Ecumenical Council. This trip was undertaken after the National Jewish organizations arrived at a conclusion which, categorically, was opposed to such begging. The editorial, not being a vehicle of newspaper reporting but rather of opinion, merely states that such action on the part of Professor Heschel was of disservice to the Jewish community.

We wish to go behind the scenes and ask on whose behalf did Dr. Heschel speak? Did he speak on behalf of the Seminary, the American Jewish Committee, his own name? Diverse rumors link many of the extremes of the Jewish community on the one side and the Chassidic movement on the other side. When Dr. Heschel was asked by the *Viewpoint* editor on whose behalf and in whose name he spoke, he answered, "No comment."

We spoke out once before about the distaste in lay leaders paying homage to the pope. How much more so is it degrading to have spiritual leaders lower themselves to beg.

As we write this editorial we are informed that Dr. Heschel will be one of the speakers at the New York rally for Russian Jewry.[21] In all frankness, Young Israel did not want to sit at a public meeting with people who flagrantly violate the decisions reached by unanimity of all organizations. We were tempted not to participate in this rally. However, we must face the very cold facts. When Russian Jewry is at stake, we must at all costs present a unified Jewry. We must show the Russian government that on the issue of the persecution of our people, we set aside all differences and we work together. When it comes to alleviating the pain of a fellow Jew behind the Iron Curtain, we are compelled to swallow our pride and overlook the hurt. Therefore, our presence at the rally for Russian Jewry was merely an indication of our desire for unity, but should not be interpreted to acquiesce to Dr. Heschel's visit to the pope.

Confrontation

Joseph B. Soloveitchik | 1964

In 1964 Rabbi Joseph Soloveitchik responded to calls from Catholics and Jews in the wake of the Second Vatican Council to restart a dialogue between the two faiths. Soloveitchik argued for borders and limitations to these conversations, which restricted religious discourse. "The confrontation," as he was wont to describe it, "should occur not at a theological, but at a mundane human level." He delivered this message at the RCA's Mid-Winter Conference in February 1964. Soloveitchik's standing in the Orthodox community ensured that most of its leaders abided by his position. This is an excerpt from those remarks.

It is self-evident that a confrontation of two faith communities is possible only if it is accompanied by a clear assurance that both parties will enjoy equal rights and full religious freedom. We shall resent any attempt on the part of the community of the many to engage us in a peculiar encounter in which our confronter will command us to take a position beneath him while placing himself not alongside of but above us. A democratic confrontation certainly does not demand that we submit to an attitude of self-righteousness taken by the community of the many which, while debating whether or not to "absolve" the community of the few of some mythical guilt, completely ignores its own historical responsibility for the suffering and martyrdom so frequently recorded in the annals of the history of the few, the weak, and the persecuted.

We are not ready for a meeting with another faith community in which we shall become an object of observation, judgment, and evaluation, even though the community of the many may then condescendingly display a sense of compassion with the community of the few and advise the many not to harm or persecute the few. Such an encounter would convert the personal Adam-Eve meeting into a hostile confrontation between a subject-knower and a knowable object. We do not intend to play the part of the object encountered by dominating man. Soliciting commiseration is incongruous with the character of a democratic confrontation. There should rather be insistence upon one's inalienable rights as a human being, created by God.

In light of this analysis, it would be reasonable to state that in any confrontation we must insist upon four basic conditions in order to safeguard our individuality and freedom of action.

First, we must state, in unequivocal terms, the following. We are a totally independent faith community. We do not revolve as a satellite in any orbit. Nor are we related to any other faith community as "brethren" even though "separated." People confuse two concepts when they speak of a common tradition uniting two faith communities such as the Christian and the Judaic. This term may have relevance if one looks upon a faith community under an historico-cultural aspect and interprets its relationship to another faith community in sociological, human categories describing the unfolding of the creative consciousness of man. Let us not forget that religious awareness manifests itself not only in a singular apocalyptic faith experience but in a mundane cultural experience as well. Religion is both a divine imperative which was foisted upon man from without and a new dimension of personal being which man discovers within himself. In a word, there is a cultural aspect to the faith experience which is, from a psychological viewpoint, the most integrating, inspiring, and uplifting spiritual force. Religious values, doctrines, and concepts may be and have been translated into cultural categories enjoyed and cherished even by secular man. All the references throughout the ages to universal religion, philosophical religion, *et cetera*, are related to the cultural aspect of the faith experience of which not only the community of believers but a pragmatic, utilitarian society avails itself as well. The cultural religious experience gives meaning and directedness to human existence and relates it to great ultimates, thus enhancing human dignity and worth even at a mundane level.

Viewing the relationship between Judaism and Christianity under this aspect, it is quite legitimate to speak of a cultural Judeo-Christian tradition for two reasons: First, Judaism as a culture has influenced, indeed, molded the ethico-philosophical Christian world-formula. The basic categories and premises of the latter were evolved in the cultural Judaic orbit. Second, our Western civilization has absorbed both Judaic and Christian elements. As a matter of fact, our Western heritage was shaped by a combination of three factors, the classical, Judaic, and Christian, and we could readily speak of a Judeo-Hellenistic-Christian tradition within the framework of our Western civilization. However, when we shift the focus from the dimension of culture to that of faith—where total unconditional commitment and involvement are necessary—the whole idea of a tradition of faiths and the continuum of revealed doctrines which are by their very nature incommensurate and related to different frames of reference is utterly absurd, unless one is ready to acquiesce in the Christian theological claim that Christianity has superseded Judaism.

As a faith individuality, the community of the few is endowed with intrinsic worth which must be viewed against its own meta-historical backdrop without relating to the framework of another faith community. For the mere appraisal of the worth of one community in terms of the service it has rendered to another community, no matter how great and important this service was, constitutes an infringement of the sovereignty and dignity of even the smallest of faith communities. When God created man and endowed him with individual dignity, He decreed that the ontological legitimacy and relevance of the individual human being is to be discovered not without but within the individual. He was created because God approved of him as an autonomous human being and not as an auxiliary being in the service of someone else. The ontological purposiveness of his existence is immanent in him. The same is true of a religious community, whose worth is not to be measured by external standards.

Therefore, any intimation, overt or covert, on the part of the community of the many that it is expected of the community of the few that it shed its uniqueness and cease existing because it has fulfilled its mission by paving the way for the community of the many, must be rejected as undemocratic and contravening the very idea of religious freedom. The small community has as much right to profess its faith in the ultimate certitude concerning the doctrinal worth of its world formula and to behold its own eschatological vision as does the community of the many. I do not deny the right of the community of the many to address itself to the community of the few in its own eschatological terms. However, building a practical program upon this right is hardly consonant with religious democracy and liberalism.

Second, the *logos*, the word, in which the multifarious religious experience is expressed, does not lend itself to standardization or universalization. The word of faith reflects the intimate, the private, the paradoxically inexpressible cravings of the individual for and his linking up with his Maker. It reflects the numinous character and the strangeness of the act of faith of a particular community which is totally incomprehensible to the man of a different faith community. Hence it is important that the religious or theological *logos* should not be employed as the medium of communication between two faith communities whose modes of expression are as unique as their apocalyptic experiences. The confrontation should occur not at a theological but at a mundane human level. There, all of us speak the universal language of modern man. As a matter of fact our common interests lie not in the realm of faith, but in that of the secular orders.[22] There, we all face a powerful antagonist, we all have to contend with a considerable number of matters of great concern. The relationship between two communities must be outer-directed and related to the secular orders with which men of faith come face to face. In the secular sphere, we may discuss positions to be taken, ideas to be evolved, and plans to be formulated. In these matters, religious communities may together recommend action to be developed and may seize the initiative to be implemented later by general society. However, our joint engagement in this kind of enterprise must not dull our sense of identity as a faith community. We must always remember that our singular commitment to God and our hope and indomitable will for survival are non-negotiable and non-rationalizable and are not subject to debate and argumentation. The great encounter between God and man is a wholly personal private affair incomprehensible to the outsider—even to a brother of the same faith community. The divine message is incommunicable since it defies all standardized media of information and all objective categories. If the powerful community of the many feels like remedying an embarrassing human situation or redressing an historic wrong, it should do so at the human ethical level. However, if the debate should revolve around matters of faith, then one of the confronters will be impelled to avail himself of the language of his opponent. This in itself would mean surrender of individuality and distinctiveness.

Third, we members of the community of the few should always act with tact and understanding and refrain from suggesting to the community of the many, which is both proud and prudent, changes in ritual or emendations of its texts. If the genuinely liberal dignitaries of the faith community of the many deem some changes advisable, they will act in accordance with their convictions without any prompting on our part. It is not within our purview to advise or solicit. For it would be both impertinent and unwise for an outsider to intrude upon the most private sector of the human existential experience, namely, the way in which a faith community expresses its relationship to God. Non-interference with and non-involvement in something which is totally alien to us is a *conditio sine qua non* for the furtherance of good will and mutual respect.

Fourth, we certainly have not been authorized by our history, sanctified by the martyrdom of millions, to even hint to another faith community that we are mentally ready to revise historical attitudes, to trade favors pertaining to fundamental matters of faith, and to reconcile "some" differences. Such a suggestion would be nothing but a betrayal of our great tradition and heritage and would, furthermore, produce no practical benefits. Let us not forget that the community of the many will not be satisfied with half measures and compromises which are only indicative of a feeling of insecurity and inner emptiness. We cannot command the respect of our confronters by displaying a servile attitude. Only a candid, frank, and unequivocal policy reflecting unconditional commitment to our God, a sense of dignity, pride, and inner joy in being what we are, believing with great passion in the ultimate truthfulness of our views, praying fervently for and expecting confidently the fulfillment of our eschatological vision when our faith will rise from particularity to universality, will impress the peers of the other faith community among whom we have both adversaries and friends. I hope and pray that our friends in the community of the many will sustain their liberal convictions and humanitarian ideals by articulating their position on the right of the community of the few to live, create, and worship God in its own way, in freedom and with dignity.[23]

The New Encounter

Irving "Yitz" Greenberg | 1967

Most Orthodox rabbis stood by Soloveitchik and the RCA's position on ecumenism. There were exceptions, most notably Rabbi Irving Greenberg. In the 1960s, he delivered a number of lectures entitled "The New Encounter of Judaism and Christianity." On one occasion, Greenberg put his thoughts into writing.

The great question for us is: can we create a community which is committed enough to live in an open situation? My own community (the Orthodox Jewish community) is full of predictions that the Catholic Church is not long for this world and that it will dissolve into secular culture. These predictions are ideological rationalizations, of course. They justify not trying the same renewal experiment—which is what the group is afraid to do. The reassurance to status quo is the claim that once a religious group yields its inner community sanctions and management of the information flow, it will not be able to maintain itself. This is, indeed, a real possibility which I am sure many Catholics have noted; some with anticipation, some with fear. Given the unprecedented nature of this effort, dialogue may play its most constructive role. Can we genuinely create a Judaism and Christianity free of in-group distortions and rewards? We will never know until we try. Insofar as Judaism has been caricatured within the Christian community, the Christian need not experience Christianity in all its depth and beauty in order to remain a Christian. If he can dismiss Judaism as legalism or tribalism or petrifaction, there is no serious alternative to match. Insofar as a Jew could dismiss Christianity as ascetic or other-worldly, he need not confront the question of the validity and significance of living in his own tradition in its grandeur. Whether, indeed, the religious communities are prepared to give up the easy sanctions of human distortions and develop a faith that is so open to God that it does not need the in-group payoffs is a big question mark. If religions cannot do this, then their future appears dim indeed. The culture will become more pervasive and the mass media can reach deeper and deeper into the groups with alternate images and models of living. Apparently films do affect people even more deeply than books and identify them with the other, *pace* Marshall McLuhan.[24] The key to religious survival and to variety and plural cultural trends in an increasingly homogenized world depends on the creative solutions of this challenge. And the only way religions can raise people in this open manner, the only way they can develop a new vocabulary and imagery that does not distort the other, is by speaking constantly and by raising people constantly in the presence of the other. It may take centuries to develop the new vocabularies and images, and they will only be done if the new encounter is open, frank, and loving.

To attempt this experiment will be to become involved in fundamental theological rethinking and changes within our own traditions. I do not believe that Christianity can seriously do this without a profound shift in its understanding of the relationships of the two covenants—Jewish and Christian. It will have to come to the recognition that God's promises are not lightly given and are not forfeited. Even as they were given by God's love rather than man's merit, so they are not lost by men's lack of merit—if indeed they did lack merit. This would mean a new Christian self-understanding which would base its validity on its own moral and religious life—not on the death or insufficiency of others. Nor will Judaism be exempt from self-consideration. The great searching point there will undoubtedly be the Gentile-Jewish dichotomy which characterizes the Jewish way and life and which can too easily slip from legitimate particularity to egocentricity and insensitivity to the fullness and claims of the other. These reconsiderations will not be quid pro quos but the fruit of the discovery and love of the other. And the range of rethinking and new language development is more staggering than may be apparent. There are thousands of areas where the simple use of words is so loaded and distorting. The word "Pharisee" is a negatively loaded word in Christian terminology; it is one of the great words of Jewish tradition.[25] The Law-Gospel dichotomy, the God of Love and God of Wrath, the universalism-particularism negative contrast are only surface examples of how widespread the problem is. And as the distortions are removed, the danger of being swept up into the other becomes great. Yet, if successful, the enterprise offers the possibility of pure service of God. This would require a trust in God so complete that I do not demand an advance pledge that I am right and the other is wrong. It means a willingness to live under the judgment of God without the easy assurances of guaranteed righteousness and salvation. In a world where men are learning the problem and need to heal other human beings, perhaps the new encounter can give us the possibility of Jew and Christian—and all men—living side by side in this encounter until the end of days.

There are indeed men who are willing to live side by side until the end of days who do so because they are fully confident that the Messiah, when he comes, will confirm their rightness all along. Of course, it is a step forward to live together until that time. But even here, we may underrate the love and wonder of the Lord. I have often thought of this as a kind of nice truism. Let us wait until the Messiah comes. Then we can ask him if this is his first coming or his second. Each of us could look forward to a final confirmation. A friend, Zalman Schachter, taught me that perhaps I was a bit too narrow in my trust in God with this conception.[26] He wrote a short story in which the Messiah comes at the end of days. Jews and Christians march out to greet him and establish his reign. Finally they ask him if this is his first or second coming. To which the Messiah smiles and replies: "No comment." Perhaps we will then truly realize that it was worth it all along for the kind of life we lived along the way.

CONCLUSION

In 1967 the Jewish Community Council of Boston asked the rabbi of the Young Israel of Brookline if his congregation would participate in a panel on "Jewish-Catholic Relations." He declined, explaining that "the major Orthodox groups are following the policy of Rabbi Joseph Soloveitchik."[27] On the whole, this was the response of most Orthodox rabbis. Yet the community was divided on other issues, some of which were addressed in the above writings. Certainly not everyone fully embraced the changing attitude toward women's advanced Torah study, nor did all Orthodox Jews accept the RCA as the rabbinical overseer of religious observance and practice. The Modern Orthodox camp inherited this uneven cohesion of the Orthodox institutions and perspectives. These challenges made it difficult for Modern Orthodox leaders to establish a sturdy foothold for their movement.

9 | The Orthodox Synagogue and Rabbinate

INTRODUCTION

In 1956 National Council of Young Israel offered space in its journal, *Viewpoint,* for a disenchanted young clergyman to explain why he had left the Orthodox rabbinate. To him, "the task of spiritual leadership soon became synonymous with bulletin editorship, raconteur of funny stories, fund-raiser, and authority of all repairs and renovations of Synagogue nature." Even worse, the anonymous writer confessed that "nowhere in my school days did I ever imagine that spiritual leadership meant the responsibility of having to answer for a delayed shipment of plumbing supplies for the Synagogue's new wing."[1] Certainly not every rabbi felt so demoralized. In the same Young Israel publication, on a different occasion, Rabbi Ralph Pelcovitz (b. 1921) of Long Island, New York, admitted that he assumed a number of those inglorious clerical responsibilities because that is what it takes to "build an orthodox shul" and to be in a position to "guard and elevate synagogue standards."[2]

After World War II, Orthodox rabbis and the congregations they led underwent considerable transition. A new generation of American-born and better educated Jews took advantage of their academic pedigree and earning potential. Like their Reform and Conservative coreligionists, Orthodox Jews moved their families to the suburbs and constructed large synagogue edifices. Orthodox affluence and the community's rising standard of Jewish education and literacy generated new social dynamics within the congregation. As well, Orthodox suburbanites positioned in closer proximity to relatively traditional Conservative synagogues started to consider "innovations" like bat mitzvah celebrations for girls and more extravagant bar mitzvah parties for boys.

The situation also accorded Orthodox rabbis and congregants with an opportunity to reevaluate the boundaries of halakhic decision making. Some believed that Orthodox Judaism's new "modern" environs should motivate its leaders to think about Jewish law in fresh terms. Others disagreed and to various degrees. In one instance, the closeness with which Orthodox Jews lived to non-Orthodox Jews pushed laypeople to ratchet up their observance of Jewish law—and commitment to modest behavior—and outlaw "social dancing" in which husbands and wives (and boyfriends and girlfriends) publicly danced with one another. Related to this, by the close of the 1960s most Orthodox congregations installed a mehitzah, thereby concluding a matter that had long blurred the lines between Conservative and Orthodox Judaism. In 1969, a Yeshiva University official wrote to the president of the Hebrew Theological College to ask for his help to "hold the line together" and stop placing graduates of the Chicago school in "mixed" synagogues.[3] Even more pervasive was the outlawing of the microphone as a forbidden use of electricity on the Sabbath, a position held most forcefully by Rabbi Joseph Soloveitchik.

Accordingly, enhanced wealth and new geographic conditions moved the Orthodox community in many religious directions. Foremost, perhaps, it transformed the professional portfolio of the rabbinate to include much more than knowledge of Jewish law and a skill for pulpit homiletics. With his new set of responsibilities, the Orthodox rabbi emerged as the multifaceted executive of the much-transformed suburban synagogue. In addition to this, the Modern Orthodox rabbi had to contend with the usually more bolstered Conservative congregation. In so doing, Orthodox leaders faced the challenge of deciding what was within the parameters of their Modern Orthodox viewpoint and what lay beyond those borders.

The Friday Night Bat Mitzvah

Oscar Z. Fasman | 1944

In 1922 Rabbi Mordecai Kaplan's daughter, Judith, became the first Jewish girl to celebrate a bat mitzvah in the United States. Yet the diffusion of the bat mitzvah ceremony was slow to stick. Significant numbers of Conservative and Reform congregations (which had preferred communal confirmation ceremonies to personal celebrations) started to adopt bat mitzvah in the 1950s. Orthodox leaders resisted the "innovation" and impulse to be "with it." In fact, as late as the 1970s, only the most accommodating Orthodox rabbis permitted bat mitzvah ceremonies, and they allowed just the most modest sort of occasions. In 1944 Rabbi Oscar Fasman (1908–2003) advocated for the introduction of bat mitzvah ceremonies into "Late Friday night" synagogue programs. Whereas Conservative congregations used Friday night services to draw Jews who would not attend earlier, afternoon worship around sunset (especially during the winter), the future president of Chicago's Hebrew Theological College suggested that Orthodox congregations establish "Friday Night Forums" for other programs. This, then, was an early push for the Orthodox bat mitzvah, and the Orthodox Union offered Fasman space in its journal to express his views.

Among the subjects that trouble and perplex synagogue leaders, both rabbis and laymen, few have assumed such vast proportions as the question: What kind of activity should the synagogue carry on every Friday evening? Opinions vary from the one extreme that the late Friday evening gathering should consist of the entire Kabbolath Shabboth and Maariv services, plus a sermon or lecture, to the other extreme that only a lecture or a sermon should be delivered.[4] It is possible, too, to gather Halachic evidence to support almost any viewpoint advanced, so that the real issue is the wisdom or danger in one policy or another. Hence, the decision that a synagogue reaches regarding the kind of Forum to conduct is tremendously dependent upon the circumstances in which its program functions. Where, for example, a synagogue is so unhappily situated that hardly any of its members can attend a Friday night gathering without using a car or bus, it is clear that the Friday night Forum should be held on a weekday night; or as Punch delivered its famous advice to those about to be married; "Don't."[5]

. . . We must be realistic in our synagogue work. Whether justly or wrongly, the majority of people who are affiliated with orthodox congregations deem themselves unable to attend the regular Sabbath service. The true cause of this inability may be the pressure of circumstances or a sad lack of will-power to solve the problems of the American business world but the inability is unquestionably there. I am not in accord with the opinion that people who refuse to make sacrifices in order to be present in the synagogue on the Sabbath do not deserve to have their spiritual interests protected. It is an error that proves costly to allow synagogue contacts to be reduced to the three Y's (Yom Tov, Yizkor, and Yahrzeit).[6] Not that I am so naïve as to think that all members who do not come for early services Friday evening will be present at the Forum later that night, but the point I desire to make is that the synagogue should offer them an opportunity to mark the Sabbath in a religious atmosphere.

. . . Among the more recent suggestions that may be mentioned with the opportunities afforded by the social hour is a method for marking the entrance of Jewish girls into the obligations under the provisions of our code.[7] Since many of our educators consider that the modern scene necessitates the creation of a ceremony by which the girl who becomes twelve years of age will be impressed with the importance of her status and will feel that Judaism does not ignore her, as contrasted with her thirteen-year-old brother who becomes Bar Mitzvah, a congregation may be taking a wise step by instituting some form of Bat Mitzvah procedure. While the rabbi takes some moments from his sermon to address the girl herself, instructing her in a manner similar to the well-known address to a Bar Mitzvah, she herself would have a chance at the social hour to read and translate selected verses from the

Torah portion of the Sabbath, or she might deliver a short speech suitable for the event. The party in her honor would help to make her feel that her role in Jewish life is no less respected than that of the boys in her family. And just as the Sabbath morning of a Bar Mitzvah usually brings more congregants to the synagogue, the Friday night Forum at which a girl celebrates her Bat Mitzvah will undoubtedly attract members of the family and friends, so that the attendance will be improved.

Fancy Parties and Busy Fathers

Joseph Speiser | 1961

Many of the Orthodox rabbis who resisted the girls' bat mitzvah innovation were cognizant that non-Orthodox critics found the decision sexist, due in large measure to the lavish bar mitzvah parties often hosted to fete Orthodox sons. In 1961, in the thick of the bat mitzvah debate, the Rabbinical Council of America published Rabbi Joseph Speiser's strong rebuke of those extravagant galas, which he perceived to be devoid of much religious meaning.

Last week a young lad asked me when the ceremony of Bar Mitzvah first began in Judaism. This innocent question focused my attention upon a tragic aspect of American Judaism which threatens to destroy the very vitals of our religion and must receive our ever-increasing attention.

Our Sages may have had this in mind in the following comment: Don't do as the Egyptians do, nor as the Canaanites do, and in their statutes you shall not walk. The last phrase seems redundant. It refers, say the Sages, to theatres, circuses, and stadiums (see Rashi, Lev. 18:3).

That so much of our religious activity revolves around the sale of theatre tickets and the like is sad, but can at least be justified on the grounds that with the funds thus realized we are *marbitz torah* [disseminating Torah] and *machzik das* [strengthening religion]. But what justification can there be for making a three-ring circus of Torah and Mitzvos themselves?

To our young lad, Bar Mitzvah was merely a ceremony followed by an extravagant party and expensive gifts. Nothing he had ever seen could indicate to him that this was the moment when one becomes obligated legally and morally to the fulfillment of Mitzvos Hashem, the precepts of Judaism. *He got lost at the Bar and never reached the Mitzvah.*

Not that I am opposed to Bar Mitzvah parties. On the contrary, Abraham approved it and I surely do. "And the child grew, and was weaned. And Abraham made a great feast on the day that Isaac was weaned" (Gen. 21:8). Abraham, however, made a party only *"on the day that Isaac was weaned."* Nowhere do we find that he made a party for Ishmael. When the child was delivered and he saw that it was an *Isaac*, then he made a party.

How tragic it is that in America the *Isaacs* rarely get the party. The Ishmaels are treated to extravaganza. "What a Bar Mitzvah I made for my son; I spared nothing!" is one of the proudest statements American Jews make.

This statement is the height of vanity. The son is usually deprived of the "main course"—his father. American fathers are too busy: too busy to go to *shul*, too busy to learn, too busy to teach their children— just too busy. They are preoccupied with making money for fancy Bar Mitzvah parties. "So they went both of them together. And they came to the place which God had told him" (Gen. 22:8–9).

Every father means well and wants the best for his son. He ought to know, then, that our G-d appointed goals can only be reached when we walk together with our sons, not only at the Bar Mitzvah but before and after as well. "And he said: 'My father.' And he said: 'Here I am, my son'" (Gen. 22:7).

Abraham gave his son a "fancy party," but he also gave himself. Will we?

Law Is Law

William N. Ciner | 1952

In the 1960s, many Orthodox congregations hosted "mixed dancing" events. Young Israel congregations, it was alleged, "closed their eyes to such activities as mixed dancing," despite the fact that "few rabbinic authorities would sanction" them. It was not infrequent that at synagogue functions rabbis would knowingly depart early from events. Their departure would signal to the laypeople that husbands and wives were now free to dance together. By the 1980s, just a few Orthodox congregations allowed mixed dancing in the synagogue. One of the first to outlaw the practice was Kneseth Israel (the "White Shul") in Far Rockaway, New York. In 1952 William Ciner (1913–88) wrote a forceful letter in the synagogue bulletin that urged fellow members to end "social dancing" in favor of fidelity to Jewish law and rabbinic authority. A businessman for most of his career, Ciner served in a number of leadership positions in his Long Island congregation and within educational institutions.

Desecration of Jewish law and ritual by organizations, within the walls of the synagogue proper, represents one of the greatest hypocrisies current in present-day Jewish life. A wrong perpetrated by an individual may at times be ignored or considered uncontrollable. But what about group infidelity?

Shocking, would be the word, were we to permit a social gathering, within our building proper, on Sabbath eve. Deplorable, the word, were we not to take every precaution regarding Kashruth, in permitting an affair to take place in our synagogue. We, particularly, we orthodox Jews, would consider any such action outrageous and inexcusable, for we know the law. Any and all arguments to the contrary would only indicate ignorance of the law, for "law is law" and there is no deviation. Some would label us as fanatics, and we would resent it bitterly, for no arguments by any individual, or group of individuals, could compromise our laws. We expect to be respected for our sincerity and true belief. Yet do we respect the sincerity and true belief of others, as we expect to be respected?

There are many who are opposed to dancing in the synagogue. Their argument, the same as ours, is that "law is law." Shall we present arguments to the contrary? Shall we call them fanatics? Or shall we respect their sincerity and true belief?

We, as an orthodox congregation, profess to be the standard-bearers of Jewish traditions and principles. It is high time that we took cognizance of the fact that self-ridicule, amongst ourselves, ultimately leads to self-destruction. By scoffing at that which is precious, to others, in Judaism, are we not defeating the very purpose of our organization and our existence as a distinct people?

Let us not come to a hasty conclusion on this subject, but rather review it over carefully in our minds. For the records permit me to state that I have danced in synagogues. However, as your president, I should like to think that we all respect the belief of others, as we would like to have others respect ours, particularly when it is a question of law, for "Law is Law."

The Reacculturation of the "Yeshiva Student"
Ralph Pelcovitz | 1960

Ordained at Torah Vodaath in Brooklyn, New York, Rabbi Ralph Pelcovitz was one of the preeminent congregational rabbis in American Orthodox Judaism. In 1960 he described the difficulties he had encountered at Kneseth Israel (the "White Shul") in Far Rockaway with an emerging group of laypeople. Unlike the previous generation, this new crop of Orthodox men received an extensive Jewish education and did not feel that the social and educational programs that took place in Pelcovitz's "synagogue-center" catered to their needs. These young people consulted with scholars and heads of their yeshivot rather than turn to local congregational rabbis. Below is an excerpt from Pelcovitz's much-discussed article.

When a young man who has lived many years in a yeshivah environment moves into the newer city neighborhood or suburbia, he brings with him views and attitudes molded and fostered in that milieu. Among them is a certain *bitul* [nullification], a belittlement and disparagement of the modern manifestations of the American Jewish community. A major target of this attitude is the Synagogue-Center. The evolution of the modern shool [*sic*] into a social center, with religious activity shunted to the periphery, is an image firmly embedded in the mind-eye of the yeshivah student. His negative, almost antagonistic attitude borders on contempt, coupled with a determination to escape this distasteful communal affiliation and identification. This image is not dispelled, alas, in most cases and the alumnus, strengthened in his preconceived prejudices, shuns the shool and strikes his community roots elsewhere.

He would be pained and shocked if one would intimate that his point of view is one that could be termed "peace unto my soul and a plague on all your houses." It is so, nonetheless. Secession may grant him comfort and a cozy sense of superiority, but it creates more problems than it solves. Above all, it is a shattering of the fond dream entertained for years by responsible Jewish leaders, namely, that some day the yeshivah-trained layman would revolutionize our synagogue and change the face of our communities; within, not without, the framework of the synagogue.

In addition to the antipathy engendered in some yeshivoth toward the modern synagogue, regardless of its traditional structure and spirit, there is a characteristic of the yeshivah alumnus which serves as an added barrier between himself and orientation to a shool. This implanted yeshivah trait is an impatience with pomp and ceremony, formality, and ritual. One who has participated in a so-called yeshivah-davening for many years in the beth-hamidrosh [study hall] finds the average synagogue services quite uncomfortable. This service, with its attendant congregational singing, sermon, lengthy Torah reading, and insistence upon decorum, to name but a few encumbrances, is distasteful and tedious to the yeshivah-trained worshipper.

There are other motivations which are perhaps not as apparent or discernable, nor are they, in all candidness, usually admitted or expressed.

There may well be an understandable reluctance to do so. The *talmid cho-chom*, American style, finds it a mite unpleasant to be part of the mass, to be submerged and thereby lose his unique identity. He is disciplined to become indistinguishable from other members of the community.

This is, indeed, a form of intellectual snobbery, stemming from a sense of religious and academic superiority. Nonetheless, it is quite understandable and should be commiserated with rather than condemned. The yeshivah alumnus hungers for a degree of recognition. If a niche can be found for his talents he will usually emerge from his glorious isolation to receive his recognition and honor.

One should also mention in this connection an inherent unwillingness to accept the prosaic role of *baal-habayis* [layman], for it is somehow difficult for him to accept authority and discipline. It is paradoxical that the person who gladly accepts the authority and discipline of Torah finds it so difficult to accept the disciplines of society and the community. Since the discipline is perforce mandatory in any reputable, responsible synagogue it becomes a difficult obstacle, in the path of the yeshivah-trained layman, to overcome and surmount. Maturity is desperately needed to accept the role and rule of rabbi and lay leadership. Unfortunately, maturity is a rare attribute in today's world.

The Social Politics of Shul

Samuel C. Heilman | 1976

Two of the major social components of the Orthodox community are the post-Sabbath service "kiddush" and private Sabbath meals. After the conclusion of Sabbath prayers, male and female worshippers in most congregations retire to the synagogue social hall to recite the "kiddush" blessing over wine and liquor, chat, gossip, and snack on refreshments. In addition, families and couples host other Orthodox Jews at their homes for meals on Friday night and Saturday afternoon. Long ago, sociologist Samuel Heilman (b. 1946) described the social dynamics of these food forums in his study of the pseudonymous suburban congregation, Kehilath Kodesh.

The subject of Sabbath dinners deserves closer scrutiny. Rather than serendipitous events, invitations to such dinners are subject to a whole set of unspoken yet unbreachable conventions and procedures. Like a prestation, each invitation is subject to repayment, although not always in kind. Members of the same clique usually repay dinner for dinner. For every invitation received, another is tendered, always in alternating order; each succeeding invitation ensures that host and guest will be tied together in obligation.

Repayment for invitations from members who are not within the same clique may take other forms. Thus when a guest brings along a bottle of wine, flowers, chocolates, or some other gift, he is both repaying his host and signaling him not to expect a reciprocating dinner invitation. (Not all gifts guarantee this message, but gifts given by members of other cliques do.) In accepting the gift, the host acknowledges that the obligation has been paid off, with no other response expected.

The prestational quality of meals often requires one to take into account the menu. As Mary Douglas remarks, "Drinks are for strangers, acquaintances, workmen, and family. Meals are for family, close friends, honored guests."[8] At Kehilath Kodesh one might say: kiddush (cold meal, standup, an occasional hot hors d'oeuvre) is for all members of the shul; dinner (hot meal, several courses, sitdown) is for the members of one's clique. Repayment for an invitation to a meal may be made in the frame of a kiddush. No matter how lavish or filling the kiddush, it does not require repayment and serves to close an obligation that no material gift has closed. It is interesting to note that kiddush is the sort of meal tendered to the entire congregation. When a member sponsors a kiddush in shul, he does not impose invitation obligations on all those present. The lengthy discussion of the menu of such a kiddush is the members' way of evaluating the respect shown the group by the donor. However, the kiddush has become so standardized that little room is left for individual expression. Kiddush at home still allows for some expression of relationship. Some kiddushes may express little more than minimum necessary repayment (a few crackers, an alcoholic drink, a piece of cake); others express a closer bond between host and guest (a hot dish, herring, expensive foods); while, finally, the full-course meal expresses the closest linkage.

SECTION 3 | The "New" Orthodox Rabbi

My Return to the Rabbinate
Anonymous | 1968

The Orthodox rabbinate has evolved over time. In the immediate postwar period, Orthodox congregations hired rabbis to serve as eloquent preachers and teachers. In the 1960s, the Orthodox rabbinate developed a more intellectual bent while assuming other administrative responsibilities. For some, these pastoral and executive positions had little to do with the training they had received in rabbinical school. In 1968 an anonymous writer shared his odyssey from rabbinical disillusionment to an eventual return to the pulpit.

Preparing this paper has been a great effort for me. I am undertaking this task only because I feel that many of my younger colleagues and perhaps even a few of the older ones are engaged in an inner battle questioning the worthwhileness of their life's work. I shall try to analyze the reasons for my leaving the rabbinate, my experiences outside the rabbinate, and finally my decision to return to the pulpit.

An inventory of external circumstances cannot possibly have explained my inner quest. On the contrary, everything pointed to a most successful career. I was just completing my ninth year of service in a large congregation on the Eastern Seaboard. A year before my leaving, we completed the building of a million dollar structure; I was located a stone's throw from a prominent university; my salary was far above average; and a new contract made my position secure. I enjoyed the confidence of membership, and my wife and children were completely integrated into the life of the community. My dissatisfaction was not with the congregation but obviously with the rabbinate.

In retrospect, I now see that, undoubtedly, the inner tensions began with my Semicha. I had good cause to ask myself the fundamental question, "Am I really a Rov?" How could I answer in the affirmative? I always had with me a living image of a Rov. I didn't have to search hard; it was my father, a true talmid chochom filled with great piety, and ethical beyond all compromise. The comparison was literally frightening. I must admit that I considered myself unsuited. In knowledge, I was tolerably conversant with Halacha but, in no sense, a talmid chochom. In Yiras Shomayim [fear of heaven], I was well-intentioned but without the old-time fervor. Whenever I spent time with rabbonim [rabbis] of the old school, I was overwhelmed with their spirituality, wisdom, and total involvement in Torah.

I know that "Yiftach B'doro Kishmuel B'doro," that each generation creates the leaders best suited for its needs.[9] I am also aware that America's Jewry sorely needed leadership for which I was better qualified than the European-trained rov. Certainly, I possessed the means of communication, in terms of language and culture, best suited to establish a dialogue with the estranged. Yet I have always felt that these areas of proficiency did not excuse my tenuous rootedness in scholarship and piety. Precisely, because our modern generation is so alienated and illiterate, it behooves the rabbi to have greater Torah resources and deeper spiritual anchorage. Perhaps, I pondered, I would be a greater influence for Yiddishkeit as a layman. This then was my initial source of restlessness, my feelings of unworthiness compared to the Torah personalities we have been taught to admire.

This attitude of denigration of my role, together with the normal questions about the worthwhileness of my work, formulated my decision to leave. Attendance at Sabbath morning service remained nominal. Of a community of many hundreds, only a minute percentage attended. We tried various gimmicks which spurred attendance only sporadically. Our Friday night gatherings were much more substantial, but this was due to the guest speaker and alternating organizational sponsorship, together with the spirit of comradeship it generated. The actual religious phase was limited and diluted. In a word, in this area and in others, I did not regard my achievements as sufficiently noteworthy.

Personal counselling and hospital visitations took up my time. Was I effective? The members appreciated my efforts. But was it because of my effectiveness, I asked myself, or was it because in their minds I had some magical powers. Dozens of such questions gave me no rest.

It is strange, but the more successful I became, the more agonizing it became for me to remain in the rabbinate. The more honor and praise were heaped upon me, the cheaper I felt. I began to yearn for the peace and quiet of an anonymous existence. I dreamt of a job from 9:00 a.m. to 5:00 p.m. five days a week, living in suburbia, surrounded by a few good friends and making a comfortable living. The more I thought of the possibility, the more the thought appealed to me. When the opportunity came to me to enter the brokerage business, I broke the news to my wife and she reluctantly went along with my madness, and I abruptly handed in my resignation to the Synagogue.

I must admit that at first the novelty of my new world was exhilarating. We moved into a beautiful home, joined a synagogue, and I sat back enjoying the lack of pressure. The six-month training course was fun; it was going back to school with challenging and stimulating instructors in a totally new area of learning. I cannot say the same about the rough and tumble world of business. I believe that by now you recognize that this paper is written with the utmost frankness, and so you must take my word for the statement that is to follow. My disillusionment in business had nothing to do with the hardships of making a living. On the contrary, with each passing day the financial picture looked brighter. The day I left the brokerage business, I was the number one producer in my training class of forty-two brokers, and the firm offered me all types of inducements to remain in the business. At the most, it would have taken me two or three years to duplicate my rabbinic salary. I did not leave the rabbinate to become rich, nor did I return to the rabbinate to regain economic security. I came back because in a short time the pew taught me lessons which I couldn't possibly learn from the pulpit.

I must confess that it was a revelation that I didn't expect. I would like to share with you the following observations:

1. Only from the pulpit can you appreciate the great role of the rabbinate. I found that the rabbi in my congregation was very much like myself and very different from my father. He became a central figure in my life and in the life of my family. He did not overwhelm me with his Talmudic background, but he did teach me through his sermons and his classes. I found that they often became topics of conversation around the Sabbath table. We took his insights seriously, and his interpretations of the tradition did influence our thinking and our lives. His warmth and understanding made him a welcome figure in our home. We were delighted when he and his wife came to visit us, and our children were proud of our association with him. I doubt if he knows it, but he did have a positive effect upon our family.

2. When I attended services I found that I was bored with my "attendance game." My family and I were there; who cared how many other people were in the pews. The center was the Ark, the cantor, the rabbi.

3. The Synagogue school was no better and no worse than other religious schools. True, most children unfortunately will not be great Talmudists, but would they be better off without the Synagogue school? They were inspired to participate in the services, chant a Haftorah, and many were influenced to attend a Yeshiva. They developed love for Israel, ceremonies, holidays—that is, a general love for Judaism. Without a doubt we would have been much poorer without the rabbi, synagogue, or school.

4. I said that I craved anonymity, but it wasn't really the truth. Stay out of the rabbinate and see how you miss the prestige and the status. I recall how grateful I was to any colleague who asked me to preach or to teach. I even liked the pat on the back from the congregants. Lay activities simply do not take the place of leadership and influence in the community, though I did value working for the local Yeshiva. I just couldn't get myself to attend a Men's

Club smoker, or become an usher, or even join a ritual committee. I couldn't get myself to talk to them about the business world—it simply bored me. If not for my colleagues, I don't know what I would have done. I only felt sorry that they couldn't appreciate their important position.

5. I said that I wasn't sure about my effectiveness in involving myself in the lives of people. I found out that in normal circumstances the rabbi, because of his great prestige, could guide them to the proper sources for help. I began to miss the contact and involvement in the personal problems of people. I missed the satisfaction of meeting a couple before a marriage ceremony, of a teenager dropping into my study and unburdening himself, of consoling a mourner, of cheering up an invalid, and the many other opportunities of personal service. It is much more satisfying than the humdrum routine of selling and buying. I also became aware that I had been overly critical of my past achievements in the rabbinate in terms of spiritual accomplishments.

6. I also learned the great lesson that in every field of endeavor there are frustrations. How much creative activity is a doctor engaged in during the course of a day? I am told that ninety percent of the patients would get well if nature would take its course. It is the ten percent of usefulness that gives satisfaction to the physician. In years of practice, how many people does a psychiatrist help? How many pupils does a teacher inspire? How many exciting moments are there in the routine of business? Why should we demand constant satisfaction and fulfillment in our calling? Isn't it more than enough if a handful of our youngsters do go on to higher Jewish learning, communal leadership, and love for Judaism?

7. I felt guilty that whatever talents I had were being wasted. I merely substituted one set of pressures for other pressures. I no longer believe that there is a nine to five job. Sure, there are pressures of sermons, lectures, teaching, meetings, bulletin deadlines, etc. These, however, are for the most part pressures that stimulate the intellect. I could now understand why men in the business

world hardly ever read or relax. Believe me, the mind continues to work way beyond five o'clock. The guilt of leaving the rabbinate took on some unusual forms. I recall my determination to attend a Board of Rabbis meeting, and I got as far as the door and then turned back. I constantly lived with the thought that I had betrayed a sacred task.

8. The "Rov" has his place and we have our role. My father is a scholar and saint, but he is not the Gaon of Vilna. Professional roles change in every generation. I am a product of the modern generation, and I can cope with the problems of my contemporaries. My children and their friends respect my father, but they don't understand him. I am convinced now that they need me.

I swallowed my pride and decided after one year in the business world to return to the rabbinate. I spent a year working with a Jewish organization, but I knew that it was only a temporary arrangement.

Today I am back in the pulpit much more sober and much more grateful for the opportunity to serve again. I relish every moment of it. I love the preaching, teaching, counselling, administering, and all the other manifold demands. I find that the two years of leave were a blessing in disguise. Nothing seems burdensome and everything seems meaningful. There are bound to be frustrations, pettiness, but all these will add up to a day's work.

A Hero for the "Religiously Apathetic"
Steven "Shlomo" Riskin | 1972

In 1964 Steven "Shlomo" Riskin (b. 1940) was appointed the founding rabbi of Lincoln Square Synagogue on New York's Upper West Side. Earlier Riskin had established himself as one of the leading outreach and educational leaders within the Orthodox orbit. At Lincoln Square, the rabbi recruited hundreds of religiously disenchanted young people to attend Sabbath and holiday prayer services. In short order, Jewish and non-Jewish observers took notice of Riskin's ability to bring young adults to Orthodox Judaism, including Time *magazine, which published an article on Riskin in 1971. Unlike Chabad and other Ultra-Orthodox outreach organizations, Riskin enchanted his followers with his Modern Orthodox point of view. "The rabbi is something that God has given to us" was a refrain rehearsed by many Lincoln Square worshippers. In the essay below, Riskin explained the motivation for his outreach work.*

In the contemporary American orthodox Jewish scene there have emerged two distinct attitudes towards the non-orthodox: the one may be called isolationist and the other expansionist. The former maintains that, like the Biblical Noah, we have neither the strength nor the resources to concern ourselves with the non-committed. All that we can hope to achieve is the establishment of our own ark, our own sectarian institutions and even communities, in the hope of rescuing ourselves and our families from the flood of secularism seeking to inundate us. The expansionists, on the other hand, seek to emulate our Patriarch Abraham by reaching out actively to the non-orthodox in an attempt to convince them of our divine *Weltanschauung* and persuade them to adopt our way of life. . . .

. . . The concept of *onus* (one who has been forced to commit a transgression against his will) may very well be extended to include those who have rejected aspects of Jewish law and theology due to the emotional pressures of our age or even due to heterodox intellectual conviction. If one would draw this concept to its logical conclusion it might mean a total rethinking of our category of culpability and punishment. At the very least it demands that we have neither the moral nor legal right to exclude the majority of American Jewry from our agonizing concern. We dare not build Noah's ark merely for the preservation of our orthodox colleagues. We dare not encourage an attitude of cynicism and disdain towards those Synagogue rabbis, educators, and laymen attempting to call back our wayward brethren.[10] And most important, each and every orthodox Jew must awaken to his personal responsibility to enter into religious fields of endeavor and, at the very least, to attempt to reach out to those who are Jews in name only.

And there is no question in my mind that we can succeed.

We are living in an age of unprecedented religious interest and concern alongside of the radical theologians and secular city–situation ethic enthusiasts. The Yavneh organization which has successfully brought Torah Study and kosher kitchens to countless campuses, the Orthodox Union's NCSY movement and its events, and Yeshiva University's youth seminars, which have introduced so many youngsters to Torah-true Judaism, as well as the honest search for values and meaning which lies behind the hippie movement and many LSD tripsters all point towards the opportunities which lie before us. First we must have the will and then we must create the vocabulary and the means to speak persuasively to those waiting for our message. . . . In our modern age of religious apathy and intellectual turmoil, we must contain every Jew—despite his avowed heresies and intemperate behavior—within the banner of K'lal Yisroel and never yield our obligation and privilege to restore for him the vital teachings of his religion.

Needed: Clinical Pastoral Training

Sherman P. Kirshner | 1988

In the 1980s, rabbis and congregants replaced the "scholar-rabbi" with the "pastor-rabbi." With greater frequency, rabbinic search committees asked Orthodox seminaries to supply them with candidates who possessed excellent pastoral skills and deemphasized the importance of intellectual attainment. This point was made in its clearest form by Rabbi Sherman Kirshner (1934–2011), who was ordained at the Hebrew Theological College in Chicago and served a number of pulpits in the Midwest.

Jewish seminaries of all trends have been relatively slow to teach "Pastoral Psychology and Counseling."[11] Although random courses in Behavioral Sciences are offered by some, I am very proud that my Alma Mater, The Hebrew Theological College—Jewish University of America, Skokie, Illinois, foresaw the great need and the urgency of Master's and Doctoral programs in Pastoral Counseling. Our Yeshivot and Seminaries would do well to seriously consider the establishment of such programs as part of the curriculum. Our rabbinic students would derive great benefit by learning to counsel skillfully and successfully.

Several years ago, I sat on a Placement Committee for rabbis. Almost every discussion entered into with a variety of congregational representatives portrayed a snag in personalities with rabbi and congregants. Never was there mention made of the candidate's inability to preach effectively, to conduct a class for adults or youngsters, or to perform any of the rabbinic duties normally expected. Rather, the committee would complain of a gross lack of understanding between personalities.

What troubles me especially is that we Jews were always at the forefront of new and exciting ways of learning. I believe that the time has come for our institutions of Higher Jewish Learning to teach a total program of Pastoral Psychology and Counseling leading to a degree in this field. Rabbis and other Jewish professionals are entitled to a deeper insight and understanding of the human psyche. It will prove invaluable to them in their daily dealings with community members and to understand them better and counsel effectively.

CONCLUSION

In 1956 Rabbi Emanuel Rackman was one of the first to recognize Orthodoxy's shift away from the synagogue to fund and focus on schools and other institutions. He described the move as conscious, a way to "prevent the institutionalized synagogue from turning Judaism into a temple cult," a condition that Rackman believed was well under way in Conservative and Reform circles. To curtail this, explained the rabbi, "Orthodoxy today is transferring its prime emphasis from the synagogue to the school."[12] Despite Rackman's claims, most Orthodox Jews did not notice the change for another decade. In the 1960s, a number of Orthodox writers weighed in on the transfer of rabbinic authority from the congregational rabbi to the deans—*roshei yeshiva*—of the leading yeshivot and advanced academies.[13] For the next decade, rabbis fought to remain relevant in the lives of congregants who viewed their "synagogue-centers" as a place to network and socialize with fellow Orthodox Jews as well as a religious space for prayer and study. A few like Rabbi Shlomo Riskin managed to spark interest and recruit young Jews to the synagogue. Increasingly, though, Orthodox Jews encountered their religion in their children's day schools and at night as they reviewed their sons' and daughters' homework assignments. In response, the rabbinate attempted to assert itself in the far more private sphere of the Jewish home.

10 | The State of Orthodox Belief

After World War II, Orthodox Jews ventured into the suburbs and competed with the other religious movements for adherents. Often suburban Jews invited representatives of Orthodox, Reform, and Conservative Judaism to sit on panels and publicly advocate for their respective movements. In most cases, the middle-of-the-road Conservative rabbi held a viewpoint that was most in concert with his audiences.[1] Still, this did not stop Orthodox leaders from formulating theological expositions that could resonate with the impressionable Jewish hinterland communities.

Like their Christian counterparts, rabbis felt the need to offer manuals that provided accessible "introductions" to Jewish religion. Orthodox writers participated in this enterprise, and the most successful by far was Pulitzer Prize–winning novelist Herman Wouk (b. 1915). His best-selling *This Is My God* (1959) was syndicated in major newspapers like the *Los Angeles Times* and reviewed in nearly every Jewish periodical. In 1960 a journalist reported that Wouk's Orthodox Jewish manual had "won such wide acceptance during the pre-holiday buying that it is safe to assume both Christians and Jews welcomed it."[2] In response, hundreds of rabbis of all types addressed the author's descriptions of a religion that portended to represent all of Judaism but in reality spoke for Orthodoxy. Accordingly, it was the Orthodox community that heaped the greatest praise on Wouk's work. In short order, one rabbinic writer produced a "study guide" to *This Is My God,* to be used by Jewish book clubs.[3] Other writers attempted to aid the Orthodox cause with their own religious manuals. No doubt, some Orthodox ideologues knew more about Jewish literature and dogma than Wouk, and they did their best to share their knowledge at various symposiums and forums. Yet it was Wouk, with his clever prose, who was most successful.

In many instances, Orthodox writers proffered their views on Halakhah rather than theology, for they understood Judaism as a religion of "deed," not "creed." Most notably, this was evident in the writings of Rabbi Joseph Soloveitchik. However, the discussions on the flexibility and rigidity of Jewish law stood out in this period as the liveliest form of religious debate within the Orthodox camp. Consequently, the second section in this chapter addresses the debates that surrounded interpretation of Jewish law. True, this issue was not appealing to the suburban congregations who had other priorities, such as determining with what denomination their newly built synagogues should identify. For Orthodox insiders, though, this was the most daunting philosophical quest for Modern Orthodox Judaism to consider.

SECTION 1 | What Does Orthodoxy Believe?

The Core of Judaism

Herman Wouk | 1959

In the late 1950s, Herman Wouk was perhaps the best known Orthodox Jew in the United States. In 1959 the famed novelist published a nonfiction portrait of Jewish life. The work, unmistakably Orthodox in its presentation, was celebrated by Orthodox rabbis but sharply criticized by non-Orthodox leaders who believed the book to be misleading and unrepresentative of the majority of America's Jews. Consequently, Wouk's This Is My God *signaled the beginning of Orthodox triumphalism. The book remained on the* New York Times Best Sellers *list for several months and was syndicated in the* Los Angeles Times. *In this excerpt, Wouk offered his reasons for belief.*

I have on my desk a letter from an agnostic friend, part of a running correspondence many years old. Says he, "What is the *core* of being a Jew: to be different in living habits, or to practice a moral way of life based on behavior toward other people? To imply that in some significant measure the terrible problems of social existence on a crowded planet are solved by refusing to eat lobsters seems irretrievably petty to me."

The pious reader may not agree, but I think this is excellently put. Once I think I made a similar point, though much more crudely, about naval service. I had been a midshipman for a couple of weeks, and I was nailed with a demerit for incorrect use of words. I growled to my roommate as the tyrannical ensign walked off, "How will it help beat the Japanese if I call a staircase a ladder?"

I eventually learned to do so. It is not my impression that I thereby advanced the surrender ceremonies in Tokyo Bay, say from September fifth to September second. But I am pretty sure that I became a useful naval officer in part by learning the lingo; and whatever minute service I gave toward that surrender, I gave it as a naval officer.

Possibly because the navy meant so much in my life, I have always thought that the Jewish place among mankind somewhat resembles the position of navy men among other Americans. Are the sailors and officers less American because they are in the navy? They have special commitments and disciplines, odd ways of dress, sharp limits on their freedom. They have, at least in their own minds, compensations of glory, or of vital service performed. The Jews are not cut off from mankind by their faith, though they are marked different. They have their special disciplines, and—at least in their own minds—their rewards.

I remember being looked up to as a naval officer in wartime; then when peace came and I travelled to take my Reserve cruises, people in trains and planes tended to regard me as an unfortunate misfit. One or two actually said, "How come you're still in?" I think that is essentially the question that agnostics address to observant Jews.

We are still in, I suppose, because we take it on faith that the law of Moses is from God, and our observation tells us that the patterns of the law help keep our tiny folk in life, in the grand sweep of history. We share the hope of our fathers that out of our tiny folk, in some way none of us can foresee, the light of lasting peace will someday come. I cannot produce the Messiah. But in my sons, as Providence allows, I can produce two informed Jews who will keep alive that hope beyond my life.

My friend's question, then, answers itself. The core of Judaism is right conduct to other people. The Talmud (if I am not growing too anecdotal here) tells that a Gentile came to the Rabbi Hillel and asked to be taught all Judaism while standing on one foot. Hillel's colleague, Shammai, had driven the man from his door, taking the question for a baiting impertinence. Hillel amiably replied, "What is offensive to you do not do to others. That is the core of Judaism. The rest is commentary. Now carry on your studies." The man became a convert (Shabbat 31a).

The core of a nuclear reactor, or of an apple, or of a religion, is not all of it. We make few core-decisions day by day. Life is too packed with running trivialities, with mechanical repetition. Judaism does not let that part of life go. It weaves commitment, and therefore at least formal significance, all through one's day. It is perfectly true that Gentile and Jew alike have sometimes taken the forms for the core. Hence on one hand the agnostic disapproval of the faith because of its "petty concern with ceremony." Hence on the other hand the ultra-orthodox who will not recognize the State of Israel because its government members are not all pious. But if a way of life be judged by its misinterpreters, which way will stand?

Minimal Set of Principles

Leonard B. Gewirtz | 1961

Rabbi Leonard Gewirtz (1918–2003) was the longtime spiritual leader of Adas Kodesch Shel Emeth Congregation in Wilmington, Delaware. A graduate of Hebrew Theological College in Chicago, the self-professing "Traditional" rabbi studied ethics at the University of Chicago. In his 1961 manual on Judaism, Gewirtz outlined a "set of principles" on God, Torah, and the Jewish people that he believed conformed to the "authentic" beliefs of Judaism. His more rigid presentation was typical of the Orthodox rabbinate in this period and probably less appealing than Herman Wouk's more colorful prose.

Here is a set of minimal principles for authentic Jews who are not yet prepared to accept and follow maximal traditional Judaism. Unlike other declarations of minimal principles, these are designed to help the average American Jew come closer to Judaism to return to God and His Torah. They are, of course, not final, but only tentative.

God—In our mystical literature, we have this profound statement: "God, Torah, and Israel are One." We believe in the reality of God because we see His influence in the beauty and orderliness of nature. "The heavens declare the glory of God and the firmament showeth his handiwork," says the psalmist (Ps. 19:2). The rabbis in a deeply religious mood taught: "The non-believer even when alive is considered dead, because he sees the sun rise and does not pronounce the blessing, 'Blessed art Thou, O Lord Our God, King of the Universe, who formest light and created darkness, who makest peace and createst all things.' He eats, drinks, and does not bless the Name. But the believers—the *Tzadikim*—bless everything they eat, drink, see, and hear."[4] Do the Rabbis really mean that merely by refraining from pronouncing any blessing a man becomes a Rosha [wicked] and is considered dead? Rather this seems to be the true meaning: The non-believer is dead *spiritually* to the extent that he does not sense the mystery inherent in the rising and setting of the sun and does not feel the need to recite a blessing to God. The non-believer is spiritually dead because he looks upon a wonder of nature as a mechanical thing; he does not behold the divine interlaced in all that is about him. Elizabeth Barrett Browning expressed the spiritual death of him who does not see in the following words:

> "Earth's crammed with heaven and every common bush afire
>   with God.
> But only he who sees, takes off his shoes."[5]

The God we believe in as Jews is the Creator. "In the beginning God created Heaven and earth" (Gen. 1:1). Yet our God is not a distant Being who once created a vast universe and is now indifferent to its needs. He is *Avinu*, Our Father. He is not only our God, but the God of Abraham, of Isaac, and of Jacob. He is the God who took our forefathers out of Egypt, who gave us our Torah. He is our Father in

Heaven who is "near to those who call upon Him, to all who call upon Him sincerely" (Ps. 145:18).

Torah—We also believe in Torah because we feel that God, Who is good and Who created man, would want to help man by showing him how to live. God has done this, as we believe, through the Torah.

The Orthodox believe that the *Chumash*, the Five Books of Moses, word for word, was dictated by God to Moses, and these words are divine. The non-orthodox consider the Torah "divinely inspired," written by men under a spell of inspiration. Divine inspiration, to the non-orthodox, is a figure of speech. Shakespeare, too, was truly inspired when he wrote his great dramas, as is any poet or philosopher, or any writer in his moments of creativity. Does this mean we must try to live by the words of every artist in language, every teller of tales?

The *Chumash*, though written by Moses, is the result of a "dialogue," a meeting between God and man. When a man under the impact of God's presence sees the "burning bush" and takes off his shoes, surely this man is receiving a revelation. And when, through all Jewish history, the great spiritual leaders of Judaism saw the "Earth crammed with heaven and every common bush afire with God," surely the Torah they helped create and write, the Torah they taught and lived by, is as revealed as anything can ever be revealed by God to Man.

When our God-intoxicated men, our spiritual giants, wrote down their great pronouncements under the impact of their encounter with God, they left us documents of a direct personal meeting. These documents contain eyewitness information of a revelation, of a God given truth. This is our Torah as it was studied through all generations. And those who studied and imbibed it were themselves seared and singed in their hearts and souls. For this is the power of the revealed word that comes from God.

This Torah—the term includes both our Bible and our Talmudic-rabbinic literature—is the link connecting man to God. Between man and God there are for us no saints, no sons, no mothers. As Jews, we believe there is nothing between man and God other than the Torah, the most perfect revelation of God to man, to bind man to God.

Israel—We also believe in Israel. In classic Jewish theology this concept is based on the "Election" of Israel or Israel as the "Chosen People." Reform Judaism accepts the Orthodox doctrine of the chosenness of Israel. Mordecai Kaplan rejects this view for a very naïve reason: the world, he says, has too much chauvinism and we Jews ought to set a good example of tolerance by discarding our doctrine of the "Chosen People." But this whole approach is irrelevant as well as irreverent.[6]

. . . Authentic Judaism emphasizes unity among God, Torah, and Israel. Israel loves God and Torah, God loves Torah and Israel, Torah loves God and Israel. To be an authentic Jew, then, means loving Israel (Ahavas Yisroel), loving the Torah of Israel (Ahavas Toras Yisroel), and loving the God of Israel (Ahavas Elokai Yisroel).

These three loves are the basis for a minimal program for authentic Jews who take their Jewishness seriously, who are willing to ponder and study as they make their way back to Judaism.

The State of Orthodox Belief—An Open View
Marvin Fox | 1966

In 1966 a popular Jewish monthly magazine, Commentary, *submitted surveys to fifty-five rabbis; one-fifth of those queried identified as Orthodox Jews. The editors posed five questions. They asked the religious leaders about the role of Judaism in politics and about the differences between Judaism and other religions like Christianity and Islam and Buddhism. The editors also queried rabbis on the viability of Judaism in the modern secular age. Yet perhaps two questions were the most confrontational. First: "In what sense do you believe that the Jews are the chosen people of God?" Second: "How do you answer the charge that this doctrine is the model from which various theories of national and racial superiority have been derived?" One of the respondents was Marvin Fox (1922–96), a philosopher at Ohio State University. He was also a leading member of a group of young academics who paved important inroads for Orthodox Jews in American universities. In 1974 Fox moved to Brandeis University, where he maintained a larger public profile. His answers to the magazine revealed the philosopher's open-mindedness to major tenets of Jewish faith and a modest hesitation to offer firm positions on these matters.*

(1) It is essential to distinguish between the metaphysical aspects of revelation and the practical implications of revelation. With respect to both I believe in the traditional doctrine of *Torah min ha-shamayim*, the teaching that the Torah is divine. I also follow the tradition which allows great latitude in our theological understanding of the nature of revelation while insisting on rigorous adherence to fixed norms of behavior.

No one can reasonably claim to understand how God reveals Himself to man. The very idea of revelation leads us to paradoxes which defy rational explanation. We cannot make fully intelligible in the language of human experience how the eternal enters into the temporal world of man, or how the incorporeal is apprehended by corporeal beings. Yet we affirm in faith what we cannot explicate, for our very humanity is at stake. I believe, because I cannot afford not to believe. I believe, as a Jew, in the divinity of Torah, because without God's Torah I have lost the ground for making my own life intelligible and purposeful.

To believe because life demands it is not peculiar to religious men. It is something that reasonable men do as a matter of course in other areas. For example, most men in Western society believe that there is some necessary relationship between reason and reality, though no decisive evidence can be offered for this conviction. They hold to it because if the world does not conform to human reason, then it is unintelligible, and we find that an unbearable state of affairs. Rather than face the pain of an unintelligible world, we affirm, as an act of faith, that it must be rationally ordered. We insist that whatever reason finds necessary must be the case in reality and whatever reason finds impossible can never be the case in reality. And we do so rightly, for with anything less our lives would become a hopeless chaos. The same holds true of the Jew who believes in the Torah as divine, even while acknowledging that he has and can have no decisive evidence. He believes because the order, structure, direction, and meaning of his life are at stake, because the alternative is personal and moral chaos. He believes because all that he finds precious hangs in the balance—the quality, substance, and texture of his own existence. His belief is not formulated as a set of dogmatic propositions. It is, rather, *emunah*, trust in God and in the tradition of the community of Israel. In that trust the believing Jew finds the ground of his own existence and opens himself to unique and exalted possibilities. In that trust he discovers that the truly human is a reflection of the divine, a discovery which has the power to transform and sanctify man and his world.

In affirming such a belief in revelation, I make no specific claim about the way in which revelation took place, except the traditional one that the biblical prophets are its only valid channel. Moses holds a unique place among these prophets, and through him the Torah was transmitted to the community of Israel. Because prophecy transcends my own experience, I cannot read the biblical descriptions of the prophetic vision in simple literal terms. Jewish tradition offers ample precedent for understanding the Torah in symbolic or metaphorical terms. The text, of course, must be studied perceptively and with meticulous care, but this is not to say that it is to be read in literal or fundamentalist fashion. . . .

In effect this suggests a wide range of ways in which we might formulate our admittedly inadequate ideas of revelation. Presumably, a highly sophisticated philosopher or theologian will view the matter differently from an unlearned man of simple faith. What all affirm, if they stand in the normative tradition, is that God has addressed us through His prophets. I share fully this classical Jewish belief.

In noting the latitude and diversity of theological understanding, it was not my intention to suggest that there are no limits or boundaries. As a believing Jew, I conceive of revelation as including *Torah she-be'al peh,* the oral tradition. Here we find the valid Jewish guides to understanding the theological as well as the legal teachings of the Torah. The range of possible approaches to revelation is rooted in and defined by this oral Torah.

While allowing diversity of theological insight, I also follow the tradition in holding that all the commandments of the Torah are binding upon every Jew. To know what these commandments are, we must again appeal to the oral tradition which continues to unfold through all the generations of Jewish history. The judgments and decisions of recognized and qualified Torah scholars have the binding force of law, for they are the very substance of Torah. Hence, I accept not only the 613 commandments of the written Torah, but equally the explication of those commandments through the oral Torah. In fact, we cannot know clearly what is intended by the commandments of the Torah except through the teaching of the oral tradition. Here, in contrast to the abstractions of theology, we have a clear and concrete pattern of practice. Of course, there are disputed questions concerning practice also, but for these there is a clear technique for decision. It is this unified pattern of religious behavior which binds us as Jews. Through the fulfillment of God's commandments we serve Him, express our love for Him, and achieve the ultimate purpose of Jewish existence—the sanctification of our lives. . . .

(2) Just as I do not claim to understand revelation, I do not claim to understand fully how the Jews were chosen by God, for this is itself an element of revelation. However, I believe in the chosenness of the Jewish people, both because the Torah affirms it and because our history justifies it. For the Jews to have been chosen suggests nothing whatsoever about their superiority. Nowhere in the Torah is the doctrine of the chosen people based on claims of special merit or natural superiority. On the contrary, the people of Israel are depicted in all of their human weakness. Consider the first generation after the Exodus from Egypt. They worship the golden calf immediately after the revelation at Sinai. They are exposed as a nation of whining complainers constantly dissatisfied with life in the desert. They are so lacking in faith that a whole generation must perish before they are fit to enter their promised land. Surely these are not claims to national or racial superiority. What was true of the first generation was, unhappily, all too often true of later generations, and for their sinfulness they earned the rebukes and the chastisement of the prophets. This supposedly superior people blames itself for its exile and the devastation of its land and records this blame in its own official literature.

As to the claim that this doctrine is the model for modern racialist theories, one can only dismiss it as a malicious distortion. The evidence is so well known and so commonplace that one hesitates to cite it. There is a long list of outstanding Jewish sages—men whose names are honored and whose teachings are revered—who were not of Jewish birth but became converts to the Jewish faith. Others of great eminence are held to be descended from converts. Above all, the biblical record speaks for itself. King David, ancestor of the Messiah, is a direct descendant of Ruth, a Moabite woman converted to the Jewish faith. It is hard to imagine any more vigorous rejection of racialism.

What, then, is intended in the doctrine that the Jews are a people chosen by God? They were chosen, for reasons we cannot fully fathom, to bring mankind the message of God's existence and His teachings. "Ye are my witnesses saith the Lord" (Isa. 43:10). It is the task of the Jews to serve as teachers and models for mankind. Their duty is to bear witness to the truth of God both by their explicit teaching and by the quality of their lives. If this is a privilege it is also a burden. It confers no special rights, only special responsibilities. We were chosen to receive the Torah, commanded to live in accordance with its precepts, and thereby to bring divine truth into the world.

It is only honest to recognize that Jews have sometimes been guilty of arrogance and self-satisfaction. They have at times imagined that they were chosen because of their innate superiority. Such distasteful attitudes deserve only contempt and condemnation, though they are an understandable reaction to the oppression which Jews have so often suffered. Patriotism is easily distorted into ultranationalism or chauvinism, but this should not lead reasonable men to reject honest patriotism as evil. Nor should we feel forced to reject the classical image of the Jews as chosen to witness to God, merely because it can be distorted into racialism or smugness and pride.

The State of Orthodox Belief—A Less-Open View
Immanuel Jakobovits | 1966

In contrast to Marvin Fox, Rabbi Immanuel Jakobovits (1921–99) of the Fifth Avenue Synagogue in New York shared his more forceful answers to the Commentary *questions. Like Fox, the future Chief Rabbi of the British Commonwealth was a "moderate" within Orthodox Judaism's rabbinic and scholarly ranks. However, in this presentation Jakobovits reflected a trend among Orthodox leaders to espouse their beliefs in more definitive terms.*

(1) To me the belief in *Torah min ha-shamayim* (the divine revelation of the Torah), in its classical formulation by Maimonides, represents a definition of the essence of Judaism as inalienable as the postulate of monotheism. Until the rise of the Reform movement in 19th-century Germany, this axiom of Judaism was never challenged or varied by any Jewish thinker or movement, whether traditional or sectarian.

Torah min ha-shamayim essentially means that the Pentateuch as we have it today is identical with the Torah revealed to Moses at Mount Sinai and that this expression of God's will is authentic, final, and eternally binding upon the Jewish people. Immaterial to this belief is the mode in which the Torah was communicated to Moses—whether by "dictation," "verbal inspiration," or some other mystic communion peculiar to prophecy.

But intrinsic to this doctrine, as painstakingly emphasized by Maimonides, is the equal sanctity of all parts of the Torah and of all its laws. To my mind, this is dictated by reason no less than by the explicit claims of the Torah and its classic exponents. Any substantive division between ethical and ritual laws is arbitrary and altogether foreign to the text and religious philosophy of the Scriptures. Both types of laws are featured quite indiscriminately in the Ten Commandments and throughout the Torah (see especially Leviticus 19) as well as in the Prophets and the Talmud. In Judaism's penal legislation, too, ritual and ethics are treated alike; every offense against man at the same time constitutes a sin against God requiring ritual atonement, while any religious transgression is also a crime against society. All biblical laws equally derive their validity from their revelation by God. "Love thy neighbor as thyself" is a norm of virtue only because "I am the Lord [who commands it]" (Lev. 19:18), and the social statutes of the Torah have the same Sinaitic origin and *raison d'être* as the ritual precepts (*par excellence*) about the altar (Ex. 20:21), as several exegetes are careful to stress.

This is fundamental rather than purely fundamentalistic. If ethical laws were good, immutable, and divine because their virtue is manifest to reason, intuition, conscience, or any other human faculty, or if the validity of any law in the Torah were subject to human discrimination— accepting those as "divine" which appeal to our present-day notions and rejecting as "man-made" those we do not understand—the whole structure of Judaism as a revealed religion would collapse. We would create a god in man's own image; for man, not God, would determine what is "divine" law, using Him only as a rubber stamp to "authenticate" purely human judgments. Judaism stands or falls by the heteronomy of the law: "*He* hath told thee, O man, what is good" (Mic. 6:8), not the reverse.

Moreover, any system of ethics contingent upon the arbitrary and fickle whims of the human consensus (which varies from time to time and from one individual to another) would lack all virtue as well as true religiosity. Relying on man's reason, intuition, or utility as its source and compulsion, such a system would make the interests of man and his faculties the ultimate object of his service. In the significant words of Maimonides, good conduct determined by "the verdict of the intellect" rather than by revelation might be "wise" (expedient) but could never be "saintly" (meritorious) (Hil. Melakhim 8:11).

(2) Yes, I do accept the chosen people concept as affirmed by Judaism in its holy writ, its prayers, and its millennial tradition. In fact, I believe every people—and indeed, in a more limited way, every individual—is "chosen" or destined for some distinct purpose in advancing the designs of Providence. Only some fulfill their assignment and others do not.

Maybe the Greeks were chosen for their unique contributions to art and philosophy, the Romans for their pioneering services in law and government, the British for bringing parliamentary rule into the world, and the Americans for piloting democracy in a pluralistic society.

The Jews were chosen by God to be "peculiar unto Me" as the pioneers of religion and morality; that was and is their national purpose. From this choice flow certain privileges (above all, the perennial survival of Israel and its role in the messianic consummation of man's final destiny) and obligations (such as self-discipline through the *mitzvot* and frequently martyrdom). This concept, more than any other, has sustained the Jewish resolve to remain distinct in the face of endless persecution and in defiance of tempting (or violent) inducements to merge with the majority. And this concept has inspired the will to submit to a severely exigent code of laws (hence the mention of the "chosen people" promise, and not of any other reward, immediately prior to the revelation at Sinai [Ex. 19:5]).

I think few factors are more deleterious to Jewish life today than the widespread rejection of this "chosen-ness." The humblest Jew in the Middle Ages had a greater awareness of his and his people's indispensable part in realizing the prophetic vision of human perfection than most Jewish leaders have in our times.

Without the incentive of serving a (religiously and morally) superior purpose, the Jewish commitment to that purpose—individually and nationally—was bound to give way to leading an "ordinary" existence like others, just as Americans, deprived of the belief in the superiority of "the American way of life," would lose the distinctiveness of their national genius and cease to shoulder their special burdens in the world. Only the promise of a "chosen" role can educe the ambition and energy needed for exacting tasks and ideals.

The Jewish "chosen people" idea has nothing to do with national or racial superiority as currently understood. The idea never justified, or led to, discrimination against strangers in Jewish law, expansionism or political domination in Jewish history, or conversionist aspirations in Jewish theology. It was invariably directed at exacting greater sacrifices from the Jew, not at imposing them on the non-Jew.

Halakhic Man and the Mathematician

Joseph B. Soloveitchik | 1944

In 1944 Rabbi Joseph Soloveitchik authored perhaps his most important essay. In his book Halakhic Man *the "Rav" argued for a Jewish theology that was based on the process of fulfillment and study of Halakhah. His non-Orthodox critics accused Soloveitchik of restating traditional Jewish positions in updated Kantian terms. Yet those who managed to grasp the 1944 essay in its original Hebrew form understood that Soloveitchik had accomplished much more. As this excerpt indicates, Soloveitchik compared the halakhist's quest for truth with the mathematician. Both make use of a system of rules and postulates to "examine empirical reality." For Soloveitchik, the "halakhic man" is not merely someone who observes the dictates of Jewish law, but rather an individual who rigorously studies his reality with the "apparatus" supplied to him by the Talmud and other rabbinic codes. In this view, the "halakhic man" is similar to other scientists and philosophers who work within a specific system and frame of reference.*

When halakhic man approaches reality, he comes with his Torah, given to him from Sinai, in hand. He orients himself to the world by means of fixed statutes and firm principles. An entire corpus of precepts and laws guides him along the path leading to existence. Halakhic man, well furnished with rules, judgments, and fundamental principles, draws near the world with an a priori relation. His approach begins with an ideal creation and concludes with a real one. To whom can he be compared? To a mathematician who fashions an ideal world and then uses it for the purpose of establishing a relationship between it and the real world, as was explained above. The essence of the Halakhah, which was received from God, consists in creating an ideal world and cognizing the relationship between that ideal world and our concrete environment in all its visible manifestations and underlying structures. There is no phenomenon, entity, or object in this concrete world which the a priori Halakhah does not approach with its ideal standard. When halakhic man comes across a spring bubbling quietly, he already possesses a fixed, a priori relationship with this real phenomenon: the complex of laws regarding the halakhic construct of a spring. The spring is fit for the immersion of a *zav* (a man with a discharge); it may serve as *mei ḥatat* (waters of expiation); it purifies with flowing waters; it does not require a fixed quantity of forty se'ahs, etc. When halakhic man approaches a real spring, he gazes at it and carefully examines its nature. He possesses, a priori, ideal principles and precepts which establish the character of the spring as a halakhic construct, and he uses the statutes for the purpose of determining normative law; does the real spring correspond to the requirements of the ideal Halakhah or not?

Halakhic man is not overly curious, and he is not particularly concerned with cognizing the spring as it is in itself. Rather, he desires to coordinate the a priori concept with the a posteriori phenomenon.

When halakhic man looks to the western horizon and sees the fading rays of the setting sun or to the eastern horizon and sees the first light of dawn and the glowing rays of the rising sun, he knows that this sunset or sunrise imposes upon him anew obligations and commandments. Dawn and sunrise obligate him to fulfill those commandments that are performed during the day: the recitation of the morning *Shema, tzitzit, tefillin,* the morning prayer, *etrog, shofar, Hallel,* and the like. They make the time fit for the carrying out of certain halakhic practices: Temple service, acceptance of testimony, conversion, *ḥalitzah,* etc., etc.[7] Sunset imposes upon him those obligations and commandments that are performed during the night: the recitation of the evening *Shema, matzah,* the counting of the *omer,* etc.[8] The sunset on Sabbath and holiday eves sanctifies the day: the profane and the holy are dependent upon a natural cosmic phenomenon—the sun sinking below the horizon. It is not anything transcendent that creates holiness but rather the visible reality—the regular cycle of the natural order. Halakhic man examines the sunrise and sunset, the dawn and the appearance of the stars; he gazes into the horizon—Is the upper horizon pale and the same as the lower?—and looks at the sun's shadows—Has afternoon already arrived? When he goes out on a clear, moonlit night (until the deficiency of the moon is replenished) he makes a blessing upon it. He knows that it is the moon that determines the times of the months and thus of all the Jewish seasons and festivals, and this determination must rely upon astronomical calculations.

. . . Halakhic man explores every nook and cranny of physical-biological existence. He determines the character of all of the animal functions of man—eating, sex, and all the bodily necessities—by means of halakhic principles and standards: the bulk of an olive (ke-zayit), the bulk of a date (ke-kotevet), the time required to eat a half-loaf meal (kedai akhilat peras), the time required to drink a quarter log (revi'it), eating in a normal or nonnormal manner, the beginning of intercourse, the conclusion of intercourse, normal intercourse and unnatural intercourse, etc., etc.[9] Halakhah concerns itself with the normal as well as abnormal functioning of the organism, with the total biological functioning of the organism: the laws of menstruation, the man or woman suffering from a discharge, the mode of determining the onset of menstruation, virginal blood, pregnancy, the various stages in the birth process, the various physical signs that make animals or birds fit or unfit for consumption, etc., etc.

There is no real phenomenon to which halakhic man does not possess a fixed relationship from the outset and a clear, definitive, a priori orientation. He is interested in sociological creations: the state, society, and the relationship of individuals within a communal context. The Halakhah encompasses laws of business, torts, neighbors, plaintiffs and defendant, creditor and debtor, partners, agents, workers, artisans, bailees, etc. Family life—marriage, divorce, halitzah, sotah, conjugal refusal (mi'un), the respective rights, obligations, and duties of a husband and a wife—is clarified and elucidated by it.[10] War, the high court, courts and penalties they impose—all are just a few of the multitude of halakhic subjects. The halakhist is involved with psychological problems—for example, sanity and insanity, the possibility or impossibility of a happy marriage, miggo [i.e., the principle that a party's plea gains credibility when a more advantageous plea is available], and assumptions as to the intention behind a specific act (*umdana*), the presumption that a particular individual is a liar or a sinner, the discretion of the judges, etc., etc. "The measure thereof is longer than the earth and broader than the sea" (Job 11:9).

Halakhah has a fixed a priori relationship to the whole of reality in all of its fine and detailed particulars. Halakhic man orients himself to the entire cosmos and tries to understand it by utilizing an ideal world which he bears in his halakhic consciousness. All halakhic concepts are a priori, and it is through them that halakhic man looks at the world. As we said above, his world view is similar to that of a mathematician: a priori and ideal. Both the mathematician and the halakhist gaze at the concrete world from an a priori, ideal standpoint and use a priori categories and concepts which determine from the outset their relationship to the qualitative phenomena they encounter. Both examine empirical reality from the vantage point of an ideal reality. There is one question which they raise: Does this real phenomenon correspond to their ideal construction?[11]

Authentic Halakhah and the "Teleological Jurist"
Emanuel Rackman | 1954

In 1954 Rabbi Emanuel Rackman published a critique of a "static" approach to Jewish law in favor of a more "dynamic" attitude that encouraged thoughtful consideration of both the traditional rabbinic texts and the "philosophies" that underpinned those writings. To support his position, the writer (with permission) reproduced private letters sent to him by Rabbi Joseph Soloveitchik. Below is an excerpt from Rackman's article.

The only authentic Halachic approach must be that which approximates the philosophy of the teleological jurist. The teleological jurist asks: what are the *ends* of the law which God or nature ordained and how can we be guided by these ideal ends in developing the Law?[12]

The Torah, to the devotee of Halachah, is God's revealed will, not only with respect to what man shall do but also with respect to what man shall fulfill. To apprehend these ends, however, requires more than philosophical analysis of some general ideals set forth in the Bible. It is not enough to say that the Sabbath is a day of rest. One must also study the detailed prescriptions with respect to rest so that one may better understand the goals of the Sabbath *in the light of the prescriptions*, for if one considers the ends alone, without regard to the detailed prescriptions, one will be always reading into the Bible what one wants to find there. It is God's ends we are to seek, not our own. The Halachic scholar must probe and probe, and his creativity must itself be a religious experience supported by the conviction that in what he is doing he is fulfilling a divine mandate—a divine responsibility. Thus in seeking to understand the Law he is seeking to understand God, and in developing the law he is discovering God's will more fully for the instant situation. Needless to say, his results must meet the challenge of revelation in the Bible, the challenge of history in general and Jewish history in particular, and also the challenge of Jewish life in the present.

The teleological approach is to be found at its best in the work of Dr. Joseph B. Soloveitchik of Yeshiva University. For him, the Halachah is "an *a priori* idea system. [In other words,] it postulates a world of its own, an ideal one, which suits its particular needs."[13] To begin with, therefore, any rejection of the revealed character of both the Written and the Oral Law constitutes a negation of the very essence of the Halachah. Jews who thus reject would do better to regard their interest in Halachah as comparable to the antiquarian's interest in antiquity. They may become historians of the Halachah, or borrowers from the Halachah; they cannot regard themselves as actors within the Halachic tradition.

But once one concedes the divine character of the *a priori* idea-system, one can turn to the second phase of Halachic creativity—in which the Law begins "to realize its ideal order within a concrete framework and tries to equate its pure constructs and formal abstractions with a multi-colored transient mass of sensations." On the level of application and realization, the Halachic scholar has God's revealed method, "a *modus cogitandi*, a logic, a singular approach to reality which the community [instead of accepting] had to learn to understand, to convert into an instrument of comprehension of which man, notwithstanding frailties and limitations, could avail himself. [On the first level God appears to the members of His community as king and commands them; on the second, as teacher and instructs them. Thus, the halakhic a priori thinking was humanized, conditioned to man's mentality, and embedded in finitude and concreteness.] Man's response to the great Halachic challenge asserts itself not only in blind acceptance of the divine imperative but also in assimilating a transcendental content disclosed to him through an apocalyptic revelation and in fashioning it to his peculiar needs." There is objectivity and stability in the Halachah. "Yet these do not preclude diversity and heterogeneity as to methods and objections. The same idea might be formulated differently by two scholars; the identical word accentuated differently by two scribes [and Halakhah, regardless of its identic content, could also be expressed in a variety of ways]. Halacha mirrors personalities; it reflects individuated *modi existentiae* [and it conveys a message otherwise inexpressible]."

The observance of the Sabbath is one area in which the teleological approach is of special significance. Simply to assert that God wanted man to rest one day in seven, as the physician prescribes a vacation, is to oversimplify. Even to assert that God wanted the day to be a holy day on which man will come closer to Him is to rush hastily to conclusions on the basis of a few Biblical verses and to ignore a tremendous Halachic tradition which begs for philosophical analysis. Yes, rest and relaxation, as well as consecration, are ends of the Sabbath. But what do the prescriptions with regard to work imply? What is the unity in the thirty-nine types of labor traditionally prohibited?[14] What is the point of the Rabbinic additions? To answer these questions will not only bring us closer to understanding what the Law *is*; it will also show us how the Law can be creatively developed.

The Letter and the Spirit of the Law

Immanuel Jakobovits | 1962

Rabbi Emanuel Rackman's provocative essay on Jewish law gained wider circula-
tion when it was republished in 1961. The following year, Rabbi Immanuel Jako-
bovits penned an implicit response to Rackman's more liberal stance. Jakobovits
regularly contributed the "Review of Recent Halakhic Periodical Literature" in
the RCA's journal, Tradition. *One commentator dubbed Jakobovits's writing the*
"most popular feature" and the "showpiece" of Tradition. *Below is an excerpt*
from that feature, in which Jakobovits asked for a modern but more conservative
view of Jewish law than the one advanced by Rackman.

In common with most oriental systems of legislation, Jewish law is
generally defined in terms of concrete illustrations representing the
rules and principles to be expressed. For instance, the Mishnah, in
dealing with the Sabbath laws, does not speak of the ban on carrying
an object from one domain to another; it speaks of a householder who
seeks to hand a gift from within his home to a poor man outside. Jewish law draws pictures, as it were, of personal and actual experiences
to convey the abstraction of legal rules. This contrasts with Western
legislation which is phrased in abstract terms; its laws appear as dis-
embodied, impersonal ideas and principles. The Jewish tendency to
represent abstract concepts by the symbolic use of concrete things or
acts is also reflected in the characteristic trait of Hebrew etymology in
which abstract words are derived from concrete roots; e.g., *rachamim*
("compassion") from *rechem* ("mother's womb," the object exempli-
fying the most complete empathy or attachment of one human being
to another); or *chet* ("sin") from *chata* ("to miss the mark," "overshoot
the target").

This feature is indeed symptomatic of Judaism in a more general
sense. As a Halakhah-centered system, it employs laws to convey and
inculcate concepts in much the same way as the artist uses his material
for the communication of his notions. The ideas, feelings, and attitudes
which he expresses in terms of poetry, music, painting, or other arts

we portray primarily in the form of "do's" and "don'ts." The practical regulations governing Jewish conduct define our theology, our philosophy, our ethics, and our attitude vis-à-vis any intrinsically abstract subject or problem.

While the Halakhah, then, speaks in terms of action, it bespeaks a line of thought. Looking at rabbinical responsa, we often see purely technical arguments, with predominantly ritual and legalistic undertones. The concrete letter of the law is more apparent than its abstract spirit. But that is the way Jewish law operates. It abhors the vacuum of abstractions; yet it aims at their definition by erecting a legal structure around them. We may compare it to a building. Only the concrete walls and floors are visible; yet these exist only for the sake of the empty space encompassed by them, the "abstract" shelter provided in the building's rooms which in themselves contain no intangible matter. The room is such a space *minus* the walls, etc.

Usually in halakhic dissertations and decisions there are visible only the legalistic bricks with which laws are constructed, i.e., the letter of the law. These indispensable features of the halakhic edifice exist for the sake of forming Jewish attitudes and convictions—the spirit of the law. But one can no more generate that spirit without the letter than one can create a room without a floor, a ceiling, and walls.

It is not always easy, or even possible, to extract the spirit from the law, at least not with any degree of precision and certainty. Being abstract, the spirit may be too intangible and elusive; it may defy all attempts at clear definition. Indeed it may be capable of diverse definitions to different people or at different times, just as a great masterpiece of art may suggest different notions to different viewers. "While several biblical verses can never convey one meaning, one verse can convey several meanings" (Sanhedrin 34a). In its religious, economic, social, and philosophical significance, the Sabbath no doubt *meant* something different to the generations of Moses or Hillel or Maimonides from what it means to us today. The spirit of the law can vary; the letter cannot. But imbedded in the concrete structure of every law is an abstract idea.

An instructive example of this fundamental feature of Jewish law may be found in the discussions on liturgical and synagogue usages reviewed in this volume. Placing the *bimah*, from which the Torah is publicly read, in the center of the synagogue is obviously meant to emphasize the centrality of the law in Judaism—an abstraction suggested by a concrete regulation.

Of more profound significance, and serving as a most far-reaching illustration of this principle, may be the decisions on the use of microphones in synagogue worship.

The use of microphones on the Sabbath or for transmitting the sound of the *Shofar* and the *Megillah* raises questions concerning the activation of electrical currents and discharges, the need to perform religious precepts by a human agency, the distinction between a natural echo and artificial amplification, etc.—all questions of a more or less technical and *physical* nature. Yet the composite *idea* which emerges from these concrete particulars deals with the *attitude* towards the increasing mechanization of life—one of the foremost moral problems besetting our age.

With the advancing tide of technology, man is today threatened by the very machine his genius has created. Human life is in danger of being reduced to an artificial, synthetic existence in which he relegates his work, often his thinking, and sometimes even his generation to mechanical devices. The process, if unchecked by some controls, is bound to stifle the free development of man's personality, his sense of responsibility and moral judgment.

Science is of necessity impersonal and undemanding. It is uncritical of man, for it deals with life as it is, not as it should be, thus nursing a spirit of complacency. By seeking to eliminate work and to exchange the struggles and hardships of life for prefabricated pleasures, it tends to make human life mechanical, materialistic, soulless, and hedonistic.

True religion works in the opposite direction. It is personal and exacting. It offers constant criticism, pointing up the gap between life as it is and life as it should be. Far from making life easier, it calls for ever more sacrifices and self-imposed privations. It posits service, not comfort and amusement, as the highest ideal, and it promises rewards for effort rather than for success. It aims to maintain the supremacy of man's dignity and unique personality by insuring that the machine will be his servant, not his master.

How can our religious experience promote the attainment and constant awareness of these ideals? Judaism, true to its aversion for creedal or philosophical abstractions unrelated to rules of conduct, can do so only in terms of law.

Man was created to harness and exploit the forces of nature—to "subdue the earth and have dominion over . . . every living thing" (Gen. 1:28). To exercise such mastery over the universe and its immense forces is man's privilege. But only within limits. In two areas—one, of place and the other, of time—the Jew must renounce the assertion of his mastery over nature and return it to God, to be reminded that there is a Master above him after all. By proscribing for the Jew the operation of machines on the Sabbath—the sanctuary of time—and in the synagogue—the sanctuary of space, Judaism seeks to secure one impregnable refuge from the tyranny of automation.

We do not object to easing the drudgery of life by utilizing the mechanical aids provided by science. On the contrary, Orthodox Jews are probably the greatest beneficiaries of such wonderful gadgets as time-switches, electrical shavers—and fully automatic elevators. But in the contemporary struggle for the heart and mind of man between the worship of science and the science of worship, religion must preserve the spiritual area from mechanization and artificiality if it is not to surrender its function as the guardian of the Divine in man. Worship must be purely personal; it cannot be replaced by push-button devices. The medium of microphones may vitiate the personal element in worship. (Moreover, we would compromise the indispensability of synagogues if we could fulfill our religious duty by listening to services on phonographs or loudspeakers, which can be installed at home.) On the Sabbath and in the synagogue we are to be creatures, not creators; for once we are to be servants, not masters, so that we shall remember always to subordinate the scientific urge for mastery to the religious urge for service. Thus the Sabbath and the synagogue are to remind us that the highest achievement of the human intellect lies less in our ability to create than in our knowledge of how to control our creations and preserve our supremacy over them. On such knowledge, as we now realize, the survival of mankind will ultimately depend.

New York's Most Powerful Rabbi?

Ronald I. Rubin | 1979

In 1979 sociologist Ronald I. Rubin (b. 1942) penned an article for the popular New York Magazine, which identified the "most powerful rabbis in New York." The first listed was Rabbi Moshe Feinstein. Feinstein did not identify as Modern Orthodox; he was a leading rabbinic figure in the right-wing Agudath Israel and lived a modest life on New York's Lower East Side. Yet, as evidenced by the questioners cited in his many responsa volumes, Modern Orthodox rabbis and laypeople turned to Feinstein for their "modern" and "complex" queries on Jewish law. He also satisfied Rackman's desire for "halakhic creativity." In 1964 Rackman applauded the first of Feinstein's tomes, "which reveals not only erudition of exceptional breadth and depth but also courage worthy of a Gadol in an age of unprecedented challenge to our cherished Halachah." Below is Rubin's portrait of Feinstein in the latter's waning years.

Does Judaism countenance test-tube babies? May one twin be killed so that another may live? Does Judaism's ban on posthumous surgery apply in the case of plutonium-powered cardiac pacemakers, which are required under federal guidelines to be removed after death?

These are among the scores of technical questions for which Jews daily turn to 83-year-old Rabbi Moshe Feinstein (affectionately called "Rav Moishe" by his followers), one of the world's leading authorities on Jewish law. While the Lower East Side "world of our fathers" belongs mostly to the past, Rabbi Feinstein's East Broadway yeshiva, Mesivtha Tifereth Jerusalem, continues to hold a pivotal place for devout Jews. A joke among clergymen is that at the back of every young rabbi's ordination certificate, for a quick answer to any religious question, is Rabbi Feinstein's phone number.[15]

In tackling the problems posed by the new technology for observant Jews, the rabbi has left his imprint on Jewish life for generations to come. His five books of responsa—answers to contemporary questions of religious observance—form a link in the chain of Jewish law beginning with the Torah, the Five Books of Moses, and continuing with the Talmud and succeeding commentaries. Indigenous to each work, regardless of the century in which it was written, is the belief that the Torah is as immutable today as when it was first given by God on Mt. Sinai.

Rabbi Feinstein's responsa treat subjects ranging from sex therapy and artificial insemination to the use of automated elevators on the Sabbath. (One recent decision, for instance, was that Orthodox Jews, who may not use appliances on the Sabbath, may set a timer to turn on a lamp—because light is necessary for the holiness of the day— but they may not use it to turn on a dishwasher or oven.)[16] The rabbi's writings are the best guide for a religious Jew seeking to uphold the letter of the law despite complex scientific challenges.

CONCLUSION

In 1989 Rabbi Yehuda Parnes (b. 1928) affirmed that the tenets of Orthodox Judaism had been decided by Moses Maimonides in the twelfth century. Anything added to or subtracted from the medieval philosopher's Principles of Faith was beyond the boundaries of Orthodoxy.[17] Of course, Parnes was not the first Orthodox rabbi or leader in the United States to put forward this view. A number of documents in this anthology share a similar point of view. However, Orthodox Judaism's venture into the religiously uncharted suburbs forced many to reconsider the theological underpinnings of their beliefs. Their reappraisals took on many forms and set different constraints on theological limitations. Ultimately, Orthodox Judaism's theological presentations broke down into two categories. There were those who dared to speak and write about God, Revelation, and other traditional religious questions. Others wished to address Halakhah, as that was the major concern of past rabbinic writers. In all probability, the vantage point depended on the readers and audiences just as much as it did the writer and speaker.

11 | Responding to Tragedies and Triumphs

INTRODUCTION

In 1968 Rabbi Walter Wurzburger submitted that "Orthodox Jewry is frequently accused of not facing up to the religious implications of the establishment of the State of Israel." He added, "As yet we have not formulated a proper response to the holocaust nor have we reacted in religious terms to the realities of Israel's independence."[1] Wurzburger's conclusion was less than charitable to the Orthodox ideologues in the United States. In 1956 Rabbi Joseph Soloveitchik delivered an important discourse at Yeshiva University on Israel Independence Day. Five years later, his widely acclaimed lecture that offered a theological response to both the Holocaust and the State of Israel was published in Hebrew.[2] He also delivered a number of important Yiddish-language speeches before the Religious Zionists of America, and some were swiftly printed in pamphlet form. Younger scholars like Rabbi Norman Lamm had also put their sophisticated thoughts on the Holocaust and Israel into writing.[3]

Yet it is certainly the case that Orthodox Jews in the United States interpreted the tragedies of Europe and the triumphs of Israel in different ways. In fact, one observer noted that Modern Orthodox Judaism's interpretations and reactions to the Holocaust and the State of Israel served as its greatest forms of demarcation from more right-wing sectors of American Orthodoxy.[4] Take, for example, the divergent views of Rabbis Meir Kahane (1932–90) and Irving Greenberg on the proper reaction to the Holocaust, positions that became all too apparent when the two men debated one another in the 1980s.[5] Kahane challenged his coreligionists to become more self-reliant and to remain distant from non-Jewish politicians in America and Arabs in Israel. This was the major lesson that he had learned from the Nazi terror. On the other hand, Greenberg championed pluralism. For him, the Holocaust signaled a call for Jews and Christians to work together to ensure peace. In contrast to Kahane, Greenberg pointed a finger at God, who, the theologian alleged, had abandoned His Chosen People and broken the biblical covenant that He had consecrated with Abraham. Most Orthodox Jews found both interpretations rather extreme and instead sided with the more moderate views articulated by Soloveitchik and the Lubavitcher Rebbe.

This chapter examines the variety of Orthodox Jewish responses to the major events of the Holocaust and the creation and formative years of the State of Israel. These documents demonstrate the many perspectives that were available to Modern Orthodox Jews. In addition, the final section explores the Orthodox reaction to the Soviet Union and communism. The Soviet Union impelled Jews to consider grave matters of antisemitism and political activism. Once again, Orthodox Jews were not of one mind on how to react to recent events and politics. Most profoundly, they disagreed on whether to package their opposition to the Soviet Union in religious or political terms.

SECTION 1 | The Holocaust

Never Again!

Meir Kahane | 1971

In 1968 the Orthodox rabbi Meir Kahane founded the Jewish Defense League to combat antisemitism. The organization was strongest in New York and among his fellow Orthodox Jews. Kahane claimed that his group was neither militant nor racist, but federal officials and fellow Jews disagreed, and Kahane was jailed for a short time for conspiring to manufacture explosives. Yet he continued to express his views, attacking Arabs, African Americans, the Soviet Union, and leading New York politicians. At the end of his life Kahane organized Kach (The Way), a short-lived political party in Israel. In 1990 he was assassinated in New

York by an Arab gunman. In 1971 Kahane published Never Again, *a manifesto that outlined his right-wing political philosophies and his vow to prevent anything similar to the Holocaust. This excerpt is taken from the end of the book and demonstrates the importance that Kahane placed on the Holocaust, the State of Israel, and the importance of Jewish self-reliance in the formation of his beliefs.*

Our problems are that we live lives of quiet fears. We are afraid of countless things that are mostly nonexistent or unimportant. What we are most afraid of is being in a minority. We tend to assume that because a majority believes a certain way it must be correct. When that majority is composed of wealthy and prestigious people and organizations, we are convinced of it. Power intimidates us, and powerful people, with supreme contempt for commoners, know this and utilize it.

But majorities are not always right, and the fact that the same running of a democratic society calls for the minority to accept the mandate of the majority still does not mean that the mandate is blessed with truth. Indeed, when it comes to the question of principles and ideals, there is a rebuttal presumption that the ruling powers are correct. Those who hold the seat of power seek to cleave to that power and are motivated, not so much by truth but by self-interest. This is not the surest guarantee of attaining truth.

Let us never fear being a minority. We are the minority *par example* and have survived it with honor. Let us not be terrified or intimidated by the thought of being alone, the one person in the crowd who disagrees, the one who is convinced of the truth of his position and who cries out his opposition. Let us not back down before the fury and storm of prestige and power. It is not easy to stand alone against the crowd or the power brokers. It means derision, threats, defamation, and loneliness. It is so much easier to drift with the tide rather than swim against it. Man is happier that way; he has fewer problems.

That is not the way of man; that is certainly not the way of a Jew. If the Jew had accepted the premise that the majority must be right, he would long since have disappeared from the stage of history. If he had capitulated before the power and prestige of kings and churchmen, he would have long ceased being a Jew. If he had been intimidated by numbers and reputation, he would not have been the son of Abraham that he is.

They called our father Avraham HaIvri—Abraham, the Hebrew (Gen. 14:13). And the word Ivri, Hebrew, comes from the word *eyver* or "side." The whole world stood on one side and Abraham on the other. The whole world said that theirs was the way, and Abraham dissented. In the end he was right and all the others wrong. In the end he was proven right only because he had the courage to endure the loneliness of the long distance rebel. We are his children.

To dissent is not easy and to be a rebel is more than difficult, but no great revolution has ever taken place in Jewish history that was not begun and concluded by rebels willing to risk that loneliness and the storm of hatred and attack that was leveled at them.

"'Everybody is wrong, you alone are right.' No doubt this question springs by itself to the reader's lips and mind. It is customary to answer this with apologetic phrases to the effect that I fully respect public opinion, that I bow to it, that I was glad to make concessions. All that is unnecessary and untrue. You cannot believe in anything in this world if you admit even once that perhaps your opponents are right, and not you. This is not the way to do things. There is but one truth in the world and it is all yours. If you are not sure of it, stay at home; but if you are sure, don't look back and it will be your way."[6]

These are the words of Ze'ev Jabotinsky, the supreme Jewish rebel of our time.[7] Only because of such words and such a stubborn Jew did all the outrageous concepts he advanced and all the rebellious ideas that he propagated finally come into being. There is a Jewish state today because Theodor Herzl, when refused a permit to hold the Zionist Congress in Munich because of Jewish Establishment pressure on the authorities, refused to abandon the idea, he held it in Basle instead.[8] He was a rebel. There is a State of Israel today because the Jewish underground, Irgun and Sternists, were attacked and assaulted by Jewish leaders, but they insisted to the end they were right. They were rebels.

"You alone are right?" If you believe so, shout it forth: "Yes, I am right and I will fight for the day when you, too, understand." Such a man must be prepared to look at the angry, hate-filled faces of his opponents, those who cannot forgive his defiance and courage. He must look at them and choose greatness together with loneliness, enmity, and opposition!

It is not important.

He must have within him the iron and steel to move forward against obstacles that will be placed in his path at all times; to move against the fierce storm of opposition; to fly in the face of personal attacks and insults; to stand up to the slings and arrows of his opponents and the protests of even those he loves. Little men cannot abide giants in spirit; they remind them of their own weaknesses. They envy and resent those who carry within them the gift of vision; they must be destroyed. No matter.

He must have within him the unbending strength to move forward resolutely in spite of those attacks. He must have within him a sense of values and must understand that which is truly important—not by bread alone shall man live (Deut. 8:3). He will be discouraged. He will be depressed by failures. He must learn that patience that comes from iron. He must have the confidence that comes from the steel within him.

Why? Because he loves Jews and because Jews need him and because someone must do what has to be done. Because he cares about his brother and loves his sister and is moved by some compelling force to help even while being condemned.

Because in his mind he has seen the mounds of corpses and visited the camps where they killed us. Because he stands in the now empty rooms where once Jews were driven to stand in their nakedness and breathe their last. Because while he stands alone he does not stand alone. Because, by his side, are the ghosts of those who are no longer, whose blood was shed like water because Jewish blood was considered cheap. Because he has seen their outstretched hand and looked into the burning and soul-searing eyes of tragedy that peered into his very being and heard them say:

"Never again. Promise us, *never again.*"

The Voluntary Covenant

Irving Greenberg | 1982

In the 1960s, Rabbi Irving Greenberg started to formulate his view of the Holo-
caust's impact on Jewish theology, one that called for Jews and Christians to recon-
sider their theological tenets after the Nazi horror. In 1982 Greenberg published
his Voluntary Covenant, *which furthered his post-Holocaust theology. Inspired*
by novelist and activist Elie Wiesel (b. 1928), Greenberg argued that God had
broken his covenant with the Jewish people by not sparing them from the Holo-
caust. He claimed that Jews have "voluntarily" reaccepted their bond with God
and emerged with a "more active role" in the covenant.

But do the Jews keep the covenant? There were a significant number
of suicides among survivors who so despaired that they could not live
on without their lost loves, lost families, lost faith.[9] Still others converted or ran away from the Jews to assimilate and pass among the Gentiles and so tried to shake off the danger and pain of being a Jew. But
the overwhelming majority of survivors, far from yielding to despair,
rebuilt Jewish lives and took part in the assumption of power by the
Jewish people. For many of them, refusal to go anywhere but Israel
meant years of waiting in DP [displaced persons] camps, or a miserable risky trip in crowded, leaky, and unseaworthy boats to Israel or
internment in refugee camps in Cyprus and Mauritius. Was there ever
faith like this faith?

The Jewish people overwhelmingly chose to re-create Jewish life,
to go on with Jewish testimony after the Holocaust. What is the decision to have children but an incredible statement of hope, of unbroken
will to redemption, of belief that the world will still be perfected—so
that it is worth bringing a child into this world. When there was no
hope, as in Kovno or Warsaw in 1943–44, the birth rate dropped pre-
cipitously to a ratio of less than 1 to 30 deaths. Logically, assimilated
Jews should have gone ever further with assimilation once they heard
about the Holocaust for thus they could try to rid themselves of the
dangers of being Jewish. Instead, hundreds of thousands of them opted

to become more Jewish. Committed Jews have responded by the largest outpouring of charity and concern for other Jews in history. Observant, learned Jews have re-created *yeshivot* and Torah study so that today more people study *Torah/Talmud* full time than ever before in Jewish history, and that includes the Golden Age of Spain and the heyday of East European Jewry.

By every right, the Jews should have questioned or rejected the covenant. If the crisis of the First Destruction was whether God had rejected the covenant, then the crisis that opens the third stage of the covenant is whether the Jewish people would reject the covenant.[10] In fact, the bulk of Jews, observant and non-observant alike, acted to re-create the greatest Biblical symbol validating the covenant, the State of Israel. "The reborn State of Israel is the fundamental act of life and meaning of the Jewish people after Auschwitz. . . . The most bitterly secular atheist involved in Israel's upbuilding is the front line of the messianic life force struggling to give renewed testimony to the exodus as ultimate reality."[11]

What then happened to the covenant? I submit that its authority was broken, but the Jewish people, released from its obligations, chose voluntarily to take it on again.[12] We are living in the age of the renewal of the covenant. God was no longer in a position to command, but the Jewish people was so in love with the dream of redemption that it volunteered to carry on its mission.

When the Jewish people accepted the covenant, they had no way to measure what the cost might be. The *Midrash* repeatedly praises the Israelites' response to the offer of the covenant, "We will do and we will listen" (Ex. 24:7), as amazing.[13] As the cost of faithfulness increased, the Jews might have withdrawn and cut their losses. In fact, in this era, their faithfulness proved unlimited. Their commitment transcended all advantages of utilitarian considerations. They had committed their very being.

In [Joseph] Soloveitchik's words, the covenant turned out to be a covenant of being, not doing. The purpose of the Jewish covenant is to realize the total possibility of being.[14] It is not like a utilitarian contract designed to achieve limited ends where, if the advantage is lost, the agreement is dropped. The Jewish covenant is a commitment, out of faith, to achieve a final perfection of being. Faith sees the risks but knows that without the risks the goal can never be realized. Covenanted living, like marriage or having children, is an open-ended commitment, for the risks are great and one never knows what pain, suffering, danger, or loneliness one is taking on. Faith in the final perfection involves seeing what is, but also what could be, precisely because life is rooted in the ground of the Divine and we do have a promise of redemption. Out of this faith comes the courage to commit.

The crisis of the Holocaust was that not in their wildest dreams did Jews imagine that this kind of pain and destruction was the price of the covenant. Nor did they realize that the covenant might unfold to the point where God would ask them to take full responsibility and unlimited risks for it. Yet, in the ultimate test of the Jews' faithfulness to the covenant, the Jewish people, regardless of ritual observance level, responded with a reacceptance of the covenant, out of free will and love. For some, it was love of God; for others, love of the covenant and the goal; for others, love of the people or of the memories of the covenantal way. In truth, it hardly matters because the three are inseparable in walking the covenantal way.

If the covenant is not over, then what does the Holocaust reveal about the nature of the covenant? What is the message to us when the Divine Presence was in Auschwitz, suffering, burning, starving yet, despite the most desperate pleas, failing to stop the Holocaust?

The Divine Presence need not speak through prophets or Rabbis. The Presence speaks for itself. If the message of the Destruction of the Temple was that the Jews were called to greater partnership and responsibility in the covenant, then the Holocaust is an even more drastic call for total Jewish responsibility for the covenant. If after the Temple's destruction, Israel moved from junior participant to true partner in the covenant, then after the Holocaust, the Jewish people is called upon to become the senior partner in action. In effect, God was saying to humans: You stop the Holocaust. You bring the redemption. You act to ensure that it will never again occur. I will be with you totally in whatever you do, wherever you go, whatever happens, but you must do it. And the Jewish people heard this call and responded by taking responsibility and creating the State of Israel. Thereby, the people took power into its hands to stop another Holocaust as best it could.

SECTION 2 | Zionism and the State of Israel

The Religious Zionist's Responsibilities in "Galut" to "Eretz Israel"
Bessie Gotsfeld | 1941

In 1925 Bessie Gotsfeld (1888–1962) founded the Mizrachi Women's Organization. For many years she was the leading female voice of religious Zionism in the United States. She initiated a number of programs that encouraged migration to Palestine and helped organize religious schools in the Jewish settlements there. Often Gotsfeld delivered the principal speech at the annual convention of the women's organization. In this 1941 discourse, the Mizrachi leader stressed the importance of developing a religious culture in Palestine and charged her listeners to consider how this mission exceeded similar challenges they faced in the United States.

In the present period of transition when the fate of the Jewish people hangs in the balance and the political prospects of the Zionist movement are shrouded by a veil of uncertainty, it is incumbent upon all Zionists to reaffirm the fundamental objectives which underlie all their efforts. If the impact of future events is not to drive us from our course, we must gain a clear and distinct view of our goal. Otherwise, in the nebula of world disorganization and reconstruction we are likely to be guided by false starts or to lose our orientation altogether.

What is true of the Zionist movement as a whole is true to no less a degree of the various aspects of Zionism which constitute the specific spheres of the several Zionist parties and bodies. The conditions of work are in constant flux. New needs to be satisfied and new problems to be solved arise almost daily. The tide of changing events brings a constant wash of fresh slogans and ambitions to our shores, and unless we cling closely to the line set by us, we are in danger of being swept away by the backwash, and efforts which were once organized to achieve maximum effectiveness will be turned into random strokes against the angry waves. Thus, we as a particular organization must also clearly define to ourselves the specific aims and principles upon which our work is predicated.

As Zionists we aim at nothing less than the achievement of all the conditions of normal nationhood for the Jewish people in Eretz Israel [Land of Israel]. This means freedom of entry, the maintenance of institutions of self-government, national education, and, above all, the existence of a well-balanced Jewish society in Eretz Israel performing all the functions and maintaining all the services of an organized community. It means creating a Jewish economy which shall embrace all aspects of productive endeavor and to this end requires free settlement on the land and the creation of a well-rooted Jewish rural class.

These objectives are determined by our positive aspirations as a nation and remain valid whether Hitler drives refugees to the Palestinian shores or not. Moreover, as Zionist experience has shown, they are attainable in spite of all the political obstacles which may be placed in our way.

In the past twenty years, we have made great strides in this direction in spite of the fluctuation in the political fortunes of Zionism and the sabotage of the mandate. There is no better testimony to this effect than that included in the report of the Peel Commission.[15] Our dissent from their conclusions arises only from the fact that what they regard as a National Home we consider a mere kernel for the national Jewish community which we envisage in Eretz Israel.

The secret of Zionist successes during the past two decades has been in the constant emphasis upon practical construction. At every juncture the predominant concern was how best to build at the moment so that the results may best fit into the pattern of the great structure at whose completion we aim. It was thus possible to put to profitable use even those periods when the combination of forces was against us. In this manner, the four years of political unrest and economic recession which were not propitious for private enterprise saw an unprecedented expansion of the agricultural basis of the Yishuv [Jewish residents in Palestine] brought about by the joint effort of our national institutions (the Keren Kayemet and the Jewish Agency) and our labor and youth movements.[16] As a result, not only has the area under Jewish settlement been enlarged and its strategic distribution been improved, but this expansion has left the socioeconomic structure of the Yishuv far sounder than in any previous period in its history. In considering our future path, we must constantly keep in mind that all this was possible only because the work was carried out along clear constructive lines as part of an organized program. Had the great efforts and sums which were expended upon the great settlement program of 1936–40 been scattered in diverse uncoordinated directions, we would probably have had nothing to show for them.

As Mizrachists, it is necessary that we learn to distinguish clearly between religious questions in the Galut [Exile], especially in America, and the same questions as they arise in Eretz Israel. Our religious problems in the Galut are those of individuals and associations who desire to maintain the tradition of our religious practices and beliefs. Questions of religious education, services, spiritual leadership, the satisfaction and regulation of various ritual needs and practices such as Shehita, Tahara [ritual purity], etc., practically exhaust the specific interests of religious institutions and organizations in the Galut.

Not so in Eretz Israel. Here, the fact that we are concerned with the creation of a self-sufficient national community expands the proper region of Mizrachi activity far beyond that of education or the supplying of religious services. We are confronted in Eretz Israel with the existence of a Jewish environment which in spite of its Jewishness is alien to Torah. We cannot combat such an environment as we do the Galut environment by devoting our efforts to purely religious matters.

It is necessary that we set up a counter-environment embracing almost all phases of endeavor in which every religious individual may find his place. The eventual goal of the Mizrachi in Eretz Israel must be to convert the religious Yishuv or as large a portion of it as possible into an organized community which can control the general conditions of its existence as far as possible. The task confronting us at the moment is the development of a nucleus for such a community—a nucleus of which one aspect has already been called into being in our agricultural settlements—and to satisfy those needs which the religious Yishuv has in so far as it may be regarded as a community.

We, the Mizrachi Women's Organization of America, embarked upon our career with the recognition that a maximum utilization of our potentialities could be achieved only by devoting all our efforts to a clearly outlined set of objectives. As an organization of Mizrachi Women interested primarily in constructive contribution to the upbuilding of Eretz Israel in the Mizrachi spirit, we had no interest in embracing any specific political line within the Mizrachi movement. We would contribute towards whatever was intrinsically of constructive value. But at the same time, it would have been a waste of our capacity for achievement had we become a mere auxiliary of the general Mizrachi organization with activities limited to raising funds and turning them over. The path that lay open before us was that of choosing a particular aspect of Mizrachi work and carrying it out as completely as possible by means of concrete projects.

The effect of such a policy was twofold. By concentrating upon a certain set of problems, we could hope, by a gradual development, to reach a stage where our achievements would constitute a considerable contribution towards their resolution. A scattering of our efforts in various directions could at most have helped out a little here or patched up a situation there. In the final summing up there would have been nothing of permanent value or of far-reaching significance to show. Centralization of endeavor, however, makes it possible to point to a given aspect of Mizrachi work in Palestine where the function performed by the projects of the Mizrachi Women's Organization of America is of major significance.

A Few Words of Confession

Joseph B. Soloveitchik | 1962

In 1953 the Religious Zionists of America (Mizrachi) appointed Rabbi Joseph Soloveitchik honorary president. In that role, Soloveitchik delivered Yiddish-language discourses at Mizrachi's annual conventions. In this excerpt from his 1962 discourse, he questioned his colleagues and students who relied on him to render halakhic decisions but refused to ally with their teacher on the matter of Zionism.

How must American Jewish Orthodoxy respond to such a movement? Logically, all religious Jews ought to belong to the Mizrachi, since the Mizrachi's worldview—to defend the "tents of Jacob" by penetrating the "field," the area of Esau, and transforming it into "the field which the lord has blessed"—is the generally accepted point of view of the Jewish community in America. Religious Jews in America are not locked up in tents. Their children, thank God, attend the finest educational institutions in the country; they do not associate exclusively with religious people, but also with non-religious, and even with non-Jews. They speak English; they participate in all professions, etc. The American Jew—and I mean religious Jew—cannot understand how it is possible to be isolated from his environment. He is a part of the economic-political society in America. Therefore, he ought to be consistent and support the same position for Israel. However, unfortunately, many of them stand aside, many others search for faults.

I want to say to my colleagues and students, rabbis who occupy seats of Torah: why do you not join the movement? Is it not sufficiently religious for you? Are you really cloistered in the tents of Jacob and do you not in fact venture out into the "field" to influence it? Let me ask a little sarcastically: Are the American synagogues—even those with the tall mehitzot—tents of Jacob, or are they not also to be found in the "field?" Are your presidents and other synagogue officers all Sabbath observers? Are not your bar mitzvah innovations somewhat secular in nature? Do you not need politics to hold on to your prestige and influence? I am not criticizing you, heaven forbid. I know that you are the guardians of the walls and that without you the wave of reform would engulf everything. However, I want to put forward a question to you: Why do you begin to hesitate when it comes to Israel, and think that the expansionist program of the Mizrachi—the position that holds "see the smell of my son, as the smell of the field with which God hath blessed him"—is incorrect (Gen. 27:27)? Suddenly you become righteous and adopt the principles of isolation, adherents of Jacob sitting only in tents! It is true that there were Torah giants [Gedolei Torah] who believed in this way of life, but they were Torah giants who practiced what they preached. They lived as ascetics [Nazarites], apart from this world. In this manner, they educated and reared their children, and in truth so did most of their followers. But you, with your children in American colleges, with sermons, manuals, book reviews, and Thanksgiving services, with ministerial associations (I am criticizing nothing)—you are in the "field!" So I ask you, why can you not understand the importance of our work in Israel? Why do you maintain your distance? Believe me, in the last thirteen years Mizrachi has achieved a thousand times more than all the rabbinical organizations of America combined. I call upon all my students, wherever you are, to join the Mizrachi and recruit the members of your communities to our movement. On a daily basis, you send me questions in different areas of Jewish law—matters of kashrut, divorce, marriage, conversion, the Sabbath, liturgy, the synagogue, lending and borrowing, monetary affairs, etc., and you rely on my decisions and rulings. The formulation of a correct attitude toward Israel is just as important an issue as the other questions. In this also, you may rely on me. I say to you, our movement is good enough for American laypeople and rabbis.

An Expression of the "Jewish Soul"

Joel B. Wolowelsky | 1970

In 1970 Yavneh's collegiate leadership produced a thin pamphlet of prayer services for a number of new Jewish and Zionist holidays. The National Jewish Religious Students Association represented hundreds of Orthodox collegians,

including Joel Wolowelsky (b. 1946). This pamphlet, then, represented a signifi-
cant attempt to firmly incorporate Israel's national holidays into the American
Jewish calendar and, to some extent, assign greater rabbinic authority to the
Chief Rabbinate in Israel.

We are all aware of the great impact that the establishment of the State of Israel has had on world Jewry. But while many see the revival of the Jewish state in nationalistic terms, others see in it the *atchalta d'g'ula*, the beginning of the redemption. Needless to say, those who see the State in religious terms expect to see their feelings mirrored in the words of the siddur, which has always been an expression of the "Jewish soul." For these people, Yavneh has published *Veheveti*.

While many rabbis enjoy the respect of large segments of religious Jewry, only the Chief Rabbis of Israel and Tsahal [Israel Defense Force], by virtue of their official position, can make claim to being the national rabbinate of Israel. Therefore, with regard to Yom Ha-Zikaron, Yom Ha-Atzma'ut, and Yom Yerushalayim, we have limited ourselves to their opinions. . . .[17]

The ritual of the Matzah of Hope has been included with some trepidation, lest some individuals think that they have fulfilled their responsibility towards Russian Jewry by merely reciting a paragraph at the Seder.[18] Rather, it is hoped that the sensitive reader will see it as a call to action and work throughout the year on behalf of his brothers in the Soviet Union. The text was prepared by the American Jewish Conference on Soviet Jewry, a coordinating organization for twenty-six national American Jewish organizations.[19]

While 27 Nissan has been designated by the Israeli Knesset as Yom Hashoah Ve-Hagvurah [Holocaust Remembrance Day] in commem-oration of the victims of the Holocaust and the fighters of the ghetto uprisings, no religious service has been developed as yet.[20] The rabbin-ate observes 10 Tevet as the commemoration date of the Shoah; those who lost relatives in the Holocaust but do not know the exact date of their deaths observe 10 Tevet as their *yahrzeit* . . . .

Yavneh presents *Veheveti* [literally, "And I have delivered you"] in appreciation of the religious dimension in the establishment of *Medi-nat Yisrael* [State of Israel]. As we have been privileged to witness the *atchalta d'g'ula*, may we be privileged to hear *kol shofro shel mashiach* [the sound of the Messiah's shofar].

The Six-Day War
Eliezer Berkovits | 1973

In June 1967 Israel launched a preemptive attack on Egypt and other Arab neigh-bors after intelligence revealed that the Arab countries were planning their own military operations against the Jewish state. Israel achieved great success and significantly expanded its borders, including the reunification of Jerusalem. The Israeli victory inspired much Jewish pride among Americans. For Orthodox Jews, the events triggered religious triumphalism. Rabbi Eliezer Berkovits was one of the members of this community who felt impelled to articulate the theological significance of the Six-Day War, which for him could not be separated from the despair of the Holocaust.

When in the early spring of 1967 we decided to set down our thoughts on the problem of faith raised by the European holocaust, we could not anticipate that by the time the task was brought to a conclusion, a threat, in its consequences even more fateful than Auschwitz itself, would becloud the skies of Jewish existence. The Arab nations resolved to wipe the small state of Israel off the map of the earth. If the threat in all its seriousness could in no way have been surmised, the fact that the frightening drama of perhaps ultimate extinction would find its redemptive denouement in the awe-inspiring return of the Jewish people to Zion and Jerusalem could not have been visualized by the wildest imagination as being within the realm of historical possibilities. We started our discussion with the theological and religious problems arising from the darkest hour in the history of Israel's exile. Soon after our task was finished, we stepped into the brightest hour that God, in His unexpected mercy, bestowed upon Israel since the inception of its dispersion. But, of course, that is the question. Was it indeed "from

God"? Was it in truth—to use the phrase of Isaiah—the "hiding" God of Israel who acted as the savior? How are the events and the results of Israel's Six-Day War to be seen in the context of the position we have tried to develop in the previous pages? Did we really experience one of those rare occasions when God—almost as in biblical times—made his presence manifest as the Redeemer of Israel?

It was probably helpful that what we had to say on the problem of the European holocaust was developed independently of the impact of the Israeli victory. If our analysis of the Jewish affirmations in the face of the challenge of Auschwitz is valid, it must be so independently of Jewish military victories. On the other hand, if our analysis has no validity, no feat of arms, however magnificent, could change that. Military victory alone does not prove divine involvement in history, just as the crematoria are no proof of divine indifference. Defeat and suffering need not mean being abandoned by God, and worldly success in the affairs of man is no proof of divine support. Nevertheless, the Jews the world over, and especially in the state of Israel, experienced the speedily developing crisis, followed by the lightning transformation of the Six-Day War as history on a metaphysical level. This was not a conscious reaction to what had happened, nor an interpretation of the events, nor a considered judgment. As a conscious reaction, the sensing of metaphysical meaning might be questioned. But the realization that through the events of those few days all Israel was addressed from beyond the boundaries of time was not in the realm of conscious reaction. It was a spontaneous experience, borne in upon the Jew with the power of inescapable revelational quality. Can this revelational character of the experience be proved? Revelation is never provable. One can only testify to its occurrence: "Ye are my witness! says God" (Isa. 43:10). Once again the words of Isaiah have found their realization in world history. Nevertheless, after the event it is incumbent upon us to render an account of the experience in the context of Judaic teachings and expectations. In order to do this we might do well to recall the theological relevance of a state of Israel, to examine the place that a Jewish state holds within the system of Judaism.

A vital aspect of Jewish messianism is the faith in Israel's return to its ancestral land. All the prophets that prophesy concerning Israel's redemption see it materialize in the land of Israel. God comforts Zion through the return of her children. Nothing could be further from the truth than to interpret these messianic hopes as a nationalistic aspiration. The prophetic mood belies such misconceptions. The messianic goal is a universal one. The Messiah ushers in universal justice and world peace. But the universal expectation is inseparable from Israel's homecoming. The very passage that directs man's hope to the time when "nation shall not lift up sword against nation, neither shall they learn war any more" also envisages that "out of Zion shall go forth Torah and the word of God from Jerusalem" (Isa. 2:3–4). There can be little doubt that Zion and Jerusalem have no mere symbolical significance in this universalistic text, but are historic places in the land of the Jews. The prophets look forward to a time when God's plan for mankind is fulfilled, when peace and brotherhood prevail among all nations, when God's blessing embraces "Egypt My people and Assyria the work of My hands, and Israel Mine inheritance" (Isa. 19:25). But the realization of all these expectations will find Israel reestablished in the land of its ancestors. The redemption of mankind includes the redemption of the Jewish people in the land of the Jews. Wherein lies the messianic significance of the land?

. . . Without return to Zion, Judaism and Jewish history become meaningless. The return is the counterpart in history to the resolution in faith that this world is to be established as the Kingdom of God. The thought has its roots in the very foundation of Judaism, but might have been mere wishful thinking had it not been supported by the reality of Israel, its existence, its survival, its return to Zion. One must appreciate the irrationality of it all before one can grasp its significance. In terms of exclusively man-made history, Israel's existence is irregular—a people like that of the Jews is not supposed to exist; its survival, anomalous—a people as irregular as the Jews is not expected to survive; its return to Zion, absurd—the irregular and the anomalous compounded into the impossible realization of a delusion. . . . For Israel history is messianism on the way to the Kingdom of God on earth. Because of that Israel knows Auschwitz, because of that Israel, all through its history, has been on the way to Zion.

In our days it has arrived there. It may very well be that a majority of the contemporary generation of Jews may not consciously subscribe either to our interpretation of Judaism or to that of the Kingdom of God, yet the overwhelming majority of them experienced the recent confrontation between the state of Israel and the Arab nations as a moment of messianic history. It was an event not on the purely man-made level of history, but one that took place in conformity with the divine plan. Especially in the land of Israel the widest section of the population were convinced that "this is God's doing; it is marvelous in our eyes" (Ps. 118:23). What justification was there to see events in such a light? Apparently, those who lived through them could not see them in any other. Generals and commanding officers were unable to render a purely military account of what happened. It was the secularist in Zion who insisted that not to recognize the miraculous would not be realistic. People who never prayed were overwhelmed by the desire to turn to God in prayer. It was not the prayer in the trenches where, supposedly, there are no atheists. It was the prayer beyond the trenches, in the clear air of victory; no prayer of fear, but prayer in its pristine spontaneity, as the elementary desire of the soul to reach out to God. The Jew has found himself. Hard-boiled paratroopers were embracing the cold stones of the West[ern] Wall of the ancient temple as lovers embrace the most beloved. There was a Presence about in the land.

SECTION 3 | Communism, Vietnam, and Soviet Jewry

The Rosenberg Case
National Council of Young Israel | 1953

In 1953 Julius (1918–53) and Ethel Rosenberg (1915–53) were executed for conspiracy to commit espionage. The Rosenbergs were American citizens who had worked as spies for the Soviet Union, passing along atomic secrets to the Communists. Jews in the United States feared an antisemitic backlash from the highly publicized case. In a resolution approved shortly after the Rosenberg affair, the National Council of Young Israel professed that its brand of Orthodox Judaism was incompatible with the values of communism.

Whereas, Communism and Traditional Judaism are unalterably opposed to one another, both in principle and in practice, it being well recognized by all concerned that no adherent of Traditional Judaism can possibly be devoted to, or in sympathy with, the Communist Movement; and

Whereas, loyalty to the Government is a principle of Traditional Judaism; and

Whereas, the Soviet Union has always advocated atheism and opposed religious practices, even at those times when it sought the support of Jewish people; now, therefore, be it

Resolved, that

The National Council of Young Israel condemns the attempts of the Communist Movement to make the recent execution of Julius and Ethel Rosenberg a religious issue, as a hypocritical and cynical attempt by an avowedly atheistic group to exploit and hide behind deep religious feelings for their own ulterior advantage; and, be it further

Resolved, that

Copies of this Resolution be sent to the newspapers.

The Student Struggle for Soviet Jewry
Jacob Birnbaum | 1964

In 1964 the German-born Jacob Birnbaum (1926–2014) founded the Student Struggle for Soviet Jewry, which spearheaded the Movement to Free Soviet Jewry. The Soviet Union had imposed severe religious and economic restrictions on Jews there, and their coreligionists, especially in the United States, sought to liberate them. Although Birnbaum and most of his fellow activists were Orthodox Jews, this invitation to attend the founding meeting did not describe their efforts in Orthodox or Jewish terms. Two hundred and fifty Jewish students attended this first meeting at Columbia University, and four days later, more than a thousand attended a rally organized by the group.

Dear Friend:

There is overwhelming evidence to show that in recent years the Soviet Government has greatly speeded up its attempts at forcible assimilation of Russian Jewry. The screw is being turned swiftly and inexorably tighter. Just one example: in the last few years alone well over 300 synagogues have been closed down, leaving only 60 or so synagogues for a population of 3,000,000 Jews. Furthermore, autonomous cultural life is almost completely banned. By contrast, tiny Soviet minorities of less than half a million have flourishing cultural institutions of every kind, and most other religious denominations continue to lead a very visible and active, if limited, existence.

We are able to document a concerted effort at spiritual and cultural strangulation, very often shot through with vicious "anti-semitism." The net result is that masses of Jews are in an increasingly ambiguous position, neither assimilating nor living self-respecting Jewish lives, nor yet being able to emigrate.

This is an intolerable situation and a moral blot on humanity. Justice is indivisible. Just as we, as human beings and as Jews, are conscious of the wrongs suffered by the Negro and we fight for his betterment, so must we come to feel in ourselves the silent, strangulated pain of so many of our Russian brethren.[21] A recent visitor to Russia was approached by a man with glowing eyes, who whispered: "Why do you keep silent?"

We, who condemn silence and inaction during the Nazi holocaust, dare we keep silent now?

The time has come for a mass grass-roots movement— spearheaded by the student youth. A ferment is indeed at work at this time. Groups of students all over New York are spontaneously coming together, and hundreds of signatures have been collected.

There is a time to be passive and a time to act. We believe most emphatically that this is *not* a time for quietism. We believe that a bold, well-planned campaign, to include some very active measures, can create a climate of opinion, a moral power, which will become a force to be reckoned with.

A meeting has, therefore, been arranged of students from all parts of the metropolitan area.

Monday evening next—April 27—at 8 p.m.
at Columbia University
in the Graduate Students Lounge of Philosophy Hall

The agenda will be as follows:

After brief introductory remarks, the meeting will be thrown wide open for the purpose

1. of clarifying the issues

2. of examining possible courses of action, and

3. of appointing a pro-tem city-wide college committee for Soviet Jewry

Your care, your concern for a suffering portion of Klal Yisroel [Jewish people], united with the concern of your fellows, will surely wing its way through the ether, leap over frontiers, and penetrate into the heart of many a discouraged Russian Jew.

Come! Bring your friends!

Jacob Birnbaum, Bernard Caplan,
Moses Stambler, James Torczyner

Rabbi Ahron Soloveichik's Opposition to the Vietnam War

Hamevaser | 1968

In September 1968 the Orthodox collegiate leaders of Yavneh invited Rabbi Ahron Soloveichik to address 300 members at the organization's annual convention. Soloveichik shared his belief that American involvement in the Vietnam War

Beginning in the 1960s, the Student Struggle for Soviet Jewry adopted Rabbi Shlomo Carlebach's "Am Yisrael Chai" as its anthem. Carlebach had written the song in honor of the Movement to Free Soviet Jewry. The organization provided the (slightly inaccurate) sheet music for Carlebach's song in its many pamphlets and brochures. Reprinted with the permission of the Estate of Rabbi Shlomo Carlebach.

was *"immoral,"* although he condemned draft evasion. In the past, the rabbinic head of the Hebrew Theological College and younger brother of Rabbi Joseph Soloveitchik (they spelled their surnames differently) had emerged as an Orthodox voice on behalf of African American civil rights and other sociopolitical issues. In his remarks on Vietnam in the RIETS student publication Hamevaser, Soloveichik contextualized them in rabbinic categories, as was his typical fashion.

Rabbi Ahron Soloveichik, formerly Rosh Yeshiva at RIETS and presently Dean of the Hebrew Theological College at Skokie, Ill., recently decried the United States' involvement in the Vietnam War. Speaking before hundreds of students at the national Yavneh Convention earlier this month, Rabbi Soloveichik declared that the war is "unjust" and "immoral."[22]

Following a three-hour discourse on the Jewish attitude towards war which drew from the classic Talmudic sources and commentaries, Rabbi Soloveichik related the concepts he had elaborated to the Vietnam conflict.

Since the United States does not face clear and present danger against which it must defend itself in Vietnam, the war cannot be categorized as a *milchemet mitzvah,* an obligatory war. At best, the conflict may be considered as a *milchemet reshut* (which in a national Jewish context is a war declared by a Jewish king and sanctioned by the Great Sanhedrin as a long-range deterrent to aggression).[23]

In a general (non-Jewish) context, Maimonides concedes the legitimacy of any war declared by a government, although he expresses scorn of such a war which is not justified by moral criteria (Hil. Melakhim 6:1). The Vietnam War is legally legitimate because it is waged as the official policy of the U.S. government. Consequently, draft evasion is not acceptable Halachically.

However, since the Vietnam conflict is at best a *milchemet reshut,* it is regulated by the laws of this category of war. Thus, killing civilians (prohibited in *milchemet reshut*) is not permitted under any circumstances. If a Jewish soldier in Vietnam is assigned to a napalm bombing operation which will probably result in civilian deaths, he must refuse it. He must similarly refuse to participate in "search-and-destroy" missions if the probability points to civilian deaths. Rabbi Soloveichik pointed out that killing of civilians in a *milchemet reshut* is classified in the group of cardinal sins which a Jew must avoid, even if his life will be at stake as a result.

On the basis of a political analysis of the events which led to the present situation, Rabbi Soloveichik maintained that the contention of the U.S. government that the war is stemming the tide of communism in Asia is unjustified. He was especially critical of the corrupt South Vietnamese government which the United States supports as an alternative to the Communists.

Rabbi Soloveichik suggested that the response of Jewish organizational bodies to the present moral dilemma must concentrate on a campaign for selective conscientious objection. Under the law, a person may claim conscientious objection only if he is opposed to all wars. Judaism, however, is not opposed to all wars. The war waged against the Nazis was certainly a *milchemet mitzvah*. This present war certainly is not, the Rabbi maintained. The law, therefore, must respect a person's moral code, and make possible discriminating dissent, instead of general arbitrary dissent.

Rabbi Soloveichik's address was frequently punctuated by impassioned appeals to the audience's moral sensitivities. He criticized those Jewish rabbis and lay leaders who support the war while remaining oblivious to the death and misery inflicted upon innocent women and children.

A Prayer for Soviet Jews

Haskel Lookstein | 1981

From 1979 through 2015, Rabbi Haskel Lookstein (b. 1932) served as the senior rabbi of Congregation Kehillath Jeshurun on the Upper East Side of Manhattan. He was also the principal of Ramaz School, founded by his father, Rabbi Joseph Lookstein. The younger Lookstein also served as chairman of the Greater New York Conference for Soviet Jewry and emerged as one of the leading rabbinic

*exponents on behalf of the Soviet Jewry movement. Unlike Jacob Birnbaum,
Lookstein was very eager to contextualize his efforts in a religious viewpoint. In
October 1981 he composed a special prayer on behalf of Soviet Jews for his con-
gregation that was recited on Yom Kippur and other Jewish holidays.*

Merciful father:

Have mercy upon the remnant of Thy people who are victims of
repression and persecution in the Soviet Union. Bless them
with courage and fortitude in their determination to live freely
as Jews and to leave the land of their oppression.

Strengthen our resolve to stand in solidarity with them, to strive
for their deliverance, and to struggle for their freedom.

Help us to understand that as we dedicate our efforts for their
redemption we simultaneously redeem ourselves. The battle for
their survival assures our survival. The uncompromising fight
for their right for Aliyah raises our sense of purpose, uplifts our
lives, and gives noble meaning to our existence.

May redemption come to our beleaguered brothers and sisters.
May they be restored to Israel: the people, the nation, and the
destiny.

May the prophetic promise be fulfilled in our time. "For I shall
redeem you from afar and your children from the land of their
captivity. And Israel shall return in peace and security, with
none to make them afraid" (Jer. 46:27).

CONCLUSION

In March 1968 Charles Liebman polled members of the Rabbinical
Council of America on their views of the Vietnam War. Most respondents held a middle-of-the-road position that favored gradual "de-
escalation" of American participation in Vietnam. More important, the
vast majority of Orthodox rabbis indicated that they had expressed their
positions in sermons or in private communications with their congre-

gants.[24] In fact, Orthodox rabbis and laypeople freely took stands on a number of Jewish and non-Jewish issues.[25] In general, Modern Orthodox Judaism supported Zionism and strongly advocated on behalf of disenfranchised Jews in the Soviet Union. Yet they were divided on some more particular aspects of social justice and political activism. In all probability, this lack of consensus gave the impression that as a community Modern Orthodox Judaism was not, as Walter Wurzburger stated it, "facing up to the religious implications" of the world around it.

12 | The Orthodox Family

In 1960 Rabbi Joseph Grunblatt (1927–2013), then of Montreal, confessed that "it still takes a certain amount of daring to speak candidly on the subject of sex." Still, explained the rabbi, "the subject must be dealt with openly and thoroughly so that an often confused and bewildered young generation may be guided to face itself, to face its biological makeup, and to correlate it to the requirements of social values and social stability."[1] Grunblatt and other Orthodox rabbis recognized what they were up against. Many Jews, even Orthodox ones, were repelled by the frigid and "emotionally distant" protocol for menstruating women (Niddah) to follow during their nearly two-week window of "impurity." According to the rabbinic laws that govern the rules of "family purity," husbands and wives must refrain from physical contact and maintain other minor barriers from one another. After this, the woman immerses herself in a ritual bath, a mikvah, and may resume physical contact with her spouse. The Orthodox rabbinate also felt compelled to oppose the use of birth control, which it believed threatened the composition of the Jewish family. In late 1960 a Hasidic rabbi appeared on a televised debate and declared that "according to Jewish law it is forbidden to use contraception."[2] By and large, Orthodox rabbis took this stance, despite ample rabbinic sources that offered at least some legal leeway.

The most successful rabbinic leaders to engage with "family matters" were those who maintained a conservative position that placated their rabbinical colleagues but also demonstrated a measure of sophistication and sensitivity to the private nature of Jewish family life. A case in point is the commotion over the discovery of Tay-Sachs disease in the early 1970s. Just a few authorities permitted conditional abortion for a woman known to be pregnant with a fetus identified with the "Ashkenazic" genetic abnormality.[3] On the other side, a number of leading scientist-rabbis prohibited genetic screening for couples. While blood tests could reveal whether the woman or man was in fact a carrier of the Tay-Sachs abnormality, these authorities ruled against the testing, out of fear for the psychological welfare of the couples. Rabbi J. David Bleich (b. 1936) offered a middle-of-the-road approach that discouraged abortion but advocated genetic screening for young people and marriage-age adults. In 1972 he persuaded Orthodox Jews with an essay that featured a sophisticated treatment of Halakhah: science, common sense, and sensitive reasoning.

The final section in this chapter addresses two important documents related to Jewish divorce. To assist women whose husbands refused to issue them bills of divorce, Orthodox rabbis negotiated the limits of Halakhah and politics to maintain order in family life. Perhaps no issue highlighted the tension between rabbinic authority and the Jewish family life more than this one. Unlike the prior cases, however, rabbis held complete control. The so-called chained Orthodox women who suffered in these instances could not remarry and understood that children born to them in future relationships would be labeled mamzerim [bastards] and incapable of marrying most Jews. All this unless, of course, the Orthodox rabbinate could devise a method to effect a divorce from recalcitrant husbands.

SECTION 1 | Ritual Purity and Birth Control

Five Reasons Why Every Jewish Woman Should Adhere to Family Purity

Women's Branch of the Union of Orthodox Jewish Congregations of America | 1941

For decades, Orthodox leaders had tried to convince Jewish women to frequent the mikvah for religious and scientific reasons. In 1941 the Women's Branch of the Orthodox Union prepared a list of reasons for women to observe mikvah. At the end of the list, the editors of the journal included a directory of "modern ritualariums" in the New York area.

1. THE TORAH COMMANDS IT. Any Jewish woman who violates Taharath Hamishpachah [family purity] by neglecting to observe the ritual of Mikveh transgresses one of the fundamental precepts of the Torah. *This violation is as serious as eating on Yom Kippur.*

2. FOR YOUR CHILDREN'S SAKE. The future spiritual destiny of your children demands it. Born in traditional purity your children will be afforded spiritual recognition, a life of health and G-d given immunity from disease which will ultimately lead them to love you and regard you with devoted honor and respect.

3. MEDICAL OPINION SUPPORTS IT AND SCIENCE HAS PROVED IT. The greatest medical authorities, both Jews and non-Jews, bear witness to the great value of Taharath Hamishpachah for health and happiness. The practice and observance of the laws of Taharath or Family Purity have contributed largely to the survival of the Jews these thousands of years despite all adversity. *Destroy our family purity and G-d forbid we destroy the Jewish people.*

4. THE BATHTUB IS NOT A MIKVEH. No bathtub or modern shower can take the place of the Mikveh. Only a specially con-structed pool can satisfy all religious requirements. Since the observance and the regulations encompass more than mere matters of cleanliness, the woman who uses a bathtub as a means of purification is still according to the Jewish law not purified. She remains a Niddah and lacks the Jewish ideal of holiness necessary for marital sanctity. Only when she goes through the process of a formal and ordained T'vilah or ritual immersion in a proper Mikveh has she adhered to the principles of traditional moral purity.

5. MODEL MIKVEH SOLVES THE PROBLEM OF FAMILY PURITY. It is the answer to all needs of the scrupulous and observant Amer-ican Jewish woman. Its ideal facilities, its exquisite beauty, its

sanitary features, its modernity, make the observance of family purity a joy and enhance thereby the traditional respect for Jewish womanhood.

Hedge of Roses
Norman Lamm | 1966

In 1966 Rabbi Norman Lamm published a thin tract on the laws and morals of Jewish marriage. Borrowing from Song of Songs, Lamm's Hedge of Roses *was one of the first English-language manuals to treat the laws of Niddah with both sophistication and sensitivity. Instantly, the work became a popular wedding gift for young couples. It was also warmly greeted as a useful teaching device for rabbis to discuss sexuality with their marriage-age congregants, a tool that they had lacked in the past. Since then, it has been republished in English six times as well as in Hebrew and Portuguese. Below is an excerpt from the manual.*

That Judaism's view on these most intimate aspects of married life is worthy of consideration by modern young couples is indicated by the striking record of domestic happiness characteristic of Orthodox Jewish homes even in the midst of an environment where the breakdown of family life becomes more shocking with each year. After describing the felicity that has distinguished the observant Jewish family since the Middle Ages, a noted Reform leader writes:

> Particularly in those households where Orthodox Judaism is practiced and observed—both in Europe and in cosmopolitan American centers—almost the entire rubric we have drawn of Jewish home life in the Middle Ages may be observed even today.
>
> In those homes where the liberties of Emancipation have infiltrated there exists a wide variety of family patterns, conditioned by the range of defection from Orthodox tradition. . . .
>
> It was possible for a historian, viewing the whole of the present-day Jewish scene, to say, only a few years ago, "The family possesses

more than ordinary importance in Jewish life, for it is the bond of cohesion which has safeguarded the purity of the race and the continuity of religious tradition. It is the stronghold of Jewish sentiment, in which Jewish life unfolds itself in its most typical forms and intimate phases."[4] This is certainly true of those families in which concern for religious tradition exists, even in most unorthodox expression.[5]

This typical Jewish family cohesion is surely not the result of any indigenous ethnic or racial virtue of the Jewish people. Nor does it derive from some general, well-intentioned but amorphous "concern for religious tradition." It is, most certainly, the product of the specific "Orthodox" tradition—the Halakhah or Jewish "way of life." It is this codified tradition, this obligatory Law, that has bestowed the gift of stability upon the Jewish family.

There are, no doubt, many elements among those that constitute the halakhic "way" that, together, strengthen the fabric of Jewish family life. But there can be little doubt that foremost among them is that body of laws that treats directly of conjugal relations. The code prescribed by Jewish Law for husband and wife is generally referred to as *taharat ha-mishpahah*, "the purity of the family." It is, as we have already seen, a most appropriate euphemism, for it addresses itself to the aspiration for that form of self-transcendence known as *taharah* or purity, and provides marvelous and magnificent safeguards for the integrity of the *mishpahah* or family.

We have discussed, above, the sense of psychological purification that is attained by observance of immersion in the *mikvah* by the bride. But the psychological implications of Family Purity are not restricted to the general nature of sex as it expresses itself in the early years of marriage. *Taharat ha-mishpahah* is also crucial in protecting the marital bond from one of its most universal and perilous enemies which comes to the fore soon after the newness of married life has worn off: the tendency for sex to become routinized.

It is easy enough to get married. It is quite another thing to stay married. The Talmud considers the pairing of couples as difficult as the splitting of the waters of the Red Sea; and the miracle there was not so much the separation of the waters as the keeping them apart so that the Exodus might proceed successfully (Sotah 2a). So with the joining of husband and wife. The *wedding*, for all the problems it presents to the young couple and their families, is comparatively simple. Far more significant, far more difficult, and a far greater miracle to achieve in this turbulent society is—the *marriage*, staying married.

Sexual attraction plays a major role in bringing a man and woman to the bridal canopy and keeping the couple together in the early months and years of marriage. But if this attraction wanes and withers in the years following, the permanence of the marriage itself is imperiled and may likewise slowly disintegrate.

So often—so unfortunately!—that is exactly what happens! What to the young, recently married couple is such an exciting and fulfilling adventure soon becomes just another dull experience to be re-enacted almost mechanically as part of the whole marital complex. The charm and the delight, the thrill and the beauty of young love is soon replaced by the stale and the prosaic, the plain and the profane. There is hardly a more deadly poison that so threatens the existence of happy marriage!

For marriage to thrive, the attractiveness of wife and husband for each other that prevailed during the early period of the marriage must be preserved and even enhanced. And it is the abstinence enjoined by Family Purity that helps keep that attraction and longing fresh and youthful. This is how the Talmud explained the psychological ramifications of *taharat ha-mishpahah*:

> Because a man may become over-acquainted with [his wife] and thus repelled by her, therefore the Torah said that she should be considered a *niddah* for seven days, i.e., after the end of her period, so that she might become beloved of her husband on the day of her purification even as she was on the day of her marriage (Niddah 31b).

Unrestricted approachability leads to over-indulgence. And this over-familiarity, with its consequent satiety and boredom and *ennui*, is a direct and powerful cause of marital disharmony. When, however, the couple follows the Torah's sexual discipline and observes this period of separation, the ugly spectre of over-fulfillment and habituation is banished and the refreshing zest of early love is ever-present.

There is so much insight in this comment of the Rabbis! Familiarity does indeed breed contempt, and a little absence does make the heart grow fonder. As Chief Rabbi [Isser Yehudah] Unterman of Israel has pointed out, it has been the experience of people who deal in marriage counseling that sometimes a husband will ask for a legal separation on the way to divorce.[6] Then, after he has been separated a while from his wife, he suddenly discovers that he needs her and wants her and even loves her! The separation is a prelude to reunion. This separation, too, which Judaism commands, as part of the observance of Family Purity, is that which puts the poetry back into the marriage, which retains the charm, the elegance, the excitement. It is the pause that refreshes all of married life.

Commandment Number One: Birth Control

Herbert S. Goldstein | 1959

Advances in contraception in the 1950s worried the Orthodox rabbinate. Notably, Rabbi Moshe Feinstein ruled against the use of birth control as a means for a couple to delay having children. Rabbi Herbert Goldstein of New York's Upper West Side concurred. Rather than a halakhic argument, the New York rabbi put forward a moral rationale. He believed that birth control was detrimental to marital happiness and, in most cases, a violation of Judaism's principles on family life.

The Bible contains 613 Commandments. The first commandment is found in the First Chapter of Genesis, Verse 28: "Be fruitful and multiply."

"Be fruitful" is both a blessing and a command to have children; "and multiply" means that we must leave the race more numerous than we found it. The prophet Isaiah gave a generalization of the Divine policy on this subject as follows: "For thus hath said the Lord who created the heavens; God Himself who formed the earth and made it. He hath established it. Not in vain hath He created it. He formed it to be inhabited" (Isa. 45:18). The Rabbis point out in the Talmud, Niddah 13a, that the gravest sin, and the one which was responsible for the destruction of the generation of the Flood, was the custom of husbands and wives living the married life without the possibility of propagation.

At first the female was called "Ishah," "Woman," that companion to Adam; later she was called "Chava," "Eve," the mother of all living. Woman reaches her highest and most exalted function in motherhood. This lofty and eternal privilege of woman cannot be degraded because of ignoble and selfish ease on the part of our young people.

Often the legitimacy of birth control is justified because of the economic question. As a matter of fact, birth control is usually practiced by those of the middle and well-to-do classes. Judaism recognizes, however, exceptional cases where birth control is permitted. In certain cases, to be sure, where health is involved, the Rabbis have indicated methods for legitimate birth control. In such cases, the laity should not take the law into their own hands, but should seek counsel from the proper religious authorities. Indiscriminate birth control is against the law of God, "Be fruitful and multiply."

It has often been stated that the mother who bears many children loses her health. There are statistics to prove that maternal longevity is associated with large families. Not the bearing of children, but ignorance and the lack of medical care have in most cases been the real causes of disease and death. A physician of standing wrote in one of the British medical reviews as follows: "An experience of well over forty years convinces me that the artificial limitation of the family causes damage to a woman's nervous system. It makes her not only sterile, but also nervous, and generally poor in health."[7] Fibroids and neuroses of various kinds are traceable, according to the testimony of leading physicians, to birth control.

I have found that birth control is largely responsible for the breakdown of the stability of the marriage bond. And one-room hotel suites or expensive two-room apartments occupied by tens of thousands of married people are evidences of a preconceived determination on the part of the so-called better classes for birth control. As a result, there is no real home life and a total lack of the joy and rejuvenation of spirit that children bring into a home.

SECTION 2 | Tay-Sachs: An Ashkenazic "Disease"

Tay-Sachs Disease

Allan Kaplan | 1973

In the early 1970s, scientists alerted Jews of a newly identified "Ashkenazic disease." Geneticists assured Jews that they could screen fetuses in utero for the Tay-Sachs disorder in sufficient time for pregnant women to consider abortion. To Orthodox experts in Jewish law, this was not an acceptable recourse, even if a child suffering with Tay-Sachs would not live past his or her fourth year of life. Instead, scholars like Rabbi J. David Bleich advocated early screening for young women and men. In his pioneering treatment of Tay-Sachs and Jewish law, Bleich offered a thorough response to a more learned generation of Orthodox Jews who demanded that halakhic decision-makers possess mastery in Jewish codes, complex medical knowledge, and sensitivity to the social conditions of Jewish family and personal life. Yeshiva College student leaders adopted his position as they arranged for genetic testing on their Manhattan campus.

With the upcoming Tay-Sachs program at Yeshiva [College] only a short while away, the nature of the disease and the goals this program hopes to achieve were discussed recently with Rabbi J. David Bleich, a rosh yeshiva in RIETS.

Rabbi Bleich, in his survey of recent halachic periodic literature published in *Tradition Magazine*, volume 13 #1, discussed the background and causes of the disease.[8] He stated that although there were descriptions of the disorder dating back to 1881, an explanation of the nature of the disease was not found until 1969. Research has discovered that the disease is caused by the absence of an enzyme which normally exists in the breakdown of certain fatty substances. Since the enzyme is absent, these substances accumulate in the cells and tissues of the affected child and ultimately lead to the destruction of brain cells. The disease results from a union of genes in which both are defective.

In the same discussion, Rabbi Bleich stated that centers in Johns Hopkins University in Baltimore, Montreal's Children's Hospital, and the Hospital for Sick Children in Toronto have begun campaigns to identify potential victims and to eliminate the disease. A carrier can be identified by means of a simple blood test, since the enzyme responsible for the condition can be found in the plasma of the blood and in fetal amniotic fluid. Absence of this enzyme indicates the presence of a carrier.

With this in mind, Rabbi Bleich affirmed the validity and necessity for the testing of college-age people for this condition.[9] Physicians in the communities carrying out this testing urgently recommend rabbis to refer prospective couples for testing, but Rabbi Bleich believes that testing should be carried out before the people are ready to get married at an earlier stage of adolescence.

Rabbi Bleich believes that such testing must be undertaken only in conjunction with a mass scale of education. "Only those students capable of coping with the possibility of a positive test should undergo examination. Any stigma that exists is based on ignorance only."

If such early testing is not carried out, Rabbi Bleich says we will be faced with the grave problem of abortion. In his article he writes, "The fear that a child may be born physically malformed or mentally deficient does not justify recourse to abortion. Amniocentesis cannot be performed prior to the fourth month of pregnancy and all halachic authorities agree that at so late a stage of pregnancy, abortion is permissible if continuation of pregnancy threatens the life of the mother. This procedure for the detection of Tay-Sachs is therefore not permissible and also constitutes an act of chavalah—an unwarranted assault upon the mother." Thus he believes the only way to prevent abortion later is to test earlier.

In conclusion, Rabbi Bleich reaffirmed his strong feelings concerning the need to counsel and educate those people undergoing testing. "This would serve to dispel any possible misconceptions and stigmas that could arise from a positive test. He himself will sit in on the counselling that will be undertaken in Yeshiva, and the student will thus be made aware of the religious and psychological ramifications of a positive test.

An Official Policy for Genetic Screening

Association of Orthodox Jewish Scientists | 1973

In 1973 the Yeshiva College student council organized a program that offered genetic screening and counseling for students. The event raised a "storm of controversy" and provoked a number of leading rabbis and organizations to clarify their positions. One of the more important viewpoints was shared by the Association of Orthodox Jewish Scientists. In contrast to Rabbi Bleich, this organization was wary of the psychological impact of Tay-Sachs screening. To mollify all sides, student leaders arranged for the screening at the end of the spring semester and the testers sent the results to private homes rather than to dormitory addresses.

To the editor:

This is to clarify the position of the Association of Orthodox Jewish Scientists regarding Tay-Sachs screening programs.

The Association supports, and indeed originally proposed in 1972 under the then presidency of Dr. M. Tendler, a voluntary screening of young adults of an age in which marriage has become a serious consideration but before definite marital commitments have been made.[10] The screening of younger individuals years before marriage yields no immediate benefits and might result in a longer period of anxiety in carriers than is warranted. We feel that all screening must be linked to both genetic and religious personal counseling. Emotionally immature individuals may be traumatized psychologically if they learn of their carrier state, and these individuals must be provided with the opportunity for additional professional psychological support. Genetic counseling must be in consonance with Torah principles.

The Association is unalterably opposed to amniocentesis, whose natural and logical consequence is abortion. It likewise feels that screening of married couples or those whose marriage is imminent and who are not committed to disruption of their mutual marital commitments, were both partners to be discovered to be Tay-Sachs carriers, is unwise, again because virtually the only consequences would be abortion or a childless marriage. We are also concerned that any program be absolutely voluntary and that the nature of any educational drive be informational rather than coercive. There must also be absolute assurance that the confidentiality of all carriers will be safeguarded.

The AOJS records with pleasure the interest of the student population in devoting time and energy for the betterment of their fellow man and joins with them in the hope that the Almighty free us from the pain and anguish of genetic disease.

Association of Orthodox Jewish Scientists

The Pros and Cons of "Mass Hysteria"
Moshe D. Tendler | 1977

The Association of Orthodox Jewish Scientists' anti-screening position was based on the conclusions of Rabbi Dr. Moshe Tendler. Several years later, Tendler, who had earned a doctorate in biology from Columbia University, offered a fuller articulation of his view. His opposition to testing moved well beyond Jewish law and medicine and into the realms of psychology.

Let us examine the problem for its halachic consequences. If one is tested and determines that he or she is a carrier, there is no problem if one's mate is a non-carrier. But how does one handle this information? The social implications are quite obvious. Carriers would be discriminated against in cases even where one's potential mate is a certain non-carrier. Why should one introduce to his family's genetic pool a possible defective gene that would require testing by future generations prior to marriage? Are we to declare all carriers unmarriageable?

There is also great concern for the import of this knowledge on a teenager whose self-image is just being fashioned. It is a time when any "blemish" is magnified to become a psychological stress with unknown consequences. Mass screening in schools, where confidentiality is difficult to maintain, is particularly objectionable. Students, if only frivolously, often reveal intimate details of their family life, since they are unware of the social consequences.

Of greater significance is the fact that mass screening is objectionable because it creates a mass hysteria that pressures people to undergo testing. The pro-testing group, namely, the Tay-Sachs organization, holds a pro-abortion viewpoint. It reassures people that even when both are carriers, the genetic status of the fetus can be determined and a defective one aborted. However, such an abortion is halachically not permissible. The fetus will be born perfectly normal, and becomes ill only after approximately one year of life. If one advocates destroying this fetus, because ethical-moral considerations define this child as no longer a child after six months of life, must we not then say that a man with only six months to live is no longer a man? How does one distinguish between such an abortion and euthanasia?

SECTION 3 | The Prenuptial Agreement

Creativity in "Family Law"

Emanuel Rackman | 1973

According to Jewish law, a husband must willingly issue his wife a writ of divorce (get) in order to dissolve their marriage. For many years, American rabbis struggled to solve the issue of agunah, literally the "chained" woman, whose recalcitrant husband refuses to provide the writ of divorce. In 1953 the Conservative Rabbinical Assembly accepted the so-called Lieberman Takana proposed by Rabbi Saul Lieberman of the Jewish Theological Seminary, which inserted a clause into the marriage contract (ketubah) that empowered both the wife and Conservative rabbis to effect a divorce without the consent of the husband. The Orthodox rabbinate rejected this position. Nevertheless, Rabbi Rackman urged his colleagues to consider ways to "annul" marriages in an acceptable fashion. In 1973 Rackman articulated the crux of his views at a symposium on "Halakha in Modern Life," held in Switzerland. A section of Rackman's remarks are reproduced below. Two years later, at the RCA convention, Rabbi Joseph B. Soloveitchik publicly attacked Rackman and what he declared to be his unorthodox position. He declared: "I want to be frank and open. Do you expect to survive as Orthodox rabbis? Do you expect to carry on the mesorah [tradition] under such circumstances?"

The major problems of the Halacha today are created as much by its supporters as by its resisters. The Halachists are keeping the Halacha frozen and I cannot be content with the freeze.

We cannot ask people forever to be patient. And I don't fight to solve the Agunah problem or the problem of illegitimacy because I want to silence opposition to the Halacha. I fight for solutions because as an Orthodox Jew I want the Halacha to cause no agony to any human being. I am fighting because of my own conscience and my own empathy with suffering fellow-Jews. The freeze has been tragic and we must confess our sin. The fact that there are many great rabbis who are frightened by the thought of solutions that may divide the Jewish community is no answer. The Talmud tells us that the destruction of the Temple came about because one rabbi didn't have the "guts" in the year 70 to do that which he should have done (Bava Metzia 30b). And Orthodoxy now bears the burden of doing some very constructive things.

What are the areas in which something must be done? What are the areas of critical concern for the future of the Halacha—areas that require bold creativity? First and foremost, we have the area of family law. We Jews must bear in mind that up until a century ago, it would have been difficult to find a system of law that was as progressive as the Halacha in safeguarding the dignity of every member of the family. But now there is need for creativity, not only for the sake of Israeli Jews but even more for Diaspora Jews. We must bear in mind that some progress has been made by Chief Rabbis Herzog, Uziel, and Nissim.[11] But there is need for much more rapid development. The literature and the techniques are available. What is required is a bold Chief Rabbinate that will not panic because some Jews will not want to take advantage of the legislation and may even scream that the Halacha is being subverted. There have always been Jews who didn't want to take advantage of "Heterim," and they can continue to refuse to take advantage of them. Even in Tannaitic times not all Jews accepted the "Heterim" that were given.[12] One reason for optimism in this connection is that Orthodox women themselves are now beginning to clamor for action. And this is a very hopeful sign on the horizon.

In the Matter of Prenuptial Agreements
Rabbinical Council of America | 1993

In the 1980s, members of the RCA proposed a method that appeared similar to the Lieberman clause and Rackman's proposals, and this was likewise rejected. In 1993 Rabbi Mordechai Willig (b. 1947) authored a "prenuptial agreement" that stipulated that "every day that husband and wife are separated, even prior to divorce, the wife is entitled to demand of her husband a specified per diem sum for her support." The RCA and the Orthodox Caucus sponsored the proposal because it did not augment the traditional marriage contracts but levied tremendous financial burden upon recalcitrant husbands who would in time seek religious divorce from their "chained" wives. Below is the RCA's resolution that formally accepted Willig's contract.

1. Whereas it was clearly the desire of God that couples live together in peace and harmony, in love and devotion all of their lives, so that strong marriages could serve as the heart of a strong Jewish community; but

    Whereas the Torah recognizes that some marriages could not be sustained and therefore provided procedures for the termination of those marriages, so that husband and wife could then be freed to create new and stronger marriages; but

Whereas in some unfortunate instances husbands or wives, for reasons of spite or venality, refuse to cooperate with the appropriate instructions of a *bet din* regarding the termination of their marriages with a *get*, thereby preventing the spouse from rebuilding family life.

2. Therefore, be it resolved that every member of the Rabbinical Council of America will utilize prenuptial agreements, which will aid in our community's efforts to guarantee that the *get* will not be used as a negotiating tool in divorce procedures. We realize that there are several prenuptial agreements and many may raise halakhic or legal difficulties. We, therefore, call upon the Executive Committee of the Rabbinical Council of America to disseminate a list of approved prenuptial agreements with procedures of implementation to the *chaverim* [members]. All prenuptial agreements must be approved by the Rabbinical Council of America's *bet din*. To this date, only Rabbi [Mordechai] Willig's prenuptial agreement has been accepted and this document will be distributed immediately to the Rabbinical Council of America members.

Why Orthodox Rabbis Should Insist on a Prenuptial Agreement

Saul J. Berman | 1993

Despite the resolution passed by the RCA, not every member of the rabbinical group embraced the document as a viable means to reduce cases of agunot. Some felt that the document, while supported by leading authorities, was still too much of an innovation. To persuade them otherwise, Rabbi Saul Berman (b. 1939) of Stern College for Women published the following essay in the RCA's monthly newsletter.

Many of my rabbinic colleagues have told me that they are reluctant to use a prenuptial agreement related to assurance of issuance of a *Get* upon dissolution of the marriage by civil divorce. I am deeply dismayed by the reluctance, albeit I have some understanding of why such resistance exists.

Why a Prenuptial Agreement Altogether?

The inability of Jewish courts in the United States to compel a husband to issue a *Get* to his wife, because of lack of jurisdiction and enforcement powers, has resulted in a powerful advantage held by the husband. Unfortunately, some husbands, often cruelly and unethically advised to do so by their attorneys, choose to exploit this advantage by using the issuance of the *Get* as leverage for the achievement of other purposes, such as monetary extortion or reordering child custody arrangements.

Great Jewish minds have devoted not insignificant amounts of energy to produce a solution to this problem. As the dust settles after almost forty years of deliberation and debate, both Orthodoxy and the Conservative movement have elected a common approach, albeit in differing frame-works. The Conservative movement, under the guidance of the late Rabbi Saul Lieberman, added a clause to the *ketubah* which would make an order of a *Bet Din* enforceable in civil courts in the manner of binding arbitration.

Orthodoxy, with great fanfare, rejected this particular device, but affirmed the approach of using the American civil courts as the means of resolving this problem. Thus, Agudath Israel, under the leadership of their *Mo'etzet Gedolei HaTorah* [Council of Torah Sages], went the legislative route and successfully supported the passage of the *Get* Statute in the State of New York.[13] The Rabbinical Council of America, under the leadership of the late Rav Yosef Dov Soloveitchik, elected rather the use of a prenuptial agreement which would bind the parties through their own prior consent to be subjected to significant financial loss through their failure to issue a *Get* in a timely fashion. The struggle within Orthodoxy to fine tune the prenuptial agreement into a document capable of being assented to by virtually all Torah circles has taken almost fifteen years and has left many sacrificed *agunot* by the wayside of life during the struggle. This has been an infuriating and almost intolerable time for sensitive Orthodox Jews. But it now appears that a document having the consensus of most Orthodox *halakhic* leaders is truly at hand.

The New Agreement

Rabbi Mordechai Willig of Yeshiva University has, under the aegis of the Orthodox Caucus, and with the timeless strength of great Jewish leaders, shepherded through the hands and hearts of the leaders of the *halakhic* community a new prenuptial document. With, I am sure, some minor changes soon to come, the documents have been approved for use by Ashkenazic and Sephardic scholars in Israel [and] by a very diverse set of *Haredi* [Ultra-Orthodox] and American Orthodox *poskim* here in the United States. Whether one takes the attitude of "it's about time" or of "patience has finally been rewarded," the time seems now to be at hand for the universal adoption of the use of these documents.

The Next Steps

The next and most crucial step in the resolution of this problem now lies in the power of the rabbinate. If we, all of us together, can interpret the importance of, and insist on the use of, these documents at every Jewish marriage, then we will rid Jewish society of this scourge which now afflicts our moral condition as a people. This is one time when our united energies are essential. Only when every Jewish couple has such a document will those who will need it be protected.

I understand the sense of reluctance which many rabbis have about discussing divorce and possible extortion in the midst of premarital counseling. Yet, is not the entire *ketubah* precisely a contract in contemplation of divorce or death of the husband? And people hang illustrated texts of the *ketubah* over their beds! The point is that the very universality of the *ketubah* allows people to accept without feeling that they are making a negative statement about the expected longevity of their marriage. The same can eventually be true of these prenuptial documents.

What, I believe, will ease the process of use of these documents is their use in place of the traditional *tennaim*, which are now in any case almost always used only to increase the number of honors available for distribution at the wedding. We ought also transfer over to these new *tennaim* the custom of the active presence of the mothers, either still breaking a plate, or performing some other act indicating the protective responsibility of mothers.

As rabbis, we only rarely have the opportunity to shape a new and universal Jewish practice while simultaneously helping to prevent Jewish immorality. Such a joint opportunity is now before us. Our creativity can mold the practice, our capacity as teachers and leaders will be tested in the process of convincing this coming first generation of users to be comfortable with the process, and our ethical vigor will leave a lasting mark on all future generations of Jews.

CONCLUSION

In 1986 a researcher found that about 70 percent of so-called Young Israel mothers used birth control before they became pregnant with their first child. These women admitted that birth control practice was in fact governed by Halakhah, but they also insisted that their "personal decision" overrode the dictates of Jewish law.[14] The same was probably true for Orthodox responses to genetic diseases. Fortunately, genetic testing since the 1970s has largely reduced the number of infants born with the Tay-Sachs disease. However, like contraception, many Modern Orthodox Jews facing this struggle bypassed the rabbinical queries that govern this matter and elected for abortion, despite more "expert" rulings to the contrary. To be sure, Orthodox women and men could find rabbis who permitted both birth control and abortion under a number of circumstances. However, the majority opinion among Orthodox clergymen was frequently disregarded if it did not suit the likings of the Modern Orthodox family.

Again, the exception was agunah, a matter that carried wide consequences for more than just the suffering woman: it impacted her children's ability to marry other Orthodox Jews. On this score, too, the Orthodox rabbinate remained staunchly conservative. In 1975, for example, Rabbi Joseph Soloveitchik led a vociferous outcry against Rabbi Emanuel Rackman's proposals for "marriage annulments" that would retroactively solve the matter of agunah. Soloveitchik argued that such innovations would betray the "Orthodoxy" of the rabbinate.[15] In 1993 Rabbi Mordechai Willig resolved some of the angst with his solution that attacked the recalcitrant husband's financial resources rather than augmented any religious contract. All of this points to the religiously conservative viewpoint of the Orthodox rabbinate and its attempt to remain relevant in the domestic lives of the Modern Orthodox community.

13 | From Rebbetzin to Rabbah

INTRODUCTION

In June 2009 Rabbi Avi Weiss (b. 1944) of the Hebrew Institute of Riverdale conferred the title of Maharat (a Hebrew acronym that stands for halakhic, spiritual, and Torah leader) to his assistant, Sara Hurwitz (b. 1977). For years Hurwitz had studied with Weiss and mastered the material required in the curriculum of Weiss's rabbinical school, Yeshivat Chovevei Torah. Still, the liberal-oriented Orthodox rabbi was yet unwilling to offer his student rabbinical ordination.[1] In fact, the watershed event to bestow Hurwitz with her new title was announced as a "conferral" rather than an "ordination" ceremony. That soon changed. Seven months after the initial designation, Weiss changed Hurwitz's title to "Rabba," a feminized version of his own rabbinical title. Later on, however, Weiss retreated. Faced with much criticism from within Orthodox rabbinical circles, he pledged to henceforth ordain women with the Maharat moniker rather than the Rabba designation that Hurwitz maintained.[2]

The position of the female synagogue leader is a complicated one in the history of Orthodox Judaism. In the United States, the rabbi's wife—known as the rebbetzin—was reluctant to stand at the forefront of synagogue politics and religious matters. Rather, she preferred to remain a spouse who occasionally played the role of hostess but primarily worked to support her harried "all-too-important" rabbinic husband. In time, the rebbetzin's portfolio evolved, according her with sizable leadership but circumscribed to the realm of Orthodox women. The platform that she assumed (the rabbi's wife could instead choose a more private life or another profession) enabled her to counsel her female coreligionists and support other feminine initiatives. The rebbetzin has remained a focal leader within feminine spheres, although the parameters of her job description have most certainly increased. In all probability, the "traditional" and unofficial status of the rabbi's wife has shielded it from considerable critical examination.

Concomitantly, a growing number of Orthodox women agitated for leadership roles beyond that of the rebbetzin. In 1984 feminist activist Blu Greenberg (b. 1936) posed the possibility of female ordination in Orthodox circles.[3] Inspired by the decision of Conservative leaders to ordain women at the Jewish Theological Seminary, Greenberg appeared recurrently in the Jewish press (as did her opponents) to voice her interest in enlarged female representation in the synagogues in which she was most comfortable praying. To date, Greenberg's vision has not quite met reality. Instead, Orthodox Jews have offered compromises. Since 1997, a number of congregations have installed female "congregational interns" and "community scholars" who functioned as clergy without rabbinical titles. More daring leaders like Weiss have explored female congregational empowerment with labels like "Maharat" and "Rabba." On some level, the women who occupy these more radical positions perform the same duties as the traditional-minded rebbetzin, but with greater responsibilities to the male sphere within their congregations.

SECTION 1 | The Rabbi's Wife

The Rabbi's Wife

Sara Hyamson | 1925

Sara Hyamson (1871–1950) was married to Rabbi Moses Hyamson (1862–1949) of Congregation Orach Chaim on New York's Upper East Side. Previously the couple had lived in London where Rabbi Hyamson served as a judge and as acting Chief Rabbi of the British Empire (1911–13). In New York Sara Hyamson periodically wrote for Orthodox magazines about the role of women in the traditional Jewish community. In 1925 the New York Board of Ministers asked her to outline the professional responsibilities of the rabbi's wife. In her view, the rebbetzin should support her husband in his private life and do her best to maintain a distance from public matters.

The President of The New York Board of Jewish Ministers has asked me three questions, which I will try to answer.[4]

The first question is, "Are there any phases in the scope of the Jewish Ministry, which can and should exclusively be entrusted to the Rabbi's wife?"

To this question I reply emphatically that there are. The scope of activity in the Jewish ministry which, I humbly submit, should *primarily* be the function of the Rabbi's wife is the care of the Rabbi. I will be told, of course, that that privilege belongs to all wives in relation to their husbands. I contend, however, that there is a very great difference between the Rabbi's wife and other men's wives. The layman's wife can arrange her life to suit herself and make it as busy and as quiet as she likes. The Rabbi's wife lives in a hurly-burly of congregational activity and communal service, and therefore it is most necessary to remind her to make the care of her husband her first and paramount duty. She must watch over him that he shall not overwork, that he shall have time for study, that he shall not fritter his energies on insignificant trivialities, nor allow well-meaning congregants to fritter them away. She must jealously guard him from needless interruptions, so that he shall have time to concentrate on the important duties which are peculiarly his and which no one else can carry out.

She must discover the special abilities latent in her husband, of which he himself may be unconscious, and bring out the best that in him lies. She must overcome his diffidence and spur him on and stimulate him to develop and realize these abilities.

By her cheerfulness she must save him from the disappointments and despondency to which the minister's calling is particularly prone, because the reality achieved falls so often short of the ideal desired and taught. She must be his private censor and his general critic, pointing out to him the slight shortcomings and the foibles from which even he is not entirely free. But she must do this more tactfully than did the famous Mrs. Caudle in her nagging curtain lectures.[5]

Her ever ready sympathy, encouragement, and stimulation will be of utmost benefit not only to the Rabbi but indirectly to his congregation, to the community at large, and to Judaism.

The second question put by the President is, "What precautions and what don'ts would you urge with regard to the participation of the Rabbi's wife in the problems of his ministry?" In my opinion the Rabbi's wife should take no part in the solution of such problems. An experience of 33 years as a minister's wife and many years longer as a minister's daughter have shown me conclusively that the Rabbi's wife must steer clear of openly taking part in settling of any problems. She must avoid everything which may be looked upon as interference. She may, however, be the power behind the throne, but she must be *behind* the throne and not *apparent*. The lay mind is peculiar. It will courteously and tolerantly receive suggestions, ideas, and even rebuke from the Rabbi's lips, but will impatiently resent any suggestions, no matter how valuable, from his wife.

My dear colleagues need not be uneasy: There are many positive duties which we are permitted and are practically expected to carry out. Among them I would mention the privilege of preserving peace in the congregation. The exceedingly difficult task needs so much tact and patience and delicate handling that the Rabbi's wife can often do more in this direction than the Rabbi himself. I contend, perhaps conceitedly, that the peace of the home, of the congregation, of the country lies in the hands of the women. They can so often soothe irritation and smooth difficulties which do arise. The Rabbi's wife knows so much of what is happening in her congregation that she often has the opportunity, in an unobtrusive way, to prevent misjudgments, and to clear up misunderstandings. To this end, she must scrupulously carry out her social duties and react sympathetically to the life of the congregation and to that of its members. She must visit her congregants as much as her time and energy permit. Here youth will score. I regret I have to restrict myself to visit only on special occasions, joyous and sad. Her members must feel that they can easily have access to her and that their visits to her home are welcome. The Rabbi's wife must endeavor to be the friend and, if called upon, the confidante of every family in her congregation. In this connection, however, unnecessary as it may be, I take the liberty of warning her against a *faux pas*. She must scrupulously respect the confidence reposed in her and never be tempted in the slightest way to give hints to others of what she has confided to her.

The Rabbi's wife will sometimes be requested to perform peculiar tasks. And if so asked, she must use the utmost tact, discretion, and understanding to carry them out effectively. Many mothers view with anxiety and trepidation the modern outlook of the young towards marriage; and their callousness in not regarding it as a life partnership fills parents with dread and foreboding. There are still old-fashioned mothers who believe that if the ordinances of our Jewish Law were better observed, they might create greater stability and sanctity in family life. But these mothers stand in awe of their up-to-date daughters, and therefore turn to the Rebbetzin and ask her help. They may request her to explain to their daughters the special duties which have been given to the Jewish women to help them preserve the beauty, the purity, the modesty, and holiness of the Jewish family. These duties, they believe, are the bulwark of protection against outside evil influences, and undoubtedly have been the strongest pillar in the preservation of our people. They remember that their own mothers had no difficulty in teaching them their religious observances, because they were obedient to parental authority and example, faithful and God-fearing, and had no doubts and no questionings. They fear, however, the skeptical influences and indifference of the present age, and feel themselves incapable of teaching their own daughters what they learned from their mothers—that privileges entail responsibilities, that the restrictions imposed upon us are for our good, and that obedience to God's Law will bring its own reward. The Rabbi's wife has a wonderful opportunity of helping our young daughters to understanding. She may rest assured that if she succeeds in this, it will be love's labor well spent. If our young daughters will be taught sympathetically and intelligently, they will understand. And if they will understand what is required of them by our Holy Law, they will, I am certain, obey and observe it.

The Rabbi's wife has a greater power than she is conscious of in forming the character and strengthening the faith of the daughters of Israel. If she can only surround herself with the young girls of the congregation at their impressionable age and enlist them in her work, she will gain their love and their admiration, and then it will be easy, very easy for her to exert her influence upon them and impress upon them her own outlook on life and regard for our Faith. She will have good material at hand to mold into noble Jewish lives.

Still another duty, which is particularly the province of the Rabbi's wife, is her encouragement and promotion of all movements which make for improvement in the condition of the poor. In fact, charity is one of her chief domains. As the wise King puts it: "The law of kindness is on her lips" (Prov. 31:26). The work of her sisterhood will occupy a great deal of her time, thought, and energies. It will be her privilege to place this self-sacrificing work on a high plane and to make the sisterhood an efficient instrument to answer the needs of her congregation and calls from without.

If it possibly can be avoided, she should not be the president of her sisterhood. If circumstances force this office and this honor upon her, she must be very circumspect and carefully divide the work and still more carefully distribute the honors. Whether president of her sisterhood in name or in fact, she has to see to it that that organization takes its full share in the larger organization of which it forms a constituent and which represents its religious viewpoint, and also in the still larger community of charitable endeavor. She herself must give her support to all good movements and foster cooperation wherever possible and necessary.

There is so much overlapping in our community that I cannot refrain from bringing in my hobby horse—organization and cooperation in the various districts. With all due respect to the stronger sex, when it comes to details in arrangements, most women have more patience and therefore are specially fitted to do work in this much needed direction. Each of you will know just which branch of philanthropy or education needs your efforts in cooperation. I found the distribution of Passover relief in a very chaotic state when we arrived here nearly thirteen years ago. Thanks to the willing service and kindly and generous cooperation of the Rabbis' wives in Yorkville, we have now a strong United Yorkville Joint Passover Relief Fund, which is of utmost benefit to the poor and much appreciated by them.

The third question which was put to me is, "Would you draw any distinctions in connections with this subject between the small town congregation and the big city congregation?" To my mind the small town congregation is the miniature of the large one. The negative and positive counsels I have given apply just as much and perhaps more to the small congregation than to the large one. One advantage there may be that, the field being smaller and the problems lesser, the work might be easier. But here, probably, it will be necessary for the Rabbi's wife to take part in the teaching in the religious school, particularly if she has special qualifications for such work and if the congregation is not blessed with too much wealth.

All these multifarious duties will certainly duly occupy the time and engage the mind and energies of the Rabbi's wife. Therefore, I will add only one more duty, and that is *self-preservation*. She must not overtax her strength. Her health and good spirits are the best assets which she can give her husband and her congregation. In her zeal and enthusiasm she must not be carried away into overwork. She must always remember that the staunchest friend the Rabbi has, and the most reliable worker the congregation has, is the Rabbi's wife.

"My Occult Powers"

Channa Gerstein | 1947

After World War II, the rebbetzin's portfolio began to change, as did the role of women in American society. In this period, the Orthodox rabbi's wife took on a larger role as the matriarch of the Orthodox congregation. She mentored young brides and looked after ill women and others in distress. In turn, the rebbetzin emerged as a public figure within her synagogue and a role model for female congregants. Channa Gerstein of the Passaic Park Jewish Community Center in New Jersey articulated this position, and an excerpt from her "Reflections of a Rebbitzen" is provided below.

There is a school of thought which holds that the rabbi's wife should stay out of the public picture as much as possible. I did not share that viewpoint. The Rabbi's wife can perform greatly in the furtherance of traditional Judaism by standing forth as a symbol of the woman's place in the synagogue. The notion is currently that the traditional synagogue relegates the woman to a subordinate position. Such an impression if allowed to stand and gain currency may prove ruinous to the synagogue in a land of woman's suffrage. The Rebbetzin's participation in the affairs of the synagogue may be eloquent testimony to the role a woman may play in the synagogue.

I for one never held any particular office in the Sisterhood or any other organization, but in my unofficial capacity I did suggest, guide, and encourage action along certain lines. Because of my position, I was able to lend effective assistance to the membership drive, programming, sick visiting, and in the Mitzvah of welcoming newcomers. . . .

The path a Rebbetzin has to tread is not all a bed of roses. The feeling of having to live up to certain expectations, of leading a sort of goldfish existence, may prove burdensome at times. These disadvantages, however, were more than compensated for by the genuine respect, admiration, and love that were showered upon me. In some cases there was an almost superstitious faith in my occult powers. I recall the episode told to me by a devoted friend who was nevertheless a member of the Reform group. She had treasured a miniature Torah I had given her, and how much that scroll meant to her came home to me when she related in utter seriousness that her infant grandchild had taken sick in a rather mystifying manner. Checking back on her diet and outdoor activity to determine the causes of her illness, they could find nothing to account for it. Then they happened to come upon the little Torah standing in its ark—it was in an upside down position. Ever since they took good care of that little scroll!

Let me not omit mention of another feature which contributed to the sweetness of life—that of serving as *unterführer* for bride or groom during the war days when marriages were consummated under emergency conditions.[6] Nor should I fail to mention the many truly stimulating acquaintances that were made when the Rabbi and I had the privilege and pleasure of being hosts to distinguished guests who came on various missions.

In short, whenever anyone lacking full appreciation of my position as Rebbetzin would attempt to commiserate with me and offer me sympathy, I would tell them: Save your sympathy for someone that really needs it. I am grateful to the Almighty for my portion.[7]

The Role of the Rabbi's Wife

Theodore L. Adams | MARCH 1959

Rabbi Theodore L. Adams (1915–84) held a number of pulpit positions, including one at Congregation Ohab Zedek on New York's Upper West Side. He also served terms as the president of the Rabbinical Council of America and the interdenominational Synagogue Council of America. In the late 1950s, Adams was appointed to the editorial board of the RIETS alumni magazine and consistently penned columns in its pages. In 1959 he offered his perspective on the role of the rabbi's wife, a position that promoted domesticity, one that was far more in vogue decades earlier.

There is an old cliché which states that behind every successful man, there is a woman. More often than not, this woman is a self-effacing modest woman. In the rabbinate this saying holds especially true, for a rabbi's wife has a prominent but difficult role. If a woman contemplated marrying a rabbi merely because of the superior position she will have in relation to other women or because of the glamour of being in the public's eye, both she and her husband's profession, upon analysis, are seen to suffer. The rabbinate is one profession in which a successful man must be backed by his wife.

The position of a rabbi's wife is a very complicated one. A constant dilemma of how to act presents itself to her. Must she remain the influ-ence at home only, inspiring her husband *behind* the scenes, or should she extend her influence to the various aspects of congregational life that would present her as an individual and entity in the community? If she is too withdrawn she runs into the danger of being judged as indifferent. If she is too forceful she might incur the displeasure of the members of the congregation. The writer, judging from observation and analysis, has arrived at a pattern which he believes is the proper one. The rabbi's wife, talented or not, should be very careful in consent-ing to be drawn into positions of leadership for one of many reasons.

First, the rabbi has so little time to spend at home and in many instances sees very little of his children. He must have someone in the family capable of dispensing the deep moral and religious influences that only a mother can give. If his wife is engaged in communal affairs to the extent her husband is, the family must be neglected.

Secondly, capable workers are constantly sought by all organizations, communal and congregational. The number of communal and congre-gational demands made by these organizations upon the rabbi's wife is too great to have her do justice to all. She therefore must discriminate. In this process offending one organization or another is inevitable.

Thirdly, the rabbi's wife, in addition to her responsibility of being a mother of children and making the rabbi's home in appearance and conduct a reflection of everything he teaches, has a responsibility to the rabbi as "the woman behind the rabbi." Every man has latent special abilities and it takes only a little encouragement and careful prodding to bring them out. When the rabbi's wife uses her abilities to spur on her husband, stimulate him to develop and realize faculties he may be quite unaware he possesses, she is helping herself as well as her hus-band. In this area she is appreciated to a greater degree. Through ever-ready sympathy, encouragement, and stimulation she is indirectly of greater assistance to the community through her husband than if she took over certain activities and did them herself. In the congregation self-effacement, tact, cordiality, and courtesy are sure paths of suc-cess for the rabbi's wife. This rule applies to Sisterhood matters, too.

The rabbi's wife should seek to be active but not president, taking second place to other women possessing, or believing they possess, equal ability.

There is another factor that should influence the conduct of the rabbi's wife in a community—the psychological well-being of the rabbi. Many capable men have been relegated to second place in the minds of community members because of the overwhelming personality of their wives. In many cases brought to the attention of this writer, even sermons have been credited to the rabbi's wife, while ideas and programs presented were surreptitiously discussed as the "brain children" of the "rebitzen." Respect for a rabbi's judgment is considerably impaired in such cases. The community's confidence in the rabbi's abilities is badly shaken and the rabbi himself soon loses confidence in his own capacities through such an outgoing, overwhelming, though talented spouse. So much more good can be accomplished for the rabbi, the family, the community, and all concerned when the rabbi's wife having ability and talent is able to utilize them to enhance her husband's prestige and position. The lay mind is peculiar in this respect. It can appreciate and even tolerate criticism from a rabbi, but it impatiently resents any recommendation by the rabbi's spouse, no matter how valuable the advice. Every rabbi's wife should note this.

In order to prepare the ground for a pleasant relationship between rabbi, rabbi's wife, and community, a rabbi should impress upon his congregation at the outset that his wife's services are not contracted for when he assumes spiritual leadership. This is equally valid in small-town communities as in large ones. With a clear-cut knowledge of one's own goals and ideals, approached with a sensible understanding, the rabbi and his wife can enjoy normal and happy relationships within their communal and social life. The rabbi is deserving of no less privacy and mastery over his life than anyone else. If it is clear to all what his role and his wife's role are, the community will respect his definition and develop a healthy relationship with all concerned. The rabbi's wife herself is the best instrument for consolidating the pattern of a judicious and satisfying relationship that produces lasting results.

A Rebbitzen Respectfully Dissents

Helen Felman | NOVEMBER 1959

Rabbi Adams's column did not resonate with the Orthodox rebbetzin. In particular, it provoked Helen Felman (1914–2003), the rebbetzin of Congregation Judea Center of Brooklyn, to publish a dissent on behalf of "many other rebitzens" in the RIETS magazine. Far from relating a feminist viewpoint, Felman argued for her place as a female leader in the congregation that did not conflict or seek to emulate the Orthodox (male) rabbi.

In a recent issue, Rabbi [Theodore] Adams projected the ideal role of the rebitzen as that of non-involvement in the programmatic and administrative aspects of the synagogue.

I would like to take exception to this viewpoint and I am probably echoing the sentiments of many other rebitzens who have chosen a course of active participation in synagogual and community affairs.

I feel that a rebitzen, in addition to being a devoted wife and mother, is, by virtue of her inescapable status, the first lady of the congregation. Her counsel will inevitably be sought by the Sisterhood; her unique abilities by virtue of her Jewish rooting especially qualify her to assist in many vital areas. She can desist or she can become an active force for good in the synagogue, believing firmly that thereby, she is aiding and advancing her husband and the cause of Judaism.

It is no wonder that a rabbi's wife is honored by a unique title, "Rebitzen," denoting an inescapable community role. If she is truly to be a source of psychological strength to her husband, to encourage and to counsel, then she must have a realistic understanding of synagogual affairs which can only come from a rebitzen who is involved. Like Mrs. Roosevelt who was the eyes and ears of her husband, so can a rebitzen be similarly helpful.[8]

Attendance at Sabbath services is very important. Here she can be helpful in evaluating her husband's sermons and possible procedural failings which are not discernible from the altar. Greeting people with "Gut Shabbos" after service is excellent public relations, certain to evoke good will.

I believe that a rebitzen's primary role should be in cultural activities in Sisterhood and in outside organizations. She is uniquely qualified for this role and has a positive contribution to make. In this capacity, she will find herself a member of the Sisterhood Board and thus exercise a voice of restraint or encouragement in matters crucial to our ideology. Deviationist tendencies can thus be curbed, trefa affairs sidetracked, and traditional Judaism encouraged.

Of course, a rebitzen should never permit herself to outshine her husband by word or deed. In her every endeavor, she must ask herself, "Will this further the welfare of my husband and thereby redound to the benefit of the organization as well?" Her role is strictly auxiliary; the rabbi is always the shining luminary.

Some rebitzens may feel timid, fearful in assuming roles for which they have had no formal training. I can state that it's not the training but rather the sincerity, the warmth, the love of people, and the desire to serve that really count . These qualities will, unquestionably, bring honor to herself and to her husband while, in general, evoking good will.

Rabbi Adams is entitled to his opinion, but this rebitzen respectfully dissents.

Helen Felman (Mrs. Meir Felman)
Brooklyn, New York

SECTION 2 | A Female Synagogue Leader

Is Now the Time for Orthodox Women Rabbis?
Blu Greenberg | 1993

In 1984 writer and feminist Blu Greenberg publicly posed a question to her Ortho-
dox community in the wake of the Conservative Movement's decision to ordain
women: "Will there be Orthodox women rabbis?" Herself a rebbetzin (Rabbi
Yitz Greenburg's wife), Greenberg was unsatisfied with this less official synagogue

leadership position, and she continued to agitate for larger and more professional-
ized roles for women in Orthodox life. In 1993 Greenberg wrote another essay on
this topic. In it, she explained that the currents of American Orthodox Judaism
had encouraged her to redouble her efforts to advocate for women's ordination.

Today there are no Orthodox women rabbis to serve as role models. No equivalent status of leadership is conferred upon Orthodox
women. No one asks a woman's opinion on halachic matters. Nor are
there community expectations. In fact, the lines have hardened. Once
not an issue within Orthodoxy—so remote was it from communal
consciousness—the matter has now come closer to home with the
ordination of traditional Conservative women. And the response from
centers of Orthodox authority tends to be: Not Permissible!

Moreover, Orthodox women themselves are largely inhospitable
to the idea. This despite the growth of a curious new form of discrimination against them: Because the title "rabbi" is required for certain
non-congregational positions, such as hospital chaplaincy (in which
Reform, Conservative, and Reconstructionist women rabbis figure
prominently), Orthodox women who might otherwise qualify are
simply out of the loop. Another example: the Women's Cabinet of the
UJA ought to—and probably soon will—have a woman rabbi in its
service.[9] I can think of several Orthodox women who would be excellent religious mentors for the cabinet, but lacking the title "rabbi," their
names would never be considered.

Similarly, Orthodox women are left out of the networking that goes
on between religious women leaders. Orthodox women are not nour-
ished by intergroup dialogue, nor do they contribute to others the
unique insights of Orthodoxy.

On the other hand, we do have role models. There has been an
explosion of women's learning within Orthodoxy, intensive learning
of sacred texts and—particularly new—study of Talmud. Whereas a
generation ago, only a handful of women were taught Talmud—among
them the two daughters of the great Rabbi Joseph B. Soloveitchik, of

blessed memory—today thousands of Orthodox women study Talmud, some making it their life's work.

Institutions of higher learning of religious texts have been created for women, among them Drisha, the first and most established (Manhattan); Machon N'shei Torah (Brooklyn); Shalhevet (Queens); Ma'ayan (Boston); and many in Israel. Add to this list long-standing institutions that have reshaped their curricula to accommodate women's new learning, such as the *yeshiva* day and high school system and the Stern College Kollel program. Add again the university doctoral programs in Talmud in which substantial numbers of Orthodox women are enrolled, and you have a virtual transformation of the intellectual potential of the community. Shortly we shall have a critical mass of learned women who have mastered the qualifying texts for rabbinic ordination.

Moreover, the numbers of noteworthy female teachers of religious texts has risen. A generation ago, there was but one—the incomparable Nechama Leibowitz.[10] Her vast knowledge of rabbinic commentary on the Torah inspired many thousands of students. Today there are Orthodox women who teach Scriptures, commentary, *halachah*, *midrash*, codes, and even Talmud. And contrary to the stereotypes some hold of Orthodoxy, there has been communal appreciation of women in these roles not in every instance, but in enough to make it apparent that the love of Torah prevails, no matter the gender source. Thus Nechama Leibowitz, Naomi Cohen, Chanah Beilinson, Oshra Enker, Aviva Zornberg, Menucha Chwat, Tamar Ross, Chanah Henkin, Devora Steinmetz, Dena Weiner, Malka Bina, Esther Krauss, Rivka Haut, Beruriah David, Maidy Katz, and several dozen others may not carry the title "rabbi," but they serve in similar ways. These women have different areas of specialization and different depths of knowledge, but all are totally dedicated to Torah learning within the tradition.

In an open society, role models can come from outside one's community. The existence of women rabbis and the honorable ways they serve speaks more powerfully than a thousand debates on the subject. In Riverdale not long ago, a Reform rabbi, Shira Milgrom, taught a class in *Mishnayot* to a group of Orthodox women.[11] That she was friend and neighbor was her entrée. But in the encounter itself, in the acceptance of her as teacher, new ideas about women rabbis were surely replacing old diffidences.

I believe the ordination of Orthodox women is close at hand. The cumulative impact—of a critical mass of students of Talmud and *halachah*, a plethora of rising-star teachers, the support of educational institutions, and the presence of respected women rabbis in the liberal denominations—will be to transform the expectations of Orthodox women. This will be a powerful agent for change.

The Female "Congregational Educator"

Richard Kestenbaum | 1997

In December 1997 Rabbi Adam Mintz (b. 1961) of Lincoln Square Synagogue in Manhattan hired the first female congregational intern to serve an Orthodox congregation. Mintz tapped Julie Stern Joseph (b. 1973), a fellow at the nearby Drisha Institute, to occupy a role in which she would teach adult education, provide pastoral counseling, and visit women in the hospital. In a letter to the congregation, Mintz stressed the congregational intern's ability to "expand both the educational and pastoral components within the synagogue" and "provide an opportunity for women in the congregation to utilize the services that another woman can provide more fully and appropriately." Later on, Lincoln Square and other Orthodox congregations employed female "community scholars" and "congregational educators" to aid the clergy. In a letter to Lincoln Square's lay leaders, President Richard Kestenbaum (b. 1956) announced Joseph's appointment and the implications it had for Orthodox Judaism.

To All Officers and Honorary Presidents:
I am delighted to announce that Lincoln Square Synagogue will be adding a new position of Congregational Intern. The new position will be held by Julie Stern Joseph and she joins us on January 1, 1998.

Julie Stern Joseph is currently studying for her certificate at The Drisha Institute (graduation expected in 2000). Concurrently, she is working towards her Master's Degree in Medieval Jewish History which she expects to earn in 1999. She graduated from Barnard College with a B.A. in Jewish History in 1996 (Cum Laude, Dean's List all three years). She is also a graduate of Midreshet Lindenbaum, which she attended from 1991 to 1993. Over the last four years she has taught courses at Barnard College, Machon Gold, and Congregation Beth Shalom in Lawrence NY, where her husband is currently the Rabbinical Intern. During 1994 and 1995, Julie was a member of two special programs at Barnard and Columbia-Presbyterian during which she trained with social workers, physicians, and government prosecutors to deal with emergencies in homes including abuse of drugs, alcohol, or other persons.

The new position of Congregational Intern will allow the Synagogue to offer better religious and pastoral services to women in our community. Julie's immediate functions will be to visit women who are ill or giving birth, counsel women or families that require assistance, and teach. Since our teaching schedule is already in place, Julie's immediate function will be to teach on an ad hoc basis. Her first public comments will be at Seudah Shlishit [Sabbath afternoon meal, lit., "third meal"] on January 17, 1998. She will be added to the teaching schedule on an as-needed basis for the immediate future.

Julie will be the first woman in the world to hold such a position in an Orthodox Synagogue.

For the first six months, the cost of Julie's employment to Lincoln Square Synagogue will be zero as she will be working on a volunteer basis. At the end of six months, Julie's position will be evaluated and if she continues on a paid basis at that time, additional funds outside of our normal fundraising channels will be obtained.

I am very excited about this opportunity for Lincoln Square Synagogue to once again lead by providing outstanding services to our community within our fiscal constraints.

Kindest regards.
Richard Kestenbaum

New Roles for Rebbetzins

Abby Lerner | 1998

The 1990s introduced some new opportunities for Orthodox women in the synagogue, and others agitated for even larger, more "rabbinic" roles for them. In fact, the long-established position of rebbetzin underwent further change in this period. In 1998 Abby Lerner (b. 1952) offered her assessment of this metamorphosis. She and her husband had arrived at the Young Israel of Great Neck in 1975 and were involved in the changes that occurred over the ensuing decades. More than two decades later, the "new role" or expectation of the rabbi's wife was apparent. As Lerner shared in her article, the Orthodox rebbetzin was now called on to play an even larger role in shepherding the women of her congregation, at times assuming roles in halakhic, pastoral, and educational spheres of Jewish life. Unlike the other "newer" female congregational roles, this expanded, yet traditional position never faced similar levels of scrutiny among observers.

As the role of women continues to change and become more complex, the traditional role of the *rebbetzin* is also undergoing a transformation. Being merely a "hostess" is not enough for *rebbetzins* or their communities. Although few *rebbetzins* neglect the task of providing a warm, welcoming atmosphere in their homes for congregants, most recognize that the "job" has become much more.

In the last two decades or so, rabbis and *rebbetzins* have become educational resources. We are asked to lecture and give classes. These requests are a result of better secular and Jewish educational experiences for both *rebbetzins* and other women in present society and the desire for more learning. Many *rebbetzins* have found it necessary to further their education and learn more to stay ahead of their eager students.

Another crucial area requires more preparation from the *rebbetzin*. The community rabbi is often the first line of defense in answering *halachic* questions and dealing with problems of interpersonal relationships, but the *rebbetzin* also plays an important part in these issues, especially among women in the community. It is very possible that the *rebbetzin* may receive the first call when there are personal problems between parents and children and husbands and wives. Although what may really be needed at this point is the advice of a mental health professional or the *halachic* perspective that the rabbi can offer, it may seem much less threatening to call the *rebbetzin* who after all is a "friend." As problems in the religious community become more complicated, we are obligated to read as much as possible on parenting, marital relationships, and general psychology. We must learn not only so we can help, but so we will know when we can't help, and when we are in over our heads. Staying in touch on some level with psychologists, psychiatrists, and educators is a requirement to learn and expand our base of information, and discussing ideas ensures that we are on the proper course of action. It is important to keep a list of these professionals and their telephone numbers handy. Sometimes the very best suggestion is to encourage outside help and then back it up with a referral to someone you know.

Rebbetzins can have an invaluable function as liaisons in the area of *taharat hamishpachah*. Although it is gratifying to note that more women now are asking questions of their *poskim* [experts in Jewish law] regarding this very personal subject, most women still do not. It seems that the most religious women would much rather suffer than ask a question of a rabbi. I believe quite strongly that we must educate ourselves much more extensively, but even without a sophisticated background in this area, a *rebbetzin* can still field a woman's questions and, if necessary, call the *posek*. Of course, it is better if the woman makes the call, but if she cannot be convinced, so much anguish can be alleviated if the *rebbetzin* intervenes. When her knowledge of *halacha* is more comprehensive, she can do an even better job. The *rebbetzin* can question the woman more intimately to get the pertinent facts and the detailed information that may allow the *posek* to decide more leniently in a particular situation. Often a woman will not share these details with her *posek* because of embarrassment or because she is unaware of their significance. Sometimes the *posek* himself doesn't ask all the necessary questions. It is natural for a woman to feel more comfortable speaking to a *rebbetzin*. Our involvement can make a serious and important contribution to the well-being of the families in our communities.

For those *rebbetzins* who choose to fully participate in the community life that we have been thrust into by our husbands' jobs, there is so much to do. Our "new" roles are much more taxing—but so much more significant and that much more rewarding.

Yes, We Are Orthodox, and Yes, We Hired a Female Member of Our Clergy!
Adam Scheier | 2013

In 2013 Congregation Shaar Hashomayim in Montreal hired Rachel Kohl Finegold (b. 1980) to serve as a member of the clergy. Finegold was one of the first graduates of Yeshivat Maharat, a New York school that trains women for Orthodox clerical positions. In May 2013 Rabbi Adam Scheier (b. 1978) explained to his congregation the reasons for Finegold's appointment and justified the move within the parameters of Modern Orthodox Judaism. An excerpt of the Yeshivat Chovevei Torah–trained rabbi's sermon is below.

We have been blessed to see a great deal of wisdom as of late. We have engaged in a thoughtful conversation about the role of women in Orthodox Judaism, and we should be proud that, on an international level, Shaar Hashomayim has played a central role in this conversation. We have played a role because our members care about the place of women in Jewish leadership, and we have played a role because we are a congregation that adheres to the practices and teachings of Modern Orthodoxy.

And we should be proud of both of these. We are *unapologetically* Orthodox, while at the same time a home for Jews of all levels of observance; and we are *unapologetically* modern, embracing the social challenges presented to us by our Canadian values and society.

And we should be proud of the *chochma* [wisdom] inherent in our conversation. We respect the wisdom of our ancestors. We listen. We respond thoughtfully. And we progress forward.

Part of this progress has led to the hiring of a Maharat—a Madricha Hilchatit Ruchanit v'Toranit—a guide in matters of Jewish law and spirituality. A recent editorial in the *Canadian Jewish News* "applaud[ed] Montreal's Shaar Hashomayim Congregation, which snapped up Rachel Kohl Finegold, one of Yeshivat Maharat's first three graduates.... Shaar Hashomayim [is] blazing the trail of the future."[12] With all of the incredible support, and with all of the voices that have applauded this significant step for our congregation, it is important to acknowledge that not all have enthusiastically supported us.

Consider that, over the past few months, there have been two avenues of opposition to our decision. The first has been to discredit us as an institution that cares about Jewish Law. The second has been to discredit the overall initiative to promote women's involvement in the spiritual leadership of the Orthodox community.

A few months ago, an article was posted on the Internet which asserted that Shaar Hashomayim should stop billing itself as a traditional congregation: "Nothing could be further from the truth. Yes, they have a mechitzah and use the orthodox siddur, but that's where it stops.... The rabbi there, Adam Scheier, is a product of Chovevei Torah, the controversial rabbinical seminary headed by Rabbi Avi Weiss."[13]

I believe that it's been quite some time since my "controversial" rabbinical school, of which I am proud to have been a member of the first graduating class, entered the mainstream of the North American Orthodox conscience. Included in its graduates are rabbis of major Orthodox congregations in North America, countless Orthodox educators in schools, Hillels, and other organizations, and even the Chief Rabbi of Finland. Each and every day, tens of thousands of individuals are being inspired and are learning from compassionate Open Orthodox rabbis. The only thing controversial—no, scandalous—related to the rabbinical school is the reluctance of the Rabbinical Council of America to accept these rabbis into its club of Orthodox Rabbis. But I am proud that, in my nine years in Montreal and in my nine years as a member of the Rabbinical Council of Canada, my courageous Canadian Orthodox colleagues have never questioned my Orthodoxy, nor have they considered me particularly controversial.

The article continues: "Scheier recently attended the installation ceremony of the new 'rabbi' . . . at Montreal's Reform Temple. . . . Even worse, Rabbi Scheier recently invited her to lecture at the Shaar's adult continuing education program." In other words, as proof to the fact that I—that we—are not traditional, that we are rebellious reformers of Jewish law, that we are dangerous threats to the unbroken chain of halakhic tradition, they cite something that I'm so deeply proud of. To have respectful relationships with colleagues of other denominations is a value of Open Orthodoxy. Upholding the value of Am Yisrael [people of Israel], unity amongst the Jewish people, doesn't detract from our Orthodoxy—rather, it enhances and strengthens it.

Rabbi David Hartman would often speak to us, to his students who were rabbis, about how Orthodox rabbis who willingly engage in dialogue with other denominations demonstrate tremendous faith in their Judaism.[14]

Our Judaism, he would remind us, is one that won't crumble under the influence of divergent opinions. He suggested that those who withdraw from dialogue believe that the moment one allows outside influences to compete with the life of Torah, the Torah will lose. But those of us who know and love our tradition, our halakha: we know that our tradition will not only survive any challenge or change, but will grow stronger from it.

The article continues: "On the home page of their website, the Shaar says that they adhere to traditional halacha! Just to add to the confusion, Rabbi Adam Scheier's wife is attending Rabbi Avi Weiss's seminary for women 'rabbis.'" Years ago, when there was a particularly painful comment made about me on a Haredi website, I turned to a colleague from another denomination for moral support.[15] He said something that comforted me. He said, "Take it as a compliment. They don't criticize me like that."

"I believe a red line has been crossed, and people should be informed of the true nature of the Shaar and its rabbi. They are definitely NOT traditional. Tevye the Milkman said it best: 'Without our traditions, our lives would be as shaky as—as a fiddler on the roof!'"[16]

. . . Many have opposed Yeshivat Maharat and this new era of Orthodox women's leadership by saying that it is a break from tradition. In fact, the rabbinic wing of the Orthodox Union, the RCA, recently published a statement opposing Abby and Rachel and their classmate Ruth's upcoming ordination from Yeshivat Maharat.[17] The final sentence of the statement is the following: "The RCA views this event as a violation of our mesorah and regrets that the leadership of the school has chosen a path that contradicts the norms of our community."[18]

Friends, don't be fooled. This is a not a break from tradition. If you look closely enough, the women have been there all along. It's just now that we're recognizing their presence, and it's just now that we're stepping aside just a little bit to create a place for that voice to be heard in our Beit Midrash, from our pulpit, and from the other areas of Jewish life which are not halakhically limited to men, but have been traditionally perceived as the domain of men.

. . . But I would argue, as a proudly Orthodox rabbi, that our open and modern Orthodox identity is enriched and deepened by the trailblazers, by those leaders who saw and acted upon the need to do things just a little bit differently than had been done in the past.[19] And it is following their example that we can proudly say, "Yes, we are Orthodox, and yes, we have hired a female member to serve on our clergy!"

CONCLUSION

In May 2000 Julie Stern Joseph left her position as congregational intern of Lincoln Square Synagogue in New York, and her departure left questions about the viability of nonrabbinical female leadership in the Orthodox synagogue. "The idea worked out well at the beginning," explained Rabbi Adam Mintz to the New York press, "then it was less successful."[20] Since then, Lincoln Square has appointed women to serve the rank of "community scholar," while others hired female "congregational educators" to fill a gender vacuum. Stability, though, remains elusive. Likewise, it remains uncertain whether Avi Weiss's Maharat movement will persevere. Only the most progressive-leaning Orthodox congregations in the United States and Canada have hired graduates of Weiss's Yeshivat Maharat for women. Perhaps somewhat too hastily, observers note that the students at Weiss's Yeshivat Chovevei Torah have also struggled to obtain pulpit positions and that the market for an Orthodox female clergywoman might not be sufficient to support the future graduates of Yeshivat Maharat.[21] Still, it is far too soon to offer conclusions. On the other hand, the nonprofessionalized rebbetzin remains a pillar of her Orthodox community. To be sure, some rabbinic wives elect other fulfilling careers, but in other instances, rabbinical spouses have sought out education to help facilitate their congregational role. Yet the most important credential for such Orthodox women remains her marriage to a rabbi and the "traditionalism" that is typically associated with it.

14 | Sliding to the Right and to the Left

INTRODUCTION

In 1977 Rabbi Joseph Soloveitchik told an Israeli journalist that the "new generation is more stubborn than the older one." He saw this among his students at Yeshiva University's rabbinical school and considered it his duty to move them toward "moderation." To Soloveitchik, his "more recent students were not similar to those who preceded them by thirty years. They are not prepared for any compromise." True, he admitted, the new crop of Orthodox rabbis demonstrated a "devotion toward Torah . . . sevenfold what it was in the past" but did not possess the same worldview as their rabbinic master.[1] In part, this was the impact of the "winnowing of American Orthodoxy."[2] Earlier Rabbi Joseph Lookstein referred to the "non-observant Orthodox" who despite their miscreant religious behavior still identified with Orthodox Judaism. When they performed rituals, they did so in Orthodox synagogues and in Orthodox fashion.[3] Yet, by the late 1970s, many of these individuals moved out of Orthodoxy altogether, either to a different movement or to none at all. This winnowing left a stronger core that often gravitated rightward. The "Rav" was not the only one who observed this movement away from the center. To close ranks, Orthodox Jews in the mainstream rebranded themselves as part of a "Centrist Orthodox Movement." Modern, then, was too far to the left.

Much of the commotion over Modern Orthodox and Centrist Orthodox Judaism took place within the walls of Yeshiva University, the undisputed flagship of this movement, regardless of the adjectives used. The "Centrist," Yeshiva University president Norman Lamm, had in mind "moderation" rather than a plotted position between so-called leftists and rightists.[4] Yet others chose to interpret Centrist Orthodox in longitudinal terms, and this new reconfiguration of Modern Orthodox Judaism became more vulnerable to attacks by critics on either flank.[5] In the late 1980s, a cohort of left-leaning clergymen formed the short-lived Fellowship of Traditional Orthodox Rabbis. Members of this group resented the appellation "Centrist" that had replaced "Modern" in Orthodoxy's ranks; a good number of this new cohort were also HTC graduates who led midwestern "Orthodox" congregations that featured family-style seating.[6] Some "liberal rabbis" like Rabbis Irving Greenberg, now president of CLAL (National Jewish Center for Learning and Leadership), and Avi Weiss of the Hebrew Institute of Riverdale accused the RCA of deploying McCarthy-like tactics to silence them on matters of women's leadership and ecumenism.[7] What is more, Greenberg accused Lamm and his Centrists of succumbing to the "powerful intimidation" of the right wing.[8] Others in Greenberg's camp, like Weiss and Rabbi Saul Berman, agreed and launched initiatives outside of Yeshiva University, which they believed no longer could support their work. For instance, in 1997, Blu Greenberg and likeminded women founded the Jewish Orthodox Feminist Alliance (JOFA) to explore women's leadership in the community. Those to the right who had spent much time considering the "embarrassment and degradation" heaped on Orthodox Judaism by Greenberg retargeted their guns to "aim at Lamm."[9] Even the president of the typically middle-of-the-road Orthodox Union told an audience that Lamm's Centrist proposition was "not a helpful idea."[10]

The texts featured in this chapter describe more than just the besiegement of Centrist Orthodoxy. They also point to a "sliding" to both the religious right and left that simultaneously weakened the Center but also expanded the boundaries of the broader Modern Orthodox community. In 1985 Soloveitchik retired from public life and left few other than Lamm to articulate a moderate vision. Two years earlier, Rabbi Shlomo Riskin moved to Israel to establish a settlement in Efrat. Although he still maintained ties to the United States, Riskin and his critics started to posture the once-celebrated centrist closer to the left.[11] In addition, Rabbi Aharon Lichtenstein left Yeshiva University for Israel in the early 1970s and did not feel compelled (one exceptional instance follows at the end of this chapter) to speak up for American Orthodoxy as he had in his 1960s bout with Greenberg. All this impacted the trajectory of Modern Orthodox Judaism and the rank-and-file American Orthodox Jews in the final decades of the twentieth century.

SECTION 1 | The Center under Siege

An American Zionist Lives a "Schizoid Life"
David Landesman | 1976

In the wake of the Six-Day War, many Orthodox Jews in the United States immigrated to Israel. A large number of these Jews were educated in the newly established day schools and attended Zionist summer camps. Their teachers and parents had impressed upon them the importance of the Holy Land; the Zionist triumphalism released by Israel's military victories convinced young Religious Zionists to leave the comforts of American suburbia. On the other hand, the departure of these impassioned and bright young people severely depleted Modern Orthodoxy's ranks. Most prominently, Rabbi Aharon Lichtenstein, the leading light of Yeshiva University, left New York in 1971 to take up a leading role in Yeshivat Har Etzion. In 1976 David Landesman (1949–2015) published a thin pamphlet for Israel's Ministry of Absorption that was distributed by the Orthodox Union. In it, Landesman explained his reasons for resettling in Israel, an excerpt of which is below.

My family came on Aliyah in October of 1972. We had the usual (and sometimes unusual) problems in adjusting to "our" country. But from the first day we were here, we considered it ours. There are many things I find distasteful in Israel; most of them manifestations of the fact that Israel is a secular Jewish state. Yet, despite the secularism, I find Israel to be a very Jewish country. In the United States my religious life had little to do with my political beliefs. I lived a schizoid life—full-fledged Orthodox Jew and at the same time full-fledged American. I do not mean to imply that the two are incompatible; for me they were simply two distinct parts of my being. Israel has united my "several parts" into me, for whatever I do here has Jewish meaning. The thought might very well be hackneyed, but for me it is true. I "kvell" when I see soldiers with payis [sidelocks] and I feel good when I hear the bus driver wish me Shabbat Shalom on Friday afternoon. Emotional? Maybe. But a good many of men's deepest and most basic human needs and life forces are emotional!

We were lucky as we were eligible for housing in Jerusalem. From our bedroom windows we can see Nebi Samuel—the traditional burial place of Shmuel Ha-Navi. A ten-minute walk up the hill takes us to Ramat Eshkol—one of Jerusalem's newer neighborhoods. They coexist with each other—old Nebi Samuel with its religious connotations and Ramat Eshkol with its secular manifestations—for they are both part of the eternity and destiny of Israel. In Israel we've become sentimentalists though we were pragmatists in the America of the 60's and 70's. There is very little that words can express when one attempts to explain the attachment a Jew feels for his land. In truth, though, there is very little that needs explanation. I belong here and that is what made me come.

. . . I tell the following story only for the point it proves to me. I was offered a job in Miami two years after we came. The work would have been rewarding and the financial terms were better than I could hope for in Israel. After much soul-searching we decided to accept the position because it meant building something that was Jewishly important. When the time came to give my affirmative answer I found myself saying "no" with great relief. Until that point I had never realized just how much Eretz Yisrael meant to me. My wife and I have often looked back upon the decision, but without regret. Instinctively, I know that I made the right decision. Whatever contribution I might have made in America is less important than the contribution I made to myself by staying. I'd rather be a Jew without a national prefix.

A Modern Orthodox Utopia Turned to Ashes
David Singer | 1982

In 1982 the editors of the RCA-sponsored Tradition *published a symposium on the "State of Orthodoxy." The contributors offered varied responses, some more optimistic than others. David Singer (b. 1941), editor of the* American Jewish Year Book, *vividly expressed his personal disillusionment with the Modern Orthodox movement. Bothered by what he perceived as a lack of intellectual rigor and experimentation at Yeshiva University and other Modern Orthodox centers, Singer conceded that his teachers and rabbis had surrendered to more "right-wing" elements.*

If Rabbi Joseph B. Soloveitchik is correct in arguing that loneliness is the defining characteristic of the religious Jew, then it is fair to say that I am super *frum*.[12] I am (may God have mercy on me) a modern Orthodox Jew and thus a man without a community. Having crossed a bridge into the modern world, I now find myself stranded there together with a handful of Orthodox intellectuals while the Orthodox community as a whole goes marching off in a traditionalist direction (the widely noted "move to the right").

When I was an undergraduate at Yeshiva College in the early 1960s, I had no idea that things would turn out this way. Then it seemed clear to everyone I knew (the perils of in-group parochialism!) that modern Orthodoxy was here to stay; that, indeed, it was only a matter of time before all the Orthodox joined the modernist camp. Who could resist something as appealing as modern Orthodoxy? Who in his right mind would spurn a form of Orthodoxy which held out the promise of a successful integration of Judaism and Western culture, tradition and modernity, Jewish and American living? Who could be so hopelessly narrow-minded as to choose to live in one world—the world of Jewish tradition—when modern Orthodoxy offered the best of two worlds— the truths of Torah combined with the insights of secular knowledge? This was "synthesis," or as the Yeshiva University motto had it, "Torah and science."[13] It was an inspiring vision, and one that my friends and I fully expected to become a universal reality in Orthodox life.

What went wrong? Why did the dream of a modern Orthodox utopia turn to ashes? For a time I was convinced that modern Orthodoxy had failed the acid test: it had been tried and had been found wanting. Now I know better: modern Orthodoxy did not fail, it never happened.

With few exceptions (perhaps the most notable being Emanuel Rackman), the spokesmen for the movement had been engaged in an elaborate charade. While they talked bravely about modern Orthodoxy representing the true ideal of Torah (à la Maimonides and the like), they really regarded it as a survival strategy—this was America; in America one had to compromise; and that compromise was secular studies. In their heart of hearts, most modern Orthodox leaders felt guilty about what they were saying and doing. Their model of authentic Jewishness remained that of the East European yeshivah world—a total absorption in Judaism's sacred texts. Hence, when Orthodox traditionalism reared its head, the spokesmen for modern Orthodoxy immediately retreated. Who were they to argue with "Torah-true" Jews? How could they (with their PhDs no less!), stand up to the *gedolim*? The battle to determine the future shape of Orthodoxy in America came to an end even before it began.

If what I am saying seems wildly exaggerated, consider for a moment that Frankenstein of modern Orthodoxy: compartmentalization. Yeshiva College claimed to be offering its students "synthesis"—the mutually enriching interaction of Judaism and Western culture. In fact, however, the two spheres were almost never permitted to come into contact with each other. The yeshivah was the yeshivah and the college was the college; Bible and Talmud were taught with no reference to modern scholarship; the social sciences and the humanities were presented without the slightest regard for Judaic teaching. Had the leadership of modern Orthodoxy been serious about what it was preaching, it would never have permitted this state of affairs—this compartmentalization of reality into sacred and secular realms—to exist. . . . While insisting that it was building bridges between cultures and world views, Yeshiva College was in reality busy erecting intellectual *mehitsot*.

The disastrous consequences of a compartmentalized education are everywhere apparent in what passes for modern Orthodox circles. These Jews are almost invariably religiously observant secularists. They may be meticulous in their observance of the Law, but their values and attitudes are shaped by the surrounding secular culture (on most social issues, they could be card-carrying members of the ACLU [American Civil Liberties Union]). The current crop of modern Orthodox Jews have made a sociological reality out of Louis Ginzberg's famous *bon mot*: act kosher and think *treif*. The only time they do not think *treif* is when they are studying a Jewish text (Bible, Talmud, and so forth). Then, sad to say, they do not think at all! Nothing they have learned in any secular discipline—history, psychology, literature, anthropology, and the like—is ever brought to bear on their understanding of the affirmations of Judaism. All in all, today's modern Orthodox types lead consistently inconsistent lives.

... It would be nice to think that those Jews who remain committed to the creation of an authentic modern Orthodoxy might yet win over the larger Orthodox community to their cause. I am afraid, however, that this is just not in the cards. History, almost certainly, has passed us by. We are pathetically few in number, lack a sound institutional base, and are largely without leadership. Of course, we will persevere in our cause; first, because we believe in it; secondly, because there is no viable alternative on the current Orthodox scene. But we should not fool ourselves: our children—my children—will grow up in an Orthodox world in which talk about "synthesis" will seem totally alien. No wonder, then, that I feel lonely—and profoundly sad.

"Centrist Orthodoxy"

Gilbert Klaperman | 1984

In February 1984 Gilbert Klaperman (b. 1921), president of the Rabbinical Council of America, delivered the major address at the rabbinical group's Midwinter Conference in Upstate New York. Rather than speak about his "Modern Orthodox" circle, the Long Island–based rabbi positioned himself and the RCA as the leaders of "Centrist Orthodoxy." Observers took careful note of this change, as well as Klaperman's impatient stance toward the right-wing sector of Orthodox Judaism, a group that Klaperman described as the "Yeshiva World." A segment of the RCA president's remarks are below.

Although RCA members like to consider themselves as "Centrists," we are being drawn to the right by the adamant inflexibility of those who are at the right.[14] We are intimidated by the right. We react to events and ideologies around us but frequently lack the courage to initiate because of the fear that we may be challenged by our brethren on the right.[15]

Why, for example, if I daven [pray] daily, Shabbos, Yom Tov, and Yomim Noraim [High Holidays] in a yarmulke, must I put on a black hat to officiate at a wedding with other rabbis who are thus attired? We do not have to collapse into miserable surrender because someone who claims greater piety favors a certain form of dress. There is a tyranny in self-declared piety that is as objectionable as the scorn of the left.

There is a belittling in the "yeshiva world," as well as in its graduates who frequent the shtiblach and some Young Israel congregations that are undermining the institution of the synagogue. I know of no major theological difference or religious belief that separates us from the so-called right-wing Orthodox groups. My kashrut is as good as theirs—if not better. I wear the same t'fillin and observe the same mitzvot. And I am prepared to say that among our chaverim there are greater Talmidei Chachamim than there are in that camp. Certainly, we are Talmidei Chachamim enough and intelligent enough to justify our being more secure in our practices.

I therefore call upon the membership of the Rabbinical Council of America to emerge as the leaders of Orthodoxy and the defenders of our faith. For if the Centrist position is lost, then we will, by abdication, establish the supremacy of the sects of the right that will legislate us and all those to the left of us out of the fold. We must develop more tactics and strategy in dealing affirmatively with the problems that face us.

Gifter Slaughters Lamm for Passover

Mordechai Gifter | 1988

On Passover 1988, Rabbi Mordechai Gifter (1915–2001) lectured at the Young Israel of Cleveland. A month earlier, President Norman Lamm of Yeshiva University delivered a speech at the Fifth Avenue Synagogue in New York. The press

reported on Lamm's articulation of "Centrist Orthodoxy" (he was now more com-
fortable with this terminology than Modern Orthodoxy) and criticism of "right-
wing" Orthodox leaders. Gifter, the rosh yeshiva (rabbinic head) of Cleveland's
Telshe Yeshiva and a leading member of the Agudath Israel's Moetzes Gedolei
HaTorah (Council of Torah Sages), responded in scathing fashion. His speech
was delivered on the intermediate days of Passover and cleverly titled (by oth-
ers) "Gifter Slaughters Lamm for Passover." Audio recordings of Gifter's remarks
reached into many Jewish circles. A portion of his rebuke is produced here.

I specifically do not like to use the word "Orthodox" because that has
nothing to do with Torah. "Orthodox" is a Greek term that has nothing
to do with Torah. I am interested in the "Torah community." And the
Torah community means those who live by the dictates of God's Torah.

And now let me unburden myself of something that has been both-
ering me for a long time. We carry a terrible responsibility. Now, let
us read an article in the media—the *New York Times*, March 24, 1988.
It happened not too long ago. This is a report by a reporter named Ari
Goldman in the *New York Times*.[16] It begins:

> Ultra-orthodox Jews (you know what that means? The extremists),
> including the Hasidim, have set the religious agenda for too long in
> both the United States and in Israel, the president of Yeshiva Uni-
> versity said Tuesday, calling on moderate Orthodox elements to
> reassert themselves.[17]

This was a major speech on "Centrist Orthodoxy." Centrist Orthodoxy, says our good friend Lamm, "follows the Halakhah." I do not know
what that means. Do you follow behind it or does the Halakhah govern what you should do? What is Halakah? "Traditional law," explains
Lamm, is "spelling out the authoritative norms of daily conduct, including Sabbath observance and adherence to kosher dietary laws, as well
as moral and ethical behavior."

This is the "Centrist" philosophy—once you do that you are okay.
You do not have to measure whether your business dealings are in

order. But your "moral behavior"—whatever that is—and your "ethical behavior"—whatever that is—and you observe kashrut. You do not observe it to the point that you get the best "hekhsher" you can.

He argues for "Kashrut observance and Sabbath observance." It is said that these people turn on their radios and televisions on a clock to work the entire *Shabbes*. They cannot live without it. I leave it to you to tell me if this is a *Shabbes*, or if that is a joke—not a *Shabbes*.

The article continues: "But unlike what [Lamm] calls the right wing"—I belong to that wing—"Dr. Lamm said the centrist group is open to secular culture, is unabashedly Zionist and values tolerance of different opinions." Now let's take this one by one. In other words, I, the rightist, am not open to secular culture. That is an outright lie. Secular culture can add a great deal to the proper understanding of Torah. The question is: when should the student go to college? Is he first to become a Torah scholar and then go to college, or should he go to college and then try to become a Torah scholar? If he does it that way, there is no hope for him. You do not need to bring proof from Torah for that. It is just common sense.

Now, "who is unabashedly Zionist?" I am not a Zionist? The audacity. Who is a Zionist? Who is the Jew who recites: "May our eyes behold Your return to Zion in mercy"?[18] Who says that? The Zionist Organization? Or, these terrible fanatics—the rightists? Their entire lifeblood is Zion. So if someone is a Zionist, the question is what does he mean he is a "Zionist"? Is he a member of a Zionist organization? Or, is he a member of God's Zionist organization? Is he a part of the World Jewish Congress or American Jewish Congress, who declare themselves as leaders of the American Jewish public and the world Jewish public?

... This individual we have been quoting here has absolutely no contact with that type of individual [a "right-wing" Orthodox Jew]. He does not know what it is all about. And he makes the mistake of thinking that we are not "Centrists." He makes the mistake of thinking that we are against secular knowledge. He makes the mistake of thinking that we are intolerant because we do not stand for Reform and we cannot sit at one table with them. If you want to know who is right, see what the Synagogue Council has done for American Jewry since it was organized and see what "Torah Jewry" has done for American Jewry. From that angle, measure what is truth and what is not truth!

I would like everything we have said here tonight to reach Lamm. Not Rabbi Lamm, but Dr. Lamm. It should reach him so that he can understand where we come from. It is our duty to give thought to what is demanded of us. And to tell Lamm and all his cohorts: "Mind your own business. Go away. We are not disturbing you in the least. Do not try to disturb us."

Baruch Lanner Will Be Your Rabbi
Elie Hiller | 1989

In 1989 Elie Hiller (b. 1964) wrote an open letter to the Orthodox Jewish community in Teaneck, New Jersey, to oppose the appointment of the charismatic Rabbi Baruch Lanner (b. 1949) to lead a local upstart congregation there. Two years earlier, Hiller had resigned as Lanner's assistant at NCSY's New Jersey Region, after Lanner had instigated a violent altercation with Hiller's younger brother. In addition to this, Hiller was aware of Lanner's track record of physical, psychological, and sexual abuse. He outlined all this in his public letter, and Lanner did not assume his position in the congregation. However, Lanner maintained a senior position (though he was moved from New Jersey to the national headquarters) at NCSY, and Hiller was censured by Orthodox rabbis (who later apologized) for damaging the rabbi's reputation. In June 2000 journalist Gary Rosenblatt (b. 1947) published an exposé on Lanner, prompting the swift resignations of Lanner and other leading officers at the youth organization and its parent body, the Orthodox Union. Afterward, the OU appointed Richard Joel (b. 1950) to lead an investigation into the organization's role in the scandal. Coverage of Joel's commission elevated his own status and catapulted him into the presidency of Yeshiva University. In 2002 Lanner was convicted of sexually abusing two teenage girls when he served as principal in a New Jersey high school. He was sentenced to seven years in prison. The Lanner affair raised unprecedented awareness of abuse in the Orthodox community, and much like in Catholic cir-

cles, the Lanner incident was a sea change in the manner in which the Modern Orthodox community addresses and reacts to abuse.

Dear Members of the Jewish Community of Teaneck,
I was one of many residents of the Teaneck Jewish community to receive the most recent update from the Roemer Synagogue announcing the selection of Baruch Lanner as the new, and first, Rabbi of the fledgling synagogue.[19]

This open letter to you is to voice one man's moral outrage over this development and to alert others of what is about to fall upon my fellow Jews of Teaneck, Bergen County and, indeed, the total Jewish community.

To be a Rabbi in the Orthodox community, one is expected to have S'micha (a proper rabbinical teaching and ordination), a firm knowledge of Torah and commitment to its values, and Yirat Shamayim ("fear in G-d who is above"). The specific role and function of a pulpit Rabbi in a community demands other qualities and values that go beyond, yet are merely outgrowths, of the aforementioned virtues.

Baruch Lanner will be expected to speak the words of Torah to parent and child at weekly sermons and ongoing lectures. . . .

Yet, in seven years in NCSY, where I worked alongside him, I have heard Baruch constantly call myself and others "s—heads," "big b—s," "d—face," and "f—," and refer to such anatomical features as the "p—y," the "ba—," the "t-ts," and the "shv—zel" to myself, other advisors, and even children. Baruch would often ask girls, "How big are your breasts?" or if they "gave good bl——bs."

Baruch Lanner will be asked for marital counseling by congregants and their youngsters. . . .

Yet here is what he told one of "his" engaged NCSYers: "Once he sticks it between your legs, you're used material and you can't turn back." He would often ask me if I was "doing it," "sht—ing," or "sticking it up" my wife.

Baruch Lanner will be looked upon as the standard of a Torah home and family values. . . .

Yet, in my presence, I have heard Baruch Lanner yelling at his wife, calling her a "w—e," a "s—t," and a "stupid b—h" on several occasions. He would also, in front of my eyes and to my embarrassment, slam her against the refrigerator and pinch her breasts.[20]

Baruch Lanner will be trusted to insure the privacy of a congregant with regard to delicate affairs and sensitive issues that may be discussed. . . .

Yet a resident of our community can tell you of the times when, as a young lady studying at the Frisch School and boarding at the Lanner residence, Baruch would often sit on her, or search through her drawers to show off her undergarments, or walk into her room while she was undressed and attempt to lift the blankets off her bed where she lay hiding from his probing eyes.[21]

Baruch Lanner will be looked upon to provide guidance and gently lead his flock. . . .

Yet this is the same Baruch Lanner who violently kneed me in the groin, punched me on the back of my neck, and kicked me in the head on countless occasions, and has perpetrated these acts on other advisors and youngsters as well.

Less than two years ago, in an act that precipitated my immediate resignation from NCSY and the job that I loved dearly, Baruch Lanner attacked my brother, Jonah, grabbing and punching him repeatedly and lunging at him with a sharp knife.[22]

I am guilty of, for years, allowing these actions to go unreported. I am not the only one. As a young man committed to the cause and ideals of NCSY, I had rationalized that here was a case of the good outweighing the bad. "Look at all the good work he has accomplished." Baruch had also, on numerous occasions, threatened to withhold my paycheck and my health insurance benefits, and I was married with a month-old daughter to support. Now I am older, wiser, and not afraid of Baruch Lanner.

My family and I have attempted to resolve this matter in quieter fashion. This letter to you is my final recourse, after being ignored by the various parties involved, who could have rectified the situation but, instead, have chosen to look the other way.

The time for silence and pretending to look the other way is over.

At stake is our Jewish community. It will be our children that Baruch Lanner addresses at Roemer's open youth lectures. Our sons and daughters that he invites to his home for a weekend. Our colleagues and neighbors who he will refer to in his preferred choice of words. Our RCBC [Rabbinical Council of Bergen County] which he may someday join.

At issue is not his talents or accomplishments but sensitivity, integrity, and human decency. His appointment will affect our physical and spiritual lives and reflect this community's views of what is to be expected of an Orthodox Rabbi and religious leader.

I write this letter with total candor and utter shame. I write with only the power of my words and what I know to be true and the hope that others express their moral outrage and disapproval to the powers that be. I have spoken up before, and I speak up once again. Can you afford not to?

Respectfully,
Elie Hiller

"Frum from Birth"

Anonymous | 1993

In 1993 researchers published a collection of "portraits" that depicted Jewish life in the United States. In one chapter titled "The Resilience of Orthodoxy," the interviewers included the anonymous testimony of a self-described "Modern Orthodox Jew." This account threw light on the "social" aspects of the Orthodox community that help retain members. In contrast, this source related that the intellectual arguments of Modern Orthodoxy were not sufficiently compelling to retain some of the more intellectually inquisitive Orthodox day school graduates of the 1970s and 1980s.

I'm "F.F.B." It stands for *frum* from birth. It's a term I'd never heard until I read it in that *New York* magazine piece on the "new Orthodox" on the Upper West Side.[23] But I think it's a good term because it points to something interesting. My sense is that people who became Orthodox after not being so tend to be much more serious about things. They don't have a kind of sense of perspective that people who have always been Orthodox tend to have. Because, you know, no one can keep all of the commandments of the Torah; you know, you do the best you can. But it is easy to spot someone who wasn't Orthodox from birth; for example, they'll say much more often, "*im yirzeh Hashem,*" that's like, "I'll see you tomorrow, *if God is willing.*" Fine OK, that's always implicit in anything anybody does, but these newly Orthodox tend to say noticeably more things like that.

I grew up in a dense Orthodox community in Queens. My parents were modern Orthodox; my father is a history professor and my mother works as a consultant on early childhood education at an Orthodox day school. I went to the same shul the whole time, from when I was born until I got married and even for the first seven years of [my] marriage. Now that we've moved to Forest Hills, we are part of an Orthodox community, and we go to the shul there.

Pretty much everyone I grew up with was Orthodox. I had very little contact with the rest of the city, the non-Jewish part, until I went to college. That was really the first time I got to know people who weren't Orthodox or who weren't even Jewish. College can be a difficult time. You come across many different influences, you learn about all the great Western thinkers, and if you're from my kind of background, you have a sense of your insularity. It's natural to question. I saw many of my Orthodox friends from Flatbush Yeshiva become less Orthodox.[24] You are exposed to biblical criticism, and you think, maybe everything in the Torah isn't 100 percent true, or you wonder whether God really cares if I turn on a light on Shabbos, or whether the Torah was really written by God or by people. You can make a good argument that it was written by people. Or Evolution—I think there are ways that Orthodox Jewish scholars have attempted to rationalize, to say that the Torah is right *and* that science is right.[25] Like "years" means thousands or millions of years—things like that. I'm a little skeptical of all that. I just don't know. I've had problems on an intellectual level. In a way, I'm close to an agnostic. I don't *know* if God exists—there are good arguments for it and against it. But I've lived my life on the basis that He does exist, and I guess we'll find out at the end. Who knows? Take AIDS—you know some people say it is a punishment from God. I say, maybe it is and maybe it isn't. Some people get annoyed at that—how can you *possibly* say, even suggest, that AIDS could be a punishment from God? But I just don't know. I'm not God. I think there are things in the world that may point to the existence of God—the creation of the State of Israel, the Six-Day War, other things.

But I view the intellectual side of religion and the practicing emotional part as two completely different things. None of the intellectual questions would make me give up this life. I think the strength of modern Orthodoxy for those who stay Orthodox is that it is like their skin—they don't think about it much, it is just daily life. You don't hear much discussion about the metaquestions, the deeper questions. About practice and law, people do talk and argue. And doing is more important than pure belief—that idea is in the Talmud.

I think questions are there for me and for a lot of people. But it hasn't affected my practice, in part because I'm not sure and there is a good chance that God does exist, but mainly because I derive tremendous emotional satisfaction and comfort from doing these things I've always done. I value very highly having order in my life, and doing everything the way I've always done it gives me a tremendous sense of order. Take Shabbos: I'll come home Friday afternoon, I'll take the kids to shul; most of our friends from the neighborhood are there with their kids; it's a special time for all of us. We'll come home, I'll make Kiddush, my wife will light the candles, we'll sing songs. We won't answer the phone or watch TV or use the car. It's a time when the family is together, doing things together. Like the holidays, which are very satisfying, the repeating of the cycles of the Jewish year. You look forward to each, and the year goes by that way. It is very different from the secular world and its calendar. Here there are real events, the cycle of Jewish time.

An "Unorthodox" Ad?

Haskel Lookstein | 1984

In 1984 Rabbi Haskel Lookstein wrote in the name of "Centrist Orthodoxy" to defend his position on Jewish ecumenism. In response to an advertisement (reproduced after this text) placed in the Jewish press by the Agudath Ha-Rabbonim, Lookstein argued for tolerance toward non-Orthodox Jews, a trait that observers understood as a fleeting quality among America's Orthodox Jews.

The unorthodox advertisement placed by the Agudas Harabonim in the Rosh Hashanah issue of the *Jewish Week*, which "warns Jews not to pray in Reform or Conservative Temples," should not go unchallenged by Orthodox Jews. Many of us are greatly offended by the gratuitous public slap in the face to our friends and co-workers in the Jewish community. We are also deeply disturbed by the advertisement's divisive message at a time when Jewish unity is harder to achieve and more essential than ever to maintain.

The festival of Sukkot provides the Orthodox view of the sanctity, dignity, and inherent worth of every Jew. In a comment about the four species we use during the holiday, the ancient text of the Midrash Rabbah (Lev. Rabbah 30:12) asserts that each represents a different type of Jew with different levels of observance.

The *etrog* (citron) has both taste and fragrance, representing the Jew who reflects both Torah and good deeds. The *lulav* (palm) has taste but no fragrance, representing the Jew who is steeped in Torah but devoid of good deeds. The *hadas* (myrtle) has no taste but has a fragrance, representing the Jew who is poor in Torah but rich in good deeds. The *aravah* (willow) has neither taste nor fragrance, representing the Jew who has neither Torah nor good deeds to his or her credit.

And what are we to do with these species—and the Jews they represent? The Midrash states our responsibility clearly: "Let them be bound together in one unit and they will atone for each other."

The explicit message of this well-known and oft-quoted Midrash is that every Jew is important and that he or she contributes to the wholeness and sanctity of the Jewish people in an essential manner. Some will contribute through Torah scholarship and observance. Some will offer good deeds as their contribution. Some will bring both, while still others will contribute simply by being part of the Jewish people. In the aggregate, we all merit God's forgiveness for our inadequacies and His love for our choosing to be His people, however that choice is manifested.

It is sad when so august a body as the Agudas Harabonim undermines this fundamental unity of all Jews by a public pronouncement on the eve of the holiest season of the year which brought pain and embarrassment to so many. Why did hundreds of thousands of Jews who chose to worship in Reform and Conservative temples and synagogues have to be admonished not to do so but rather to stay home instead? Did they ask a *shaila* (a religious inquiry) to which a response was necessary? Was there anyone, anywhere, who stayed home because of that ad? No, the only thing the ad accomplished was to publicly slap the faces of Reform and Conservative Jews and their rabbis.

Why did they deserve such an insult? Many of them are very heavy contributors in the realm of good deeds. Many of them are deeply involved in perpetuating Jewish life and in saving Jewish lives all over the world. One cannot imagine UJA, Federation, Israel Bonds, and an entire network of Jewish services without these Jews and the rabbis who inspire them to lead Jewish lives. Why repudiate them and their form of Judaism in so insulting a manner?

The answer, presumably, is that the ad proposed to tell New York Jews what was wrong in the eyes of the framers of that ad and to warn them against "sin" and "error." If so, then this form of public teaching is not only insulting; it is also ineffective. Nobody responds to such teaching. No one responded to it when it was the fashion in Eastern Europe 50 years ago. Surely today, in a time of greater freedom and pluralism, this negative approach can only be counterproductive. There are groups which advertise to promote candle-lighting and to urge Jews to pray and to hear the shofar. These are constructive pronouncements. But to tell Jews where not to pray? Such advice, far from being heeded, will only be resented.

Unfortunately, the real result of the ad was to inflame non-orthodox Jews and to create an almost unbridgeable gulf between Orthodox Jews and all other Jews. The anger and vituperation which are evident in the letters published by the *Jewish Week* are a tragic consequence of the inflammatory rhetoric in the ad. The opinions and legal decisions of revered sages like Rabbi Moshe Feinstein and Rabbi Joseph B. Soloveitchik are suddenly grist for the mill of all kinds of writers, most of whom lack the requisite expertise to be able to cite their words accurately and all of whom are, understandably, too angry to represent their views fairly.

We have come to expect such divisiveness between religious and secular and between Orthodox and non-orthodox in Israel. But in America we have learned to live with religious pluralism. We can compete ideologically and religiously without repudiating those with whom we disagree. We are committed to mutual respect and civil discourse, both of which are important Jewish values. We accept boundaries, but we reject barriers. We should not allow an unfortunate advertisement to change these ground rules for our relationships with each other.

This writer is part of a very large constituency of centrist Orthodox Jews—rabbis and lay people—who deeply regret the submission and publication of the Agudas Harabonim's advertisement and who are determined to maintain Jewish unity.[26] We feel that internal strife has no place in k'lal Yisrael at any time. It is utterly unacceptable today when the Jewish people face the most critical challenges and problems locally, nationally, and internationally.

The sainted Rabbi Abraham Isaac Ha-Kohen Kook, of blessed memory, once commented orally on the term "Sukkah shalom." Why, he asked, is the Sukkah a symbol of peace? His answer: The Sukkah need not be perfect; its walls may tilt; they need not touch the ground; they need not even be four in number—two and a fraction suffice. And so it

This advertisement, penned by the Agudath Ha-Rabbonim, appeared in the September 28, 1984, edition of the *Jewish Week*. Courtesy of the editor and publisher of the *Jewish Week*.

is with peace, said Rabbi Kook. It need not be perfect. Even a partial, imperfect peace should be pursued and is worthwhile.[27]

The Misleading Salesmen of Torah u-Madda
Paul Eidelberg | OCTOBER 7, 1988

In 1987 political scientist Paul Eidelberg (b. 1928) served as a visiting professor at Yeshiva College. Shortly after his return to Israel's Bar Ilan University, Eidelberg published a critique of liberal arts education in the New York Jewish press. His rebuke of the Yeshiva College curriculum was part of a much larger assault on

humanities studies taught in American colleges. At YU, more students in the 1980s
preferred to concentrate their studies in the newly established business school and
science programs than focus on literature, history, and philosophy. This intellectually
conservative "Closing of the American Mind" was a deeply troubling trend for Nor-
man Lamm and other advocates of Torah u-Madda (Torah and secular wisdom)
who had grown accustomed to justifying the school's ideology in liberal arts terms.

Having taught in a three-year PhD program on "Politics and Literature,"
I believe I can speak without prejudice about the value or disvalue of
combining literature with Torah education.

The first thing to bear in mind is that virtually all fictional literature
is an escape from reality. Consider the greatest tragic poets, Sophocles and Shakespeare. As the Oedipus cycle indicates, Sophocles was
obsessed with the inability of man to overcome fate. Shakespeare, a
disguised pagan, was disgusted with Christianity and its corruption of
Roman greatness. He really believed that "life is a tale told by an idiot,
full of sound and fury, signifying nothing."

Swift's *Gulliver's Travels* reeks with pessimism. The same may be said
of Kierkegaard, Flaubert, Yeats, and Eliot. Matthew Arnold's *Dover
Beach* reflects the poet's nostalgia for the "sea of faith" desiccated by
science and the industrial revolution.

And in the literature of Conrad, Camus, Sartre, and Hemingway,
one finds little more than the horror, absurdity, and meaninglessness
of human life. No one put it more subtly than Plato. In his dialogue in
the *Symposium*, after a festive night of drinking, only three banqueters
remain sober: Agathon the tragic poet, Aristophanes the comic poet,
and of course the ironic Socrates. Human life is tragic-comedy.

Finally, consider "deconstructive criticism," a French school of literary criticism that has conquered Yale and is sweeping across the USA.
This avant-garde piece of madness makes utter nonsense of language,
denying that language conveys truth, if only because there is no such
thing as "truth." Indeed, for deconstructive critics there is no such thing
as an "author," only readers who read into books their own moods and
feelings. (Apply this to the relationship between psychiatrists and their

clients, and Goethe's prediction that modernity would become one big mental hospital was prophetic.)

Now go to virtually any university in the West. There the quest for truth has been replaced by warring and decrepit ideologies. When Nietzsche defined philosophy as a "species of autobiography," he was anticipating deconstructive criticism which makes truth, including ideas regarding good and bad, purely subjective or relative. No wonder nihilism, homosexuality, and cheating flourish on almost any campus in the democratic world.

Nevertheless, one prominent Jewish university boasts of its program of Torah u-Madda. If *madda* meant science in the rigorous sense of the term, all would be well. But the purveyors of this program include the humanities and social sciences under that honorific category.

Now, as I pointed out in a previous article, the social sciences are not sciences at all but organized common sense—at best.[28] Not only are they based on atheism, but they are permeated by the pernicious doctrine of moral relativism. I have seen the influence of this doctrine on orthodox Jewish students; it dilutes their dedication to truth, hence to Torah. It is clear to me that institutions of Jewish education are oblivious of the corrosive effect of moral relativism.

As for the humanities, obviously they are not sciences. And as I have shown above, they are based on a false conception of man and human history. Hence the salesmen of Torah u-Madda are misleading Jewish students and, of course, philanthropists who support such programs.

The only sound reason for including courses in the humanities and social sciences in any institution of Jewish education is to expose the falsity and pernicious character of the doctrines in question, i.e., moral relativism and subjectivism.

Trashing Torah u-Madda

Behnam Dayanim and Dov Pinchot | OCTOBER 25, 1988

The Eidelberg article deeply troubled a number of Yeshiva College students, including the editors of the student newspaper, the Commentator. *Moreover, it*

*struck a tender chord for the collegiate journalists, since Eidelberg's opposition
to liberal arts was a view shared by a number of the school's leading rabbis and
students. Accordingly, Behnam Dayanim (b. 1967) of Virginia and Dov Pinchot
(b. 1967) of Maryland took up the charge to defend the intellectual openness of
their college and the ideological forces that had long supported it.*

The Commentator will not sit idly by as Yeshiva University takes in attack
after attack to her philosophic foundation, Torah u-Madda—whether
the aggressor be found without or within the University itself. The latest recreant assault was an article in the October seventh issue of *The
Jewish Press*, written by last year's visiting professor at YU, Paul Eidelberg. Professor Eidelberg, claiming the ability to speak without prejudice, expressed not the slightest humility in viciously discrediting a
philosophy supported by such men of immense stature as Rav Joseph
B. Soloveitchik, YU President Norman Lamm, and Rav Aharon Lichtenstein. The Professor of political science seems quite at home lecturing
these Rabbonim (all of whom have received PhDs in the humanities)
on what truths may be gleamed from a purely Judaic education. Professor Eidelberg pretentiously accuses these men, and in fact all who
support the ideal of Torah u-Madda, of obliviousness to the corrosive effect of moral relativism. But he cannot withhold himself from
going one step further: "The salesmen of Torah u-Madda are misleading Jewish students and, of course, philanthropists who support such
programs." Ironically, by presenting his oversimplified analysis in such
a surprisingly unprofessional manner, it is the vainglorious and opin-
ionated Professor Eidelberg who is culpable of misleading.

There exists a different but nevertheless serious challenge to Torah
u-Madda festering within the walls of the University itself. This sour-
ing and in some cases outright rejection of the Yeshiva's philosophy
by certain Roshei Yeshiva is an affront to the Moreh D'Asrah [halakhic
authority] of YU, Rabbi Norman Lamm. The Torah u-Madda lecture
series has, more often than not, provided a forum for speculation on
the validity and utility of Torah u-Madda, rather than an exploration
of positive approaches to this philosophy.[29]

Torah is, without any question, primary in the cultural synthesis espoused by YU. If the individuals who teach the Torah side reject the desirability of this synthesis, the philosophic foundation of this unique Yeshiva University will never attain the greatness to which it aspires.

The Israel Experience
Esther Krauss | 1990

Since the 1960s, many American-born Orthodox Jews traveled to Israel to study in a yeshiva or women's seminary before entering college. Some elected to study in Israel as a semester or year abroad during their college experience. By the late 1980s, the practice had become more popular, and students frequently opted for an additional second year of yeshiva study. Further, parents and teachers noticed that students who had studied in Israel returned to their American homes "flipped out," fervently pious and punctilious in Jewish law. And young people came back uninterested in participating in their parents' brand of Modern Orthodox Judaism. One of the first to notice this phenomenon and put her thoughts into writing was Esther Krauss (b. 1938), principal of Yeshiva University High School for Girls ("Central") in Queens, New York. The educator found much "success" in the Israel experience but also cautioned against unadulterated praise for the "Year in Israel."

On a trip to Israel last January, as one in a throng of parents visiting with their children during intersession (*our* intersession, not theirs), but also as an educator visiting with former students, I was both moved and disturbed by an enlightening discussion I had with a young woman who was in the midst of her second year of study at one of the prestigious educational institutes for women in Jerusalem.

I was touched by the sincerity and, yes, naiveté of her account of the soul-searching that the Israel experience had evoked in her; by the hyper-critical, somewhat jaundiced view of American orthodoxy that had emerged from her limited contacts with a parallel Israeli orthodoxy, and by the concomitant process of religious self-evaluation that comparison had stimulated in her. She was a particularly sensitive and serious young woman for whom Israel had been an appropriate catalyst for the kind of spiritual questioning and growth that every Jew should undergo on the road to maturity. I'm not sure that it could or would have happened in the same way, with the same intensity in America.

I was equally impressed by the intellectual growth, by the satisfaction from "*shteiging*" [rise, or study with intensity] in learning, in *bekiut* [breadth of study], in textual skills, in the use of *sifrei kodesh* [holy books] and reference materials that she so eagerly described to me.

I was disturbed, however, by her statement that much of her growth had taken place in this, her second year. Although I've always maintained that the Israel experience ideally requires a second year, because it takes students at least half a year to adjust to the cultural changes and to find their niche, that was not her explanation. She explained the disparity between the first and second year in other terms, most notably that this year she did not have the "distraction" of her American friends, nor did she now have to deal with constant visits by well-meaning parents interrupting the momentum of her studies with two months of nightly forays to the beckoning local restaurants that exist in such delectable abundance in Jerusalem. As a result, she felt free this year to become totally involved in and absorbed by an authentic, comprehensive, and intensive learning program, conducted solely in Hebrew this time, together with Israeli students for whom studying was serious business.

This conversation substantiated many of my previously held, often unorthodox, and certainly unpopular opinions about the educational "success" story of the American yeshiva student studying in Israel. It also provoked me to examine more carefully what the phenomenon represents and what its potential is for American Jewish education, were we to become more actively involved in exploiting it. We hesitate to criticize the Israel experience for fear of being considered anti-Israel, anti-learning, or just plain anti-religious. The argument goes that in spite of the acknowledged fact that the streets and eating places of Jerusalem are filled with our students at all hours of the day and night, engaged in less than serious or particularly uplifting activities, it is still better and more Jewishly productive than what they would be doing on

American campuses. That sounds like a big compromise and, incidentally, also a devastating critique of what we are all about educationally.

"I Never Saw the Rav Read a Secular Book"
Abba Bronspigel | 1993

In April 1993 Rabbi Joseph B. Soloveitchik died in Boston. For years he had suffered from a protracted illness that prevented him from maintaining his leadership role in the American Orthodox community. In the weeks that followed, Yeshiva University provided a prominent evening forum for Soloveitchik's disciples to share their memories of their fallen teacher. One of the more controversial memoirists was Rabbi Abba Bronspigel (b. 1939), a senior member of the RIETS faculty. Several years later he departed YU to serve as a founding rabbinic head of Lander College in Queens, New York. Toward the conclusion of his lengthy remarks, Bronspigel downplayed his teacher's commitment to non-Jewish knowledge and asserted that he never witnessed Soloveitchik opening up a secular book.

If you should ask me: Who was the Rav? What was he? So, of course the Rav was many things. Did he know philosophy? The answer is yes. Was he a literary person? The answer is yes. Was he well educated in various fields? The answer is yes. But if you ask me: Was this the Rav? The answer is no. The great part of his life, what did the Rav do? He learned Torah. The Rav basically was a *lamdan* par excellence. He was a *Gadol be-Yisrael* in the true sense of the word. It so happened, he also knew many other things. However, his character was as someone who sat and learned for the great part of his life—and that was his joy. I came into his apartment many times, here in the dormitory.[30] I never saw the Rav read a secular book. I know he did, but I never saw it. I saw him read a newspaper sometimes. He had a library in his apartment. There were some secular books. Whenever I came in, there were not that many Jewish books on the table either. There was a Gemara, a Rambam, a Tur, a Rashba.[31] I asked a number of other students who went into the apartment here [in New York]—I do not know about Boston—and they told me the same thing.

In the mid-1980s, Rabbi Joseph B. Soloveitchik (juggling above) was about to retire and his intellectual heir was far from apparent. On May 8, 1985, the Yeshiva College student newspaper published this cartoon to show how reliant many of its school's leaders were on their teacher's ideas (clockwise from the top, Rabbis Moses Tendler, Yehuda Parnes, and Norman Lamm). The illustration also suggests the students' impression that Soloveitchik's students were not capable of reaching their master's stature. Courtesy of the *Commentator*.

My impression is that whenever he had to speak or deliver a special lecture he may have looked up something [in a secular book] but it is not the case the he studied it routinely—he just knew it. His main involvement was Torah. Therefore, if you ask me: Who was the Rav? What was the Rav? In his personality, the Rav learned Torah in the great part of his life. He was also thinking of Torah. This gave him his life. . . . Despite the fact that he lived in the Modern Era and was considered by the outside world as a modern person, if you really knew him you understood that he was not modern at all. It is true, as I said before, he was very educated. But as for his basic character—and this I will always remember about him—I will always remember the shiurim [lectures] he gave and how he inspired me to learn and how he instilled in me a tremendous love for Torah. . . . We should remember him like this.

SECTION 3 | Sliding to the Left

Modern Orthodoxy Goes to Grossinger's
Shlomo Riskin | 1976

To some extent, Modern Orthodox Judaism's shift to the "left" includes more than just left-leaning ideologies. For many, this trend represented a shift in emphasis with regard to religious observance. In 1976 Rabbi Shlomo Riskin lamented the lack of piety and punctiliousness that he had observed among his followers. This was not necessarily a matter of "non-observance," but rather a lack of focus on religion among Modern Orthodox Jews. A portion of Riskin's remarks are included here.

Emunah and *Kedushah*, Faith and Sanctity, are not easily achieved. Their temporal absence is understandable. But the absence of a striving after *Emunah* and *Kedushah*, which is widespread within the modern Orthodox community, is symptomatic of spiritual failure and goes to the heart of many of the practical shortcomings that are more visible to the eye. Many of our synagogue "services" are sterile and noisy, devoid of the straining for *Kavannah*, for direction, which characterize the authentic effort to achieve an awareness of the Divine Presence. The closing prices on the New York Stock Exchange have a greater impact on the worshipper at the Shabbos morning service than the cry of *Sh'ma Yisrael* climaxing with the emphatic "ECHAD."[32] The siddurim, once stained by tears, are now marked with lipstick. The man or woman who musters tears during prayer—even on the Days of Awe—is looked upon as strange. Having lost our talent for the art of prayer, it is not surprising that many congregants arrive in the middle of the Torah reading on Shabbos morning and begin to show signs of boredom after the *Mussaf Kedusah*. And despite all of the *kippot* [yarmulkes] at Grossinger's, how many have the commitment to attend daily minyan?[33]

A person shows his true mettle by how he spends his "spare time"—if one can properly speak of time, the very essence of our lives, as being superfluous. How many of us spend our evening hours with a *seifer* [religious book]?—and how many of us spend our evening hours watching Johnny Carson?[34] The plethora of kosher eating places in New York City offering Chinese, Italian, and French cooking may well be a legitimate sign of more sophisticated American Orthodoxy, but is a nightclub, replete with all the trappings of modern-day hedonism, a proper environment for an Orthodox Jew—even though the meat served is Glatt Kosher?[35]

How many modern Orthodox Jews pride themselves on their children's "early admission" to an Ivy League school and aspire to their becoming scientists, attorneys, or physicians?—and how many look forward to a son who is a *talmid chachom*, a Torah educator, or a Rosh Yeshiva? Do we really believe that sitting in Grossinger's nightclub or at the pool while wearing a *kippah* will inspire our children to be vibrant and committed Jews who will passionately accept their Jewish heritage and reject the valueless world of secularism? And is it any wonder that with all of our yeshivos, American Orthodoxy has produced so few genuine *Talmidei Chachemim*? Producing authentic Torah scholars requires the single-minded intensity of purpose and total devotion to G-d and his Torah, which modern Orthodoxy hardly reflects.

The RIETS Responsum on Women's Prayer Groups

Five Yeshiva University Roshei Yeshiva | 1984

In 1984 Rabbi Louis Bernstein (1927–95) accepted the presidency of the Rabbinical Council of America, the second stint for Bernstein as the RCA's top officer. He replaced Rabbi Gilbert Klaperman, who closed his term with a plea to find meaningful places for women in Orthodox synagogues. In the late 1970s, a number of women had initiated private "prayer groups." In these prayer settings exclusively for women, worshippers recited the parts of the traditional liturgy that did not require a quorum of men and chanted from the Torah scroll. Bernstein did not adhere to his predecessor's call. Instead, he petitioned five leading rabbinical scholars at Yeshiva University to determine the rabbinical organization's position toward women's prayer groups. This is the response that Bernstein received from the panel of RIETS rabbis.

We were asked by Rabbi Eliezer Zalman [Louis] Bernstein, president of the Rabbinical Council, the following question:[36]

A few Orthodox synagogues have adopted the practice of hosting special hakafot for women on Simhat Torah and women's prayer groups that include Torah reading and the reading of the Megillah [on Purim].[37] Is this permitted or forbidden?

These practices are forbidden for a number of reasons. First, since women do not count toward a religious quorum, [the ritual] is found to be a destructive institution, as there is neither the Hazarat ha-Shatz, Kaddish, Kedushah, nor the formal blessing that precedes the recitation of the Shema.[38] Accordingly, none of these mitzvot are fulfilled in its entirety. Moreover, regarding the notion that these groups meet to form a "minyan," as if to demonstrate that they join together as a true quorum, this is a falsification of the Torah (Ziyuf ha-Torah). Second, this practice also reflects a complete and very apparent transformation of the tradition of our forefathers, and an affront to the customs

of Israel and a separation from the ways of the community, in specific, the considerable strictness that regards the customs of the synagogue. Third, there is a concern that these practices are intended to emulate the ways of the gentiles [Hukat ha-Goyim], since these customs are derived from the feminist movement, a domain that is principally committed to elements of depravity; this, in specific, according to Nahmanides, violates the particular proscription against forming mitzvot according to their [non-Jewish] behavior.[39] Owing to all of these reasons, it appears to us that according to [Jewish] law that all of these practices mentioned above are prohibited. It is forbidden to initiate them. In places that have already enacted them—it is correct to abolish them for now and in the future.

It is well known that the two great sages of our generation—to whom all of us and all of our colleagues adhere—Rabbi Yosef Dov Soloveitchik and Rabbi Moshe Feinstein, both adamantly opposed all of these aforementioned ideas.

"Blessed is he who keeps the word of this Law to fulfill them" (Deut. 27:26). This refers to the Jewish courts in this world. We beseech the leaders of the Rabbinical Council to stand up with all their might in opposition to this breach, and to urge all of our students and all of our like-minded colleagues not to succumb to the trends of the time, and not to conduct [their communities] in this manner, as who can know what will be in the end? We caution only those who are cautious of themselves.[40]

In witness hereof we hereby sign on Thursday, 19 of Kislev, 5745 [December 13, 1984]:

Nisson Lipa Alpert, Abba Bronspigel, Mordechai Willig, Yehuda Parnes, Zvi Schachter

(*opposite*) For decades, Modern Orthodox Jews (and other Orthodox types) have migrated to Florida and other balmy environs to vacation and celebrate Passover. As this 1980 ad indicates, many Passover programs advertise annually in Jewish newspapers, promising top hotel accommodations, scholars-in-residence, and acclaimed cantors. Large and consistent turnouts to these pricey programs reflect the relative affluence of the Modern Orthodox community.

The Affairs of the Rabbinical Council

Louis Bernstein | 1985

On November 14, 1984, Rabbi Louis Bernstein of the Rabbinical Council of Amer-
ica debated with Rabbi Avi Weiss on the topic of women's prayer in the latter's
Riverdale synagogue. The public event drew many interested parties. Bernstein
dismissed women's prayer groups as a fleeting trend, while Weiss pushed for its
permanence in Orthodox Jewish life. After the debate, a group of women wrote
to the president of the RCA to share with Bernstein their impressions of the Riv-
erdale affair. They described Bernstein's remarks as "demeaning and presump-
tuous" and his selection of rabbinic authorities as unbalanced. The letter writers
therefore asked Bernstein to open up the halakhic discussion to other prominent
Modern Orthodox leaders like Rabbi Saul Berman. Below is Bernstein's response.

Dear Friends,
Please excuse my not addressing all five of you properly. I couldn't
decipher most of the signatures. What the Rabbinical Council does
is its own affair, as are the reasons for my posing a question to five
learned colleagues. Since you took the trouble to write to me, I shall
respond briefly.

My decision to ask for the responsum followed a talk and correspondence with a young rabbi who grew up in my community,
weeks after my returning into the lionesses' den.[41]

Permit me to correct the misimpression of what I said that evening which will help you understand why I asked for guidelines to
open a halachic discussion. I kept pressing my colleague, "Who are
your authorities? What are your sources?" I further asked the rabbi
why he doesn't submit his halachic rationale to his peers or to a halachic publication. Rabbi [Avi] Weiss replied that he did not want to
because he feels that the only way to get the establishment to move
is by pressuring it from the outside. One cannot remain outside the
establishment and reap the advantages of remaining within it.

Appointing commissions is the president's responsibility. While
I appreciate your concern and suggestions, I prefer to make my

own choices. I did appoint a commission of five very erudite and respected scholars. With due respect for all our other colleagues in the Rabbinical Council, few enjoy the respect for erudition and scholarship that these men have. Those of us in the pulpit cannot aspire to their expertise. Nonetheless, Rabbi [Saul] Berman can and should respond with the same kind of a responsum. I am urging him to do so. A main goal of our question was to stimulate debate and discussion within our ranks. I restate what I said in Riverdale. Halacha requires expertise, and it cannot be discussed in the marketplace.

It is clear to me that you are unaware that Rabbi [Hershel] Schachter has prepared an exhaustive responsum which should be available in a few days.[42] It explains the position of the Roshei Yeshiva in great detail. Judgment really cannot be rendered on a decision without reading this complete brief. You might be surprised to find that he is aware of all women's sentiments.

Sincerely,
    Rabbi Louis Bernstein, President

Piety Not Rebellion
Rivka Haut | 1985

The 1984 RIETS responsum reverberated throughout the Modern Orthodox community. In particular, the issuance of this public statement set off the leaders of women's prayer groups, who believed that their efforts sat comfortably within the confines of Modern Orthodox Judaism. Despite the earlier responsum, the women never described their mission to form a "minyan," or halakhic quorum. Led by Rivka Haut (1942–2014) of the Flatbush, New York, women's prayer group, a number of Orthodox females organized the Women's Tefilah Network. More than sixty, women convened a conference in Riverdale, New York, but could only recruit a single Orthodox rabbi to speak at and support the endeavor.

Recently, my sister became engaged. After many years of being unhappily single, she was going to be married! Three weeks before her wedding, on *Shabbat,* she celebrated by being called up to the Torah, surrounded by her mother, her aunts, her sister (me), her nieces, and her closest friend. As her name was called out for her *Aliyah,* everyone present burst into song. The *d'var torah* that morning was specifically in her honor. After the services, there was a festive *kiddush.* Instead of partying with her friends, my sister was able to express her joy in her forthcoming marriage in a spiritual, religious format, by attending monthly *Shabbat* services in a women's *Tefillah* group.

Halachic women's prayer groups enable Jewish women to commemorate important events in their lives in a synagogue setting. Women receive *aliyot* in order to celebrate engagements, marriages, receiving degrees, buying homes, getting new jobs. Women are able to name their babies in *shul. Bat Mitzva* girls are able to actively participate in the prayer services by reading the *Torah,* reciting the *Haftarah,* delivering a *d'var torah.* Women can recite the "*Mi Shebayrach*" prayer for people who are ill. Orthodox women have, through women's prayer groups, developed a mode whereby women no longer have to vicariously experience religious expression in the synagogue through their fathers or husbands; they can participate actively and directly in all aspects of synagogue services, and they can do so in an halachically acceptable way.

What exactly are women's prayer groups? They consist of groups of women who meet regularly, in most cases once a month, on *Shabbat,* to conduct prayer services. These groups are no *minyanim,* though they have been persistently and erroneously called so by many rabbis. They scrupulously avoid reciting any prayer for which a *minyan* of men is necessary. The prayers said are exactly and only those that are recited by any woman, or any man for that matter, when praying alone. There is, however, one major difference between private prayer and the women's *tefillah*—the Torah reading.

Reading from a *sefer Torah* is at the heart of every women's prayer service. The *Torah* is carried about the room, so that every woman present may reach out and kiss it. The entire *Torah* portion for that week is read. This *Torah* reading is the basic innovation of women's *tefillah* groups. For the reality of women praying together is not new. Indeed, in most girls' *yeshivot*, the girls pray together daily and have been doing so for many years without arousing any controversy. It is, therefore, or seems to be, the addition of the *Torah* reading that is the cause of the bitter invectives directed against women's prayer groups by various rabbis.

Ironically, there is no halachic impediment to *Torah* reading by women. The *Tosefta*, at Berachot 2:12, states: "Males and females who have unclean issues, menstruant, and women who have given birth, are permitted to read from the *Torah* and to study *Mishna*." Maimonides, in his *Mishna Torah*, Hilchot Sefer Torah 10:8, codified this ruling and stated: "All ritually impure people, even menstruants, and even Samaritans, are permitted to hold a *sefer Torah* and to read from it." His ruling was brought down in the Shulchan Aruch, Yoreh Dayah 282:9. In a recent *teshuva* written by . . . Rabbi Moshe Feinstein, it is made quite clear that, in Rabbi Moshe Feinstein's opinion, women are not prohibited from reading from a *sefer Torah*.[43]

And yet in Orthodox *shuls*, women have no contact with a *sefer Torah*. In many *shuls*, women cannot even see it. Even in those *shuls* that do allow women visual access to the *Torah*, they cannot hold it or look inside it.

Many women today feel the need for close, physical contact with a *sefer Torah*. They want to be able to look inside, to see the holy words, and to read them. I am sure that there are few *Torah* scrolls that are treated more lovingly, and with more reverence, than those used by women's prayer groups.

A women's prayer service is, as we have seen, a complete *Shabbat* morning prayer service, with the omission of those prayers for which a *minyan* is necessary, and including a complete *Torah* reading. Surely, there can be nothing wrong with this. Women have never been encouraged to attend daily *minyan*, rather than to pray individually. Those Rabbis who are vociferously opposed to women's prayer groups have not been exhorting women to attend synagogue prayer services, so that they can attain a "higher level *mitzvah*." Most daily *minyanim* are not even set up to accommodate women. Orthodox rabbis have never actively encouraged women to attend prayer services. It is the women themselves who are motivated, and are motivating other women, to participate regularly and actively in prayer services.

Women today have been provided with more *Torah* education than ever before. They are no longer content to be mere onlookers in the synagogue, careful to remain out of sight and to keep their voices muted. Women's *tefillah* groups provide women of all ages with the opportunity to participate directly in the prayer service. In many groups, the *Torah* portion is read by seven different women, one for each *Aliyah*, thus maximizing participation. Even the youngest girls participate, by opening and closing the ark, and by leading in the singing of the concluding songs. Anyone seeing the radiant faces of the little girls, as they perform these activities which have hitherto been denied them, would not question the right of women's *tefillah* groups to exist.

Fortunately, women's *tefillah* groups have received support and guidance from individual rabbis.[44] However, some rabbinic organizations, most notably the Rabbinical Council of America, and its incumbent president, Rabbi Louis Bernstein, have expended much energy towards attempting to destroy existing groups and insuring that new ones not arise. A publication of the Agudah, the *Jewish Observer*, recently contained an article critical of women's prayer groups.[45] In a recent *teshuva*, signed by five Yeshiva University rabbis, women's *Megillah* reading, *hakafot* for women on *Simchat Torah*, and women's "*minyanim*" were all denounced and pronounced to be in violation of *Halacha*. All this in a one-page document! One of the five, Rabbi Hershel Schachter, has recently written an article which is an elaboration of that *teshuva*, with the same conclusion.[46] In this article, he maintains that the motivation of the women involved is not the love of *mitzvot* but, rather, for personal "honor" and publicity. A representative of the Women's Tefillah Network, which is an organization of halachic women's prayer groups, attempted to meet with Rabbi Schachter before publication of his article to discuss the matter with him. He responded that he was too busy.[47]

How sad it is that these rabbis have chosen this issue for their particular attention. At a time when the religious community is faced with so many serious problems, such as the *get* (divorce) issue and the rising rate of intermarriage, today's rabbinic "leaders" have chosen to attack the very groups that are instrumental in bringing so many women closer to Torah observance.

I cannot presume to understand the motivations of these rabbis who so eagerly, and without proper knowledge, oppose women's prayer groups. I am not really sure what it is that they are so afraid of. Various women's groups have written to the president of the RCA, requesting that the organization set up halachic guidelines for women's prayer groups, in order for there to be unity in the practices of the different groups. These requests have been rejected. There are now signs that some individual rabbis are forming a committee to deal with this issue. Hopefully, they will do so before it is too late, before the women involved decide that the rabbinic leadership of today has forfeited its right to lead.

"Very Little Halachic Judaism"

Eliezer Berkovits | 1985

While some supporters of women's prayer groups tried to placate their opposition and push for dialogue, others rejected the legitimacy of the RIETS responsum. Rabbi Eliezer Berkovits, who had retired from the Hebrew Theological College in Chicago to settle in Israel, was one such critic.

Sir,

I read with interest your article of September 11, "Orthodox Women Fume at Rabbis."[48] One may no longer remain silent. I have read carefully the responsum of the five talmudists at Yeshiva University, forbidding prayer services by women. I wish to state unequivocally that their "T'shuva" has nothing to do with Halacha.

People will have to realize that knowledge and understanding are not identical. One may know a lot and understand very little.

There may be a great deal of Orthodoxy around. Unfortunately, there is only very little halachic Judaism.

May God grant to the women of Women's Tefilla Network strength and courage to continue their efforts to the best of their abilities.

Rabbi Eliezer Berkovits, Jerusalem

"Modern Orthodox" and "Traditional Conservative": Is an Alliance Possible?
Avi Weiss | 1989

On June 11, 1989, Rabbi Avi Weiss delivered a provocative lecture at the annual convention of the Union for Traditional Conservative Judaism (UTCJ) in Highland Park, New Jersey. His remarks were "enthusiastically received" by the organization that had for several years identified as the right wing of the Conservative Movement. (It had emerged after the Rabbinical Assembly resolved to ordain women in 1984.) Weiss was well known for his leadership in the Movement to Free Soviet Jewry, a role that was acclaimed by most within the Orthodox community. However, Weiss had also publicly identified as part of the Modern Orthodox rabbinate that resisted a so-called shift to the right. In this realm, Weiss encountered more opposition than sympathy from his Orthodox rabbinical colleagues. Despite his minority status, Weiss was cautious to quickly embrace an alliance with the right-wing section of the Conservative Movement. To do this, he believed, the Conservative counterparts would need to make considerable compromises with regard to their more liberal religious practices. In the end, such a coalition between Weiss and the UTCJ went unrealized. Below is the final portion of Weiss's speech; it reflected the consideration of some to merge parts of the Orthodox and Conservative movements as well as the unwillingness of Orthodox leaders to meet others halfway on matters of Halakhah.

Both the Modern/Centrist Orthodox and the Traditional Conservative movements are experiencing similar challenges. In most Orthodox Yeshivot—even at Yeshiva University, where I have been a rebbe of Torah for 20 years—the Roshei Yeshiva are pulling right (many of the children of Roshei Yeshiva at Yeshiva University attend more right-wing Yeshivot) as Rabbi Lamm and others like him struggle to hold the center. At the Jewish Theological Seminary, the movement is left as the Roshei Yeshiva and the Traditionalists struggle to maintain the integrity of the halakha.[49]

A new alignment is emerging. The Orthodox are moving further to the right; the Conservative are veering left close to Reform; and in the center, an alliance between the Modern/Centrist Orthodox and the Conservative Traditionalist is no longer impossible. There are, of course, differences between the Modern/Centrist Orthodox and the Traditional Conservative camps. For example, there is no accepted halakhic responsum which sanctions mixed seating or the use of a microphone on Shabbat. For an alliance to surface, it would be necessary to accept the normative halakhic position on these issues. The Traditionalists would, in addition, have to drop the term "Conservative" from their title.[50]

Still, there are enough points in common on key issues for serious discussions to take place. Where the dialogue will take us, how it will develop, what kind of formal alliances will emerge, is difficult to predict. But dialogue in earnest should begin. What unites us is far greater than what divides us.

If we succeed, I can envision a fusion into "The Movement of Halakhic Judaism." We're far from that day, but the seeds have been planted. A natural offspring of such a "Movement" would be a rabbinical school.[51]

Jewish Women Hear Muffled Voices
Laura Shaw | 1990

With the exception of outspoken leaders like Blu Greenberg, most of the founders of women's prayer groups in the 1970s and 1980s tried to express their efforts in traditional Orthodox terms. However, the subsequent generation adopted a "feminist" rhetoric that posed a challenge to the established (male) Modern Orthodox guard and moved to widen the boundaries of the community, rather than fit somewhere within it. This was evident in Columbia law student Laura Shaw's (b. 1968) column in the university's student newspaper. Shaw had just graduated from Columbia College, where she served as a leader in the Orthodox community there. Later, she assumed an important role in the Women's Tefila Network and in the founding of the Jewish Orthodox Feminist Alliance (est. 1997).

"My brother and I were at Sinai / He kept a journal / of what he saw / of what he heard / of what it all meant to him / I wish I had such a record / of what happened to me there."—Merle Feld in "We All Stood Together."[52]

As a religious Jewish feminist, these words strike the deepest chords in my soul. The Rabbis tell us that every Jew that ever lived and ever will live was at Mount Sinai to witness the giving of the Ten Commandments. The Torah tells us that, before God gave us the Ten Commandments, God told Moses to tell the Children of Israel not to go near a woman for three days. Not to go near a woman? Why wasn't Moses told to tell the Children of Israel not to go near a member of the opposite sex for three days? Was the Torah only meant to be given to the male Israelites? Maybe Moses was told to inform the women as well as the men, but because a man told the story, the woman's point of view got lost. I'd rather believe this than that the term "Children of Israel" refers only to men.

I feel a burning need to go back in time inside my head to hear the voices of my foremothers, so that I can truly feel my place in the endless chain of tradition that is the Jewish people. I have so many questions about my foremothers that the text of the Torah simply does not answer for me. My Hebrew name is Na'ama, and when I looked to the Torah to see who Na'ama was, I found her among a genealogy in Genesis—a list of fathers begetting sons. Na'ama is the only female in the list. Who was this Na'ama that she was mentioned in this list of men? Was she a leader of some sort? Why is she so important? I'm her namesake—I want to know. But the text doesn't tell me, so I must crawl deep into my memory, all the way back to when I stood at Sinai so I can remember.

When the Torah tells us that after Dina was raped in Genesis 34:1, she "goes out to see the daughters of the land." What does this mean?

Who were these daughters? Did Dina go to a community of women for solace? To heal? How did Sarah feel when Abraham took Isaac to be sacrificed? Will I ever know? There are so many other women too— some that aren't mentioned by name in the text at all. What about Lilith, who according to the Rabbis was Adam's first wife?[53] The legends relate that Lilith was evicted from the Garden of Eden for refusing to submit to Adam sexually. Of course, according to these same legends, Lilith is now a demon who spends her days killing newborn babies as revenge. Maybe the Rabbis made Lilith into a demon because a powerful woman could only be dangerous and evil. What really happened to Lilith?

To begin our journey into our collective women's memory, Jewish women must look for ways to reclaim and humanize the voices of our textual foremothers. Aside from reading the text and trying to imagine who these women were and what were their hopes, dreams, and ambitions, we must allow these women to stand on their own merits as important members of our lineage. For instance, in the Amidah, or Silent Devotion, Jews say three times each day, we refer to God as the God of Abraham, Isaac, and Jacob. I add in the names of the foremothers to my prayer, referring also to the God of Sarah, Rebecca, Rachel, and Leah. But then I get angry with myself, in chronological order, Leah would come before Rachel. Do I only say Rachel before Leah because Rachel was Jacob's more beloved and beautiful wife? So obviously, just mentioning the names of the foremothers is not enough if I am doing it through the male point of view. How can I train my ear to hear the female rhythms in the text?

Maybe the way to tune ourselves into these rhythms is to start training ourselves to hear and feel them at birth. A new ceremony that has become popular among Jews from different affiliations is the Simchat Bat—a ceremony for the welcoming of a new daughter. Because this is a relatively new ritual, there is nothing canonized and parents therefore have a lot of freedom in composing a text for their own daughter's Simchat Bat. Perhaps through our telling the stories of our foremothers to welcome our daughters we will set a precedent of being sensitive to the female voices we so often miss. Perhaps by beginning our daugh-

AN OPEN LETTER TO THE VA'AD HARABONIM OF QUEENS

The brief and unfortunate statement prohibiting women's tefillah (prayer groups made up of women only) issued by the Va'ad Harabonim of Queens should be challenged by all who love halacha and are zealous for *kavod hatorah*.

Although the Va'ad acknowledges that many women have a sincere devotional inspiration that calls out for expression, they attempt to shut down a halakhicly legitimate communal enterprise that gives voice to those spiritual feelings. They defend themselves with attribution to *Gadolei Hador* (leading halakhic authorities) whose words they have taken out of context. Those supporting women's tefillah groups have found equal basis in the writing and pronouncements of the *Gadolei Hador.*

The Va'ad also mistakenly supports its position by referring to a 1984 statement of five RIETS Roshei Yeshiva as a p'sak. That statement was clearly not issued as a p'sak. Rather, that document was a condemnatory statement which argued that women's tefillah was nothing more than a radical political enterprise not directed towards a genuine heavenly purpose. Inasmuch as women have participated in women's tefillah for over 20 years and clearly know that the experience is altogether one of *l'shem shamayim*, the pronouncement of the RIETS rabbis had little impact. In fact, now a single women's tefillah in the United States nor anywhere else in the world closed its doors in response to that document.

The parallel between the two pronouncements is that neither group saw fit to enter into a discussion with women of the women's tefillah, never came forward to observe such a gathering though invitations were extended, never showed the courtesy to hear women's objections to such pronouncements. Which is why, sadly, that this conversation must be carried out in print.

The rabbis of the Va'ad would do well to reconsider both the content and the manner of their deliberations. The resolution violates the principle of respect for p'sak of the *moreh deatra* (rabbinic rulings of individual rabbis) inasmuch as it seeks to ban existing groups which now meet with full authority and support from their local rabbi. Additionally, women's tefillah meets all the standards of halakha.

Many orthodox women and men are of the firm conviction that this is an *halakhic* way to come nearer to G-d in a sacred community. Women's tefillah meets all the tests of *"hatzneah lechet im Hashem elokecha:* Walking humbly with your G-d" (Micha 6:8) it is wrong to say that is a break with tradition. Not only is it not *"poretz geder b'mesorah"*, it is rapidly becoming *mesorah b'yisrael.* At a time when the modern orthodox community is dramatically raising the level of learning and religious expression of its women, those who fear these developments should exercise restraint and allow others, equally committed, to develop vehicles of religious expression which bring Jews closer to the love and service of G-d.

THE WOMEN'S TEFILLAH NETWORK
40 GROUPS AND 4000 WOMEN
IN NORTH AMERICA, ENGLAND, AUSTRALIA AND ISRAEL

ters' lives with emphasis on women's voices in our tradition, our daughters will grow up able to hear things we were unable to hear ourselves.

When we raise a generation of daughters that can feel their female ancestors' part in the shaping of our tradition, and can incorporate the lost influences these heroic women once had, we will be able to round out our Judaism. Instead of only reading about those things which affected men, we will learn of our people as a whole. I think when this happens we will reach new spiritual heights. As Ecclesiastes tells us, "Two are better than one." By including women in the story of our people, we will only strengthen the chain that binds our past to our future.

"If we remembered it together / we could re-create holy time / sparks flying."—Merle Feld.

Take Rav Soloveitchik at Full Depth

Aharon Lichtenstein | 1999

In 1996 Rabbi Saul Berman founded Edah as a Modern Orthodox organization and think tank. Berman's motto for his institution was "The Courage to Be Modern and Orthodox." In February 1999 journalist Eve Kessler (b. 1961) reported on the inaugural Edah Conference, writing that the "ghost of Rabbi Joseph Soloveitchik loomed over New York this week as former students" tried to "wrest his legacy away from those they called 'revisionists.'" Soloveitchik had retired from public work in 1985 and passed away in 1993. The conference on "Orthodoxy Encounters a Changing World" attracted more than 1,500 people. Most prominently, Rabbi Shlomo Riskin, now chief rabbi of Efrat, broke from his earlier moderate position to denounce those Orthodox leaders who utilized the "Rav" to project more conservative attitudes toward women's issues and modern culture. In turn, Soloveitchik's son-in-law, Rabbi Aharon Lichtenstein, now head

(*opposite*) In 1997 a group of Queens Orthodox rabbis issued a ban against women's prayer groups. The declaration was in response to well-circulated invitations to a women-only bat mitzvah celebration at the Young Israel of Hillcrest. The Women's Tefillah Network was compelled to respond. This advertisement appeared in the January 31, 1997, edition of the *Jewish Week*. Courtesy of the editor and publisher of the *Jewish Week*.

INTERNATIONAL CONFERENCE ON FEMINISM&ORTHODOXY

*Exploring the impact of feminist values
on traditional Jewish women's lives*

PROGRAM

Sunday, February 16 – Monday, February 17, 1997
9-10 Adar I 5757

Grand Hyatt Hotel

Park Avenue at 42 Street • New York City

Sponsored by
AMIT • EDAH • THE DRISHA INSTITUTE • THE WOMEN'S TEFILLAH NETWORK

*of Yeshivat Har Etzion in Alon Shvut, Israel, penned a rebuttal to what he per-
ceived as a too-narrow presentation of his teacher.*

Having read, with a mixture of interest and discomfiture, E. J. Kessler's
"Edah Conference Claims Legacy of Rav Soloveitchik," I feel impelled,
as a disciple, to respond to its central thesis.[54] That thesis in sum is that,
first, the Rav's "philosophical writings show him to be the quintessen-
tial Modern Orthodox figure," and that, second, Edah-affiliated rabbis
can therefore justifiably regard him as "the founder of their movement,
the man whose life and thought embodied their quest for an engagement with the best elements of the larger culture." Both assertions,
while partially correct, are also partially incorrect. Clarification, in the
interest of both the memory of the Rav, may his memory be a blessing,
and the current Jewish scene, is therefore in order.

If Modern Orthodoxy—and Edah, as its presumptive plenipo-
tentiary—are to be defined purely as a quest for engagement with culture, in Matthew Arnold's sense, these claims can probably pass muster.[55] The Rav favored engagement—cultural, social, and political—and
rejected, as did Milton, "a fugitive and cloistered virtue," and he acknowledged the energizing potential of secular studies as a source of richness,
power, sensitivity, and depth.[56] However, conventional wisdom assumes
that these entities represent much more than modernism is not only an
abstract conception but a social reality and that Edah not only embraces
philosophic perspectives but emblazons a manifesto and an agenda.
With some of their salient details, the Rav's name certainly cannot be
associated. I fully believe Rabbi Saul Berman and some of his colleagues
when they assert that they drew inspiration for their work from the Rav's
personality and teachings. However, the contention that this subjective

(*opposite*) In 1997 the Orthodox feminist Blu Greenberg convened the first international conference of the Jewish Orthodox Feminist Alliance. Proudly feminist and
aligned with many liberal Orthodox leaders, JOFA emerged as a major symbol of a
progressive breed of Orthodox Judaism. This was the cover of the program for the
inaugural event. Courtesy of the Jewish Orthodox Feminist Alliance.

favor lends credence to the converse claim that his imprimatur can be affixed to their positions is both fallacious and unfair.

It is not enough to speak of engagement in the abstract. One must concurrently define the character and parameters of that engagement so as to determine what ramifications and conclusions can legitimately flow from it. In this context, it is critical to bear in mind that the Rav's essence was manifested not only in philosophical writings he authored, but in theological principles to which he was committed and, above all, in a rigorous halachic discipline, which was both his patrimony and his legacy. These, as the Rav's innermost being, were forged in the tradition of Brisk rather than in Berlin; lamentably they are not sufficiently shared by significant segments of our contemporary community and its spokesmen.[57] While innovative in some areas, the Rav was highly conservative with respect to the text and context of *tefillah* (prayer) as traditionally constituted in its classical corpus and in the fabric of a shul. He was unstintingly tenacious in insisting upon the autonomy of Halacha and the rejection of historicism, in placing *lamdut* (knowledge), in the realms of theory and practice both, at the epicenter of Jewish life and in predicating the authority of Hazal as its polestar.[58] The absolutely binding character of the covenant, after the Holocaust no less than before, was the linchpin of his life and thought, the quintessence of his conceptual *tractatus thelogico-politicus*.[59] Do these positions, as a sample, conform to the rhetoric and substance of those now striving to assume his mantle? If so, let them, by all means, claim the Rav's lineage. If not, let them, in all fairness, desist.

"The Rav," Ms. Kessler quotes Eugene Korn as stating, "hated spiritual shallowness." Indeed he did. Shallowness is, however—and I say this as a devoted friend rather than as an adversary—the Achilles' heel of much of Modern Orthodoxy.[60] As such, it elicited some of the Rav's sharpest critiques of religious modernism. Flaccid prayer, lukewarm commitment to learning, approximate observance, tepid experience—anything that reflected comfortable mediocrity in the quality of acculturated American Judaism, he deplored and sought to ennoble. This is not to suggest that he regarded the anti-modernists as his ideal. He had high standards of spirituality, and few met them fully. But with respect to this particular failing, I believe it is fair to state that, both intellectually and emotionally, he regarded it as afflicting the modern community more than others. His ideological commitment to the cardinal concerns of Modern Orthodoxy—an integrated view of life, the value of general culture, and the significance of the State of Israel—and his genuine pride in some of its accomplishments did not prevent him from demanding that it hold a mirror to its face and probe for intensity and depth.

Finally, the shallowest cut of all is the attempt to pigeonhole the Rav within the confines of a current narrow "camp." At the recent Edah conference, a paper decrying right-wing revisionism concerning the Rav was widely circulated. Surely, however, left-wing revisionism—in the form of convenient conjectural hypotheses regarding what would have been his position with respect to certain current flashpoints—is no less deplorable. Had the Rav been compelled to choose between what Ms. Kessler describes as "the fervently Orthodox yeshiva world" and its denigrators, there is not a shadow of a doubt as to what his decision would have been. The point is, however, that he did not want to make that choice, and he did not need to make it. He sought, as we should, the best of the Torah world and the best of modernity. For decades, sui generis sage that he was, the Rav bestrode American Orthodoxy like a colossus, transcending many of its internal fissures. Let us not now inter him in a Procrustean sarcophagus.

> Rabbi Aharon Lichtenstein, Rosh Hayeshiva,
> Yeshivat Har Etzion

CONCLUSION

In 1995 Rabbi Chaim Landau (b. 1953) of Baltimore's Ner Tamid Synagogue warned that "Modern Orthodoxy's vibrancy as a movement would vanish unless it receives an infusion of new direction and leadership."[61] Instead, the rabbis and laypeople who championed some version of Modern Orthodox Judaism typically spoke about it through the lens of the late Rabbi Joseph Soloveitchik. There is ample evidence from the documents in this chapter that elements representative of all streams of Modern Orthodoxy positioned the spirit and teachings of Soloveitchik at the forefront of their ideologies and causes. Some argued that he would have ruled against movement toward the left while others accused their opponents of hijacking the sainted rabbi and stripping him of his more progressive tendencies. Still, David Singer and other disillusioned members of the Orthodox Centrist group bemoaned that their teacher had not adequately prepared them for life without the "Rav."

Accordingly, Modern Orthodox Jews entered the new century with a measure of insecurity. Now an aged leader, Norman Lamm abandoned "Centrism" and returned to "Modern Orthodoxy."[62] In truth, though, for more than a decade the much-battered Lamm preferred to speak about the safer intellectual realm of Torah u-Madda than to stake claims for the religious or communal concept of Modern Orthodox Judaism. Others followed suit. In England, the bright and articulate Chief Rabbi Jonathan Sacks (b. 1948) also spoke about Torah u-Madda and favored his wider-reaching "Inclusive Orthodoxy" over the far more exclusive "Modern Orthodox" designation.[63] It was, therefore, an altogether uncertain period for Modern Orthodox Judaism.

15 | Reconsidering Modern Orthodox Judaism in a New Century

INTRODUCTION

In 2000 Modern Orthodox Judaism celebrated one of its greatest triumphs: Senator Joseph Lieberman (b. 1942) was chosen as the Democratic Party nominee for vice president in the presidential election, alongside Al Gore (b. 1948). For a short while, Modern Orthodox Jews celebrated the Gore-Lieberman campaign and forgot about the turmoil of the past decades. Yet a period of great transition in the community returned attention to unsettled issues. In 2003 Richard Joel succeeded Rabbi Norman Lamm as president of Yeshiva University. Before his appointment, Joel trained as a lawyer and served as international director of Hillel. He was the fourth president of Yeshiva and the first without a rabbinical certificate or doctoral degree. Owing to this, Joel vowed: "I'm not going to be speaking as the leader of Modern Orthodoxy. I'm going to train people to be leaders of Modern Orthodoxy."[1] Eight years later he altered his stance, but in a perplexing fashion. In 2011 Joel agreed to speak on the challenges that faced "Orthodoxy," but refused to describe his community as part of a Modern Orthodox Judaism.[2] Modern Orthodox Judaism, then, required a spokesman outside of YU.

This final chapter engages the recent history of Modern Orthodox Judaism. Much of the energy of this present incarnation has been expended in the efforts to define who is not a Modern Orthodox Jew or who is even beyond the broader Orthodox pale. The most visible target has been Rabbi Avi Weiss, who founded Yeshivat Chovevei Torah (1999) and the International Rabbinical Fellowship (2007) as liberal alternatives to RIETS and the RCA. A number of these oftentimes caustic essays appeared online while others in less formal but audience-grabbing social media forums. Few rabbis and leaders of Modern Orthodox organizations have made use of their synagogues' institutions to offer fresh visions of Modern Orthodox or Centrist Orthodox Judaism. In 2014, at the RIETS quadrennial ordination ceremony, the dean of the school chose to chide his "Open Orthodox" rivals rather than signal any sort of call to his newly minted Modern Orthodox rabbis and listeners.[3] All this is in marked contrast to the founders and furtherers of Modern Orthodoxy.

Yet there are a number of intriguing examples of women and men who have considered the current state of Modern Orthodox Judaism. More often, these voices are derived from those who do not claim seats on daises or ascend Sabbath pulpits. The primary sources included in the first section are collected from these grassroots Jews. Collectively, the documents describe a community's "loosened grip" on the brand of Orthodox Judaism that had once more clearly defined it. Finally, there is ample evidence of an attempt to "reclaim" Modern Orthodoxy by those who would have probably fit most comfortably in the "New Orthodox Left" of the 1960s or the marginalized "left wing" of Modern Orthodoxy in subsequent decades. No longer content with the "Open Orthodox" moniker, these modern-traditionalists have taken up the "Modern Orthodox" rhetoric in the absence of others who might have in prior generations.

SECTION 1 | Loosening Grip

Modern Orthodox Gedolim
Dena Freundlich | 2004

In 2004 a student at the all-girls Ma'ayanot Yeshiva High School in Teaneck, New Jersey, confessed that her fellow students were "very interested in one of the controversies on one of the many Frumteens message boards." The anonymous "Moderator" of the Frumteens.com website had discouraged his female teenage readers from attending the Modern Orthodox high school that teaches its students Talmud (also called Gemara). The online comments caused a stir in the school and compelled Dena Freundlich (b. 1978), head of Ma'ayanot's Talmud Department, to respond to the Moderator on his own website. In subsequent years, the school has used the episode and the back-and-forth between Freundlich and the Moderator to teach its students about Talmud study for women.

Moderator, I understand that you are vehemently committed to your position and that you are convinced that the other side is invalid and against Halachah. However, I think it is an irresponsible use of the Moderator role to respond to a high school student that her and her school's view is "repulsive to Hashem, and a notion not worthy of being taken seriously," that it's "despicable," "absurd," "ridiculous" just to list a few of the adjectives that you have used to belittle the students with whom you are communicating. I understand that you feel passionately about the subject, but to talk to others so disparagingly, especially to students who are turning to you for guidance, just does not seem at all in line with the Torah values you are so committed to. Please let's try to serve as role models for our students of how to talk respectfully even with those who we think are wrong.

As for the issue at hand, your primary argument is that: "In Shulchan Aruch and the Rishonim [medieval commentators], it states clearly that it is forbidden to teach girls Torah She-Ba'al Peh [Oral Law], which includes Mishnayos and Gemora, among other things. Furthermore, there is no dissenting or disagreeing opinion anywhere about this. Thus, teaching girls Gemora in class is an open and public violation of a clear Halachah."[4] I believe that the issue is not nearly as clear-cut as you portray it.

First of all, the primary response as to why it is absolutely not "an open and public violation of a clear Halachah" to teach girls Talmud in class is simply that you are incorrect in your claim that "there is no dissenting or disagreeing opinion anywhere about this." Rabbi Joseph B. Soloveitchik, whom I, along with many, many others, view as one of the greatest Gedolim of the twentieth century, ruled that it is permissible for women to learn Gemara.[5] Not only that, but he demonstrated his acceptance of women learning Gemara by he himself teaching the first women's Talmud class at Stern College for Women. And when he founded Maimonides, a Yeshiva high school in Boston, he established the curriculum so that every student, female as well as male, learned Gemara.

Furthermore, the Rav's son-in-law, Rabbi Aharon Lichtenstein, the current Rosh Yeshiva of Yeshivat Har Etzion in Israel, has maintained the Rav's endorsement of the permissibility of women learning Gemara. Rabbi Lichtenstein is the official posek of our school, whom our principal consults on all major issues. Thus, since our school is following our posek's ruling by teaching our students Talmud, not only are we not committing "an open and public violation of a clear Halachah," but we are fulfilling the halachic imperative to follow our rabbinic leader. You may choose not to follow these Gedolim's rulings for yourself or for your own daughters, but we have the halachic responsibility to follow our posek's decision for ourselves, and we certainly have the right to do so without being virulently slandered for it.

The central reason why we feel so strongly that Talmud should be a mandatory part of each of our students' curriculum is that Gemara and Tanach together make up the heart and soul of Judaism. It is impossible to fully understand Judaism without Gemara because it is the repository and the foundation of everything that we do and everything that we believe. Certainly it is clear that in order to understand the development of Halacha, one must be able to learn Talmud and understand how its logic works. But even when it comes to Jewish philosophy, hashkafah, ethics, etc., Gemara is a central player in virtually every discussion. Of course one can be a completely committed, frum, inspired, passionate, 100-percent-committed Jew without Gemara. But it is impossible to be a truly educated Jew without the Talmud.

Without Gemara, one is simply missing too critical a piece of our Mesorah. Walk into any Beit Midrash and examine the shelves—probably at least half of them are devoted to the Talmud and Talmud-related texts. Shouldn't our girls have access to them, too? As an educational institution, we feel that it is our responsibility to provide each and every one of our students with at least the basic tools to learn and understand Gemara. Even if a student ultimately decides that Talmud is not for her, we are still obligated to teach it to her while she is entrusted to us for her education, the same way as we feel responsible to teach her math and science and literature even if she ultimately decides that those subjects are not for her. In order to be an educated citizen, one must have at least a rudimentary understanding of math and science and literature. So, too, in order to be an educated Jew, one must have at least a basic understanding of the Talmud.

Stalemate at Stern College

Cindy Bernstein and Norman Lamm | 2006

In March 2006 a group of Stern College students asked the school's administration to permit an all-women Megillah reading to celebrate Purim. The Stern College deans posed the question to Rabbi Norman Lamm, who still maintained a leadership position as Chancellor and Rosh Ha-Yeshiva of Yeshiva University. He forbade the event, as he later explained, on the grounds that he did not want to conflict with the ruling of his teacher, Rabbi Joseph Soloveitchik. The matter deeply discouraged senior Cindy Bernstein (b. 1984), who wrote a letter in the student newspaper complaining that the decision to ban the event was at odds with the open-minded vision of Yeshiva University. In his response, Lamm sympathized with Bernstein but felt beholden to his teacher's conservative position.

Dear Editors:
I am writing in response to an [e-mail] I received about a women's Megillah reading. When I first received the e-mail I was surprised that the reading was being held off campus; after further investigation I discovered that the reason for this was that Rabbi [Norman] Lamm had specifically said that it could not be an official Stern College event. While I must admit that I do not know the actual events that transpired between the students and Rabbi Lamm, I wanted to write this letter to share how saddened I was when I heard this news.

At first I tried to reconcile this by telling myself that YU has a specific Hashkafa [religious viewpoint] to uphold, and therefore could not allow the reading, but in actuality, there are so many different opinions and Hashkafot within YU. In truth YU just seems to be flying the banner of Orthodoxy and learning all secular and Judaic studies within that context. So long as the action is halachically acceptable, as women's Megillah reading is, there is no reason why it should not be allowed.

Yet YU has also been flying another banner, that of "bringing wisdom to life."[6] What better example of that message than when young women take the knowledge that they have learned, wisdom that they have gleaned from halachic texts and sources, and implement it into their daily lives. Regardless of my own personal beliefs on the matter, I can only respect the young lady that takes her halachic knowledge and aspires to incorporate it into all aspects of her being. It is a shame that an endeavor such as women's Megillah reading is seen as "feminist" or too "left" for YU; in actuality, I believe their efforts should be celebrated.

Furthermore, not only do I applaud their work in making a Megillah reading happen, but I admire them for their strength and courage to do so. Kol Hakavod [Congratulations]!

Sincerely,
Cindy Bernstein, '06

Response by Rabbi Dr. Norman Lamm:

I appreciate Ms. Bernstein's distress at the decision not to permit the special Megillah service led by women at Stern College. But she has it all wrong. There is nothing in my decision that has to do with "Right" or "Left." Those terms are fundamentally political and are not germane to halakhic decision making. As Rosh Hayeshiva, it is my duty to do what is best for the students in their Jewish education at YU and to make sure that all is proper according to Halakha. I have nothing but unmitigated respect for the young women who are devoting time and energy to their studies in the Bet Midrash. I know many of them and consider them upright Jewesses, wonderful students, and devoted heart and soul to the Halakha. They are a source of pride to me—and to all of us. I recognize full well that there are a number of differing *piskei halakha* concerning the permission for a woman to read the Megillah on behalf of other women who thereby fulfill their religious obligations on Purim. There are a number of reasons for my decision that such a service *not* be held at Yeshiva, although I would not object if they were held elsewhere. The crucial issue in my decision is not Megillah per se but *kevod harav*, the reverence all of us have and ought to have for the late Rabbi [Joseph] Soloveitchik, of blessed memory—my Rav and the *rav* of all our teachers who were either his students or the students of his students. It was he who preferred that such an all-women's service not be held at Yeshiva. Whatever his reasons—it is not something we need go into here—his decision prevails, especially here where his spirit and eminence still govern as our ultimate halakhic authority, and there is nothing that has happened since he made his decision that would cause me to reconsider.

Modern Orthodoxy's Demise

Gary Bauman | 2011

In June 2011 Yeshivat Rambam of Baltimore closed its doors. Founded in 1991, the day school served the educational needs of the Modern Orthodox Jews who did not feel at ease with the transdenominational "community school" on their ideological left and the more traditional Talmudical Academy on their right. The news reports cited an insoluble financial situation for Rambam's demise. Yet insiders understood that the school's rightward shift (it began as a coeducational school but at the end separated boys and girls into different buildings) sent Yeshivat Rambam into an "identity crisis." In its final years, Rambam was positioned too far to the "right" to draw from leftward-leaning families and was not sufficiently "authentic" to compete with the local Talmudical Academy, Ner Israel High School, and Bais Yaakov. To Gary Bauman (b. 1960), of the school's parent body, the end of Yeshivat Rambam represented the demise of Modern Orthodoxy, a thought he shared in the local Jewish press.

Baltimore's Orthodox community is fond of touting its achdus, unity. This illusion of unity was laid bare for all to see recently with the announcement that Yeshivat Rambam would be closing.

As a parent of four children who attended the school for 18 years and having been involved in the school since its inception, I am dismayed that this final step was taken. Although not shocking by any means, the sad ending still caused tears, anger, and a sense that the Baltimore Jewish community will be irreversibly damaged by these developments.

Much of what has been written deals with the fiscal situation of the school. Yet there is so much more to this story. Five years ago, after years of financial mismanagement, some in the school's leadership decided the only way to survive was to move to the right of the religious spectrum to attract a larger audience. For many of us who openly support the ideals of modern Orthodoxy, it was clear that this was the wrong decision. Unfortunately from both a financial and religious perspective, these decisions made no sense.

Fiscally, separating classes by gender and splitting into two separate campuses clearly would raise costs even further. Religiously, those of us who toiled for many years to stand up for clear ideals of Torah and Mada, integrating Torah with the modern world, knew that diluting those ideals was not the way to retain families, nor would it attract any wider audience.

In a community increasingly defined by an extreme right wing, Yeshivat Rambam was always meant to serve as a beacon of a more moderate, middle-of-the-road type of religious institution. Myopic, weak leadership with no vision of what a niche school is meant to be gave in to the more base tendencies of fundamentalism, thinking this would attract huge numbers of families.

It did not. An institution that does not stand up for its stated principles eventually falls.

During the past 20 years I have lived in Baltimore, we have been asked several times to assist institutions with which we have no relationship and in some cases with whom we disagree vehemently about religious issues when they were in financial need. In at least one case, rabbis decreed from the pulpit that this was a community responsibility and every Jew had an obligation to save the school. Where were all those rabbinic leaders during the past several months when it was Yeshivat Rambam's survival on the line? Or is it only a communal responsibility when an institution aligns with their religious ideals? How sad is it that an entire segment of the Orthodox community finds itself orphaned and hundreds of children are left to scramble to find alternative arrangements for their schooling? How much sadder is it that rumors abound that several institutions have made it clear they will not accept these families, as their hashkafah, their belief system, is not appropriate for their school? At least we are fortunate that one day school is making every effort to admit as many students as possible.[7]

So what now for modern Orthodoxy in Baltimore? Sadly, I think we are done. Many families have already left Baltimore or plan on doing so in the near future. We have already heard of young families who originally intended to move here now changing their plans and looking for alternative communities. Once an attractive option, Baltimore will cease to be on the list of young professionals seeking a warm, thriving community that approximates their beliefs.[8]

Yes, there will always be small pockets of those who espouse this philosophy. But without a school and with fewer new people to reinvigorate it, any sense of rejuvenating the Yeshivat Rambam mission of full engagement with the secular world, love of the State of Israel, strict adherence to Halachah, and an enhanced role for women in Judaism will be lost.

The only conclusion that can be reached is that there is no longer any place for modern Orthodoxy in the wider Orthodox community of Baltimore. How sad for this community. How tragic for future generations. How utterly devastating for those of us who are left behind.

Social Orthodoxy

Jay P. Lefkowitz | 2014

Some Modern Orthodox Jews chose to ignore the philosophical and intellectual head-butting. In 2014 prominent lawyer Jay P. Lefkowitz (b. 1962) published his thoughts on "Social Orthodoxy." In this essay Lefkowitz stressed that his fidelity to Jewish law and behavior stems from the social capital he received as a member of the well-integrated and richly resourced New York Orthodox community. The "theology" of Modern Orthodox Judaism was far less important to him than the social aspects of the community it held together, as Lefkowitz points out in the excerpted section below.

I start my day each morning by donning my tefillin before heading to my office at a law firm. I eat out in restaurants several times a month only to pass up 90 percent of the menu in favor of vegetarian fare because I keep kosher. I occasionally find myself stuck in cities on a Friday far from home because I cannot travel back to New York City in time for the arrival of the Sabbath. I go to synagogue each week and celebrate all the Jewish holidays. My children attend a Modern Orthodox day school, and my college-age daughter served as a soldier in the Israeli army. And I am proud to be a Zionist. Unless one were to look very carefully, I would appear to be the very model of an Orthodox Jew, albeit a modern one. But I also pick and choose from the menu of Jewish rituals without fear of divine retribution. And I root my identity much more in Jewish culture, history, and nationality than in faith and commandments. I am a Social Orthodox Jew, and I am not alone.

I once asked my father why he studies Jewish texts and practices Jewish rituals so rigorously. I knew he was agnostic when it came to matters of faith. He told me that he observes the Commandments because that is what connects him to Jews across continents and centuries. He said that he views halacha as a compass and that every Jew, even if he or she chooses to take some detours along the way, should know which direction is true north.

Whether such a cultural tradition can be sufficiently transmitted to the next generation is a fair question. Certainly, a neat theological package provides parents with a more direct message to convey to their children. Yet there is also an authenticity in a dynamic Judaism that recognizes its origins as a national identity. As Leon Roth [1896–1963], the first professor of philosophy at the Hebrew University, observed, dogmalessness is "the only dogma in Judaism."

So it is with many Social Orthodox Jews. We generally choose to head north, where halacha dictates. But we live in the modern world, and occasionally we explore the pathways around the edges of halacha. Much more important to us than theology, however, is maintaining the continuity of the Jewish people.

What [Mordecai] Kaplan called "civilization" and Ahad Ha'am called a "national culture" is what moves many of us.[9] We behave as Jews so we can belong as Jews. Some of us may even come to believe. The key, however, is that we live Jewish lives so we will not be disconnected, and we will never be alone.

The Freundel Affair
Kesher Israel Board of Directors | 2014

In October 2014 Rabbi Barry Freundel (b. 1951) of Washington DC was arrested on six charges of voyeurism. In February 2015 he pled guilty to 52 counts of spying and filming women undressing before immersing in the mikvah. Freundel had helped build the National Capital Mikvah, and many women who studied for conversion with the Washington rabbi visited the mikvah to complete the final stages of their initiation to Judaism. Kesher Israel Congregation and the mikvah organization fully complied with the investigation and immediately turned over evidence to police. Two days later, after Freundel's arrest, Kesher Israel suspended its rabbi without pay. Several weeks later, the congregation terminated the rabbi's contract. The collective Orthodox rabbinate and other prominent Jewish organizations condemned Freundel, who in the 1990s had served as chairman of the RCA's ethics committee. The public letter issued by Kesher Israel's lay leadership indicated the resources and strength of the Modern Orthodox community to address these circumstances. In May 2015 Freudel was sentenced to six and a half years in prison.

Last week, the Kesher Israel Board of Directors terminated the contract of Rabbi Dr. Barry Freundel. Since the day of his arrest, Rabbi Freundel had been suspended from Kesher Israel without pay. Based on last week's action by the Board of Directors, his relationship with Kesher Israel has permanently ended. As he is required to do under his contract, Rabbi Freundel has been asked to vacate the rabbinic residence by January 1, 2015.

The decision by the Board of Directors was made under extraordinarily difficult and unfortunate circumstances. The alleged acts leading to this step were a gross violation of law, privacy, halakha, and trust. They breached the high moral and ethical standards we set for ourselves and for our leadership. Our collective heart breaks for the consequences, both seen and unseen, of these alleged acts to all the potential victims and our entire community.

This step is an important moment for our community. As we move beyond the events of last month, our community continues to come together and heal. This incident has demonstrated that the Kesher Israel community remains larger than any single individual, and we have emerged stronger than we were before. We are an engaged and hopeful community—united by common faith, beliefs, and communal bond. We will remain strong and resilient.

We take great pride that our shul has continued to operate without interruption since the arrest, including through the chagim [holidays], during recent smachot [celebrations], and through family losses. We are deeply grateful for the volunteers and community members who have stepped up during this challenging time and have worked tirelessly on behalf of the Kesher community. We are also thankful to Rabbi Kenneth Brander and Nechama Price for their continued short-term halakhic support.[10] We are committed to finding more long-term solutions to our religious needs very soon.

As Kesher continues to move forward, the Board of Directors is committed to listening to the needs of the entire congregation. We encourage members of our community to reach out to the shul's leadership to voice any concerns, provide input, or even just to talk. Please do not hesitate to share your thoughts.

We look forward to continuing to build a vibrant future for Kesher Israel and to ensuring our community remains a warm, welcoming, and safe place to gather, worship, and learn.

SECTION 2 | Modern Orthodoxy Reclaimed?

Open Orthodox Judaism

Dov Linzer and Avi Weiss | 2003

In 1999 Rabbi Avi Weiss founded Yeshivat Chovevei Torah as a liberal alternative to Yeshiva University's rabbinical school. He hired RIETS-trained Rabbi Dov Linzer (b. 1966) to serve as the rabbinic head of the Orthodox seminary. In YCT's formative years, Weiss and Linzer thought it prudent to outline the planks and pillars of their school. This 2003 essay reflects many of the ideas debated in prior decades and a belief that Yeshiva University could no longer serve the needs of rabbinical students who desired to reside on the more progressive side of an ideologically and institutionally broadening Modern Orthodox enclave. In articulating this vision, the authors sought to create a rabbinate for a new "Open Orthodox" community.

Orthodox Judaism is currently at a crossroads. In the post-Holocaust generation, Orthodoxy has shown new life, attracting and maintaining adherents and cultivating an increasing commitment to scrupulous observance and regular Torah study. The choice that Orthodoxy faces today is whether to focus on the needs of its own community or on the needs of the larger Jewish community, expanding outward, nondogmatically and cooperatively. Believing in an Orthodoxy that is open intellectually and expansive and inclusive in practice, we need a new breed of rabbis. To this end, three years ago, we created Yeshivat Chovevei Torah Rabbinical School.

Our goal is to create rabbis who are critical thinkers with intellectual integrity and who openly engage the challenges of our modern and post-modern world while living a life of faith and religious commitment. Our curriculum includes classes that explicitly address these issues. Our culture and staff encourage open discussion, and many of our students regularly participate in interdenominational and interfaith events. Our students learn that religious growth comes not through dogmatism but through questioning and struggle.

Openness in thought leads to inclusiveness in practice. We are training our students to be rabbis and leaders who will work to expand and enhance the role of women in religious leadership, the halakhic process, and ritual; to pursue positive interactions with all Jewish denominations; to impart to their congregants the deep religious significance of the State of Israel; and to see *tikkun olam* [literally, repairing the world] as a significant religious obligation. We recognize that the vast majority of Jews are unaffiliated; we are training our students to engage these Jews—not with the goal of making them Orthodox, but rather to ignite in them the spark of Jewish consciousness and inspire their spiritual striving.

To create rabbis who are spiritual leaders, a culture of openness and an innovative academic curriculum are not sufficient. What is needed is a course of study that addresses areas such as leadership, education, communication, and conducting life-cycle events. Our professional training extends beyond a comprehensive classroom experience with two years of supervised fieldwork and internships mentored by seasoned rabbis in consultation with mental health professionals. Such a curriculum is designed to produce rabbis with wisdom as well as knowledge, who can educate and spiritually nurture all Jews, aiding them in times of crisis and helping them at all times to connect meaningfully with their Judaism.

While a professional training curriculum is *de rigueur* in non-Orthodox rabbinical schools, it is virtually unheard of in Orthodox yeshivot. The goal of traditional yeshivot is to produce Torah scholars. The goal of our school, as both a yeshiva and a rabbinical school, is to produce Torah scholars who are passionate about learning and are professionally trained rabbis and leaders.

We hope to produce rabbis with professionalism and mission— rabbis who will begin to transform Orthodoxy into a more open and inclusive movement. Through such a transformed Orthodoxy that so meaningfully and respectfully interacts with all Jews, regardless of affiliation, commitment, or background, we believe that we can do our share to transform the face of the Jewish community.

The Close of Edah

Saul J. Berman | 2006

In 2006 Rabbi Saul Berman announced the close of his Modern Orthodox think tank. Billed as an organization for those with the "courage to be Modern and Orthodox," Edah would no longer persist as a stand-alone institution. Owing to financial limitations, Berman and a number of the Edah resources moved to Yeshivat Chovevei Torah. Edah's founder and director pledged that other groups would incorporate other facets of his program. Berman's farewell message was one of optimism, as the excerpted selection indicates. He did not share the grievances or caution that others conveyed in their reflections on the Modern Orthodox sphere.

We founded Edah in 1997 as a think tank to restore the essential elements of Modern Orthodox ideology. Edah was not formed as a critique of haredi Orthodoxy but as a critique of the Modern Orthodox neglect of its own distinctive ideological positions. We recognized from the outset that a strong haredi community contributed to the strength of Modern Orthodoxy as well as to the well-being of the entire Jewish people. We believed, however, with equal conviction, that a strong Modern Orthodox community, committed to tolerance and diversity, would contribute to the well-being of both the haredi community and to the entire Jewish people.

Simply put, we believed that strengthening the Torah way of life required the most honest expression of Modern Orthodox ideology. We began with a website and publications to provide a clear picture of Modern Orthodox ideology. We arranged for a small conference to explore Torah life as it applied to the reality of secular America and Israel. We hoped open discourse between rabbis, scholars, and lay people was the best way to help the Modern Orthodox community reconstitute itself and address its problems.

Our plan in February 1999 for a gathering of 300 people snowballed into a two-day conference of 1,500 men and women, at which more than 75 study and discussion sessions were overwhelmed by the number of people clamoring for attendance and by the intensity and openness of the debate they brought to the sessions. Samuel G. Freedman later described that conference in his book *Jew vs. Jew* as the moment "the Modern Orthodox movement climbed back up from its knees."[11] It was the beginning.

. . . Nine years later, what has Edah accomplished? As to our first goal, to clarify and disseminate the integrationist ideology, we believe Edah has changed the conversation in the Modern Orthodox community. Through conferences—four international, four in Israel, eight regional—five years of courses at the Manhattan JCC, and regular publication of the *Edah Journal*, Edah has created a new arena of thought on issues of Modern Orthodoxy, validated the legitimacy of Modern Orthodox positions within the *mesoret*, and presented them with a persuasive power previously lacking.

Now that the Edah think tank has achieved many of its original objectives, and the Modern Orthodox community has matured and stabilized, Edah is electing to wind down. We founded Edah when Modern Orthodoxy's identity had become thin and its energy weak. The current reality is different. . . . We take pride in knowing that Edah has served its purpose well—and that its message and outlook will continue to be pursued energetically by those whom Edah inspired. The organization will close; the vision will continue to grow.

Shirah Hadashah

Tova Hartman | 2007

In 2002 a group of Jerusalem residents founded Kehillat Shirah Hadashah. The congregation aimed to provide a space for "partnership between men and women in leading the service" that would be governed by a plausible interpretation of Jewish law. The congregation uses the traditional Jewish liturgy and permits women to lead services in certain parts of the worship. This includes, for example, the opening sections of the daily and Sabbath prayers and the Kabbalat Shabbat service on Friday evenings. In short order, the "Shirah Hadashah phenomenon" migrated to the United States. In 2015 JOFA's website listed twenty-seven "partnership minyanim" in the United States that meet on a weekly or monthly basis. A number have emerged on college campuses as well. In 2007 the gender studies scholar and Shirah Hadashah cofounder Tova Hartman (b. 1957) published a memoir of her experiences in establishing the new congregation. For many years Hartman has stood out as a leading Orthodox feminist for cohorts in Israel and North America. An excerpt is provided here.

I first met Elie Holzer, one of the founders of Shirah Hadashah, at a JOFA conference in 2001.[12] By sheer coincidence, we had both come to speak about the same topic: Rabbis [Mayer] Twersky and [Moshe] Meiselman's responses to the phenomenon of women's prayer groups.[13] Each of us reclaimed the intrinsic value of a person's religious subjectivity as something that cannot and should not be a priori defined by authority, whether textual or human. Elie drew his claim from an analysis of Rabbi [Joseph] Soloveitchik's hermeneutic and philosophy of religion and I did so from a feminist-psychological perspective. After our sessions we began brainstorming about what a serious prayer community—one that acknowledged and honored the spiritual dignity and desires of women—could like look.

In light of both our general experiences within the Modern Orthodox community and the specific topic that had brought us to the conference, Elie and I understood quite keenly how charged this issue was.

The preceding years had been characterized by intense exchanges in the Modern Orthodox world about increased women's participation in public roles, particularly around prayer and the ritual life of the synagogue. Modern Orthodox women felt an increased sense of desire—and of entitlement—in this arena, and the response of many Modern Orthodox authorities was taking the shape of a classic patriarchal backlash against feminist gains. There seemed to be much at stake for those attempting to hold the line of "no change," which was reflected in their willingness to lash out quite aggressively against those calling even for changes that appeared to pose no halakhic problem (or at least could find solid halakhic ground upon which to stand).

Elie and I both had spent many years on the ritual committees of shuls, and so we were familiar with the range of responses to this call for change. We knew that we would not be confronting a purely halakhic conversation. We knew that some would attempt to make halakhic arguments, some would stress the need to maintain a unified front with Orthodoxy, and some—inevitably the loudest—would employ a range of metahalakhic, antifeminist rhetoric.[14] We knew of the deep discomfort of certain rabbinic authorities and their adherents in admitting that some religious needs are left unmet by the tradition in its current state.

The halakhic arguments against ritual changes could be met with counterarguments, and this was a welcome and legitimate conversation.[15] After all, we were not (and are not) claiming ours is the *only* halakhic way to do communal prayer or the only way to understand traditional principles like *kvod ha-tzibur* (respecting communal dignity) and *kvod ha'adam* (respecting human dignity)—which are also the central halakhic categories employed in determining such issues as the permissibility of women reading from the Torah and leading certain parts of the service.[16] Our intention was never to argue that ours was the only way to pray, but merely that it is a traditionally valid mode in which to stand before God.[17]

The argument about Orthodox unity is one to which we remain sympathetic, but which we decided cannot outweigh the considerations of human dignity. Once again, we were and are perfectly willing to view this argument as a *makhloket le-shem shamayim* (a disagreement for the sake of heaven). The metahalakhic, antifeminist conversation, on the other hand, utilized tactics of recrimination, intimidation, and delegitimation that, ultimately and ironically, undermined its own purpose: exposing the extent to which increased women's participation was not *at all* a halakhic issue (why else all the fire and brimstone, with little or no halakhic content anywhere to be found?) and undermining its own credibility with hyperbolically alarmist claims. When Rabbi Meiselman says that if we accept women's prayer groups, soon women will be dancing with pagan idols in shul, the mind races until it settles upon a profound understanding that what is at stake is something other than halakhic integrity. The intent of such rhetoric is clearly to shut down conversation, to silence opposition—and, in most cases, it succeeds.

A Statement of Principles

Nathaniel Helfgot | 2010

In December 2009 Yeshiva University hosted a panel discussion on "Being Gay in the Modern Orthodox World," an event that attracted about eight hundred students and interested listeners. The affair occasioned much discussion in the Modern Orthodox sphere, both positive and negative. Supporters of the panel were encouraged that Yeshiva University and Modern Orthodox Jews felt so obliged to encounter a thorny matter like homosexuality, which was so proscribed in the Torah but so much a part of American society. Those opposed to the public discussion wondered aloud how the Orthodox university could countenance a conversation that centered on an "abominable" sin. In fact, shortly after the event, Rabbi Mayer Twersky (b. 1960) of RIETS compared the panel to another hypothetical public discussion on adultery. Both, he surmised, were "sinful." Perhaps the most strategic response to the panel occurred seven months later. In July 2010 Rabbi Nathaniel Helfgot (b. 1963) published an online "Statement of Principles on the Place of Jews with a Homosexual Orientation in Our Community." A RIETS-trained writer and educator, Helfgot was one of the founding faculty members of the liberal-leaning Yeshivat Chovevei Torah. Yet the hundreds of sig-

natures attached to the Statement of Principles reflected its acceptance in a variety of sectors within the wider Modern Orthodox fold.

We, the undersigned Orthodox rabbis, *rashei yeshiva, ramim* [rabbinic teachers], Jewish educators, and communal leaders affirm the following principles with regard to the place of Jews with a homosexual orientation in our community:

1. All human beings are created in the image of God and deserve to be treated with dignity and respect (*kevod haberiyot*). Every Jew is obligated to fulfill the entire range of *mitzvot* between person and person in relation to persons who are homosexual or have feelings of same-sex attraction. Embarrassing, harassing, or demeaning someone with a homosexual orientation or same-sex attraction is a violation of Torah prohibitions that embody the deepest values of Judaism.

2. The question of whether sexual orientation is primarily genetic or rather environmentally generated is irrelevant to our obligation to treat human beings with same-sex attractions and orientations with dignity and respect.

3. Halakhah sees heterosexual marriage as the ideal model and sole legitimate outlet for human sexual expression. The sensitivity and understanding we properly express for human beings with other sexual orientations does not diminish our commitment to that principle.

4. Halakhic Judaism views all male and female same-sex sexual interactions as prohibited. The question of whether sexual orientation is primarily genetic or rather environmentally generated is irrelevant to this prohibition. While Halakhah categorizes various homosexual acts with different degrees of severity and opprobrium, including *toeivah* [abomination], this does not in any way imply that lesser acts are permitted. But it is critical to emphasize that Halakhah only prohibits homosexual acts; it does not prohibit orientation or feelings of same-sex attraction, and nothing in the Torah devalues the human beings who struggle with them.

(We do not here address the issue of *hirhurei aveirah,* a halakhic category that goes beyond mere feelings and applies to all forms of sexuality and requires precise halakhic definition.)

5. Whatever the origin or cause of homosexual orientation, many individuals believe that for most people this orientation cannot be changed. Others believe that for most people it is a matter of free will. Similarly, while some mental health professionals and rabbis in the community strongly believe in the efficacy of "change therapies," most of the mental health community, many rabbis, and most people with a homosexual orientation feel that some of these therapies are either ineffective or potentially damaging psychologically for many patients. We affirm the religious right of those with a homosexual orientation to reject therapeutic approaches they reasonably see as useless or dangerous.

6. Jews with a homosexual orientation who live in the Orthodox community confront serious emotional, communal, and psychological challenges that cause them and their families great pain and suffering. For example, homosexual orientation may greatly increase the risk of suicide among teenagers in our community. Rabbis and communities need to be sensitive and empathetic to that reality. Rabbis and mental health professionals must provide responsible and ethical assistance to congregants and clients dealing with those human challenges.

7. Jews struggling to live their lives in accordance with halakhic values need and deserve our support. Accordingly, we believe that the decision as to whether to be open about one's sexual orientation should be left to such individuals, who should consider their own needs and those of the community. We are opposed on ethical and moral grounds to both the "outing" of individuals who want to remain private and to coercing those who desire to be open about their orientation to keep it hidden.

8. Accordingly, Jews with homosexual orientations or same-sex attractions should be welcomed as full members of the synagogue and school community. As appropriate with regard to gender and

lineage, they should participate and count ritually, be eligible for ritual synagogue honors, and generally be treated in the same fashion and under the same halakhic and hashkafic framework as any other member of the synagogue they join. Conversely, they must accept and fulfill all the responsibilities of such membership, including those generated by communal norms or broad Jewish principles that go beyond formal Halakhah.

We do not here address what synagogues should do about accepting members who are openly practicing homosexuals and/or living with a same-sex partner. Each synagogue together with its rabbi must establish its own standard with regard to membership for open violators of Halakhah. Those standards should be applied fairly and objectively.

9. Halakhah articulates very exacting criteria and standards of eligibility for particular religious offices, such as [an] officially appointed cantor during the year or baal tefillah on the High Holidays. Among the most important of those criteria is that the entire congregation must be fully comfortable with having that person serve as its representative. This legitimately prevents even the most admirable individuals, who are otherwise perfectly fit halakhically, from serving in those roles. It is the responsibility of the lay and rabbinic leadership in each individual community to determine eligibility for those offices in line with those principles, the importance of maintaining communal harmony, and the unique context of its community culture.

10. Jews with a homosexual orientation or same-sex attraction, even if they engage in same-sex interactions, should be encouraged to fulfill *mitzvot* to the best of their ability. All Jews are challenged to fulfill *mitzvot* to the best of their ability, and the attitude of "all or nothing" was not the traditional approach adopted by the majority of halakhic thinkers and poskim throughout the ages.

11. Halakhic Judaism cannot give its blessing and imprimatur to Jewish religious same-sex commitment ceremonies and weddings, and halakhic values proscribe individuals and communities from

encouraging practices that grant religious legitimacy to gay marriage and couplehood. But communities should display sensitivity, acceptance, and full embrace of the adopted or biological children of homosexually active Jews in the synagogue and school setting, and we encourage parents and family of homosexually partnered Jews to make every effort to maintain harmonious family relations and connections.

12. Jews who have an exclusively homosexual orientation should, under most circumstances, not be encouraged to marry someone of the other gender, as this can lead to great tragedy, unrequited love, shame, dishonesty, and ruined lives. They should be directed to contribute to Jewish and general society in other meaningful ways. Any such person who is planning to marry someone of the opposite gender is halakhically and ethically required to fully inform his or her potential spouse of their sexual orientation.

We hope and pray that by sharing these thoughts we will help the Orthodox community to fully live out its commitment to the principles and values of Torah and Halakhah as practiced and cherished by the children of Abraham, who our sages teach us are recognized by the qualities of being *rahamanim* (merciful), *bayshanim* (modest), and *gomelei hasadim* (engaging in acts of loving-kindness).

Taking Back Modern Orthodox Judaism

Asher Lopatin | 2014

In October 2013 Yeshivat Chovevei Torah installed Rabbi Asher Lopatin (b. 1964) as its second president, succeeding founder Rabbi Avi Weiss. Before this, Lopatin served as rabbi of Anshe Sholom B'nai Israel Congregation in Chicago. Since taking office at YCT, Lopatin moved away from professing his predecessor's "Open Orthodox" creed and has shown less sympathy for his YCT colleagues who remain too close to the fringes of Orthodox Judaism and its fidelity to the Written and Oral Law. Instead, he has argued for the revitalization of Modern Orthodox

Judaism, with his school at the forefront. With considerable historical precision, Lopatin authored the following vision for a "rejuvenated" Modern Orthodoxy.

Modern Orthodoxy as it developed in 20th-century America was dynamic, vibrant, challenging, and filled with new insights into Judaism. This was made possible not by taking in the values of modernity wholesale but by maintaining a positive attitude toward those values and not opposing them merely because they were foreign. At its best, Modern Orthodoxy represented an embrace of the idea that the world around us could help Jews, not just hurt them. It is this Modern Orthodoxy, willing to listen to voices from without and within, that we need to revitalize.

This is the very paradigm that was under siege twenty years ago when Rabbi Avi Weiss wrote his manifesto "Open Orthodox Manifesto."[18] Important and controversial Orthodox thinkers, including Rabbis Yitz Greenberg and David Hartman, were being shunned by the so-called Modern Orthodox establishment. Even Rabbi Shlomo Riskin, the founder and former spiritual leader of New York's Lincoln Square Synagogue, was not allowed to speak at Yeshiva University. There was a sense of despair that the Modern Orthodoxy of the 1950s and 1960s—an era in which Rabbis Emanuel Rackman, Yitz Greenberg, and Eliezer Berkovits and (in Israel) the philosopher Yeshayahu Leibowitz were household names—had been lost.[19] Even as Rabbi Saul Berman's Edah initiative, noted by [Jack] Wertheimer, succeeded in restoring a certain pride in the name Modern Orthodox, there was legitimate concern that the movement was coming to represent an ossified and unimaginative type of Judaism, always looking fearfully over its right shoulder. Hence "Open Orthodoxy."[20]

Fortunately, we are in a different situation today. In certain circles Modern Orthodoxy is returning to its roots and coming back to life. After decades of struggle and hard work by the Jewish Orthodox Feminist Alliance, Aguna Inc., and many others, America now has an Orthodox rabbinical court dealing with the needs of women whose husbands have refused to give them a writ of Jewish divorce. Under the able leadership of Rabbi Simcha Krauss, the court is open to considering halakhic procedures of the past that have been lost to us in 21st-century America and Israel.[21] Rabbis associated with the new International Rabbinic Fellowship and other Modern Orthodox organizations will undoubtedly support Rabbi Krauss's rulings.

Similarly, Rabbi Marc Angel has established the Institute for Jewish Ideas and Ideals, bringing back the diversity of opinions, even the vibrancy inherent in a certain irreverence for authority, previously characteristic of Modern Orthodoxy.[22] Through the institute's journal *Conversations*, thousands of discussions have been sparked across America, and future Modern Orthodox leaders are being encouraged to appreciate and engage with challenging opinions through campus fellows' programs. Yeshivat Maharat in the United States and at least three different programs in Israel train women to be teachers, halakhic thinkers, and decisors and, in the case of Yeshivat Maharat, to go out and lead their own communities.

The Modern Orthodoxy of the past was not built solely upon controversy and irreverence for authority; it combined an awe of Judaism with an appreciation for what an engagement with modernity could do to make us better Jews and scholars of Torah. It is this balance that we need to retrieve. Indeed, there is even a great deal that the most open-minded and truly modern Orthodox Jew has to learn from the haredi world. Since the biblical prophet Isaiah bids the entire Jewish people to be "haredim," shaking at the word of God, one thinker has even proposed adopting the term "Modern Haredi" (Isa. 66:5). We need to be passionate about our Torah and our *Yiddishkeit*; we need to be in awe of the divine message and even more truly in awe of God. All this, while maintaining our engagement with the outside world and the diverse opinions that are a hallmark of our camp.

The exciting and courageous Modern Orthodoxy of yesteryear is back. It may still be most active under the surface, but the energy and potential are powerful. Rabbi Yaakov Perlow, the Novominsker Rebbe, was correct in pointing to the growing influence of the nearly 90 rabbis who have graduated from Yeshivat Chovevei Torah over the past

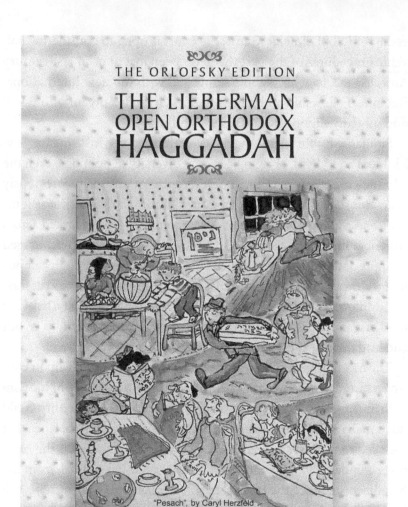

THE ORLOFSKY EDITION

THE LIEBERMAN OPEN ORTHODOX HAGGADAH

"Pesach", by Caryl Herzfeld

RABBI SHMUEL HERZFELD

 GEFEN PUBLISHING HOUSE

In 2015 Rabbi Shmuel Herzfeld (b. 1974) published an "Open Orthodox" Passover Haggadah. The book included essays and commentaries by a number of self-professed Open Orthodox women and men. The Haggadah quickly sold out its initial run of five thousand. The appearance and success of Herzfeld's work also suggests, and contrary to Rabbi Asher Lopatin's call, that there are many progressive Orthodox Jews who are more comfortable with the term *Open Orthodox* than with *Modern Orthodox*. Image courtesy of Gefen Publishing House Ltd., Jerusalem.

ten years, most of whom work in Jewish communal life and fully 40 percent of whom occupy pulpits spanning the globe.[23]

Now is indeed the time to reclaim Modern Orthodoxy as a vibrant, creative, and open movement. Accordingly, many of us no longer speak of Open Orthodoxy as a separate stream but rather of bringing back the real Modern Orthodoxy: the kind in which an Orthodox journal could print an article like Rabbi Norman Lamm's "Faith and Doubt," which claims doubt as part of our religion, or an article by Rabbi Eliezer Berkovits accompanied by a note stipulating that the content is not necessarily in consonance with editorial opinion.[24]

Jack Wertheimer has laid down a challenge: can we rejuvenate the proud tradition of Modern Orthodoxy and connect it to our generation? From my vantage point, the answer is yes. With God's help and with humility, awe, and the passion to explore the infinite depths of God's Torah, we can revitalize Modern Orthodoxy.

CONCLUSION

In 2013 the Pew Research Center released a "Portrait of Jewish Americans" that offered an extremely grim presentation of American Judaism and its denominations. The exception, perhaps, was the Orthodox community, which expressed a "level of religious commitment" that "matches or exceeds most other religious groups."[25] Orthodox Jews achieved better retention of its adherents, maintaining the highest fertility rate and the lowest measure of instances of intermarriage. A number of Orthodox pundits cheered the findings. Yet not everyone was as sanguine. Upon reviewing the data, Rabbi Jacob J. Schacter viewed the Pew report as an "indictment of Orthodoxy."[26] As one of Modern Orthodoxy's leading intellectuals, Schacter called on Modern Orthodox congregations and their institutions to seek out the "unaffiliated" Jews who were included among the more tragic figures in the research study. The high tally among these ranks represented, for Schacter, a failure to "meaningfully engage and impact the broad spectrum of *acheinu*

Bnai Yisrael [Jewish brethren] in this country." In Schacter's call were echoes of Rabbi Shlomo Riskin's outreach efforts and Rabbi Joseph Lookstein's explanation of the "non-observant Orthodox Jew," among other voices included in this Modern Orthodox anthology. Other texts in this chapter move the reader to recall the religious "identity crisis" that Norman Lamm had described in the 1960s. Viewed as a whole, the documents in these final chapters prove that the history of Modern Orthodox Judaism is one that moves in cycles and with a dynamic penchant for "change." That Yeshiva University will soon launch a search for a new leader to replace Richard Joel will ensure this. Accordingly, there will be new chapters to write in the decades that follow. So be it.

Source Acknowledgments

1. Engaging Reform

"Retrograde instead of Advancing": Mordecai Noah. "Jewish Converts." *New York National Advocate*, October 18, 1825, 2.

New Lights and Old Lights: "For the Mercury." *Charleston Mercury*, October 28, 1825, 2.

This Happy Land: Isaac Harby. *A Discourse, Delivered in Charleston, (S.C.) on the 21st of Nov. 1825, before the Reformed Society of Israelites, for Promoting True Principles of Judaism According to its Purity and Spirit, on Their First Anniversary.* Charleston: A. E. Miller, 1825, 3–5.

A Jewish Luther: Jacob Mordecai. "Remarks on Harby's discourse Delivered in Charleston (S.C.) on the 21st day of Nov. 1825 Before the Reformed Society of Israelites on their First Anniversary By a Congregationalist of Richmond, Virginia, January 1826." Transcribed by Gary P. Zola, sc-8422, 1–3, American Jewish Archives, Cincinnati. Published with permission and courtesy of the Jacob Rader Marcus Center of the American Jewish Archives, Cincinnati. americanjewisharchives.org.

An Open Letter to Gustavus Poznanski: Isaac Leeser. "Letter to the Rev. G. Poznanski." *Occident*, August 1843, 253–61.

"Some Wolves Clothed in Sheep's-Cover": Nathan M. Kaganoff. "A Historic Document." *Tradition* 7 (Winter 1965): 121–22. Reprinted with permission of *Tradition* and Rosalyn Kaganoff.

What Prevails among the Jewish People? Mordecai Noah. "Inquirer." *Sunday Times and Weekly Messenger*, September 29, 1850, 1.

This Is Religious Liberty in America: Abram Vossen Goodman. "A Jewish Peddler's Diary." *American Jewish Archives Journal* 3 (June 1951): 108–10. Republished with permission and courtesy of the Jacob Rader Marcus Center of the American Jewish Archives, Cincinnati. americanjewisharchives.org.

Our Holy Place: Letter from Trustees of Shearith Israel Banning Intermarried Men, March 21, 1847, FF-20-219, Arnold and Deanne Kaplan Collection of Early

American Judaica, Herbert D. Katz Center for Advanced Judaic Studies, Philadelphia. Published with permission and courtesy of the Arnold and Deanne Kaplan Collection of Early American Judaica. Library at the Herbert D. Katz Center for Advanced Judaic Studies, Kislak Center for Special Collections, Rare Books and Manuscripts, University of Pennsylvania.

Strange Misbehavior: L.D. "Parties—Keep Peace!" *Asmonean,* August 4, 1854, 125.

An Aunt's Admonishment: Anna Marks Allen to Her Nephew, June 28, 1858, SC-199, American Jewish Archives, Cincinnati. Published with permission and courtesy of the Jacob Rader Marcus Center of the American Jewish Archives, Cincinnati. americanjewisharchives.org.

2. The Traditional Talmud and Response to Reform Prayer Books

The Talmud Is Not Divine: "The Oral Law—Letter of the Rev. Mr. Carillon." *Occident,* October 1843, 347–48.

At the Risk of Being Considered Hyper-Orthodox: "Editorial Correspondence." *Occident,* November 1843, 395–97.

A Return to the Maimonidean View? "Letter of the Rev. Mr. Rice—The Oral Law." *Occident,* August 1844, 253–54.

The Cleveland Conference: Isaac Leeser. "Cleveland Conference." *Occident,* November 1855, 410–13.

It Is Decidedly Heretical: Morris J. Raphall. "Remarks on the Rev. Dr. Einhorn's Replies." *Asmonean,* January 26, 1856, 117.

An Ornament for Parlor-Tables: Bernard Illowy. "The Reformed Prayer-Book." *Occident,* November 1855, 414–15.

A Letter from an "Enlightened Orthodox" Jew: Benjamin Franklin Peixotto to Isaac Leeser, November 16, 1859, SC-9474, American Jewish Archives, Cincinnati. Published with permission and courtesy of the Jacob Rader Marcus Center of the American Jewish Archives, Cincinnati. americanjewisharchives.org.

On Burning Reform Prayer Books: Eliyahu M. Holzman. *Emek Refa'im,* 4, 20. New York, 1865.

Minhag Ashkenaz and Minhag Reform: Nathan Rossman vs. Anschi Chesed, filed April 6, 1866, New York County Clerk Archives, New York.

3. An Orthodox Ministry

Rabbinic Tenure: Max Lilienthal. "The Appointment of Jewish Ministers in America." *Israelite*, October 27, 1854, 124.

A New Calling: Palestine. "Communications." *Israelite*, June 27, 1862, 411.

Isaac Leeser's Successor: Alfred T. Jones. *Address*, 5–7. Philadelphia, 1869.

The Ethics: Alexander Kohut. *The Ethics of the Fathers*, ed. Barnett A. Elzas, 7–9. New York: Publishers Printing Company, 1920.

Backward or Forward? Kaufmann Kohler. *Studies, Addresses, and Personal Papers*, 201–3. New York: Bloch, 1931.

What Is Progress? Alexander Kohut. *The Ethics of the Fathers*, ed. Barnett A. Elzas, 88–90, 92–93. New York: Publishers Printing Company, 1920.

To the Hebrews of America: Henry Pereira Mendes to the Hebrews of America, 1886, acc/2805/02/01/093, acc/2805/02/01/093, London Metropolitan Archives, London. Published with the permission of the Office of the Chief Rabbi of the United Hebrew Congregations of the Commonwealth.

A School for the Intelligent Orthodox: Sabato Morais. "A Vindication." *American Hebrew*, August 5, 1887, 196–97.

To Preserve Judaism Above All Else: Jacob H. Schiff. "One Institution for Rearing Rabbis?" *American Hebrew*, May 25, 1900, 37–38.

4. The Arrival of Eastern European Immigrants

Sabbath at the Polish Shul: William M. Rosenblatt. "A Sabbath among the Orthodox Jews." *Galaxy*, September 1872, 380–81.

The Chief Rabbi's Sermon: Reprinted from *The Education of Abraham Cahan*, trans. Leon Stein, Abraham P. Conan, and Lynn Davison, by permission of the University of Nebraska Press. Copyright 1969 by the Jewish Publication Society.

The Charleston Responsum: Naftali Zvi Yehudah Berlin. Responsa *Meshiv Davar*. Warsaw: Meir Yehiel Halter, 1894, 15.

Father and Mother: Anzia Yezierska. *Bread Givers: A Novel*, 8–11. Garden City: Doubleday, 1925.

"Daughter of the Ramaz": S. N. Behrman. "Daughter of the Ramaz." *New Yorker* (November 21, 1953): 45–46. "Daughter of the Ramaz," copyright © 1953 by S. N. Behrman. Originally appeared in the New Yorker magazine. Reprinted by permission of Brandt & Hochman Literary Agents, Inc. All rights reserved.

The Bylaws of the Agudath Ha-Rabbonim: *Sefer Ha-Yovel: Agudath Ha-Rabbonim ha- Orthodoxim de-Artzot ha-Brit ve-Canada*, 24–25. New York: 1928.

The Orthodox Convention: "The Orthodox Convention." *American Hebrew*, June 10, 1898, 172-73.

What Is Orthodoxy? Henry Pereira Mendes. "What Is Orthodoxy?" *American Hebrew*, June 17, 1898, 199–200.

Modern Orthodoxy in the Light of Orthodox Authorities: Gotthard Deutsch. *Modern Orthodoxy in the Light of Orthodox Authorities*, 6–13. Chicago: Bloch & Newman, 1898.

Pictures of Jewish Home Life: Esther J. Ruskay. Hearth and Home Essays, 80–84. Philadelphia: Jewish Publication Society of America, 1902.

Young Israel: "Young Israel." *Hebrew Standard*, January 10, 1913, 9.

Proposal for a Five-Day Work Week: Bernard Drachman. *The Jewish Sabbath Question: As Presented before a Christian Convention at Oakland, California*," 12–16. New York, 1915.

The Synagogue Council of America: Abraham Burstein. "The Synagogue Council of America." *Jewish Forum* 10 (February 1927): 52–53.

5. Trailblazers

An Orthodox High School: Solomon T. H. Hurwitz. "Orthodoxy in America." *American Jewish Chronicle* 1 (June 16, 1916): 178.

The Question of the Time: Eliezer Ladizinsky. "She'elah Bi-Zmanah." *Hedenu* 1 (June 25, 1926): 2. Republished with the permission of Yeshiva University.

Yeshiva College: Bernard Revel. "The Yeshivah College: A Statement of Aims." *Jewish Forum* 11 (May 1928): 253–55. Republished with the permission of Yeshiva University.

The Hebrew Theological College of Chicago: Hyman L. Meites. *History of the Jews of Chicago*, 551–52. Chicago: Chicago Jewish Historical Society, 1924.

Is Schechter Orthodox? Emanuel Schreiber. "Is Schechter Orthodox?" *Reform Advocate*, September 13, 1902, 62–63.

The "General Religious Tendency" of the Seminary: *Inaugural Address of Solomon Schechter as President of the Faculty of the Jewish Theological Seminary of America*, 19–23. New York, 1902.

A Dangerous Situation: "A Dangerous Situation." American Hebrew, June 17, 1904, 130.

The Orthodox Rabbis and the Seminary: Judah David Eisenstein. "The Orthodox Rabbis and the Seminary." *American Hebrew*, July 1, 1904, 180.

A Reaffirmation of Traditional Judaism: Max Drob. "A Reaffirmation of Traditional Judaism." *Proceedings of the Rabbinical Assembly of the Jewish Theological Seminary of America* 3 (1929): 44–46. Reprinted by permission of the Rabbinical Assembly, publisher.

6. The Parting of the Ways

A Definition of Modern Orthodox: Henry Pereira Mendes to Cyrus Adler, February 14, 1913, MS-39, box 1, folder 3, American Jewish Archives. Published with permission and courtesy of the Jacob Rader Marcus Center of the American Jewish Archives, Cincinnati. americanjewisharchives.org.

The "Modern Orthodox" Rabbi: Solomon Zucrow. *Adjustment of Law to Life in Rabbinic Literature*, 183–85. Boston: Stratford, 1928. Republished with the permission of Congregation Mishkan Tefila.

What Is Orthodox Judaism? Leo Jung. "What Is Orthodox Judaism?" In *The Jewish Library*, ed. Leo Jung, 2:113–17. New York: Bloch, 1930.

The Rabbinical Council of America: Louis Bernstein. "The Emergence of the English-Speaking Orthodox Rabbinate," 559. PhD diss., Yeshiva University, 1977. Republished with the permission of the Rabbinical Council of America.

Orthodox–Traditional–Torah-True Judaism: Adapted and reprinted with permission from Orthodox Judaism: Joseph H. Lookstein. "Orthodox Judaism." In *Fireside Discussion Group of the Anti-Defamation League, B'nai B'rith*. Chicago: Anti-Defamation League, 1940. www.adl.org. All rights reserved. Material from the essay is excerpted from the original and any footnotes accompanying the excerpts are my own, not ADL's.

"A Modern Orthodox Congregation": Joseph Rudnick. "The President's Appeal." *Kehillath Israel Chronicle* 1 (February/March 1925): 1–2. Republished with the permission of Congregation Kehillath Israel.

May Men and Women Sit Together in Shul? Joseph B. Soloveitchik. "On Seating and Sanctification." In *Sanctity of the Synagogue*, edited by Baruch Litvin. New York: The Spero Foundation, 1959, 115–18. Originally published as Yosef Dov Soloveitchik. "May Men and Women Sit Together in Synagogue." *Der Tog*, November 22, 1954, 5. Republished with the permission of Jeanne Litvin.

A "Family Seated" Orthodox Synagogue: Yeshiva University Archives, New York, Rabbinic Placement Records, box 17, folder: "Cong. Chevra Thilim," Julius Katz to Morris H. Finer, October 27, 1956. Courtesy of Yeshiva University Archives.

A New Religious Group in American Judaism? S. Felix Mendelsohn. "The Question Box." *The Sentinel*, February 11, 1943, 9.

The Excommunication of Mordecai Kaplan: "Asefat Ha-Herem." *Ha-Pardes* 19 (July 1945): 2–3.

The Conservative Beth Din: Fabian Schoenfeld. "Sincerity behind the Conservative Beth-Din." *Young Israel Viewpoint* (January/February 1954): 26–27. Republished with the permission of the National Council of Young Israel.

The Synagogue Council Ban: Louis Bernstein. "The Emergence of the English-Speaking Orthodox Rabbinate," 556. PhD diss., Yeshiva University, 1977.

A Conservative Converts to Orthodox Judaism: C. E. Hillel Kauvar to Aaron Blumenthal, March 21, 1958, X-135, American Jewish Archives, Cincinnati. Published with permission and courtesy of the Jacob Rader Marcus Center of the American Jewish Archives, Cincinnati. americanjewisharchives.org.

A Convert within Your Gates: Samson R. Weiss to C. E. Hillel Kauvar, April 3, 1958, X-135, American Jewish Archives, Cincinnati. Published with permission and courtesy of the Jacob Rader Marcus Center of the American Jewish Archives, Cincinnati. americanjewisharchives.org.

7. Becoming Modern Orthodox Jews

The Search for a Modern Orthodox "Ideologist": Charles S. Liebman. "Orthodoxy in American Jewish Life." *American Jewish Year Book* 66 (1965): 48–49. Republished with the permission of the American Jewish Committee.

Making Orthodoxy Relevant in America: Harold Goldberg. "Dr. Greenberg Discusses Orthodoxy YU, Viet Nam & Sex." *Commentator*, April 28, 1966, 6, 8. Republished with the permission of the *Commentator*.

Dear Yitzchak: "Rav Lichtenstein Writes Letter to Dr. Greenberg." *Commentator*, June 2, 1966, 7–8. Republished with the permission of the *Commentator*.

The Radicals: Walter Wurzburger. "The 'Radicals.'" *Jewish Chronicle*, April 14, 1967, 6. Republished with the permission of the *Jewish Chronicle*.

The *College Bowl* Sensation: Yeshiva University Archives, New York, Public Relations Collection, box 1963–1977, G.E. College Bowl Folder, Student Government Organization of Yeshiva of Flatbush H.S. to Yeshiva University College Bowl Team, May 13, 1963. Courtesy of Yeshiva University Archives.

Watching with Great Enthusiasm and Excitement: Yeshiva University Archives, New York, Public Relations Collection, box 1963–1977, G.E. College Bowl Folder, Grade 5 Students of Hillel Day School to Debating Team, May 22, 1963. Courtesy of Yeshiva University Archives.

Modern Orthodoxy Is Not a Movement: Emanuel Rackman. "A Challenge to Orthodoxy." *Judaism* 18 (Spring 1969): 46. Republished with permission of the American Jewish Congress.

A Modern Orthodox Movement: Norman Lamm. "Modern Orthodoxy's Identity Crisis." *Jewish Life* 36 (May/June 1969): 5–8. Reprinted with permission from *Jewish Life* and the Orthodox Union.

8. Orthodox, Inc.

Maimonides School: Shulamith Meiselman. "For Jewish Education." *Jewish Advocate*, May 30, 1941, 4. Republished with permission of *The Jewish Advocate*.

A Rabbinical Supervisory Council for Day Schools: Doniel Z. Kramer. "The History and Impact of Torah Umesorah and Hebrew Day Schools in America," 339, 342. PhD diss., Yeshiva University, 1976. Republished with the permission of Torah Umesorah.

Orthodox Student Pride: Gwendolyn R. Buttnick. "The Hebrew Day School: Seattle." *Yavneh Review* 6 (1967): 117–18.

Camp Moshava: Lillian X. Frost. "A True Story from Life." *Chicago Sentinel*, November 8, 1945, 26.

National Conference of Synagogue Youth: Yeshiva University Archives, New York, YU Rabbinic Placement Records, box 14, folder: "Georgia, Savannah— Cong. B'nai B'rith Jacob," Abraham I. Rosenberg to Samuel Belkin, December 18, 1956. Courtesy of Yeshiva University Archives.

Drisha Institute for Jewish Education: Soshea Leibler. "Teaching Talmud to Women: Blasphemous or Blessed?" *Baltimore Jewish Times*, May 30, 1980, 10. Republished with permission of the *Baltimore Jewish Times*.

Synthesis: Samuel Belkin. "Synthesis." *Gesher* 1 (June 1963): 3. Republished with the permission of Yeshiva University.

A New Beginning: Yeshiva University Archives, New York, Stern College for Women Records, box 1, folder 6, "Look into Learning: Stern College Beit Midrash Program." Courtesy of Yeshiva University Archives.

The "OU" Symbol: Herbert S. Goldstein. "Kashruth and Union Supervision." *Orthodox Union* 1 (August 1933): 4. Reprinted with the permission of the Orthodox Union.

How Kosher Is OU? Saul C. Framowitz. "How Kosher Is OU? Rabbi Rosenberg Answers Many Loaded Questions." *Viewpoint* (March/April 1958): 7–10. Republished with the permission of the National Council of Young Israel.

The Self-Appointed Spokesman: "The Self-Appointed Spokesman." *Viewpoint* (October 26, 1964) 4. Republished with the permission of the National Council of Young Israel.

Confrontation: Joseph B. Soloveitchik. "Confrontation." *Tradition* 62 (Spring/ Summer 1964): 21–25. Republished with permission of *Tradition* and Haym Soloveitchik.

The New Encounter: Irving Greenberg. "The New Encounter of Judaism and Christianity." *Barat Review* 3 (June 1967): 123–25. Republished with permission of DePaul University.

9. The Orthodox Synagogue and Rabbinate

The Friday Night Bat Mitzvah: Oscar Z. Fasman. "This Friday Night Forum." *Orthodox Union* 11 (February 1944): 4–6. Reprinted with the permission of the Orthodox Union.

Fancy Parties and Busy Fathers: Joseph Speiser. "Fancy Parties and Busy Fathers." In *The Rabbinical Council Manuel of Holiday and Sabbath Sermons*, edited by Emanuel Feldman. New York: Rabbinical Council Press, 1961, 360–61. Republished with the permission of the Rabbinical Council of America.

Law Is Law: William N. Ciner. "Law Is Law." *Kneseth Israel Bulletin*, November 1952. Republished with the permission of Alan Ciner.

The Reacculturation of the "Yeshiva Student": Ralph Pelcovitz. "The Yeshivah Alumnus and the Synagogue." *Jewish Life* 28 (October 1960): 36–37. Reprinted with permission from *Jewish Life* and the Orthodox Union.

The Social Politics of Shul: Samuel C. Heilman. *Synagogue Life: A Study in Symbolic Interaction*, 137–38. Chicago: University of Chicago Press, 1976. Republished with the permission of the University of Chicago Press.

My Return to the Rabbinate: "My Return to the Rabbinate." *Ideas: A Handbook for Synagogue Leaders* 10 (March 1968): 69–73. Republished with the permission of Yeshiva University.

A Hero for the "Religiously Apathetic": Steven Riskin. "Reaching Out to the Non-Committed." *Jewish Life* 39 (October 1972): 8–12. Reprinted with permission from *Jewish Life* and the Orthodox Union.

Needed: Pastoral Training: Sherman P. Kirshner. "Needed: Clinical Pastoral Training." *Jewish Spectator* 53 (Fall 1988): 63. Republished with the permission of Robert Bleiweiss.

10. The State of Orthodox Belief

The Core of Judaism: Herman Wouk. *This Is My God*, 51–53. Garden City: Doubleday, 1959. Copyright © 1959 by the Abe Wouk Foundation, Inc. Copyright renews 1987 by Herman Wouk. Republished with permission.

Minimal Set of Principles: Leonard B. Gewirtz. *The Authentic Jew and His Judaism*, 24–28. New York: Bloch, 1961. Republished with the permission of Gladys Gewirtz.

The State of Orthodox Belief—An Open View: "The State of Jewish Belief: A Symposium." *Commentary* 42 (August 1966): 89–91. Republished with the permission of *Commentary*.

The State of Orthodox Belief—A Less-Open View: "The State of Jewish Belief: A Symposium." *Commentary* 42 (August 1966): 105–6. Republished with the permission of *Commentary*.

Halakhic Man and the Mathematician: Reprinted from *Halakhic Man* by Joseph B. Soloveitchik, translated by Lawrence Kaplan, by permission of the University of Nebraska Press. Copyright 1983 by the Jewish Publication Society, Philadelphia.

Authentic Halakhah and the "Teleological Jurist": Emanuel Rackman. "Can We Moderns Keep the Sabbath?" *Commentary* 18 (September 1954): 215–16. Republished with the permission of *Commentary*.

The Letter and the Spirit of the Law: Immanuel Jakobovits. "Review of Recent Halakhic Periodical Literature." *Tradition* 4 (Spring 1962): 257–60. Republished with the permission of *Tradition*.

New York's Most Powerful Rabbi? Ronald I. Rubin. "The Most Powerful Rabbis in New York." *New York Magazine* 12 (January 22, 1979) 41. Republished with the permission of Ronald I. Rubin.

11. Responding to Tragedies and Triumphs

Never Again! Meir Kahane. *Never Again! A Program for Survival.* Los Angeles: Nash, 1971, 283–87. Republished with the permission of Libby Kahane.

The Voluntary Covenant: Irving Greenberg. "Voluntary Covenant." *Perspectives* (October 1982): 16–18. © 1982 CLAL–The National Jewish Center for Learning and Leadership. Republished with the permission of CLAL–The National Jewish Center for Learning and Leadership.

The Religious Zionist's Responsibilities in "Galut" to "Eretz Israel": Bessie Gotsfeld. President's Address, 1941 National Convention of the Mizrachi Women's Organization, AMIT Archives, New York. Published with the permission of AMIT.

A Few Words of Confession: Joseph B. Soloveitchik. *Five Addresses*, 191–93. Jerusalem: Tal Orot Institute, 1983. Some of the English rendering has been slightly modified based on a review of the original Yiddish publication. Republished by permission of Atarah Twersky and Tovah Lichtenstein.

An Expression of the "Jewish Soul": *Veheveti: The Prayer Service for Yom Ha-Atzmaut and Yom Yerushalayim*, edited by Joel B. Wolowelsky, 5–6. New York: Yavneh, 1970.

The Six-Day War: Eliezer Berkovits. *Faith after the Holocaust*, 144–46, 153–54. New York: Ktav, 1973. Republished with the permission of Shalem College.

The Rosenberg Case: "The Rosenberg Case." *Viewpoint* (September/October 1953): 48. Republished with the permission of the National Council of Young Israel.

The Student Struggle for Soviet Jewry: YU Archives, New York, SSSJ Papers, box 1, folder 1, "SSSJ Founding Meeting," April 27, 1964. Courtesy of Yeshiva University Archives.

Rabbi Ahron Soloveichik's Opposition to the Vietnam War: "Rav Aaron Decries Civilian Toll in Vietnam; Questions Recent Stand of Jewish Leaders." *Hamevaser*, September 30, 1968, 1. Republished with the permission of Yeshiva University.

A Prayer for Soviet Jews: *Yizkor—Remember: A Service of Prayer, Congregation Kehilath Jeshurun*, 14–15. New York: Congregation Kehillath Jeshurun, 1981. Republished with the permission of Congregation Kehillath Jeshurun.

12. The Orthodox Family

Five Reasons Why Every Jewish Woman Should Adhere to Family Purity: "Five Reasons Why Every Jewish Woman Should Adhere to Taharath Hamishpachah or Family Purity through the Observance of Laws and Ritual of Mikveh." *Orthodox Union* (December 1941): 13. Reprinted with the permission of the Orthodox Union.

Hedge of Roses: Norman Lamm. *Hedge of Roses: Jewish Insights into Marriage and Married Life*, 51–58. New York: Philipp Feldheim, 1966. Republished with the permission of Feldheim Publishers.

Commandment Number One: Birth Control: Herbert S. Goldstein. *Between the Lines of the Bible: A Modern Commentary on the 613 Commandments*, 1–2. New York: Crown, 1959. Republished with the permission of Naomi G. Cohen.

Tay-Sachs Disease: Allan Kaplan. "Rabbi Bleich Stands Firm; Advises Tay-Sachs Testing." *Commentator*, April 11, 1973, 6. Republished with the permission of the *Commentator*.

An Official Policy for Genetic Screening: "Tay-Sachs I." *Commentator* (April 11, 1973): 6. Republished with the permission of the *Commentator*.

The Pros and Cons of "Mass Hysteria": Moshe D. Tendler. *Pardes Rimonim: A Manual for the Jewish Family*, 88. New York: Judaica Press, 1977. Republished with the permission of Moshe D. Tendler.

Creativity in "Family Law": "Presentation by Rabbi Emanuel Rackman." In *Halakha in Modern Jewish Life*, edited by Nahum Goldmann. New York: Memorial Foundation for Jewish Culture, 1974, 16–17. Republished with the permission of the Memorial Foundation for Jewish Culture.

In the Matter of Prenuptial Agreements: "Resolutions of the Rabbinical Council of America." In *The Prenuptial Agreement: Halakhic and Pastoral Considerations*, edited by Kenneth Auman and Basil Herring. Northvale: Jason Aronson Inc., 1996, 21–22. Republished with the permission of the Rabbinical Council of America.

Why Orthodox Rabbis Should Insist on a Prenuptial Agreement: Saul J. Berman. "Why Orthodox Rabbis Should Insist on a Prenuptial Agreement." *Rabbinics Today* 2 (December 1993): 1–2. Republished with the permission of Basil Herring and the Rabbinical Council of America.

13. From Rebbetzin to Rabbah

The Rabbi's Wife: Sara Hyamson. "The Rabbi's Wife." *Jewish Forum* 8 (December 1925): 383–85.

"My Occult Powers": Channa Gerstein. "Reflections of a Rebbitzen." *Jewish Life* (December 1947): 17–20. Reprinted with permission from *Jewish Life* and the Orthodox Union.

The Role of the Rabbi's Wife: Theodore L. Adams. "The Role of the Rabbi's Wife." *Chavrusa* 3 (March 1959): 5–6, 8. Republished with the permission of Yeshiva University.

A Rebbitzen Respectfully Dissents: Helen Felman. "A Rebitzen Respectfully Dissents." *Chavrusa* 4 (November 1959): 5. Republished with the permission of Yeshiva University.

Is Now the Time for Orthodox Women Rabbis?: Blu Greenberg. "Is Now the Time for Orthodox Women Rabbis?" *Moment Magazine* 18 (December 1993):

51–52. Republished with the permission of *Moment Magazine*, momentmag.com.

The Female "Congregational Educator": Richard Kestenbaum to All Officers and Honorary Presidents of Lincoln Square Synagogue, December 8, 1997. Published with the permission of Richard Kestenbaum.

New Roles for Rebbetzins: Abby Lerner. "New Roles of Rebbetzins: Teacher, Halachic Liaison, Counselor, & Friend." *Rebbetzin's Letter* (Summer 1998): 3. Republished with the permission of the National Council of Young Israel.

Yes, We Are Orthodox, and Yes, We Hired a Female Member of Our Clergy! Adam Scheier. "Yes, We Are Orthodox, and Yes, We Hired a Female Member of Our Clergy!" Sermon delivered on May 16, 2013, Congregation Shaar Hashomayim, Montreal, Canada. Published with permission of Adam Scheier.

14. Sliding to the Right and to the Left

An American Zionist Lives a "Schizoid Life": 4 *Orthodox Couples Tell Their Stories about Living in Israel*, edited by David Landesman, 29–33. New York: Union of Orthodox Jewish Congregations of America, 1976. Reprinted with the permission of the Orthodox Union.

A Modern Orthodox Utopia Turned to Ashes: David Singer. "A Symposium: The State of Orthodoxy." *Tradition* 20 (Spring 1982): 69–72. Republished with the permission of *Tradition*.

"Centrist Orthodoxy": Stewart Ain. "Rabbinical Council President Decries Holier-than-Thou Attitude of Right Wing." *Long Island Jewish World*, March 1, 1984, 14. Republished with the permission of *Long Island Jewish World*.

Gifter Slaughters Lamm for Passover: Mordechai Gifter. "Gifter Slaughters Lamm for Passover." Lecture delivered at the Young Israel of Cleveland, April 5, 1988. Published with the permission of Binyomin G. Gifter and Zalman S. Gifter.

Baruch Lanner Will Be Your Rabbi: Elie Hiller to Members of the Jewish Community of Teaneck, July 24, 1989. Published with the permission of Elie Hiller.

"Frum from Birth": Sara Bershtel and Allen Graubard. *Saving Remnants: Feeling Jewish in America*, 170–71. Berkeley: University of California Press, 1993. Republished with the permission of Sara Bershtel.

An "Unorthodox" Ad? Haskel Lookstein. "An Orthodox Response to an Unorthodox Ad." *Jewish Week*, October 19, 1984, 28. Republished with the permission of *Jewish Week*.

The Misleading Salesmen of Torah u-Madda: Paul Eidelberg. "Torah vs. the Humanities, Etc." *Jewish Press*, October 7, 1988, 10. Republished with the permission of *Jewish Press*.

Trashing Torah u-Madda: Behnam Dayanim and Dov Pinchot. "Trashing Torah U'Mada." *Commentator* (October 25, 1988): 2. Republished with the permission of the *Commentator*.

The Israel Experience: Esther Krauss. "The Israel Experience: A Closer Look from America." *Ten Da'at* 5 (Fall 1990): 32. Republished with the permission of Yeshiva University and the World Zionist Organization.

"I Never Saw the Rav Read a Secular Book": Abba Bronspigel. "Memories of the Rav." Lecture delivered on April 28, 1993, Yeshiva University, New York. Published with the permission of Elisheva Bronspigel.

Modern Orthodoxy Goes to Grossinger's: Shlomo Riskin. "Where Modern Orthodoxy Is At—and Where It Is Going." *Jewish Life* (Spring 1976): 28–29. Reprinted with permission from *Jewish Life* and the Orthodox Union.

The RIETS Responsum on Women's Prayer Groups: "Teshuvah bi-Inyan Nashim bi-Hakafot." *Ha-Darom* 54 (Sivan 1985): 51–53. Republished with the permission of the Rabbinical Council of America.

The Affairs of the Rabbinical Council: Louis Bernstein to Miriam Schachter and Associates, February 26, 1985. In *Duties of the Heart Conference Program*. New York: Women's Tefillah Network, 1985. Republished by permission of Freda Rosenfeld.

Piety Not Rebellion: Rivka Haut. "From Women: Piety Not Rebellion." *Sh'ma* 15 (May 17, 1985): 110–11. Reprinted with permission from *Sh'ma* (www.shma .com).

"Very Little Halachic Judaism": Eliezer Berkovits. "Women's Prayer Groups." *Jerusalem Post*, September 20, 1985, 18. Republished with the permission of *Jerusalem Post*.

"Modern Orthodox" and "Traditional Conservative": Is an Alliance Possible?: Avi Weiss, "Is an Alliance between the Modern or Centrist Orthodox and the Conservative Traditional Movement Possible?" June 11, 1989. Paper delivered at the convention of the Union for Traditional Conservative Judaism, Union for Traditional Judaism Archives, New York. Republished with the permission of Avi Weiss.

Jewish Women Hear Muffled Voices: Laura Shaw. "Jewish Women Hear Muffled Voices." *Columbia Daily Spectator*, November 26, 1990, 3, 6. Republished with the permission of *Columbia Daily Spectator*.

Take Rav Soloveitchik at Full Depth: Aharon Lichtenstein. "Take Rav Soloveitchik at Full Depth." *Forward*, March 22, 1999, 6. Republished with permission of Tovah Lichtenstein.

15. Reconsidering Modern Orthodox Judaism in a New Century

Modern Orthodox Gedolim: Excerpted from Dena Freundlich. "Response to Frumteens Moderator." Ma'ayanot Yeshiva High School for Girls, November 2004. Published with the permission of Dena Freundlich.

Stalemate at Stern College: "Letters to the Editors." *Observer*, March 2006, 3. Republished with the permission of the *Observer*.

Modern Orthodoxy's Demise: Gary Bauman. "Modern Orthodoxy's Demise." *Baltimore Jewish Times*, May 20, 2011, 17. Republished with the permission of *Baltimore Jewish Times*.

Social Orthodoxy: Jay P. Lefkowitz. "The Rise of Social Orthodoxy: A Personal Account." *Commentary* 137 (April 2014): 42. Republished with the permission of *Commentary*.

The Freundel Affair: "Statement by the Kesher Israel Board of Directors." November 30, 2014. Published with the permission of Kesher Israel Congregation.

Open Orthodox Judaism: Dov Linzer and Avi Weiss. "Creating an Open Orthodox Rabbinate." *Sh'ma* 33 (February 2003): 10. Reprinted with permission from *Sh'ma* (www.shma.com).

The Close of Edah: Saul J. Berman. "The Emergence, Role, and Close of Edah." *Jewish Press*, July 14, 2006, 1. Republished with the permission of *Jewish Press*.

Shirah Hadashah: Tova Hartman. *Feminism Encounters Traditional Judaism: Resistance and Accommodation*, 99–100.Waltham: Brandeis University Press, 2007. © University Press of New England, Lebanon NH. Reprinted with permission.

A Statement of Principles: Nathaniel Helfgot. "Statement of Principles." July 2010. Published with the permission of Nathaniel Helfgot.

Taking Back Modern Orthodox Judaism: Asher Lopatin. "How to Rejuvenate Modern Orthodoxy." *Mosaic* (August 19, 2014). Republished with the permission of *Mosaic*.

Notes

Foreword

1. Jacob Rader Marcus, *American Jewry: Documents, Eighteenth Century* (Cincinnati: Hebrew Union College Press, 1959), 52–53. I am frankly impressed with those Jews who did choose to come together for prayer, even if they did not dress in traditional religious garb. See also Jeffrey S. Gurock, *Orthodox Jews in America* (Bloomington: Indiana University Press, 2009), 34.
2. Sidney M. Fish, "The Problem of Intermarriage in Early America," *Gratz College Annual of Jewish Studies* 4 (1975): 89, 93.
3. Jonathan D. Sarna, *American Judaism: A History* (New Haven: Yale University Press, 2004), 66.
4. Marshall Sklare, *Conservative Judaism: An American Religious Movement* (Glencoe IL: Free Press, 1955), 43. This prediction also appears in the 1972 and 1985 reprints of Sklare's book.
5. See *Judaism's Encounter with Other Cultures: Rejection or Integration?* ed. Jacob J. Schacter (Northvale: Aronson, 1997).
6. *Yehuda Amichai: A Life of Poetry, 1948–1994,* trans. Benjamin and Barbara Harshav (New York: HarperCollins, 1994), 333.

Preface

1. "Prag," *Allgemeine Zeitung des Judentums,* June 8, 1869, 453–55.
2. "Berliner Zustände," *Der Israelit,* June 9, 1869, 441–42.
3. "Modern Orthodoxy in Germany," *Jewish Times,* July 9, 1869, 5. A leading reformer in Cincinnati jested in a similar vein at this time. See "Elements of the Jewish Faith," *Israelite,* August 7, 1857, 36, and "The Fundamental Error of Modern Orthodoxy," *Israelite,* April 30, 1869, 4.
4. "Reform's Sacrifice," *American Hebrew,* February 19, 1886, 18.
5. "The Aim of the Order," *Jewish Messenger,* January 3, 1868, 5.
6. "Reformation in Israel," *Rochester Democrat and Chronicle,* November 19, 1885, 6. See also Stuart E. Rosenberg, *The Jewish Community in Rochester, 1843–1925* (New York: Columbia University Press, 1954), 98.
7. See Jeffrey S. Gurock, "From Fluidity to Rigidity: The Religious Worlds of Conservative and Orthodox Jews in Twentieth-Century America," in *Ameri-*

can Jewish Identity Politics, ed. Deborah Dash Moore (Ann Arbor: University of Michigan Press, 2008), 159–206.

8. Luis Lugo et al., *A Portrait of Jewish Americans: Findings from a Pew Research Center Survey of U.S. Jews* (Washington DC: Pew Research Center, 2013), 48.

9. See Katherine Light, "Inside Out, Outside In: Yeshivat Chovevei Torah's Open Orthodoxy Transmitted, Absorbed, and Applied" (MA thesis, Brandeis University, 2008).

10. On a recent development, see Asher Lopatin, "How to Rejuvenate Modern Orthodoxy," *Mosaic*, August 2014.

11. Charles S. Liebman, "Orthodoxy in American Jewish Life," *American Jewish Year Book* 66 (1965): 44.

12. Emanuel Rackman to Joseph Karasick, April 13, 1966. A copy of this letter is in the author's possession.

13. There is a difference between "ideological" Modern Orthodoxy and "behavioral" Modern Orthodox Jews who willingly do not observe essential areas of Jewish law. On this, see Lawrence Kaplan, "The Ambiguous Modern Orthodox Jew," *Judaism* 28 (Fall 1979): 439–48.

14. See Norman Lamm, "Modern Orthodoxy's Identity Crisis," *Jewish Life*, (May/June 1969): 5–8.

15. See Irving Greenberg, "A Letter to the Editor," *Jewish Observer* 3 (December 1966): 16.

16. Emanuel Rackman, "A Challenge to Orthodoxy," *Judaism* 18 (Spring 1969): 146.

17. Solomon Roodman, *The Suburbs of the Almighty: Sermons and Discourses* (New York: Jonathan David, 1962), 202.

18. See Zev Eleff, "The Decline of the Rabbinic Sermon," *Jewish Action* 74 (Fall 2013): 44–46.

19. Norman Lamm, "Furthermore," April 6, 1972, Lamm Archives, Yeshiva University, New York.

20. See Zev Eleff, "'Viva Yeshiva!' The Tale of the Mighty Mites and the *College Bowl*," *American Jewish History* 96 (December 2010): 287–305.

21. On the early reception of Hirsch and Hildesheimer's teachings in the United States, see Zev Eleff, "American Orthodoxy's Lukewarm Embrace of the Hirschian Legacy, 1850–1939," *Tradition* 45 (Fall 2012): 35–53, and Gil Graff, "Toward an Appreciation of the American Legacy of Rabbi Esriel Hildesheimer: The U.S. Rabbinate of Three Hildesheimer Students," *Modern Judaism* 31 (May 2011): 166–87.

22. See, for example, Samson Raphael Hirsch, *Der Pentateuch* (Frankfurt am Main: J. Kauffmann, 1899), 5:250.

23. See David Ellenson, *Rabbi Esriel Hildesheimer and the Creation of a Modern Jewish Orthodoxy* (Tuscaloosa: University of Alabama Press, 1990), 85, 142.

24. See Zev Eleff, "Between Bennett and Amsterdam Avenues: The Complex American Legacy of Samson Raphael Hirsch," *Tradition* 46 (Winter 2013): 8–27.

25. Gideon Aran, "Jewish Zionist Fundamentalism: The Bloc of the Faithful in Israel (Gush Emunim)," in *Fundamentalisms Observed*, ed. Martin Marty and Scott Appleby, 296 (Chicago: University of Chicago Press, 1991).

26. See Yoel Finkelman, "On the Irrelevance of Religious-Zionism," *Tradition* 39 (Spring 2005): 21–44.

27. On this, see Yehudah Mirsky, *Rav Kook: Mystic in a Time of Revolution* (New Haven: Yale University Press, 2014), 218–39.

28. See Charles S. Liebman, "Orthodox Judaism Today," *Midstream* 25 (August/September 1979): 24.

29. There is no reliable data on the number of Modern Orthodox synagogues. For a tabulation of schools, see Marvin Schick, *A Census of Jewish Day Schools in the United States, 2008–2009* (New York: Avi Chai Foundation, 2009), 6.

30. On the term "symbolic exemplar," see Jack Bloom, "The Rabbi's Family," *Central Conference of American Rabbis* 86 (1976): 105–14.

31. See Jeff Ifrah, "The Rav in Perspective," *Commentator*, November 8, 1988, 7.

32. "Rav's Teachings Enhance Upper School Curriculum," *Kol Rambam*, Spring 2014, 3. Along with his wife, Tonya Soloveitchik, the Rav founded Maimonides School in 1937, then in the Roxbury area.

33. Lawrence Grossman, "Modern Orthodoxy's Human Pillar," *Forward*, September 2, 2011, 9.

34. See Julie Weiner, "What Kind of Kipa Do You Wear?" *Jewish Week*, April 9, 2004, 14.

35. See, for example, Gary Rosenblatt, "Tolerance, Tradition Collide in Same-Sex Union Row," *Jewish Week*, October 15, 2010, 1, 7.

36. See Hannah Dreyfus, "Birth Control, Jewish Law Collide at Stern," *Jewish Week*, February 20, 2015, 1, 18, and Sarah Silver Bunim, "Religious and Secular Factors of Role Strain in Orthodox Jewish Mothers" (PhD diss., Yeshiva University, 1986), 88–93.

37. See Michael A. Meyer, "Where Does the Modern Period of Jewish History Begin?" *Judaism* 24 (Summer 1975): 329–38.

38. Gary Phillip Zola, *Isaac Harby of Charleston, 1788–1828: Jewish Reformer and Intellectual* (Tuscaloosa: University of Alabama Press, 1994), 112–49.

39. *The Sabbath Service and Miscellaneous Prayers: Adopted by the Reformed Society of Israelites* (Charleston: J. S. Burges, 1830), 6–7. See also Gary Phillip Zola, "Isaac Harby of Charleston: The Life and Works of an Enlightened Jew during the Early National Period" (PhD diss., Hebrew Union College, 1991), 565–68.

40. On the question of Reform Judaism and earlier precedents in Europe, see Michael A. Meyer, *Response to Modernity: A History of the Reform Movement in Judaism* (Oxford: Oxford University Press, 1988), 3–9.

41. See Jacob Katz, "Orthodoxy in Historical Perspective," *Studies in Contemporary Jewry* 2 (1986): 3–17.

42. See J. D. Eisenstein, "The History of the First Russian-American Jewish Congregation: The Beth Hamedrosh Hagadol," *Publications of the American Jewish Historical Society* 9 (1901): 63–74.

43. Ordained "rabbis" did not appear in the United States until the 1840s. Before then, congregations described their religious functionaries as "ministers" or "reverends," much like their Protestant counterparts. In fact, these titles were still very much in use well into the latter half of the nineteenth century to describe untrained congregational hirelings as well as learned rabbis.

44. See J.N., "Orthodoxy is My Doxy, Heterodoxy Is Another Man's Doxy," *Jewish Messenger*, March 4, 1859, 66.

45. See Jonathan D. Sarna, *American Judaism: A History* (New Haven: Yale University Press, 2004), 375.

46. See Tobias Brinkmann, "'German Jews'? Reassessing the History of Nineteenth-Century Jewish Immigrants in the United States," in *Transnational Traditions: New Perspectives on American Jewish History*, ed. Ava F. Kahn and Adam D. Mendelsohn (Detroit: Wayne State University Press, 2015), 144–64.

47. See Richard L. Bushman, *The Refinement of America: Persons, Houses, Cities* (New York: Knopf, 1992), 313–52.

48. Simon Kuznets, "Immigration of Russian Jews to the United States," *Perspectives in American History* 9 (1975): 35–124.

49. See Jacob Rader Marcus, *To Count a People: American Jewish Population Data, 1585–1984* (Lanham: University Press of America, 1990), 241.

50. See Arthur Hertzberg, "'Treifene Medina': Learned Opposition to Emigration to the United States," *Proceedings of the Eighth World Congress of Jewish Studies* (1984): 1–30, and Israel Bartal, "Heavenly America: The United States

as an Ideal Model for Nineteenth-Century East European Jews," in *Following Columbus: America, 1492–1992*, ed. Miriam Eliav-Felton (Jerusalem: Zalman Shazar, 1996), 511–22.

51. See Jeffrey S. Gurock, "Resisters and Accommodators: Varieties of Orthodox Rabbis in America, 1886–1983," *American Jewish Archives Journal* 35 (November 1983): 100–187.

52. See, for example, H. Pereira Mendes, "What Is Orthodoxy?" *American Hebrew*, June 17, 1898, 199, and "Modern Orthodoxy," *American Hebrew*, April 7, 1916, 630.

53. See Christine Stansell, *American Moderns: Bohemian New York and the Creation of a New Century* (New York: Metropolitan Books, 2000).

54. "Prominent Rabbi," *American Hebrew*, November 5, 1920, 758.

55. See Shulamith Berger, "Insights from the Archives," *Hamevaser*, October 1990, 12.

56. See Eugene Kohn, *The Future of Judaism in America* (New Rochelle: Liberal Press, 1934), 98.

57. S. Felix Mendelsohn, "The Question Box," *The Sentinel*, February 11, 1943, 9.

58. David Luchins, "In Reply," *Commentator*, December 22, 1966, 6.

59. See Lucy Dawidowicz to Milton Himmelfarb, November 4, 1958, box 21, folder 38, Marshall Sklare Papers, Robert D. Farber University Archives of Brandeis University, Waltham MA.

60. Shimon Schwab, *Selected Speeches: A Collection of Addresses and Essays on Hashkafah, Contemporary Issues, and Jewish History* (New York: CIS, 1991), 74.

1. Engaging Reform

1. "To the President and Members of the Adjunta of Kaal Kadosh Beth Elohim of Charleston, South-Carolina," *Israel's Advocate*, January 1826, 13. See *The Jews of the United States, 1790–1840: A Documentary History*, vol. 2, ed. Joseph L. Blau and Salo W. Baron (New York: Columbia University Press, 1964), 554–60.

2. *The Constitution of the Reformed Society of Israelites, for Promoting True Principles of Judaism According to Its Purity and Spirit* (Charleston: B. Levy, 1825), 4.

3. Isaac Harby, *A Discourse, Delivered in Charleston, (S.C.) on the 21st of Nov. 1825, before the Reformed Society of Israelites, for Promoting True Principles of Judaism According to Its Purity and Spirit, on Their First Anniversary* (Charleston: A. E. Miller, 1825), 6–8.

4. Harby, *A Discourse, Delivered in Charleston*, 4.

5. See Emily Simms Bingham, "Mordecai: Three Generations of a Southern Jewish Family, 1780–1865" (PhD diss., University of North Carolina, 1998), 299n57.

6. For one of the first uses of this phrase, see "Pioneering Reform Congregation to Celebrate Centennial of Movement in America," *American Israelite*, November 13, 1924, 4.

7. See Allan Tarshish, "The Charleston Organ Case," *American Jewish Historical Quarterly* 54 (June 1965): 411–49. See also Jacob Katz, *Divine Law in Human Hands: Case Studies in Halakhic Flexibility* (Jerusalem: Magnes Press, 1998), 265–80.

8. "A Retrospect and an Expectation," *Occident*, April 1845, 5. See also "Reforming and Deforming," *Occident*, May 1850, 61.

9. On early American intermarriage, see Malcolm H. Stern, "Jewish Marriage and Intermarriage in the Federal Period (1776–1840)," *American Jewish Archives Journal* 19 (November 1967): 142–43, and Jonathan D. Sarna, "Intermarriage in America: The Jewish Experience in Historical Context," in *Ambivalent Jew: Charles Liebman in Memoriam*, ed. Stuart Cohen and Bernard Susser (New York: Jewish Theological Seminary of America, 2007), 125–33.

10. Noah was likely referring to "Worship of the Jews," *Israel's Advocate*, May 1825, 71. The article was derived from the *Religious Intelligencer*, April 2, 1825, 697. The evangelical weekly described how "The greater part of the service is to be performed in English, many Rabbinical institutions and useless ceremonies are to be laid aside, and music is to be introduced, as in Christian Churches." However, the journal stopped short of Noah's "conversion" claims.

11. In fact, Harby publicly expressed his dismay for the Christian missionizing of Jews.

12. Noah's attack was directed specifically at Harby. The latter had emerged as a vocal critic of Noah's Ararat plan to establish a colony for Jews on Grand Island, near Buffalo, New York. Noah proposed this "asylum" as a measure to rescue Jews in Europe from oppression.

13. Of course, Noah was not the most staunchly Orthodox Jew, and at times he flouted the same sacred texts that Harby denounced. In 1845 he recommended that his coreligionists should "shut the Talmud and open the Bible." Two years later, he denounced a rabbi in Baltimore who presumably used talmudic sources to write a "tract upon dancing, which he repudiates as 'unholy,' and invented by the world to gratify its 'unholy dispositions.'" Noah

criticized the (no longer extant) pamphlet, insisting that "dancing in Scripture is not prohibited."

14. See Common Sense, "M. M. Noah, a Judge of Israel," *Charleston Mercury*, October 4, 1825, 2.

15. "Miscreated fronts" is a reference to Methodist John Wesley's essay "Thoughts upon Liberty" (1772), which dealt with the festering disharmony between Britain and the American colonists.

16. Harby's "this Happy land" developed into a rhetorical refrain used in polemics between Orthodox and Reform exponents. Particularly in Charleston, the phrase was repeated and alluded to by reformer Gustavus Poznanski as well as traditionalists Jacob Rosenfeld and Morris J. Raphall.

17. The original protest submitted to Beth Elohim included forty-seven signatures.

18. This is the opening sentence of the Shema prayer recited twice daily and on other religious occasions.

19. The "adjunta" was the executive committee of the synagogue, often involving the wealthiest members of the congregation. By this, Mordecai may refer to a letter he sent to the reformers shortly after the memorial was disseminated. See Myron Berman, *The Last of the Jews?* (Lanham MD: University Press of America, 1998), 50.

20. The writer probably had in mind the theologian Abraham Ruchat's multivolume history, *Die Religion in Geschichte und Gegenwart*.

21. In April 1843 Poznanski delivered a sermon that advocated for the deletion of the second festival day of the major Jewish holidays. Rather than fight with upset congregants, Poznanski resigned his salaried post. He retained his position on a volunteer basis thereby evading future reprimands from the congregation. Poznanski could afford this luxury because his wife, Esther Barrett (1820–70), was the only daughter of Isaac Barrett (1791–1834) and heir to his fortune. Other ministers at this time were at the mercy of their congregation's trustees.

22. Leeser refers to the Thirteen Principles of Faith formulated by Moses Maimonides (1138–1204). The Philadelphia minister implied that the Maimonidean creed had by the nineteenth century achieved a consensus among Jews. He did not mean that Maimonides's formulation was in fact divine.

23. See "Literary Notices," *Occident*, July 1843, 209.

24. Benjamin Gildersleeve (1791–1875) was a Presbyterian editor in the South. He edited the *Charleston Observer* and later the *Watchman and Observer* and the *Central Presbyterian* in Richmond VA.

25. In 1841, Poznanski delivered a sermon at the dedication of a new synagogue building. In that speech, the minister declared that "this synagogue is our *temple*, this city our *Jerusalem*, this happy land our *Palestine*, and our fathers defended with their lives *that* temple, *that* city, and *that* land, so will our sons defend *this* temple, *this* city, and *this* land." His bold words elicited reaction from traditional Jews and reverberated within Charleston's Jewish community many years afterward.

26. "The Israelites of Charleston—Once More," *Charleston Observer*, June 17, 1843, 95.

27. William Theophilus Brantly Sr. (1787–1845) was a Baptist scholar and minister who served churches in Georgia, Pennsylvania, and South Carolina. William Hazzard Barnwell (1806–63) was minister of St. Peter's Church in Charleston.

28. Earlier Poznanski directed a committee to furnish a "somewhat altered" form of the Maimonidean Principles of Faith. "Poznanski's version," as it was characterized by Charleston's Jews, was displayed in the synagogue on two large plaques with golden lettering, and deleted the arrival of the Messiah and belief in the resurrection of the dead as tenets of Jewish faith.

29. There exists no record that Poznanski responded to Leeser's open letter.

30. In December 1848 Isaac Mayer Wise of Albany's Congregation Beth El called for a conference of "ministers and other Israelites" to unite and improve American congregations. Leeser published Wise's notice and lent his support to the meetings.

31. Yehudah ha-Levi, *Sefer ha-Kuzari*, ed. A. Tzifroni (Tel Aviv: Mosad ha-Rav Kook), 3.

32. Rabbi Yosef Karo (1488–1575) published his *Shulhan Arukh* in 1565. In time, Karo's four-volume legal code has emerged as the leading digest of Jewish law.

33. In Europe, a number of Reform rabbis convened three conventions between 1844 and 1846. The meetings were held in Brunswick, Frankfurt, and Breslau. In those proceedings, delegates considered the "ways and means for the preservation of Judaism, and the awakening of the religious spirit." They debated changes to liturgy and the use of Hebrew in worship, marriage ceremonies, Sabbath laws, and the requirement of circumcision.

34. Rice refers here to the "ritual baths" in which Jewish women immerse themselves after their menstruation period.

35. Noah, of course, had no way of knowing Wise's true intent. Still, Wise developed a reputation for equivocation. See Henry Iliowizi, *Through Morocco to Minnesota: Sketches of Life in Three Continents* (Minneapolis, 1888), 90–91.

36. This is not true. In fact, the lay leaders of Beth Elohim offered Wise the vacant position. Wise initially accepted the call but turned it down out of fear of a yellow fever outbreak in the region.

37. In 1833, William Miller (1782–1849) announced his belief in the Second Coming of Jesus in the near future. With the assistance of a massive journalistic movement to spread the gospel of its founder, Millerism gained a rapid following. In 1844, despite Miller's prediction, the Second Advent did not occur, leaving most of the denomination's followers disillusioned and in search of other religious movements.

38. Joseph Smith (1805–44) was the founder of the Church of Jesus Christ of Latter-day Saints. In 1830, Smith published the Book of Mormon, the sacred text of the movement that claims to contain the writings of ancient North American Christian prophets. The charismatic Smith recruited tens of thousands of followers.

39. According to traditional (Geonic) practice, Jewish men may not trim their beards or cut their hair during the days preceding the fast of the Ninth of Av. According to a number of authorities, Jewish men are not permitted to shave during the intermediate days (Hol Ha-Mo'ed) of Jewish holidays.

40. In this paragraph, Allen alluded to three items that Jewish men adorn during worship. The "Mantle that Envelopes" refers to the *talit* (prayer shawl) with its *tzitzit* (fringes) attached to each corner of the shawl. Male worshipers also wrap *tefilin* (phylacteries) on their forehead and arms.

41. William Rayner, *Address Containing the History of the Har Sinai Congregation, of Baltimore City* (Baltimore: Guggenheimer, Weil, 1892), 4.

2. The Traditional Talmud

1. "Editorial Correspondence," *Occident*, November 1843, 395.

2. Moshe Halbertal, *People of the Book: Canon, Meaning, and Authority* (Cambridge: Harvard University Press, 1997), 54–72.

3. Moses Maimonides, *Mishneh im Perush Rabeinu Moshe ben Maimon*, vol. 1, ed. Yosef Kapah (Jerusalem: Mosad ha-Rav Kook, 1963), 11.

4. See Samson Raphael Hirsch, *Horeb: Versuche über Jissroéls Pflichten in der Zerstreuung, zunächst für Jissroéls denkende Jünglinge und Jungfrauen* (Frankfurt: J. Kauffmann, 1889), 19.

5. See Jonathan D. Sarna, "The Debate over Mixed Seating in the American Synagogue," in *The American Synagogue: A Sanctuary Transformed*, ed. Jack Wertheimer (New York: Cambridge University Press, 1989), 363–94.

6. Leo Merzbacher, *The Order of Prayer for Divine Services* (New York: J. Muhlhauser, 1855).

7. See David Einhorn, *Gebetbuch für Israelitische Reform-Gemeinden: im Verlag der Har Sinai-Gemeinde zu Baltimore* (New York: H. Frank, 1856).

8. See "Cincinnati," *Israelite*, October 2, 1857, 102.

9. Aaron Wolff (1795–1872) was one of the highest ranking officials on the Danish island of St. Thomas and, as Carillon made clear, was one of the most involved members of the local Jewish community.

10. Isaac Leeser, *Catechism for Younger Children, Designed as a Familiar Exposition of the Jewish Religion* (Philadelphia: Adam Waldie, 1839) was based on Eduard Kley's *Catechismus der Mosaischen Religion* (Berlin: Mauer, 1814).

11. In 1759 Denmark passed a royal decree that rendered confirmation compulsory for children between fourteen and nineteen years old.

12. In order to establish better decorum during services, a number of congregations eliminated the sale of honors during worship.

13. Founded in 1840, the West End Synagogue was the first Reform congregation in England. It was immediately opposed by Rabbi Solomon Hirschell and communal lay leader Moses Montefiore. In 1841 the Reform congregation issued a relatively moderate Reform prayer book that shortened some minor portions of the worship and translated the Aramaic Kaddish prayer into Hebrew.

14. David Woolf Marks (1811–1909) was an English Reform minister at West London Synagogue. He held that post from 1840 to 1895. He responded to the *Occident* in a series of letters. For the first, see "Letter from the Rev. Mr. Marks," *Occident*, April 1844, 53–56.

15. Hyman Hurwitz (1770–1844) was a professor of Hebrew at the University of London. In this reference, Carillion probably had in mind Hurwitz's *Hebrew Tales from the Writings of the Hebrew Sages* (London: Morrison and Watt, 1826), 36–38.

16. Abraham Ibn Ezra (1089–1164), David Kimhi (1160–1235), Rashi (1040–1105), and Moses Maimonides were all scholars and biblical commentators whose interpretations of Scripture at times departed from the explanations offered in the Talmud and other earlier Jewish texts.

17. Before this letter, Rice penned a more technical note that was published in the *Occident*. See "Letter of the Rev. A. Rice," *Occident*, February 1844, 559–60.

18. Rice referred to a second and shorter letter submitted by Goldsmith. See "Letter from Mr. H. Goldsmith," *Occident*, May 1844, 94–96.

19. Rice's translation is imperfect. The Talmud does not mention Purim.

20. The *Yad Ha-Hazakah* is another name for the *Mishneh Torah*, Maimonides's code of Jewish law.

21. On October 17, 1855, sixteen rabbis and ministers attended the so-called Cleveland Conference, convened by Isaac Mayer Wise, then of Cincinnati. Their agenda was to compose a set of religious principles that could unite American Jewish congregations. Afterward, both Orthodox and Reform observers rejected the decisions voted on at the Cleveland meetings.

22. The actual text of the second proposed plank read: "That the Talmud is acknowledged by all as the legal and obligatory commentary of the Bible."

23. A number of traditional rabbis initially committed to attending the Cleveland convention but ultimately did not, probably due to anti-Orthodox sentiments printed in Wise's newspaper in the months leading up to the conference. The most notable was Bernard Illowy (1814–71) of St. Louis, who had initially endorsed the convention. In the end, most of the Orthodox delegates hailed locally, from Cleveland.

24. Leo Merzbacher was a Bavarian rabbi. He served as minister of Temple Emanu-El in New York, a leading Reform congregation in the United States, and he composed one of the first (moderate) Reform prayer books in America.

25. The official published platform stated: "The Talmud contains the traditional, legal and logical exposition of the biblical laws which must be expounded and practised according to the comments of the Talmud."

26. See "A Reply to M.J.R.," *Israelite*, January 11, 1856, 222.

27. Although the letter "ought by rights to have been sent at once" to Wise's newspaper, Illowy submitted the letter to Leeser's since "Dr. W. is absent at the conference at Cleveland, and might thus leave it unpublished for some time."

28. Founded in 1845, Temple Emanu-El in New York quickly emerged as one of the most affluent and leading Reform congregations in the United States. In 1855 its minister, Leo Merzbacher, introduced his *Order of Prayer for Divine Service*. Merzbacher's prayer book retained nearly all of the traditional services and in the original Hebrew, but parted ways with the Sabbath Mussaf service and some of the extraneous and repetitive sections of the service. His additional German prayer recited after the chanting of the Torah was already a staple in the Emanu-El service. The prayer book was later revised in more radical form by Merzbacher's successor, Samuel Adler (1809–91).

29. Peixotto referred to Anshe Chesed and Tifereth Israel. The latter congregation was founded in 1850 by reformers and former members of Anshe

Chesed. The two congregations did not merge, but the leaders of Anshe Chesed enacted reforms shortly after Peixotto's letter reached Leeser.

30. In 1851, Isaac Mayer Wise's congregation, Anshe Emeth of Albany, introduced mixed seating into the American synagogue. Peixotto also alluded to Wise's prayer book, *Minhag America*, which he published later on in Cincinnati.

31. The letter-writer referred to Jewish law's strictures on a Jewish woman during menstruation (niddah). In fact, none of the traditional rabbinic writers offers this as an explanation for separate seating in the synagogue.

32. Schachne Isaacs (1811–87) was a fervently Orthodox Jew in Cincinnati. Sometime before Holzman published his book, Isaacs publicly burned Wise's prayer book in a stove. In 1867, Wise referred to Isaacs as a "fanatic" but never responded at length to his opponent's demonstration.

33. Holzman referred to the prophet Elijah's actions described in 1 Kings 18.

34. See Shulhan Arukh, Yoreh De'ah 281:1.

35. This is probably the reason that Holzman dedicated his book to Schachne Isaacs, who incinerated Wise's *Minhag America* as an act of protest against the reformer.

36. In 1866 Nathan Rossman filed for an injunction to stop Anshi Chesed's trustees and their rabbi, Moses Mielziner (1828–1903), from revising the German congregation's worship. Each side presented learned affidavits to argue the merits of their respective cases. In addition to Isaacs, the Orthodox plaintiff submitted letters from Jonas Bondi (1804–1874) and Morris Raphall.

37. Isaacs refers to Isaac Mayer Wise, David Einhorn, and Samuel Adler. All three men composed prayer books and also submitted letters of support for the Reform defendants at Anshi Chesed.

38. See Joseph Buchler, "The Struggle for Unity: Attempts at Union in American Jewish Life, 1654–1868," *American Jewish Archives Journal* 2 (June 1949): 28–31.

39. "The Conference at Cleveland," *Israelite*, October 26, 1855, 132.

40. Max Lilienthal, "The Parties," *Israelite*, March 14, 1856, 292.

41. See, for example, "The Dedication of the New Temple in Lafayette," *Israelite*, November 15, 1867, 4.

3. An Orthodox Ministry

1. "Cincinnati, Ohio," *Jewish Chronicle*, January 18, 1850, 115–16.

2. "The Rev. H. A. Henry," *Asmonean*, September 12, 1851, 180.

3. Jay Henry Moses, "Henry A. Henry: The Life and Work of an American Rabbi, 1849–1869" (Ordination thesis: Hebrew Union College–Jewish Institute of Religion, 1997), 41–42.

4. See Zev Eleff, *Who Rules the Synagogue? Religious Authority and the Formation of American Judaism* (New York: Oxford University Press, 2016).

5. Morris J. Raphall of B'nai Jeshurun, Leo Merzbacher of Emanu-El, Samuel Myer Isaacs of Shaaray Tefila, Jacque Judah Lyons (1813–77) of Shearith Israel, Isaac Mayer Wise of B'nai Yeshurun, and James K. Gutheim (1817–86) of Congregation Dispersed of Judah.

6. Actually, Wise was the first Jewish minister in the United States to receive a lifetime contract. Years later, Lilienthal corrected himself when he recalled the "noble" decision of Cincinnati's B'nai Yeshurun to empower its rabbi with tenure.

7. According to one contemporary estimate, there existed about one hundred Jewish congregations and minyans in the United States.

8. Like many American Protestants and Jews in the nineteenth century, Lilienthal was vocal of his prejudice toward Catholics and their hierarchical religious structure.

9. The plan for the Emanu-El Theological Seminary began in earnest in 1865, three years after this conversation took place. However, as the letter-writer indicated, the establishment of a seminary or fund to help train young men for the rabbinate was an idea conjured up by Samuel Adler when he first accepted the ministry of Emanu-El in 1857. Unfortunately for Adler, his seminary plan never materialized. In 1875, Adler retired the plan for good after Isaac Mayer Wise founded Hebrew Union College.

10. This was something of a generalization. Protestant ministers also suffered from low stature in this period and only the most fortunate and talented Christian clergymen claimed the level of stature that this Jewish woman assigned to them. Still, her impression is most valuable for detecting a change in the American Jewish laity's view of the rabbinate.

11. See Palestine, "Communications," *Israelite*, July 25, 1862, 26.

12. Born in Jamaica, George Jacobs immigrated to Virginia in 1854. He apprenticed for a short time before assuming the rabbinic functions of the then-traditional Congregation Beth Shalome in Richmond.

13. Before assuming the position of hazzan at Mikveh Israel in Philadelphia, Isaac Leeser lived in Richmond from 1824 to 1829. He left Mikveh Israel in 1850. In 1857, he returned to the pulpit as minister of Beth El Emeth.

14. In 1828, Leeser published a well-publicized essay in the *Richmond Whig* that defended Jews against bigoted charges levied at them in London. This article garnered the attention of Philadelphia's Jews and helped Leeser secure a prominent pulpit in that community.

15. In Philadelphia, Leeser edited a monthly periodical, established the first Jewish publication society, translated the Jewish prayer book and the Bible, and was very instrumental in a number of other literary and organizational projects.

16. Historian Jacob Rader Marcus estimated the New York Jewish population in 1885 at 100,000.

17. In this period, Reform congregations did not celebrate an individual boy's bar mitzvah. Rather, reformers instituted a group "confirmation" ceremony held on the springtime holiday of Shavuot. Confirmation acknowledged that young women and men had completed a curriculum of Jewish studies and were prepared to affirm their commitment to Judaism.

18. In 1884, Isaac Mayer Wise and Kohler considered furnishing a new English translation of the Bible. Nothing came of this project but Kohler maintained his interest and led a similar project for the Jewish Publication Society in the early twentieth century.

19. The New York *Jewish Messenger* supported Kohut upon his arrival to America. Also in Manhattan, the editors of the *American Hebrew* were cool to Kohut but emerged as his greatest supporters during the Kohut-Kohler controversies.

20. Isaac Luria (1534–72) was a very influential Kabbalist in Safed. The so-called Lurianic Kabbalah offered Jewish mystics a fresh understanding of the Zohar, a fundamental kabbalistic work.

21. Moses Montefiore (1784–1885) was a British financier and the leading figure among British Jewry in his lifetime. He also served as sheriff of London. In 1837 Montefiore was knighted by Queen Victoria (1819–1901).

22. Nathan Rothschild (1840–1915) was a banker and the first Baron Rothschild of that banking dynasty. His father, Baron Lionel de Rothschild (1808–79), was voted to the British House of Commons in 1847. However, he resigned his seat because he refused to be sworn in with a Christian oath. In 1858, Rothschild was reelected and permitted by law to take a non-Christian oath, which he did with a covered head. His son, Nathan, did so upon taking office as well.

23. In 1881, Eastern European Jews began to migrate westward in large numbers to flee antisemitic violence. Rioters blamed Jews for the assassination of Tsar Alexander II (1818–1881). As a result, millions of Russian Jews resettled in the United States. The Jewish population in the United States grew from about 250,000 in 1880 to more than a million at the turn of the twentieth century.

24. Morais was responding to an editorial published by Richard Gottheil (1862–1936), who had criticized seminary leaders for attacking Hebrew

Union College in Cincinnati and their refusal to identify the seminary as an "Orthodox" rabbinical school. See Richard Gottheil, "Under Which Flag?" *American Hebrew*, July 29, 1887, 179–80.

25. On other occasions, Morais employed the term "Enlightened Orthodoxy."

26. Julius Wellhausen (1844–1918) was a German Bible scholar and the founder of the "Documentary Hypothesis," which proposes that the Pentateuch was the product of independent human narratives and eventually redacted rather than transmitted by a heavenly force at Sinai.

27. Morais delivered the major discourse at the seminary's opening on January 2, 1887. For his speech, see S. Morais, "The Work in Hand," *American Hebrew*, January 7, 1887, 132–33.

28. Morais alluded to Kaufmann Kohler. See "Dr. Kohler on the Seminary," *American Hebrew*, January 14, 1887, 146.

29. In 1875, Isaac Mayer Wise founded Hebrew Union College in Cincinnati. Although it was not overtly intended to be a "Reform" rabbinical school, it failed to attract more religiously conservative young men to its campus.

30. In 1873, Moritz Loth and other lay leaders of B'nai Yeshurun and Bene Israel, the two premier Reform congregations in Cincinnati, founded the Union of American Hebrew Congregations. The chief task of this organization was to unify congregations to support the soon-established Hebrew Union College.

31. In 1890, JTS inquired into Solomon Schechter's interest in assuming a leadership position. JTS pursued him repeatedly and offered him the position shortly after Morais's death in 1897. In 1902 Schechter finally accepted the call.

32. Wise died on March 26, 1900. Wise and Hebrew Union College failed to initiate a succession plan and as a result, the College struggled immediately after Wise's death.

33. The newspaper editors sent the same letter to at least nine other leading American Jews. The list included legal scholar Lewis Dembitz (1833–1907), political lobbyist Simon Wolf (1836–1923), and lawyer and philanthropist Louis Marshall (1856–1929). However, Schiff's was the lengthiest letter and the first published in the *American Hebrew*.

34. The attempt to merge failed. Shortly after the newspaper published Schiff's letter, a number of seminary leaders convinced him to support an effort to reorganize JTS under different leadership. The result was the appointment of Solomon Schechter of England's Cambridge University.

35. Schiff wrote this letter to Bernhard Bettmann (1834–1915), president of HUC's Board of Governors. Bettmann responded in German: "*Wir haben auch Lokalstolz,*" we too have local pride.

36. Adolf Jellinek (1821–93), Samuel Holdheim (1806–60), Abraham Geiger (1810–74), Leopold Stein (1810–82), Samuel Adler, David Einhorn, Adolph Huebsch (1830–84), Max Lilienthal, Samuel Hirsch (1815–89), and Isaac Mayer Wise were all Reform rabbis in Europe and the United States.

37. In 1950, HUC opened a campus in New York, a result of its merger with rival seminary, Jewish Institute of Religion (est. 1922). Since then, the school and its affiliate organizations have moved their headquarters to New York.

38. See Lance J. Sussman, "The Myth of the Trefa Banquet: American Culinary Culture and the Radicalization of Food Policy in American Reform Judaism," *American Jewish Archives Journal* 57 (2005): 29–52.

39. See "Dr. Kohler's Rejoinder to Dr. Kohut," *Jewish Messenger*, June 19, 1885, 4.

40. See Kaufmann Kohler to David Philipson, July 3, 1885, box 1, folder 1, MS-35, American Jewish Archives, Cincinnati OH.

41. See Richard Gottheil, "Under Which Flag?" *American Hebrew*, July 29, 1887, 179–80.

4. The Arrival of Eastern European Immigrants

1. Marcus, *To Count a People*, 240–41.

2. Yisrael Meir Ha-Kohen, *Nidhei Israel* (Warsaw: Meir Yeheil Halter and Meir Eisenstadt, 1893), 84.

3. See Arthur Hertzberg, "'Treifene Medina': Learned Opposition to Emigration to the United States," *Proceedings of the Eighth World Congress of Jewish Studies* (1984): 1–30.

4. Leah Rachel Yoffie, "Yiddish Proverbs, Sayings, Etc., in St. Louis MO," *Journal of American Folklore* 33 (April–June 1920): 164.

5. See Jeffrey S. Gurock, "Resisters and Accommodators: Varieties of Orthodox Rabbis in America, 1886–1983," *American Jewish Archives Journal* 35 (November 1983): 100–187.

6. See Israel Bartal, "Heavenly America: The United States as an Ideal Model for Nineteenth-Century East European Jews," in *Following Columbus: America, 1492–1992*, ed. Miriam Eliav-Felton (Jerusalem: Zalman Shazar, 1996), 511–22.

7. See *Forty Years of Struggle for a Principle: The Biography of Harry Fischel*, ed. Herbert S. Goldstein (New York: Bloch, 1928), 14–22.

8. Meaning, toward Jerusalem.

9. Actually, the sentiment among the established Orthodox community was mixed. One advocate told the New York press that "I think it very desirable to have the office of chief rabbi instituted here, so there will be somebody in authority to give proper advice in regard to ritualistic and dietary matters."

Another complained that Joseph was "of no more importance than any rabbi in this city and he is at the head of but two hundred Hebrews."

10. Pinchas "Piney" Minkowski (1859–1924) served briefly as cantor of Kahal Adas Yeshurun Synagogue in New York. In 1887, the congregation offered Minkowski a $2,500 annual contract (today, $64,000), considerably more than typical cantorial or rabbinical salaries in that time. Three years later, the cantor returned to Odessa as chief cantor of the Brody Synagogue.

11. There is no record of a congregation by the name of Beth Jacob. Most scholars have assumed that Berlin was actually referring to nonobservant Jews in the Orthodox Congregation Brith Shalom.

12. In other words, the Talmud permitted mild violators of Jewish law to offer sacrifices to the Temple in Jerusalem. Likewise, similar miscreants are permitted to pray in the traditional synagogue, according to Rabbi Berlin.

13. The Talmud treats violators of the Sabbath and worshipers of foreign gods as more severe transgressors.

14. Berlin's responsum became well known in America's rabbinic circles and an obstacle for those who sought to issue a more lenient ruling. See Yosef Eliyahu Fried, *Sefer Ohel Yosef* (New York: A. H. Rosenberg, 1903), 9a.

15. In 1870, Eastern European Jews started to move into Worcester (forty miles west of Boston). In the late nineteenth century, the Jewish community of Worcester supported more than a dozen synagogues.

16. Known by the acronym "Ramaz," Moshe Zevulun Margolies (1851–1936) immigrated to Boston in 1889. Seventeen years later, the rabbi accepted the call of the affluent Congregation Kehilath Jeshurun in New York. The Yiddish-speaking Margolies was a noted scholar and was considered at the time of his death as the "dean of Orthodox rabbis in North America."

17. In 1918, the Yiddish novelist and playwright Peretz Hirschbein (1880–1948) published *Grine Felder* [Green fields].

18. Born in Minsk, Jacob Ben-Ami (1890–1977) was one of the best known Yiddish stage actors in the United States.

19. Rashi and Moses Maimonides were leading medieval rabbinic figures. From the time of publication, their works have been consulted regularly by students and scholars.

20. Hans Holbein the Younger (1497–1543) was a German artist known for his portrait work.

21. The Jewish month of Tamuz occurs in the summer and Tevet in the winter.

22. The "principles" included support for a "Jewish Synod" of rabbis to decide religious matters, belief in Divine revelation, and adherence to the "codes of

our Rabbis and Maimonides's thirteen principles of faith." The Union also pledged fidelity to the Restoration of Zion and denounced "intermarriage between Jew and Gentile." See "The Orthodox Jewish Congregational Union of America," *American Jewish Year Book* 1 (1899–1900): 99–100.

23. Born in Posen, Lewis N. Dembitz was a legal scholar and political activist in Louisville KY. He wrote for many of the American Jewish periodicals and served on a number of Jewish organizations. In addition to the Union of Orthodox Jewish Congregations, Dembitz also played a role in the early years of the Hebrew Union College in Cincinnati and the Jewish Theological Seminary in New York.

24. Bernard Drachman (1861–1945) was a university-trained, American-born rabbi. His religious studies in Europe moved his theological outlook from Reform to Orthodox. In 1890, he accepted a rabbinical post at the well-heeled Park East Synagogue on Manhattan's Upper East Side.

25. Portuguese-trained Rev. Meldola de Sola (1853–1918) was minister of Shearith Israel in Montreal, known for his public support of Zionism. Born in New York, Henry W. Schneeberger (1848–1916) traveled to Esriel Hildesheimer's (1820–99) Orthodox rabbinical seminary in Berlin. Upon return, the rabbi aligned with what one observer described as "Positive Judaism" and accepted a call in 1876 to serve at Chizuk Amuno Congregation in Baltimore.

26. Born into an "uptown" New York family, Max Cohen (1853–1943) was a lawyer and communal leader. In addition to his work for the "Union," he was also a member of the close circle that founded the *American Hebrew* and supported the Jewish Theological Seminary.

27. In 1516, the Ottoman Empire conquered Palestine. It remained under Turkish rule until World War I, when it was placed under the control of the British Empire.

28. In 1898, the USS *Maine* exploded in the Havana Harbor. The ship was sent to the region to protect American interests during the Cuban revolt against Spain. Although investigators could not determine the reason for the demise of the *Maine*, American journalists were quick to blame the Spanish.

29. Gotthard Deutsch, "The Orthodox Convention from a Liberal Point of View," *American Hebrew*, July 15, 1898, 322–23.

30. Rabbi Tobias Shanfarber (d. 1942) wrote that Deutsch's questions "were worthy of a reply, and we had hoped would be dignified with such by the president [Mendes] of the Orthodox Convention, but no such reply was forthcoming. Shall we draw the conclusion that Dr. Deutsch's queries were unanswerable and is it henceforth to be said that Orthodoxy is not Ortho-

doxy, but some other kind of doxy? That is the way it looks." See T.S., "The Pertinent Questions," *Jewish Comment*, July 29, 1898, 4.

31. In 1646, the Church of England convened the Westminster Assembly to establish official doctrines for the reformation of the Church.

32. Charles Briggs (1841–1913) and Henry Preserved Smith (1847–1927) were Presbyterian theologians. In 1892 the Presbytery of Cincinnati expelled Smith for questioning the "historic truths" in the Book of Chronicles. One year later, the General Assembly of the Presbyterian Church excommunicated Briggs, also for higher biblical criticism.

33. In 1565, Rabbi Yosef Karo of Safed published his *Shulhan Arukh*, an expansive, four-volume code of Jewish law. Since its appearance and the insertion of an additional gloss authored by Moshe Isserles (1520–72) to accommodate Ashkenazic practices, Karo's work has achieved a consensus as the leading text authority of Halakah. The legal code was successful despite vocal sixteenth-century opposition from leading rabbinic figures.

34. Kaufmann Kohler published his *Guide for Instruction in Judaism: A Manual for Schools and Homes* (New York: Philip Cowen, 1898) as a "school-book" to impart the "religious and ethical teachings of Judaism in a comprehensive, clear and systematic form."

35. In 1869, Pope Pius IX (1792–1878) convened the First Vatican Council, which was the first meeting to officially decree the doctrine of papal infallibility.

36. Ignaz von Döllinger (1799–1890) was a German priest who rejected the First Vatican Council's declaration of papal infallibility.

37. Isaac Mayer Wise, Kaufmann Kohler, Samuel Hirsch, and Gustavus Gottheil were all prominent American Reform rabbis. Henry Pereira Mendes, Philip Klein (1849–1926), Jacob Joseph, and Shmuel Salant (1816–1909) were Orthodox rabbis. Deutsch confused Salant with the earlier Israel of Salant (1810–83).

38. Sir Isaac Newton (1643–1727) and Galileo Galilei (1564–1642) were pathbreakers in the fields of science and mathematics who shaped the modern understanding of the Earth and its spatial and physical realities.

39. The traditional Jewish liturgy includes the mourner's Kaddish, an Aramaic prayer that bereaved family members recite as a reaffirmation of their belief in God. According to Jewish mystical teachings, the recitation of the Kaddish can elevate the soul of the deceased.

40. Zacharias Frankel (1801–75) was a moderate reform rabbi and scholar in Breslau. For Deutsch's reference, see S. Bernfeld, "Zacharias Frankel in Berlin," *Allgemeine Zeitung des Judentums*, July 23, 1898, 343–46.

41. In addition to Mendes, the Hungarian-born Rabbi Philip Klein was viewed as an educated and worldly scholar. Still, Deutsch challenged both Orthodox leaders to align rabbinic texts with Nicolaus Copernicus's (1473–1543) accepted heliocentric model of the universe.

42. Two years earlier, journalist and communal worker Bernard G. Richards (1877–1971) employed the phrase "Young Israel" to describe Judah Magnes's retirement sermon from Temple Emanu-El in New York. In all likelihood, Magnes borrowed "Young Israel" and other points that echo in the later Young Israel mission statement. Magnes delivered a number of lectures on behalf of Young Israel. See "An Inspiration to Young Israel," *Hebrew Standard*, May 27, 1910, 7.

43. For instance, the Seventh-day Adventist Church.

44. The five-day work week did not take hold until the 1940s.

45. In fact, Orthodox institutions hesitated before entering into the Synagogue Council's ranks. Orthodox Union leaders wished that cases in which "questions of Jewish Law shall be involved, the Orthodox view shall prevail." No such deal was agreed upon, but the Orthodox Union joined anyway.

46. See Bernard Drachman, "Orthodox Judaism in Accord with Modern Thought," *Jewish Exponent*, February 21, 1908, 9.

47. See "An Interview between Hon. Lincoln C. Andrews and Rabbi Simon Glazer," November 12, 1925, box 1, folder 3, MS-269, American Jewish Archives, Cincinnati OH.

5. Trailblazers

1. Herbert S. Goldstein, "A Tribute," *Orthodox Union*, November/December 1940, 5.

2. See Jeffrey S. Gurock, "Yeshiva Students at the Jewish Theological Seminary," in *Tradition Renewed: A History of the Jewish Theological Seminary*, ed. Jack Wertheimer (New York: Jewish Theological Seminary of America, 1997), 1:486–87.

3. See Arnold Rothkoff, *Vision and Realization: Bernard Revel and His Era* (PhD diss., Yeshiva University, 1967), 55.

4. See Zev Eleff, "Jewish Immigrants, Liberal Higher Education, and the Quest for a Torah u-Madda Curriculum at Yeshiva College," *Tradition* 44 (Summer 2011): 22.

5. S. Felix Mendelsohn, "Topics of the Week," *Chicago Sentinel*, November 10, 1922, 10.

6. Moses Lipshutz, *Yidei Moshe* (St. Louis: Moinester Printing, 1921), 7.

7. "Yeshiva Seminary and College in New York Praised by American University Presidents," *Jewish Exponent*, April 17, 1925, 7.

8. Henry Hurwitz to Nathan Isaacs, February 13, 1929, box 1, folder 1, MS-184, American Jewish Archives, Cincinnati OH. Rabbi Leo Jung (1892–1987) was the leader of the Jewish Center on Manhattan's Upper West Side. He maintained an enlarged public profile as a busy writer and spokesman for traditional Jews in America.

9. "An Appreciation of Schechter the Humanist," *Menorah Journal* 1 (December 1915): v.

10. Tobias Schanfarber, "Dr. Schechter's Inaugural," *Reform Advocate*, December 6, 1902, 345.

11. Bernard Revel was the president of the Rabbi Isaac Elchanan Theological Seminary and all of the schools and programs, including the Talmudical Academy, within its constellation. He held ties to the Agudath Ha-Rabbonim (Union of Orthodox Rabbis) and Mizrachi, a Religious Zionist movement.

12. Rabbi Jacob Joseph School was founded in 1903, in memory of the recently deceased Jacob Joseph, the so-called chief rabbi of New York. In 1886, Eastern European migrants founded the Etz Chaim Yeshiva on New York's Lower East Side to educate young boys in traditional Jewish learning.

13. In the early 1920s, the United States passed legislation that severely restricted migration from Eastern Europe as well as other regions. The Immigration Act of 1924 all but halted the once-steady flow of Jewish migration from Europe to America.

14. By this, the writer meant the "clay" to represent American society and the "spirit" to stand for Orthodox Judaism.

15. The Yeshivath Etz Chaim in Chicago was founded in 1899. It labored under financial difficulties and inadequate facilities until it finally merged with the Hebrew Theological College in 1921. Ephraim Epstein (1876–1960) was a prominent rabbi and community organizer, Abraham I. Cardon (1882–1945) was rabbi of the Sawyer Street Synagogue, and Hayyim Rubenstein (1872–1943) was a rabbinical scholar and educator.

16. Little is known of Ben Zion Lazar (b. 1859), who was president of the Moses Montefiore Hebrew School and involved in other matters of Jewish education in Chicago.

17. A contemporary news report stated that the amount was $135,000 (today, $1,740,000). The article also claimed that the new building could facilitate six hundred students.

18. Saul Silber (1881–1946) was the rabbi of Anshe Sholom in Chicago and the president of the Hebrew Theological College.

19. In 1921 the rabbinical school's articles of incorporation proposed that the object of the organization was to "own, operate, conduct and maintain schools and colleges for Hebrew training and educational purposes, and to create and maintain general and special funds for the support thereof and students therein."

20. Beth Hamedrash L'Torah (Academy for Torah) is the Hebrew name for the Hebrew Theological College, although the latter title is the official name of the institution.

21. In 1902 Solomon Schechter arrived in the United States to take the helm of the Jewish Theological Seminary in New York. He was well known for his pathbreaking work on medieval Jewish manuscripts. Many American Jews viewed Schechter's move to the United States as a signal of American Judaism's prominence and a religious leader for traditional-minded Jews.

22. In truth, Jacob Schiff supported the Jewish Theological Seminary. In particular, he underwrote the seminary's teachers' training program and purchased many books for its library.

23. In 1879 Schechter enrolled in the Reform-minded Hochschule rabbinical seminary in Berlin.

24. Solomon Schechter, *Studies in Judaism* (New York: Macmillan, 1896), xii.

25. Schreiber had in mind Rabbi Emil G. Hirsch (1851–1923) of Sinai Congregation in Chicago. Hirsch was perhaps the leading radical Reform figure in the United States and Kaufmann Kohler's brother-in-law.

26. Sabato Morais (1823–97) of Philadelphia's Mikveh Israel served as the founding president of the Jewish Theological Seminary.

27. Isaac M. Wise, *Pronaos to Holy Writ and the Authenticity of the Pentateuch* (Cincinnati: Robert Clarke, 1891), 4.

28. Wise, *Pronaos to Holy Writ*, 5–6.

29. Leopold Zunz (1794–1886) is considered the founder of modern critical Judaic studies (Wissenschaft des Judentums), a frequent subject in Solomon Schechter's writings.

30. The Know Nothing Party was an American political movement in the mid-nineteenth century that supported nativism. In particular, its members strongly opposed the immigration of Irish Catholics to the United States.

31. Sir Boyle Roche (1736–1807) was an Irish politician known for issuing "Irish bulls," in other words, logically absurd statements in public discourses.

32. Abraham Lincoln (1809–65) spoke these words at his annual message to Congress on December 1, 1862.

33. It is not entirely clear what Schechter meant by "Catholic Israel," a term he returned to repeatedly. It was likely inspired by the notion of "Klal Yisrael," or the communal unity of the Jewish people.

34. Michel de Montaigne (1533–92) was a popular writer and essayist during the French Renaissance.

35. See "A Word of Caution," *American Hebrew*, May 13, 1904, 794.

36. Rabbi Bernard Levinthal of Philadelphia was president of the Agudath Ha-Rabbonim. By herem, the editors referred to the rabbinic ban discussed at length in the Talmud and its commentators. Such excommunications were typically reserved for idolaters and extreme flouters of rabbinic legislation.

37. Rabbi Louis Ginzberg (1873–1953) was a European-trained Talmudist. In 1903 Schechter brought Ginzberg to JTS, where the latter emerged as the school's leading intellectual and halakhist. Earlier Ginzberg was turned down by Hebrew Union College in Cincinnati. The Reform school judged Ginzberg's openness to biblical criticism as too radical for its institution.

38. L.G., "Law, Codification of," *The Jewish Encyclopedia* (New York: Funk and Wagnalls, 1904), 7:636. Eisenstein, it should be noted, was a very vocal opponent of the *Jewish Encyclopedia* project.

39. L.G., "Law, Codification of," 637.

40. See Wise, *Pronaos to Holy Writ*.

41. Drob referred to the Reform rabbinical conference held in Pittsburgh in November 1885. In truth, the platform decided at the conference rearticulated radical religious views stated earlier by reformers. Nonetheless, the planks garnered the attention and ire of traditional Jews.

42. In 1913 Solomon Schechter founded the United Synagogue—borrowing a name and template of already established Anglo Jewish organization—as a synagogue body for communities that wished to identify with the Jewish Theological Seminary and its affiliated rabbis.

43. Established in 1901 as the Alumni Association of the Jewish Theological Seminary, the rabbinical body changed its name to the Rabbinical Assembly in 1918 to incorporate non-seminary rabbis.

44. The Sanhedrin was the legislative body that governed Israel and decided Jewish law during the Second Temple period.

45. The Talmud relates that Rabbi Eliezer was certainly correct in his position. However, Rabbi Joshua prevailed on him to accept the majority decision that sided against Rabbi Eliezer.

46. An Agunah, literally "anchored" or "chained" woman, is a wife whose husband cannot (e.g., he is missing) or refuses to deliver her a bill of divorce. According to Jewish law, the woman is not allowed to remarry, and any future children would be declared mamzerim, bastards, and would also not be permitted to marry under ordinary circumstances.
47. "Modern Orthodoxy," *American Hebrew*, April 7, 1916, 630.
48. "Jewish Theological Seminary," *Yiddisches Tageblatt*, April 4, 1905, 8.
49. See Aaron Rothkoff, *Bernard Revel: Builder of American Jewish Orthodoxy* (Philadelphia: Jewish Publication Society of America, 1972), 142–48.

6. The Parting of the Ways

1. "Congregation Shaarey Tefilla of the Southwest," *B'nai B'rith Messenger*, April 18, 1913, 5.
2. "Congregation Beth Itzchok Notes," *Chicago Sentinel*, February 18, 1921, 31.
3. "Prominent Rabbi," *American Hebrew*, November 5, 1920, 758.
4. Samuel Rabinowitz, "What Is 'Middle Termism,'" *American Hebrew*, July 1, 1910, 227.
5. Louis Finkelstein, "The Present and Future of Traditional Judaism in America," *Proceedings of the Rabbinical Assembly* 4 (1933): 12.
6. Eugene Kohn, *The Future of Judaism in America* (New Rochelle: Liberal Press, 1934), 98.
7. Aaron M. Rine, "What is an Orthodox Synagogue?," *Shofar* (1949-1950) 20.
8. See Jenna Weissman Joselit, "In the Driver's Seat: Rabbinic Authority in Postwar America," in *Jewish Religious Leadership: Image and Reality*, ed. Jack Wertheimer (New York: Jewish Theological Seminary of America, 2004), 2:659–70.
9. Cyrus Adler was a Semitics scholar and librarian of the Smithsonian Institute. In his lifetime, Adler served as president of the American Jewish Committee, the American Jewish Historical Society, Dropsie College, and the Jewish Theological Seminary (after Solomon Schechter).
10. Jacob Kohn (1881–1968) was a rabbi in Chicago and vice president of the United Synagogue. He was also a close disciple of Solomon Schechter and aided him in forming the congregational body that Mendes referred to in his letter to Adler. In 1913 the plan for the organization was transformed and renamed the United Synagogue.
11. The "Shaital" referred to by Mendes is a wig that many Orthodox Jewish women wear to conform to the Talmud's proscription against married women appearing bareheaded in public (Ketuvot 72a).

12. Zucrow was motivated to publish this essay in response to an article that appeared in a magazine published by a local Jewish congregation's men's club. Temple Mishkan Tefila of Boston printed an anonymous correspondence between a woman and a rabbi whom she wanted to officiate at her upcoming wedding. The rabbi refused on the grounds that the woman was still wedded to her first husband and could not remarry without a religious divorce. The woman explained that her husband had abandoned her (while she was pregnant), and there was no way to obtain a divorce from him. This was still insufficient for the rabbinic correspondent. To his mind, Zucrow believed that the new breed of "modern Orthodox rabbis" could figure out a method to "free" this woman and maintain their fidelity to Jewish law. See "An Appeal to Justice," *Jewish Center* 2 (March 1922): 3–4.

13. The books of the Midrash are rabbinic collections from the talmudic and post-talmudic periods. Rabbis Samson Raphael Hirsch and Meir Leibush Malbim (1809–79) wrote extensively in defense of traditional Judaism and emerged as vocal opponents of Reform in the nineteenth century.

14. The "Authorized Version" refers to the English translation of the Bible commissioned by King James of England and published in 1611.

15. The writer's father, Rabbi Meir Zvi Jung (1858–1921) was heavily influenced by Samson Raphael Hirsch. The latter utilized the philosophies of the German thinkers Georg Wilhelm Friedrich Hegel (1770–1831) and Immanuel Kant (1724–1804).

16. Samson Raphael Hirsch frequently referred to "Torah im Derekh Eretz" as his motto to represent his embrace of Jewish and secular knowledge.

17. Exodus 20 details the Revelation at Sinai and the subsequent chapter deals with a number of laws regarding slavery, damages, and torts.

18. Hirsch used the phrase "Gesetzestreuer Juden." A literal translation is "Jews faithful to the law."

19. Both points are historical oversimplifications but not incorrect. Reform Judaism emerged in Central Europe before it migrated to the United States. In 1870 Chief Rabbi Nathan Marcus Adler (1803–90) founded (via an Act of Parliament) the United Synagogue, a congregational body that formally united three London synagogues. In 1913 Solomon Schechter borrowed the name and nature of the organization when he founded the United Synagogue in the United States.

20. Rashi and Maimonides were perhaps the major rabbinic figures of the eleventh and twelfth centuries. The French Tosafists was a prominent school of Talmudists that spanned the twelfth through the fifteenth centuries.

21. Pinkhos Churgin (1894–1957) served as dean of the Teachers Institute of Yeshiva University. Originally founded by the Religious Zionist organization Mizrachi, the Teachers Institute aimed to train educators for Hebrew schools. In 1955 Churgin founded Bar Ilan University in Israel.

22. Both journals founded by Yeshiva College scholars, *Horev* (est. 1934) and *Scripta Mathematica* (est. 1932), were well-regarded academic journals in Jewish and non-Jewish circles.

23. In other words, a secret ballot.

24. For years, Mishkan Tefila in nearby Roxbury had identified as a "Conservative" congregation. In addition to mixed seating, this synagogue boasted an organ and admitted female singers into its choir. Kehillath Israel had no intention of implementing these innovations and therefore did not see itself as Conservative; its members were therefore "Modern Orthodox."

25. Soon after, the congregation elected Louis M. Epstein (1887–1949) as its rabbi. Epstein was president of the Rabbinical Assembly and a leading member of that organization's Committee on Jewish Law. In 1925 Epstein identified as "Orthodox." In 1940, in response to Orthodox backlash against his proposal to modify Jewish marriage ceremonies, Epstein finally and fully identified with Conservative Judaism.

26. The leading member of the departing party was textile manufacturer Samuel C. Feuerstein (1893–1983). In 1926 Feuerstein founded Congregation Sons of Israel in Brookline, establishing it on the basis of "Strict Orthodoxy." In 1947 the congregation evolved into the Young Israel of Brookline.

27. In this early stage, Kehillath Israel did not employ a rabbi, but this would not last for long. In July 1925 the newspapers announced the hiring of Rabbi Louis Epstein at the Brookline congregation.

28. Gus Singerman (1909–92) was the leading member of the defendants in *Katz v. Singerman*.

29. Rabbi Isadore Goodman (d. 1962) was the longtime spiritual leader of the Baron Hirsch Synagogue in Memphis TN.

30. Leo Jung, "Orthodox Judaism," *The Universal Jewish Encyclopedia* (New York: Universal Jewish Encyclopedia, 1942), 6:239.

31. The author referred to the ninth of Moses Maimonides's thirteen principles of faith.

32. "Conservative Movement to Inaugurate National Beth Din," *United Synagogue Review* 7 (September 1953): 5. All subsequent quotations were derived from this document.

33. The balance of Schoenfeld's essay addresses the technical matters of "conditional marriage" and offers an in-depth view of relevant sources in the Talmud.

34. Formed in 1881, the New York Board of Rabbis is composed of clergymen from all major American Jewish movements.

35. In 1959 Rabbi Menachem Mendel Schneerson (1902–94), the Lubavitcher Rebbe, issued the same ruling. According to him, "The doctrines and ideology of the Conservative and Reform movements can only be classed in the category of heretical movements."

36. Aaron H. Blumenthal (1907–82) served as rabbi of Congregation Emanuel in Mount Vernon NY and was president of the Rabbinical Assembly. In 1954 he authored the Conservative responsum permitting women to receive aliyot in the synagogue (published in 1955).

37. Around this time, Kauvar had publicly complained about Conservative rabbis' willingness to ease up on kosher standards and alter parts of the traditional liturgy.

38. Ivan Salomon (1881–1972) was a leading figure within Shearith Israel in New York and the Orthodox Union. A philanthropist, much of his efforts were engaged in elevating the status of Sephardic studies in the United States and Europe. Solomon J. Sharfman (1915–2004) was the rabbi of the Young Israel of Flatbush and president of the Rabbinical Council of America (1956–58).

39. See "'Little Caesar' Dolgin Refers to Conservative and Reform Jews as 'Goyim,'" *California Jewish Press*, July 21, 1961, 1–2.

40. Simon Dolgin, "Beth Jacob Congregation," in *The Sanctity of the Synagogue*, ed. Jeanne Litvin (Hoboken: Ktav, 1987), 489–92. In 1954 Dolgin's congregation agreed to separate men and women on Sabbath and holidays but retain mixed pews for the High Holidays.

7. Becoming Modern Orthodox Jews

1. Milton Himmelfarb, "An Unknown Jewish Sect," *Commentary* 33 (January 1962): 66.

2. See Marshall Sklare, *Conservative Judaism: An American Religious Movement* (Glencoe IL: Free Press, 1955), 42, and Nathan Glazer, *American Judaism* (Chicago: University of Chicago Press, 1957), 142.

3. See Yosef Dov Soloveitchik, *Fir Derashot* (New York: Orot, 1967), 29.

4. See David Luchins, "In Reply," *Commentator*, December 22, 1966, 6.

5. Jacob Neusner, "The New Orthodox Left," *Conservative Judaism* 20 (Fall 1965): 10.

6. Eliezer Berkovits, "Orthodox Judaism in a World of Revolutionary Transformation," *Tradition* 7 (Summer 1965): 68.

7. Shelomoh E. Danziger, "Modern Orthodoxy or Orthodox Modernism," *Jewish Observer* 3 (October 1966): 9.

8. Irving Greenberg, "A Letter to the Editor," *Jewish Observer* 3 (December 1966): 16.

9. Emanuel Rackman, "A Challenge to Orthodoxy," *Judaism* 18 (Spring 1969): 46.

10. *Speeches and Addresses Given by Rabbis and Religious Lay Leaders at the First World Conference of Ashkenazi and Sephardi Synagogues* (Jerusalem: World Conference of Ashkenazi and Sephardi Synagogues, 1972), 94.

11. Earlier in this essay, Liebman explained that the "church" embraces secular culture and attempts to thrive within it. The "sect," a smaller group, typically prefers isolation from the secular culture.

12. The writer had in mind a number of articles authored by Rackman as well as his *Jewish Values for Modern Men* (New York: Jewish Education Committee, 1962).

13. Emanuel Rackman, "Can We Moderns Keep the Sabbath?" *Commentary* 18 (September 1954): 212.

14. After the excitement generated over the interview, Greenberg issued a letter of "clarification." See "Greenberg Clarifies and Defends His Views," *Commentator*, May 12, 1966, 8–9.

15. Fulton Sheen (1895–1979) was an American Catholic bishop and popular radio preacher. A similar sentiment was also offered by the Anglican priest William Ralph Inge (1860–1954).

16. See Neusner, "The New Orthodox Left."

17. Cardinal John Henry Newman (1801–90) was a leader of the Oxford Movement, which sought to reinstall older traditions into the Anglican theology and worship. In 1852 Newman published his philosophies of university education (*The Idea of a University*), in which he wrote about "a pure and clear atmosphere of thought, which the student also breathes, though in his own case he only pursues a few sciences out of the multitude."

18. See Joseph B. Soloveitchik, "Confrontation," *Tradition* 6 (Spring/Summer 1964): 20.

19. In the 1960s, the Rabbinical Council of America supported a bill passed in Pennsylvania that required slaughter houses to employ "humane" methods. In the previous decade, the rabbinical group had fought legislation that would effectively prohibit ritual slaughter but eventually worked with other

groups to develop a procedure that could assuage concerned activists and maintain the standards of Jewish law. Other Orthodox groups were dissatisfied with this concession.

20. In its first match, the Yeshiva College team defeated University of Louisville, 335–140.

21. According to the trivia show's rules, the team that won five matches in a row was declared the season's champion. Unfortunately, the YU team lost the subsequent duel against Temple University. However, the outpouring of letters and editorials continued and boasted of Orthodox Judaism's triumph.

22. Rackman held to this position for the remainder of his life. See, for example, Emanuel Rackman, "Religious Revolution," *Jewish Week*, November 3, 1989, 36.

23. Jacques Maritain was a French Catholic philosopher. Lamm referred to Maritain's discussion on the "worship of modernity" in *Le paysan de la Garonne* (Paris: Desclée de Brouwer, 1966).

24. Rabbi Samson Raphael Hirsch was the leading figure in his Frankfurt community. His Orthodox followers continued to read his works and teachings and held to his separatist positions for many years after he died and was succeeded by his son-in-law and grandchildren.

25. Rabbi Abraham Isaac Kook (1865–1935) was a towering Talmudist and Zionist ideologue. He served as the first Ashkenazic Chief Rabbi of Palestine.

26. Rabbi Akiva ben Joseph was the leading sage in the Tannaitic period in the first and second centuries.

27. Students of the Satmar Hasidic group and those of Rabbi Yitzhak Ze'ev Soloveitchik (1886–1959)—the "Brisker Rav"—adopt the respective schools' very particular styles of Torah study and fervent religious behavior.

28. Chaim Dov Keller, "Modern Orthodoxy: An Analysis and a Response," *Jewish Observer* 6 (June 1970): 4.

29. Yet the idea was clearly in Lamm's mind. See Norman Lamm, "Religion with a Future," sermon delivered at the Jewish Center, January 5, 1963, Lamm Archives, Yeshiva University, New York.

30. See Norman Lamm, "The Voice of Torah in the Battle of Ideas," *Jewish Life* 34 (March/April 1967): 23–31.

31. Norman Lamm, "The Arrogance of Modernism," sermon delivered at the Jewish Center, May 23, 1969, Lamm Archives.

8. Orthodox, Inc.

1. Arthur Hertzberg, "The Changing American Rabbinate," *Midstream* 12 (January 1966): 29.

2. Alvin I. Schiff, *The Jewish Day School in America* (New York: Jewish Education Committee Press, 1966), 48–65.

3. See Jeffrey S. Gurock, *The Men and Women of Yeshiva: Higher Education, Orthodoxy, and American Judaism* (New York: Columbia University Press, 1988), 142–62, 186–212.

4. Morris Max, "The Making of a Modern Siddur," *Jewish Life* 27 (August 1960): 40, 43.

5. See, for example, Paltiel Birnbaum, "Siddur Hadash ba La-Medinah," *Hadoar*, December 9, 1960, 85–86, and Simcha Elberg, "The Court of the Rabbinical Council," *Ha-Pardes* 35 (Tevet 1961): 2–3.

6. See "Executive Passes Siddur's Revision," *Rabbinical Council Record* 6 (February 1961): 1, 3.

7. Clarence Newman, "Kosher Label Covers More Name Brands from Aspirin to Pizza," *Wall Street Journal*, April 8, 1963, 1.

8. In 1939, Rabbi Joseph Soloveitchik founded the Heichal Rabenu Hayim Halevi as an institute for advanced Torah study. However, it did not last long, as Soloveitchik struggled to maintain both the Boston school and his new position at RIETS in New York.

9. Rabbi Moses Soloveitchik (1879–1941) was a Talmud scholar and a leading member of the RIETS faculty.

10. Hyman E. Cline (1888–1952) was a construction contractor and a leading figure in Boston Jewish communal life.

11. In 1946, the director of the camp, Rabbi Moshe Litoff (1923–2014) opined: "The success of Camp Moshava can be measured by the fact that so many of its campers return year after year. Children who come from completely unorthodox homes have become integrated to the life of Camp Moshava and speak with great enthusiasm of the 'swell' time they have had at Camp Moshava."

12. Hapoel Hamizrachi was a political party in Israel. In the United States in 1912, its supporters established the Religious Zionists of America (American Mizrachi). The leaders of this organization founded the first Moshava camps.

13. Other camps did not label themselves as "Orthodox" but were still very hospitable to Orthodox Jews. One observer noted the following about Camp Massad in Pennsylvania: "I have heard it said that the comparatively important place religion has in the total program stems primarily from the fact that so many of the children come from Orthodox or Quasi-Orthodox homes. My own observation convinced me that this explanation does not pass muster. From the earliest days of the Massad idea its founders put their accent on all those forms of Jewish life which are instrumental in the preservation

of Judaism. Few students of Jewish history doubt the tremendous importance of religious precept and practice in the survival scheme. At Massad the
prayers, the observance of *Shabbat*, the impressive rites of *tishah b'av*, and
other religious observances become integral and functional because they
assume their natural place in the totality of Jewish living. For example, the
whole community of Massad prepares for the Sabbath; camper and counsel-
lor alike engage in transforming the area of the profane into holy ground. It
is hard to exaggerate the positive effect of such participation on the child."
See Maurice M. Shudofsky, "Massad—An Experiment in Hebrew Summer
Camping," *Jewish Frontier* 18 (December 1951): 29.

14. New York attorney and lay leader Harold Boxer (1907–73) founded NCSY.
Still, Rosenberg was an important rabbinic leader and resource to Boxer and
the Orthodox Union when the synagogue organization founded the youth
movement in the 1950s.

15. In 1951 the United Synagogue founded the United Synagogue Youth to serve
young Conservative Jews.

16. Of course, NCSY and all coeducational Orthodox youth movements had
detractors. In 1963 the Ultra-Orthodox Rabbi Uriel Zimmer (1921–61) wrote
that "there is no difference between a nationwide or even world-wide organization and between a local, say, Synagogue-Youth organization. The 'Modern
Orthodox' type in its American edition and its 'made in Israel' (Bnei Akiva)
equivalent are equally wrong from the Torah viewpoint."

17. Literally: "If there are no kids, there will be no goats." The text is from Lev.
Rabbah (11:7), which continues: "If there are no goats, there will be no flock.
If there is no flock, there will be no shepherd. If there is no shepherd, there
will be no world."

18. In 1954 Yeshiva University established its Youth Bureau. Its major program
was the Torah Leadership Seminar, first held during high school winter vacation and later during the summer. YU took advantage of this endeavor. In
1956 the school opened its Jewish Studies Program, which catered to public
school graduates with minimal Jewish studies education.

19. In 1935 chemist Abraham Goldstein left the Orthodox Union to found Organized Kashruth Laboratories (OK Labs).

20. Rabbi Eliezer Silver was a well-known rabbi in Cincinnati OH, and head of
the Agudath Ha-Rabbonim. He was a leading voice of American Orthodoxy, especially during the first half of the twentieth century. The Iggud Ha-
Rabbonim (Rabbinical Alliance of America) was founded in 1942 as a right-
wing alternative to the RCA.

21. Beginning in the 1960s, American Jews demonstrated on behalf of Soviet Jewry. The Soviet government furthered a long-standing campaign against Jews, closing down synagogues, issuing antisemitic propaganda, and inciting violence against Jews.

22. In a footnote, Soloveitchik clarified: "The term 'secular orders' is used here in accordance with its popular semantics. For the man of faith, this term is a misnomer. God claims the whole, not a part of man, and whatever He established as an order within the scheme of creation is sacred."

23. After Soloveitchik's address, the RCA passed a resolution that stated in part: "Any suggestion that the historical and meta-historical worth of a faith community be viewed against the backdrop of another faith, and the mere hint that a revision of basic historic attitudes is anticipated, are incongruous with the fundamentals of religious liberty and freedom of conscience and can only breed discord and suspicion. Such an approach is unacceptable to any self-respecting faith community that is proud of its past, vibrant and active in the present, and determined to live on in the future and to continue serving God in its own individual way. Only full appreciation on the part of all of the singular roles, inherent worth, and basic prerogatives of each religious community will help promote the spirit of cooperation among faiths."

24. Marshall McLuhan (1911–80) was a communications theorist. In 1964 he wrote *Understanding Media: The Extensions of Man*, a book on the relationship between media and its creator's ability to connect with viewers and readers.

25. The Pharisees were a sect of Judaism during the Second Temple period. Their views served as the foundation for the teachings in the Talmud.

26. Rabbi Zalman Meshullam Schachter-Shalomi (1924–2014) was a Jewish intellectual and founder of the so-called Jewish Renewal Movement.

27. Minutes of the Jewish Community Council Meeting, April 6, 1967, 1-123, box 7, folder 1, American Jewish Historical Society, New England Archives, Boston.

9. The Orthodox Synagogue and Rabbinate

1. "Why I Left the Rabbinate," *Young Israel Viewpoint* (March/April 1956): 15.

2. Ralph Pelcovitz, "Why I Chose the Pulpit," *Young Israel Viewpoint* (September/October 1954): 36.

3. See Zev Eleff, "From Teacher to Scholar to Pastor: The Evolving Postwar Modern Orthodox Rabbinate," *American Jewish History* 98 (October 2014): 304.

4. By this, Fasman referred to the traditional liturgy for the "greeting of the Sabbath" and the special evening prayers that directly follow it.

5. See John Leech, *Mr. Punch's Book of Love* (London: Educational Book, 1910), 5.

6. Yizkor is the traditional memorial service recited on Jewish holidays by worshippers to remember deceased relatives. Yahrzeit is the Yiddish term that marks the yearly anniversary of the death of a close relative. On this occasion, Jews usually recite the Kaddish prayer and some lead prayer services.

7. Elsewhere in this essay, Fasman noted that "many synagogues have found it advisable to institute a social hour in their community hall after the Friday night Forum."

8. Mary Douglas, "Deciphering a Meal," *Daedalus* 101 (Winter 1972): 66.

9. The Talmud (Rosh Hashanah 25b) records the adage that for his generation, the biblical Jephthah held the same rabbinic standing that Samuel did in his lifetime, although Samuel was indisputably wiser and more knowledgeable than Jephthah.

10. Riskin, of course, was the most exceptional and best known among this group. In a 1971 *Time* article, the magazine wrote that "Rabbi Riskin is a charismatic speaker, flexing his voice like a Bible Belt preacher, punctuating his ideas with his hands. He is also a widely respected Talmudic scholar who stresses that the most important function of the synagogue is to be a *Bet Midrash*—a 'house of study.'" As many as 250 students regularly attended his many adult classes on Jewish law and philosophy.

11. While this was true of Orthodox schools, pastoral counseling was offered much earlier in Reform and Conservative seminaries. See Martin A. Hoenig and Stuart H. Gilbreath, "The Counseling and Pastoral Role of the Rabbi in the American Jewish Community," *Jewish Social Studies* 31 (January 1969): 20–24.

12. Emanuel Rackman, "From Synagogue toward Yeshiva," *Commentary* 21 (April 1956): 356.

13. See, for example, Nosson Scherman, "The Rabbi and the Rosh Yeshiva," *Jewish Observer* 1 (June 1964): 14–16.

10. The State of Orthodox Belief

1. See Albert I. Gordon, *Jews in Suburbia* (Boston: Beacon, 1959), 97–98.

2. Harry Hansen, "Publishing House Finds Huge Sales of Its Books," *Chicago Daily Tribune*, June 3, 1960, G6.

3. See Maurice Lamm, *I Shall Glorify Him: A Study Guide to Herman Wouk's "This Is My God"* (New York: Bloch, 1960).

4. See Hayyim Greenberg, "Yahadut, Emunah, u-Mitzvot Ma'asiyot," Megillot 12 (May 1953): 66.

5. Elizabeth Barrett Browning (1806–61) was an English Victorian poet whose works were well received in Britain and America. See Elizabeth Barrett Browning, *Aurora Leigh* (New York: C. S. Francis, 1857), 275.

6. See Mordecai M. Kaplan, The Future of the American Jew (New York: Macmillan, 1948), 211.

7. All of these examples center on activities based on the Temple in Jerusalem or the courts, institutions that operate exclusively during the daytime.

8. The "counting of the omer" refers to the daily count that traditional Jews begin on Passover and continue until the holiday of Shavuot fifty days later.

9. For areas of Jewish law that require individuals to consume food (e.g., matzah) or drink (e.g., four cups of wine during the Passover Seder), the Halakhah regulates the minimum amount to fulfill the mitzvah based on the measurements listed by the author.

10. The "sotah" is a woman suspected of adultery who, after several important preceding steps, must undergo an ordeal to prove her innocence or guilt. "Mi'un" refers to the procedure in which an underage, fatherless girl who has been married by her mother or brothers may annul her marriage without requiring a formal writ of divorce.

11. In a note at the end of this paragraph, Soloveitchik wrote: "When epistemological doctrine speaks of the a priori nature of mathematics, it is not approaching the subject from a psychogenetic vantage point but rather from the perspective of a symmetric, transcendental outlook concerning the nontemporal nature of mathematical knowledge and its inherent necessity and truth. This approach is particularly exemplified by the transcendental method of [Immanuel] Kant as interpreted by the philosophy of Hermann Cohen."

12. Orthodox Judaism's right-wing sector strongly criticized Rackman for his essay because it posed a grave "danger" when "it is presented to the public." In 1964 Rabbi Joseph Elias (1919–2014) complained that "such an approach, in effect, does away with the immutability of Halachah. Torah law will have to change with the times, in order to make sure that the purpose of the Creator will be attained under the changing historical conditions."

13. Rackman reproduced excerpts from a letter sent to him by Soloveitchik, who was responding to an earlier draft of Rackman's 1954 essay. See Joseph B. Soloveitchik, *Community, Covenant, and Commitment: Selected Letters and*

Communications, ed. Nathaniel Helfgot (Jersey City: Ktav, 2005), 273–78. Portions of Soloveitchik's letter not included in Rackman's original essay are added within brackets.

14. The Mishnah recorded in Shabbat 73a refers to thirty-nine categories of "work" that observant Jews do not perform on the Sabbath.

15. In 1970, another writer offered a similar quip but also included Rabbi Joseph Soloveitchik (who resided in Boston) in the joke: "A wag once quipped that stamped on the back of every American yeshivah semichah certificate is Rabbi Moshe Feinstein's telephone number for just such emergencies. Perhaps for Y.U. musmachim it is a Boston number."

16. See Moshe Feinstein, *Iggerot Moshe* (New York, 1974), 6:91.

17. Yehuda Parnes, "Torah u-Madda and Freedom of Inquiry," *Torah u-Madda Journal* 1 (1989): 70–71. See also Marc B. Shapiro, *The Limits of Orthodox Theology: Maimonides' Thirteen Principles Reappraised* (Oxford: Littman Library, 2004).

11. Responding to Tragedies and Triumphs

1. "The Religious Meaning of the Six-Day War: A Symposium," *Tradition* 10 (Summer 1968): 6.

2. Joseph B. Soloveitchik, "Kol Dodi Dofek," in *Torah u-Melukhah: Al Makom ha-Medinah be-Yahadut*, ed. Simon Federbush (Jerusalem: Mosad ha-Rav Kook, 1961), 11–41.

3. See Norman Lamm, "Tisha B'av Today," *Jewish Life* 23 (July/August 1956): 44–51.

4. See Charles Selengut, "Between Tradition and Modernity," *Midstream* 39 (January 1993): 12.

5. Jonathan Mark, "The Greenberg-Kahane Debate: Crimes of Passion," *Long Island Jewish World*, February 12, 1988, 8–9.

6. Vladimir Jabotinsky, *The Story of the Jewish Legion*, trans. Samuel Katz (New York: Bernard Ackerman, 1945), 63.

7. Ze'ev "Vladimir" Jabotinsky (1880–1940) was the founder of the Jewish Self-Defense Organization in Odessa and emerged as the leading ideologue for the Revisionist Zionist Movement. Kahane credited Jabotinsky's writings for inspiring his right-wing politics and the need for an armed self-defense organization to serve Jews.

8. Theodor Herzl (1860–1904) was an Austrian journalist and the leading voice of Political Zionism in the later stages of his life. In 1897 Herzl convened the First Zionist Congress and established the World Zionist Organization that set in motion events that led to the founding of the State of Israel.

9. Greenberg referred here to the immediate post-Holocaust period.

10. In Greenberg's view, the first and second stages closed with the destruction of the various Jewish temples in Jerusalem.

11. See Irving Greenberg, "Cloud of Smoke, Pillar of Fire: Judaism, Christianity, and Modernity after the Holocaust," in *Auschwitz: Beginning of a New Era? Reflections on the Holocaust*, ed. Eva Fleischner (New York: Ktav, 1977), 43.

12. In a note found in the original text, Greenberg stressed: "The term 'broken covenant' must be properly understood. A broken covenant may still exercise a powerful magnetism. While its brokenness reflects the wound inflicted on the covenantal people and the damage done to the credibility of hope and redemption, paradoxically enough the shattering also witnesses to the profound bond between the covenant and the Jewish people. The covenant shares Jewish fate; the Torah is not insulated from Jewish suffering. Thus its brokenness makes the covenant more adequate insofar as it relates more totally to the human condition. This helps account for the extraordinary pull it exerts on this generation of Jews. Elsewhere, I have cited Rabbi Nachman of Bratislav's famous dictum that 'nothing is so whole as a broken heart' and I argued that, after the Holocaust, 'no faith is so whole as a broken faith.' By this logic, no covenant is so complete as a broken covenant."

13. See Babylonian Talmud, Shabbat 88a.

14. See Joseph B. Soloveitchik, "Lonely Man of Faith," *Tradition* 7 (Summer 1965): 23–30.

15. In 1937 the Palestine Royal Commission (known as the Peel Commission) concluded that the British Mandate of Palestine was unsustainable and that the area should be partitioned, thereby offering Jews a chance at national sovereignty.

16. The Jewish National Fund (Keren Kayemet) was founded in 1901 to purchase and develop land in Palestine. In 1908 the Jewish Agency opened in Jaffa to represent Jewish interests in Palestine to the governing Turkish authorities.

17. Yom Ha-Zikaron is the national day of remembrance of Israeli soldiers and victims of terror that falls on the Hebrew date 4 Iyar. It directly precedes Yom Ha-Atzma'ut, Israel Independence Day. This day is observed on 5 Iyar and commemorates Prime Minister David Ben-Gurion's (1886–1973) public reading of the Israeli Declaration of Independence in 1948. Yom Yerushalayim, Jerusalem Day, is an Israeli holiday that commemorates the reunification of Jerusalem on the Hebrew date 28 Iyar 1967.

18. During the 1960s through the 1980s, many Jews recited a prayer over an additional fourth matzah at their Passover Seder table in solidarity with Jews suffering in the Soviet Union.

19. In 1964 activists founded the American Jewish Conference on Soviet Jewry to establish firmer lines of contact with U.S. politicians.

20. In 1959 the Israeli government established Holocaust Remembrance Day on the Hebrew date 27 Nissan, the supposed anniversary of the Warsaw Ghetto Uprising (1943).

21. Note that "Negro" was a typical description of African Americans in this period and not yet viewed as a politically incorrect designation.

22. A 1968 survey of Orthodox rabbis revealed that most held a more moderate position. They supported "de-escalation" of the American effort but did not go as far as Soloveichik had in describing U.S. participation as "unjust."

23. In contrast, Michael Wyschogrod (1928–2015) argued in 1966 that there was a "Jewish interest" in the Vietnam War. Specifically, the Orthodox intellectual noted Jewish opposition to communism and the Soviet Union's negative stance toward Israel.

24. Charles S. Liebman, "The Orthodox Rabbi and Vietnam," *Tradition* 9 (Spring 1968): 30.

25. See, for example, Zev Eleff, "Brown v. Board: An Orthodox Cause?" *Jewish Action* 75 (Winter 2014): 56–62.

12. The Orthodox Family

1. Joseph Grunblatt, "Sex Questions and Tz'niuth," *Jewish Life* 27 (August 1960): 33.

2. See Isaac Alon, "The Problem of Birth Control in Light of the Halakhah," *Ha-Doar*, December 16, 1960, 105.

3. See J. David Bleich, *Contemporary Halakhic Problems* (New York: Ktav, 1977), 1:112–15.

4. Israel Cohen, *Jewish Life in Modern Times* (London: Methuen, 1914), 40.

5. Stanley R. Brav, *Marriage and the Jewish Tradition* (New York: Philosophical Library, 1951), 98–99.

6. Rabbi Isser Yehudah Unterman (1886–1976) served as the Ashkenazi Chief Rabbi of Israel from 1964 through 1973. Known as a moderate, Unterman spent much time discussing and writing about Jewish marriage and divorce laws.

7. Mary Scharlieb, "Birth Control," *British Medical Journal* 2 (July 16, 1921): 93.

8. J. David Bleich, "Tay-Sachs Disease," *Tradition* 13 (Summer 1972): 145–48.

9. In his treatment on the subject, Bleich wrote: "Blood testing programs as a screening method for the identification of carriers of Tay-Sachs disease are certainly to be encouraged. However, sensitivity to the dictates of Halakhah, which precludes both abortion and a sterile union, would indicate that the most propitious time for such screening is childhood or early adolescence. Early awareness of a carrier state, particularly when determination can be made on a mass scale and accompanied by a public information campaign, would contribute greatly to alleviating the gravity of the situation."

10. Rabbi Dr. Moshe D. Tendler (b. 1926) is a leading rabbinical scholar at RIETS and Bella Tendler Professor of Jewish Medical Ethics and Professor of Biology at Yeshiva College. He is also the son-in-law of leading halakhist Rabbi Moshe Feinstein.

11. In 1950 the Israeli Chief Rabbinate led by Rabbi Yitzhak Herzog (1888–1959) and Rabbi Ben-Zion Uziel (1880–1953) banned polygamy. In the 1960s Sephardic Chief Rabbi Yitzhak Nissim (1896–1981) worked to standardize marriage and divorce practices in Israel.

12. Rackman meant the period of the teaching and editing of the Mishnah in the first two centuries of the Common Era.

13. In 1980 New York passed the so-called Get Bill that prevented state courts from entering into a judgment on civil annulments or divorces if there exist "barriers to remarriage" for either spouse. The law was revised by the state legislature in 1992.

14. See Sarah Silver Bunim, "Religious and Secular Factors of Role Strain in Orthodox Jewish Mothers" (PhD diss., Yeshiva University, 1986), 172.

15. See David Singer, "Emanuel Rackman: Gadfly of Modern Orthodoxy," *Modern Judaism* 28 (May 2008): 140.

13. From Rebbetzin to Rabbah

1. See Elicia Brown, "Mahawhat? A Rabbi by Any Other Name," *Jewish Week*, April 10, 2009, 50

2. See Darren Kleinberg, "Orthodox Women (Non-)Rabbis," *CCAR Journal* 59 (Spring 2012): 80–99.

3. See Blu Greenberg, "Will There Be Orthodox Women Rabbis?" *Judaism* 33 (Winter 1984): 23–33.

4. Israel Goldstein (1896–1986) was rabbi of B'nai Jeshurun in New York and served as president of the New York Board of Jewish Ministers. He was an

ardent Zionist and one of the leading voices of the Conservative Rabbinical Assembly in the interwar era.

5. In the 1840s Douglas William Jerrold published a series of comics entitled "Mrs. Caudle's Curtain Lectures" in the British magazine *Punch*. The collection consists of more than thirty "nagging" lectures that Jerrold's Mrs. Caudle directed toward her husband. The popular series was later published in book form.

6. In Yiddish, an *unterführer* is the person who leads the bride to the wedding canopy and subsequently escorts the bride and groom to a private room directly after the marriage ceremony.

7. Elsewhere in her essay, Gerstein wrote that at the beginning of her marriage she had read Rebekah Kohut's *My Portion* (1925). Her conclusion alluded to this point.

8. Eleanor Roosevelt (1884–1962) held a very public profile as First Lady of the United States. The wife of Franklin Delano Roosevelt (1882–1945), Eleanor Roosevelt remained a prominent activist throughout her lifetime. In addition, women invoked Roosevelt's image and legacy to further their feminine causes.

9. From 1939 until 1999, the United Jewish Appeal served as the umbrella organization for local Jewish federations and philanthropic organizations.

10. Nechama Leibowitz (1905–97) was a renowned Bible scholar and Israeli professor. A prolific writer and popular teacher, she mentored several generations of male and female Orthodox scholars.

11. Shira Milgrom (b. 1951) is rabbi of Congregation Kol Ami in White Plains, New York. Throughout her career, Milgrom has remained a prominent voice for Jewish feminism.

12. Daniel Held, "Welcoming Women into Religious Leadership," *Canadian Jewish News*, May 9, 2013, 21.

13. "Opinion: What Tradition," *Bill613*, April 7, 2013, http://www.bill613.com /opinion/opinion-shaar-hashomayim-congregation (accessed Sept. 15, 2014).

14. Rabbi David Hartman (1931–2013) was a scholar and philosopher. In 1971 he founded the pluralistic Shalom Hartman Institute to offer advanced education to scholars, rabbis, and Jewish educators.

15. "Haredi" (literally, to tremble) refers to the Ultra-Orthodox sector of Judaism.

16. Joseph Stein, *Fiddler on the Roof: Based on Shalom Aleichem's Stories* (New York: Crown, 1964), 9.

17. In addition to Finegold, the inaugural graduating class of Yeshivat Maharat included Ruth Balinsky Friedman (b. 1985) and Abby Brown Scheier (b. 1978). Friedman serves on the clergy of the National Synagogue in Washington DC and Scheier is a Jewish educator in Montreal.

18. "RCA Statement Regarding Recent Developments at Yeshivat Maharat," May 7, 2013. Available at http://www.rabbis.org/news/article.cfm?id=105753 (accessed December 29, 2014).

19. Elsewhere in his sermon, Scheier compared his congregation's efforts to other pathbreaking initiatives in Jewish history. Among those he included Sarah Schenirer's (1883–1935) founding of Bais Yaakov in Poland and Dr. Tonya and Rabbi Joseph Soloveitchik's establishment of the coeducational Maimonides School in Boston.

20. Jonathan Mark, "Reassessing an Experiment," *Jewish Week*, May 26, 2000, 8.

21. See Anne Cohen, "As Maharats Cheer Milestone, Split over Women's Role Widens among Orthodox," *Forward*, June 28, 2013, 1, and Uriel Heilman, "So You've Decided to Become a Rabbi," Jewish Telegraphic Agency, March 14, 2014.

14. Sliding to the Right and to the Left

1. Levi Yitzhak Ha-Yerushalmi, "Sihah me-Yuhedet im ha-Rav Yosef Dov Soloveitchik," *Ma'ariv*, October 28, 1977, 25.

2. See Jeffrey S. Gurock, "The Winnowing of American Orthodoxy," in *Approaches to Modern Judaism*, ed. Marc Lee Raphael (Chico: Scholars Press, 1984), 2:41–53.

3. See Robert Gordis, "'Unobservant,' 'Modern,' and Orthodox Jews," *Judaism* 30 (Summer 1981): 384.

4. Norman Lamm, "Some Comments on Centrist Orthodoxy," *Tradition* 22 (Fall 1986): 1–12.

5. See "Centrist: Between the 'Right Wing' and Whom?" *Jewish Observer* 17 (April 1984): 34–35.

6. "Jewish Communal Affairs," *American Jewish Year Book* 90 (1990): 274.

7. Jonathan Mark, "Modern Orthodox Rabbis Claim Assault from RCA Right Wing," *Jewish Week*, July 13, 1990, 4.

8. Irving Greenberg, "Fighting for the Soul of Orthodoxy," *Jewish Week*, July 13, 1990, 20.

9. Mark, "Modern Orthodox Rabbis Claim Assault from RCA Right Wing," 29. See also Jonathan Mark, "Yeshiva U.'s Lamm: A Rabbi under Siege," *Jewish Week*, August 18, 1989, 24.

10. Greenberg, "Fighting for the Soul of Orthodoxy," 20.

11. See "Approaching the Avos—Through Up-Reach or Drag-Down?" *Jewish Observer* 24 (March 1991): 48–51. See also Shlomo Riskin, *Confessions of a Biblical Commentator: The Rights—and Wrongs—of Individual Interpretations in Biblical Exegesis* (Efrat: Ohr Torah Stone, 1997).

12. See Joseph B. Soloveitchik, "The Lonely Man of Faith," *Tradition* 7 (Summer 1965): 5–67. "Frum" is Yiddish for fervently religious.

13. Actually, Yeshiva University president Samuel Belkin explained "synthesis" in very different terms. To him, Jewish and secular knowledge were independent spheres, never meant to interact with each other. See Samuel Belkin, "Synthesis," *Gesher* 1 (June 1963): 3.

14. In 1986 Rabbi Norman Lamm also adopted "Centrist Orthodox Judaism," albeit with some hesitation: "We seem to be suffering from a terminological identity crisis. We now call ourselves 'Centrist Orthodoxy.' There was a time, not too long ago, when we referred to ourselves as 'Modern Orthodox.' Others tell us that we should call ourselves simply 'Orthodox,' without any qualifiers, and leave it to the other Orthodox groups to conjure up adjectives for themselves. I agree with the last view in principle, but shall defer to the advocates of 'Centrist Orthodoxy.'" See Lamm, "Some Comments on Centrist Orthodoxy," 1.

15. At another RCA conference held a few months later, in May 1984, Klaperman reiterated his position, decrying "pressures upon us from the so-called right wing. We cannot constantly be threatened that if we do not follow their line completely we will be rebuffed."

16. Ari L. Goldman (b. 1949) served as religion writer for the *New York Times* and later as professor of journalism at Columbia University. His uncle is Rabbi Norman Lamm.

17. Ari L. Goldman, "Jewish Moderate Urges Believers to Take Stand," *New York Times*, March 24, 1988, A16.

18. This is the opening of one of the blessings in the thrice-daily traditional Jewish liturgy.

19. In 1987 Orthodox Jews in North Teaneck founded a synagogue association that evolved into Congregation Keter Torah, sometimes known as the Roemer Synagogue. The congregation's synagogue building is located on Roemer Avenue.

20. In 2000 Lanner's wife divorced her husband, thereby empowering a number of witnesses of Lanner's behavior who had remained silent out of fear that "any negative publicity before the divorce proceedings were complete may

have jeopardized its resolution." The new testimony prompted the watershed article on Lanner. See Gary Rosenblatt, "Stolen Innocence," *Jewish Week*, June 23, 2000, 1.

21. Founded in 1972, the Frisch School is a coeducational Orthodox high school in Paramus NJ.

22. In 1987 Lanner attempted to break up the engagement of Hiller's younger brother, who was battling cancer. Jonah Hiller (1965–91) confronted Lanner. In response, Lanner attacked Hiller with a knife and cut him in the neck and arm. Jonah Hiller was married soon thereafter. He died three years later.

23. See Cathryn Jakobson, "The New Orthodox," *New York Magazine*, November 17, 1986, 52–60. The article focused on the popularity of Lincoln Square Synagogue on New York's Upper West Side.

24. Founded in 1927, Yeshivah of Flatbush is a coeducational Modern Orthodox day school in Brooklyn.

25. In 1966 the Orthodox Jewish Scientists published an article on Orthodox Judaism and Evolution, and much has been written on this subject since then. See L. M. Spetner, "A New Look on the Theory of Evolution," *Proceedings of the Association of Orthodox Jewish Scientists* 1 (1966): 79–85.

26. However, not everyone in this camp agreed with Lookstein's position on ecumenism. Two years earlier, Rabbi Shubert Spero (b. 1923), a member of the so-called Centrist group, published an essay that criticized Reform and Conservative rabbis for expecting full toleration from Orthodox Jews.

27. See Avraham Yitzhak Kook, *Ma'amrei ha-Re'iyah* (Jerusalem: Keren Golda Katz, 1984), 1:149–50.

28. See Paul Eidelberg, "The Torah vs. the Social 'Sciences,'" *Jewish Press*, May 13, 1988, 18.

29. In 1986 President Norman Lamm launched the Torah U'Mada Project to fill the "absence of clear lines of demarcation" of Yeshiva University's motto and philosophy. Lamm appointed Rabbi Jacob J. Schacter (b. 1950) the director of the initiative. Among the Project's activities was a lecture series on Torah u'Madda. Nearly all of the presenters were sympathetic to the cause, but a few offered some limitations. See, for example, Ahron Soloveichik, *Logic of the Heart, Logic of the Mind: Wisdom and Reflections on Topics of Our Times* (Jerusalem: Genesis Jerusalem Press, 1991), 35–60.

30. For more than forty years, Soloveitchik commuted from his hometown, Boston, to Yeshiva University in New York. The school supplied the renowned teacher with a private apartment in one of the dormitory buildings.

31. In other words, Bronspigel claimed that his teacher devoted most of his time to the Talmud and its classical commentaries and codes.

32. The Shema prayer recited twice daily commences with the declaration "Shema Yisrael," Hear O Israel, and concludes with the affirmation "Ehad," that God is "One."

33. Throughout the twentieth century, Grossinger's Catskill Resort Hotel in Upstate New York was the iconic vacation resort for kosher eating and other Jewish accommodations.

34. Comedian Johnny Carson (1925–2005) was the host of the very popular *Tonight Show*. He led the program from 1962 until 1992.

35. Literally, "Glatt Kosher" refers to kosher meat from animals with smooth lungs. However, the term has evolved to indicate higher standards of kosher products.

36. Bernstein asked five senior scholars at RIETS to address his question. They included Rabbis Nisson Lipa Alpert (1927–86), Abba Bronspiegel, Mordechai Willig, Yehuda Parnes, and Hershel (Zvi) Schachter (b. 1941). In a subsequent meeting of the RCA's executive committee, an embattled Bernstein explained that he posed the question as an "individual" and not "in the name of the RCA."

37. Hakafot, literally, "circuits" or "laps," refers to the dancing that takes place on the Simhat Torah holiday that circumnavigates the bima at the center of the room.

38. This refers to the repetition of the major portion of the traditional liturgy, the Kaddish recitation and the section of the liturgy that is said aloud responsively by the prayer leader and the other worshippers.

39. Rabbi Moshe ben Nahman (1194–1270) was a major Spanish rabbinic scholar. In addition to his kabbalistic writing, Nahmanides wrote commentaries on the Talmud and treatises on Jewish law. He also authored a major commentary to the Pentateuch. The above reference refers to his commentary on Deut. 12:30.

40. See Makkot 23a.

41. Previously Bernstein had served as president of the RCA from 1972 to 1974. In all, Bernstein served as president of the rabbinical body three times. To date, no other president has served for more than a single term.

42. See Zvi (Hershel) Schachter, "Tzei Likha bi-Ikvei ha-Tzon," *Beit Yitzchak* 17 (1985): 118–34.

43. The unpublished responsum was written by Feinstein (with the assistance of his grandson) in 1983. Feinstein ruled in favor of women's prayer groups on a

theoretical basis, when they were conducted "for the sake of heaven." However, he judged that the ones he knew of were "not for this purpose, rather
the desire comes out of a rebellion against God and His Torah" and is therefore "forbidden."

44. In fact, few Modern Orthodox rabbis supported the movement at this time. The
exceptions were Rabbis Avi Weiss and Saul Berman of New York.

45. See Yaacov Amitai, "Sanctity and Self-Expression," *Jewish Observer* 18 (February 1985): 23–25.

46. Rabbi Hershel Schachter is one of the leading rabbinic scholars at Yeshiva
University and serves as the head of RIETS's Marcos and Adina Katz Kollel.
A prolific writer, Schachter has authored a number of books on the teachings
and thoughts of his mentor, Rabbi Joseph Soloveitchik.

47. The writer rejected the accusation that her program was "feminist" or in
line with the "Conservative Movement." Elsewhere, Haut told a newspaper reporter, "I'm sorry, I can't help what it looks like. If we wanted that, we
could go to Conservative shuls. We're doing this precisely because we want
to remain within *halacha*."

48. See Larry Cohler, "Orthodox Women Fume at Rabbis," *Jerusalem Post*, September 11, 1985, 1.

49. In the early 1980s, the Conservative Movement was divided on whether or
not to ordain women at the Jewish Theological Seminary. The vast majority
of the Talmud faculty was opposed to the decision, while other leading Conservative rabbinic leaders and laypeople were in favor of the change.

50. The "Conservative" designation was soon dropped. In 1990 an "overwhelming majority" voted to change the organization's name to the Union for Traditional Judaism.

51. At the time of Weiss's remarks, there was much talk within the Union for
Traditional Conservative Judaism about founding a rabbinical school. In
1990 the organization established the Institute of Traditional Judaism as a
"bridge seminary" and reestablished the "center" of American Judaism. In
1999 Weiss founded Yeshivat Chovevei Torah as an Orthodox rabbinical
school.

52. On this poem written in the early 1980s, see Merle Feld, *A Spiritual Life: A
Jewish Feminist Journey* (Albany: State University of New York Press, 1999),
243–47.

53. On Lilith and her many interpreters and mythic transformations, see Ilana
Schwartzman, "Lilith from the Pre-Biblical and Biblical Periods until Today"
(rabbinic thesis, Hebrew Union College, 2007).

54. E. J. Kessler, "Edah Conference Claims Legacy of Rav Soloveitchik," *Forward*, February 19, 1999, 3.

55. Matthew Arnold (1822–88) was an acclaimed Victorian poet and literary critic in England.

56. John Milton (1608–74) was an English poet and political critic. The quotation above is derived from Milton's *Areopagitica*, a polemical tract published in 1644 in defense of freedom of speech.

57. Soloveitchik hailed from a rabbinic family that achieved much esteem as the leading scholars of Brest-Litovsk, a Belarusian city known in Yiddish as "Brisk." Later on, Soloveitchik studied at the University of Berlin, where he earned a PhD.

58. "Hazal" is a Hebrew acronym that refers to the sages of the Mishnah and Talmud.

59. In 1670 philosopher Barukh Spinoza (1632–77) anonymously published his *Tractatus Theologico-Politicus*, a controversial philosophical tract that challenged the authority of the Bible. Spinoza meant for this work to establish the foundations of his worldview. Lichtenstein's reference to this tract was meant to underscore the total viewpoint of his father-in-law, rather than to imply anything heretical about Soloveitchik's philosophies.

60. Rabbi Eugene Korn (b. 1947) is a noted scholar and writer in Israel. Much of his work concerns Jewish-Christian relations. He is academic director of the Center for Jewish-Christian Understanding and Cooperation in Efrat, Israel. In 1999 Korn served as adjunct professor of Jewish thought in the program for Christian-Jewish Studies at Seton Hall University.

61. Rona Hirsch, "A Movement without a Leader," *Baltimore Jewish Times*, December 1, 1995, 20.

62. See Norman Lamm, *Seventy Faces: Articles of Faith* (Hoboken: Ktav, 2002), 1:1.

63. Jonathan Sacks, *Community of Faith* (London: Peter Halban, 1995), 109.

15. Reconsidering Modern Orthodox Judaism

1. Richard Joel, "Twenty-First Century Judaism," *Sh'ma* 33 (February 2003): 13.

2. Shlomo Zuckier, "Kelei Kodesh and Lay Kodesh: An Interview with President Richard M. Joel," *Kol Hamevaser* 5 (September 27, 2011): 6.

3. See Menachem Penner, "Open to Embracing Jews; Open to Embracing Mesorah," *Chavrusa* 48 (June 2014): 15–17.

4. The Frumteens.com Moderator posted this message on his message board on November 15, 2004.

5. The recent rise of women's leadership in the synagogue has moved at least one leading rabbinic figure within the Modern Orthodox community to question the propriety of maintaining Rabbi Soloveitchik's position. In August 2015 Rabbi Mordechai Willig caused much commotion when he published an online essay that stated: "the inclusion of Talmud in curricula for all women in Modern Orthodox schools needs to be reevaluated." Willig did not deny Soloveitchik's ruling but wondered aloud whether it should still be followed. See http://www.torahweb.org/torah/2015/parsha/rwil_ekev.html (accessed September 13, 2015).

6. The "Bring Wisdom to Life" motto was introduced at Yeshiva University shortly after Richard Joel succeeded Lamm as president of the school in 2003.

7. Shortly before the close of Yeshivat Rambam, the nearby Beth Tfiloh Dahan Community School told the Rambam parents that it would "consider opening another class in various grades to accommodate Rambam students who might be a good match for the school."

8. In response, one letter writer wrote the following in the subsequent week's edition of the newspaper: "Dr. Gary Bauman's grief caused by the closure of Yeshivat Rambam does not justify his hateful speech toward those who are more Orthodox than he in culture or observance. It is surprising that the *Jewish Times* would print such biased speech. Would his comments have been printed had he written about people with black skin instead of people with black hats?"

9. The writer refers to Rabbi Mordecai Kaplan's *Judaism as a Civilization* (1934) and then Zionist writings of Asher Zvi Hirsch Ginsberg (1856–1927), more commonly known by his pen name, Ahad Ha'am.

10. Rabbi Kenneth Brander (b. 1962) is vice president of University and Community Life at Yeshiva University and rabbi emeritus of the Boca Raton Synagogue. Nechama Price (b. 1980) is director of Stern College's Graduate Program in Advanced Talmudic Studies. She is a certified Yoetzet Halachah, a female advisor on Jewish laws pertaining to family purity.

11. Samuel G. Freedman, *Jew vs. Jew: The Struggle for the Soul of American Jewry* (New York: Simon & Schuster, 2000), 226.

12. Elie Holzer (b. 1962) is a practice-based philosopher of Jewish education, senior lecturer at Bar Ilan University, and co-president of Shma Kolenu: The Center for Prayer and Community.

13. See Mayer Twersky, "Halakhic Values and Halakhic Decisions: Rav Soloveitchik's Pesak Regarding Women's Prayer Groups," *Tradition* 32 (Spring 1998): 5–18, and Moshe Meiselman, "The Rav, Feminism, and Public Policy: An Insider's

Overview," *Tradition* 33 (Fall 1998): 5–30. The authors of both articles are right-ward-leaning students of the Rav. The former is Rabbi Soloveitchik's grandson.

14. In February 2014 the RCA released a seven-page responsum authored by Rabbi Hershel Schachter forbidding attendance at a "partnership minyan." Much of Schachter's rationale was similar to the reasoning he offered in his 1984 responsum on women's prayer groups.

15. See Aryeh Frimer and Dov Frimer, "Women, *Keri'at ha-torah,* and *Aliyyot,*" *Tradition* 46 (Winter 2013): 67–238.

16. See Mendel Shapiro, "*Qeri'at ha-torah* by Women: A Halakhic Analysis," *Edah Journal* 1 (Sivan 2001): 1–52.

17. In 2015 Rabbi Heshie Billet (b. 1949) cautioned that "it would be an error to launch a crusade against these minyanim. This is not a non-Orthodox ven-ture. We should not lose sight of the fact that, while the people involved in these minyanim may be mistaken, they are primarily Orthodox Jews com-mitted to halakhic Judaism. They have chosen their *posekim* and act accord-ingly. They deserve to be seriously critiqued but not delegitimized."

18. See Avraham Weiss, "Open Orthodoxy! A Modern Orthodox Rabbi's Creed," *Judaism* 46 (Fall 1997): 409–21.

19. Yeshayahu Leibowitz (1903–94) was a professor of science at Hebrew Uni-versity and a major Israeli intellectual. Despite his training and professional career as a scientist, Leibowitz became known for his outspokenness on Israeli politics and philosophy of Jewish law.

20. See Jack Wertheimer, "Can Modern Orthodoxy Survive?" *Mosaic,* August 3, 2014.

21. Simcha Krauss (b. 1937) was a leading rabbinic figure in Queens, New York. In June 2014 Krauss established the International Beit Din to think "cre-atively" about Jewish divorce and annulment to free agunot from their recal-citrant husbands.

22. Marc Angel (b. 1945) is the rabbi emeritus of Shearith Israel in New York and a former president of the Rabbinical Council of America.

23. On May 27, 2014, Rabbi Yaakov Perlow (b. 1931) addressed an Agudath Israel dinner. In his remarks, Perlow, the leading rabbinic figure of the organization, warned of the growing influence of YCT rabbis, a group he dubbed "heretics."

24. See Norman Lamm, "Faith and Doubt," *Tradition* 9 (Spring/Summer 1967): 14–51, and Eliezer Berkovits, "Orthodox Judaism in a World of Revolution-ary Transformations," *Tradition* 7 (Summer 1965): 68.

25. Luis Lugo et al., *A Portrait of Jewish Americans: Findings from a Pew Research Center Survey of U.S. Jews* (Washington DC: Pew Research Center, 2013), 71.

26. Jacob J. Schacter, "The Pew Report: What Really Matters," *Jewish Action* 74 (Summer 2014): 58. Schacter was the longtime rabbi of the Jewish Center in Manhattan and is currently University Professor of Jewish History and Jewish Thought and Senior Scholar at the Center for the Jewish Future at Yeshiva University.

Author's Note on Sources

In 1973 Rabbi Gilbert Rosenthal lamented that "regrettably, Orthodox Judaism in the United States has not yet found its historian" (*Four Paths to One God*, 26). In that time, historians of American Jews desired to trace their religious and cultural legacies back to their earliest incarnations in the United States. Most of these writers did not identify as Orthodox Jews and were uninterested in that sort of history. They probably also agreed with the sentiments of one noted author: for Orthodox Judaism "there is little to say. It has survived—barely" (Glazer, *American Judaism*, 142). However, Rosenthal's dreary survey of the historical literature was not entirely true. In the 1940s, Hyman Grinstein (1945) and Jeremiah Berman (1947) wrote on Orthodox Judaism. Abraham Karp took time out from his busy schedule as a congregational rabbi to write an essential and substantial article on Orthodox immigrants to America (1955). Likewise, Reform Congregation Keneseth Israel offered its pulpiteer, Rabbi Bertram Korn, ample time to devote toward his studies in American Jewish history, a goodly portion of which concentrated on Orthodox Judaism in the nineteenth century (1954, 1967). In 1962 Harvard-trained Moses Rischin published the most comprehensive book on New York's Eastern European Jewish immigrants and the Orthodox faith they brought with them from the Old World. Also, a number of Yeshiva University graduate students wrote biographies of important nineteenth-century Orthodox rabbis or institutional histories of Orthodox organizations, in fulfillment of their graduate studies (see Markovitz, "Henry Pereira Mendes"; Nussenbaum, "Champion of Orthodox Judaism"; and Simon, "Samuel Myer Isaacs"). In fact, a number of these theses were later published as monographs (e.g., Klaperman, *Story of Yeshiva University*, and Rothkoff, *Bernard Revel*). Still, it was certainly the case that Orthodox Judaism in the United States had not yet received the same sort of systematic treatment that was afforded to its Reform and Conservative counterparts (e.g., Davis, *Emergence of Conservative Judaism*, and Philipson, *Reform Movement in Judaism*).

A moment of maturation occurred in the late 1970s. In large measure, the unprecedented interest in the historical study of Orthodox Jews was due to the religious revival of this rejuvenated community. In 1979 Nathan Kaganoff committed an entire issue—six articles in total—of the American Jewish Historical Society's quarterly journal to the subject of Orthodox Judaism in America ("Introduction," 157). This was a project that had long been on Kaganoff's mind. Three years earlier, the editor of the journal had lamented that this field had "been almost completely untouched" ("American Rabbinic Books," 235). He therefore seized the opportunity in this special edition of *American Jewish History* on the grounds that observers had predicted "that the latter half of the 20th century may witness the blossoming of Orthodoxy in America" ("Introduction," 157).

Soon after, the other major journal on American Jewish history looked to help fill the void of American Orthodox scholarship. Based at Cincinnati's Hebrew Union College, the American Jewish Archives entrusted a special edition of its journal to two promising historians. For this 1983 installment, the editorial reins were handed to Jonathan Sarna, while the nearly one hundred pages were offered to Yeshiva University's Jeffrey Gurock to theorize about the "Resisters and Accommodators" who had shaped the Orthodox rabbinate and the communities they led over the course of the twentieth century. Others contributed lengthy expositions on the Conservative and Reform rabbinates, but it was Gurock's that was described as especially "pathbreaking" and has stood as the seminal article in that edition (Sarna, "Introduction," 92).

In short order, Gurock emerged as the specialist in American Orthodox history, even as he continued to write on other areas of American Jewish history. In truth, Gurock's first book and his articles that had preceded "Resisters and Accommodators" offered new perspectives on New York's Jews and not always the most traditional type (see Gurock, *When Harlem Was Jewish*). Yet, since the appearance of this essay, Gurock has authored more than two dozen scholarly articles focused primary on America's Orthodox Jews, some of which were collected into a single volume (1996). In addition, Gurock published monographs on a history of Yeshiva University, the Orthodox encounters of Mordecai Kaplan, and a synagogue history of the Orthodox Congregation Brith Sholom Beth Israel in Charleston (the Mordecai Kapan biography was coauthored with Jacob J. Schacter). The majority of these works concentrated on the social history of Orthodox Jews after the Eastern European migration in the 1880s. In 2009 Gurock synthesized these works and further developed them with new material as a historical survey on Orthodox Jews in America. (On some changes in perspective offered in Gurock's survey, see his "Rethinking the History of Nonobservance.")

In time, other historians offered their contributions to the growing scholarship on Orthodox Judaism in the United States. To be sure, some writers like Aaron Rakeffet started to produce pertinent work on American Orthodoxy in the 1970s and 1980s. However, the most fruitful period arrived later on. Jenna Weissman Joselit produced two important monographs that threw light on the Orthodox Jewish home and on the changing cultural identities of Orthodox Jews in the interwar era (1990, 1994). In Canada, Ira Robinson produced a series of essays on Orthodox Jewish life (2008). Israeli scholars Menahem Blondheim (1998) and Kimmy Caplan (2002) made good use of sermonic literature to explore the experiences of immigrant rabbis at the turn of the twentieth century, a subject that is at the core of Jonathan Sarna's translation and annotated memoir of Rabbi Moses Weinberger (1981). As well, Caplan (1998) and Jeffrey Shandler (2012) have each produced articles that throw light on the importance of the cantor in Orthodox Jewish life. In another critical area of research, Seth Farber (2004) wrote a history of Maimonides School in Boston, while Gil Graff's (2008) survey of Jewish education contains much information on Orthodox day schools. This was also a topic addressed by Jeffrey Gurock (1989), as was Orthodox Jewry's engagement with Zionism (1998). As well, Yaakov Ariel's article on Shlomo Carlebach and his fringe group (groupies) in the Bay Area is the best treatment on this important topic (2003). As for the "Ultra-Orthodox" enclave, Sue Fishkoff (2003) and Jerome Mintz (1992) wrote on Hasidim while Yoel Finkelman authored several articles on Rabbi Aharon Kotler and his Lakewood yeshiva (2002, 2007).

A popular subject among historians is the long and sometimes painful break between Conservative and Orthodox Judaism. Again, it was Gurock who first explored this topic in a lecture delivered at the University of Michigan (2008). Most recently, Michael Cohen published a monograph on the "parting of the ways" of Orthodoxy and Conservativism (2012), but from the perspective of the latter. Then there is the more focused attention on Modern Orthodox Judaism after World War II. The late Benny Kraut contributed a monograph on the history of Yavneh, the collegiate organization that along with rabbinic elites helped revive Orthodox Judaism in the 1960s (2011). A number of my publications also explore this so-called "golden age" of Modern Orthodox Judaism (2009, 2010, and 2014). (For an assessment of this period in American Orthodox Judaism, see Sacks, *Future Tense*, 210.) From their perch at the American Jewish Committee, researchers Lawrence Grossman (2009, 2010) and David Singer (2006, 2008) have written fine essays on the history of Modern Orthodox Judaism they had observed since childhood. Finally Adam Ferziger has studied, among other themes, Modern Orthodoxy's encounter with the Soviet Jewry and feminist movements (2015). A student of Jacob Katz's sociology of religion school, Ferziger's work offers fresh perspectives viewed from lenses not too often worn by historians of American Jewish history.

Individual synagogue histories are valuable for their attention to the historical details of congregations and their insight into local archives so often unavailable to researchers. In addition to Gurock's book on Charleston's Jews, there is David and Tamara de Sola Pool's on Shearith Israel, the oldest congregation in North

America (1955). Much more recently, Edward Abramson published an interesting work on Lincoln Square Synagogue in New York and his mentor Rabbi Shlomo Riskin (2008).

The history of Orthodox Judaism in the nineteenth century remains understudied. Most of the literature on this topic centers on the Orthodox Jews in Philadelphia. Dianne Ashton (1997), Arthur Kiron (1999), and Lance Sussman (1995) each wrote biographies on the leading figures who shaped Philadelphia's Orthodox community. Other biographers contributed studies on other defenders of Orthodox Judaism in this century, but there is much work to be done in this epoch of American Orthodox Judaism (Moses 1997, Sharfman 1988, and Sherman 1991). Likewise, while a few scholars have studied the transmission of European rabbinic legacies to America (Graff 2011, 2014, Eleff 2012, 2013), there is not much written on the migration of European Orthodox Judaism to the United States, nor is there an abundance of writing on the history of Orthodox Halakhah in the New World (Mintz 2009).

A number of important books and articles were the output of writers whose work usually resides somewhere beyond the direct scope of American Jewish history. The writings of historians David Ellenson (1979), Steven Lowenstein (1989), David Myers (2013), Marc Shapiro (2006), and Haym Soloveitchik (1994) usually concern Judaism in Europe but found occasion to relate their work on Europe's Jews to the Orthodox experience in the New World. In addition, "organization men" like the Rabbinical Council of America's Louis Bernstein (1982), the Orthodox Union's Saul Bernstein (1997), and Yeshiva University's Victor Geller (2003) published institutional histories that offer episodes and data unavailable in other, more scholarly works. Similarly, there is much to be gleaned from popular—if sometimes hagiographical—biographies published by Orthodox presses like ArtScroll (Rosenblum 1993) and Feldheim (Kranzler and Landesman 1998).

In tandem with all this, sociologists have long observed the interesting tendencies and acculturation of America's Orthodox Jews. In 1965 Charles Liebman published a lengthy and highly regarded sociological essay on Orthodox Jews in the United States that is rich with historical material. (For one exceptional case of a sociological study of Orthodox Jews that preceded the Liebman essay, see Polsky, "A Study of Orthodoxy in Milwaukee.") Several years later, Samuel Heilman published an anthropological study of the Orthodox synagogue (1976), and later he produced more ethnographical researches of the Modern Orthodox (1981, 2006) and Ultra-Orthodox communities (1992), as did William Helmreich (1982). (In 1989 Heilman coauthored a quantitative study on Modern Orthodox Jews, *Cosmopolitans and Parochials*, but the work was deeply flawed in its data-gathering.

See Berger, "Modern Orthodoxy in the United States," 261–72.) Shalom Berger's work on the "Year in Israel" (2007) is the only treatment of that subject to date, and the same goes for Etan Diamond's book on the suburbanization of Orthodox Jews (2000). Much of Sylvia Fishman's (1993) and Chaim Waxman's (1989) scholarship will be very useful to students of Orthodox feminism and family life, and Religious Zionism, respectively. And in the area of Orthodox Jewish thought, Reuven Bulka's edited volume (1983) contains a comprehensive bibliography of popular-style articles on this subject and essays that hold important insights on Orthodox Judaism in the United States, as do a number of articles in Yosef Salmon's collection (2006).

Finally, a word on reference works and primary sources: Moshe Sherman's dictionary of Orthodox rabbis and institutions offers students of American Orthodox Judaism important data and bibliographical references (1996). Other encyclopedic works like Jacob Rader Marcus's biographical dictionary (1994) and Yosef Goldman's two volumes on Hebrew printing in the United States (2006) are not specific to Orthodox Judaism but contain invaluable material for study of religiously traditional Jews. Many of the books listed in Goldman's volumes are available for public access at Hebrewbooks.org. Published primary sources are available in the pages of the *American Jewish Year Book* as well as Orthodox-minded periodicals such as *Ha-Pardes, Jewish Life, Jewish Observer,* and *Tradition.* The most extensive collection of unpublished materials can be found at the American Jewish Archives in Cincinnati. The nearby Klau Library of Hebrew Union College holds many English, Hebrew, and Yiddish-language newspapers. The Gershwind-Bennett Isaac Leeser Digital Repository, a project of the University of Pennsylvania's Herbert D. Katz Center for Advanced Judaic Studies, has digitized thousands of valuable letters and correspondences related to Orthodox Judaism in the nineteenth century. Researchers should consider the materials held at the Center for Jewish History, National Orthodox Jewish Archives of the Agudath Israel, and the Archives and Special Collections at Yeshiva University. My own scholarship on Orthodox Judaism in the United States has benefited greatly from these primary sources and the secondary literature reviewed above. No doubt, the merits of this book would be much diminished without the efforts of the scholars and archivists who preceded me.

Selected Bibliography

Abramson, Edward. *Circle in the Square: Rabbi Shlomo Riskin Reinvents the Synagogue.* Jerusalem: Urim, 2008.

Ariel, Yaakov. "Hasidism in the Age of Aquarius: The House of Love and Prayer in San Francisco, 1967–1977." *Religion and American Culture* 13 (Summer 2003): 139–65.

Ashton, Dianne. *Rebecca Gratz: Women and Judaism in Antebellum America.* Detroit: Wayne State University Press, 1997.

Berger, David. "Modern Orthodoxy in the United States: A Review Essay." *Modern Judaism* 11 (May 1991): 261–72.

Berger, Shalom et al. *Flipping Out? Myth or Fact? The Impact of the "Year in Israel."* New York: Yashar Books, 2007.

Berman, Jeremiah J. "The Trend in Jewish Religious Observance in Mid-Nineteenth-Century America." *Publications of the American Jewish Historical Society* 37 (1947): 31–53.

Bernstein, Louis. *Challenge and Mission: The Emergence of the English-Speaking Orthodox Rabbinate.* New York: Shengold, 1982.

Bernstein, Saul. *The Orthodox Union Story: A Centenary Portrayal.* Northvale: Jason Aronson, 1997.

Blondheim, Menahem. "Divine Comedy: The Jewish Orthodox Sermon in America, 1881–1939." In *Multilingual America: Transnationalism, Ethnicity, and the Languages of American Literature,* ed. Werner Sollors, 191–214. New York: New York University Press, 1998.

Bulka, Reuven. *Dimensions of Orthodox Judaism.* New York: Ktav, 1983.

Caplan, Kimmy. *Orthodox Judaism in the New World: Immigrant Rabbis and Preaching in America, 1881–1924.* Jerusalem: Merkaz Zalman Shazar, 2002.

———. "In God We Trust: Salaries and Income of American Orthodox Rabbis, 1881–1924." *American Jewish History* 86 (March 1998): 77–106.

Cohen, Michael R. *The Birth of Conservative Judaism: Solomon Schechter's Disciples and the Creation of an American Religious Movement.* New York: Columbia University Press, 2012.

Davis, Moshe. *The Emergence of Conservative Judaism: The Historical School in Nineteenth-Century America.* Philadelphia: Jewish Publication Society of America, 1963.

Diamond, Etan. *And I Will Dwell in Their Midst: Orthodox Jews in Suburbia.* Chapel Hill: University of North Carolina Press, 2000.

Eleff, Zev. "American Orthodoxy's Lukewarm Embrace of the Hirschian Legacy, 1850–1939." *Tradition* 45 (Fall 2012): 35–53

———. "Between Bennett and Amsterdam Avenues: The Complex American Legacy of Samson Raphael Hirsch." *Tradition* 46 (Winter 2013): 8–27

———. "From Teacher to Scholar to Pastor: The Evolving Postwar Modern Orthodox Rabbinate." *American Jewish History* 98 (October 2014): 289–313.

———. *Living from Convention to Convention: A History of the NCSY, 1954–1980.* Jersey City: Ktav, 2009.

———. "'Viva Yeshiva!' The Tale of the Mighty Mites and the College Bowl." *American Jewish History* 96 (December 2010): 287–305.

Ellenson, David. "A Jewish Legal Decision by Rabbi Bernard Illowy of New Orleans and Its Discussion in Nineteenth-Century Europe." *American Jewish History* 69 (December 1979): 174–95.

Farber, Seth. *An American Orthodox Dreamer: Rabbi Joseph B. Soloveitchik and Boston's Maimonides School.* Hanover: Brandeis University Press, 2004.

Ferziger, Adam S. *Beyond Sectarianism: The Realignment of American Orthodox Judaism.* Detroit: Wayne State University Press, 2015.

Finkelman, Yoel. "An Ideology for American Yeshiva Students: The Sermons of R. Aharon Kotler, 1942–1962." *Journal of Jewish Studies* 58 (Autumn 2007): 314–32.

———. "Haredi Isolation in Changing Environments: A Case Study in Yeshiva Immigration." *Modern Judaism* 22 (February 2002): 61–82.

Fishkoff, Sue. *The Rebbe's Army: Inside the World of Chabad-Lubavitch.* New York: Schocken Books, 2003.

Fishman, Sylvia Barack. *A Breath of Life: Feminism in the American Jewish Community.* New York: Free Press, 1993.

Geller, Victor B. *Orthodoxy Awakens: The Belkin Era and Yeshiva University.* Jerusalem: Urim, 2003.

Glazer, Nathan. *American Judaism.* Chicago: University of Chicago Press, 1957.

Goldman, Yosef. *Hebrew Printing in America, 1735–1926: A History and Annotated Bibliography.* 2 vols. Edited by Ari Kinsberg. Brooklyn: YG Books, 2006.

Graff, Gil. *"And You Shall Teach Them Diligently": A Concise History of Jewish Education in the United States, 1776–2000.* New York: Jewish Theological Seminary of America, 2008.

———. "Toward an Appreciation of the American Legacy of Rabbi Esriel Hildesheimer: The U.S. Rabbinate of Three Hildesheimer Students." *Modern Judaism* 31 (Spring 2011): 167–88.

———. "Giving Voice to 'Torah-true Judaism' in the U.S., 1922–1939: Leo Jung and the Legacy of the Rabbinerseminar." *Modern Judaism* 34 (Spring 2014): 167–87.

Grinstein, Hyman B. *The Rise of the Jewish Community of New York, 1654–1860.* Philadelphia: Jewish Publication Society of America, 1945.

Grossman, Lawrence. "American Orthodoxy in the 1950s: The Lean Years." In *Rav Chesed: Essays in Honor of Rabbi Dr. Haskel Lookstein,* ed. Rafael Medoff, 1:251–69. Jersey City: Ktav, 2009.

———. "The Kippah Comes to America." In *Continuity and Change: A Festschrift in Honor of Irving (Yitz) Greenberg's 75th Birthday,* ed. Steven T. Katz and Steven Bayme, 129–49. Lanham: University Press of America, 2010.

Gurock, Jeffrey S. *American Jewish Orthodoxy in Historical Perspective.* Hoboken: Ktav, 1996.

———. "American Orthodox Organizations in Support of Zionism, 1880–1930." In *Zionism and Religion,* ed. Shmuel Almog, Jehuda Reinharz, and Anita Shapira, 219–34. Hanover: Brandeis University Press, 1998.

———. "From Fluidity to Rigidity: The Religious Worlds of Conservative and Orthodox Jews in Twentieth-Century America." In *American Jewish Identity Politics,* ed. Deborah Dash Moore, 159–206. Ann Arbor: University of Michigan Press, 2008.

———. *The Men and Women of Yeshiva: Higher Education, Orthodoxy, and American Judaism.* New York: Columbia University Press, 1988.

———. *Orthodox Jews in America.* Bloomington: Indiana University Press, 2009.

———. *Orthodoxy in Charleston: Brith Sholom Beth Israel and Orthodox Jewish History.* Charleston: College of Charleston Library, 2004.

———. "The Ramaz Version of American Orthodoxy." In *Ramaz: School, Community, Scholarship, and Orthodoxy,* ed. Jeffrey S. Gurock, 40–82. Hoboken: Ktav, 1989.

———. "Resisters and Accommodators: Varieties of Orthodox Rabbis in America, 1886–1983." *American Jewish Archives Journal* 35 (November 1983): 100–187.

———. "Rethinking the History of Nonobservance as an American Orthodox Jewish Lifestyle." In *New Essays in American Jewish History: Commemorating the Sixtieth Anniversary of the Founding of the American Jewish Archives,* ed. Pamela S. Nadell, Jonathan D. Sarna, and Lance J. Sussman, 305–23. Cincinnati: American Jewish Archives, 2010.

———. *When Harlem Was Jewish.* New York: Columbia University Press, 1979.

Gurock, Jeffrey S., and Jacob J. Schacter. *A Modern Heretic and a Traditional Community: Mordecai M. Kaplan, Orthodoxy, and American Judaism*. New York: Columbia University Press, 1997.

Heilman, Samuel C. *Defenders of the Faith: Inside Ultra-Orthodox Jewry*. New York: Schocken Books, 1992.

———. *Sliding to the Right: The Contest for the Future of American Jewish Orthodoxy*. Berkeley: University of California Press, 2006.

———. "Sounds of Modern Orthodoxy: The Language of Talmud Study." In *Never Say Die! A Thousand Years of Yiddish in Jewish Life and Letters*, ed. Joshua A. Fishman, 227–53. The Hague: Mouton, 1981.

———. *Synagogue Life: A Study in Symbolic Interaction*. Chicago: University of Chicago Press, 1976.

Heilman, Samuel C., and Steven M. Cohen. *Cosmopolitans and Parochials: Modern Orthodox Jews in America*. Chicago: University of Chicago Press, 1989.

Helmreich, William B. *The World of the Yeshiva: An Intimate Portrait of Orthodox Jewry*. New Haven: Yale University Press, 1982.

Joselit, Jenna Weissman. *New York's Jewish Jews: The Orthodox Community in the Interwar Years*. Bloomington: Indiana University Press, 1990.

———. *The Wonders of America: Reinventing Jewish Culture, 1880–1950*. New York: Hill and Wang, 1994.

Kaganoff, Nathan M. "American Rabbinic Books Published in Palestine." In *A Bicentennial Festschrift for Jacob Rader Marcus*, ed. Bertram Wallace Korn, 235–61. New York: Ktav, 1976.

———. "Introduction." *American Jewish History* 69 (December 1979): 157–58.

Karp, Abraham J. "New York Chooses a Chief Rabbi." *Publications of the American Jewish Historical Society* 44 (March 1955): 129–98.

Kiron, Arthur. "Golden Ages, Promised Lands: The Victorian Rabbinic Humanism of Sabato Morais." PhD diss., Columbia University, 1999.

Klaperman, Gilbert. *The Story of Yeshiva University: The First Jewish University in America*. New York: Macmillan, 1969.

Korn, Bertram Wallace. *Eventful Years and Experiences: Studies in Nineteenth-Century American Jewish History*. Cincinnati: American Jewish Archives, 1954.

———. "Isaac Leeser: Centennial Reflections." *American Jewish Archives Journal* 19 (November 1967): 127–41.

Kranzler, David, and Dovid Landesman. *Rav Breuer: His Life and His Legacy*. Jerusalem: Feldheim, 1998.

Kraut, Benny. *The Greening of American Orthodox Judaism: Yavneh in the Nineteen Sixties*. Cincinnati: Hebrew Union College Press, 2011.

Liebman Charles S. "Orthodoxy in American Jewish Life." *American Jewish Year Book 66* (1965): 21–92.

Lowenstein, Steven M. *Frankfurt on the Hudson: The German-Jewish Community of Washington Heights, 1933–1983, Its Structure and Culture.* Detroit: Wayne State University Press, 1989.

Marcus, Jacob Rader. *The Concise Dictionary of American Jewish Biography.* Brooklyn: Carlson, 1994.

Markovitz, Eugene. "Henry Pereira Mendes (1877–1920)." PhD diss., Yeshiva University, 1961.

Mintz, Adam. "Is Coca-Cola Kosher? Rabbi Tobias Geffen and the History of American Orthodoxy." In *Rav Chesed: Essays in Honor of Rabbi Dr. Haskel Lookstein,* ed. Rafael Medoff, 2:75–90. Jersey City: Ktav, 2009.

Mintz, Jerome R. *Hasidic People: A Place in the New World.* Cambridge: Harvard University Press, 1992.

Moses, Jay Henry. "Henry A. Henry: The Life and Work of an American Rabbi, 1849–1869." Rabbinic thesis, Hebrew Union College–Jewish Institute of Religion, 1997.

Myers, David N. "Commanded War: Three Chapters in the 'Military' History of Satmar Hasidism." *Journal of the American Academy of Religion* 81 (June 2013): 311–56.

Nussenbaum, Max Samuel. "Champion of Orthodox Judaism: A Biography of the Reverend Sabato Morais, LLD." PhD diss., Yeshiva University, 1964.

Philipson, David. *The Reform Movement in Judaism.* London: Macmillan, 1907.

Polsky, Howard W. "A Study of Orthodoxy in Milwaukee: Social Characteristics, Beliefs, and Observances." In *The Jews: Social Patterns of an American Group,* ed. Marshall Sklare, 325–35. New York: Free Press, 1958.

Pool, David, and Tamara de Sola. *An Old Faith in the New World: Portrait of Shearith Israel, 1654–1954.* New York: Columbia University Press, 1955.

Rakeffet-Rothkoff, Aaron. *Bernard Revel: Builder of American Jewish Orthodoxy.* Philadelphia: Jewish Publication Society of America, 1972.

———. *Rakafot Aharon: A Collection of Published Scholarship in the Fields of Halakhah and Jewish History.* Jerusalem: Shvut Ami, 1991.

———. *The Silver Era in American Jewish Orthodoxy: Rabbi Eliezer Silver and His Generation.* Jerusalem: Feldheim, 1981.

Rischin, Moses. *The Promised City: New York's Jews, 1870–1914.* Cambridge: Harvard University Press, 1962.

Robinson, Ira. *Translating a Tradition: Studies in American Jewish History.* Boston: Academic Studies Press, 2008.

Rosenblum, Yonason. *Reb Yaakov: The Life and Times of HaGaon Rabbi Yaakov Kamenetsky*. Brooklyn: Mesorah, 1993.

Rosenthal, Gilbert. *Four Paths to One God: Today's Jew and His Religion*. New York: Bloch, 1973.

Rothkoff, Aaron. *Bernard Revel: Builder of American Jewish Orthodoxy*. Philadelphia: Jewish Publication Society of America, 1972.

Sacks, Jonathan. *Future Tense: Jews, Judaism, and Israel in the Twenty-First Century*. New York: Schocken, 2009.

Salmon, Yosef et al. *Orthodox Judaism: New Perspectives*. Jerusalem: Magnes Press, 2006.

Sarna, Jonathan D. "Introduction." *American Jewish Archives Journal* 35 (November 1983): 91–99.

———. *People Walk on Their Heads: Moses Weinberger's Jews and Judaism in New York*. New York: Holmes and Meier, 1981.

Shandler, Jeffrey. "The Sanctification of the Brand Name: The Marketing of Cantor Yossele Rosenblatt." In *Chosen Capital: The Jewish Encounter with American Capitalism*, ed. Rebecca Kobrin, 255–71. New Brunswick: Rutgers University Press, 2012.

Shapiro, Marc B. *Saul Lieberman and the Orthodox*. Scranton: University of Scranton Press, 2006.

Sharfman, Harold. *The First Rabbi: Origins of Conflict between Orthodox and Reform*. Malibu: Pangloss Press, 1988.

Sherman, Moshe. "Bernard Illowy and Nineteenth-Century American Orthodoxy." PhD diss., Yeshiva University, 1991.

———. *Orthodox Judaism in America: A Biographical Dictionary and Sourcebook*. Westport: Greenwood Press, 1996.

Simon, E. Yechiel. "Samuel Myer Isaacs: A Nineteenth-Century Jewish Minister in New York City." PhD diss., Yeshiva University 1974.

Singer, David. "Debating Modern Orthodoxy at Yeshiva College: The Greenberg-Lichtenstein Exchange of 1966." *Modern Judaism* 26 (May 2006): 113–26.

———. "Emanuel Rackman: Gadfly of Modern Orthodoxy." *Modern Judaism* 28 (May 2008): 134–48.

Soloveitchik, Haym. "Rupture and Reconstruction: The Transformation of Contemporary Orthodoxy." *Tradition* 28 (Summer 1994): 64–130.

Sussman, Lance J. *Isaac Leeser and the Making of American Jewry*. Detroit: Wayne State University Press, 1995.

Waxman, Chaim I. *American Aliya: Portrait of an Innovative Migration Movement*. Detroit: Wayne State University Press, 1989.

Index

Page numbers in italic indicate illustrations

abortion, 304–5, 312, 313, 314–15, 316, 322
Abraham (patriarch), 280
Abramson, Edward, 492
abstract concepts and Jewish law, 143, 270–72
Adams, Theodore L., 332–34, 335
adjunta, 447n19
Adler, Cyrus, 141, 464n9
Adler, Nathan Marcus, 465n19
Adler, Samuel, 46, 71, 451n28, 452n37, 453n9, 456n36
Agudath Ha-Rabbonim. *See* Union of Orthodox Rabbis of America
Agudath Israel, 178, 274, 320, 493
agunot, 316–17, 319–20, 322–23, 464n46, 487n21
Ahad Ha'am (pen name), 407, 486n9
Ahawath Chesed, 56–57
Akiva ben Joseph, 193, 469n26
Alexander II, 454n23
Allen, Anna Marks, 24–25, 449n40
Alpert, Nisson Lipa, 379, 483n36
American Hebrew: Alexander Kohut and, 454n19; Jewish Theological Seminary Association and, 65–68; Max Cohen and, 458n26; Orthodoxy and, 98, 130–33, 137, 463n36; potential seminary merge and, 68–73, 455n33
American Jewish Archives, 490, 493
American Jewish Conference on Soviet Jewry, 291, 477n19

American Jewish Historical Society, 489–90
American Jewish History, 489–90
American Jewish Year Book, 173, 352, 493
American Jewry, building, 116–21
amniocentesis, 313, 314
"Am Yisrael Chai" (Carlebach), 299
Angel, Marc, 421, 487n22
annulment, marriage, 316–22, 323, 478n11. *See also* divorce
Anshe Emeth Congregation, 452n30
Anshi Chesed Congregation, 41–43, 45–46, 451–52nn29–30, 452nn36–37
antisemitism, 278, 297, 454n23, 472n21
Ariel, Yaakov, 491
Arnold, Matthew, 368, 393, 485n55
ArtScroll, 492
Ash, Abraham, 82
Ashkenazic disease. *See* Tay Sachs disease
Ashton, Dianne, 492
Association of American Orthodox Congregations, 82
Association of Orthodox Jewish Scientists, 314–15
authority, religious, xxxvi, 27, 30–39, 99–100

bar mitzvah, 79, 81, 198, 229, 232–34, 454n17
Barnwell, William Hazzard, 13, 448n27
bat mitzvah, 229, 231, 232–33

Bauman, Gary, 403–5, 486n8
beards, 23, 449n39
"Be fruitful and multiply," 310–11
Behrman, Samuel Nathaniel, 88–92
"Being Gay in the Modern Orthodox
World" panel, 415
Beirack, Michael, 83
beit din, 161–63, 319–20, 487n21
Beit Midrash Program, 209–10, 210
Belkin, Samuel, 196, 204, 204, 207–9,
481n13
Ben-Ami, Jacob, 89, 457n18
Bene Israel Congregation, 455n30
Berger, Shalom, 493
Berkovits, Eliezer, 171, 292–95, 385–86,
423
Berlin, Naftali Zvi Yehudah, 85–86,
457nn11–12, 457n14
Berman, Jeremiah, 489
Berman, Saul J., 210, 319–22, 349, 391,
411–12, 484n44
Bernstein, Cindy, 401–2
Bernstein, Louis, 377–81, 384, 483n36,
483n41, 492
Bernstein, Saul, 492
Beth El Emeth Congregation, 54, 453n13
Beth Elohim Congregation, 3–4, 447n17,
449n36
Beth Hamedrash L'Torah. See Hebrew
Theological College of Chicago
Beth HaMedrosh Hagadol Congrega-
tion, 164
Beth Jacob Congregation, 85, 166, 457n11
Beth Tfiloh Dahan Community School,
486n7
Bettmann, Bernhard, 455n35
Bible: interpretations of, 145, 268,
465n14; Mosaic origin of, 126–27;
Orthodoxy and, 97–98, 177–78; Pres-
byterianism and, 99; Radical Reform

and, 142; Reform Judaism and, 35–
36, 59, 60, 454n18
Billet, Hershel, 487n17
Birnbaum, Jacob, 296–98
birth control, 304, 310–13, 322
Bleich, J. David, 305, 312–14, 478n9
Blondheim, Menahem, 491
blue laws, 104, 107
Blumenthal, Aaron H., 164, 467n36
B'nai Yeshurun, 453n6, 455n30
Boxer, Harold, 471n14
Brander, Kenneth, 408, 486n10
Brantley, William T., Sr., 13, 448n27
Bread Givers (Yezierska), 86–88
Briggs, Charles, 99, 459n32
Brith Shalom Congregation, 85, 457n11,
490
Bronspigel, Abba, 373–75, 379, 483n31,
483n36
Browning, Elizabeth Barrett, 254, 474n5
Bulka, Reuven, 493
Burstein, Abraham, 107–9
Buttnick, Gwendolyn R., 200–202

Cahan, Abraham, 82–85
Camp Massad, 470–71n13
Camp Moshava, 202–3, 204, 470nn11–12
camps, summer, 202–3
Canadian Jewish News, 344
Caplan, Kimmy, 491
Cardon, Abraham I., 122, 461n15
Cardozo, Isaac Nunes, 6
Carillon, Benjamin Cohen, 27, 28–32
Carlebach, Shlomo, 299, 491
Carvalho, David Nunes, 6
Catholicism: Judaism and, 218, 219, 225–
27; Max Lilienthal and, 453n8; papal
infallibility and, 99, 100; parochial
schools of, 114, 115
"Catholic Israel," 127, 129, 133, 137, 463n33

Center for Jewish History, 493

Centrist Orthodoxy, 348–50, 354–58, 364–67, 386–87, 396, 481n14

charity, 329–30, 336

Charleston Observer, 12–13, 447n24

cheder (school), 113–14, 115

Chief Rabbi: of Israel, 291; Jacob Joseph as, 78, 82–85, 456–57n9; position of, 83, 456n9

chosenness, Jewish, 177, 256, 259–60, 262–63

Christianity: church seating and, 155; dogma of, 99–100; Judaism and, 221–22, 225–27; Sabbath and, 104–5, 107, 460n43; stature of clergy of, 453n10. *See also* Catholicism; Mormonism; Protestantism

Church of England, 459n31

Church of Jesus Christ of Latterday Saints, 20, 449n38

Churgin, Pinkhos, 151, 466n21

Ciner, William N., 235–36

classes of American Jewry, 108, 117, 460n45

clergy, stature of, 53–56, 453n10. *See also* rabbinate

Cleveland Conference, 35–39, 47, 451n21, 451n23, 451n25

Cline, Hyman, 199, 470n10

Cohen, Harold, 205

Cohen, Max, 95, 458n26

Cohen, Michael, 491

College Bowl, 186–87, *188*, 469nn20–21

commandments of the Torah, 256, 258–59, 261, 265, 388

Commentary, 256

Commentator, 369–71, 374

communism, 295–96, 301, 477n23

community scholars, female, 325, 339, 346

compartmentalized education, 353–54

Conference of Presidents of Major American Jewish Organizations, 172

confirmation, 29, 450n11, 454n17

congregational educators, female, 339–40, 347

congregations, number of, 453n7

conjugal refusal, 266, 474n10

conscientious objection, 301

Conservative Judaism: divorce and, 161–63, 320; Irving Greenberg on, 175–76, 177; meaning of, 139–40, 141, 150; movement of, 386–87, 484nn49–50; Orthodox Judaism parting ways with, xxxvii, 159–67, 491; post World War II, 250

contraception, 304, 310–13, 322

convention of German rabbis, 17, 448n33

Conversations, 421

Copernican system, 100–101

Copernicus, Nicolaus, 460n41

Cosmopolitans and Parochials (Heilman and Cohen), 492

culture and Judaism, 120–21, 221

dancing, 230, 235–36, 446–47n13, 483n37

Dati Le'umi Jews, xxxii

"Daughter of the Ramaz" (Behrman), 88–92

Dayanim, Behnam, 370–71

day schools, Orthodox, xxxiii, 113–16, 119, 196, 197–202, 491. *See also specific day schools*

deconstructive criticism, 368–69

deficit of clergy, 50–53, 453n9

Dembitz, Lewis, 95, 455n33, 458n23

Der Tog, 154

de Sola, Meldola, 95, 458n25

Deutsch, Gotthard, 98–101, 458–59n30, 459n37, 460n41

Diamond, Etan, 493
Divine Presence, 284, 376
divorce: beit din and, 161–63, 319–20,
  420–21, 487n21; Get Bill and, 478n13;
  prenuptial agreements and, 318–22;
  writ of, 142, 161, 305, 316–17, 464n46,
  465n12, 474n10
Documentary Hypothesis, 125, 127, 132–
  33, 135, 455n26
Dolgin, Simon, 166
Douglas, Mary, 239
Dover Beach (Arnold), 368
Drachman, Bernard, 95, 104–7, 109,
  458n24
draft evasion, 300
Drisha Institute for Jewish Education,
  206–7, 338
Drob, Max, 134–37, 463n41

ecumenism, 220–25, 364–66, 482n26
Edah, 391–95, 411–12, 420
"Edah Conference Claims Legacy of
  Rav Soloveitchik" (Kessler), 393
Educational Alliance, 101
Eidelberg, Paul, 367–70
Einhorn, David, 28, 46, 71, 452n37,
  456n36
Eisenstein, Judah David, 132–33, 463n38
Elias, Joseph, 474n12
Elijah (prophet), 45, 452n33
Ellenson, David, 492
Emanu-El Theological Seminary, 453n9
Emek Refa'im (Holzman), 43
encyclopedic works on Judaism, 493
Epstein, Ephraim, 122, 461n15
Epstein, Harry, 144
Epstein, Louis M, 466n25, 466n27
Eretz Israel. *See* Israel, State of
"The Ethics of the Fathers" (Kohut),
  57–58

evolution, 362, 482n25
excommunication, 131–32, 160–61,
  463n36

"Faith and Doubt" (Lamm), 423
family purity, 304, 305–7, 308–10, 342–43
Farber, Seth, 491
Fasman, Oscar Z., 231–33, 473n4, 473n7
fathers, busy, 101, 234
Feinstein, Moshe, 163, 274–75, 310, 379,
  383, 475n15, 483–84n43
Feld, Merle, 388, 391
Feldheim Publishers, 492
Fellowship of Traditional Orthodox
  Rabbis, 349
feminist movement, 387–91, 392–93,
  413–15, 491, 493
Ferziger, Adam, 491
Feuerstein, Moses, 172
Feuerstein, Samuel, 466n26
Finegold, Rachel Kohl, 343, 344, 346
Finer, Morris, 157
Finkelman, Yoel, 491
Finkelstein, Louis, 139, 164
Fischel, Harry, 78
Fishkoff, Sue, 491
Fishman, Sylvia, 493
five-day work week, 104–7, 460n44
flag ceremony, mifkad, 204
four species of Sukkot, 364–65
Framowitz, Saul C., 212–18
Frankel, Zacharias, xxxii, 100, 459n40
Freedman, Samuel G., 412
Freundel, Barry, 407–9
Freundlich, Dena, 399–401
Friday night forums, 231–33, 473n7
Friedman, Ruth Balinsky, 346, 480n17
Frost, Lillian X., 203
Frumteens.com, 398–401, 485n4
fundamentalism, 145–46, 149

Galician Jews, 117

Galilei, Galileo, 100, 459n38

Geffen, Tobias, *144*

Geiger, Abraham, 71, 456n36

Geller, Victor, 492

genetic screening for Tay-Sachs. *See*
Tay-Sachs disease

Gershwind-Bennett Isaac Leeser Digital
Repository, 493

Gerstein, Channa, 330–32, 479n7

get, 319–20, 478n13. *See also* divorce

Gewirtz, Leonard B., 253–56

Gifter, Mordechai, 355–58

Gildersleeve, Benjamin, 13, 447n24

Ginzberg, Louis, 132–33, 354, 463n37

Glatt Kosher, 376, 378–79, 483n35

Glazer, Simon, 109

Goldberg, Harold, 174

Goldman, Ari, 356, 481n16

Goldman, Yosef, 493

Goldsmith, Henry, 31–35, 450n18

Goldstein, Abraham, 212, 471n19

Goldstein, Herbert S., 111, 211–12, 310–12

Goldstein, Israel, 478–79n4

Goodman, Isadore, 158, 466n29

Gotsfeld, Bessie, 285–88

Gottheil, Richard, 454–55n24

Graff, Gil, 491

Greenberg, Blu, 325, 336–39, 349, 392–93

Greenberg, Irving "Yitz": Aharon
Lichtenstein and, 178–82; Christianity and, 225–27; Modern Orthodoxy and, 420; New Orthodox Left
and, 171–72; on Orthodoxy, 174–
79, 468n14; Rabbinical Council of
America and, 349; *Voluntary Covenant,* 277–78, 282–85, 476nn9–10,
476n12

"Green Fields" (Hirschbein), 89, 457n17

Grinstein, Hyman, 489

Grossinger's Catskill Resort Hotel, 376,
483n33

Grossman, Lawrence, 491

Grunblatt, Joseph, 304

"Guide for Instruction in Judaism"
(Kohler), 99, 459n34

Gurock, Jeffrey, 490, 491

hakafot (Simhat Torah dancing), 377,
384, 483n37

Halakhah. *See* Jewish law

"Halakha in Modern Life," 317

Halakhic Man (Soloveitchik), 264–67,
474n11

Hamevaser, 298–301

Ha-Pardes, 493

Hapoel Hamizrachi, 203, 470n12

Harby, Isaac, 3–4, 7–9, 446nn11–13,
447nn15–16

Hartman, David, 345, 420, 479n14

Hartman, Tova, 413–145

Hasidim, 356, 491

Haut, Rivka, 381–85, 484n47

Hebrew Standard, 103–4

Hebrew Theological College of Chicago: graduates of, 158, 171, 247, 253;
leaders of, 300, 385; opening of, 111,
122–24, 462nn18–20; pastoral counseling and, 247; Rabbinical Council
of America and, 148; Yeshivath Etz
Chaim and, 461n15

Hebrew Union College: about, 454–
55n24, 455n30, 458n23, 490, 493;
founding of, 49, 73, 134, 455n29;
Jewish Institute of Religion merge
with, 456n37; Jewish Theological
Seminary and, 68–73, 455nn29–30,
455n32, 455nn34–35; leaders of, 59,
98, 458n23; Louis Ginzberg and,
463n37

Hechsher (kosher certification), 211–17
Hedge of Roses (Lamm), 307–10
Hegel, Georg Wilhelm Fredrich, 146, 465n15
Heichal Rabenu Hayim Halevi, 199, 470n8
Heilman, Samuel C., 238–40, 492
Helfgot, Nathaniel, 415–19
Helmreich, William, 492
Henry, Henry A., 48
Herbert D. Katz Center for Advanced Judaic Studies, 493
herem, 131–32, 160–61, 463n36
Hertz, Joseph, 103
Hertzberg, Arthur, 196
Herzl, Theodor, 280, 475n8
Herzog, Yitzhak, 317, 478n11
Herzfeld, Shmuel, 422
Heschel, Abraham Joshua, 218–19
hierarchical religious structure, 50, 453n8
Hildesheimer, Esriel, xxxi–xxxii
Hillel (talmudic sage), 62, 253
Hillel Day School, 187
Hiller, Elie, 358–61
Hiller, Jonah, 360, 482n22
Himmelfarb, Milton, 171
Hirsch, Emil G., 126, 462n25
Hirsch, Samson Raphael: about, 465nn15–16, 469n24; American Judaism and, xxxi–xxxii, 27, 47, 149, 465n13, 465n18
Hirsch, Samuel, 71, 456n36
Hirschbein, Peretz, 89, 457n17
Hirschell, Solomon, 450n13
Holbein, Hans, 91, 457n20
Holdheim, Samuel, 71, 456n36
holidays, Israeli, 290–92, 476n17, 477n20
Hollander, David, 163
Holocaust, 277–85, 291, 292–93, 476nn9–10, 477n20

Holocaust Remembrance Day, 291, 477n20
Holzer, Elie, 413–14, 486n12
Holzman, Eliyahu M., 43–45, 44, 452n33, 452n35
home life, Jewish, 101–3, 307–8, 490–91, 493
Horeb, 151, 466n22
hospital chaplaincy, 337
hotels, kosher, 376, 379–80, 483n33, 483n35
Huebsch, Adolph, 71, 456n36
humanities, study of, 118, 353, 368–69
Hurwitz, Henry, 112, 461n8
Hurwitz, Hyman, 30, 450n15
Hurwitz, Sara, 324
Hurwitz, Solomon T. H., 112–16
Hutner, Yitzchak, 163
Hyamson, Moses, 325
Hyamson, Sara, 325–30

Ibn Ezra, Abraham, 33, 450n16
Iggud Ha-Rabbonim, 471n20
Illowy, Bernard, 39–40, 451n23
immigrants, Jewish: adaptation of, 109–10, 114; assistance to, 68, 77–78, 101, 103; from Europe, xxxv, xxxvi; to Israel, 350–51; literature on, 489, 491, 492; restriction of, 116, 461n13, 462n30
Immigration Act of 1924, 461n13
immortality of soul, 14, 15
Inclusive Orthodoxy, 396
Independent Order of B'nai B'rith, xxix
Institute for Jewish Ideas and Ideals, 421
Institute of Traditional Judaism, 484n51
interdenominational participation, 163–64, 174, 183, 345, 467n35
interfaith dialogue, 218–27; Irving Greenberg and, 225–27; Joseph B.

Soloveitchik and, 219–24, 472nn22–23; National Council of Young Israel and, 218–19

intermarriage, 4–5, 20–21, 423, 458n22

International Beit Din, 487n21

International Rabbinical Fellowship, 397, 421

Isaacs, Samuel Myer, 45–46, 50, 453n5

Isaacs, Schachne, 43–45, 44, 452n32, 452n35, 452n37

isolationists, 246

Israel, State of: Bessie Gotsfeld and, 285–88; holidays of, 290–92, 476n17, 477n20; immigration to, 350–51; Irving Greenberg and, 283, 285; Joseph B. Soloveitchik and, 289–90; Meir Kahane and, 280; Modern Orthodoxy and, 277; Orthodox doctrine on, 256; Six-Day War and, 292–95; study by Americans in, 371–73

Israelite, 38, 39, 52–53

Isserles, Moshe, 459n33

Jabotinsky, Ze'ev, 280, 475n7

Jacob Joseph School, 114–15, 461n12

Jacobs, George, 54, 55, 453n12

Jakobovits, Immanuel, 260–63, 270–74

Jellinek, Adolf, 71, 456n36

Jerrold, Douglas William, 479n5

Jewish Agency, 287, 476n16

Jewish-Catholic relations, 218–27

Jewish Comment, 98

Jewish Community Council of Boston, 227

Jewish Daily Forward, 82

Jewish Defense League, 278

Jewish Encyclopedia, 132–33, 463n38

Jewish Forum, 108, 134

Jewish Fundamentalism, 145–46

Jewish Institute of Religion, 456n37

Jewish law: Aharon Lichtenstein and, 179–80, 182; Centrist Orthodoxy and, 356; Emanuel Rackman and, 173–74, 267–69, 474n12; food and, 266, 474n9; homosexuality and, 416–19; Immanuel Jackobovits and, 270–74; Irving Greenberg and, 176, 178; Joseph Karo and, 459n33; Joseph B. Soloveitchik on, 264–67, 474n9; marriage and family life and, 308, 316–22; mixed dancing and, 235–36; Modern Orthodoxy and, xxxii–xxxiv, xxxvii, 387, 421; nineteenth century observing of, 4–5, 19–25, 27–28; Orthodox Judaism and, 147, 460n45, 465n17; post World War II, 229–30; Solomon Zucrow on, 142–44, 465n12; Talmud and, 85–86, 143–44, 457nn12–13; women and, 402–3, 414–15

Jewish Library, 145

Jewish Life, 493

Jewish Messenger, 45, 454n19

Jewish Observer, 384, 493

Jewish Orthodox Feminist Alliance (JOFA), 349, 388, 392–93, 413, 420

The Jewish Press, 370

Jewish Record, 54

Jewish Sabbath Alliance of America, 109

Jewish Theological Seminary Association (JTS): about, xxxvi–xxxvii, 103, 458n23, 458n26; *American Hebrew* on, 137; Conservative movement and, 387, 484n49; divorce and, 161–62; founding of, 49, 63–68, 73–74, 454–55nn24–25, 455n27; Hebrew Union College and, 68–73, 455nn34–35; Jacob Schiff and, 462n22; Louis Ginzberg and, 463n37; Max Drob and, 134–37, 463n41; Orthodox Union and, 140–42; Solomon Schechter and, 112, 127–30, 455n31

Jewish Times, 486n8

Jewish Week, 364, 366, 367, 390–91

Jew vs. Jew (Freedman), 412

Joel, Richard, 358, 397, 486n6

JOFA (Jewish Orthodox Feminist Alliance), 349, 388, 392–93, 413, 420

Joint Kashruth Commission, 213

Jones, Alfred T., 54–56

Joselit, Jenna Weissman, 490–91

Joseph, Jacob, 78, 82–85, 456–57n9, 461n12

Joseph, Julie Stern, 339–40, 346

JTS (Jewish Theological Seminary Association). *See* Jewish Theological Seminary Association (JTS)

Judaism: culture and, 120–21, 221; Herman Wouk on, 251–53; Irving Greenberg on, 175–76; Joseph Lookstein on, 149–51; Leo Jung on, 145–47; Leonard Gerwitz on, 253–56; Max Drob on, 135–37; Solomon Schechter on, 128–29; Walter Wurzburger on, 185

Jung, Leo, 139, 144–48, 159, 461n8

Jung, Meir Zvi, 465n15

Kabbalah, 60, 454n20

Kaddish, 100, 377, 459n39, 473n6, 483n38

Kagan, Yisrael Meir, 77

Kaganoff, Nathan, 489

Kahal Adas Yeshurun, 457n10

Kahane, Meir, 277–81, 475n7

Kamenetsky, Yaakov, 163

Kant, Immanuel, 146, 465n15, 484n11

Kaplan, Allan, 312–14

Kaplan, Judith, 231

Kaplan, Mordecai, 103, 140, 160–61, 256, 407, 486n9, 490

Karo, Yosef, 448n32, 459n33

Karp, Abraham, 489

Kashruth Division of Orthodox Union, 94, 197, 211–17

Katz, Julius, 157–58

Katz v. Singerman, 157, 466n28

Kauvar, Charles Eliezer Hillel, 164–66, 467n37

Kedushah, 375

Kehilath Jeshurun Congregation, 90, 149

Kehilath Kodesh Congregation, 238–40

Kehillath Israel, 152–53, 466nn24–27

Kehillat Shirah Hadashah, 413

Keller, Chaim Dov, 194

Keren Kayemet, 287, 476n16

Kesher Israel Congregation, 407–9

Kessler, Eve J., 391, 393, 394, 395

Kestenbaum, Richard, 339–40

Keter Torah Congregation, 359, 481n19

ketubah, 161, 316–17, 320–21

kiddush, 238–40

killing civilians, 300–301

Kimhi, David, 33, 450n16

Kiron, Arthur, 492

Kirshner, Sherman P., 247–48

Klaperman, Gilbert, 354–55, 377, 481n15

Klau Library, 493

Klein, Philip, 100, 459n37, 460n41

Kneseth Israel (the "White Shul"), 235, 236

Know Nothing Party, 128, 462n30

Kohler, Kaufmann, 49, 59–61, 73, 99–100, 454nn18–19, 455n28, 459n34

Kohn, Abraham, 19–20

Kohn, Jacob, 141, 464n10

Kohut, Alexander, 49, 56–59, 61–63, 73, 454n19

Kohut, Rebekah, 479n7

Kook, Avraham Yitzhak, xxxii, 193, 366–67, 469n25

Korn, Bertram, 489

Korn, Eugene, 394, 485n60

Kosher Certification Service, 211–17, 214–15

kosher food, 94, 197, 211–17, 214–15, 379, 483n34

Kotler, Aharon, 163, 199, 491

Krauss, Esther, 371–73

Krauss, Simcha, 421, 487n21

Kraut, Benny, 491

Ladizinsky, Eliezer, 116–18

Lamm, Norman, 210; Centrist Orthodoxy and, 348–49, 355–58, 396, 481n14; "Faith and Doubt," 423; Holocaust and Israel and, 277; on marriage, 307–10; Megillah readings by women and, 401–3; Modern Orthodoxy resurrection by, xxxi, 172, 189–95, 469n23, 469n29; Torah u-Madda and, 368, 370, 374, 482n29

Landau, Chaim, 395

Landesman, David, 350–51

language use for preaching, 130, 132, 136

Lanner, Baruch, 358–61, 481–82n20, 482n22

Lazar, Ben Zion, 123, 461n16

Leeser, Isaac: about, 4, 55, 453–54nn13–15; Abraham Rice and, 17–18, 25–26; Benjamin Carillon and, 27, 28–29; Benjamin Peixotto and, 41–43; Cleveland Conference and, 35–38; Gustavus Poznanski letter from, 12–16, 447n22, 448n30

Lefkowitz, Jay P., 406–7

Leibler, Soshea, 206–7

Leibowitz, Nechama, 338, 479n10

Leibowitz, Yeshayahu, 420, 487n19

Lerner, Abby, 341–43

Levinthal, Bernard, 92, 131–32, 463n36

Levy, Joseph, 37

liberal arts education, 151, 208, 367–71

Lichtenstein, Aharon, 178–82, 349–50, 391–95, 400, 485n59

Lieberman, Joseph, 397

Lieberman, Saul, 161, 316, 320

The Lieberman Open Orthodox Haggadah (Herzfeld), 422

Lieberman Takana, 316

Liebman, Charles, 171, 172–74, 187, 302, 468n11, 492

life appointment of clergy, 49–52, 453nn5–6

Lilienthal, Max: about, 21–22, 71, 456n36; at Cleveland Conference, 36–37, 38; on Orthodox Jewish life, 22–24, 26; on rabbinic tenure, 49–52, 453n6, 453n8

Lilith (midrashic figure), 389

Lincoln, Abraham, 129, 463n32

Lincoln Square Synagogue, 245–46, 339–40, 346–47, 492

Linzer, Dov, 409–11

literature on Orthodox Judaism, 489–93

Lithuanian Jews, 117

Litoff, Moshe, 470n11

Lookstein, Haskel, 301–2, 364–67

Lookstein, Joseph, 139, 149–51, 348, 424

Lopatin, Asher, 419–23

Los Angeles Times, 251

Loth, Moritz, 455n30

Lowenstein, Steven, 492

Lubavitcher Rebbe, 278, 467n35

Luria, Isaac, 60, 454n20

Luther, Martin, 3, 10

Ma'ayanot Yeshiva High School, 398–99

Magnes, Judah, 103, 460n42

Maharat moniker, 324–25

Maimonidean Articles of Faith, xxxiv, 12–15, 159, 275, 447n22, 448n28, 458n22

Maimonides, Moses: about, 60, 90, 150, 450n16, 457n19, 465n20; on good conduct, 262; religious authority and, 27, 34–35, 174, 451n20; Torah and, 133, 150, 261, 383; on war, 300

Maimonides School, xxxiii, 197–99, 400, 443n32, 470n8, 491

Maine, uss, 98, 458n28

Malbim, Meir Leibush, 145, 465n13

Marcus, Jacob Rader, 454n16, 493

Margolies, Mose Zevulun, 89–90, 92, 457n16

Maritain, Jacques, 189, 469n23

Marks, David Woolf, 30, 33, 450n14

marriage, Jewish, 307–10, 314–15, 328, 416, 477n6. *See also* divorce; intermarriage

Marshall, Louis, 455n33

mashgichim (kosher supervisors), 211–12, 216–17

Masmid, 122

matchmaking, *xxxix*, 92

Matzah of Hope, 291, 477n18

McLuhan, Marshall, 226, 472n24

"The Meaning and Scope of the Jewish Theological Seminary" (Schechter), 127–30

mehitzah. See mixed seating

Meiselman, Moshe, 413, 415

Meiselman, Shulamith Soloveitchik, 197–99

Meites, Hyman L., 122–24

Mendelsohn, Samuel Felix, 159–60

Mendes, Henry Pereira, 63–65, 94–95, 96–98, 100, 140–42, 458n30

Mendlowitz, Shraga Feivel, 199

menstruation, 266, 304, 305–7, 309, 452n31

Merzbacher, Leo, 28, 37–38, 50, 451n24, 451n28, 453n5

Mesivtha Tifereth Jerusalem, 274

Messiah, 13–14, 18–19, 42, 227, 294–95, 448n28

microphone usage, 230, 272, 273

Midrash, 145, 283, 364–65, 465n13

Mielziner, Moses, 452n36

mikvah, 17, 304–7, 308–10, 407, 448n34

Mikveh Israel, 12, 65, 109, 453n13

milchemet mitzvah, 300–301

milchemet reshut, 300–301

Milgrom, Shira, 338–39, 479n11

Miller, William, 449n37

Millerism, 20, 449n37

Milton, John, 393, 485n56

minhag, 45–46, 47

Minhag America (Wise), 28, 45, 452n30, 452n35

Minhag Amsterdam, 46

Minhag Ashkenaz, 45–46

minister moniker, 444n43

Minkowski, Pinchas, 83, 457n10

minority, Jews as a, 279–80

Mintz, Adam, 339–40, 346

Mintz, Jerome, 491

minyanim, 377, 382, 383–84, 413, 453n7, 487n14, 487n17

Mishkan Tefila Temple, 465n12, 466n24

Mishna Torah, 34, 383, 451n20

mi'un, 266, 474n10

mixed dancing, 230, 235–36, 446–47n13

mixed marriage, 4–5, 20–21, 423, 458n22

mixed seating: opposition to, 28, 41, 42, 140, 152, 158, 452nn30–31; support of, 116, 230, 467n40

Mizrachi, 113, 289–90, 461n11, 466n21, 470n12

Mizrachi Women's Organization, 285–88

modernity and Orthodoxy, 98–101, 458n30

Modern Orthodoxy: Conservative Judaism and, 159–67, 171; defined, 139–40, 141, 159–60, 173; disillusionment with, 351–54; life of, 361–63; movement away from center of, 350–55, 386–87; as a movement, question of, 187–89, 469n22; Norman Lamm and, xxxi, xxxviii, 172, 189–95, 469n23, 469n29; overview of, 171–72, 397–98; rabbis and Jewish law and, 142–44, 465n12; rejuvenating, 420–23; Shlomo Riskin on, 375–77; Traditional Conservatism and, 386–87. *See also* New Orthodox Left; Orthodox Union (OU)

Montaigne, Michel de, 130, 463n34

Montefiore, Moses, 62, 450n13, 454n21

Morais, Sabato: about, 48, 65, 462n26; Jewish Theological Seminary and, 65–68, 69, 134, 454–55nn24–25, 455nn27–28

moral relativism, 369, 370

Mordecai, Jacob, 3–4, 9–11, 447n19

Mormonism, 20, 449n38

Mosaico-Rabbinical Judaism, 57, 58, 59, 60–61, 73

motherhood, Jewish, 101–3, 311, 328

Movement to Free Soviet Jewry, 296–98, 299

"Mrs. Caudle's Curtain Lectures" (Jerrold), 327, 479n5

Myers, David, 492

My Portion (Kohut), 479n7

Nachman of Bratislav, 476n12

Nahmanides, 379, 483n39

National Conference of Synagogue Youth (NCSY), 203–5, 247, 358–60, 471n14, 471n16

National Council of Young Israel. *See* Young Israel

National Jewish Fund, 287, 476n16

National Jewish Population Survey, xxxviii

National Orthodox Jewish Archives, 493

National Society for Hebrew Day Schools, 199–200

NCSY (National Conference of Synagogue Youth), 203–5, 247, 358–60, 471n14, 471n16

Neusner, Jacob, 171

Never Again (Kahane), 279–81

The New Encounter of Judaism and Christianity (Greenberg), 225–27

Newman, John Henry, 183, 468n17

New Orthodox Left, 172–85; Aharon Lichtenstein and, 178–82; Charles Liebman and, 172–74, 187, 468n11; Emanuel Rackman and, xxxi, 171–74, 184, 187–89, 194, 468n12, 469n22; Irving Greenberg and, 174–79, 468n14; Modern Orthodoxy and, 398; overview of, 171–72; Walter Wurzburger on, 182–85

Newton, Isaac, 100, 459n38

New York Board of Jewish Ministers, 325–26, 478n4

New York Board of Rabbis, 163, 467n34

New Yorker, 88

New York Magazine, 274

New York Times, 356, 481n16

niddah, 266, 304, 305–7, 309, 452n31

Nissim, Yitzhak, 318, 478n11

Noah, Mordecai, 3–4, 5–7, 18–19, 446n10, 446–47nn12–13, 448n35

non-believers as spiritually dead, 254

Occident, 12–16, 29–35, 450n14, 450n17

Olat Tamid (Einhorn), 28

omer, counting of the, 265, 474n8

onus, concept of, 246

Open Orthodoxy, 344–45, 398, 409–10, 420, 422, 423

Oral Torah, xxxv–xxxvi, 27, 32, 38–39, 57, 399

Order of Prayer for Divine Service (Merzbacher), 39–40, 451n28

Orthodox high school, 111, 113–16, 398–401, 482n21. *See also* day schools, Orthodox

Orthodox Jewish Congregational Union of America. *See* Orthodox Union (ou)

Orthodox Judaism: background and overview, xxix–xl; day schools, xxxiii, 113, 119, 196, 197–202, 491; defined, xxx, xxxvi–xxxviii, 97–99, 140, 145–47, 149–50, 189, 442n13; as ghetto Judaism, 150, 176; modernity and, 98–101, 458n30; nineteenth century, xxix–xxx, xxxi–xxxii, xxxiv–xxxvi, 25–26; parting ways with Conservative Judaism, xxxvii, 159–67, 491; post–World War II transition of, 229–30, 250–51; shift from synagogue focus of, 196–97, 248–49; survey of state of belief of, 256–63; twentieth century, xxxi, xxxii–xxxiii, xxxvi–xl, 149–51, 171–72, 228, 250; twenty-first century, xxx–xxxi, xxxiv, xxxix, 409

Orthodox Modernism, 172, 183

Orthodox Union (ou): background and overview of, xxx, xxxvi–xxxvii, 78, 150; first convention of, 94–96, 457–58nn22–23; Henry Mendes and, 96–98, 140–41; Jewish day schools and, 113; Judah Eisenstein and, 132–

33; kosher food and, 197, 211–17, 214–15; National Conference of Synagogue Youth of, 203–5, 247, 358–60, 471n14, 471n16; Norman Lamm and, 189, 194, 349; Oscar Fasman and, 231; Samson Weiss and, 165; Synagogue Council and, 460n45; women's branch of, 211, 305–7; Zionism and, 350. *See also* Rabbinical Council of America (rca)

"Orthodoxy Encounters a Changing World" conference, 391

"Orthodoxy in American Jewish Life" (Liebman), 172–74, 468n11

Palestine (pseudonym), 52–54

Palestine, 95–96, 285, 286–87, 458n27, 476nn15–16

Palestine Royal Commission, 286, 476n15

papal infallibility, 99, 459nn35–36

Parnes, Yehuda, 275, 374, 379, 483n36

parochial school, 113–16, 151, 198

Passover programs, 378–79

pastoral counseling, 247–48, 473n11

Paul VI, Pope, 218–19

Peel Commission, 286, 476n16

Peixotto, Benjamin Franklin, 41–43, 451–52nn29–30

Pelcovitz, Ralph, 229, 236–38

Pentateuch, 79–80, 125, 126–27, 133, 261, 455n26

Perlow, Yaakov, 421–23, 487n23

Pew Research Center, xxx, 423

Pharisees, 226, 472n25

Pinchot, Dov, 370–71

Pius IX, Pope, 100, 459n35

Plato, 368

Polish Jews, 79, 117

Pool, David and Tamara de Sola, 491–92

population: of Jews in New York, 454n16; of Jews in U.S., xxx, xxxv, xxxvi, 77, 454n23; of Orthodox Jews, xxx, xxxviii

Portuguese Jews, xxxv, 20

Poznanski, Gustavus: about, 4, 447n16, 447n21, 448n25; Isaac Leeser and, 12–16, 448nn28–29

prayer books: of Isaac Wise, 28, 45, 452n30, 452n32; of Mordecai Kaplan, 160–61; Reform Judaism and, 27–28, 30–35, 39–40, 43–45, 44, 47, 450n13, 451n28; standardization of, 196–97

prayer for Soviet Jews, 301–2

prayer groups of women, 377–85, 387, 390–91, 413, 415, 483–84n43

prenuptial clause, 316–22

Presbyterianism, 99, 459nn31–32

Price, Nechama, 408, 486n10

Principles of Faith, Maimonides', xxxiv, 12–15, 159, 275, 447n22, 448n28, 458n22

progress in religion, 60–63

Pronaos to Holy Writ (Wise), 126

Protestantism, xxxv, 39, 99, 453n10

Rabba moniker, 324–25

Rabbi Isaac Elchanan Theological Seminary (RIETS): about, 118, 150, 211; modern Orthodoxy and, 398; publications of, 300, 332, 335; Rabbinical Council of America and, 148; terminology and, xxxvii; women prayer groups and, 377–79, 381, 483n36, 483n38

rabbi moniker, 444n43

rabbinate: clergy deficit of, 50–53, 453n9; nineteenth century overview of, 73–74; pastoral training and, 247–48, 473n11; post–World War II tran-

sition of, 229–30, 240; stature of, 53–56, 453n10; synagogue focus shift of, 240–49; tenure of, 49–52, 453n56; women in, 324–25, 336–39, 343–47, 413, 484n49

Rabbiner-Seminar für das Orthodoxe Judentum, xxxii

Rabbinical Alliance of America, 471n20

Rabbinical Assembly of America, 135, 161, 164–66, 316, 463n43, 466n25, 467n36

Rabbinical Council of America (RCA): bar mitzvah and, 233; Centrist Orthodoxy and, 354–55, 481n15; Eliezer Berkovits and, 171; founding of, 147–48; interdenominational participation and, 163–64; interfaith dialogue and, 472n23; kosher certification and, 212, 213, 217; Mid-Winter 1964 Conference of, 219–24; *minyan* and, 487n17; prayer book standardization and, 196–97; prenuptial agreement and divorce and, 318–19, 320, 478n13; religious unevenness of, xxx; slaughter and, 468–69n19; *Tradition,* 171, 182, 270, 312, 351, 493; Vietnam War and, 302; women clergy and, 344, 346; women's prayer groups and, 377–79, 380–81, 384, 483n36

Rabbinical Council of the Union of Orthodox Jewish Congregations of America, 147–48

Rabbinical Supervisory Council, 199, 200

Rabbinic Kashruth Commission, 213, 217

Rackman, Emanuel: on Halakhah, 184, 267–70, 274, 474nn12–13; on marriage annulment, 317–18, 323, 478n12;

Rackman, Emanuel (*continued*)
  Modern Orthodoxy and, xxxi, 171–
  74, 187–89, 194, 353, 468n12, 469n22;
  Orthodoxy in schools and, 248
Radical Orthodoxy, 182, 183–85
Radical Reform, 142
Rakeffet, Aaron, 490
the Ramaz, 89–90, 92, 457n16
Raphall, Morris J., 18, 38–39, 44, 48,
  447n16, 452n36
Rashi, 33, 90, 150, 450n16, 457n19,
  465n20
Rav. *See* Soloveitchik, Joseph B.
RCA (Rabbinical Council of America).
  See Rabbinical Council of America
  (RCA)
rebbetzin. *See* wives, rabbi's
"Reflections of a Rebbitzen" (Gerstein),
  331–32, 479n7
Reform Advocate, 98
Reformed Society of Israelites: Isaac
  Harby and, 7–9, 447nn15–16; opposition to, 5–6, 9–11, 447n19; overview of, xxxiv, 3–4, 447n17; support
  for, 6–7
Reform Judaism: Cleveland Conference
  and, 35–39, 451n21, 451n23n, 451n25;
  defined, 141, 150, 465n19; division
  of Jewish community and, 48–49,
  108; Emanuel Schreiber and, 124–27;
  Irving Greenberg on, 175–76; Jewish law and responsibility and, 19–
  25, 29, 449nn39–40, 454n17; Kohut
  and Kohler exchange on, 56–63, 73,
  454n19; Minhag reform and, 45–46,
  47, 452n37; Orthodox Union and, 97,
  98; overview of, xxxiv–xxxv; prayer
  books and, 27–28, 30–35, 39–40, 43–
  45, 44, 47, 450n13; religious beliefs of,
  13–15, 18–19, 41–43, 448n28. *See also*

Hebrew Union College; Reformed
  Society of Israelites
"Resisters and Accommodators"
  (Gurock), 490
Reichman, Solomon, 147–48
religion: science and, 208, 272–75, 362–
  63, 482n25; secularism and, 207–9
religious authority, xxxvi, 27, 30–39,
  99–100
Religious Zionists of America, 113, 289–
  90, 461n11, 466n21, 470n12
responsibility to uphold faith, 24–25,
  449n40
resurrection of the dead, 13, 15, 18–19, 42,
  448n28
"Retrograde instead of Advancing"
  (Noah), 5–6, 446nn10–11
Revel, Bernard, 111–12, 113, 118–21, 122,
  137–38, 461n11
revelation: Orthodoxy and, 147, 159, 178,
  255–59, 261, 457n22, 465n17; Six-Day
  War and, 293
reverend moniker, 444n43
"Review of Recent Halakhic Periodical
  Literature" (Jakobovits), 270–74
Rice, Abraham, 16–18, 25–26, 33–35,
  448n34, 450nn17–19
Richards, Bernard G., 460n42
Richmond Whig, 453n14
RIETS (Rabbi Isaac Elchanan Theo-
  logical Seminary). *See* Rabbi Isaac
  Elchanan Theological Seminary
  (RIETS)
Rischin, Moses, 489
Riskin, Steven "Shlomo": about, 245–46,
  349, 391, 473n10, 492; outreach work
  of, 245–47; shift in Modern Ortho-
  doxy and, 375–77, 420
ritual slaughter, 185, 468–69n19
Robinson, Ira, 491

Roche, Boyle, 129, 462n31
Roemer Synagogue, 359, 481n19
Roosevelt, Eleanor, 335, 479n8
Rosenberg, Abraham I., 203–5, *204*, 471n14
Rosenberg, Alexander, 212–18
Rosenberg case, 295–96
Rosenblatt, Gary, 358
Rosenblatt, William M., 79–82
Rosenfeld, Jacob, 447n16
Rosenthal, Gilbert, 489
Rossman, Nathaniel, 452n36
Roth, Leon, 407
Rothschild, Lionel de, 454n22
Rothschild, Nathaniel, 62–63, 454n22
Rothstein, Joshua, 82
Rubenstien, Hayyim, 122–23, 461n15
Rubin, Ronald I., 274–75
Rubin, Sallie, 203
Ruderman, Yaakov, 163
Rudnick, Joseph, 152–53
Ruskay, Esther J., 101–3
Russian Jewry, 65, 68, 79, 219, 397, 454n23. *See also* Soviet Jewry
Russian Orthodoxy, 141

Sabbath: bat mitzvah and, 231–33; five-day work week and, 104–7; Jewish law and, 272, 273–74, 275; meals of, 238–40; Mussaf service, 451n28; observing, 85–86, 91, 102–3, *144*, 457n13; Orthodox Union and, 94, 97; prayer service of, 79–82; teleological approach to observance of, 269, 475n14; Temple Emanu-El and, 39; women's prayer groups and, 382
Sabbath Prayer Book (Kaplan), 160–61
Sacks, Jonathan, 396
Salmon, Yosef, 493
Salomon, Ivan, 166, 467n38

Sanhedrin, 136, 300, 463n44
Sarna, Jonathan, 490, 491
Satmar Hassidic group, 193, 469n27
Schachter, Hershel, 381, 384, 483n36, 484n46, 487n14
Schachter-Shalomi, Zalman Meshullam, 227, 472n26
Schacter, Hershel, 172
Schacter, Jacob J., 423–24, 482n29, 488n26
Schechter, Solomon: about, 112, 455n34, 462n21, 462n23; Emanuel Schreiber on, 124–27; Jewish Theological Seminary and, 127–30, 132–35, 137, 455n31, 463n33; United Synagogue and, 141, 463n42, 465n19
Scheier, Abby Brown, 346, 480n17
Scheier, Adam, 343–46, 480n19
Schiff, Jacob H., 68–73, 125, 455n33, 455n35, 462n22
Schneeberger, Henry, 95, 458n25
Schneerson, Menachem Mendel, 467n35. *See also* Lubavitcher Rebbe
Schoenfeld, Fabian, 161–63, 467n33
schools, Orthodox day, xxxiii, 113, 119, 196, 197–202, 491
Schreiber, Emanuel, xxix, 124–27
Schwab, Shimon, xl
science and religion, 208, 272–75, 362–63, 482n25
Scripta Mathematica, 151, 466n22
seating. *See* mixed seating
Second Vatican Council, 218, 219
secularism: interfaith relationships and, 223, 472n22; in Israel, 350; in Jewish day schools, 114–15, 200–201; Joseph B. Soloveitchik and, 373–75, 374; Modern Orthodoxy and, 180, 352–54, 357, 481n13; religion and, 207–9; Sabbath and, 105, 106

Seder Tefilot (Kaplan), 160–61

Sephardim, xxxv, 20

sex, 174, 304, 307–10

Shaaray Tefila, 45, 48, 139

Shaar Hashomayim Congregation, 343–46, 480n19

Shabbat. See Sabbath

shaitel (woman's head covering), 141, 464n11

Shakespeare, William, 255, 368

Shandler, Jeffrey, 491

Shanfarber, Tobias, 98, 458n30

Shapiro, Marc, 492

Sharfman, Solomon J., 166, 467n38

Shari Emouna Congregation, 85

shaving, 23, 449n39

Shaw, Laura, 387–91

Shearith Israel Congregation, 5, 20–21, 63, 96, 491–92

Sheen, Fulton, 181, 468n15

Shema prayer, 9, 447n18

Sherman, Moshe, 493

Shulhan Arukh, 17, 40, 85, 99, 100, 178, 448n32, 459n33

Silber, David, 206

Silber, Saul, 123, 462n18

Silver, Eliezer, 163, 217, 471n20

simchat bat, 389

Singer, David, 351–54, 396, 491

Singerman, Gus, 157–58, 466n28

sisterhood, synagogue, 329–30, 331, 333–34, 335–36

Six-Day War, 292–95

slaughter, ritual, 185, 468–69n19

Smith, Henry Preserved, 99, 459n32

Smith, Joseph, 20, 449n38

Social Orthodoxy, 406–7

social sciences, study of, 369

Soloveichik, Ahron, 179, 298–301

Soloveitchik, Haym, 492

Soloveitchik, Joseph B.: Abba Bronspigel on, 373–75; about, xxxiii, 171, 184, 349, 373, 374, 483n31, 485n57; on congregation seating, 154–57; on the covenant, 283; divorce and, 317, 323; halakhic writings by, 251, 264–67, 268, 474n11, 474n13; Holocaust and Israel and, 277, 278; interdenominational participation and, 163; interfaith dialogue and, 219–24, 227, 472n22; legacy of, 391–95, 396, 403, 485n59; Maimonides school and, 197, 198, 199; on "new generation," 348; standardized prayer book and, 197; Stern College and, 209, *210*; use of microphone on Sabbath and, 230; women's reading of Talmud and, 196, 399–400, 486n5; on Zionism, 289–90

Soloveitchik, Moses, 199, 470n9

Soloveitchik, Tonya, 197

Soloveitchik, Yitzhak Ze'ev, 469n27

sotah, 266, 474n10

Soviet Jewry, 291, 296–98, 301–3, 472n21, 477nn18–19, 491. *See also* Russian Jewry

Soviet Union, 278, 291, 296–98, 302, 303, 477n23

Specific Orthodox, xxix

Speiser, Joseph, 233–34

Spero, Shubert, 482n26

Spinoza, Barukh, 485n59

spirit of the law, 271

"Statement of Principles on the Place of Jews with a Homosexual Orientation in Our Community" (Helfgot), 415–19

State of Orthodox Belief survey, 256–63

"State of Orthodoxy" symposium, 351–52

Stein, Leopold, 71, 456n36

Stern College for Women, 196, 209–10, 210, 338, 400, 401–3

St. Thomas, congregation in, 28–31

Student Struggle for Soviet Jewry, 296–98, *299*

"Studies in Judaism" (Schechter), 125–26

suburban synagogues, 229–30, 250–51, 493

sukkah, 366–67

Sukkot festival, 364–65

summer camps, 202–3

Sunshine Company, *214–15*

superiority of Jews, 259–60, 263

Sussman, Lance, 492

Symposium (Plato), 368

Synagogue Council of America, 107–9, 140, 164, 174, 460n45

synagogue dedication in Charleston, 13, 448n25

synthesis of Orthodoxy and secularism, 207–9, 352–54, 481n13

taharat ha-mishpahah, 304, 305–7, 308–10, 342–43

Talmud: Jewish law and, 85–86, 143–44, 457nn12–13; Mordecai Noah and, 446n13; Reform Judaism and, 27, 30–39, 40, 47, 451n22; scientific matter and, 100–101; women's reading of, 399–401, 486n5

Talmudical Academy, 111, 113, 114–15, 403, 461nn11–12

Tay-Sachs disease, 304–5, 312–16, 322, 478n9

Teachers' Institute of Yeshiva College, 151, 466n21

Tefillah groups, women's. *See* prayer groups of women

teleological approach to Halakhah, 267–69, 474n12

Temple Emanu-El, 28, 39–40, 48, 68, 451n28

Tendler, Moshe D., 314, 315–16, *374*, 478n10

tenure, rabbinic, 48–52, 453nn5–6

This Happy Land discourse (Harby), 7–9, 447nn15–16

This Is My God (Wouk), 250, 251–53

"Thoughts upon Liberty" (Wesley), 447n15

Tifereth Israel, 41–43, 451–52n29

Time, 245–46, 473n10

Torah: divineness of, 257–59, 261–62; mikvah and, 306; oral, xxxv–xxxvi, 27, 32, 38–39, 57, 399; Orthodox Judaism and, 145–47, 159, 255–56; study of, 193, 469n27; Traditional Judaism and, 129, 133, 136; women's prayer services and, 382–85

"Torah im Derech Eretz," 146, 465n16

Torah Leadership Seminar, 471n18

Torah min ha-shamayim, 257, 261

Torah she-Ba'al Peh, xxxv–xxxvi, 27, 32, 38–39, 57, 399

Torah-true Judaism, 139, 145, 149, 165, 465n18

Torah u-Madda, 367–71, 396, 482n29

Torah Umesorah, 199–200

Tosafists, 150, 465n20

Tosefta, 383

tractatus theologico-politicus, 394, 485n59

Tradition, 171, 182, 270, 312, 351, 493

Traditional Conservatism, 386–87, 484n51

Traditional Judaism, 134–37, 296

Trefa Banquet, 73

Twersky, Mayer, 413, 415

UJA (United Jewish Appeal), 337, 479n9

Ultra-Orthodox, xxvii, xl, 253, 356, 479n15, 491, 492

Union for Promoting Traditional Judaism in America. *See* United Synagogue (U.S.)

Union for Traditional Conservative Judaism (UTCJ), 386–87, 484nn50–51

Union of American Hebrew Congregations, 69, 455n30

Union of Orthodox Jewish Congregations of America. *See* Orthodox Union (OU)

Union of Orthodox Rabbis of America: about, 78, 110, 151, 463n36, 471n21; advertisement of, 364–66, 367; *American Hebrew* on, 130–32; by-laws of, 92–94; Mordecai Kaplan and, 160–61; Solomon Schechter and, 137–38

Union of Traditional Torah-Faithful Rabbis, xxxii

United Jewish Appeal (UJA), 337, 479n9

United Synagogue (London), 136, 465n19

United Synagogue (U.S.), 135, 141–42, 164, 463n42, 464n10, 465n19

United Synagogue Review, 162

United Synagogue Youth, 205, 471n15

Universal Jewish Encyclopedia, 159

unterführer, 332, 479n6

Unterman, Isser Yehudah, 310, 477n6

UTCJ (Union for Traditional Conservative Judaism), 386–87, 484nn50–51

Uziel, Ben-Zion, 317, 478n11

Va'ad Ha-Rabbonim of Greater New York, 160, 390–91

vacation resorts, 376, 379–80, 483n33, 483n35

Veheveti, 290–92

Vereinigung traditionell-gesetzestreuer Rabbiner, xxxii

Vietnam War, 298–301, 302, 477nn22–23

Viewpoint, 212–19, 229

Voluntary Covenant (Greenberg), 282–85, 476nn9–10, 476n12

von Doellinger, Ignaz, 100, 459n36

Wall Street Journal, 197

Waxman, Chaim, 493

"We All Stood Together" (Feld), 388, 391

Weinberger, Moses, 491

Weiss, Avi: about, 386, 397, 409; Conservative Movement and, 386–87; Open Orthodoxy and, 409–11, 420; women's prayer groups and, 380, 484n44; women synagogue leaders and, 324, 325, 345, 349; Yeshivat Chovevei Torah and, 347, 484n51

Weiss, Samson R., 165–66

Wellhausen, Julius, 66, 455n26

Wertheimer, Jack, 420, 423

Wesley, John, 447n15

Westminster Assembly, 459n31

Wiesel, Elie, 282

Willig, Mordechai, 210, 318–19, 321, 323, 379, 483n36, 486n5

wine, sacramental, 109

Wise, Isaac Mayer: about, 49, 50, 133, 448n30, 448n35, 449n36, 453nn5–6; Benjamin Peixotto and, 41, 452n30; Bernard Illowy and, 39, 451n27; Bible translation and, 454n18; Cleveland Conference and, 35–38, 47, 451n21; Eliyahu Holzman and, 43–45; Hebrew Union College and, 69, 70, 71, 455n29, 455n32; *Minhag America,* 28, 46, 452n30, 452n32, 452n35, 452n37; Principles of Faith and, 18–19; *Pronaos to Holy Writ,* 126; Schachne Isaacs and, 452n32

Wissenschaft des Judentums, xxxi, 462n29

wives, rabbi's, 324–36; Abby Lerner on, 341–43; Chana Gerstein on, 330–32; Helen Felman on, 335–36; overview of, 324–25; Sara Hyamson on, 325–30; Theodore Adams on, 332–34

Wolf, Simon, 455n33

Wolff, Aaron, 29, 450n9

Wolowelsky, Joel B., 290–92

women, Jewish: as clergy, 324–25, 336–39, 343–47, 413, 484n49; expectations and responsibilities of, 24–25, 86–88, 91; feminist movement of, 387–91, 392–93, 413–15, 491, 493; institutions of higher learning for, 206–7, 209–10, 338, 343, 346, 347; menstruation and mikvah and, 17, 266, 304–10, 448n34, 452n31; Orthodox Union branch of, 211, 305–7; prayer groups of, 377–85, 387, 390–91, 413, 415, 483–84n43; Russian Orthodoxy and, 141, 464n11. *See also* wives, rabbi's

Women's Branch of the Orthodox Union, 211, 305–7

Women's Tefilah Network, 381–86, 388, 390–91, 484n47

Worcester, MA, 88, 457n15

Wouk, Herman, 250, 251–53

Wurzburger, Walter, 182–85, 277, 303

Wyschogrod, Michael, 477n23

Yad Ha-Hazakah (Maimonides), 34, 383, 451n20

Yahrzeit, 232, 291, 473n6

Yavneh, 290–92, 298–300, 491

Yeshiva College: about, 150–51, 207; establishment of, 111, 118–21, 122; Samuel Belkin and, 207–9; secular and religious synthesis at, 352–53, 481n13; student newspapers of, 174–82, 370–71, 374, 466n22; Tay-

Sachs and, 312, 314; Teachers' Institute of, 151, 466n21; Torah u-Madda and, 367–71, 482n29. *See also* Yeshiva University

Yeshivah of Flatbush High School, 186, 362, 482n24

Yeshiva Rabenu Hayim Halevi, 199, 470n8

Yeshivat Chovevei Torah: about, xxx, 324, 397, 415, 419, 484n51; Edah and, 411; graduates of, 347, 421–23, 487n23; positions of, 409–11

Yeshivath Etz Chaim, 122, 461n15

Yeshivat Maharat, 343, 346, 347, 421, 480n17

Yeshivat Rambam, 403–5, 486nn7–8

Yeshiva University: about, xxx, *xxxix*, 118, 158, 207, 486n6, 489; Archives and Special Collections at, 493; Centrist Orthodoxy and, 348–49; College Bowl and, 186–87, *188*, 469nn20–21; homosexuality and, 415–19; Joseph B. Soloveitchik and, xxxiii, 277, 348, 373; literature and research material and, 490, 493; matchmaking program of, *xxxix*; Megillah reading and, 402–3; Richard Joel and, 397; Samuel Belkin and, 196, 207–9, 481n13; secularism and, 352–53, 481n13; Stern College for Women, 196, 209–10, *210*, 338, 400, 401–3; women's prayer groups and, 377, 384; youth programs and, 204–5, 247, 471n18. *See also* Yeshiva College

Yezierska, Anzia, 86–88

Yom Ha-Atzma'ut, 291, 476n17

Yom Hashoah Ve-Hagvurah, 291, 477n20

Yom Ha-Zikaron, 291, 476n17

Yom Yerushalayim, 291, 476n17

Young Israel: about, xxx, 103–4, 235, 460n42; communism and, 295–96;

Young Israel (*continued*)
Conservative Beth Din resolution
and, 161–63; movement of, 78, 103–4;
Viewpoint, 212–19, 229
Young Israel Institute for Jewish Studies, 165
Youth Bureau of Yeshiva University, 204,
471n18
youth programs, 202–5, 204, 247, 358–
60, 470–71nn14–16

Zimmer, Uriel, 471n16
Zionism: Bessie Gotsfeld and, 285–88;
Charles Liebman and, 173; immi-
gration to Israel and, 350; Joseph B.
Soloveitchik on, 289–90; literature
on, 491, 493; Mizrachi and, 113, 289–
90, 461n11, 466n21, 470n12; Mizrachi
Women's Organization and, 285–88;
Modern Orthodoxy and, xxxi, xxxii,
303, 357; Orthodox Union and, 94–
96, 458n22; supporters of, 458n25,
469n25, 475nn7–8, 478–79n4, 486n9;
youth and, 203
Zohar, 60, 454n20
Zola, Gary, 6
Zucrow, Solomon, 142–44, 465n12
Zunz, Leopold, 128, 462n29